OBSERVER'S HANDBOOK 2001

EDITOR
RAJIV GUPTA

NINETY-THIRD YEAR OF PUBLICATION

© THE ROYAL ASTRONOMICAL SOCIETY OF CANADA
136 DUPONT STREET, TORONTO, ONTARIO M5R 1V2
2000

ISSN 0080-4193
ISBN 0-9695804-8-7

PRINTED IN CANADA
BY THE UNIVERSITY OF TORONTO PRESS

CANADIAN PUBLICATIONS MAIL REGISTRATION NO. 09818
US PERIODICALS REGISTRATION NO. 010-751

CONTENTS

The Sky Month by Month

The Sun

The Moon

Planets and Satellites

THE OBSERVER'S HANDBOOK

The *Observer's Handbook* is one of Canada's oldest scientific publications. Created by C. A. Chant, Professor of Astronomy at the University of Toronto, it first appeared nearly a century ago as *The Canadian Astronomical Handbook for 1907*, a small (13 × 17 cm), 108-page publication. A second edition covered the year 1908, but for the following two years most of the information that would have appeared in it was published in instalments in the Society's *Journal*. The Council of the Society decided to return to a separate publication for 1911 with a new name—the *Observer's Handbook*—and it has been published annually ever since.

Each year some 12 000 copies of the *Handbook* are distributed to many countries throughout the world, to amateur and professional astronomers, to educators at school and university levels, and to many observatories, planetaria and libraries. The *Handbook* is the main source of income for The Royal Astronomical Society of Canada. Since the first edition in 1907, the various *Handbook* Editors, Assistant Editors, and Contributors (see the inside front cover) have voluntarily contributed their time and expertise to produce this unusual book.

EDITORS OF THE OBSERVER'S HANDBOOK

		Position	Editions	President RASC
C. A. Chant	(1865–1956)	Editor	1907–1957	1903–1907
Frank Hogg	(1904–1951)	Assistant Editor	1939–1951	1940–1942
Ruth Northcott	(1913–1969)	Assistant Editor	1952–1957	1962–1964
		Editor	1958–1970	
John Percy	(1941–	Editor	1971–1981	1978–1980
Roy Bishop	(1939–	Editor	1982–2000	1984–1986
Rajiv Gupta	(1958–	Editor	2001–	

The *Observer's Handbook* is intended to be "a companion which the observer would wish always to have in his pocket or on the table before him."

C. A. Chant, Toronto, 1906

"We believe that the *Observer's Handbook* is a truly significant contribution that Canadian astronomy in general and our Society in particular has been making to the dissemination of astronomical knowledge for half a century. I trust that it will still occupy the same position of respect after the first hundred years."

Ruth Northcott, Ottawa, 1964

"The more one knows, the more one can benefit from the *Handbook*. It inspires all who leaf through its pages to learn and question what the tables, graphs and data mean, perhaps to speculate on the mysteries of the Universe, and above all, to get out and look beyond our world. You have in your hands a key to the Universe—a key which will fit many doors. Please use it well and treasure it."

Peter Broughton, Toronto, 1992
Author of: *Looking Up, A History of the RASC*

"The *Observer's Handbook* is the single most useful publication for the observational astronomer. Its combination of authoritative data, informative diagrams, and concise text is unique. Anyone interested in astronomy, beginner or expert, amateur or professional, student or teacher, will find the *Observer's Handbook* indispensable. Its international reputation for quality is a credit both to its many contributors and to Canadian astronomy."

Roy Bishop, Halifax, 2000

HOW TO USE THIS HANDBOOK

This Handbook is high-density synopsis of the observer's sky in 2001. By reading the following key points, you will allow yourself to reap maximum benefit from it.

(1) The Handbook is composed of various *sections*. Related sections are grouped into chapters, as listed in the CONTENTS. Chapter titles are given in large dark-grey boxes and section titles against light background shades, both of which extend into the outside margin of the page. The section title and chapter title are given in headers at the top of the pages. These identifiers are meant to facilitate the quick location of desired material.

(2) References to other sections are given in SMALL CAPITAL TYPE, and this type is generally reserved for this purpose. Page numbers are included when relevant. Internet email addresses and web sites are also given in a **distinctive font**. A SELECTED INDEX OF WEB ADDRESSESS is given on p. 287.

(3) The INDEX at the back contains a short listing of keywords.

(4) Long tables are broken into blocks, either with the insertion of horizontal spaces between lines or the shading of blocks of rows, to facilitate location of entries. Every table has a shaded header with the titles of the various columns given in **bold**. Detailed explanation of the meaning of the columns is usually given in accompanying text.

(5) SI symbols and abbreviations are used throughout. See pp. 24 and 27 in the section SOME ASTRONOMICAL AND PHYSICAL DATA for the most common abbreviations. The letter "m" is used to denote both minutes of right ascension and metres; the meaning will be clear from the context. Minutes of time are usually abbreviated "min."

(6) The time scale Universal Time is generally used. Times of day are generally given in the 24-hour clock, using numerals separated by colons. The section TIME AND TIME SCALES on pp. 30–34 explains the various time scales used in astronomy.

(7) The section TERMINOLOGY AND SYMBOLS on p. 17 lists Greek letters (and other symbols) and defines some basic terms.

(8) The section TEACHING AND THE OBSERVER'S HANDBOOK on pp. 14–16 gives an overview of the contents of this Handbook.

Acknowledgements

In addition to the 36 contributors listed on the inside front cover, several other individuals and organizations played a role in the production of this Handbook.

Much of the data contained herein comes from the publications *Astronomical Phenomena for the Year 2001* and *The Astronomical Almanac 2001*, both prepared jointly by the U.S. Naval Observatory's Nautical Almanac Office and Her Majesty's Nautical Almanac Office. Also, the Bureau des Longitudes in Paris provided ephemerides for Jupiler's Galilean satellites.

The Editor would like to express gratitude to his spouse, Anuradha Nayar, for her patience and support during the rather intense production period. Patrice Scattolin provided several detailed and helpful comments. Mark Bratton, David Lane, Richard Langley, and Mary Lou Whitehorne also provided corrections and suggestions.

Particular thanks is extended to Betty Robinson for her expert proofreading. The advice of an amiable and capable professional makes the undertakings of an amateur considerably easier and also more rewarding and enjoyable.

EDITOR'S COMMENTS

I have long regarded the *Observer's Handbook* as the most important tangible contribution the Royal Astronomical Society of Canada makes to the astronomical community. I, along with most members of the Society, held its previous Editor, Roy Bishop, in awe. For 19 years, longer than I had been a member, he had tirelessly edited our *Handbook*, a concise and authoritative observer's companion that had become the most important publication of its type worldwide. When Dr. Bishop announced his retirement last fall, I was very surprised and honoured when the Nominating Committee of the Society asked me to become his successor. The position *Editor of the Observer's Handbook* carries with it a great deal of responsibility, and it involves a tremendous amount of work. My passion for my hobby runs too deep for me to have declined; thus, I have, somehow, become the 5th Editor of the *Observer's Handbook* in its 93rd year of publication.

True to the form he practised as Editor, Dr. Bishop provided invaluable assistance as I assumed my new role. He not only left me with impeccable content and a host of reliable, knowledgeable contributors (not the least of whom was himself—see the inside front cover), but also provided a detailed "how to" manual. I merely had to follow the recipe that Roy had perfected over his long tenure, with a few modifications to the method of assembly (notably the use of current digital technology).

The *Observer's Handbook 2001* is very similar in content to its recent second-millenium cousins. Updates have been made as required; in particular, the sections dealing with eclipses and planets have been significantly expanded over the 2000 edition to reflect the (more interesting) circumstances in 2001.

The new sections in this edition are the one to the left, an attempt to help readers get the most from the *Handbook*, and the index of web addresses on p. 287. I hope that readers will find these additions useful.

Working on this edition has taught me a great deal about astronomy, desktop publishing, style, and grammar. It has been a most enriching experience, and I look forward to the continuing education that future editions will provide.

Rajiv Gupta, Vancouver, 2000 August 26
gupta@interchange.ubc.ca

Cover photo

The Pleiades cluster is one of the most prominent astronomical objects. Its allure makes for a rich presence in literature, mythology, and art, and it also receives an inordinate amount of attention from both amateur and professional astronomers. Excluding this caption, the Pleiades or its components are mentioned in no fewer than six sections of this Handbook. This 2001 Handbook is indeed "full of stars," not to mention nebulae, moons, planets, asteroids, meteors, comets, galaxies...

The photo was taken by the Editor using a 130-mm f/6 refractor. Three separate medium-format exposures, two on black-and-white film and one on colour film, were digitally combined. Further details and a full-size version of the photograph appear in the award winning RASC Observer's Calendar, *which may be purchased by contacting the RASC.*

AN INVITATION FOR MEMBERSHIP IN
THE ROYAL ASTRONOMICAL SOCIETY OF CANADA

The beginnings of The Royal Astronomical Society of Canada go back to the middle of the nineteenth century. The Society was incorporated within the province of Ontario in 1890, received its Royal Charter from King Edward VII in 1903, and was federally incorporated in 1968. The National Office of the Society (containing the business office and library) is located at 136 Dupont Street, Toronto, ON, M5R 1V2, phone: (416) 924-7973 or (888) 924-7272 from within Canada, email: rasc@rasc.ca, web site: http://www.rasc.ca.

The RASC consists of two employees, the Society's Executive Secretary Bonnie Bird and Membership and Publications Coordinator Isaac McGillis, plus more than 4200 members. RASC members are from many countries and from all walks of life. Members receive the *Observer's Handbook* (published in September for the next calendar year) and the bimonthly *Journal of the RASC*, which contains review articles, research papers on historical and contemporary topics, education notes, general notes of astronomical interest, book reviews, news items concerning the Society and its Centres, informal articles, and letters. Also included in a membership is Canada's popular bimonthly astronomy magazine *SkyNews*.

Membership fees are $40 per year, or $25 for persons under 21 years of age. Life membership is $800. (To cover higher mailing costs, these figures are to be read as U.S. dollars for members outside of Canada.) An applicant may affiliate with one of the Centres of the Society across Canada or join the Society directly as an unattached member (some Centres levy a surcharge above the regular membership fee).

Mailing, email, and web site addresses of the 25 RASC Centres in Canada, listed in the order that the stars rise, are given below.

St. John's: c/o 206 Frecker Drive, St John's NF A1E 5H9, randy@morgan.ucs.mun.ca, http://www.rasc.ca/stjohns

Charlottetown: 38 Mt Edward Road, Charlottetown PE C1A 5S2, cperryphoto@pei.sympatica.ca, http://www.rasc.ca/charlottetown

Halifax: P.O. Box 31011, Halifax NS B3K, halifax@rasc.ca, http://halifax.rasc.ca

Moncton: 66 Meadowbank Avenue, Saint John NB E2K 2C6, bordagea@nbnet.nb.ca

Québec: 2000 boul. Montmorency, Québec QC G1J 5E7, srac_quebec@hotmail.com, http://www.rasc.ca/quebec

Montréal: (Centre Francophone) C.P. 206, Station St-Michel, Montréal QC H2A 3L9, sam@cam.org, http://www.rasc.ca/montrealf

Montreal: P.O. Box 1752, Station B, Montreal QC H3B 3L3, rascmtl@altavista.net, http://www.rasc.ca/montreal

Ottawa: P.O. Box 33012, 1974 Baseline Rd., Nepean ON K2C 0E0, afraser@magma.ca, http://ottawa.rasc.ca

Kingston: P.O. Box 1793, Kingston ON K7L 5J6, rascexec@cliff.path.queensu.ca, http://www.rasc.ca/kingston

Niagara: P.O. Box 4040, St. Catharines ON L2R 7S3, jvandwil@vaxxine.com or rascniag@vaxxine.com, http://www.rasc.ca/niagara

Toronto: c/o Ontario Science Centre, 770 Don Mills Road, Don Mills ON M3C 1T3, http://www.rasc.ca/toronto

Hamilton: P.O. Box 1223, Waterdown ON L0R 2H0, http://www.rasc.ca/hamilton

Kitchener-Waterloo: 157 Thornberry Lane, Waterloo ON N2T 2C8, neil@mitra.com, http://kw.rasc.ca

London: P.O. Box 842, Station B, London ON N6A 4Z3, pjedicke@fanshawec.on.ca, http://www.rasc.ca/london

Sarnia: c/o Jim Selinger, 160 George St., Sarnia ON N7T 7V4, jselinge@mnsi.net, http://www.rasc.ca/sarnia

Windsor: c/o Frank J. Shepley, 671 Inman Sideroad, RR #2, Ruthven ON N0P 2G0, fshepley@wincom.net, http://www.rasc.ca/windsor

Thunder Bay: 286 Trinity Crescent, Thunder Bay ON P7C 5V6, http://www.rasc.ca/thunderbay

Winnipeg: P.O. Box 2694, Winnipeg MB R3C 4B3, http://winnipeg.rasc.ca

Regina: P.O. Box 20014, Cornwall Centre, Regina SK S4P 4J7, http://www.rasc.ca/regina

Saskatoon: P.O. Box 317, RPO University, Saskatoon SK S7N 4J8, keser@duke.usask.ca, http://www.rasc.ca/saskatoon

Edmonton: c/o Edmonton Space & Sciences Centre, 11211-142 St., Edmonton AB T5M 4A1, rascedm@worldgate.com, http://www.rasc.ca/edmonton

Calgary: c/o Calgary Science Centre, P.O. Box 2100, Station M, Loc.#73, Calgary AB T2P 2M5, http://www.rasc.ca/calgary

Okanagan: P.O. Box 20119 TCM, Kelowna, BC V1Y 9H2, http://www.rasc.ca/okanagan

Vancouver: c/o Gordon Southam Observatory, 1100 Chestnut St., Vancouver BC V6J 3J9, http://www.rasc.ca/vancouver

Victoria: c/o Bill Almond, 4734 Lisandra Road, Victoria BC V9C 4G1, sbarta@pinc.com, http://www.rasc.ca/victoria

REPORTING OF ASTRONOMICAL DISCOVERIES

To report a possible significant discovery (e.g. a new comet, nova, or supernova), a message should be sent to the International Astronomical Union's Central Bureau for Astronomical Telegrams. Send electronic mail to cbat@cfa.harvard.edu. Messages are monitored at all times. If this preferred method of communication is unavailable, a telephone call may be made to (617) 495-7244 or -7440 or -7444, but telephone calls are discouraged and these numbers will not be answered at all times. Also, a follow-up letter should be sent to the Central Bureau (60 Garden St., Cambridge, MA 02138, USA). Inexperienced observers should have their observation checked before contacting the Central Bureau.

For any new object, specify the date and time of observation, RA and Dec (with epoch), magnitude, and some physical description. For photographic discoveries, confirmation with a second image is highly desirable. In the case of a new comet, the rate of motion in RA and Dec should also be indicated.

Reports may instead be filled out at http://cfa-www.harvard.edu/iau/cbat.html. Recent IAU circulars and subscription information are also available at this web address.

VISITING HOURS AT SOME CANADIAN OBSERVATORIES AND PLANETARIA
By Mary Lou Whitehorne

OBSERVATORIES

Burke-Gaffney Observatory, Saint Mary's University, Halifax NS B3H 3C3. The observatory will be closed during the first half of 2001 due to major renovation of the building that houses the observatory. In the second half of the year, public tours will be held on many Saturday evenings, weather permitting. (902) 496-8257, bgo@ap.stmarys.ca, http://apwww.stmarys.ca/bgo

Canada-France-Hawaii Telescope (CFHT), Mauna Kea, Hawaii, USA. RASC members visiting the "Big Island" of Hawaii may arrange daytime group tours of the CFHT installations by contacting, at least one month in advance, the Canada-France-Hawaii Telescope Corporation, either by letter (CFHT Corp., P.O. Box 1597, Kamuela, HI 96743, USA) or by telephone ((808) 885-7944). username@cfht.hawaii.edu, http://www.cfht.hawaii.edu

David Dunlap Observatory (DDO), Box 360, Richmond Hill ON L4C 4Y6. Wednesday mornings throughout the school year, 10 a.m.; Saturday evenings, April–October; Friday evenings, June–October. Call or visit web site for information on tour times and dates. (905) 884-2112, http://ddo.astro.utoronto.ca

Dominion Radio Astrophysical Observatory, Penticton BC V2A 6K3. Conducted Tours: Sundays, July and August only, 2 to 5 pm. Visitors' Centre: Open every day April 1 to October 15, 10 am to 5 pm. Open weekdays only October 16 to March 14. (250) 490-4355, http://www.drao.nrc.ca

Gordon MacMillan Southam Observatory, 1100 Chestnut St., Vancouver BC V6J 3J9. Open Fri. and Sat., 7 to 11 p.m., weather and volunteer staff permitting. Extended hours during school holidays. 150-mm refractor for H-alpha solar views, 0.5-m reflector. (604) 738-STAR, ddodge@hrmacmillanspacecentre.com, http://hrmacmillanspacecentre.com

Helen Sawyer Hogg Observatory, National Museum of Science & Technology, P.O. Box 9724, Stn. T, 1867 St. Laurent Blvd., Ottawa ON K1G 5A3. 380-mm refractor (from the Dominion Observatory) and Starlab Planetarium. "Discover the Universe" public visits by appointment only and group tours Monday to Thursday from October to May, rain or shine. Reservations: (613) 991-9219, http://www.science-tech.nmstc.ca

Herzberg Institute of Astrophysics (National Research Council of Canada), 5071 West Saanich Road, Victoria BC V8X 4M6. May–August: Daily 9:15 a.m. to 4:30 p.m.; September–April: Monday–Friday 9:15 a.m. to 4:30 p.m. Public observing, Saturday evenings, April–October inclusive, 7:00 to 11:00 p.m. Visits: (250) 363-0030, school tours: (250) 363-0012, office: (250) 363-0001, http://www.hia.nrc.ca, http://scienceweb.hia.nrc.ca

Hume Cronyn Observatory, Department of Physics and Astronomy, The University of Western Ontario, London ON N6A 3K7. Summer Open Houses (slide show and viewing with a 250-mm refractor) are held Saturdays in June, July and August 8:30 to 11:00 p.m. A winter public program is available to groups and individuals by appointment. (519) 661-3183, http://phobos.astro.uwo.ca

Ken Odaisky Memorial Observatory, Sudbury Astronomy Club, Suite M250, 800 Lasalle Blvd., Sudbury ON P3A 4V4. Free private and group tours through the observatory, housing a 150-mm refractor. April through October. Reservations: Karen or Garry Lalonde, (705) 858-4343, garry@cyberbeach.net, http://ww2.isys.ca/astroclub

Observatoire astronomique du mont Mégantic, Notre-Dame-des-Bois QC J0B 2E0. An interpretation centre, ASTROLab du Parc du mont Mégantic, with an exhibition hall, a multimedia show, observing nights with 35-cm and 60-cm telescopes, is open daily to the public during the summer (May–September), and on weekends during spring and fall. Inquire for updates about the schedule and for reservations (required for observations). Information: (514) 343-6718, observatory: (819) 888-2941, fax: (819) 888-2943, astrolab@interlinx.qc.ca, http://astrolab.qc.ca

Prince George Astronomical Society Observatory, c/o 3330 22nd Ave., Prince George BC V2N 1P8. 610-mm Cassegrain telescope. Public viewing Fridays 8 p.m. to midnight from March–May and August–October. Group tours available. (250) 964-3600, http://www.pgweb.com/astronomical, nelson@cnc.bc.ca

Science North Solar Observatory, 100 Ramsey Lake Road, Sudbury ON P3E 5S9. Two heliostats provide viewing of the Sun in hydrogen-alpha and white light in a darkened theatre where a multi-media interpretation of the Sun is also presented. Open every day except Dec. 24, 25, 26 and Jan. 1. (705) 522-3701, http://sciencenorth.on.ca/astrosphere.html

University of British Columbia Observatory, 2219 Main Mall, Vancouver BC V6T 1Z4. Free public observing on clear Saturday evenings: (604) 822-6186, tours: (604) 822-2267, fax: (604) 822-6047, http://www.astro.ubc.ca

University of Saskatchewan Observatory, c/o Dept. of Physics & Engineering Physics, 116 Science Place, Saskatoon SK S7N 5E2. Public viewing on Saturday evenings. (306) 966-6429

York University Observatory, Dept. of Physics and Astronomy, 4700 Keele St., Toronto ON, M3J 1P3. Tours are run all year, each Wednesday, rain or shine, and for special events. Use the Steeles entrance of York University, in the Petrie Science Building. Hours vary depending on the season. (416) 736-2100 Ext. 77773, http://www.astro.yorku.ca/observatory

PLANETARIA

Calgary Science Centre, 701-11 Street SW. Mailing address: P.O. Box 2100, Station M, Calgary AB T2P 2M5. Features Discovery Dome, with Canada's only Digistar projector and Super-70-mm dome movies. Program and sky information: (403) 221-3700, fax: (403) 237-0186, http://www.calgaryscience.ca, discover@calgaryscience.ca

Doran Planetarium, Laurentian University, Ramsey Lake Road, Sudbury ON P3E 2C6. Shows in English and French. Information: (705) 675-1151, group reservations: ext. 2227, fax: (705) 675-4868, plegault@nickel.laurentian.ca, http://www.laurentian.ca/www/physics/Planetarium/Planetarium.html

Edmonton Space & Science Centre, Coronation Park, 11211-142 Street, Edmonton AB T5M 4A1. Features Margaret Zeidler Star Theatre, IMAX ® Theatre, public observatory and exhibit galleries, Science Magic gift shop featuring telescopes. Advance ticket sales: (780) 451-3344, program information: (780) 451-3344, recorded astronomy information: (780) 493-9000/4254, gift shop: (780) 452-9100, http://www.edmontonscience.com

The Halifax Planetarium, The Nova Scotia Museum of Natural History, 1747 Summer St., Halifax NS B3H 3A6. Public shows are no longer offered. School classes are booked through a lottery system each September and January. (902) 424-6512, http://www.ednet.ns.ca/educ./museum/

H. R. MacMillan Space Centre, 1100 Chestnut St., Vancouver BC V6J 3J9. Open daily July and August; otherwise open Tues.–Sun. and holidays (except Christmas). Star theatre, motion simulator, exhibit gallery, multi-media theatre. (604) 738-STAR (738-7827), fax: (604) 736-5665, lKomori@hrmacmillanspacecentre.com, http://hrmacmillanspacecentre.com

The Lockhart Planetarium, 394 University College, 220 Dysart Road, The University of Manitoba, Winnipeg MB R3T 2M8. Group reservations and public show schedule: (204) 474-9785

Manitoba Planetarium, 190 Rupert Ave. at Main St., Winnipeg MB R3B 0N2. Victoria Day to Labour Day shows daily. Rest of year: Tuesday to Sunday and holidays, closed Mondays. The Planetarium is part of the Manitoba Museum of Man and Nature, which includes a Science Centre as well as a Starlab mobile planetarium program. The Museum Shop carries science books for all ages. Planetarium show times: (204) 943-3139, inquiries: (204) 988-0615, general: (204) 956-2830, fax: (204) 942-3679, info@manitobamuseum.mb.ca, http://www.manitobamuseum.mb.ca

Ontario Science Centre, 770 Don Mills Road, Toronto ON M3C 1T3. Open every day except December 25. Live planetarium shows daily. (416) 696-3127, http://www.osc.on.ca

Planétarium de Montréal, 1000 St. Jacques St. W., Montreal PQ H3C 1G7. Live shows in French and in English every open day. (514) 872-4530, fax: (514) 872-8102, http://www.planetarium.montreal.qc.ca

Royal Ontario Museum, Education Department, 100 Queen's Park, Toronto, Ontario M5S 2C6. Operates three mobile planetariums for "Travelling Stars" educational programs both at the Museum and in the community. Topics from grades K–13 cover basic astronomy to the astronomy of ancient civilizations, complementing Ontario school curriculum, and are presented by trained astronomy teachers. (416) 586-5801, fax: (416) 586-5807, schoolv@rom.on.ca, http://www.rom.on.ca/schools

Solar Wind Portable Planetarium, Toronto, ON, offers curriculum-based presentations. For information: Kathy McWatters, (416) 221-7375. solar.wind@pathcom.com

W. J. McCallion Planetarium, Department of Physics and Astronomy, McMaster University, 1280 Main Street West, Hamilton ON L8S 4M1. (905) 525-9140, ext. 27777, fax: (905) 546-1252, http://physun.physics.mcmaster.ca/institutes/fs3_institutes.html

The Night Sky with its beautiful stars
and its message of our place in the Universe
is a precious treasure of all humanity,
on which we rely for our knowledge and understanding
of our origins and destiny.†

† The International Astronomical Union, Exposition on Adverse Environmental Impacts on Astronomy, Paris, 1992 [I.A.U. Information Bulletin 69, January 1993, p. 10].

RECOMMENDED READING AND ATLASES

Astronomy, a popular, non-technical, monthly magazine for amateur astronomers (phone: (800) 446-5489, fax: (414) 796-0126).

The Backyard Astronomer's Guide†, by Terence Dickinson and Alan Dyer. Firefly Books (Canada: (800) 387-6192, United States: (800) 387-5085), 1991. The best guide to equipment and techniques for amateur astronomers, by two experienced observers.

Catalogue of the Astronomical Society of the Pacific (A.S.P., 390 Ashton Ave., San Francisco, CA 94112, USA, 415-337-2624), an excellent source of astronomical educational resources such as books, slides, videos, globes, posters, software, teacher's classroom activity guides and more.

Catalogue of Sky Publishing Corporation†, a good source of astronomical books, atlases, globes, slide sets, software, and posters.

Exploring the Night Sky, by Terence Dickinson. Firefly Books (see above), 1987. A guide to stargazing, recommended for children.†

The Guide To Amateur Astronomy† (2nd edition), by Jack Newton and Philip Teece. Cambridge University Press, Cambridge, 1995. A valuable introduction to many diverse aspects of amateur astronomy.

Nightwatch† (3rd edition), by Terence Dickinson. Firefly Books (see above), 1998. An excellent, introductory observing guide.

SkyNews, the (bimonthly) Canadian magazine of astronomy & stargazing. Send $24 Cdn ($31 Cdn outside Canada) to: SkyNews, P. O. Box 2050, Stn LCD Malton, Mississauga, ON L4T 9Z9; by credit card call (800) 267-3999.

Starlight Nights†, by Leslie Peltier (1900–1980), 1965. Sky Publishing Corporation. Anyone who enjoys the night sky should read this book.

Sky & Telescope†, a monthly magazine widely read by both amateur and professional astronomers (phone: (800) 253-0245, fax: (617) 864- 6117).

Atlas of the Moon†, by Antonín Rükl. Kalmbach Books, Waukesha, 1992, or Hamlyn Publishing, London, 1991. A first-rate lunar atlas for amateur astronomers.

Bright Star Atlas 2000.0†, by Wil Tirion. Contains 9000 stars to magnitude 6.5 and 600 clusters, nebulae and galaxies on 10 charts.

Sky Atlas 2000.0† (2nd edition), by Wil Tirion and Roger Sinnott, 1998. Large format and well done. Contains 81 000 stars to magnitude 8.5 and 2700 clusters, nebulae and galaxies on 26 charts.

Uranometria 2000.0†, by W. Tirion, B. Rappaport, and G. Lovi. A comprehensive star atlas. Volume 1 covers the northern sky to declination $-6°$. Volume 2 covers the southern sky to declination $+6°$. Contains 332 000 stars to magnitude 9.5 and more than 10 000 clusters, nebulae and galaxies on 473 charts.

Millennium Star Atlas†, by R. Sinnott and M. Perryman. A recent sky atlas based on data from the European Space Agency's HIPPARCOS satellite. Three volumes, each covering 8 hours in RA. Contains more than 1 000 000 stars to magnitude 11 and more than 10 000 clusters, nebulae and galaxies on 1548 charts.

Computer-based Planetarium Programs: Several are available, for example, *ECU* (Earth Centered Universe), *Redshift 3*, *TheSky*, *Voyager II*, *Starry Night Deluxe*. For information on the last four, see the two catalogues listed above; for *ECU* see the web site http://www.nova-astro.com.

† Available from Sky Publishing Corp., 49 Bay State Rd., Cambridge MA 02138-1200, USA; (800) 253-0245, http://www.skypub.com.

TEACHING AND THE OBSERVER'S HANDBOOK
BY JOHN R. PERCY

You are holding in your hand a valuable resource for teaching astronomy. Every user of this Handbook, whether amateur or professional astronomer or teacher in any setting, at any level, can contribute to education in astronomy. Partnerships and coalitions between scientists and educators are especially effective and enjoyable.

As a result of curriculum renewal in Canada, the United States, and other countries, astronomy is now taught in many elementary and secondary schools; see *JRASC*, *92*, 38, February 1998.

In the United States, the National Science Foundation has an annual education budget of over half a billion dollars, and some of this has been used to develop curriculum, activities and materials for the teaching of astronomy. Some of these are listed at the end of this article: the *Project STAR* text and materials and *The Universe at Your Fingertips*, all of which have been carefully researched and tested.

The Night Sky

Teachers should make sure that their students are aware of what can be seen in the night sky, even though "the stars come out at night, but the students don't." THE SKY MONTH BY MONTH section of this Handbook (pp. 56–81) provides an excellent guide. Star charts can be found in many books and magazines (see Resources on p. 16) as well as in the section MAPS OF THE NIGHT SKY (pp. 276–283). (Study the first page of this section to get the most out of these maps.) Make sketches, including the horizon and compass points, to record the appearance and changes of the sky.

Night and Day, Seasons, and the Phases of the Moon

These basic astronomical concepts are misunderstood by most people, as many surveys have found. One of the common misconceptions about the seasons is that it is hottest in the summer because of the shape of Earth's orbit—we are closest to the Sun in the summer. But does this explain why the seasons are reversed in the Southern Hemisphere? Even those who "know" that the seasons are due to "the tilt of Earth's axis" may think that, because of the tilt, the hemispheres are closer to the Sun during their respective summers.

Other misconceptions relate to a lack of knowledge of the scale of the solar system. Assuming a high speed that we are familiar with, say that of a commercial jet plane, how long would it take to travel to the Moon? To the Sun? If a beach ball represents the Sun, the solar system fits in your town, but the next nearest star is another beach ball on the opposite side of Earth! The sections BASIC DATA (pp. 18–29), THE BRIGHTEST STARS (pp. 220–230), and THE NEAREST STARS (pp. 231–235) are useful references for constructing such models.

Here is an example of a useful "hands-on" activity: choose a day when the Sun and Moon are both visible in the sky (in the afternoon when the Moon is near first quarter or in the morning when the Moon is near last quarter—see THE SKY MONTH BY MONTH section). Hold a ball in your hand so that the Sun shines on it, and extend it toward the Moon. You will see the ball and the Moon illuminated by the Sun in the *same* way—a clear demonstration that the Moon is a spherical, non-luminous body floating in space.

These concepts are so basic that it is worth teaching them correctly, that is monitoring the students' preconceptions through interviews and discussions, and being absolutely sure that they understand the concepts and can explain them from their understanding—not just from memorization.

The Sun

(1) Track the path of the Sun in the sky during one day and over successive days and weeks. This may be done safely and simply by using the shadow of a pole (or a student). Sunrise/sunset data and the changing position of the Sun in the heavens are given in THE SUN section of this Handbook (pp. 90–92 and p. 83, respectively).

(2) Project an image of the Sun on a sheet of white cardboard, using binoculars or a small telescope. Observe sunspots, and watch the Sun rotate from day to day. Practise setting up such a demonstration ahead of time. Once you get the hang of it, it can be set up very quickly. **Warning**: Never observe the Sun directly, especially not by looking through binoculars or a telescope. Permanent eye damage could result. When projecting a solar image, use a barrier to prevent anyone from looking directly into the light beam. See the sections FILTERS (pp. 48–50) and VIEWING A SOLAR ECLIPSE—A WARNING (p. 143) in this Handbook.

The Moon

(1) Keep a "Moon journal": Observe and record where the Moon is, what shape it is, when it rises and sets. Note how these variables change over several days and weeks. (Don't forget that the Moon is often visible in daytime.)

(2) Draw the general appearance of the Moon's surface as seen with your naked eye. Many features, including the regions of the Apollo landing sites, can be identified using the MAP OF MOON on pp. 96–97. A film or video of one of the Apollo missions is worth showing to a class.

(3) Eclipses: a three-dimensional model, to the correct scale, is a great aid in explaining eclipses and why there is not an eclipse every two weeks. See the ECLIPSES DURING 2001 section in this Handbook (pp. 115–138) for information on eclipses that may be visible from your locality this year.

(4) If ocean tides occur in your area, correlate the times and the range of the tide with the Moon's position in your sky, its phases and distances. Lunar phases, perigees, and apogees are tabulated in THE SKY MONTH BY MONTH section, and an overview of tides appears in the TIDES AND THE EARTH–MOON SYSTEM article in this Handbook (pp. 159–161).

The Planets

(1) Nothing can stimulate students' interest like direct experience, so observe the planets when they are visible! See THE SKY MONTH BY MONTH and PLANETS sections (pp. 162–181 for the latter) for the visibility of the planets during the year.

(2) Develop an awareness of Earth as a planet. Study photographs of Earth from space. For a "hands-on" experience, place an Earth globe in sunlight with its north pole oriented northward. Then rotate and tilt the globe so your locality is at the "top" of the globe (the globe will then be oriented the same way in space as is planet Earth). The regions on Earth where the Sun is rising or setting at that moment will be apparent. Note which pole is experiencing 24 hours of daylight. Slowly turn the globe eastward about its axis to show a sped-up day/night progression.

(3) Use slides, films, videos, and posters to capture the excitement of planetary exploration (see the catalogues in RECOMMENDED READING AND ATLASES on p. 13).

Comets and Asteroids

These are interesting topics, especially as it now appears that collisions between these objects and Earth may explain the extinctions of species such as dinosaurs. Use the section METEORITE IMPACT CRATERS OF NORTH AMERICA (pp. 207–210) to have students locate nearby impact craters on geographical maps. See THE BRIGHTEST ASTEROIDS (p. 193) for a finder chart to locate a bright asteroid in the night sky (only binoculars are needed). There is a classic demonstration of "Creating a Comet" (out of dry ice and sand) described at http://www.noao.edu/education/crecipe.html.

Is a Telescope Necessary?

Binoculars and telescopes can be useful but are not essential; much interesting astronomy can be done with the unaided eye. However, binoculars are often available and should be used when helpful. See the section BINOCULARS (pp. 43–47) for a guide to their selection and use. The inexpensive, make-it-yourself *Project STAR* telescopes are highly recommended. See TELESCOPE PARAMETERS (p. 39) and TELESCOPE EXIT PUPILS (pp. 40–43) for a summary of some quantitative aspects of telescopes.

Resources

In addition to the list of reading material that follows, you may be able to make use of the following:

(1) See the VISITING HOURS AT SOME CANADIAN OBSERVATORIES AND PLANETARIA article in this Handbook (pp. 10–12). Take your students to visit one of these.

(2) The Royal Astronomical Society of Canada is the largest organization of amateur astronomers in Canada. Their 25 branches across Canada (see the section AN INVITATION FOR MEMBERSHIP IN THE ROYAL ASTRONOMICAL SOCIETY OF CANADA on pp. 8–9) present a wide variety of activities that might be interesting to you and your students. A member of the RASC might be willing to visit your class and demonstrate a telescope. The Astronomical Society of the Pacific's *Project ASTRO Manual* can facilitate such visits. See http://www.aspsky.org/project_astro.html.

*Astro Adventures: An Activity-Based Astronomy Curriculu*m, by Dennis Schatz and D. Cooper. Pacific Science Center, 200 2nd Ave. N., Seattle WA 93109-4895, USA.

Astronomical Society of the Pacific, 390 Ashton Ave., San Francisco CA 94112, USA. In addition to their excellent astronomical slides and other such material (send for their catalogue), the ASP publishes a free quarterly teachers' newsletter; to order it, write on your school letterhead, or download current and back issues from http://www.aspsky.org.

Astronomy Adventures (Ranger Rick's NatureScope). National Wildlife Federation, 1412 16th St. NW, Washington DC, USA. Excellent fun activities for younger children in schools or youth groups. *Project SPICA: A Teacher Resource to Enhance Astronomy Educatio*n, edited by N. Butcher Ball et al. Kendall/Hunt Publishing Co. 1994. An excellent compilation of activity and resources for teaching grades 3–12.

*Project STAR Textboo*k. Kendall/Hunt Publishing Co. 1993. See also http://www.learner.org/teacherslab/pup/.

Project STAR Hands-on Science Materials: Learning Technologies, Inc., 40 Cameron Ave., Somerville MA 02144, USA, (800) 537-8703; http://www.starlab.com. Unique, high-quality, low-cost materials for introducing students (and teachers) to astronomy.

*SkyNew*s, P.O. Box 2050, Stn. LCD Malton, Mississauga, ON L4T 9Z9; (800) 267-3999. Bimonthly. General astronomy from a Canadian perspective.

*The Universe at Your Fingertip*s, and *More Universe at Your Fingertip*s, edited by Andrew Fraknoi et al. Astronomical Society of the Pacific, 390 Ashton Ave., San Francisco CA 94112, USA. Another excellent collection of teaching activities and resources for grades 3–12. See also http://www.aspsky.org/education/astroacts.html.

TERMINOLOGY AND SYMBOLS

COORDINATE SYSTEMS

Astronomical positions are usually measured in a system based on the *celestial poles* and *celestial equator*, the intersections of Earth's rotation axis and equatorial plane, respectively, and the infinite sphere of the sky. *Right ascension* (RA or α) is measured in hours (h), minutes (m), and seconds (s) of time, eastward along the celestial equator from the vernal equinox (see below). *Declination* (Dec or δ) is measured in degrees (°), minutes ('), and seconds (") of arc, northward (N or +) or southward (S or −) from the celestial equator toward the N or S celestial pole.

Positions can also be measured in a system based on the *ecliptic*, the intersection of Earth's orbital plane and the infinite sphere of the sky. The Sun appears to move eastward along the ecliptic during the year. *Longitude* is measured eastward along the ecliptic from the vernal equinox; *latitude* is measured at right angles to the ecliptic, northward or southward toward the north or south ecliptic pole. The *vernal equinox* is one of the two intersections of the ecliptic and the celestial equator; it is the one at which the Sun crosses the celestial equator moving from south to north.

Two objects are in conjunction if they have the same longitude or RA, and are in opposition if they have longitudes or RAs that differ by 180°. If the second object is not specified, it is assumed to be the Sun. For example, a planet is "in conjunction" if it has the same longitude as the Sun and two objects other than the Sun are in conjunction if they have the same RA. Mercury and Venus are at superior conjunction when they are more distant than the Sun and at inferior conjunction when they are nearer than the Sun (see the diagram on p. 163).

If an object crosses the ecliptic moving northward, it is at the ascending node of its orbit; if it crosses the ecliptic moving southward, it is at the descending node.

Elongation is the geocentric angle between a planet and the Sun, or between a satellite and its primary, measured in the plane formed by Earth and the other two bodies.

SYMBOLS

Sun, Moon, and Planets

☉	Sun	☾	Last Quarter	⊕	Earth	♅	Uranus
●	New Moon	☾	Moon generally	♂	Mars	♆	Neptune
☺	Full Moon	☿	Mercury	♃	Jupiter	♇	Pluto
☽	First Quarter	♀	Venus	♄	Saturn		

Signs of the Zodiac

♈	Aries....................0°	♌	Leo.................120°	♐	Sagittarius.......240°
♉	Taurus................30°	♍	Virgo...............150°	♑	Capricornus.....270°
♊	Gemini..............60°	♎	Libra................180°	♒	Aquarius..........300°
♋	Cancer...............90°	♏	Scorpius..........210°	♓	Pisces..............330°

The Greek Alphabet

A, α......Alpha	H, η......Eta	N, ν.......Nu	T, τ.......Tau
B, β.......Beta	Θ, θ, ϑ..Theta	Ξ, ξ.......Xi	Y, υ......Upsilon
Γ, γ.......Gamma	I, ι.........Iota	O, o......Omicron	Φ, ϕ......Phi
Δ, δ.......Delta	K, κ......Kappa	Π, π......Pi	X, χ......Chi
E, ε.......Epsilon	Λ, λ.......Lambda	P, ρ.......Rho	Ψ, ψ......Psi
Z, ζ.......Zeta	M, μ......Mu	Σ, σ.......Sigma	Ω, ω......Omega

BASIC DATA

PRINCIPAL ELEMENTS OF THE SOLAR SYSTEM

MEAN ORBITAL ELEMENTS
for Epoch J2000.0 = JD 245 1545.0 = 2000 January 1.5

Planet	Mean Distance from Sun (a)		Period of Revolution		Eccen-tricity (e)	Incli-nation (i)	Long. of Asc. Node (W)	Long. of Peri-helion ($\tilde{\omega}$)	Long. at Epoch (L)
	AU	10^6 km	Sidereal (P)	Syn-odic* (S)					
	a		a		d	°	°	°	°
Mercury	0.387	57.9	0.2408	116	0.206	7.0	48.3	77.5	252.3
Venus	0.723	108.2	0.6152	584	0.007	3.4	76.7	131.6	182.0
Earth	1.000	149.6	1.0000	—	0.017	0.0	—	102.9	100.5
Mars	1.524	227.9	1.8808	780	0.093	1.8	49.6	336.1	355.4
Jupiter	5.203	778.3	11.86	399	0.048	1.3	100.5	14.3	34.4
Saturn	9.555	1429.4	29.42	378	0.056	2.5	113.7	93.1	50.1
Uranus	19.218	2875.0	83.75	370	0.046	0.8	74.0	173.0	314.1
Neptune	30.110	4504.4	163.73	367	0.009	1.8	131.8	48.1	304.3
Pluto	39.545	5915.8	248.03	367	0.249	17.1	110.3	224.1	238.7

These elements are taken from the *Explanatory Supplement to the Astronomical Almanac* and are referred to the mean equinox and ecliptic of J2000.0. Current osculating orbital elements appear on p. E4 of the annual *Astronomical Almanac*.
* Synodic period = (product of *P*'s of two planets) ÷ (difference of the *P*'s). Tabular values are relative to Earth.

PHYSICAL ELEMENTS

Object	Equat. Diam. km	Oblate-ness	Mass Earth=1	Den-sity t/m^3	Grav-ity Earth=1	Escape Speed km/s	Rot'n. Period d	Incl. °	Albedo
Sun	1 392 000	0	332 946.0	1.41	27.9	617.5	25–35*	—	—
Mercury	4 879	0	0.055 274	5.43	0.38	4.2	58.646	0.0	0.11
Venus	12 104	0	0.815 005	5.24	0.90	10.4	243.019	177.4	0.65
Earth	12 756	1/298	1.000 000	5.52	1.00	11.2	0.9973	23.4	0.37
Moon	3 475	0	0.012 300	3.34	0.17	2.4	27.3217	6.7	0.12
Mars	6 794	1/154	0.107 447	3.94	0.38	5.0	1.0260	25.2	0.15
Jupiter	142 980‡	1/15.4	317.833	1.33	2.53	59.5	0.4101†	3.1	0.52
Saturn	120 540‡	1/10.2	95.159	0.70	1.06	35.5	0.4440	25.3	0.47
Uranus	51 120‡	1/43.6	14.500	1.30	0.90	21.3	0.7183	97.9	0.51
Neptune	49 530‡	1/58.5	17.204	1.76	1.14	23.5	0.6712	28.3	0.41
Pluto	2 300	0?	0.0025	1.1	0.08	1.3	6.3872	123.	0.3

The table gives the mean density, the gravity and escape speed *at the equator*, and the inclination of the equator *to the orbital plane*.
* Depending on latitude.
† For the most rapidly rotating part of Jupiter, the equatorial region.
‡ At 1 bar (101.325 kPa).

SATELLITES OF THE PLANETS
BY JOSEPH VEVERKA

Name	Diam. km	Mass[a] Pt	Density t/m³	Visual Mag.	Visual Albedo	Mean Dist. from Planet 10³ km	Mean Dist. from Planet "	Orbital Period d	Eccentricity °	Orbit Incl.[†]	Discovery
Satellite of Earth											
Moon*	3476.	73490. (70)	3.34	−12.7	0.11	384.5	—	27.322	0.055	18–29.	—
Satellites of Mars											
I Phobos*	21.	0.013 (0.002)	≈2.	11.6	0.07	9.4	25.	0.319	0.015	1.1	A. Hall, 1877
II Deimos*	12.	0.0018 (0.0002)	≈2.	12.7	0.07	23.5	63.	1.263	0.0004	1.8v	A. Hall, 1877
Satellites of Jupiter											
XVI Metis	43.	—	—	17.5	≈0.05	128.	42.	0.294	0.	0.	S. Synnott, 1979
XV Adrastea	16.	—	—	18.7	≈0.05	129.	42.	0.297	0.	—	Jewitt, Danielson, Synnott, 1979
V Amalthea*	167.	—	—	14.1	0.05	180.	59.	0.498	0.003	0.4	E. Barnard, 1892
XIV Thebe**	99.	—	—	16.	≈0.05	222.	73.	0.674	0.013	—	S. Synnott, 1979
I Io*[b]	3630.	89200. (400)	3.55	5.	0.6	422.	138.	1.769	0.004	0.	Galileo, 1610
II Europa*[b]	3140.	48700. (500)	3.04	5.3	0.6	671.	220.	3.551	0.01	0.5	Galileo, 1610
III Ganymede*[b]	5260.	149000. (600)	1.93	4.6	0.4	1070.	351.	7.155	0.001	0.2	Galileo, 1610
IV Callisto*	4800.	107500. (400)	1.83	5.6	0.2	1885.	618.	16.689	0.007	0.2	Galileo, 1610
XIII Leda	≈15.	—	—	20.	—	11110.	3640.	240.	0.147	27.	C. Kowal, 1974
VI Himalia***	185.	—	—	14.8	0.03	11470.	3760.	251.	0.158	28.	C. Perrine, 1904
X Lysithea****	≈35.	—	—	18.4	—	11710.	3840.	260.	0.107	29.	S. Nicholson, 1938
VII Elara	75.	—	—	16.8	0.03	11740.	3850.	260.	0.207	28.	C. Perrine, 1905
XII Ananke****	≈30.	—	—	18.9	—	21200.	6954.	631.	0.17	147.	S. Nicholson, 1951
XI Carme	≈40.	—	—	18.	—	22350.	7330.	692.	0.21	164.	S. Nicholson, 1938
VIII Pasiphae	≈50.	—	—	17.1	—	23330.	7650.	735.	0.38	148.	P. Melotte, 1908
IX Sinope***	≈35.	—	—	18.3	—	23370.	7660.	758.	0.28	153.	S. Nicholson, 1914
XVII 1999J1	≈10.	—	—	21.0	—	24160.	7920.	768.	0.124	142.	Spahr et al., 1999

Pronunciations of the names of the satellites are given on p. 164.

Visual Magnitude and angular Mean Distance from Planet are at mean opposition distance.

[†] Inclinations of inner satellites (those closer than 100 planetary radii) are relative to the planet's *equator*. As customary, inclinations for outer satellites (J6–J13, J17, S9, U16, U17, U19–U21, N2) are relative to the planet's *orbital plane*. Outer satellite inclinations relative to planet's equator vary due to precession effects. For our Moon, the inclination relative to Earth's orbital plane is 5°; relative to Earth's equator it varies between 18° and 29° in an 18.61-year cycle. A value >90° indicates retrograde motion.

* synchronous motion; ** probably synchronous; *** non-synchronous; **** chaotic motion; (no asterisk) rotation unknown

[a] The numbers in parentheses are possible errors.

[b] Laplace resonance. Longitudes satisfy: $L(\text{Io}) - 3L(\text{Europa}) + 2L(\text{Ganymede}) = 180°$. Also, the mean motions are such that the three periods are nearly 1:2:4.

SATELLITES OF THE PLANETS (continued)

Name	Diam. km	Mass[a] Pt	Density t/m³	Visual Mag.	Visual Albedo	Mean Dist. from Planet 10³ km	"	Orbital Period d	Eccentricity °	Orbit Incl.†	Discovery
Satellites of Saturn											
XVIII Pan[c]	≈20.	—	—	≈19.	≈0.5	134.	22.	0.577	≈0.	≈0.	M. Showalter, 1990
XV Atlas	30.	—	—	≈18.	0.4	137.	23.	0.601	0.002	0.3	R. Terrile, 1980
XVI Prometheus** [d]	100.	—	—	≈15.	0.6	139.	23.	0.613	0.002	0.1	S. Collins, D. Carlson, 1980
XVII Pandora** [d]	90.	—	—	≈16.	0.5	142.	24.	0.628	0.004	0.1	S. Collins, D. Carlson, 1980
X Janus* [e]	190.	—	—	≈14.	0.6	151.	25.	0.695	0.009	0.3	A. Dollfus, 1966
XI Epimetheus* [e]	120.	—	—	≈15.	0.5	151.	25.	0.695	0.007	0.1	J. Fountain, S. Larson, 1966
I Mimas*	390.	38. (1)	1.2	12.5	0.8	187.	30.	0.942	0.02	1.5	W. Herschel, 1789
II Enceladus*	500.	80. (30)	1.1	11.8	1.0	238.	38.	1.37	0.004	0.02	W. Herschel, 1789
III Tethys*	1060.	760. (90)	1.2	10.3	0.8	295.	48.	1.888	0.	1.1	G. Cassini, 1684
XIII Telesto	25.	—	—	≈18.	0.7	295.	48.	1.888[f]	≈0.	≈0.	Smith, Larson, Reitsema, 1980
XIV Calypso**	25.	—	—	≈18.	1.0	295.	48.	1.888[g]	≈0.	≈0.	Pascu, Seidelmann, Baum, Currie, 1980
IV Dione*	1120.	1050. (30)	1.4	10.4	0.6	378.	61.	2.737	0.002	0.02	G. Cassini, 1684
XII Helene	30.	—	—	≈18	0.6	378.	61.	2.737[h]	0.005	0.2	P. Laques, J. Lecacheux, 1980
V Rhea*	1530.	2490. (150)	1.3	9.7	0.6	526.	85.	4.517	0.001	0.4	G. Cassini, 1672
VI Titan**	5550.	134570. (30)	1.88	8.4	0.2	1221.	197.	15.945	0.029	0.3	C. Huygens, 1655
VII Hyperion****	255.	—	—	14.2	0.3	1481.	239.	21.276	0.104	0.4	W. Bond, G. Bond, W. Lassell, 1848
VIII Iapetus*	1460.	1880. (120)	1.2	11.0v	0.08–0.4	3561.	575.	79.331	0.028	14.7	G. Cassini, 1671
IX Phoebe***	220.	—	—	16.5	0.05	12960.	2096.	550.46	0.163	150.	W. Pickering, 1898
Satellites of Uranus											
VI Cordelia[j]	25.[k]	—	—	24.2	<0.1	49.8	3.7	0.333	≈0.	≈0.	Voyager 2, 1986
VII Ophelia[j]	30.[k]	—	—	23.9	<0.1	53.8	4.0	0.375	≈0.	≈0.	Voyager 2, 1986
VIII Bianca	45.[k]	—	—	23.1	<0.1	59.2	4.4	0.433	≈0.	≈0.	Voyager 2, 1986
IX Cressida	65.[k]	—	—	22.3	<0.1	61.8	4.6	0.463	≈0.	≈0.	Voyager 2, 1986

[c] Orbits within the Encke gap.

[d] Prometheus and Pandora are shepherds of the F-ring.

[e] Co-orbital satellites. Horseshoe libration, L(Janus) − L(Epimetheus) ≈180°.

[f] Telesto librates about the trailing (#5) Lagrangian point of Tethys' orbit.

[g] Calypso librates about the trailing (#4) Lagrangian point of Tethys' orbit.

[h] Helene librates about the leading (#4) Lagrangian point of Dione's orbit with a period of ≈790 d.

[i] Titan's cloud-top diameter. Solid-body diameter equals 5150 km.

[j] Cordelia and Ophelia are shepherds of the ε-ring.

[k] Diameter assuming the same albedo (0.07) as Puck.

SATELLITES OF THE PLANETS (continued)

Name	Diam. km	Mass[a] Pt	Density t/m³	Visual Mag.	Visual Albedo	Mean Dist. from Planet 10³ km	"	Orbital Period d	Eccen-tricity °	Orbit Incl.†	Discovery
Satellites of Uranus (continued)											
X Desdemona	60.[k]	—	—	22.5	<0.1	62.6	4.7	0.475	≈0.	≈0.	Voyager 2, 1986
XI Juliet	85.[k]	—	—	21.7	<0.1	64.4	4.9	0.492	≈0.	≈0.	Voyager 2, 1986
XII Portia	110.[k]	—	—	21.1	<0.1	66.1	5.0	0.513	≈0.	≈0.	Voyager 2, 1986
XIII Rosalind	60.[k]	—	—	22.5	<0.1	70.0	5.2	0.558	≈0.	≈0.	Voyager 2, 1986
XIV Belinda	68.[k]	—	—	22.1	<0.1	75.3	5.6	0.621	≈0.	≈0.	Voyager 2, 1986
XVIII 1986U10	40.[k]	—	—	23.6	<0.1	76.4	5.8	0.638	≈0.	≈0.	E. Karkoschka, 1999‡
XV Puck	155.	—	—	20.4	0.07	86.0	6.5	0.763	≈0.	≈0.	Voyager 2, 1985
V Miranda*[1]	485.	75. (22)	1.3	16.5	0.34	129.9	9.7	1.413	0.017	3.4	G. Kuiper, 1948
I Ariel*[1]	1160.	1340. (240)	1.6	14.	0.4	190.9	14.3	2.521	0.003	0.	W. Lassell, 1851
II Umbriel*[1]	1190.	1270. (240)	1.4	14.9	0.19	266.0	20.0	4.146	0.004	0.	W. Lassell, 1851
III Titania*	1610.	3470. (180)	1.6	13.9	0.28	436.3	32.7	8.704	0.002	0.	W. Herschel, 1787
IV Oberon*	1550.	2920. (160)	1.5	14.1	0.24	583.4	43.8	13.463	0.0007	0.	W. Herschel, 1787
XVI Caliban	60.	—	—	21.1	<0.1	7169.	538.	579.	0.082	140.	Gladman et al., 1997
XX 1999U2	20.	—	—	23.5	<0.1	7920.	594.	674.	0.146	141.	Gladman et al., 1999
XVII Sycorax	120.	—	—	20.6	<0.1	12214.	917.	1289.	0.509	153.	Nicholson et al., 1997
XXI 1999U3	30.	—	—	22.4	<0.1	16670.	1252.	2057.	0.323	145.	Holman et al., 1999
XIX 1999U1	30.	—	—	22.5	<0.1	17810.	1337.	2271.	0.528	147.	Kavelaars et al., 1999
Satellites of Neptune											
III Naiad	60.	—	—	24.6	≈0.06	48.0	2.3	0.3	≈0.	4.5	Voyager 2, 1989
IV Thalassa	80.	—	—	23.9	≈0.06	50.0	2.4	0.31	≈0.	0.4	Voyager 2, 1989
V Despina	150.	—	—	22.5	0.06	52.5	2.5	0.33	≈0.	<1.	Voyager 2, 1989
VI Galatea	160.	—	—	22.4	≈0.06	62.0	2.9	0.43	≈0.	<1.	Voyager 2, 1989
VII Larissa**	190.	—	—	22.	0.06	73.6	3.5	0.55	≈0.	<1.	Voyager 2, 1989
VIII Proteus**	420.	—	—	20.3	0.06	117.6	5.5	1.12	≈0.	<1.	Voyager 2, 1989
I Triton*	2700.	21400. (200)	2.07	13.6	0.8	354.	17.	5.877	<0.0005	160.	W. Lassell, 1846
II Nereid***	340.	—	—	19.7	0.16	5510.	260.	365.21	0.76	27.6	G. Kuiper, 1949
Satellite of Pluto											
Charon*	1200.	—	—	17.	—	19.1	0.9	6.387	≈0.	≈0.	J. Christy, 1978

[1] Near resonance(?). L(Miranda) – 3L(Ariel) + 2L(Umbriel) drifts slowly (period ≈12.5 a).
‡ In Voyager 2 (January 1986) images.

SATELLITES OF THE ASTEROIDS
By Joseph Veverka

Recently two asteroids have been discovered to have satellites. S/1998(45)1 was discovered using the Canada-France-Hawaii Telescope (CFHT) on Mauna Kea, Hawaii. Dactyl was discovered in images taken by the space probe *Galileo*.

Asteroid	**(45) Eugenia**	**(243) Ida**
Satellite	**S/1998(45)1**	**Dactyl**
Diameter (km)	13. ± 3.	1.4
Visual Magnitude (mean opposition)	16.6	20.3
Visual Albedo	0.04	0.2
Mean Dist. from Asteroid (km)	1200. ± 30.	85.
Orbital Period (days)	4.691 ± 0.004	—
Eccentricity	≈0	—
Orbit Inclination	≈0°	172°
Discovery	W. Merline et al., 1998 (CFHT)	*Galileo*, 1994

ORBITAL MOTION
By Roy Bishop

An understanding of orbital motion is central to an appreciation of the heavens. Whether you are observing a distant galaxy, the stars in a globular cluster, the waltz of Jupiter's Galilean satellites, the drift of the Moon during an occultation, or merely uttering an expletive as an artificial satellite passes through the field of your camera, an understanding of orbital motion adds a deep insight to all of these views.

Among early cosmologies were those of **Aristotle** (340 BC) and **Ptolemy** (140 AD), and the superior heliocentric one proposed by **Copernicus** (1543). These attempts at modelling the heavens used complex systems of circles upon circles, of epicycles, eccentrics, and deferents. John Milton, a contemporary of Galileo, wrote the following lines in his epic poem "Paradise Lost" (1674), possibly expressing his discontent with the Ptolemaic and Copernican systems of compounded circles:

> To ask or search I blame thee not, for Heav'n
> Is as the Book of God before thee set,
> Wherein to read his wond'rous Works, and learn
> His Seasons, Hours, or Days, or Months, or Years:
> This to attain, whether Heav'n move or Earth,
> Imports not, if thou reck'n right; the rest
> From Man or Angel the great Architect
> Did wisely to conceal, and not divulge
> His secrets to be scann'd by them who ought
> Rather admire; or if they list to try
> Conjecture, he his Fabric of the Heav'ns
> Hath left to thir disputes, perhaps to move
> His laughter at thir quaint Opinions wide
> Hereafter, when they come to model Heav'n
> And calculate the Stars, how they will wield
> The mighty frame, how build, unbuild, contrive
> To save appearances, how gird the Sphere
> With Centric and Eccentric scribbl'd o'er,
> Cycle and Epicycle, Orb in Orb.

Kepler (1609), using observations accumulated by Tycho, broke with the 2000-year preoccupation with circles when he discovered that the planets move in an elegantly simple way along elliptical paths. Although he had discovered *how* the planets move, Kepler was unable to explain quantitatively *why* they move in this way. **Galileo** (1632) achieved brilliant insights concerning the motion of objects; however, he ignored Kepler's ellipses and did not apply his mechanics to the sky.

Newton united the heavens and Earth by showing that the laws governing motions on Earth also apply to the heavens. In his *Principia* (1687), the greatest book in the physical sciences, Newton presented his three laws of motion and the first ever physical force law, his law of gravitation. He used these to explain the motions not only of bodies on Earth, but also of the planets, comets, stars, equinoxes, tides, etc. Newton was the first to realize that the Moon is falling toward Earth just as freely as does an apple and that the elliptical orbit of the centre of mass of the Earth–Moon system is the path that results (as he described it) as these two bodies free-fall under the action of the Sun's gravitational force.

A common misconception concerning orbits is that the inward gravitational force is balanced by an outward "centrifugal force." Newton's view is simpler: there is only one force, the inward pull of gravity. There is *no physical agent* to cause an outward force, and if there *were* an outward supporting force, the two forces would cancel and, as Galileo realized, the body would then move along a straight line. If you choose a rotating reference frame and then ignore the rotation (mistake no. 1), you have to pretend there is a "centrifugal force" (mistake no. 2) in order to make sense of motions occurring within this frame. The two mistakes effectively cancel, but understanding is compromised.

Einstein's General Theory of Relativity (GTR) of 1915 superseded Newton's description of gravity. The arbiter of which is a good theory and which theory is wrong is nature. Newton's laws are accurate enough for most of NASA's calculations, but they do not work exactly. In the case of strong gravitation and/or speeds approaching the speed of light, Newton's laws fail dramatically. The GTR may be wrong too, but so far it has passed all experimental tests.

According to Einstein's GTR, gravitation is not a mysterious force that one mass exerts upon a distant mass; gravitation is the geometry (non-Euclidean) of the 4- dimensional space-time within which we and the stars exist. Golf balls (if air friction is ignored), satellites, planets and stars follow *geodesics*, the straightest possible, force-free paths through a space-time whose geometry is shaped by mass-energy. The difficulty in intellectually grasping a non-Euclidean space-time originates with us. Common sense is inadequate. This is not surprising, given that our common sense is based on the Euclidean, 3-dimensional geometry of straight lines, rectangles, and spheres we learned in the crib by age 2.

Gravitation is geometry. This is why no one has ever felt a force of gravity. Like the centrifugal force, it never did exist. A force of gravity was the glue Newton invented to make his naive Euclidean model of space-time approximate the real universe. (Newton himself was well aware of the unsatisfactory nature of several of his assumptions, far more so than most people who came after him.) When you release a coin from your hand, you see the coin "fall" because the contact force of the ground on your feet (the *only* force you feel) accelerates you the other way. An orbiting astronaut experiences no such force, so he remains beside a released coin. Orbital motion could not be simpler—*no* forces are involved.

What would Milton have written had he been familiar with the conjectures of Newton and Einstein?

SOME ASTRONOMICAL AND PHYSICAL DATA
By Roy Bishop

Many of the numbers listed below are based on measurement. Exceptions include defined quantities (indicated by ≡), quantities calculated from defined quantities (e.g. m/ly, AU/pc), and numbers of mathematical origin such as π and conversion factors in angular measure. Of those based on measurement, some are known to only approximate precision and the equal sign is reduced to ≈. Many others are known to quite high precision (the uncertainties occur after the last digit given) and several are from "the 1998 CODATA recommended values of the fundamental physical constants" (see the web site http://physics.nist.gov/constants). The units *(Système International* (SI) where possible), symbols and nomenclature are based on recommendations of the *International Astronomical Union* and the *International Union of Pure and Applied Physics.*

LENGTH

1 metre (m) = the distance travelled by light in a vacuum in $(299\ 792\ 458)^{-1}$ s
1 astronomical unit (AU) = $1.495\ 978\ 707 \times 10^{11}$ m = 499.004 784 light-s
1 light-year (ly)   = $9.460\ 536 \times 10^{15}$ m (based on avg. Gregorian year)
                        = 63 239.8 AU
1 parsec (pc)   = $3.085\ 678 \times 10^{16}$ m
                        = 206 264.8 AU = 3.261 631 ly
1 mile*   ≡ 1.609 344 km
1 micron*   ≡ 1 μm   * Indicates deprecated unit.
1 Angstrom*   ≡ 0.1 nm   Unit on right is preferred.

TIME

1 second (s) ≡ 9 192 631 770 periods of the radiation involved in the transition between the two hyperfine levels of the ground state of the ^{133}Cs atom at mean sea level.

Day:	Mean sidereal (equinox to equinox)	= 86 164.092 s
	Mean rotation (fixed star to fixed star)	= 86 164.100 s
	Day (d)	≡ 86 400. s
	Mean solar	= 86 400.001 s
Month:	Draconic (node to node)	= 27.212 221 d
	Tropical (equinox to equinox)	= 27.321 582 d
	Sidereal (fixed star to fixed star)	= 27.321 662 d
	Anomalistic (perigee to perigee)	= 27.554 550 d
	Synodic (New Moon to New Moon)	= 29.530 589 d
Year:	Eclipse (lunar node to lunar node)	= 346.620 075 d
	Tropical (equinox to equinox) (a)	= 365.242 190 d
	Average Gregorian	≡ 365.242 5 d
	Average Julian	≡ 365.25 d
	Sidereal (fixed star to fixed star)	= 365.256 363 d
	Anomalistic (perihelion to perihelion)	= 365.259 635 d

EARTH

Mass = 5.974×10^{24} kg   Age ≈ 4.6 Ga   Central T ≈ 5000 to 6000 K
Radius: Equatorial, a = 6378.140 km   Polar, b = 6356.755 km
           Mean = $(a^2 b)^{1/3}$ = 6371.004 km   Of metallic core = 3475 km

Solar parallax = 8.794 148″ (Earth equatorial radius ÷ 1 AU)
1° of latitude = 111.13295 − 0.55982 cos 2ϕ + 0.00117 cos 4ϕ km (at latitude ϕ)
1° of longitude = 111.41288 cos ϕ − 0.09350 cos 3ϕ + 0.00012 cos 5ϕ km
1 knot = 1 nautical mile (1′ of latitude) per hour = 0.5148 m/s = 1.853 km/h
Distance of sea horizon for eye h metres above sea level
  (allowing for refraction) ≈ $3.9h^{1/2}$ km
Standard atmospheric pressure (1 atm) ≡ 101.325 kPa (≈ 1 kg above 1 cm²)
Speed of sound in standard atmosphere = 331 m/s ≈ 1 km/3 s ≈ 10^{-6} c
Magnetic field at surface ≈ 5×10^{-5} T (**B** field comes out of a N-seeking pole)
Magnetic poles: 76°N, 101°W; 66°S, 140°E
Standard acceleration of gravity ≡ 9.806 65 m/s²
Meteoric flux ≈ 1×10^{-15} kg/(m²s) ≈ 10^4 t/a over entire Earth
Obliquity of ecliptic = 23.4393° (2000.0)   Constant of aberration = 20.495 52″
Annual general precession = 50.29″ (2000.0); Precession period ≈ 25 800 a
Escape speed from Earth = 11.2 km/s   Mean orbital speed = 29.786 km/s
Escape speed at 1 AU from Sun = 42.1 km/s (= $\sqrt{2}$ × orbital speed)

SUN

Mass = 1.9891×10^{30} kg   Radius = 696 265 km   Eff. Temp. ≈ 5780 K
Output: Power = 3.85×10^{26} W, M_{bol} = 4.79
        Luminous intensity = 2.84×10^{27} cd, M_v = 4.82
At 1 AU outside Earth's atmosphere:
        Energy flux = 1.37 kW/m², m_{bol} = −26.82
        Illuminance = 1.27×10^5 lx, m_v = −26.75
Inclination of the solar equator on the ecliptic of date = 7.25°
Longitude of ascending node of the solar equator on the ecliptic of date = 76°
Period of rotation at equator = 25.38 d (sidereal), 27.275 d (mean synodic)
Solar wind speed near Earth ≈ 450 km/s (travel time, Sun to Earth ≈ 4 d)
Solar velocity = 19.4 km/s toward α = 18.07h, δ = +30° (solar apex)
Location in Milky Way Galaxy: ≈ 25 kly from centre, ≈ 50 ly N of galactic
  plane, on the inner edge of the Orion arm.

MILKY WAY GALAXY

Mass ≈ 10^{12} solar masses   Diameter ≈ 300 kly (including the galactic halo)
Centre: α = 17h 45.7m, δ = −29°00′; N pole: α = 12h 51m, δ = 27°08′ (2000.0)
Rotation speed at Sun ≈ 230 km/s, period ≈ 200 Ma
Velocity relative to 3K background radiation ≈ 600 km/s toward α ≈ 10h, δ ≈ −20°

CONSTANTS

Speed of light, c ≡ 299 792 458 m/s (This, in effect, defines the metre.)
Planck's constant, h = $6.626\ 07 \times 10^{-34}$ J s = $4.135\ 667 \times 10^{-15}$ eV s
Gravitational constant, G = 6.673 (± 0.010) $\times 10^{-11}$ Nm²/kg²
Elementary charge, e = $1.602\ 176 \times 10^{-19}$ C
Constant in Coulomb's law ≡ 10^{-7} c^2 (SI units) (This defines the Coulomb.)
Avogadro constant, N_A = $6.022\ 142 \times 10^{26}$ kmol⁻¹
Boltzmann constant, k = 1.38065×10^{-23} J/K = 8.617×10^{-5} eV/K ≈ 1 eV/10^4K
Stefan-Boltzmann constant, σ = 5.6704×10^{-8} W/(m²K⁴)
Wien's Law: $\lambda_m T$ = 2.8977×10^{-3} m K (per dλ)
Hubble constant, H ≈ 50 to 80 km/(s Mpc)
−273.15°C (degree Celsius) = 0 K (kelvin) (lowest thermodynamic temperature)
Volume of ideal gas at 0°C, 101.325 kPa = 22.4140 m³/kmol

Water: fusion at 0°C: 0.333 MJ/kg   vaporization at 100°C: 2.26 MJ/kg
specific heat & density (near 20°C): 4.18 kJ/(kg C°) & 1.00 t/m^3

MASS AND ENERGY

Mass is a measure of sluggishness of response to a net force. (SI unit: kg)
Weight ($\neq$ mass) is the force required to support a body. (SI unit: N)

1 kilogram (kg) $\equiv$ mass of a platinum-iridium cylinder stored in Paris, France
1 atomic mass unit (u) $\equiv$ 1/12th of the mass of an atom of ^{12}C
$$= 1.660\ 539 \times 10^{-27} \text{ kg} = N_A^{-1} = 931.4940 \text{ MeV}$$
1 joule (J) $\equiv$ work done by a force of 1 N acting through a distance of 1 m
$\approx$ the kinetic energy gained by this Handbook in falling freely 0.4 m
1 electron-volt (eV) $\equiv$ the kinetic energy gained by a particle carrying one unit
of elementary electrical charge (e) in falling through an
electrical potential difference of one volt (V).
$$= 1.602\ 176 \times 10^{-19} \text{ J}$$

Electron mass $= 9.109\ 38 \times 10^{-31}$ kg $= 548.579\ 91$ μu $= 0.510\ 9989$ MeV
Proton mass $\ \ = 1.672\ 622 \times 10^{-27}$ kg $= 1.007\ 276\ 467$ u $= 938.2720$ MeV
Neutron mass $= 1.674\ 927 \times 10^{-27}$ kg $= 1.008\ 664\ 92$ u $\ = 939.565$ MeV

Some atomic masses:
^{1}H $= 1.007\ 825$ u ^{5}Li $= 5.012\ 5$ u ^{16}O $= 15.994\ 915$ u
^{2}H $= 2.014\ 102$ u ^{8}Be $= 8.005\ 305$ u ^{56}Fe $= 55.934\ 940$ u
^{4}He $= 4.002\ 603$ u ^{12}C $\equiv 12.000\ 000$ u ^{235}U $= 235.043\ 928$ u

Thermochemical calorie* (cal) $= 4.184$ J
1 erg*/s $= 10^{-7}$ J/s $= 10^{-7}$ W
1 BTU*/h $= 0.2930$ W   * Indicates deprecated unit.
1 horsepower* $= 745.7$ W   Unit on right is preferred.
1 eV per event $= 23\ 060$ cal/mol
C + $O_2 \rightarrow CO_2$ + 4.1 eV   4 ^{1}H $\rightarrow$ 4 He + 26.73 MeV

Highest cosmic ray energy (carried by protons) $\approx 10^{20}$ eV
Power output (average) of an adult human ≈ 100 W
1 kg of TNT or milkshake releases 4.20 MJ ≈ 1 kWh

Relation between rest mass (m), linear momentum (p), total energy (E), kinetic
energy (KE), and $\gamma \equiv (1 - v^2/c^2)^{-0.5}$ where c is the speed of light and v is the
speed of the object: $E = \gamma mc^2 = mc^2 + \text{KE} = [(mc^2)^2 + (pc)^2]^{0.5}$

MAGNITUDE RELATIONS

Log of light intensity ratio $\equiv 0.4$ times magnitude difference
Distance Modulus (D) $\equiv$ apparent magnitude (m) $-$ absolute magnitude (M)
Log of distance in ly $= 0.2D + 1.513\ 435$ (neglecting absorption)
Magnitude of sum of magnitudes $m_i = -2.5 \log \Sigma_i\ 10^{-0.4\ m_i}$

DOPPLER RELATIONS FOR LIGHT

$\alpha \equiv$ angle between velocity of source and line from source to observer
$\beta \equiv v/c$
$\gamma \equiv (1 - \beta^2)^{-0.5}$
Frequency: $\nu = \nu_0\ \gamma^{-1}(1 - \beta \cos \alpha)^{-1}$
$z \equiv (\lambda - \lambda_0)/\lambda_0 = \gamma (1 - \beta \cos \alpha) - 1$
For $\alpha = \pi$ radians: $z = (1 + \beta)^{0.5}(1 - \beta)^{-0.5} - 1$ ($\approx \beta$ if $\beta \ll 1$)
$\beta = [(1 + z)^2 - 1][(1 + z)^2 + 1] - 1$

OPTICAL WAVELENGTH DATA

Bright-adapted (photopic) visible range ≈ 400 – 750 nm
Dark-adapted (scotopic) visible range ≈ 400 – 620 nm
Wavelength of peak sensitivity of human eye: ≈ 555 nm (photopic)
 ≈ 510 nm (scotopic)
Mechanical equivalent of light: 1 lm ≡ 1/683 W at 540 THz (λ ≈ 555 nm)
i.e. 1.46 W/klm (A 60 W incandescent light bulb emits about 1 klm = 1000 lm. Compared to an optimum light source that delivers all its energy as light at 540 THz, a 60 W incandescent light bulb is 1.46/60 ≈ 2.4% efficient.)
Colours (representative wavelength, nm):
violet (420), blue (470), green (530), yellow (580), orange (610), red (660)

Some useful wavelengths (element, spectral designation or colour and/or (Fraunhofer line)):

H Lyman α	121.6 nm	N_2^+ blue†	465.2	Hg yellow	579.1
Ca (K solar)	393.4	Hβ (F solar)*	486.1	Na (D_2 solar)	589.0
Ca (H solar)	396.8	O^{++} green*	495.9	Na (D_1 solar)	589.6
Hg violet	404.7	O^{++} green*	500.7	O red†	630.0
Hδ (h solar)	410.2	Hg green	546.1	He-Ne laser	632.8
Hγ (g solar)	434.0	O yel.-green†	557.7	O red†	636.4
Hg deep blue	435.8	Hg yellow	577.0	Hα (C solar)	656.3

* Strong contributor to the visual light of gaseous nebulae.
† Strong auroral lines

ANGULAR RELATIONS

2π radians = 360° π = 3.141 592 653 589 793 2... ≈ $(113 \div 355)^{-1}$
Number of square degrees on a sphere = 41 253.

For 360° = 24 h, 15° = 1 h, 15′ = 1 min, 15″ = 1 s

Relations between sidereal time t, right ascension α, hour angle h, declination δ, azimuth A (measured east of north), altitude a, and latitude ϕ:
$h = t - \alpha$
$\sin a = \sin \delta \sin \phi + \cos h \cos \delta \cos \phi$
$\cos \delta \sin h = -\cos a \sin A$
$\sin \delta = \sin a \sin \phi + \cos a \cos A \cos \phi$
Annual precession in α = 3.0730 + 1.3362 sin α tan δ seconds   (α must be
Annual precession in δ = 20.043″ cos α in degrees)

SOME SI SYMBOLS AND PREFIXES

m	metre	N	newton (kg m/s^2)	f	femto	10^{-15}
kg	kilogram	J	joule (N m)	p	pico	10^{-12}
s	second	W	watt (J/s)	n	nano	10^{-9}
min	minute	Pa	pascal (N/m^2)	μ	micro	10^{-6}
h	hour	t	tonne (10^3 kg)	m	milli	10^{-3}
d	day	Hz	hertz (s^{-1})	c	centi	10^{-2}
a	year	C	coulomb (A s)	k	kilo	10^3
A	ampere	V	volt (J/C)	M	mega	10^6
rad	radian	T	tesla (Wb/m^2)	G	giga	10^9
sr	steradian	lm	lumen	T	tera	10^{12}
K	kelvin (temperature)	cd	candela (lm/sr)	P	peta	10^{15}
ha	hectare (10^4 m^2)	lx	lux (lm/m^2)	E	exa	10^{18}

VOYAGES IN OUR PLANETARY SYSTEM
BY ROY BISHOP

A topic of considerable interest is the remarkable series of spacecraft that have explored our Moon and all but one of the other planets during the past half century. These explorations are significant for what they have revealed of our solar system, for the technological progress they represent, and for the broad awareness they have generated of humanity's place in the heavens. A knowledge of these achievements provides an invaluable historical perspective of this unique era.

The following chronological list should be a useful reference. No attempt has been made to record all space missions, nor even all space "firsts." Missions were carried out by the former Soviet Union (*), by the USA (no mark), by the European Space Agency (†), and jointly by the European Space Agency and the USA (‡).

Year	Name	Significance
1957	*Sputnik 1**	First artificial satellite of Earth (October 4)
1957	*Sputnik 2**	First living being in space (a dog named Laika)
1959	*Luna 1**	First spacecraft to escape Earth's gravity
1959	*Luna 2**	First spacecraft to impact on the Moon
1961	*Vostok 1**	First human in space (Yuri Gagarin) (April 12)
1962	*Mariner 2*	First successful flyby of another planet (Venus)
1965	*Mariner 4*	First successful flyby of Mars
1966	*Luna 9**	First soft landing on the Moon
1966	*Venera 3**	First spacecraft to impact on another planet (Venus)
1966	*Luna 10**	First spacecraft to orbit the Moon
1968	*Apollo 8*	First human voyage to the Moon (and orbit, without landing) (Frank Borman, James Lovell, William Anders) (Dec. 24)
1969	*Apollo 11*	First humans on the Moon (July 20) (Neil Armstrong, Edwin Aldrin)
1970	*Venera 7**	First soft landing on another planet (Venus)
1971	*Mariner 9*	First spacecraft to orbit another planet (Mars)
1971	*Mariner 9*	First close views of other satellites (Phobos, Deimos)
1972	*Apollo 17*	Last human visit to the Moon (Dec. 14)
1973	*Pioneer 10*	First flyby of Jupiter
1973	*Pioneer 10*	First spacecraft to achieve escape speed from the Sun
1974	*Mariner 10*	First flyby of Mercury
1976	*Viking 1*	First successful Mars landing
1979	*Voyager 1*	First close-up study of Jupiter and its satellites
1979	*Pioneer 11*	First flyby of Saturn
1980	*Voyager 1*	First close-up study of Saturn and its satellites
1981	*STS-1*	First reusable spacecraft for humans (Space Shuttle, Columbia)
1985	*ICE*	First cometary encounter (Comet Giacobini-Zinner)
1986	*Giotto†*	First good image of a cometary nucleus (Comet Halley)
1986	*Voyager 2*	First flyby of Uranus
1989	*Voyager 2*	First flyby of Neptune
1991	*Galileo*	First flyby of an asteroid (951 Gaspra)
1994	*Galileo*	First satellite of an asteroid (243 Ida) discovered
1994/5	*Ulysses‡*	First flyby above the Sun's south/north poles
1995	*Galileo*	First probe into Jupiter's atmosphere
1997	*Pathfinder*	First roving vehicle on another planet (Mars)
2000	*Shoemaker*	First spacecraft to orbit an asteroid (Eros)

TABLE OF PRECESSION FOR ADVANCING 50 YEARS

Precession in right ascension for declination in row immediately below

RA for Dec− (h m)	RA for Dec+ (h m)	Prec in Dec (′)	85° (m)	80° (m)	75° (m)	70° (m)	60° (m)	50° (m)	40° (m)	30° (m)	20° (m)	10° (m)	0° (m)	Prec in Dec (′)	RA for Dec+ (h m)	RA for Dec− (h m)
12 00	0 00	16.7	2.56	2.56	2.56	2.56	2.56	2.56	2.56	2.56	2.56	2.56	2.56	−16.7	12 00	24 00
12 30	0 30	16.6	4.22	3.39	3.10	2.96	2.81	2.73	2.68	2.64	2.61	2.59	2.56	−16.6	11 30	23 30
13 00	1 00	16.1	5.85	4.20	3.64	3.35	3.06	2.90	2.80	2.73	2.67	2.61	2.56	−16.1	11 00	23 00
13 30	1 30	15.4	7.43	4.98	4.15	3.73	3.30	3.07	2.92	2.81	2.72	2.64	2.56	−15.4	10 30	22 30
14 00	2 00	14.5	8.92	5.72	4.64	4.09	3.53	3.22	3.03	2.88	2.76	2.66	2.56	−14.5	10 00	22 00
14 30	2 30	13.3	10.31	6.41	5.09	4.42	3.73	3.37	3.13	2.95	2.81	2.68	2.56	−13.3	9 30	21 30
15 00	3 00	11.8	11.56	7.03	5.50	4.72	3.92	3.50	3.22	3.02	2.85	2.70	2.56	−11.8	9 00	21 00
15 30	3 30	10.2	12.66	7.57	5.86	4.99	4.09	3.61	3.30	3.07	2.88	2.72	2.56	−10.2	8 30	20 30
16 00	4 00	8.4	13.58	8.03	6.16	5.21	4.23	3.71	3.37	3.12	2.91	2.73	2.56	−8.4	8 00	20 00
16 30	4 30	6.4	14.32	8.40	6.40	5.39	4.34	3.79	3.42	3.15	2.94	2.74	2.56	−6.4	7 30	19 30
17 00	5 00	4.3	14.85	8.66	6.57	5.52	4.42	3.84	3.46	3.18	2.95	2.75	2.56	−4.3	7 00	19 00
17 30	5 30	2.2	15.18	8.82	6.68	5.59	4.47	3.88	3.49	3.20	2.96	2.76	2.56	−2.2	6 30	18 30
18 00	6 00	0.0	15.29	8.88	6.72	5.62	4.49	3.89	3.50	3.20	2.97	2.76	2.56	0.0	6 00	18 00
0 00	12 00	−16.7	2.56	2.56	2.56	2.56	2.56	2.56	2.56	2.56	2.56	2.56	2.56	16.7	24 00	12 00
0 30	12 30	−16.6	0.90	1.74	2.02	2.16	2.31	2.39	2.44	2.48	2.51	2.54	2.56	16.6	23 30	11 30
1 00	13 00	−16.1	−0.73	0.93	1.49	1.77	2.06	2.22	2.32	2.39	2.46	2.51	2.56	16.1	23 00	11 00
1 30	13 30	−15.4	−2.31	0.14	0.97	1.39	1.82	2.05	2.20	2.31	2.41	2.49	2.56	15.4	22 30	10 30
2 00	14 00	−14.5	−3.80	−0.60	0.48	1.03	1.60	1.90	2.09	2.24	2.36	2.46	2.56	14.5	22 00	10 00
2 30	14 30	−13.3	−5.19	−1.28	0.03	0.70	1.39	1.75	1.99	2.17	2.31	2.44	2.56	13.3	21 30	9 30
3 00	15 00	−11.8	−6.44	−1.90	−0.38	0.40	1.20	1.62	1.90	2.11	2.27	2.42	2.56	11.8	21 00	9 00
3 30	15 30	−10.2	−7.54	−2.45	−0.74	0.13	1.03	1.51	1.82	2.05	2.24	2.41	2.56	10.2	20 30	8 30
4 00	16 00	−8.4	−8.46	−2.91	−1.04	−0.09	0.89	1.41	1.75	2.00	2.21	2.39	2.56	8.4	20 00	8 00
4 30	16 30	−6.4	−9.20	−3.27	−1.28	−0.27	0.78	1.33	1.70	1.97	2.19	2.38	2.56	6.4	19 30	7 30
5 00	17 00	−4.3	−9.73	−3.54	−1.45	−0.39	0.70	1.28	1.66	1.94	2.17	2.37	2.56	4.3	19 00	7 00
5 30	17 30	−2.2	−10.06	−3.70	−1.56	−0.47	0.65	1.25	1.63	1.92	2.16	2.37	2.56	2.2	18 30	6 30
6 00	18 00	0.0	−10.17	−3.75	−1.59	−0.50	0.63	1.23	1.63	1.92	2.16	2.36	2.56	0.0	18 00	6 00

If declination is positive, use inner RA scale; if declination is negative, use outer RA scale and reverse the sign of the precession in declination. To avoid interpolation in this table, which becomes increasingly inaccurate for large |Dec|, precession formulae may be used (see p. 27).

TIME

TIME AND TIME SCALES
By Roy Bishop

Time has been said to be nature's way of keeping everything from happening at once. Isaac Newton (1687) perceived time as being separate from and more fundamental than the spinning of changeable planets or the oily mechanisms of clocks: "Absolute, true, and mathematical time, of itself, and from its own nature flows equably without regard to anything external." This is the common sense or intuitive view most people have of time.

Albert Einstein was the first to understand that time is but an abstraction that does not exist independently of clocks. In his special theory of relativity (1905), Einstein predicted that clocks moving relative to an observer tick slower (time dilation). A decade later in his theory of gravitation, the general theory of relativity, Einstein predicted that clocks lower or higher than the observer in a gravitational field run slower or faster, respectively, than the observer's clock. In the case of a lower clock, this is called the gravitational redshift. These counterintuitive effects are not only real, but in recent years they have found their way into the consumer marketplace in the form of GPS (Global Positioning System) receivers. These handheld units receive signals from orbiting atomic clocks and rely on programs that allow for time dilation and gravitational redshift.

As to understanding time, Lord Kelvin said that you know a physical quantity if you can measure it. Time can indeed be measured, with mind-boggling precision. For those who feel compelled to state: "We still don't know what time actually is," perhaps the mystery resides merely in the meaning of this statement.

The essence of time is that isolated material changes occur in invariant ratios one with respect to another. That is, as Sir Hermann Bondi has put it: "Time is that which is manufactured by clocks." Thus, to deal with time, clocks must be devised and units established.

Periodic Time Intervals and Clocks

There are three obvious, natural, periodic time intervals on Earth: the seasonal cycle (year); the cycle of lunar phases (month); and the day–night cycle (day). The cycle of the seasons is called the *tropical year* and contains 365.242 190 days. The cycle of lunar phases is known as the *synodic month* and equals 29.530 589 days. The average day-night (diurnal) cycle is the *mean solar day* and presently contains approximately 86 400.001 s. Other types of year, month, and day have been defined and are listed along with brief definitions and durations on p. 24.

The problem of accurately subdividing these natural intervals to make time locally available at any moment (i.e. timekeeping) was satisfactorily solved in 1657 by Christiaan Huygens, who invented the first practical pendulum clock. Through successive refinements the pendulum clock reigned supreme for nearly three centuries, until it was surpassed in precision by the quartz oscillator in the 1940s. Within another 20 years the quartz clock was, in turn, superseded by the cesium atomic clock which today has a precision near 2 in 10^{15} (one second in 16 million years) using the technique of *laser cooling* of atomic beams (see *Physics Today*, December 1997, p. 17, and February 1998, p. 21).

Earth's Rotation and Time Scales

Of the three obvious, natural, periodic time intervals on Earth (year, month, and day), the day dominates our lives and determines the various time scales we have created. The day is caused primarily by Earth's rotation on its axis. To count rotations a reference or fiducial point is required. Four such points are of interest, and three of these are the basis of five time scales:

(1)   Earth's rotation relative to the distant stars: Although the distant stars (or better, extragalactic sources) provide a reference frame to determine the "true" period of Earth's rotation (presently about 86 164.100 s), because of Earth's orbital motion and its rotational precession, this true period is not that of either the solar day or the RA/Dec coordinate grid used to specify astronomical positions. Hence no time scales are based on Earth's true rotational period.

(2)   Earth's rotation relative to the equinox: The equator and poles of the RA/Dec celestial coordinate grid are aligned with Earth's mean equator and poles. ("Mean" denotes that small, periodic variations caused by the nutation of Earth's axis have been averaged out. Nutation involves the true pole moving relative to the mean pole with an amplitude of about 9″ and a variety of short periods up to 18.6 years.) Hence the RA/Dec grid slowly shifts relative to the distant stars as Earth's rotation axis precesses—a motion caused primarily by the torques exerted by the Moon and Sun on Earth's equatorial bulge. The gravitational influence of the other planets causes the plane of the ecliptic also to precess, although this *planetary precession* is far smaller than the *lunisolar precession* of the mean equator. The sum of these two precessions is called *general precession*. General precession causes the zero point of right ascension (the "Greenwich of the skies," the vernal equinox, or "first point of Aries") to drift westward along the ecliptic about 50″ per year. As a result Earth's rotation period relative to the equinox (called the *mean sidereal day*, currently 86 164.092 s) is about 8.4 ms shorter than the time for one rotation. At any longitude on Earth, the RA of a star on the meridian (corrected for nutation) is the **Local Mean Sidereal Time** (**LMST**) at that instant. At the Greenwich meridian (0° longitude) this is called **Greenwich Mean Sidereal Time** (**GMST**). LMST may be used to set a telescope on an object of known right ascension. The hour angle of the object equals the sidereal time less the right ascension. LMST may be available from a sidereal clock, or it can be calculated as explained in the middle of p. 35. Because Earth makes one more rotation with respect to the other stars than it does with respect to the Sun during a year, sidereal time gains relative to time scales linked to the Sun (see below) by about 3 min 56 s per day, or 2 hours per month.

(3)   Earth's rotation relative to the real Sun: It is a common misconception that the Sun is highest in the sky and lies on the local north-south meridian at 12:00 noon. However, time based on the position of the Sun in the sky, known as local *apparent solar time* or *sundial time*, can differ by up to an hour or more from civil time (the time that we normally use). There are two reasons for this discrepancy. One reason is that the Sun's eastward annual apparent motion around the sky is far from uniform both because of Earth's elliptical orbit and because of the inclination of the celestial equator to the ecliptic. Thus apparent solar time does not have a uniform rate (see the next paragraph). The second reason for the difference between sundial time and civil time is addressed in the penultimate paragraph of this section.

(4)   Earth's rotation relative to the mean Sun: If the Sun is replaced by a fictitious mean sun moving uniformly along the celestial equator, Earth's rotation relative to this mean sun defines **Local Mean (solar) Time** (**LMT**). Apparent solar time can differ by up to 16 min from LMT depending upon the time of year (see the section

SUNDIAL CORRECTION on p. 82). Small, periodic shifts of Earth's crust relative to the axis of rotation *(polar motion)* affect astronomical time determinations through the resulting east–west shift in the meridian at latitudes away from the equator. LMT at the Greenwich meridian (0° longitude) when corrected for this polar motion is called *Universal Time* (**UT1**, or often simply **UT**). UT1 is determined using very long baseline interferometry, satellite laser-ranging, lunar laser-ranging data, and GPS data (via the International GPS Service).

All of the above mean time scales (LMST, GMST, LMT, and UT1), being based upon Earth's rotation, are only as uniform as this rotation. By the mid-19th century, discrepancies between theory and the observed motion of the Moon indicated that, over the long term, Earth's rotation is slowing down. However, not until clocks became better timekeepers than the spinning Earth (c.1940 when crystal-controlled clocks exceeded precisions of 1 in 10^{10}) was it realized how complex is the variable rotation of our planet. There are (i) long, (ii) medium, and (iii) short-term accelerations:

(i)   Over many centuries there is a *secular* slowing caused by tidal friction of about 8 parts in 10^{13} per day (i.e. the day becomes one second longer about every 40 000 years).

(ii)   Over a few decades there are *random* accelerations (positive and negative), apparently caused by core–mantle interactions. These are about 10 times larger than the tidal deceleration and thus completely obscure the latter effect over time intervals of less than a century or so.

(iii)   The largest accelerations in Earth's rotation rate are short-term ones: *periodic components* are associated mainly with lunar-induced tides (over two-week and monthly intervals) and seasonal meteorological factors (over semiannual and annual intervals); *nonperiodic* (chaotic) high-frequency variations are associated mainly with the global atmospheric wind and pressure distributions. These short-term accelerations are typically one or two orders of magnitude larger again than the random, decade fluctuations on which they are superimposed (see the article by John Wahr in the June 1986 issue of *Sky & Telescope*, p. 545).

Uniform Time Scales

(1) Based on orbital motion: Although Earth's axial rotation is not sufficiently predictable to serve as a precise clock, the orbital motions of our Moon, Earth, and the other planets are predictable to high accuracy. Through the dynamical equations describing these motions plus extended astronomical observations, a uniform time scale can be derived. Such a scale, known as *Ephemeris Time* (**ET**), was for several years (1952–1984) the basis of astronomical ephemerides. Early in the 20th century the UT1 and ET scales coincided, but since Earth's rotation rate has been generally slower than the ET rate, by 1970 UT1 was 40 s behind ET and was losing more than one second per year. During the next 15 years, Earth's rotation rate increased (part of the random decade fluctuations). During the 1990s UT1 lost about 0.7 s per year relative to ET (actually TT, see two paragraphs ahead).

(2) Based on atomic motion: Atoms display a permanence and stability that planets, quartz crystals, and pendulums cannot. The idea of an atomic clock was proposed by the American physicist Isidor Rabi in 1945. In 1967, *the second became the basic unit of time* when it was given an atomic definition: 9 192 631 770 periods of the radiation involved in the transition between the two hyperfine levels of the ground state of the cesium 133 atom at mean sea level. This is known as the SI (for Système International) second (abbreviation s, *not* sec). The number 9 192 631 770 was chosen so that the SI second is identical to the older ET second to within the precision of measurement.

Because of several difficulties surrounding both the original concept of ET and its determination, and because atomic clocks had become readily available, in 1984 ET was abandoned in favour of **Terrestrial Dynamical Time** (**TDT**). The unit of TDT is the SI second, and its scale was chosen to agree with the 1984 ET scale. In 1991 when the general theory of relativity was explicitly adopted as the theoretical background for defining space-time reference frames, TDT was renamed simply **Terrestrial Time** (**TT**). The unit of TT is the SI second on the geoid (i.e. as would be produced by a perfect SI clock located at mean sea level on Earth). TT is the time reference for apparent geocentric ephemerides, and it is realized via TAI (see below).

International Atomic Time (**TAI** = Temps Atomique International) is based on a weighted average of atomic clocks in many countries and is the most precise *achievable* time scale. Because not even atomic clocks are perfect timekeepers, TAI shifts unpredictably relative to the ideal SI rate (the TT rate) by a few microseconds over several years. TAI was arbitrarily set to agree with UT1 at the beginning of 1958, which led to the definition that TT be exactly 32.184 s ahead of TAI on 1977 January 1.0 TAI. This ensured continuity of TT with ET.

Two other SI-based time scales are in use: **Geocentric Coordinate Time** (**TCG**) and **Barycentric Coordinate Time** (**TCB**) for non-rotating coordinate grids located at the centres of mass of Earth and of the solar system, respectively. Both use the SI second, but because of the gravitational redshift, relative to an observer at sea level on Earth both have rates slower than TT (TCG and TCB lose about 22 ms per year and 489 ms per year, respectively, relative to TT). TCG and TCB were arbitrarily set to agree with TT at Earth's centre at the beginning of 1977. Like TT, TCG and TCB are realized via TAI.

(3) Based on pulsars: Millisecond radio pulsars (old, rapidly spinning neutron stars) display extraordinary stability in their periods of rotation, comparable with the best atomic clocks. However, given the elaborate equipment needed to observe pulsars and the data analysis required, it is unlikely that, as the basis for a uniform time scale, a laboratory-based reproducible physical phenomenon like the cesium atomic transition will be abandoned in favour of a pulsar.

Uniform Time Scales with Steps (to track the mean Sun)

Closely related to UT1 (which follows Earth's variable rotation relative to the mean Sun) is **Coordinated Universal Time** (**UTC**), introduced in its present form in 1972 as the basis of the world system of civil time. UTC runs at the SI rate and is offset an integral number of seconds from TAI so that it approximates UT1. When required (at the end of June 30 or December 31), "leap seconds" are inserted into (or, if necessary, deleted from) UTC so that the difference UT1 − UTC = ΔUT1 does not exceed ±0.9 s. UTC now lags TAI, and as of 1999 January 1, 0h UT (when a leap second was last inserted) TAI − UTC = ΔAT = 32 s. Thus as this edition of the *Observer's Handbook* goes to press (summer 2000), TT + UTC = 32 s + 32.184 s = 64.184 s exactly (see the diagram on the next page). In late 1998 Earth's rotation sped up slightly; as a consequence another leap second will likely not be needed until at least the end of June 2001. UTC is readily available via radio time signals or GPS receivers. (Note: The term *Greenwich Mean Time* (GMT) over the years has had three different meanings: the same as UT1, UTC, or mean solar time at the Greenwich meridian with 0 hours corresponding to noon. To avoid confusion, the term Greenwich Mean Time should not be used.)

Anyone in North America can keep track of Earth's varying rotation by listening to the CHU or WWV radio time signals in which is coded the difference $\Delta UT1 = (UT1 - UTC)$ (see TIME SIGNALS at the right). It is interesting to record $\Delta UT1$ about once a month and use these data to make a graphical display of (TT – UT1) as a function of time over several years. Note that during 2000 and probably at least until 2001 July 1, TT – UT1 = 64.184 – (UT1 – UTC).

This diagram displays the rate and scale relations between time scales that run at or near the SI rate and which are not longitude dependent.

Local Mean (solar) Time (LMT) would suffice for the inhabitants of an isolated village, but with the advent in the 19th century of rapid travel and communication (railways, steamships, and the telegraph), it became essential that clocks over a range of longitudes indicate the same time. To keep these clocks reasonably in phase with the day-night cycle and yet to avoid the inconvenience to travellers of a local time that varies continuously with longitude, in 1884 Earth was divided into 24 *standard time* zones, adjacent zones generally differing by one hour and each ideally 15 degrees wide (see the time zone map on p. 37). All clocks within the same zone read the same time. The Canadian railway surveyor and construction engineer Sir Sandford Fleming (1827–1915) was instrumental in establishing this system of standard time zones. The zero zone is centred on the Greenwich meridian (longitude 0°), and, since 1972, standard time in that zone is UTC. Thus the world system of civil time is based on UTC and includes the "leap seconds," which keep UTC near UT1. Depending upon an observer's location within his or her standard time zone, standard time may differ by up to an hour or so from LMT (see the third paragraph on p. 89). This is the second reason why the Sun seldom, if ever, is on the observer's meridian at 12:00 noon, standard time.

Some countries observe *daylight savings time* during the summer months. In Canada and the United States, clocks are generally* set one hour ahead of standard time at 2 a.m. local time on the first Sunday in April, and return to standard time at 2 a.m. local time on the last Sunday in October: "spring ahead, fall back." *(Saskatchewan, Arizona, Indiana, and Hawaii do *not* observe daylight saving time.)

TIME SIGNALS

National time services distribute Coordinated Universal Time (UTC). UTC is coordinated through the Bureau International des Poids et Mesures (BIPM) in Sèvres, France so that most time services are synchronized to a tenth of a millisecond. Radio time signals available in North America include:

CHU Ottawa, Ontario, Canada 3.330, 7.335, 14.670 MHz;
WWV Fort Collins, Colorado, USA 2.5, 5, 10, 15, 20 MHz.

For CHU, each minute starts at the *beginning* of the tone following the voice announcement, the tone for the 29th second is omitted, and the tones for seconds 31 through 39 have a different sound from the others.

The difference ΔUT1 = UT1 − UTC to the nearest tenth of a second is coded in the signals. If UT1 is ahead of UTC, second markers beginning at the 1 second mark of each minute are doubled, the number of doubled markers indicating the number of tenths of a second UT1 is ahead of UTC. If UT1 is behind UTC, the doubled markers begin at the 9 second point.

Time signals also are available by telephone from the National Research Council in Ottawa, Canada. Call (613) 745-1576 (English) or (613) 745-9426 (French).

MEAN SIDEREAL TIME, 2001

The following is the Greenwich Mean Sidereal Time (GMST) in hours on day 0 at 0h UT of each month ("day 0" is the last day of the previous month):

Jan. 6.6486	Apr. 12.5625	Jul. 18.5421	Oct. 0.5874
Feb. 8.6856	May 14.5338	Aug. 20.5791	Nov. 2.6244
Mar. 10.5255	Jun. 16.5708	Sep. 22.6161	Dec. 4.5957

GMST (in hours) at hour t UT on day d of the month =
GMST at 0h UT on day $0 + 0.065710d + 1.002738t$
LMST (Local Mean Sidereal Time) = GMST − west longitude (or + east longitude)

LMST calculated by this method will be accurate to ±0.2s provided t is stated to ±0.1s or better and the observer's longitude is known to ±1″. (Note that t must be expressed in decimal hours UT. Also, to achieve ±0.1s accuracy in t, the correction ΔUT1 must be applied to UTC. See the TIME SIGNALS section above.)

JULIAN DATE (JD), 2001

The Julian Date (JD) is commonly used by astronomers to refer to the time of astronomical events, because it avoids some of the annoying complexities of the civil calendar. Julian Date 0.0 was the instant of Greenwich mean noon on January 1, 4713 BC (see: "The Origin of the Julian Day System" by G. Moyer in *Sky & Telescope*, April 1981).

The Julian day **commences at noon** (12h) UT. To find the Julian Date at any time during 2001, determine the day of the month and time at the Greenwich meridian, convert this to a decimal day, and add it to one of the following numbers according to the month (these numbers are the Julian Dates for 0h UT on the 0th day of each month):

Jan. ...245 1909.5	Apr. ...245 1999.5	Jul. 245 2090.5	Oct. ...245 2182.5
Feb. ...245 1940.5	May ..245 2029.5	Aug. ..245 2121.5	Nov. ..245 2213.5
Mar. ..245 1968.5	Jun. ...245 2060.5	Sep. ...245 2152.5	Dec. ..245 2243.5

For example, 21:36 EDT on May 18 = 1:36 UT on May 19 = May 19.07 UT = 245 2029.5 + 19.07 = JD 245 2048.57.

The Julian Dates for 0h UT January 0 for the three previous years are 245 0000.5 plus: 813 (1998), 1178 (1999), 1543 (2000).

STANDARD TIME ZONES

The map at the right shows the world system of standard time zones. It was prepared and provided by Her Majesty's Nautical Almanac Office. Over the open oceans, the time zones are uniformly spaced and are bounded by lines of longitude 15° apart. In populated regions, political and other considerations have considerably modified the ideal geometry.

As Earth rotates with sunlight shining from one side, at some line of longitude the day of the week must jump discontinuously ahead by one day (otherwise, Monday would be followed by Monday!). The line chosen for this jump is in the relatively-unpopulated central part of the Pacific Ocean and approximates longitude 180°. It is called the International Date Line. A person travelling westward across this line has to advance the calendar date by one day, while an eastward-bound traveller moves back one day on the calendar.

The standard time zones are generally designated by letters of the alphabet. The zero time zone, centred on the longitude zero meridian passing through the Airy Transit Circle at the Old Royal Observatory in Greenwich, England, is denoted Z. Standard time within this zone is Coordinated Universal Time (UTC). Zones A, B, C, ..., M (J excluded), run eastward at one-hour intervals to the International Date Line, while zones N, O, P, ..., Y run westward to the same boundary. Zones M and Y are only one-half hour wide. Also, as indicated on the map, there are several partial zones that are one-half hour different from the adjacent main zones.

In North America there are seven standard time zones. In terms of their name (and letter designation, hours behind the Greenwich zone, and the west longitude of the reference or standard meridian), these are:

(1) Newfoundland (P*, 3h30m, 52.5°),

(2) Atlantic (Q, 4h, 60°),

(3) Eastern (R, 5h, 75°),

(4) Central (S, 6h, 90°),

(5) Mountain (T, 7h, 105°),

(6) Pacific (U, 8h, 120°),

(7) Alaska (V, 9h, 135°).

A change not depicted on this World Map of Standard Time Zones took place on October 31, 1999. Nunavut, Canada's newest and largest territory (larger than Alaska) adopted Central time, even though its range in longitude (61° to 120°) spans five time zones.

WORLD MAP OF TIME ZONES

STANDARD TIME ZONES
Corrected to June 2000
Zone boundaries are approximate
Daylight Saving Time (*Summer Time*),
usually one hour in advance of Standard
Time, is kept in some places
Map outline © *Mountain High Maps*
Compiled by *HM Nautical Almanac Office*

Standard Time = Universal Time + value from table

	h m		h m		h m		h m
Z	0	E*	+5 30	K	+10	N	−1	T	−7
A	+1	F	+6	K*	+10 30	O	−2	U*	−8
B	+2	F*	+6 30	L	+11	P	−3	U*	−8 30
C*	+3 30	G	+7	L*	+11 30	P*	−3 30	V	−9
D*	+4 30	H	+8	M	+12	Q	−4	V*	−9 30
E	+5	I	+9	M*	+13	R	−5	W	−10
		I*	+9 30	M†	+14	S	−6	X	−11
								Y	−12

† No Standard Time legally adopted

ASTRONOMICAL TWILIGHT AND SIDEREAL TIME
By Randall Brooks

The diagram gives for any day of the year: **(1)** *the local mean time (LMT) of the end and beginning of astronomical twilight at seven specified northern latitudes (curved lines);* **(2)** *the local mean sidereal time (LMST = right ascension at the observer's meridian) as a function of LMT (diagonal lines).*

OPTICS AND OBSERVING

TELESCOPE PARAMETERS

Equations

Objective: f_o = focal length   *Eyepiece*: f_e = focal length
          D = diameter d_f = diameter of field stop
          FR = focal ratio θ_p = apparent angular field

Whole Instrument: M = angular magnification
                   d_p = diameter of exit pupil
                   θ_c = actual angular field

$$M = f_o/f_e = D/d_p \approx \theta_p/\theta_c \qquad FR = f_o/D \qquad d_f{}^* = f_o\theta_c \approx f_e\theta_p$$

*(θ_c and θ_p must be expressed in radians.)

Performance

D is assumed to be expressed in millimetres.

Light Grasp (LG) is the ratio of the light flux intercepted by a telescope's objective lens or mirror to that intercepted by a human eye having a 7-mm-diameter entrance pupil.

Limiting Visual Magnitude $m \approx 2.7 + 5 \log D$, assuming transparent, dark-sky conditions and magnification $M \geq 1D$. (See *Sky & Telescope, 45,* 401, 1973; *77,* 332, 1989; *78,* 522, 1989).

Smallest Resolvable Angle $\alpha \approx 120/D$ seconds of arc. However, atmospheric conditions seldom permit values less than 0.5″.

Useful Magnification Range $\approx 0.2D$ to $2D$. The lower limit ($0.2D$) guarantees that, for most observers, all the light exiting a telescope can reach the retina (The reciprocal of the coefficient to D is the diameter (in mm) of the telescope's exit pupil. Also, see the next section concerning exit pupils and magnification.) The upper limit ($2D$) is determined by the wave nature of light and the optical limitations of the eye, although atmospheric turbulence usually limits the maximum magnification to 400× or less. For examination of double stars, detection of faint stars, and studying structure in bright nebulae, magnifications of up to $3D$ are sometimes useful.

Values for some common apertures are:

D (mm):	60	100	125	150	200	250	330	444
LG:	73	200	320	460	820	1300	2200	4000
M:	11.6	12.7	13.2	13.6	14.2	14.7	15.3	15.9
α:	2.0″	1.2″	1.0″	0.80″	0.60″	0.48″	0.36″	0.27″
$0.2D$:	12×	20×	25×	30×	40×	50×	66×	89×
$2D$:	120×	200×	250×	300×	400×	500×	660×	890×

TELESCOPE EXIT PUPILS
By Roy Bishop

The performance of a visual telescope is constrained by Earth's atmosphere, by the wave aspect of light, by the design of the telescope, by imperfections in its optical system, and by the properties of the human visual system. Telescope and eye meet at the *exit pupil* of the telescope, which is the image of the telescope's objective lens or mirror formed by its eyepiece. When a telescope is pointed at a bright area, such as the daytime sky, the exit pupil appears as a small disk of light hovering in the space just behind the eyepiece. (Insert a small piece of paper in this vicinity to demonstrate that this disk of light *really is* located behind the eyepiece.) Since the exit pupil is the narrowest point in the beam of light emerging from the telescope, it is here that the observer's eye must be located to make optimum use of the light passing through the telescope.

Diagram

On p. 43 is a diagram that may be used to display the relation between the diameter of the exit pupil (d_p) of a telescope and the focal lengths (f_e) of various eyepieces. Both d_p and f_e are expressed in millimetres. The numbered scale around the upper right-hand corner of the diagram indicates the focal ratio (FR) of the objective lens or mirror of the telescope. (FR equals the focal length of the objective divided by its diameter—see the previous page.) To prepare the diagram for a particular telescope, locate the FR of the telescope's objective on the FR scale, and draw a straight diagonal line from there to the origin (the lower left-hand corner). The diagram provides a visual display of the standard relation: $d_p = f_e/\text{FR}$.

To determine, for example, the eyepiece focal length required to give an exit pupil of 3 mm on a certain telescope, locate $d_p = 3$ on the ordinate, run horizontally across to the diagonal line corresponding to the FR of that telescope, and from there drop vertically downward to the abscissa to find f_e. This procedure may, of course, be reversed: for a given f_e, find the corresponding d_p.

Magnification Ranges

The ranges H, M, L, and RFT blocked off along the ordinate of the diagram break the d_p scale into four sections, starting at 0.5 mm and increasing by factors of 2. Although this sectioning is somewhat arbitrary, it does correspond closely to what are usually considered to be the high (H), medium (M), low (L), and "richest-field telescope" (RFT) magnification ranges of any visual telescope—and the associated d_p ranges are easy to remember.

High Magnifications: In the case of the Moon, the planets, and all but the dimmest stars, the highest useful magnification is the point at which blurring due to diffraction (caused by the wave nature of light) begins to become noticeable. This corresponds approximately to $d_p = 0.5$ mm, assuming good optics and negligible atmospheric turbulence (i.e. excellent "seeing"). Higher magnifications will not reveal any more detail in these images and cause reductions in four desirable features: sharpness, brightness, field of view, and eye relief (the space between the eye and eyepiece). Also, as d_p is made progressively smaller, imperfections and debris in the interior of the eye (in the *vitreous humour* in front of the retina) become more noticeable and interfere with clear vision. However, for objects requiring the use of averted vision (e.g. faint stars, nebulae, and galaxies), the acuity of the eye is much reduced and very high magnifications ($d_p < 0.5$ mm) can sometimes be used to advantage (although only the brightest areas of nebulae and galaxies will still be visible at such magnifications).

Very Low Magnifications: Magnifications in the RFT range are useful because they yield wide fields of view, the brightest (highest luminance) images of extended objects, and for common telescope apertures, the most stars visible in one view (hence the term "richest field"). The lowest magnification that still makes use of the full aperture of a telescope is determined by the point at which the diameter of the telescope's exit pupil matches the diameter of the *entrance pupil* of the observer's eye.

For the dark-adapted eye, the entrance pupil diameter seldom equals the often-quoted figure of 7 mm, but depends, among other things, upon the age of the observer as indicated by the scale in the upper left portion of the diagram (See Kadlecová et al., *Nature, 182*, 1520, 1958; *Sky & Telescope*, May 1992, 502.) Note that this scale indicates *average* values; the maximum diameter of the entrance pupil of the eye of any *one* individual may differ by up to a millimetre from these values. A horizontal line should be drawn across the diagram corresponding to the maximum diameter of one's own entrance pupil. This line will be an upper bound on d_p in the same sense that the line at $d_p = 0.5$ mm is a lower bound. Note that in daylight, the entrance pupil of the eye has a diameter in the range of 2 to 4 mm. Thus for daylight use of telescopes, the upper bound on d_p will be correspondingly reduced.

Ultra-Low Magnifications: If a d_p value larger than the entrance pupil of the eye is used, the iris of the observer's eye will cut off some of the light passing through the telescope to the retina. That is, the iris will have become the light-limiting aperture *(aperture stop)* of the system rather than the edge of the telescope's objective. In this case, the cornea of the eye together with the lenses of the telescope's eyepiece form an image of the observer's iris at the objective of the telescope: to the incoming starlight, a highly magnified image of the iris hovers as an annular skirt covering the outer region of the objective of the telescope! A telescope can be used at such "ultra-low" magnifications, but obviously a telescope of smaller aperture would perform as well. However, ultra-low magnifications on any telescope *do* have two advantages:

(1) A wider actual field of view, assuming the field stop of the eyepiece will permit this (an eyepiece requiring a 2-inch-diameter focuser is usually necessary).

(2) Ease of alignment of the entrance pupil of the eye with the exit pupil of the telescope, an aspect of viewing that is usually troublesome when these two pupils are nearly the same size. An oversize exit pupil provides "slop," making alignment less critical. This is particularly helpful when using binoculars during activities involving motion, such as boating or bird-watching. This is one advantage of using 7×50 (= $M \times D$) binoculars rather than 7×35 binoculars for daytime activities, although less than half of the light entering the larger binoculars can reach the observer's retinas.

Optimum Low Magnification: A value of d_p a millimetre or two *smaller* than the entrance pupil of the eye has several advantages:

(1) Viewing is more comfortable, since the observer can move a bit (move the head and/or scan the field) without cutting into the light beam and dimming the image. As mentioned above, ultra-low magnifications have the same advantage, but light is wasted.

(2) Light entering near the edge of the pupil of the dark-adapted eye is not as effective in stimulating the rod cells in the retina—the "scotopic Stiles-Crawford effect" (see VanLoo and Enoch, *Vision Research, 15*, 1005, 1975). Thus the smaller d_p will result in more effective use of the light.

(3) Aberrations in the cornea and lens of the eye are usually greatest in the peripheral regions and can distort star images. The smaller d_p will avoid the worst of these regions and produce sharper star images.

(4) With the higher magnification, structure in dim, extended objects, such as galaxies and bright and dark nebulae, will be more easily seen. (Our ability to see detail is greatly reduced in dim light, since the retina organizes its cells into larger units, thereby sacrificing resolution in order to improve signal-to-noise in the sparse patter of photons.)

(5) The background sky glow will be darker producing views that some observers consider to be aesthetically more pleasing.

(The only disadvantage of having d_p a millimetre or two smaller than the entrance pupil of the eye is a somewhat reduced field of view, but this will be minimal if an eyepiece having a larger apparent angular field is available at this higher magnification.)

Using the Diagram

Once the diagonal line corresponding to a telescope's focal ratio has been drawn and the upper bound on d_p is established, the diagram at the right gives a concise and convenient display of the eyepiece/exit pupil/magnification range relations for a particular telescope and observer. One can see at a glance what range of eyepiece focal lengths is suitable.

Some examples:

(1) Consider the common 8-inch Schmidt-Cassegrain telescope. These have $D = 200$ mm and (usually) FR = 10. The diagram indicates that eyepieces with focal lengths from 5 mm to 55 mm are useable for most observers. With a 32-mm eyepiece, the diagram gives $d_p = 3.2$ mm, in the L magnification range, and the magnification $M = D/d_p = 200/3.2 = 62\times$.

(2) If an observer wishes to use the full aperture of an FR = 4.5 telescope, a 40-mm eyepiece is ruled out. Similarly, a 70-year-old observer should probably not use even a 27-mm eyepiece on such a telescope, and should not bother with 7×50 or 11×80 binoculars, unless ease of eye/exit pupil alignment is the main consideration.

(3) With ordinary eyepieces ($f_e \leq 55$ mm), a telescope with FR = 15 cannot be operated in the RFT range, unless a compressor lens is added to reduce its FR.

(4) There is no point in using extremely short focal length eyepieces and Barlow lenses on telescopes having large FRs. This is a common fault (among many others!) with camera/department store "junk telescopes."

EXIT PUPILS DIAGRAM

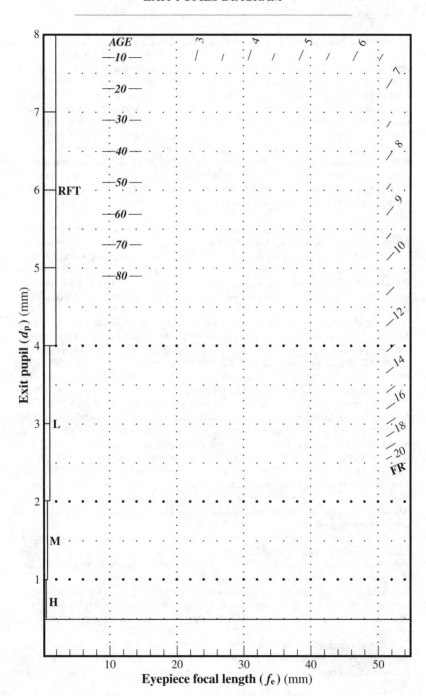

BINOCULARS
By Roy Bishop

The Role of Binoculars: Binoculars are the best choice as the first telescope for a beginner, and are indispensable for the experienced observer. For the beginner who is not familiar with the large-scale features of the sky, who cannot yet identify a dozen constellations on any clear night, a telescope with its narrow field of view and confusing image orientations will quickly cause more frustration than fun. The beginner is at a double disadvantage because he or she also does not know enough about astronomical telescopes to distinguish those that are worthy of the name from the common camera/department store "junk telescopes"—the $299 wonders with poor optics and impossibly wobbly mounts. How many such telescopes are gathering dust in closets, their young owners turned off of astronomy and their parents a few hundred dollars poorer? Far better had the same investment been made in a good pair of binoculars. With their ease of use, wide field of view, and unreversed, upright images binoculars are a great help in finding one's way around the sky, and provide many unique views of the heavens.

Binoculars magnifying 6 to 8 times are ideal for locating planets in the twilight, for scanning the constellations, for studying the larger dark nebulae and star fields of our galaxy, and for viewing large comets. Binoculars magnifying 10 to 20 times provide the best views of objects spanning a few degrees such as the Hyades, the Pleiades, the North American Nebula, the Andromeda Galaxy, and they give the finest view of the slender crescent Moon, or of the full Moon with broken clouds blowing by.

Binoculars permit us to view the universe with both eyes, thereby providing several advantages: an improved sense of reality and depth (although parallax is negligible when viewing the heavens); more relaxed viewing; a complete view in the sense that the blind areas of one eye (associated with blood vessels and the region where the optic nerve attaches to the retina) are compensated by the field provided by the other eye; and dim objects appear brighter when viewed with two eyes.

Binocular sizes are specified by numbers such as 7 × 50, 8 × 30, etc. The first number, including the "×," is the angular magnification or "power"; the second number is the diameter of the front (objective) lenses in millimetres. That is, in the notation on p. 39: $M \times D$. Thus the exit pupil diameter is easily calculated from $D \div M$ (e.g. 7 × 35 binoculars have $35 \div 7 = 5$ mm exit pupils). Another important parameter is field of view. Binoculars have apparent angular field diameters of about 50° when equipped with standard eyepieces, to near 70° with wide-angle eyepieces. The actual field of view on the sky (typically 3° to 10°) equals approximately the apparent field divided by the magnification. Thus the area of sky visible decreases rapidly with higher magnifications.

What is the best binocular size for astronomical use? There is no simple answer. Almost *any* pair of binoculars will show far more than can be seen with the unaided eyes; however, for astronomical use the objective lenses should be at least 30 mm in diameter. Also, small binoculars of high quality are more enjoyable to use than a large pair of low quality. For maximum light transmission and high contrast images, binoculars with *multicoated* optics are preferable to those with merely *coated* optics (the former give greenish or deep red reflections from their surfaces, the latter bluish or violet).

Caveat emptor! Low-quality binoculars (and telescopes) are common. Images seen through low-quality binoculars are slightly fuzzy (usually not apparent to the inexperienced observer), one's eyes will be strained in trying to compensate for imperfectly aligned optics, and the focusing mechanism is usually flexible and crackling with an excess of grease used to mask poor workmanship. Avoid both zoom (variable magnification) binoculars and binoculars not having an adjustable focus—invariably these are of low quality.

Considering that binoculars contain at least 14 pieces of glass with 36 optical surfaces, antirefection coatings on (hopefully) all air-to-glass surfaces, plus two focusing mechanisms and an interpupillary adjustment, it is not surprising that top quality instruments are in the same price range as video cameras. Such prices buy crisp, high-contrast images, accurately aligned optics, precise, rugged, dust- and moisture-proof construction, and pleasurable service for a lifetime. Nevertheless, there is a big market for $99 binoculars and $299 telescopes, and manufacturers are happy to satisfy the demand. When it comes to optical equipment, quality usually matches price.

Stability: One aspect of binocular use that often is not appreciated is how much more can be seen if the binoculars are mounted on a stable support, such as a camera tripod. This eliminates the constant jiggling associated with hand-holding. Adapters for attaching binoculars to a tripod are available, although usually it is not difficult to make your own adapter. A recent major advance in binocular design is "image-stabilization," an active optical system built into binoculars that compensates for the tremor associated with hand-holding. For example, the Canon company has introduced microprocessor-controlled binocular image stabilization, which gives near tripod-like stability with the convenience of hand-holding. Canon has produced 10×30, 12×36, and 15×45 models, the latter being particularly impressive for astronomy (see *SkyNews*, July/August 1998, p. 12; and *Sky & Telescope*, May 1998, p. 48).

Rating Binoculars

A frequently cited figure for binocular performance is "Relative Brightness," which equals the square of the diameter (in millimetres) of the instrument's exit pupils. For example, for 7×50 binoculars this figure is $(50 \div 7)^2 = 51$. Although this is a measure of the surface brightness *(luminance)* of an extended object seen through the binoculars under nighttime conditions, it is a totally inadequate measure of binocular performance on the night sky. For instance, using this figure of merit, large 14×100 binoculars have practically the same rating as the unaided eyes (which, when young and in dim light, are effectively 1×7 binoculars)!

Since seeing depends upon light, and the amount of light passing through a pair of binoculars depends primarily upon the *area* of its objective lenses (diameter D), a D^2 dependence appears reasonable. However, although the amount of light going into the point images of stars increases as D^2, assuming constant magnification the increase in the luminance of the background sky as D increases leads to a somewhat slower improvement in the visibility of these stars. A similar muted improvement occurs for dim extended images, resulting in an approximately D^1 dependence, rather than D^2.

Also, for constant D the detail that can be seen in the night sky increases with the magnification M. The resulting lower luminance of the background sky allows fainter stars to be seen, and the visibility of structure in extended images improves as M increases because the image is larger and of fixed contrast relative to the sky background.

The simplest figure of merit for the performance of binoculars in low-light conditions that combines both variables is the mathematical product $M \times D$ (which looks the same as the binocular size specification!). In the case of two pairs of binoculars, one having twice the M and twice the D of the other, $M \times D$ indicates that "four times as much" should be visible in the larger instrument (for example 16×60 versus 8×30 binoculars). This is to be expected since in the larger instrument stars will be four times brighter and extended images will have four times the area from which the eyes can glean information, with luminances being the same in both instruments.

For many decades the venerable Carl Zeiss optical company has cited $\sqrt{(M \times D)}$ as a "Twilight Performance Factor" for binoculars, its value said to be proportional to the distance at which various binoculars will show the same detail. This is equivalent to $M \times D$ being proportional to *the amount of detail that can be seen at the same distance*. The latter situation is relevant for astronomy since, unlike a bird or other object on Earth, a star or a galaxy is always at essentially the *same distance* from the observer. $M \times D$ could be called the *visibility factor*.

Binocular Performance Diagram

The diagram at the right enables one to quickly compare binoculars in terms of their ability to reveal detail in the night sky. The vertical axis is magnification M; the horizontal axis is aperture D. The uniform grid of small dots is a guide to reading the diagram. The five straight lines indicate constant exit pupil diameters of 3, 4, 5, 6, and 7 mm, as indicated both by numbers and by circles of these diameters near the top ends of the lines. The five curved arcs indicate constant values of $M \times D$ (the visibility factor), increasing by successive powers of 2 toward the upper right (100, 200, 400, 800, and 1600). Each large dot represents a common size of binoculars. The arrows in the lower right corner indicate the directions on the diagram in which various quantities increase most rapidly.

Each straight line (constant exit pupil diameter) also corresponds to constant luminance of extended areas, such as the Orion Nebula or the background sky glow, with the luminance being proportional to the square of the exit pupil diameter (provided the entrance pupils of the observer's eyes are large enough to accommodate the exit pupils of the binoculars). However, exit pupils of 3 to 5 mm ensure that all the light transmitted by the binoculars can enter the dark-adapted eyes no matter what the observer's age; that alignment of exit pupils with dark-adapted eye pupils is relatively easy to achieve; that the background sky glow will be subdued; and that star images will be less distorted by aberrations in the observer's eyes (see the previous section).

Some examples apparent from the diagram: for viewing the night sky 10×50 binoculars will show about twice as much detail as 7×35s; 11×80 and 15×60 binoculars are equally capable, as are 8×30s and 6×42s (assuming one's eye pupils can accommodate the exit pupils of the instrument with the larger D); 10×50 binoculars are appreciably better than 7×50s for visibility (although, assuming equal apparent angular fields, 7×50s will show about twice as much sky area as will 10×50s). Canon's new image-stabilized 15×45 binoculars are nearly equivalent to tripod-mounted 10×70s, with the *triple* advantage of smaller size, of accommodating observers whose pupils will not open to 7 mm, and of not requiring a tripod!

The visibility factor ($M \times D$) is applicable to the usual range of binocular sizes (exit pupils between about 3 mm and 7 mm), but should not be extrapolated indefinitely. For instance, as the magnification is increased on a telescope and the exit pupil approaches 1 mm or less, a point will be reached (dependent upon the darkness of the sky) where the background sky glow is imperceptible. A further increase in M will not cause a noticeable improvement in the visibility of stars, and the perceived contrast between an extended object and the sky will decrease. Also, the angular size of an extended object must be kept in mind. Once M is increased to the point at which the object fills the field of view of the instrument, the object may not be visible at all! For example, a large, dim comet coma may be visible in 15×60 binoculars ($M \times D = 900$) but be *invisible* in a 45×200 telescope ($M \times D = 9000$).

BINOCULAR PERFORMANCE DIAGRAM

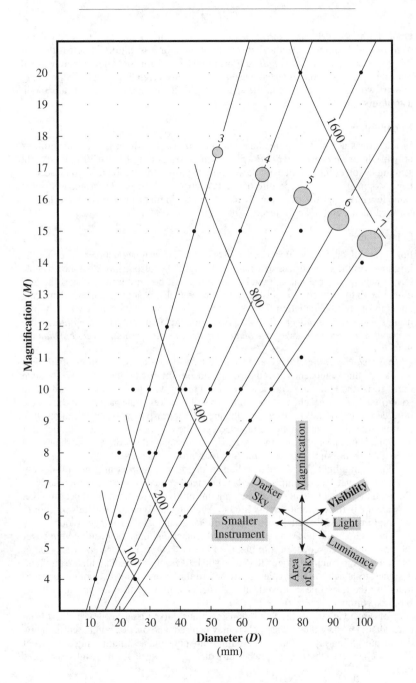

FILTERS
By Roy Bishop

Optical filters reflect and absorb some portion of the light incident upon them. *Neutral-density filters* reflect and absorb light more or less uniformly across the visible spectrum. *Coloured (dye) filters* typically pass only one or two moderately broad portions of the spectrum. *Interference filters* are more selective and typically pass only one or two narrow segments of the spectrum. All three filter types are invaluable in astronomy.

Lunar Filters

In telescopes at low to intermediate magnifications, the Moon is often uncomfortably bright. A *lunar neutral density filter*, which passes only 10% to 20% of the light striking it, solves this problem while avoiding the loss in resolution that would accompany stopping down the aperture of the telescope to decrease the brightness to the same level. A lunar filter is typically about 25 mm in diameter and is attached to the forward-facing end of an eyepiece.

Solar Filters

For observing the Sun, a filter is essential and must be designed not only to reduce the brightness of the solar surface to a comfortable level, but also to block out the invisible but damaging infrared and ultraviolet radiation. Just because a filter makes the Sun dim enough to view comfortably is no guarantee that it is not transmitting damaging amounts of invisible radiation. This is no place to experiment with do-it-yourself filter designs—use only a proper solar filter from a reputable manufacturer. *Failure to use a proper filter when observing the Sun can cause immediate and irreversible damage to vision.*

A *special warning:* Heavy atmospheric haze near sunrise or sunset often dims the Sun so that it appears as a red disk, not uncomfortably bright to the eye. At such times resist the temptation to view the Sun directly with a telescope (i.e. without a solar filter). The atmosphere at such times is still relatively transparent in the invisible infrared portion of the spectrum, and the great light grasp of a telescope can result in thermal retinal damage. With the unaided eyes the retinal solar image, although just as bright, is much smaller and the eye can better dissipate the heat. Also, with unaided vision, one is less apt to fixate on the Sun for a prolonged period.

For "white-light" views of the Sun, a dense, broad-spectrum, neutral-density *solar filter* is needed. Aluminized Mylar and metal-coated glass are common designs, although they usually do not attenuate light uniformly across the visible spectrum (i.e. they are not perfect neutral-density filters). Aluminized Mylar gives a bluish colour to the solar image, while metal-coated glass filters usually give an orange colour.

The filter should be 50 mm or more in diameter and must be positioned to cover the *front* of the telescope. Ensure that the filter is *securely* attached so that a gust of wind or a bump cannot dislodge it. (Some small telescopes are sold with a "sun filter" designed to attach to the eyepiece, just before the observer's eye. Sunlight concentrated by the telescope can overheat and shatter a filter of this design. Such filters should be thrown in the garbage.)

For direct viewing of the Sun (not using binoculars or a telescope) shade #14 (no other shade) rectangular welder's glass may be used, and may be purchased for a few dollars at welding supply shops. These filters are not suitable for attaching to the front of binoculars or a telescope simply because their poor optical quality results in a fuzzy image.

Red, flame-like prominences at the Sun's limb and much structure in its chromosphere across the solar disk can be seen in hydrogen-alpha (Hα) light, a strong spectral line emitted by atomic hydrogen. This light is totally overwhelmed by the rest of the solar spectrum, so a neutral-density filter will not work. Advances in vacuum thin-film technology have made possible filters that operate on the same principle as Fabry–Perot interferometers, involving the interference of multiply reflected beams of light. These filters can be constructed so they are transparent only to light having an extremely narrow range of wavelengths, typically 0.15 nm to 0.05 nm for solar viewing (although bandpasses up to 1 nm are used in solar prominence viewers, which are designed to occult the solar disk). If this bandpass is centred on the Hα wavelength (656.3 nm), nearly all of the Sun's light will be blocked, leaving an image in Hα light.

Hα filters are expensive, particularly for bandpasses near 0.05 nm which are needed for high-contrast images of the solar disk. Because Hα filters are usually mounted near the back end of a telescope, and because the wavelength of the centre of their narrow bandpass varies with the angle at which light rays enter the filter (a characteristic of interference filters), the focal ratio of the imaging telescope must be near f/20 for 0.15 nm bandpass filters and f/30 or higher for filters with narrower bandpasses. Temperature control is usually required to keep the bandpass centred on the Hα wavelength, although some Hα filters are designed to be tilted in order to tune them to the Hα wavelength (the wavelength of peak transmittance is shifted toward shorter wavelengths when the filter is tilted away from 90° incidence).

Hα filters are usually mounted just ahead of the eyepiece (or film holder, if photography is planned). Also, Hα filters require a broadband "energy rejection prefilter," located at the front of the telescope. The prefilter has a bandpass of about 100 nm in the red part of the spectrum and blocks essentially all of the infrared, ultraviolet, and much of the visible part of the solar radiation from entering the telescope.

Planetary Filters

Broadband "coloured" filters (usually attached at the forward end of an eyepiece) can enhance the visibility of various planetary features. For instance, a red or yellow filter will absorb light scattered in the Martian atmosphere and make the dark features on the surface of Mars easier to see. A green filter will increase the visibility of pale red and blue areas in the atmosphere of Jupiter (although the entire image will then appear green). Also, since they absorb an appreciable fraction of the light, coloured filters or polarizing filters reduce light scattering in the observer's eye when viewing bright objects such as Venus, the Moon, or Mars. With less glare, fine details are easier to see.

Nebula Filters

From the surface of Earth, the night sky is not completely dark. Even in the absence of light pollution (man-made and lunar), the air itself emits a feeble light called *airglow*. In higher latitudes, *aurorae* can also contribute to the glow of the atmosphere. This glow reduces the contrast of celestial objects and, in the case of dim galaxies and nebulae, the object may be completely obscured by the brightness of the sky.

Filters transmit only a fraction of the incident light. Thus, employing them to see faint objects may seem counterproductive. However, there are objects in the heavens that preferentially emit light only at certain wavelengths. This behaviour is characteristic of plasmas: excited gases, matter composed of separate atoms that are energized by ultraviolet radiation from nearby hot stars. Such regions are called *emission nebulae* and include star-forming regions, planetary nebulae, and some supernova remnants. A filter that selectively blocks most of the background sky glow but is transparent to the wavelengths at which such objects emit most of their visible light will darken the sky background without appreciably dimming the object of interest. With narrow-band, interference-type filters, the effect can be dramatic, improving contrast and revealing details that otherwise are completely invisible. It is the next best thing to observing these objects from above Earth's atmosphere.

Dark-adapted *(scotopic)* human vision responds to light in the 400 nm to 620 nm range. In bright light *(photopic* vision) the spectral range extends to somewhat longer wavelengths, about 750 nm. For both types of vision, the response curve (sensitivity versus wavelength) is "bell-shaped", the wavelength of maximum sensitivity being in the middle of the visible range—near 510 nm for scotopic vision and 555 nm for photopic vision. The photopic sensation produced by 555 nm light is green; for scotopic vision, colour is not produced, but at photopic levels 510 nm light appears blue-green.

Hydrogen is the predominant element in the universe. Atomic hydrogen, when excited by ultraviolet radiation from a nearby hot star, emits light in the visible spectrum at only four discrete wavelengths: 656 nm, 486 nm, 434 nm, and 410 nm (designated as $H\alpha$, $H\beta$, $H\gamma$, and $H\delta$, respectively, part of the "Balmer spectrum" of hydrogen). Scotopic vision is blind to 656 nm ($H\alpha$) light and relatively insensitive to the less intense 434 nm and 410 nm light. However, 486 nm ($H\beta$) lies near the 510 nm peak sensitivity of scotopic vision, and an **$H\beta$ ("H-beta") filter**, which has a narrow bandpass at this wavelength will greatly reduce the surrounding sky brightness and reveal $H\beta$-emitting nebulae.

The classic example is the Horsehead Nebula, a dark, silhouetted column of dust just southeast of Orion's belt. The surrounding hydrogen gas, excited probably by the nearby hot star ζ Orionis, fluoresces dimly with $H\beta$ light. If the obscuring airglow is blocked by an $H\beta$ filter, the dark Horsehead can distinctly be seen in a telescope having an aperture of 400 mm or greater.

Two other nebular emission lines lie at 496 nm and 501 nm, nearly at the peak sensitivity of scotopic vision. Originally detected in 1864 by the British astronomer William Huggins, the origin of these lines was unknown at that time, and they were attributed to a hypothetical new element, "nebulium." In 1927, the American astrophysicist Ira Bowen identified the lines as due to doubly ionized oxygen (O^{++} or "OIII"), which glows brightly when very low-density nebular gas is strongly excited (high temperature). A filter that has a narrow bandpass spanning these two wavelengths gives striking views of highly excited nebulae. A good example is the Veil Nebula, a supernova remnant in eastern Cygnus. Through an **OIII filter** on a dark, transparent night, the direct view of the Veil in a large amateur telescope is more spectacular than any photograph or CCD image. Planetary nebulae (fluorescing, low-density shells of gas surrounding hot central stars) also show up well with an OIII filter. Filters with wider bandpasses (about 20 nm, encompassing both the $H\beta$ and OIII lines) also enhance views of many nebulae, but the wider the bandpass, the brighter the sky background.

Stars emit light across the entire visible spectrum. Thus filters do not dramatically improve views of single stars, star clusters, or galaxies. Filters with wide bandpasses (near 90 nm—from about 440 nm to 530 nm) decrease the airglow and block the brighter wavelengths emitted by sodium- and mercury-vapour street lights, without dimming stars and galaxies too much. However, under dark skies the single most useful filter is probably the narrow-band OIII.

The article "Nebula Filters for Light-Polluted Skies," which includes bandpass graphs for several filters, appears in the July 1995 issue of *Sky & Telescope*, pp. 38–42.

SKY TRANSPARENCY
BY DOUGLAS PITCAIRN

One of the many difficulties with astronomical observing from the surface of our planet is the variability of the atmosphere. In any record of observations, it is important that the condition of the sky be noted. Parameters such as brightness and contrast are greatly affected by the transparency of the sky and the presence of light pollution or aurora.

One of the simplest ways to quantify local sky conditions is to note the magnitude of the faintest star visible with the unaided eye. Although individuals differ in their ability to detect faint stars, these differences are generally small, and for any one observer such observations provide a consistent measure of sky quality.

The chart below shows a 12°-wide field in the vicinity of Polaris (the brightest star on the chart), and is useful for observers at latitude 20°N or higher. For orientation, the solid lines indicate the beginning of the handle of the Little Dipper, as in the ALL-SKY MAPS on pp. 277–282. Several stars have their visual magnitudes indicated (with decimal points omitted).

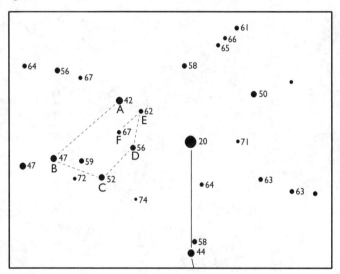

This field has several advantages: it is always above the horizon in midnorthern latitudes; its altitude does not change with the time of night or year, so the variation of atmospheric extinction with altitude is not a consideration; there are no bright stars or planets in the field to dazzle the eye; the faint stars are quite well-spaced and therefore easy to identify; and being a simple field, it can be memorized. Especially note the dashed spiral of descending magnitudes labelled "A" through "F."

Atmospheric extinction varies with altitude above the horizon. To normalize observations to the zenith (altitude 90°), the following values should be added to estimates of faintest visible magnitude obtained using the chart (format: latitude range/**correction**):

18°–20°/**0.5**; 20°–24°/**0.4**; 24°–29°/**0.3**; 29°–36°/**0.2**; 36°–52°/**0.1**; 52°–90°/**0.0**

These corrections are for near sea level, and would be less at high elevations. Also, excellent sky conditions are assumed; under less than ideal conditions the corrections are generally larger and can be quite uncertain, especially at lower latitudes where Polaris is closer to the horizon.

FREQUENCY OF CLEAR NIGHT SKIES IN JULY AND AUGUST

By Jay Anderson

The majority of users of this Handbook live in the region of North America shown in the above map. For amateur astronomers, warm weather, vacations, star parties, the presence of the Cygnus-to-Sagittarius Milky Way in the evening sky, and the Perseid meteors make the months of July and August the prime observing period of the year.

The contour lines on the map indicate the percent frequency of clear or mostly clear (≤ 3/10 cloud cover and no fog) skies for the midnight to dawn interval averaged over July and August. The map is based upon U.S. Air Force data from over 730 stations across North America over a 7- to 12-year period ending in 1990.

The map may be used to compare the probability of clear skies at various star parties, to select sites for viewing special astronomical events, or when deciding where to retire to get the best summertime night skies.

LIGHT POLLUTION
By David L. Crawford

A Lost Heritage: During this century, most people have lost the spectacular view of the universe that their ancestors enjoyed on clear nights. The development of electrical lighting technology and the increase in urban population has caused a rapid increase in sky glow above towns and cities. Few members of the general public have ever seen a prime dark sky. For urban dwellers, star-studded nights are limited to simulations at planetaria. Comets Hyakutake and Hale-Bopp, the most spectacular comets of our time, were for many people merely dim fuzz-balls because of the glare of light pollution. Even in rural areas, poorly-designed yard lights often obscure the splendour of the night sky. As Leslie Peltier, one of the most famous amateur astronomers of the 20th century, stated eloquently in his autobiography *Starlight Nights:*

> *"The moon and the stars no longer come to the farm. The farmer has exchanged his birthright in them for the wattage of his all-night sun. His children will never know the blessed dark of night."*

The increased sky glow that adversely affects the environment is called *light pollution*, for it originates mainly from excess light that does nothing to increase useful nighttime illumination. It is light that sprays horizontally and upward into the sky from poorly designed lighting fixtures. It is light that glares into the eyes of motorists and home-owners, compromising visibility, safety, and security. It is light that depresses property values by

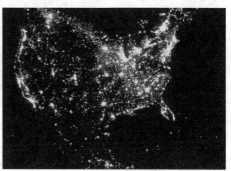

A nighttime satellite view of central North America

reducing the aesthetic quality of a neighbourhood. In the United States and Canada over a billion dollars annually plus large amounts of energy are lost in generating this wasted light.

Light pollution is a **special threat to astronomy**. Many observations, including most of those of cosmological interest, can be made only from prime observing sites, remote from centres of population. Some older observatories, such as the David Dunlap in Ontario and Mount Wilson in California, are severely affected by light pollution from nearby urban centres. New observatories usually are located at remote sites, and amateur astronomers routinely drive large distances to escape the glare of towns and cities. The argument that all astronomy can be done from space is incorrect because it does not make sense to do in space, at much higher cost, what can be done from the ground. There are observations that can only be done from space, but more than three decades of space astronomy have greatly increased the need for ground-based observatories.

Solutions exist to the problem of light pollution, and outdoor lighting ordinances have been instituted in a number of communities near large observatories, such as Tucson, Arizona and San Diego, California. *The main solution is the use of full-cutoff lighting fixtures that direct all their light below the horizontal, such that the light source itself is not directly visible from the side—an almost universal fault with street and yard lights. Since this places the light where it is needed, less total light and thus less electrical energy is required.*

Examples of inefficient street lighting

Additional major cost savings are realized by switching to light sources that are more efficient—that require less power to produce a given amount of light. In increasing order of efficiency, common types of outdoor lights are: incandescent (ordinary bulbs, 60), mercury vapour (a violet-white light, 24), metal halide (white, 17), high-pressure sodium (orange-gold, 12), and low-pressure sodium (yellow, 8). The comparative numbers are in units of watts per 1000 lumens (W/klm), and indicate the approximate amount of electrical power (watts) required to produce the same amount of visible light (1000 lm). In addition to providing light at the lowest cost, low pressure sodium (LPS) lights are nearly monochromatic with the result that much of their glare can be filtered out by astronomers. LPS is especially good for street lighting, parking lot lighting, security lighting, and any application where colour rendering is not important.

Although full-cutoff, efficient light fixtures generally have a higher capital cost than polluting fixtures, this cost is quickly recovered through the much lower operating costs. In California, the cities of Long Beach, San Diego, and San Jose each are realizing substantial savings each year through extensive use of LPS street lighting. For example, one can usually replace a 175-watt mercury vapour lighting fixture with a full-cutoff, 35-watt LPS fixture and get the same amount of useful light, with none of the glare and light trespass. The energy saving is remarkable, as is the better visibility.

An example of a full-cutoff, efficient light fixture

Even less light pollution and more savings can be realized by using *no more light than is required*. In particular, too much light and/or poorly shielded lights can ruin adaptation to night lighting, blinding us just when we need to see. When we go from too bright to too dark or vice versa, "transient adaptation" is impaired and we have poor visibility for awhile. Do not exceed IESNA (Illuminating Engineering Society of North America) recommended lighting levels. Overkill never helps, it usually just adds glare and it always wastes energy. In addition, lights should be used only when necessary (e.g. timers are useful for controlling lights).

Increased lighting generally gives a perception of greater security, yet there is no statistically significant evidence that more lighting results in less crime. Criminals need light. "Security lights" provide this, may draw attention to a house or business that would otherwise not be noticed, and mask any additional light criminals may need to do their work. Our cities and towns are far more brightly lit than ever, yet the crime rate soars. Security can best be provided by shielded, motion-activated lights which come on only when movement occurs nearby. These serve to frighten criminals, alert others that there is a potential problem, provide glare-free visibility (when properly installed so as to be glare free), and use insignificant amounts of energy.

Lack of awareness, rather than resistance, is the biggest problem in controlling light pollution. After all, it costs money to light pollute! Unlike the case with many other forms of pollution, simple solutions are available, and moreover, *everyone benefits* in applying these solutions. Most people are not yet conscious of the expense, the waste, and the harm associated with excess lighting. They put up with distant lights that shine directly into their eyes, not realizing that not only does this do *nothing* to illuminate the area near the light, but that it also produces a veiling glare. The pollution involves not only the light itself, but also other forms of environmental pollution associated with the extraction, transportation, and burning of the coal and oil which usually provides much of the energy used to supply the wasted light. This general lack of awareness has been summarized nicely by Doug Pitcairn, an astronomy teacher in Nova Scotia:

> *"It surprises me how someone who would never think of leaving a plastic bottle on the ground at a picnic site will pay extra money each month to illuminate half the neighbourhood with unnecessary, distracting light."*

Educating the public, government officials, lighting professionals, and astronomers is a major thrust of current programs. These efforts have helped. Most committees in the IESNA have been addressing these issues and upcoming Recommended Practices and other documents are fully reflecting these concerns. As they are issued, one will expect to see them implemented, albeit on a slow time schedule. Astronomers and environmentalists should do all they can to help publicize these documents when they come out, so as to help get them into existing practices in our communities.

The International Dark-Sky Association (IDA) is a tax-exempt, nonprofit, membership organization dedicated to overcoming this awareness problem, with the goal of preserving dark skies while at the same time maximizing the quality and efficiency of nighttime outdoor lighting. The IDA needs your help. Memberships begin at $30 (US) per year. To join this effort, or to obtain further information on any aspects of the issue, write to the International Dark-Sky Association, 3225 N. First Avenue, Tucson, AZ 85719, USA (phone: (520) 293-3198, fax: (520) 293-3192, email: ida@darksky.org, web site: http://www.darksky.org). Plenty of useful information is on the web site, including images, and content is being added regularly. The IDA has many information sheets available to assist you in educating others, in several languages including English and French, and can provide examples of lighting ordinances that have been enacted in many communities to enforce high quality, effective nighttime lighting. For more information, see the July 1990 (p. 23) and September 1998 issues of *Sky & Telescope*.

Within Canada, the Royal Astronomical Society of Canada has an active Light Pollution Abatement Committee under the chairmanship of Robert Dick (his address: P.O. Box 79, Rideau Ferry, ON K0G 1W0, email: rdick@ccs.carleton.ca); or you may contact the RASC directly (see p. 8). Also, some local Centres of the RASC have taken action to address poor lighting practices in their areas.

Editor's Note: An indication that the IDA is beginning to make its message heard where it counts is the recent election of IDA's (volunteer) executive director, David Crawford, as a Fellow of the Illuminating Engineering Society of North America. However, although the IDA has members in 70 countries, its total membership as of July 2000 was only about 4500 (with 146 from Canada). This is less than 5% of the community of amateur and professional astronomers. As Daniel Green of the Smithsonian Astrophysical Observatory has put it (see *Sky & Telescope*, May 1998, p. 10): *"Where are all the astronomers?"* Anyone who values the night sky should support this unique and deserving organization. An annual membership in the IDA is only about the cost of an hour's drive to a dark observing site.

THE SKY MONTH BY MONTH

LEFT-HAND PAGES BY DAVID LANE

INTRODUCTION

In the descriptions on the next 24 pages (two pages for each month), the right ascension (RA), declination (Dec) (both for epoch J2000.0), distance from Earth's centre in AU (Dist), visual magnitude (Mag), and equatorial angular diameter (Size) are tabulated for seven planets for 0h UT on the 1st, 11th, and 21st day of each month. Unless noted otherwise, the descriptive comments about the planets apply to the middle of the month. Any stated planet visibility times are in local standard time. "Northern observers" and "southern observers" are assumed to be at latitudes 45°N and 30°S, respectively. Descriptions are given first for northern observers and then for southern observers. Events of special interest are in **boldface**.

Sun—Data concerning the position, transit, orientation, rotation, activity, and rise and set of the Sun appear on pp. 82–92. For detailed information on solar eclipses during the year, see ECLIPSES DURING 2001 on pp. 115–138.

Moon

The phases, perigee and apogee times and distances of the Moon (distances from: *Astronomical Tables of the Sun, Moon, and Planets* by Jean Meeus, 2nd. ed., Willmann-Bell, 1995), and its conjunctions with the planets, are given in the monthly tables. For times of moonrise and moonset, see pp. 98–111.

Elongation, age, and phase of the Moon—The elongation is the angular distance of the Moon from the Sun counted eastward around the sky. Thus elongations of 0°, 90°, 180°, and 270° correspond to the phases: new, first quarter, full, and last quarter, respectively. The age of the Moon is the time since the new phase. Because the Moon's orbital motion is not uniform, age does not accurately specify phase. The Moon's elongation increases on the average by 12.2° per day, first quarter, full, and last quarter phases corresponding approximately to 7.4, 14.8, and 22.1 days, respectively.

The Sun's selenographic colongitude (SSC) indicates the position of the sunrise terminator as it moves across the face of the Moon, and provides an accurate method of ascertaining the angle of illumination of features on the Moon's surface. The SSC is the angle of the sunrise terminator measured toward the observer's east (i.e. westward on the Moon) starting from the lunar meridian which passes through the mean centre of the apparent disk. Its value increases by nearly 12.2° per day or about 0.5° per hour and is approximately 0°, 90°, 180°, and 270° at the first quarter, full, last quarter, and new phases, respectively. Values of the SSC are given on the following pages for the beginning of each month.

Selenographic longitude (λ) is measured toward the observer's west (i.e. eastward on the Moon) from the mean central lunar meridian. Thus sunrise will occur at a given point on the Moon when SSC = $(360° - \lambda)$, values of which for several lunar features are listed in the MAP OF MOON on pp. 96–97. The longitude of the sunset terminator differs by 180° from that of the sunrise terminator.

Libration is the apparent rocking motion of the Moon as it orbits around Earth. As a consequence, over time, about 59% of the lunar surface can be viewed from Earth (see *Sky & Telescope*, July 1987, p. 60). Libration in longitude (up to ±8°) results from the nearly uniform axial rotation of the Moon combined with its varying orbital speed along its elliptical orbit, while libration in latitude (±7°) is caused by the tilt of the Moon's equator to its orbital plane. A smaller contribution (up to ±1°), called *diurnal libration*, is associated with the shifting of the observer due to Earth's rotation.

When the libration in longitude is positive, more of the Moon's east limb, the limb near Mare Crisium, is exposed to view (in reference to the lunar limbs, *east* and *west* are used in this lunar sense. See also the "E" and "W" labels on the MAP OF MOON). When the libration in latitude is positive, more of the Moon's north limb is exposed to view. The monthly dates of the greatest positive and negative values of the libration in longitude and latitude are given in the following pages, as are the dates of greatest northern and southern declination.

The Moon's orbit is inclined at 5°09′ to the ecliptic. The gravitational influences of Earth and Sun cause the orbital plane to (1) wobble and the major axis of the orbit to (2) precess. (1) The wobble shifts the line of nodes westward (retrograde) along the ecliptic with a period of 18.61 years. During 2001 the ascending node regresses from longitude 105.7° to 86.4°, from Gemini into Taurus. Thus the ascending node is yet further from the autumnal equinox (at longitude 180°), and the monthly range of the Moon's declination increases from its 1997 minimum of ±18° to ±24° by the end of 2001. (2) The precession shifts the perigee point eastward (direct) with a period of 8.85 years, although the positions of successive perigees fluctuate considerably from the mean motion. The Moon's mean equatorial plane, its mean orbital plane, and the plane of the ecliptic intersect along a common line of nodes, the equator being inclined at 1°32′ to the ecliptic and at 1°32′ + 5°09′ = 6°41′ to the orbit (i.e. the ascending node of the equator on the ecliptic coincides with the descending node of the orbit).

Planets—See CONTENTS or the INDEX for the location of more information on each of the planets.

Jupiter's Satellites—The configurations of Jupiter's Galilean satellites, provided by Larry Bogan, are given on the right side of the monthly pages. In these diagrams, the central, vertical, straight, double line represents the equatorial diameter of the disk of Jupiter. Time is shown on the vertical scale, successive horizontal lines indicating 0h UT on the various days of the month. The relative east–west positions of the four satellites with respect to the disk of Jupiter are given by the four curves, where: I = Io, II = Europa (dashed curve), III = Ganymede, IV = Callisto. Note the "West–East" orientation given at the top of each diagram; these directions are those of the observer's sky, not Jupiter's limbs, and correspond to the view in an inverting telescope. For the various transits, occultations, and eclipses of Jupiter's Galilean satellites, see PHENOMENA OF THE GALILEAN SATELLITES on pp. 182–188. (Diagrams are also given for the five brightest satellites of Saturn. See CONFIGURATIONS OF SATURN'S BRIGHTEST SATELLITES on pp. 189–192.)

Minima of Algol—Predicted times of mideclipse are based on the formula heliocentric minimum = 244 1598.608 + 2.867315*E*, and are expressed as geocentric times for comparison with observations (the first number is the Julian date for the minimum of 1972 October 8.108 and the second is the period of Algol in days; *E* is an integer).

Occultations Involving the Moon, Stars, Planets, and Asteroids—See "Occultations" in the INDEX and the footnotes on the next 12 right-hand pages.

THE SKY FOR JANUARY 2001

		Mercury	Venus	Mars	Jupiter	Saturn	Uranus	Neptune
RA	1	19h 03m	21h 59m	14h 12m	04h 01m	03h 31m	21h 25m	20h 31m
	11	20h 14m	22h 39m	14h 35m	03h 58m	03h 30m	21h 27m	20h 32m
	21	21h 20m	23h 16m	14h 57m	03h 57m	03h 29m	21h 29m	20h 34m
Dec	1	−24° 38′	−13° 57′	−11° 59′	+19° 48′	+16° 47′	−15° 53′	−18° 46′
	11	−22° 02′	−09° 23′	−13° 53′	+19° 43′	+16° 44′	−15° 44′	−18° 41′
	21	−16° 59′	−04° 35′	−15° 37′	+19° 41′	+16° 45′	−15° 33′	−18° 36′
Dist	1	1.42	0.81	1.79	4.24	8.40	20.72	31.00
	11	1.33	0.73	1.69	4.35	8.53	20.82	31.06
	21	1.16	0.66	1.59	4.48	8.68	20.89	31.09
Mag	1	−1.1	−4.3	1.4	−2.7	−0.5	5.9	8.0
	11	−1.0	−4.4	1.2	−2.7	−0.4	5.9	8.0
	21	−0.9	−4.4	1.1	−2.6	−0.3	5.9	8.0
Size	1	4.7″	20.7″	5.2″	46.4″	19.7″	3.4″	2.2″
	11	5.1″	22.8″	5.5″	45.2″	19.4″	3.4″	2.2″
	21	5.8″	25.3″	5.9″	43.9″	19.1″	3.4″	2.2″

Moon—On Jan. 1.0 UT, the age of the Moon is 6.3 d. The Sun's selenographic colongitude is 343.81° and increases by 12.2° each day thereafter. The libration in longitude is maximum (east limb exposed) on Jan. 16 (+8°) and minimum (west limb exposed) on Jan. 4 (−8°). (See the paragraph concerning libration two pages earlier.) The libration in latitude is maximum (north limb exposed) on Jan. 3 (+7°) and Jan. 30 (+7°) and minimum (south limb exposed) on Jan. 15 (−7°). The Moon reaches its greatest northern declination on Jan. 9 (+23°) and its greatest southern declination on Jan. 22 (−23°).

There is a **total lunar eclipse** on January 9 (see p. 115 in ECLIPSES DURING 2001).

On January 10 the Moon reaches its second closest perigee distance of the year (357 130 km). With a full moon occurring about a day earlier, extra large tides will occur (see the section TIDES AND THE EARTH–MOON SYSTEM on pp. 159–161).

Mercury emerges in the evening twilight about midmonth, reaching greatest elongation east (18°) on the 28th. It can be seen very low in the southwest after sunset. Southern observers can see it with difficulty very low in the west-southwest after sunset. Near month's end Mercury fades rapidly.

Venus is at greatest elongation east on the 17th. It is about 25° high in the southwest during evening twilight and sets in midevening. Southern observers will find Venus only about 20° high in the west during evening twilight and setting about 2.5 h after the Sun.

Mars moves from Virgo to Libra early in the month. It rises near 2 a.m. in the southeast and stands about 25° high in the south-southeast at the beginning of morning twilight. For more favoured southern observers, Mars rises in the east after midnight and stands about 40° high in the east at the beginning of morning twilight.

Jupiter, in Taurus, is about 55° high in the southeast at the end of evening twilight and sets in the west-northwest near 4 a.m. For southern observers, it is 40° high and near the meridian at the end of evening twilight and sets in the west-northwest after midnight.

Saturn, in Taurus, is high in the southeast at the end of evening twilight and sets near 3 a.m. For southern observers, Saturn is near the meridian after the end of evening twilight and sets near 1 a.m. The south side of its ring system faces Earth for the next 8 years (the rings were last edge-on in 1996 February). During 2001 the tilt of the rings increases from 23.1° in January to 26.2° in early September and then closes slightly to 25.8° by late December.

Time (UT) d h m	JANUARY EVENTS	Configuration of Jupiter's Satellites

West   East

Time (UT)	JANUARY EVENTS
Mon. 1	
Tue. 2 20 05	Algol at minimum
22 31	**First Quarter**
Wed. 3 12	**Quadrantid meteors peak**
Thu. 4 9	Earth at perihelion (147 097 Mm)
Fri. 5 16 54	Algol at minimum
Sat. 6 1	**Saturn 2° N of Moon**
14	Jupiter 3° N of Moon
Sun. 7	
Mon. 8	Mercury at greatest heliocentric latitude S
3 13	**Double shadow transit on Jupiter**
13 44	Algol at minimum
Tue. 9 20 24	**Full Moon, Total Lunar Eclipse**
Wed. 10 9	Moon at perigee (357 130 km) (Large tides)
Thu. 11 10 33	Algol at minimum
Fri. 12	
Sat. 13 17	Mercury 2° S of Neptune
Sun. 14 7 22	Algol at minimum
Mon. 15 6 36	**Double shadow transit on Jupiter**
Tue. 16 12 35	**Last Quarter**
Wed. 17 4 11	Algol at minimum
6	**Venus greatest elongation E (47°)**
20	Mars 4° S of Moon
Thu. 18	
Fri. 19	Venus at ascending node
Sat. 20 1 01	Algol at minimum
Sun. 21 4	Ceres 0.7° S of Moon, Occultation†
Mon. 22 18	Mercury 0.4° S of Uranus
21 50	Algol at minimum
Tue. 23	
Wed. 24 13 07	**New Moon**
19	Moon at apogee (**406 562 km**)
Thu. 25 15	Jupiter stationary
16	Saturn stationary
18 39	Algol at minimum
Fri. 26 3	Mercury 3° N of Moon
4	Neptune in conjunction with Sun
Sat. 27	Mercury at ascending node
11	Vesta 0.8° S of Moon, Occultation‡
Sun. 28 13	**Mercury greatest elongation E (18°)**
14	Venus 6° N of Moon
15 29	Algol at minimum
Mon. 29	
Tue. 30	
Wed. 31 12 18	Algol at minimum

0.0
1.0
2.0
3.0
4.0
5.0
6.0   II   III
          I
7.0
8.0   IV
9.0
10.0
11.0
12.0
13.0
14.0
15.0
16.0
17.0
18.0
19.0
20.0
21.0
22.0
23.0
24.0
25.0
26.0
27.0
28.0
29.0
30.0
31.0
32.0

† Visible from Asia except NE.
‡ Visible from N of Africa, Europe including British Isles, Middle East, Russia except E.

THE SKY FOR FEBRUARY 2001

		Mercury	Venus	Mars	Jupiter	Saturn	Uranus	Neptune
RA	1	22h 06m	23h 52m	15h 22m	03h 57m	03h 29m	21h 32m	20h 35m
	11	21h 51m	00h 20m	15h 44m	03h 59m	03h 30m	21h 34m	20h 37m
	21	21h 13m	00h 41m	16h 05m	04h 02m	03h 31m	21h 36m	20h 38m
Dec	1	−10° 33′	+00° 42′	−17° 20′	+19° 45′	+16° 48′	−15° 21′	−18° 30′
	11	−09° 21′	+05° 15′	−18° 41′	+19° 52′	+16° 54′	−15° 10′	−18° 24′
	21	−12° 59′	+09° 15′	−19° 51′	+20° 03′	+17° 03′	−15° 00′	−18° 19′
Dist	1	0.87	0.58	1.48	4.65	8.85	20.94	31.09
	11	0.66	0.50	1.38	4.80	9.02	20.95	31.06
	21	0.67	0.44	1.28	4.97	9.18	20.93	31.00
Mag	1	−0.1	−4.5	1.0	−2.5	−0.3	5.9	8.0
	11	3.9	−4.6	0.8	−2.5	−0.2	5.9	8.0
	21	1.8	−4.6	0.7	−2.4	−0.2	5.9	8.0
Size	1	7.7″	28.9″	6.3″	42.4″	18.7″	3.3″	2.2″
	11	10.1″	33.0″	6.8″	41.0″	18.3″	3.3″	2.2″
	21	10.0″	38.3″	7.3″	39.7″	18.0″	3.3″	2.2″

Moon—On Feb. 1.0 UT, the age of the Moon is 7.5 d. The Sun's selenographic colongitude is 0.75° and increases by 12.2° each day thereafter. The libration in longitude is maximum (east limb exposed) on Feb. 13 (+8°), and minimum (west limb exposed) on Feb. 1 (−8°). The libration in latitude is maximum (north limb exposed) on Feb. 26 (+7°) and minimum (south limb exposed) on Feb. 12 (−7°). The Moon reaches its greatest northern declination on Feb. 5 (+23°) and its greatest southern declination on Feb. 18 (−23°).

On Feb. 7 the Moon reaches its closest perigee distance of the year (356 852 km). With a Full Moon occurring less than half a day later, extra large tides will occur (see the section TIDES AND THE EARTH–MOON SYSTEM on pp. 159–161).

Mercury is not easily observed this month. For northern observers, it is visible with difficulty very low in the west-southwest in the first few days of the month as it approaches inferior conjunction with the Sun on the 15th. Mercury re-emerges in the east-southeast morning sky for both northern and southern observers late in the month; however because it is faint, it is difficult to observe.

Venus is at greatest brilliancy on the 22nd. It stands about 30° high in the west-southwest during evening twilight and sets in midevening. Less favoured southern observers will find Venus only about 10° high in the west during evening twilight and setting less than 2 h after the Sun.

Mars moves from Libra to Scorpius late in the month. It rises in the east-southeast after 1 a.m. and stands about 25° high in the south-southeast at the beginning of morning twilight. For more favoured southern observers, Mars rises before midnight in the east-southeast and at the beginning of morning twilight stands about 60° high in the west.

Jupiter, in Taurus, stands about 65° high near the meridian after darkness falls and sets in the west-northwest after midnight. Southern observers will find Jupiter just over 30° above the northwestern horizon at the end of evening twilight; it sets in the west-northwest before midnight.

Saturn, in Taurus, is in the south-southwest at the end of evening twilight and sets after midnight. For less favoured southern observers, Saturn is in the northwest at the end of evening twilight and sets in late-evening.

Time (UT) d h m	FEBRUARY EVENTS	Configuration of Jupiter's Satellites
Thu. 1	Mercury at perihelion	
14 02	**First Quarter**	
Fri. 2 10	**Saturn 2° N of Moon**	
22	Jupiter 3° N of Moon	
Sat. 3 9 07	Algol at minimum	
12	Mercury stationary	
Sun. 4		
Mon. 5		
Tue. 6 5 56	Algol at minimum	
Wed. 7 22	Moon at perigee (**356 852 km**) (Large tides)	
Thu. 8 7 12	**Full Moon (Largest of 2001)**	
Fri. 9 2 46	Algol at minimum	
12	Uranus in conjunction with Sun	
Sat. 10 0	Mercury in inferior conjunction	
Sun. 11	Mercury at greatest heliocentric latitude N	
	Zodiacal Light vis. in N latitudes in W after end of evening twilight for next two weeks	
23 35	Algol at minimum	
Mon. 12		
Tue. 13		
Wed. 14 20 24	Algol at minimum	
Thu. 15 3 23	**Last Quarter**	
10	Mars 3° S of Moon	
Fri. 16		
Sat. 17 17 14	Algol at minimum	
Sun. 18 7	Ceres 0.5° S of Moon, Occultation†	
Mon. 19		
Tue. 20 14 03	Algol at minimum	
22	Moon at apogee (406 332 km)	
23	Neptune 2° N of Moon	
Wed. 21 16	Mercury 6° N of Moon	
Thu. 22	Venus at perihelion	
1	**Venus greatest brilliancy**	
Fri. 23 8 21	**New Moon**	
10 52	Algol at minimum	
Sat. 24 19	Vesta 0.2° S of Moon, Occultation‡	
Sun. 25 2	Mercury stationary	
17	Juno 1.0° N of Moon, Occultation††	
Mon. 26 7 41	Algol at minimum	
8	Venus 11° N of Moon	
Tue. 27		
Wed. 28		

West   East

0.0
1.0
2.0
3.0
4.0
5.0
6.0
7.0   III   I   IV
8.0
9.0   II
10.0
11.0
12.0
13.0
14.0
15.0
16.0
17.0
18.0
19.0
20.0
21.0
22.0
23.0
24.0
25.0
26.0
27.0
28.0
29.0
30.0
31.0
32.0

† Visible from Spain, N and central Africa, Saudi Arabia, India.
‡ Visible from central Pacific Ocean, Central America, Florida, Caribbean.
†† Visible from tip of S Africa, S Atlantic Ocean, part of Antarctica.

THE SKY FOR MARCH 2001

		Mercury	Venus	Mars	Jupiter	Saturn	Uranus	Neptune
RA	1	21h 12m	00h 52m	16h 22m	04h 05m	03h 33m	21h 38m	20h 39m
	11	21h 42m	00h 54m	16h 42m	04h 10m	03h 36m	21h 40m	20h 41m
	21	22h 29m	00h 41m	17h 01m	04h 16m	03h 39m	21h 42m	20h 42m
Dec	1	−14° 49′	+11° 48′	−20° 39′	+20° 13′	+17° 11′	−14° 51′	−18° 15′
	11	−14° 27′	+13° 41′	−21° 30′	+20° 29′	+17° 24′	−14° 40′	−18° 10′
	21	−11° 30′	+13° 27′	−22° 11′	+20° 46′	+17° 37′	−14° 30′	−18° 06′
Dist	1	0.78	0.38	1.20	5.09	9.31	20.90	30.93
	11	0.93	0.33	1.10	5.25	9.47	20.84	30.83
	21	1.07	0.29	1.01	5.40	9.62	20.75	30.70
Mag	1	0.6	−4.6	0.5	−2.3	−0.2	5.9	8.0
	11	0.2	−4.5	0.3	−2.3	−0.2	5.9	8.0
	21	0.0	−4.3	0.1	−2.2	−0.2	5.9	8.0
Size	1	8.6″	43.4″	7.8″	38.6″	17.8″	3.4″	2.2″
	11	7.2″	50.5″	8.5″	37.5″	17.5″	3.4″	2.2″
	21	6.3″	56.8″	9.3″	36.4″	17.2″	3.4″	2.2″

Moon—On Mar. 1.0 UT, the age of the Moon is 5.7 d. The Sun's selenographic colongitude is 341.41° and increases by 12.2° each day thereafter. The libration in longitude is maximum (east limb exposed) on Mar. 14 (+7°) and minimum (west limb exposed) on Mar. 1 (−7°) and Mar. 28 (−6°). The libration in latitude is maximum (north limb exposed) on Mar. 25 (+7°) and minimum (south limb exposed) on Mar. 11 (−7°). The Moon reaches its greatest northern declination on Mar. 5 (+23°) and its greatest southern declination on Mar. 18 (−23°).

Mercury is not easily observed this month by northern observers. For southern observers, it continues what becomes its **best morning apparition of the year**. It is at greatest elongation west (27°) on the 11th. At midmonth Mercury rises over 2 h before the Sun and stands nearly 10° above the eastern horizon at the beginning of morning twilight.

Venus begins the month low in the west after dark. It becomes increasingly difficult to observe in evening twilight late in the month as it approaches conjunction with the Sun on the 30th. This is a favourable inferior conjunction for northern observers; see pp. 168–169 in the section THE PLANETS FOR 2001. Less favoured southern observers will lose sight of Venus in the glare of the Sun early in the month.

Mars moves from Scorpius to Ophiuchus early in the month. It rises in the east-southeast after midnight and stands about 20° high in the south-southeast at the beginning of morning twilight. For more favoured southern observers, Mars rises in late-evening in the east-southeast and reaches a height of nearly 80° in the northeast as morning twilight begins.

Jupiter, in Taurus, stands over 40° high in the west at the end of evening twilight and sets in the west-northwest near midnight. Less favoured southern observers will find Jupiter less than 25° above the northwestern horizon at the end of evening twilight and setting about 2 h later.

Saturn, in Taurus, is in the west at the end of evening twilight and sets before midnight. For less favoured southern observers, Saturn stands about 20° above the western horizon at the end of evening twilight and sets about 3 h after the Sun.

Time (UT) d h m	MARCH EVENTS	Configuration of Jupiter's Satellites
Thu. 1 4 31	Algol at minimum	West East
18	**Saturn 2° N of Moon**	0.0
Fri. 2 9	Jupiter 3° N of Moon	
Sat. 3 2 03	**First Quarter**	1.0
Sun. 4 1 20	Algol at minimum	2.0
14	Mars 5° N of Antares	3.0
Tue. 6 22 09	Algol at minimum	
Wed. 7	Mercury at descending node	4.0
11	Venus stationary	5.0
Thu. 8 9	Moon at perigee (359 775 km)	
Fri. 9 17 23	**Full Moon**	6.0
18 58	Algol at minimum	7.0
Sat. 10 11	Mercury 0.1° N of Uranus	8.0
Sun. 11 6	**Mercury greatest elongation W (27°)**	
Mon. 12	**Zodiacal Light** vis. in N latitudes in W after end of evening twilight for next two weeks	9.0 10.0
15 48	Algol at minimum	11.0
Tue. 13 16 39	**Double shadow transit on Jupiter**	
Wed. 14		12.0
Thu. 15 12 37	Algol at minimum	13.0
21	**Mars 1.8° S of Moon**	14.0
Fri. 16	Venus at greatest heliocentric latitude N	
20 45	**Last Quarter**	15.0
Sat. 17	Mercury at aphelion	16.0
Sun. 18 7	Ceres 0.5° S of Moon, Occultation†	
9 26	Algol at minimum	17.0
22	Pluto stationary	18.0
Mon. 19		19.0
Tue. 20 8	Neptune 2° N of Moon	
11	Moon at apogee (405 474 km)	20.0
13 31	**Equinox**	21.0
19 14	**Double shadow transit on Jupiter**	22.0
Wed. 21 6 15	Algol at minimum	
14	Uranus 3° N of Moon	23.0
Thu. 22 18	**Mercury 2° N of Moon**	24.0
Fri. 23		
Sat. 24 3 04	Algol at minimum	25.0
Sun. 25 1 21	**New Moon**	26.0
Mon. 26 23 54	Algol at minimum	27.0
Tue. 27 7	Vesta in conjunction with Sun	
22 48	**Double shadow transit on Jupiter**	28.0
Wed. 28		29.0
Thu. 29 4	**Saturn 1.7° N of Moon**	30.0
20 43	Algol at minimum	
21	**Jupiter 2° N of Moon**	31.0
Fri. 30 4	**Venus in inferior conjunction (8° N of Sun)**	32.0
Sat. 31		

† Visible from Atlantic Ocean, W, central, and NE Africa, Middle East.

THE SKY FOR APRIL 2001

		Mercury	Venus	Mars	Jupiter	Saturn	Uranus	Neptune
RA	1	23h 31m	00h 18m	17h 19m	04h 24m	03h 44m	21h 44m	20h 43m
	11	00h 34m	00h 02m	17h 34m	04h 31m	03h 48m	21h 46m	20h 44m
	21	01h 46m	23h 59m	17h 45m	04h 40m	03h 53m	21h 47m	20h 44m
Dec	1	−05° 44′	+10° 30′	−22° 48′	+21° 07′	+17° 54′	−14° 21′	−18° 02′
	11	+01° 29′	+06° 47′	−23° 16′	+21° 25′	+18° 10′	−14° 13′	−17° 59′
	21	+10° 04′	+04° 01′	−23° 42′	+21° 44′	+18° 26′	−14° 06′	−17° 57′
Dist	1	1.20	0.28	0.90	5.56	9.76	20.62	30.55
	11	1.30	0.30	0.81	5.69	9.87	20.49	30.39
	21	1.33	0.35	0.73	5.80	9.96	20.34	30.22
Mag	1	−0.3	−4.0	−0.2	−2.1	−0.2	5.9	7.9
	11	−0.8	−4.3	−0.5	−2.1	−0.2	5.9	7.9
	21	−1.9	−4.5	−0.7	−2.0	−0.2	5.9	7.9
Size	1	5.6″	59.0″	10.4″	35.4″	17.0″	3.4″	2.2″
	11	5.2″	55.0″	11.5″	34.6″	16.8″	3.4″	2.2″
	21	5.0″	47.9″	12.8″	33.9″	16.6″	3.4″	2.2″

Moon—On Apr. 1.0 UT, the age of the Moon is 6.9 d. The Sun's selenographic colongitude is 359.02° and increases by 12.2° each day thereafter. The libration in longitude is maximum (east limb exposed) on Apr. 11 (+6°) and minimum (west limb exposed) on Apr. 23 (−5°). The libration in latitude is maximum (north limb exposed) on Apr. 21 (+7°) and minimum (south limb exposed) on Apr. 7 (−7°). The Moon reaches its greatest northern declinations on Apr. 1 (+23°) and Apr. 28 (+23°) and its greatest southern declination on Apr. 14 (−23°).

Mercury is not observable by northern observers until early May. For southern observers, Mercury continues to brighten, but at the same time it slowly descends further into the eastern morning twilight, becoming lost in the glare of the Sun by mid-month. It is in superior conjunction with the Sun on the 23rd.

Venus emerges in the eastern morning sky early in the month. This is a poor morning apparition for northern observers, due to the shallow angle that the ecliptic makes with the horizon and Venus' location south of the ecliptic. For northern observers, it remains in twilight throughout the month, only rising about 1.5 h before the Sun at month's end. However, southern observers will find Venus nearly 20° above the eastern horizon at the beginning of morning twilight by month's end.

Mars moves from Ophiuchus to Sagittarius in the second half of the month. Mars brightens considerably this month. It rises in the southeast before midnight and stands about 20° high, near the meridian, as morning twilight begins. For more favoured southern observers, Mars rises in midevening in the southeast and is 75° high in the west as morning twilight begins.

Jupiter, in Taurus, stands about 30° high in the west during evening twilight and sets in the west-northwest in late-evening. For less favoured southern observers, Jupiter is visible low in the west after sunset and sets about 2.5 h after the Sun.

Saturn, in Taurus, is visible early in the month low in the west after sunset. By month's end, it is visible only during evening twilight very low in the west.

Time (UT) d h m	APRIL EVENTS	Configuration of Jupiter's Satellites

d	h	m	Event
Sun. 1	2		**Daylight Savings Time begins**
	10	49	**First Quarter**
	17	32	Algol at minimum
Mon. 2			
Tue. 3			
Wed. 4	2	48	**Double shadow transit on Jupiter**
	14	21	Algol at minimum
Thu. 5	10		Moon at perigee (364 810 km)
Fri. 6			Mercury at greatest heliocentric latitude S
	21		Mercury 10° S of Venus
Sat. 7	11	10	Algol at minimum
Sun. 8	3	22	**Full Moon**
Tue. 10	2		Pallas stationary
	7	59	Algol at minimum
Wed. 11			
Thu. 12			Mars at descending node
Fri. 13	2		**Mars 1.3° S of Moon**
	4	48	Algol at minimum
Sat. 14			
Sun. 15	4		Ceres 0.9° S of Moon, Occultation†
	15	31	**Last Quarter**
Mon. 16	1	37	Algol at minimum
	14		Jupiter 5° N of Aldebaran
	16		Neptune 3° N of Moon
Tue. 17	6		Moon at apogee (404 506 km)
	17		Venus stationary
	23		Uranus 3° N of Moon
Wed. 18	22	27	Algol at minimum
Thu. 19			
Fri. 20	20		Venus 10° N of Moon
Sat. 21	19	16	Algol at minimum
Sun. 22	4		Lyrid meteors peak
Mon. 23	9		Mercury in superior conjunction
	15	26	**New Moon**
Tue. 24	16	05	Algol at minimum
Wed. 25			Mercury at ascending node
	16		**Saturn 1.4° N of Moon**
Thu. 26	13		**Jupiter 1.8° N of Moon**
Fri. 27	12	54	Algol at minimum
Sat. 28			
Sun. 29			
Mon. 30			Mercury at perihelion
	2		Juno in conjunction with Sun
	9	43	Algol at minimum
	17	08	**First Quarter**

Configuration of Jupiter's Satellites: West / East

0.0 1.0 2.0 3.0 4.0 5.0 6.0 7.0 8.0 9.0 10.0 11.0 12.0 13.0 14.0 15.0 16.0 17.0 18.0 19.0 20.0 21.0 22.0 23.0 24.0 25.0 26.0 27.0 28.0 29.0 30.0 31.0 32.0

† Visible from Europe including British Isles, North Africa, Middle East, W Russia.

THE SKY FOR MAY 2001

		Mercury	Venus	Mars	Jupiter	Saturn	Uranus	Neptune
RA	1	03h 07m	00h 10m	17h 53m	04h 49m	03h 58m	21h 48m	20h 44m
	11	04h 26m	00h 32m	17h 56m	04h 58m	04h 03m	21h 49m	20h 45m
	21	05h 26m	01h 00m	17h 53m	05h 07m	04h 08m	21h 49m	20h 44m
Dec	1	+18° 28′	+02° 57′	−24° 09′	+22° 01′	+18° 43′	−14° 01′	−17° 56′
	11	+23° 55′	+03° 26′	−24° 39′	+22° 17′	+18° 59′	−13° 58′	−17° 55′
	21	+25° 27′	+05° 03′	−25° 14′	+22° 32′	+19° 14′	−13° 56′	−17° 56′
Dist	1	1.26	0.41	0.65	5.90	10.03	20.18	30.05
	11	1.07	0.48	0.59	5.98	10.08	20.02	29.88
	21	0.85	0.56	0.53	6.04	10.10	19.85	29.72
Mag	1	−1.5	−4.5	−1.1	−2.0	−0.3	5.8	7.9
	11	−0.6	−4.5	−1.4	−2.0	−0.3	5.8	7.9
	21	0.4	−4.4	−1.7	−2.0	−0.4	5.8	7.9
Size	1	5.3″	40.8″	14.3″	33.4″	16.5″	3.5″	2.2″
	11	6.3″	34.8″	15.9″	32.9″	16.4″	3.5″	2.2″
	21	7.9″	30.0″	17.6″	32.6″	16.4″	3.5″	2.3″

Moon—On May 1.0 UT, the age of the Moon is 7.4 d. The Sun's selenographic colongitude is 4.93° and increases by 12.2° each day thereafter. The libration in longitude is maximum (east limb exposed) on May 8 (+5°) and minimum (west limb exposed) on May 21 (−5°). The libration in latitude is maximum (north limb exposed) on May 18 (+7°) and minimum (south limb exposed) on May 4 (−7°) and May 31 (−7°). The Moon reaches its greatest northern declination on May 25 (+23°) and its greatest southern declination on May 11 (−23°).

Mercury emerges rapidly in the west-northwestern evening twilight during the first half of the month. This is the **best evening apparition of the year** for northern observers. At midmonth it sets about 2 h after the Sun and stands more than 15° above the horizon at sunset. For less favoured southern observers, it sets less than 1.5 h after the Sun and stands less than 15° above the horizon at sunset. Late in the month Mercury fades rapidly. **Mercury is in conjunction with Jupiter** on the 16th, appearing about 2.8° to its north.

Venus reaches greatest brilliancy on the 4th and continues to improve its visibility in the morning sky this month. It remains low in the east during twilight, rising less than 2 h before the Sun at month's end. For more favoured southern observers, Venus is a striking object high in the east-northeast during morning twilight. By month's end, it rises over 3.5 h before the Sun.

Mars, in Sagittarius, is stationary on the 11th and begins retrograde (westward) motion. Mars continues to brighten and by month's end is even brighter than Jupiter. It rises in the southeast in late-evening and transits near the beginning of morning twilight. For more favoured southern observers, Mars rises soon after the end of evening twilight in the east-southeast and nearly reaches the zenith as it transits in early morning.

Jupiter, in Taurus, is visible low in the west-northwest after sunset early in the month. By month's end, it is lost in the glare of the Sun. **Jupiter is in conjunction with Mercury** on the 16th (see Mercury above).

Saturn can be observed with difficulty very low in the west after sunset in the first few days of the month, before being lost in the glare of the Sun. It is in conjunction with the Sun on May 25.

Time (UT) d h m	MAY EVENTS	Configuration of Jupiter's Satellites
Tue. 1		West East
Wed. 2 4	Moon at perigee (369 420 km)	0.0
Thu. 3 6 32	Algol at minimum	
Fri. 4 18	**Venus greatest brilliancy**	1.0
23	η-Aquarid meteors peak	2.0
Sun. 6 3 21	Algol at minimum	3.0
Mon. 7 13 52	**Full Moon**	
17	Mercury 4° N of Saturn	4.0
Tue. 8		5.0
Wed. 9 0 09	Algol at minimum	
Thu. 10	Mercury at greatest heliocentric latitude N	6.0
19	**Mars 1.9° S of Moon**	7.0
Fri. 11	Venus at descending node	8.0
2	Neptune stationary	
15	Mars stationary	9.0
20 58	Algol at minimum	10.0
Sat. 12 10	Mercury 8° N of Aldebaran	
Sun. 13		11.0
Mon. 14 0	Neptune 3° N of Moon	12.0
17 47	Algol at minimum	13.0
Tue. 15 1	Moon at apogee (404 144 km)	
8	Uranus 3° N of Moon	14.0
10 11	**Last Quarter**	15.0
Wed. 16 17	Mercury 3° N of Jupiter	16.0
Thu. 17 14 36	Algol at minimum	
Fri. 18 21	Ceres stationary	17.0
Sat. 19 9	Venus 4° N of Moon	18.0
Sun. 20 11 25	Algol at minimum	
21	Vesta 0.6° S of Moon, Occultation†	19.0
Mon. 21		20.0
Tue. 22 4	**Mercury greatest elongation E (22°)** (favourable for northern observers)	21.0
Wed. 23 2 46	**New Moon**	22.0
8 14	Algol at minimum	23.0
Thu. 24 7	**Jupiter 1.3° N of Moon**	
19	Mercury 3° N of Moon	24.0
Fri. 25 13	Saturn in conjunction with Sun	25.0
Sat. 26 5 03	Algol at minimum	26.0
Sun. 27 7	Moon at perigee (368 033 km)	
18	Pallas at opposition	27.0
Mon. 28		28.0
Tue. 29 1 52	Algol at minimum	29.0
22	Uranus stationary	
22 09	**First Quarter**	30.0
Wed. 30		31.0
Thu. 31 12 13	Double shadow transit on Jupiter	
22 40	Algol at minimum	32.0

† Visible from Japan, Alaska, Canada except extreme E.

THE SKY FOR JUNE 2001

		Mercury	Venus	Mars	Jupiter	Saturn	Uranus	Neptune
RA	1	05h 58m	01h 36m	17h 44m	05h 18m	04h 14m	21h 49m	20h 44m
	11	05h 53m	02h 12m	17h 32m	05h 28m	04h 20m	21h 49m	20h 44m
	21	05h 31m	02h 51m	17h 17m	05h 38m	04h 25m	21h 49m	20h 43m
Dec	1	+24° 00'	+07° 43'	−25° 53'	+22° 45'	+19° 30'	−13° 56'	−17° 57'
	11	+21° 16'	+10° 33'	−26° 24'	+22° 55'	+19° 44'	−13° 58'	−18° 00'
	21	+18° 57'	+13° 31'	−26° 43'	+23° 02'	+19° 56'	−14° 01'	−18° 02'
Dist	1	0.66	0.64	0.49	6.09	10.10	19.67	29.55
	11	0.56	0.72	0.46	6.11	10.07	19.52	29.42
	21	0.57	0.80	0.45	6.11	10.02	19.37	29.30
Mag	1	1.8	−4.4	−2.1	−1.9	−0.4	5.8	7.9
	11	4.1	−4.3	−2.3	−1.9	−0.4	5.8	7.9
	21	4.2	−4.2	−2.3	−1.9	−0.3	5.7	7.9
Size	1	10.2"	25.9"	19.3"	32.3"	16.4"	3.6"	2.3"
	11	11.9"	23.0"	20.4"	32.2"	16.4"	3.6"	2.3"
	21	11.8"	20.8"	20.8"	32.2"	16.5"	3.6"	2.3"

Moon—On Jun. 1.0 UT, the age of the Moon is 8.9 d. The Sun's selenographic colongitude is 23.48° and increases by 12.2° each day thereafter. The libration in longitude is maximum (east limb exposed) on Jun. 4 (+5°) and Jun. 30 (+6°) and minimum (west limb exposed) on Jun. 17 (−6°). The libration in latitude is maximum (north limb exposed) on Jun. 15 (+7°) and minimum (south limb exposed) on Jun. 28 (−7°). The Moon reaches its greatest northern declination on Jun. 22 (+23°) and its greatest southern declination on Jun. 8 (−23°).

There is a **total solar eclipse** on June 21 visible in the southern African countries of Angola, Zambia, Zimbabwe, Mozambique, and Madagascar. Partial phases are visible throughout much of Africa and eastern South America (see p. 116 in ECLIPSES DURING 2001).

Mercury is at inferior conjunction with the Sun on the 16th is not easily observed this month.

Venus is at greatest elongation west on the 8th. Its visibility continues to slowly improve for northern observers; however, it is still very low in the east during morning twilight. More favoured southern observers will find Venus about 25° high in the northeast as morning twilight begins.

Mars moves from Sagittarius to Ophiuchus on the 1st. It rises near sunset and sets near sunrise. It is at opposition with the Sun on the 13th. Due to its southerly declination, Mars will be poorly placed low in the southern sky for northern observers, but this is a favourable opposition of Mars for southern observers. See pp. 170–174 of the section THE PLANETS FOR 2001 for more details.

Jupiter is in conjunction with the Sun on June 14 and cannot be observed this month.

Saturn, in Taurus, emerges in the east-northeastern dawn sky late in the month for northern observers. By month's end, it rises less than 2 h before the Sun. For more favoured southern observers, it emerges about two weeks earlier—by month's end it stands nearly 10° above the northeastern horizon at the beginning of morning twilight.

Pluto, in Ophiuchus, is at opposition with the Sun on June 4. See the finder chart for Pluto on p. 181.

Time (UT)			JUNE EVENTS	Configuration of Jupiter's Satellites
d	h	m		
Fri. 1				West East
Sat. 2				
Sun. 3			Mercury at descending node	
	19	29	Algol at minimum	
Mon. 4	5		Mercury stationary	
	12		**Pluto at opposition**	
Tue. 5				
Wed. 6	1	39	**Full Moon**	
	16	18	Algol at minimum	
	19		Mars 4° S of Moon	
Thu. 7	14	52	Double shadow transit on Jupiter	
Fri. 8	5		**Venus greatest elongation W (46°)**	
Sat. 9	13	07	Algol at minimum	
Sun. 10	8		Neptune 3° N of Moon	
Mon. 11	16		Uranus 3° N of Moon	
	20		Moon at apogee (404 629 km)	
Tue. 12	9	55	Algol at minimum	
Wed. 13			Mercury at aphelion	
	18		**Mars at opposition**	
Thu. 14			Venus at aphelion	
	3	28	**Last Quarter**	
	13		Jupiter in conjunction with Sun	
Fri. 15	6	44	Algol at minimum	
Sat. 16	13		Mercury in inferior conjunction	
Sun. 17	22		**Venus 1.7° N of Moon**	
Mon. 18	3	33	Algol at minimum	
Tue. 19	22		**Saturn 0.9° N of Moon, Occultation†**	
Wed. 20				
Thu. 21	0	22	Algol at minimum	
	7	38	**Solstice**	
	11	58	**New Moon, Total Solar Eclipse**	
	23		**Mars closest approach**	
Fri. 22				
Sat. 23	17		Moon at perigee (363 132 km)	
	21	10	Algol at minimum	
Sun. 24				
Mon. 25				
Tue. 26	17	59	Algol at minimum	
Wed. 27				
Thu. 28	3	19	**First Quarter**	
	7		Mercury stationary	
Fri. 29	14	48	Algol at minimum	
Sat. 30				

† Visible from New Zealand, South Pacific Ocean.

THE SKY FOR JULY 2001

		Mercury	Venus	Mars	Jupiter	Saturn	Uranus	Neptune
RA	1	05h 24m	03h 33m	17h 04m	05h 48m	04h 30m	21h 48m	20h 42m
	11	05h 51m	04h 17m	16h 56m	05h 58m	04h 35m	21h 47m	20h 41m
	21	06h 51m	05h 04m	16h 53m	06h 08m	04h 39m	21h 46m	20h 40m
Dec	1	+18° 52′	+16° 19′	−26° 51′	+23° 07′	+20° 07′	−14° 05′	−18° 06′
	11	+20° 48′	+18° 45′	−26° 51′	+23° 10′	+20° 17′	−14° 11′	−18° 10′
	21	+22° 31′	+20° 36′	−26° 50′	+23° 10′	+20° 26′	−14° 18′	−18° 14′
Dist	1	0.68	0.88	0.46	6.09	9.95	19.24	29.21
	11	0.88	0.96	0.48	6.06	9.86	19.14	29.14
	21	1.11	1.04	0.51	6.00	9.74	19.05	29.10
Mag	1	1.7	−4.2	−2.2	−1.9	−0.3	5.7	7.9
	11	0.3	−4.1	−2.0	−1.9	−0.3	5.7	7.8
	21	−0.8	−4.1	−1.8	−2.0	−0.3	5.7	7.8
Size	1	9.9″	18.9″	20.5″	32.3″	16.6″	3.6″	2.3″
	11	7.7″	17.4″	19.7″	32.5″	16.8″	3.7″	2.3″
	21	6.1″	16.1″	18.5″	32.8″	17.0″	3.7″	2.3″

Moon—On Jul. 1.0 UT, the age of the Moon is 9.5 d. The Sun's selenographic colongitude is 30.10° and increases by 12.2° each day thereafter. The libration in longitude is maximum (east limb exposed) on Jul. 28 (+7°) and minimum (west limb exposed) on Jul. 15 (−7°). The libration in latitude is maximum (north limb exposed) on Jul. 12 (+7°) and minimum (south limb exposed) on Jul. 25 (−7°). The Moon reaches its greatest northern declination on Jul. 19 (+23°) and its greatest southern declination on Jul. 5 (−23°).

There is a **partial lunar eclipse** on July 5 (see p. 117 in ECLIPSES DURING 2001).

Mercury brightens as it emerges in the east-northeastern morning twilight early in the month. It reaches greatest elongation west (21°) on the 9th. At midmonth it rises about 1 h before the Sun. **Mercury is in conjunction with Jupiter** on the 12th, appearing about 1.9° to its south. Late in the month it becomes lost in the glare of the Sun. Both northern and southern observers have similar observing conditions this month.

Venus is low in the east-northeast during morning twilight, rising about 3 h before the Sun. For southern observers, Venus also rises about 3 h before the Sun; however, the steeper ecliptic angle allows it to stand nearly 20° high in the northeast as morning twilight begins. Venus is in conjunction with Saturn on the 15th, appearing less than 0.8° to its south. Venus makes a nice grouping with Saturn and the Moon on the 17th.

Mars, in Ophiuchus, is stationary on the 19th, then returns to direct (eastward) motion. Mars stands about 20° high in the south as darkness falls and sets after midnight. Southern observers will find Mars high in the east at the end of evening twilight. It transits in midevening and sets about 1 h before morning twilight begins.

Jupiter moves from Taurus to Gemini this month, emerging in the northeastern dawn twilight during the month. It is in conjunction with Mercury on the 12th, appearing about 1.9° to its north.

Saturn, in Taurus, rises about 3 h before the Sun but stands less than 10° above the northeastern horizon at the start of morning twilight. For more favoured southern observers, Saturn is nearly 20° above the northeastern horizon as morning twilight begins. Saturn is in conjunction with Venus on the 15th, appearing about 0.8° to its north.

Neptune, in Capricornus, is at opposition with the Sun on July 30 and was in conjunction with the Sun on January 26. Its southerly declination in 2001 makes it low in the sky for northern observers. See the finder chart for Neptune on p. 180.

Time (UT) d h m	JULY EVENTS	Configuration of Jupiter's Satellites
Sun. 1		
Mon. 2 11 36	Algol at minimum	
Tue. 3	Mercury at greatest heliocentric latitude S	
10	Mars 6° S of Moon	
Wed. 4 14	Earth at aphelion (152 088 Mm)	
Thu. 5 8 25	Algol at minimum	
15 04	**Full Moon, Partial Lunar Eclipse**	
Fri. 6	Venus at greatest heliocentric latitude S	
Sat. 7 14	Neptune 3° N of Moon	
19	Ceres at opposition	
Sun. 8 5 13	Algol at minimum	
22	Uranus 3° N of Moon	
Mon. 9 11	Moon at apogee (405 567 km)	
17	**Mercury greatest elongation W (21°)**	
Tue. 10		
Wed. 11 2 02	Algol at minimum	
Thu. 12 22	**Mercury 1.9° S of Jupiter**	
Fri. 13 8	Saturn 4° N of Aldebaran	
18 45	**Last Quarter**	
22 51	Algol at minimum	
Sun. 15 1	**Venus 3° N of Aldebaran**	
5	**Venus 0.7° S of Saturn**	
Mon. 16 19 39	Algol at minimum	
Tue. 17 13	**Saturn 0.6° N of Moon, Occultation†**	
18	**Venus 0.3° S of Moon, Occultation‡**	
Wed. 18		
Thu. 19 0	**Jupiter 0.2° N of Moon, Occultation††**	
13	**Mercury 1.0° S of Moon, Occultation‡‡**	
16 28	Algol at minimum	
23	Mars stationary	
Fri. 20 19 44	**New Moon**	
Sat. 21 21	Moon at perigee (359 027 km) (Large tides)	
Sun. 22	Mercury at ascending node	
13 17	Algol at minimum	
Tue. 24		
Wed. 25 10 05	Algol at minimum	
Thu. 26 9	Pallas stationary	
Fri. 27	Mercury at perihelion	
10 08	**First Quarter**	
15	Mercury 6° S of Pollux	
Sat. 28 6 54	Algol at minimum	
18	S δ-Aquarid meteors peak	
Sun. 29		
Mon. 30		
12	**Neptune at opposition**	
14	Mars 6° S of Moon	
Tue. 31 3 42	Algol at minimum	

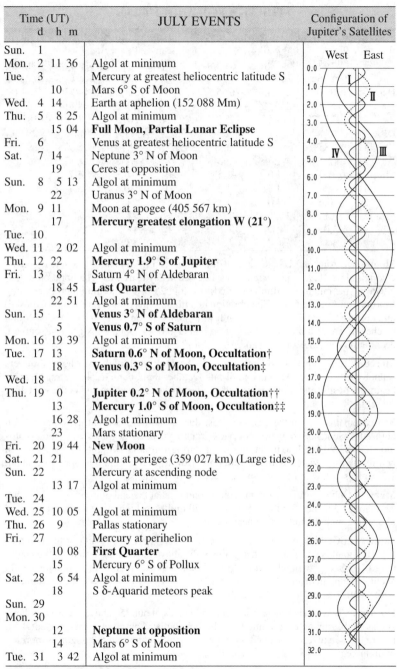

† Visible from South America except NW and extreme S.
‡ Visible from Hawaii, United States, S Canada, Caribbean.   †† Indonesia, Pacific Ocean.
‡‡ Visible from N Europe, N Russia, Arctic, Alaska, W Canada.

THE SKY FOR AUGUST 2001

		Mercury	Venus	Mars	Jupiter	Saturn	Uranus	Neptune
RA	1	08h 24m	05h 57m	16h 58m	06h 18m	04h 44m	21h 44m	20h 39m
	11	09h 47m	06h 47m	17h 08m	06h 27m	04h 47m	21h 42m	20h 38m
	21	10h 56m	07h 37m	17h 22m	06h 35m	04h 50m	21h 41m	20h 37m
Dec	1	+20° 47′	+21° 45′	−26° 52′	+23° 07′	+20° 33′	−14° 26′	−18° 18′
	11	+15° 14′	+21° 49′	−26° 57′	+23° 04′	+20° 39′	−14° 34′	−18° 23′
	21	+07° 57′	+20° 56′	−27° 01′	+22° 58′	+20° 43′	−14° 41′	−18° 27′
Dist	1	1.31	1.11	0.55	5.92	9.60	18.99	29.09
	11	1.35	1.18	0.60	5.82	9.46	18.97	29.11
	21	1.31	1.25	0.65	5.71	9.30	18.97	29.15
Mag	1	−1.7	−4.0	−1.5	−2.0	−0.3	5.7	7.8
	11	−1.4	−4.0	−1.3	−2.0	−0.3	5.7	7.8
	21	−0.6	−4.0	−1.1	−2.1	−0.3	5.7	7.8
Size	1	5.1″	15.0″	17.0″	33.3″	17.2″	3.7″	2.3″
	11	5.0″	14.1″	15.7″	33.8″	17.5″	3.7″	2.3″
	21	5.1″	13.4″	14.5″	34.5″	17.8″	3.7″	2.3″

Moon—On Aug. 1.0 UT, the age of the Moon is 11.2 d. The Sun's selenographic colongitude is 48.95° and increases by 12.2° each day thereafter. The libration in longitude is maximum (east limb exposed) on Aug. 25 (+8°) and minimum (west limb exposed) on Aug. 13 (−7°). The libration in latitude is maximum (north limb exposed) on Aug. 8 (+7°) and minimum (south limb exposed) on Aug. 21 (−7°). The Moon reaches its greatest northern declination on Aug. 16 (+23°) and its greatest southern declinations on Aug. 1 (−23°) and Aug. 28 (−24°).

Mercury is in superior conjunction with the Sun on the 5th. Northern observers cannot easily observe Mercury until late October. For southern observers, Mercury begins its **best evening apparition of the year** when it emerges low in the west after sunset in the second half of the month.

Venus remains low in the east-northeast during morning twilight, rising about 3 h before the Sun. For southern observers, Venus' visibility degrades considerably this month. It is visible low in the northeast during morning twilight, rising about 2 h before the Sun. **Venus is in conjunction with Jupiter** on the 6th, appearing about 1.2° to its south with Mu Gemini between the two planets.

Mars, in Ophiuchus, is low in the south-southwest at the end of evening twilight and sets about 2.5 h later. Southern observers will find Mars high in the north after the end of evening twilight and setting near 3 a.m.

Jupiter, in Gemini, improves its visibility considerably this month in the predawn sky. By month's end, Jupiter stands about 45° above the eastern horizon at the beginning of morning twilight. Less favoured southern observers will find Jupiter only about 20° high in the northeast at the beginning of twilight. **Jupiter is in conjunction with Venus** on the 6th (see Venus above).

Saturn, in Taurus, rises near midnight and stands about 35° above the eastern horizon at the beginning of morning twilight. For southern observers, it rises about 4.5 h before the Sun and stands about 30° above the north-northeastern horizon as morning twilight begins.

Uranus, in Capricornus, is at opposition with the Sun on Aug. 15 and was in conjunction with the Sun on Feb. 9. Its southerly declination in 2001 makes it low in the sky for northern observers. See the finder chart for Uranus on p. 179.

Time (UT) d h m	AUGUST EVENTS	Configuration of Jupiter's Satellites

Time (UT) d h m	AUGUST EVENTS
Wed. 1	
Thu. 2	
Fri. 3 0 31	Algol at minimum
19	Neptune 3° N of Moon
Sat. 4 5 56	**Full Moon**
Sun. 5 3	Uranus 3° N of Moon
21	Moon at apogee (406 269 km)
21 19	Algol at minimum
22	Mercury in superior conjunction
Mon. 6	Mercury at greatest heliocentric latitude N
0	**Venus 1.2° S of Jupiter**
Tue. 7	
Wed. 8 18 08	Algol at minimum
Thu. 9	
Fri. 10	
Sat. 11 14 57	Algol at minimum
Sun. 12 7 53	**Last Quarter**
10	**Perseid meteors peak**
Mon. 13	
Tue. 14 3	**Saturn 0.2° N of Moon, Occultation†**
11 45	Algol at minimum
Wed. 15 15	**Uranus at opposition**
20	**Jupiter 0.4° S of Moon, Occultation‡**
Thu. 16 13	**Venus 1.9° S of Moon**
Fri. 17 8 34	Algol at minimum
Sat. 18	
Sun. 19 2 55	**New Moon**
6	Moon at perigee (357 157 km) (Large tides)
Mon. 20 5 22	Algol at minimum
Tue. 21	
Wed. 22 13	Venus 7° S of Pollux
Thu. 23 2 11	Algol at minimum
Fri. 24	
Sat. 25 7	Pluto stationary
19 55	**First Quarter**
23 00	Algol at minimum
Sun. 26	
Mon. 27 12	Mars 5° S of Moon
Tue. 28 2	Ceres stationary
19 48	Algol at minimum
Wed. 29	
Thu. 30	Mercury at descending node
Fri. 31 0	Neptune 3° N of Moon
16 37	Algol at minimum

† Visible from S and E Africa, India, S China, Indonesia.
‡ Visible from E China, Japan, Alaska, SW Canada, United States.

THE SKY FOR SEPTEMBER 2001

		Mercury	Venus	Mars	Jupiter	Saturn	Uranus	Neptune
RA	1	11h 59m	08h 32m	17h 43m	06h 43m	04h 53m	21h 39m	20h 36m
	11	12h 48m	09h 21m	18h 05m	06h 50m	04h 55m	21h 38m	20h 35m
	21	13h 26m	10h 09m	18h 30m	06h 56m	04h 55m	21h 37m	20h 34m
Dec	1	−00° 12′	+18° 49′	−27° 00′	+22° 51′	+20° 46′	−14° 50′	−18° 31′
	11	−06° 53′	+15° 58′	−26° 49′	+22° 45′	+20° 47′	−14° 57′	−18° 34′
	21	−12° 10′	+12° 22′	−26° 24′	+22° 38′	+20° 47′	−15° 03′	−18° 36′
Dist	1	1.21	1.32	0.70	5.58	9.12	19.01	29.24
	11	1.09	1.37	0.76	5.44	8.96	19.07	29.34
	21	0.94	1.42	0.82	5.30	8.79	19.16	29.47
Mag	1	−0.1	−4.0	−0.9	−2.1	−0.4	5.7	7.9
	11	0.0	−4.0	−0.7	−2.2	−0.4	5.7	7.9
	21	0.2	−3.9	−0.5	−2.2	−0.5	5.7	7.9
Size	1	5.5″	12.7″	13.3″	35.3″	18.1″	3.7″	2.3″
	11	6.2″	12.2″	12.3″	36.2″	18.5″	3.7″	2.3″
	21	7.2″	11.7″	11.5″	37.2″	18.8″	3.7″	2.3″

Moon—On Sep. 1.0 UT, the age of the Moon is 12.9 d. The Sun's selenographic colongitude is 67.57° and increases by 12.2° each day thereafter. The libration in longitude is maximum (east limb exposed) on Sep. 22 (+8°) and minimum (west limb exposed) on Sep. 10 (−7°). The libration in latitude is maximum (north limb exposed) on Sep. 4 (+7°) and minimum (south limb exposed) on Sep. 17 (−6°). The Moon reaches its greatest northern declination on Sep. 12 (+24°) and its greatest southern declination on Sep. 25 (−24°).

Mercury is not easily observable by northern observers until late October. For southern observers, it continues its **best evening apparition of the year**. Mercury can be observed all month low in the west after dark. At midmonth it stands nearly 10° above the horizon at the end of evening twilight. It sets about 2 h after the Sun.

Venus is visible low in the east during morning twilight, rising about 2.5 h before the Sun. For southern observers, Venus' visibility continues to degrade this month. It is visible very low in the east-northeast during morning twilight, by month's end rising only about 1 h before the Sun.

Mars moves from Ophiuchus to Sagittarius on the 1st. It is low in the south-southwest at the end of evening twilight and sets about 2.5 h later. Southern observers will find Mars high in the north during evening twilight and setting near 2 a.m.

Jupiter, in Gemini, rises before midnight in the northeast and stands over 40° high in the east at the beginning of morning twilight. For southern observers, Jupiter rises near 2 a.m. and stands about 25° high in the northeast at the beginning of morning twilight.

Saturn, in Taurus, is stationary on the 27th and begins retrograde (westward) motion. For northern observers, it rises in late evening and is high in the southeast during morning twilight. For southern observers, it rises near midnight and stands nearly 40° high in the north at the beginning of morning twilight.

Time (UT) d h m	SEPTEMBER EVENTS	Configuration of Jupiter's Satellites
Sat. 1	Venus at ascending node	
7	Uranus 3° N of Moon	
23	Moon at apogee (406 330 km)	
Sun. 2 21 43	**Full Moon**	
Mon. 3 13 25	Algol at minimum	
Tue. 4		
Wed. 5		
Thu. 6 10 14	Algol at minimum	
Fri. 7		
Sat. 8		
Sun. 9	Mercury at aphelion	
7 03	Algol at minimum	
Mon. 10 13	**Saturn 0.2° S of Moon, Occultation†**	
18 59	**Last Quarter**	
Tue. 11		
Wed. 12 3 51	Algol at minimum	
12	**Jupiter 1.0° S of Moon, Occultation‡**	
Thu. 13		
Fri. 14		
Sat. 15 0 40	Algol at minimum	
7	**Venus 3° S of Moon**	
Sun. 16	Mars at greatest heliocentric latitude S	
	Zodiacal Light vis. in N latitudes in E before start of morning twilight for next two weeks	
16	Moon at perigee (358 128 km) (Large tides)	
Mon. 17 10 27	**New Moon**	
21 29	Algol at minimum	
Tue. 18 22	**Mercury greatest elongation E (27°)**	
Wed. 19 2	Mercury 8° S of Moon	
Thu. 20 18 17	Algol at minimum	
20	**Mercury 0.9° S of Spica**	
20	**Venus 0.5° N of Regulus**	
Sat. 22 23 04	**Equinox**	
Sun. 23 15 06	Algol at minimum	
Mon. 24 9 31	**First Quarter**	
Tue. 25 1	**Mars 2° S of Moon**	
Wed. 26 11 55	Algol at minimum	
Thu. 27 3	Saturn stationary	
5	Neptune 3° N of Moon	
Fri. 28 11	Uranus 3° N of Moon	
Sat. 29	Mercury at greatest heliocentric latitude S	
6	Moon at apogee (405 787 km)	
8 43	Algol at minimum	
Sun. 30		

† Visible from Hawaii, United States, S Canada, Caribbean.
‡ Visible from Europe except SW including British Isles, N Russia, Arctic, Alaska, N Canada.

THE SKY FOR OCTOBER 2001

		Mercury	Venus	Mars	Jupiter	Saturn	Uranus	Neptune
RA	1	13h 45m	10h 56m	18h 56m	07h 01m	04h 55m	21h 36m	20h 34m
	11	13h 27m	11h 42m	19h 23m	07h 04m	04h 55m	21h 35m	20h 33m
	21	12h 55m	12h 28m	19h 51m	07h 07m	04h 53m	21h 34m	20h 33m
Dec	1	−14° 46′	+08° 10′	−25° 43′	+22° 32′	+20° 46′	−15° 08′	−18° 38′
	11	−11° 49′	+03° 33′	−24° 43′	+22° 27′	+20° 44′	−15° 11′	−18° 39′
	21	−05° 09′	−01° 17′	−23° 23′	+22° 24′	+20° 41′	−15° 13′	−18° 40′
Dist	1	0.77	1.47	0.87	5.15	8.64	19.28	29.61
	11	0.66	1.52	0.94	4.99	8.49	19.42	29.77
	21	0.76	1.56	1.00	4.84	8.36	19.57	29.94
Mag	1	0.7	−3.9	−0.4	−2.3	−0.5	5.7	7.9
	11	3.6	−3.9	−0.2	−2.3	−0.6	5.8	7.9
	21	1.4	−3.9	−0.1	−2.4	−0.6	5.8	7.9
Size	1	8.7″	11.3″	10.7″	38.3″	19.2″	3.6″	2.3″
	11	10.1″	11.0″	10.0″	39.4″	19.5″	3.6″	2.3″
	21	8.9″	10.7″	9.4″	40.7″	19.8″	3.6″	2.2″

Moon—On Oct. 1.0 UT, the age of the Moon is 13.6 d. The Sun's selenographic colongitude is 73.59° and increases by 12.2° each day thereafter. The libration in longitude is maximum (east limb exposed) on Oct. 20 (+7°) and minimum (west limb exposed) on Oct. 8 (−6°). The libration in latitude is maximum (north limb exposed) on Oct. 1 (+7°) and Oct. 29 (+7°) and minimum (south limb exposed) on Oct. 15 (−7°). The Moon reaches its greatest northern declination on Oct. 9 (+24°) and its greatest southern declination on Oct. 22 (−24°).

Mercury is visible late in the month very low in the east before sunrise. This begins the **best morning apparition of the year** for northern observers. Southern observers can observe Mercury with difficulty in the first few days of the month very low in the west-southwest after sunset, before it is lost in the glare of the Sun. Mercury is in inferior conjunction with the Sun on the 14th and at greatest elongation east (19°) on the 29th.

Mercury and Venus are within 1° of each other for 11 days during the last week of the month and in early November; however, the planets never coincide in RA so, technically, they are never in conjunction (see. p. 17). The planets do coincide, twice, in longitude. Jean Meeus (see p. 56) has coined the term *quasi-conjunction* for close approaches such as this with no conjunction.

Venus is visible very low in the east during morning twilight, rising only about 2 h before the Sun. For southern observers, Venus is visible with difficulty very low in the east before sunrise. Venus makes a close approach with Mercury during the last week of the month (see Mercury above).

Mars moves from Sagittarius to Capricornus late in the month. It is low in the south-southwest at the end of evening twilight and sets about 2 h later. Southern observers will find Mars high in the west at the end of evening twilight and setting near 1 a.m.

Jupiter, in Gemini, rises in midevening in the northeast and is visible for the remainder of the night. Southern observers will have to wait until after midnight for Jupiter to rise, also in the northeast.

Saturn, in Taurus, rises in the east-northeast in midevening for northern observers and late evening for southern observers and is visible for the remainder of the night.

Time (UT) d h m	OCTOBER EVENTS	Configuration of Jupiter's Satellites
Mon. 1 20	Mercury stationary	West East
Tue. 2 5 32	Algol at minimum	
13 49	**Full Moon** (the *Harvest Moon*)	
Fri. 5	Venus at perihelion	
2 21	Algol at minimum	
22 26	**Double shadow transit on Jupiter**	
Sun. 7 19	**Saturn 0.5° S of Moon, Occultation†**	
23 09	Algol at minimum	
Tue. 9 11 22	**Double shadow transit on Jupiter**	
18	Vesta stationary	
Wed. 10 0	**Jupiter 1.4° S of Moon**	
4 20	**Last Quarter**	
19 58	Algol at minimum	
Fri. 12	Mars at perihelion	
Sat. 13 0 19	**Double shadow transit on Jupiter**	
16 47	Algol at minimum	
Sun. 14 2	Mercury in inferior conjunction	
23	Moon at perigee (361 860 km)	
Mon. 15	**Zodiacal Light** vis. in N latitudes in E before start of morning twilight for next two weeks	
2	Venus 4° S of Moon	
Tue. 16 13 15	**Double shadow transit on Jupiter**	
13 36	Algol at minimum	
19 23	**New Moon**	
Wed. 17 23	Neptune stationary	
Thu. 18	Mercury at ascending node	
Fri. 19 10 25	Algol at minimum	
Sat. 20 2 12	**Double shadow transit on Jupiter**	
Sun. 21 20 40	**Double shadow transit on Jupiter**	
Mon. 22 2	Orionid meteors peak	
7 13	Algol at minimum	
11	Mercury stationary	
Tue. 23	Mercury at perihelion	
15 09	**Double shadow transit on Jupiter**	
20	**Mars 0.1° N of Moon, Occultation‡**	
Wed. 24 2 58	**First Quarter**	
12	Neptune 3° N of Moon	
Thu. 25 4 02	Algol at minimum	
17	Uranus 3° N of Moon	
Fri. 26	Venus at greatest heliocentric latitude N	
20	Moon at apogee (404 935 km)	
Sat. 27 4 05	**Double shadow transit on Jupiter**	
Sun. 28 0 51	Algol at minimum	
2	**Daylight Savings Time ends**	
22 33	**Double shadow transit on Jupiter††**	
Mon. 29 17	**Mercury greatest elongation W (19°)**	
Tue. 30 17 02	**Double shadow transit on Jupiter††**	
Tue. 30 19	**Mercury 0.6° N of Venus in *ecliptic latitude***	
21 40	Algol at minimum	
Wed. 31 4	Uranus stationary	

† Visible from SW Asia, India, central and E Russia, NW China, N Japan, Alaska, W Canada.
‡ Visible from central South America, central Africa.
†† Nearly simultaneous shadow ingresses—see p. 187.

THE SKY FOR NOVEMBER 2001

		Mercury	Venus	Mars	Jupiter	Saturn	Uranus	Neptune
RA	1	13h 19m	13h 18m	20h 23m	07h 08m	04h 51m	21h 34m	20h 33m
	11	14h 13m	14h 05m	20h 52m	07h 07m	04h 48m	21h 34m	20h 34m
	21	15h 14m	14h 54m	21h 20m	07h 06m	04h 45m	21h 35m	20h 35m
Dec	1	−05° 59′	−06° 37′	−21° 33′	+22° 24′	+20° 36′	−15° 14′	−18° 39′
	11	−11° 35′	−11° 14′	−19° 33′	+22° 25′	+20° 31′	−15° 12′	−18° 38′
	21	−17° 23′	−15° 26′	−17° 16′	+22° 30′	+20° 25′	−15° 09′	−18° 35′
Dist	1	1.05	1.59	1.07	4.68	8.24	19.75	30.13
	11	1.26	1.62	1.13	4.54	8.16	19.92	30.30
	21	1.39	1.65	1.20	4.42	8.11	20.09	30.46
Mag	1	−0.7	−3.9	0.1	−2.5	−0.7	5.8	7.9
	11	−0.8	−3.9	0.2	−2.5	−0.8	5.8	7.9
	21	−0.9	−3.9	0.3	−2.6	−0.9	5.8	7.9
Size	1	6.4″	10.5″	8.8″	42.1″	20.1″	3.5″	2.2″
	11	5.3″	10.3″	8.3″	43.3″	20.3″	3.5″	2.2″
	21	4.8″	10.1″	7.8″	44.5″	20.4″	3.5″	2.2″

Moon—On Nov. 1.0 UT, the age of the Moon is 15.2 d. The Sun's selenographic colongitude is 91.27° and increases by 12.2° each day thereafter. The libration in longitude is maximum (east limb exposed) on Nov. 17 (+6°) and minimum (west limb exposed) on Nov. 4 (−5°) and Nov. 30 (−5°). The libration in latitude is maximum (north limb exposed) on Nov. 25 (+7°) and minimum (south limb exposed) on Nov. 11 (−7°). The Moon reaches its greatest northern declination on Nov. 6 (+24°) and its greatest southern declination on Nov. 18 (−24°).

Mercury continues its **best morning apparition of the year** for northern observers. Early in the month it rises in the east more than 1.5 h before the Sun; however, by about midmonth it descends further into twilight and is lost in the glare of the Sun. Mercury is not easily visible by southern observers until late December. **Mercury is in *quasi-conjunction* with Venus** early in the month (see Mercury for October).

Venus' close approach with Mercury continues early in the month, but Venus is increasingly more difficult to observe as the month progresses. It is very low in the east-southeast before sunrise. Southern observers can only glimpse Venus with difficulty very low in the east before sunrise in the first week of the month, following which it is lost in the glare of the Sun.

Mars, in Capricornus, improves in visibility slightly for northern observers this month. It stands about 25° high in the south-southwest at the end of evening twilight and sets in the late evening. For southern observers, Mars stands about 50° above the western horizon at the end of evening twilight and sets near midnight.

Jupiter, in Gemini, is stationary on the 2nd, following which it begins retrograde (westward) motion. It rises in the northeast in the early evening for northern observers and late-evening for southern observers. It is visible for the remainder of the night.

Saturn, in Taurus, rises in the east-northeast during evening twilight and is visible for the remainder of the night.

Time (UT)			NOVEMBER EVENTS	Configuration of Jupiter's Satellites
d	h	m		West East

Thu. 1	5	41	**Full Moon** (the *Hunter's Moon*)	
Fri. 2			Mercury at greatest heliocentric latitude N	
	9		Mercury 5° N of Spica	
	12		Venus 4° N of Spica	
	17		Jupiter stationary	
	18	29	Algol at minimum	
Sat. 3	2		S Taurid meteors peak	
	6	20	**Double shadow transit on Jupiter**	
Sat. 3	7		**Mercury 0.7° N of Venus in *ecliptic latitude***	
	22		**Saturn 0.6° S of Moon, Occultation†**	
Sun. 4	18		Mars 2° S of Neptune	
Mon. 5	2	29	**Double shadow transit on Jupiter**	
	15	18	Algol at minimum	
Tue. 6	7		**Jupiter 1.7° S of Moon**	
	19	37	**Double shadow transit on Jupiter**	
Wed. 7				
Thu. 8	12	07	Algol at minimum	
	12	21	**Last Quarter**	
Sat. 10	8	56	**Double shadow transit on Jupiter**	
Sun. 11	8	56	Algol at minimum	
	17		Moon at perigee (367 256 km)	
Mon. 12				
Tue. 13	1		N Taurid meteors peak	
	22	14	**Double shadow transit on Jupiter**	
Wed. 14	5	45	Algol at minimum	
Thu. 15	6	40	**New Moon**	
Fri. 16				
Sat. 17	2	34	Algol at minimum	
	11	32	**Double shadow transit on Jupiter**	
Sun. 18	10		**Leonid meteors peak I‡**	
	18		**Leonid meteors peak II‡**	
Mon. 19	23	23	Algol at minimum	
Tue. 20	21		Neptune 3° N of Moon	
Wed. 21	0	50	**Double shadow transit on Jupiter**	
	19		Mars 3° N of Moon	
Thu. 22	2		Uranus 4° N of Moon	
	20	12	Algol at minimum	
	23	21	**First Quarter**	
Fri. 23	16		Moon at apogee (404 394 km)	
Sat. 24				
Sun. 25	17	01	Algol at minimum	
Mon. 26			Mercury at descending node	
	10		Mars 0.8° S of Uranus	
Tue. 27	17		Vesta at opposition	
Wed. 28	13	50	Algol at minimum	
Thu. 29				
Fri. 30	20	49	**Full Moon**	

† Visible from Europe including British Isles, NW Africa, Arctic, Russia, Japan.
‡ Extremely high shower rates are predicted—see pp. 200–202 for details.

THE SKY FOR DECEMBER 2001

		Mercury	Venus	Mars	Jupiter	Saturn	Uranus	Neptune
RA	1	16h 19m	15h 44m	21h 48m	07h 02m	04h 42m	21h 36m	20h 35m
	11	17h 26m	16h 37m	22h 16m	06h 58m	04h 38m	21h 37m	20h 37m
	21	18h 36m	17h 31m	22h 43m	06h 53m	04h 35m	21h 38m	20h 38m
Dec	1	−21° 57′	−18° 58′	−14° 44′	+22° 36′	+20° 20′	−15° 05′	−18° 32′
	11	−24° 42′	−21° 37′	−12° 01′	+22° 44′	+20° 14′	−14° 59′	−18° 29′
	21	−25° 17′	−23° 14′	−09° 08′	+22° 52′	+20° 08′	−14° 51′	−18° 24′
Dist	1	1.45	1.67	1.27	4.32	8.08	20.26	30.61
	11	1.44	1.69	1.34	4.25	8.09	20.42	30.75
	21	1.38	1.70	1.41	4.20	8.13	20.57	30.87
Mag	1	−1.1	−3.9	0.4	−2.7	−0.9	5.8	8.0
	11	−1.0	−3.9	0.5	−2.7	−0.9	5.9	8.0
	21	−0.8	−3.9	0.6	−2.7	−0.8	5.9	8.0
Size	1	4.6″	10.0″	7.4″	45.5″	20.5″	3.5″	2.2″
	11	4.7″	9.9″	7.0″	46.3″	20.5″	3.4″	2.2″
	21	4.9″	9.8″	6.6″	46.8″	20.4″	3.4″	2.2″

Moon—On Dec. 1.0 UT, the age of the Moon is 15.7 d. The Sun's selenographic colongitude is 96.34° and increases by 12.2° each day thereafter. The libration in longitude is maximum (east limb exposed) on Dec. 14 (+5°) and minimum (west limb exposed) on Dec. 27 (−6°). The libration in latitude is maximum (north limb exposed) on Dec. 22 (+7°) and minimum (south limb exposed) on Dec. 8 (−7°). The Moon reaches its greatest northern declinations on Dec. 3 (+24°) and Dec. 30 (+24°) and its greatest southern declination on Dec. 16 (−24°).

There is an **annular solar eclipse** on December 14 visible from the Pacific Ocean and near sunset in Nicaragua and El Salvador (see p. 117 in ECLIPSES DURING 2001).

Mercury is in superior conjunction with the Sun on the 4th and is not observable by northern observers this month. For southern observers, it begins to emerge very low in the west-southwest evening sky after sunset late in the month.

Venus is only visible with difficulty very low in the east-southeast before sunrise in the first few days of the month, following which it is lost in the glare of the Sun. Venus cannot be observed this month by southern observers.

Mars moves from Capricornus to Aquarius early in the month. It stands about 30° high in the southwest at the end of evening twilight and sets in late evening. For southern observers, Mars stands about 35° above the western horizon at the end of evening twilight and sets before midnight.

Jupiter, in Gemini, is approaching opposition with the Sun, which occurs on 2002 January 1. It rises during evening twilight for both northern and southern observers, transits after midnight and sets after the Sun rises.

Saturn, in Taurus, rises near sunset and sets near sunrise. It is at opposition with the Sun on the 3rd.

Time (UT) d h m	DECEMBER EVENTS	Configuration of Jupiter's Satellites
Sat. 1 2	**Saturn 0.5° S of Moon, Occultation**†	
10 39	Algol at minimum	
Sun. 2		
Mon. 3 11	**Jupiter 1.6° S of Moon**	
14	**Saturn at opposition**	
Tue. 4 7 28	Algol at minimum	
22	Mercury in superior conjunction	
Wed. 5		
Thu. 6	Mercury at aphelion	
23	Moon at perigee (370 117 km)	
Fri. 7 4	Pluto in conjunction with Sun	
4 17	Algol at minimum	
19 52	**Last Quarter**	
Sat. 8		
Sun. 9		
Mon. 10 1 06	Algol at minimum	
Tue. 11		
Wed. 12 21 55	Algol at minimum	
Thu. 13		
Fri. 14 4	**Geminid meteors peak**	
21	**New Moon, Annular Solar Eclipse**	
Sat. 15 18 44	Algol at minimum	
Sun. 16		
Mon. 17 17	Saturn 4° N of Aldebaran	
Tue. 18 7	Neptune 4° N of Moon	
15 34	Algol at minimum	
Wed. 19 12	Uranus 4° N of Moon	
Thu. 20 20	Mars 4° N of Moon	
Fri. 21	Venus at descending node	
12 23	Algol at minimum	
13	Moon at apogee (404 633 km)	
19 21	**Solstice**	
Sat. 22 12	Ursid meteors peak	
20 56	**First Quarter**	
Sun. 23		
Mon. 24 9 12	Algol at minimum	
Tue. 25 21	Juno stationary	
Wed. 26	Mercury at greatest heliocentric latitude S	
Thu. 27 6 01	Algol at minimum	
Fri. 28 8	**Saturn 0.2° S of Moon, Occultation**‡	
Sat. 29		
Sun. 30	Jupiter at ascending node	
2 50	Algol at minimum	
10 40	**Full Moon, Penumbral Lunar Eclipse**	
14	**Jupiter 1.2° S of Moon, Occultation**††	
Mon. 31		

† Visible from Central America, United States, E Canada, Europe including British Isles, W Russia.
‡ Visible from Hawaii, S Canada, United States, Central America.
†† Visible from central Greenland.

THE SUN

EPHEMERIS FOR THE SUN

Sundial Correction

The "Greenwich Transit" time in the table at the right may be used to calculate the sundial correction at the observer's position. For example, to find the correction at Winnipeg on August 16, 2001: At Greenwich the Sun transits at 12:04:49 on August 13 and at 12:04:02 on August 17. Thus, to the nearest minute, on August 16 at both Greenwich and Winnipeg the Sun will transit at 12:04 local mean solar time (LMT), or 12:33 CST (Central Standard Time) since Winnipeg has a longitude correction of +29 min (see the 3rd paragraph on p. 89). Thus a 4 minute correction must be added to the reading of a simple sundial to obtain LMT, and an additional 29 minutes must be added to obtain CST.

A figure accurate to a second or two can be obtained by interpolating for longitude. The interpolated transit time at Greenwich for August 16 is 12:04:14, the daily change in time being −11.8 s. Adjusting this for the longitude of Winnipeg: 12 h 04 min 14 s − (11.8 s × 6 h 29 min ÷ 24 h) = 12 h 04 min 11 s. Thus the sundial correction is 4 min 11 s. To find the standard time of the Sun's transit to the nearest second or two, the observer's longitude must be known to 10″ or better. For example, suppose an observer in Winnipeg is at longitude 97°13′50″W, or 6 h 28 min 55 s W of Greenwich. The time of transit will be 12:04:11 + 28 min 55 s = 12:33:06 CST (13:33:06 CDT).

Orientation of the Sun

The table at the right gives three angles that specify the orientation of the Sun.

P is the position angle of the axis of rotation, measured eastward in the observer's sky from the north point on the disk. Note that P varies between +26° (solar north pole tilted eastward) and −26° (tilted westward) during the year. This tilt is associated mainly with the inclination of the ecliptic in the observer's sky, with a smaller contribution from the Sun's 7.2° inclination to the ecliptic (the longitude of the ascending node of the solar equator on the ecliptic is 76°).

B_0 is the heliographic latitude of the centre of the disk, and is the result of the Sun's 7.2° inclination to the ecliptic. Note that positive values of B_0 correspond to the solar equator passing south of the centre of the disk, with the solar north pole being tipped toward the observer.

L_0 is the heliographic longitude of the centre of the disk measured from Carrington's solar prime meridian in the direction of rotation. L_0 decreases about 13° per day. The dates during the year when $L_0 = 0°$ are given in the table below. The rotation period of the Sun depends upon heliographic latitude. The synodic and sidereal periods of rotation at the solar equator are 27.275 days and 25.38 days, respectively.

Commencement (UT) of Numbered Synodic Solar Rotations

No*	Commences	No	Commences	No	Commences	No	Commences
1971	'00 Dec. 21.17	1975	Apr. 9.47	1979	Jul. 27.34	1983	Nov. 13.41
1972	Jan. 17.50	1976	May 6.72	1980	Aug. 23.57	1984	Dec. 10.73
1973	Feb. 13.84	1977	Jun. 2.94	1981	Sep. 19.83	1985	'02 Jan. 7.06
1974	Mar. 13.17	1978	Jun. 30.13	1982	Oct. 17.11		

*Based on R. C. Carrington's Greemwich photoheliocentric series in which rotation number 1 commenced 1853 November 9.

EPHEMERIS FOR THE SUN, 2001

Date 0h UT	Apparent RA (2000) Dec	Greenwich Transit UT	P	B_0	L_0
Jan. 1	18 46.3 −23 01	12:03:39	+2.0	−3.0	217.3
5	19 03.9 −22 38	12:05:29	+0.1	−3.5	164.6
9	19 21.4 −22 07	12:07:11	−1.9	−3.9	111.9
13	19 38.7 −21 30	12:08:45	−3.8	−4.4	59.3
17	19 55.9 −20 46	12:10:09	−5.6	−4.8	6.6
21	20 12.9 −19 56	12:11:21	−7.5	−5.1	313.9
25	20 29.7 −19 00	12:12:22	−9.2	−5.5	261.2
29	20 46.3 −17 58	12:13:10	−11.0	−5.8	208.6
Feb. 2	21 02.7 −16 51	12:13:44	−12.6	−6.1	155.9
6	21 18.8 −15 40	12:14:05	−14.2	−6.4	103.3
10	21 34.8 −14 24	12:14:13	−15.7	−6.6	50.6
14	21 50.5 −13 04	12:14:10	−17.1	−6.8	357.9
18	22 06.0 −11 41	12:13:54	−18.4	−7.0	305.2
22	22 21.4 −10 15	12:13:28	−19.6	−7.1	252.6
26	22 36.6 −08 46	12:12:52	−20.8	−7.2	199.9
Mar. 2	22 51.6 −07 16	12:12:07	−21.8	−7.2	147.2
6	23 06.5 −05 43	12:11:14	−22.7	−7.2	94.5
10	23 21.3 −04 10	12:10:14	−23.6	−7.2	41.8
14	23 36.0 −02 36	12:09:10	−24.3	−7.2	349.1
18	23 50.6 −01 01	12:08:01	−24.9	−7.1	296.4
22	00 05.2 +00 34	12:06:50	−25.4	−7.0	243.6
26	00 19.6 +02 09	12:05:38	−25.8	−6.8	190.9
30	00 34.4 +03 42	12:04:26	−26.1	−6.6	138.1
Apr. 3	00 49.0 +05 15	12:03:14	−26.2	−6.4	85.4
7	01 03.6 +06 46	12:02:05	−26.3	−6.2	32.6
11	01 18.2 +08 15	12:01:00	−26.2	−5.9	339.8
15	01 33.0 +09 43	11:59:59	−26.0	−5.6	287.0
19	01 47.8 +11 07	11:59:04	−25.8	−5.3	234.1
23	02 02.8 +12 29	11:58:16	−25.3	−4.9	181.3
27	02 17.9 +13 47	11:57:36	−24.8	−4.6	128.5

Date 0h UT	Apparent RA (2000) Dec	Greenwich Transit UT	P	B_0	L_0
May 1	02 33.1 +15 02	11:57:03	−24.1	−4.2	75.6
5	02 48.4 +16 12	11:56:39	−23.4	−3.8	22.7
9	03 03.9 +17 19	11:56:24	−22.5	−3.3	329.8
13	03 19.6 +18 21	11:56:17	−21.5	−2.9	277.0
17	03 35.4 +19 17	11:56:21	−20.4	−2.4	224.0
21	03 51.3 +20 09	11:56:33	−19.2	−2.0	171.1
25	04 07.4 +20 55	11:56:54	−17.9	−1.5	118.2
29	04 23.7 +21 36	11:57:22	−16.5	−1.0	65.3
Jun. 2	04 40.0 +22 10	11:57:58	−15.0	−0.5	12.4
6	04 56.4 +22 38	11:58:39	−13.5	−0.0	319.4
10	05 13.0 +23 00	11:59:25	−11.9	+0.4	266.5
14	05 29.6 +23 15	12:00:14	−10.2	+0.9	213.5
18	05 46.2 +23 24	12:01:06	−8.5	+1.4	160.6
22	06 02.8 +23 26	12:01:59	−6.7	+1.9	107.6
26	06 19.5 +23 22	12:02:50	−4.9	+2.3	54.7
30	06 36.1 +23 11	12:03:39	−3.1	+2.8	1.8
Jul. 4	06 52.6 +22 53	12:04:24	−1.3	+3.2	308.8
8	07 09.0 +22 29	12:05:03	+0.5	+3.6	255.9
12	07 25.4 +21 59	12:05:37	+2.3	+4.0	202.9
16	07 41.6 +21 23	12:06:03	+4.1	+4.4	150.0
20	07 57.7 +20 41	12:06:21	+5.8	+4.8	97.1
24	08 13.6 +19 54	12:06:30	+7.6	+5.2	44.2
28	08 29.4 +19 01	12:06:29	+9.2	+5.5	351.2
Aug. 1	08 45.0 +18 03	12:06:18	+10.8	+5.8	298.3
5	09 00.5 +17 01	12:05:58	+12.4	+6.1	245.4
9	09 15.7 +15 54	12:05:28	+13.9	+6.3	192.5
13	09 30.9 +14 43	12:04:49	+15.3	+6.5	139.7
17	09 45.9 +13 28	12:04:02	+16.7	+6.7	86.8
21	10 00.7 +12 10	12:03:05	+18.0	+6.9	33.9
25	10 15.5 +10 49	12:02:03	+19.2	+7.0	341.1
29	10 30.1 +09 25	12:00:54	+20.3	+7.1	288.2

Date 0h UT	Apparent RA (2000) Dec	Greenwich Transit UT	P	B_0	L_0
Sep. 2	10 44.6 +07 58	11:59:38	+21.3	+7.2	235.4
6	10 59.1 +06 30	11:58:19	+22.3	+7.2	182.6
10	11 13.5 +05 00	11:56:56	+23.1	+7.2	129.7
14	11 27.8 +03 28	11:55:31	+23.9	+7.2	76.9
18	11 42.2 +01 56	11:54:06	+24.6	+7.2	24.1
22	11 56.5 +00 22	11:52:41	+25.1	+7.1	331.3
26	12 10.9 −01 11	11:51:18	+25.6	+6.9	278.5
30	12 25.3 −02 44	11:49:58	+25.9	+6.8	225.7
Oct. 4	12 39.8 −04 17	11:48:41	+26.1	+6.6	172.9
8	12 54.4 −05 49	11:47:31	+26.3	+6.3	120.4
12	13 09.1 −07 20	11:46:28	+26.3	+6.1	67.4
16	13 24.0 −08 50	11:45:33	+26.2	+5.8	14.6
20	13 39.0 −10 17	11:44:47	+25.9	+5.5	321.9
24	13 54.1 −11 42	11:44:12	+25.6	+5.1	269.1
28	14 09.5 −13 04	11:43:48	+25.1	+4.8	216.4
Nov. 1	14 25.0 −14 23	11:43:36	+24.5	+4.4	163.6
5	14 40.7 −15 38	11:43:36	+23.8	+4.0	110.9
9	14 56.7 −16 49	11:43:50	+22.9	+3.5	58.1
13	15 12.9 −17 55	11:44:18	+21.9	+3.1	5.4
17	15 29.4 −18 57	11:45:00	+20.8	+2.6	312.7
21	15 46.0 −19 53	11:45:54	+19.6	+2.1	259.9
25	16 02.9 −20 43	11:47:02	+18.3	+1.6	207.2
29	16 20.0 −21 27	11:48:21	+16.8	+1.1	154.5
Dec. 3	16 37.2 −22 05	11:49:50	+15.3	+0.6	101.8
7	16 54.6 −22 35	11:51:30	+13.7	+0.1	49.1
11	17 12.2 −22 59	11:53:18	+12.0	−0.4	356.4
15	17 29.8 −23 15	11:55:11	+10.2	−0.9	303.7
19	17 47.5 −23 24	11:57:09	+8.4	−1.4	251.0
23	18 05.3 −23 26	11:59:09	+6.5	−1.9	198.3
27	18 23.0 −23 20	12:01:07	+4.6	−2.4	145.6
31	18 40.8 −23 06	12:03:03	+2.6	−2.9	92.9

SOLAR ACTIVITY

By Ken Tapping

The next maximum of solar activity (for Cycle 23) should at least equal the last, but predictions that the maximum will occur in 2000 look as though they're going to be wrong. It looks as though we'll arrive at maximum in 2001. Episodes of high activity will occur over the following two or three years. On the other hand, this is only the fifth solar cycle so far that we've monitored using the 10.7 cm solar microwave flux activity index (described later in this article), so forecasting remains uncertain.

The figure below shows solar activity as represented by the adjusted 10.7 cm solar microwave flux activity index from 1947 to the present. The plotted values are averaged values of the index over each solar ($\approx$27-day) rotation; the horizontal scale shows the time in years. The $\approx$11-year activity cycle is clearly evident. The numbering system for solar activity cycles was started by Rudolph Wolf, who arbitrarily designated the activity maximum of 1750 as that of Cycle 1.

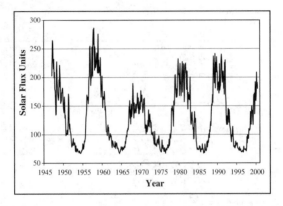

The term "solar activity" comprises all the Sun's variable aspects, such as the occurrence of sunspots and active regions, the variable emissions in soft X-rays, spectral lines such as CaII K and MgII K, and emissions at radio wavelengths. Flares are a particularly dramatic form of solar activity. Measurements made using space-borne radiometers show that as the level of solar activity increases, the Sun becomes slightly brighter. All manifestations of solar activity are driven by the same underlying engine: the varying spatial and temporal distribution of magnetic flux in the photosphere, chromosphere, and corona.

Deep below the photosphere, where the density is high enough for the solar material to drag the magnetic fields, differential rotation and convection give rise to electrical currents, which in turn produce magnetic fields. These form complex networks of twisted "magnetic flux ropes," containing enormous amounts of stored energy. It is the penetration of sections of these flux ropes through the photosphere and into the chromosphere and corona that gives rise to the many observed forms of solar activity. Above the photosphere the situation is strikingly different. The density is much lower, and the distribution and movement of the magnetic fields trap and confine the ionized gas of the solar atmosphere, supporting loops and filaments, and forming the diverse menagerie of photospheric, chromospheric, and coronal structures we are familiar with in the active Sun.

Most activity occurs in active regions: bipolar magnetic structures formed when magnetic loops emerge through the photosphere into the overlying chromosphere and corona. The formation of a new region is heralded by the formation of small pores (about 1000 km across) which coalesce into a patch a few thousand kilometres across, which is termed an emerging flux region. These eventually spread to form a patch of magnetic flux that may exceed 50 000 km in length. The average magnetic field strength in the patch is of the order of 0.01 T (100 gauss). The emergence of these magnetic fields modifies the spatial and density structure of the chromosphere giving rise to enhanced emission in the calcium and magnesium II K spectral lines. These bright patches (called plage), which stand out prominently in filtergrams, are the most conspicuous aspect of active regions.

Concentrations of magnetic flux having strengths of the order of 0.1 T locally impede the transfer of energy from deeper within the Sun, causing them to be about 3000 K cooler than the surrounding (6000 K) photosphere. Although actually quite hot, and shining quite brightly, in contrast with their hotter surroundings, these flux concentrations appear as dark spots. These (sun)spots were the first direct manifestation of solar activity to be observed. Sunspots are present in most active regions. As a region grows, one or more large spots form at the leading end, and a scattering of smaller ones form at the trailing end.

Repeated episodes of magnetic flux emergence occur during the growth phase of the active region. The size the region reaches is directly related to how much magnetic flux it accumulates. As flux emergence slows and stops, so does the growth of the region. Fragmentation sets in, the spots disappear, and the remains are left as a large area of magnetic flux arranged in a network pattern, blending in slowly with the remains of other decayed active regions.

The redistribution of magnetic flux during the evolution of active regions leads to distortion and stressing of magnetic structures in the chromosphere and corona. Energy from below the photosphere is propagated into the chromospheric and coronal magnetic fields through twisting and footpoint motions. This is stored as magnetic energy in stressed loops and flux tubes. Evolution of the host active region requires that this energy be dissipated. This occurs non-catastrophically through slow reconnection and heating, or explosively in mass ejections and flares.

The organization of the subphotospheric magnetic fields gives rise to a consistent pattern in the magnetic configuration of active regions. Each region is magnetically bipolar, with the bipoles arranged east–west on the disk. All bipoles lying in the same hemisphere are arranged with the same magnetic polarity leading (facing in the direction in which the region appears to move as it is carried across the disk by solar rotation—westward in the observer's sky). In the other hemisphere the leading and following magnetic polarities are reversed.

Exceptions do occur. Regions are sometimes formed that have a magnetic orientation perpendicular to or even the reverse of the norm for that hemisphere. Such regions usually try to move into the conventional orientation, but are impeded by the magnetic linkages they have formed with their surroundings. These regions tend to produce flares as potential energy builds up in their magnetic structures and is subsequently released catastrophically.

The "conventional" magnetic configurations for active regions reverse on alternate activity cycles. For example, during Cycle 22, active regions in the northern solar hemisphere were oriented with their "negative" (i.e. south-seeking) magnetic polarity ends leading and "positive" (north-seeking) ends following, with the reverse situation in the southern hemisphere. In Cycle 23 this arrangement is reversed. A *magnetic* activity cycle, which is probably a more realistic description of the rhythms of solar activity, is equal to two of Wolf's activity cycles and takes about 22 years to complete.

Active regions are not isolated phenomena; they occur in complexes, comprising several active regions at various stages of development, together with the network elements remaining from decayed regions. This localization of activity gives rise to a rotational modulation of the 10.7 cm flux as active region clusters are carried across the disk and disappear around the west limb. To smooth out this modulation in long-term studies of solar activity, the data are averaged over solar rotations rather than by month. Active regions can persist for one or more solar rotations and the complexes for a dozen or so.

The large-scale organization of solar magnetic activity is also apparent in the spatial distribution of active regions during the solar cycle. The first activity of the new cycle is marked by the formation of active regions at high latitudes. As activity builds toward the maximum of the cycle, the number of active regions increases, and they tend to form at lower latitudes. As the activity wanes towards the next minimum, the number of regions decreases, but the average latitude continues to decrease, until the last activity of the cycle is located near the equator. Then, as the new cycle starts, new active regions form at high latitudes.

The solar atmosphere is not stable. It is constantly flowing outwards as a stream of particles and magnetic fields—the *solar wind*. The flow is strongest where the magnetic loops are very large and impose the least drag on the outwardly flowing particles. Due to the lower coronal densities in these regions, they produce a lower flux of X-rays and appear as dark patches in X-ray images, called coronal holes. The solar wind is not homogeneous or steady; its speed, density and direction can change according to the positions of coronal holes and the nature of current solar activity.

The flow of the solar wind past Earth produces profound changes in Earth's magnetic field. The pressure of the solar wind pushes Earth's magnetic field out of its dipole shape into a long teardrop. The flow of the solar wind over the interface between it and Earth's magnetic field (the magnetopause) excites many types of waves, which move along Earth's magnetic field lines and which can be detected at high magnetic latitudes. Complex interactions between the solar wind and Earth's magnetic field accelerate particles that accumulate in the magnetosphere.

Increases in the density or velocity of the solar wind change the pressure equilibrium between the solar wind and the magnetosphere, producing fluctuations in the strength and direction of the magnetic field lines at ground level. Precipitation of charged particles (primarily electrons and protons) from the solar wind enhance and change the electrical current systems flowing in Earth's upper atmosphere. The result is magnetic storms and substorms, strong fluctuations in the strength and direction of Earth's magnetic field.

During these events, particles may leak downward along Earth's magnetic field into increasingly dense atmosphere, until they collide with the atmospheric constituents, exciting them with sufficient energy to produce light. These displays are called aurorae, or the northern and southern lights—*aurora borealis* and *aurora australis*, respectively. Views from space show that aurorae fall in a rough circle (the auroral oval), centred around the magnetic pole, that is, in a definite band of magnetic latitudes. As activity increases, the auroral oval expands, covering lower and lower magnetic latitudes. It also becomes increasingly distorted. During the period of very high activity in March 1989, auroral displays were seen as far south as the Caribbean.

Aurorae occur in many forms and can be steady, moving, or rapidly pulsating, depending upon the nature of the particle streams causing them. Aurorae can appear green or red, although if they are faint, the eye cannot respond in colour and they appear grey. The greenish colour is due to spectral lines from oxygen (558 nm) and a range of lines from nitrogen covering the band 391 nm to 470 nm. Under highly disturbed conditions, red spectral line emissions at 630 nm and 636 nm, and in a series of bands between 650 nm and 680 nm can also be seen. The green emissions are produced at a height of about 110 km. The red, 630 nm and 636 nm emissions, due to atomic oxygen, originate at heights between 200 km and 400 km; the 650 nm to 680 nm emissions are produced at about 90 km.

Solar activity has had profound effects upon Earth extending as far back in time as we have been able to look. The solar activity cycle is reflected in the growth rates of trees (determined from the study of tree rings) in recently living timber, wood from mediaeval buildings, and fossilized trees. The activity cycle has also been seen in the changes in the thickness of annual sedimentary deposits in lakes that dry up in summer.

There is extensive evidence of the dramatic effects solar activity has upon our activities. Magnetic storms due to solar activity induce currents in communications and power transmission systems using long distance wires, disrupting their operation for hours. The power blackouts in Québec and Scandinavia produced by a large flare on 1989 March 10 is a particularly outstanding example. Railway signalling systems can also be affected. Increased X-ray emissions from flares cause enhanced ionization of Earth's atmosphere at D region heights (about 90 km), producing blackouts of short wave communications.

Solar activity heats the upper atmosphere, causing it to expand further into space, increasing the drag experienced by artificial satellites in low orbits. It is ironic that the lifetime of the Solar Max satellite was dramatically shortened in this way.

Above the atmosphere, satellites have no protection from high-energy particle fluxes produced by the Sun. Their electronic systems are damaged, leading to catastrophic failures in some cases, as occurred with two Anik communications satellites in January 1994.

The oldest index of solar activity is the sunspot number. A number of techniques, many empirical, have been developed to combine observations from various observatories and observers to form the *International Sunspot Number*. This rather poor index has, however, the great advantage of forming a database extending back to at least the 17th century.

Probably the best available index of solar activity, at least covering the last 50 years or so, is the *10.7 cm flux*, or $F_{10.7}$. This index is an objective measurement of the integrated emission at the 10.7 cm wavelength (a frequency of 2.8 GHz) from all sources present on the solar disk. It has been measured daily by the National Research Council of Canada for nearly 50 years and is now used worldwide as a primary index of solar activity. It is expressed in solar flux units (1 sfu = 10^{-22} Wm^{-2} Hz^{-1}). The 10.7 cm flux has the great advantage that it can be measured in any weather and requires no human involvement or "interpretation." When quiet, the Sun produces a 10.7 cm flux of 64 sfu, due to free-free thermal emission from the quiet solar corona. This index is expressed in two main forms: the *observed* and *adjusted* flux values.

The *observed* value is what is measured, and since this represents the impact of solar activity on Earth, it is useful in studying the consequences of solar activity here on Earth and our near-Earth space environment. The *adjusted* value is what we would observe at a constant distance from the Sun of one astronomical unit. This version of the index describes the activity of the Sun as a star, with the effect of the changing Earth–Sun distance taken out.

The 10.7 cm flux can be used as an objective proxy for other activity-related quantities. For example, the *adjusted* 10.7 cm flux can be used as a proxy for sunspot number through the relation "*sunspot number*" = 1.14(*adjusted solar flux*) − 73.21, and the total *photospheric magnetic flux*, in units of 10^{22} Maxwells, equals (*adjusted flux*)/2 − 10.

We are a long way from understanding the nature and the extent of the effects solar activity has upon Earth. Some correlations, like that between the length of miniskirts and solar activity, are probably spurious; others might not be. As we exploit our environment more fully, we become increasingly sensitive to things that might affect it, even slightly.

AURORAL FORMS

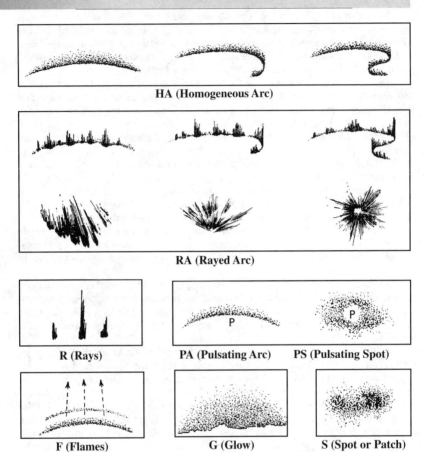

HA (Homogeneous Arc)

RA (Rayed Arc)

R (Rays)   **PA (Pulsating Arc)**   **PS (Pulsating Spot)**

F (Flames)   **G (Glow)**   **S (Spot or Patch)**

The above sketches illustrate standard auroral forms. This simplified classification was devised for visual observers during the International Geophysical Year over four decades ago (1957–58). Although there is great variety in auroral patterns, the sketches emphasize fundamental features and minimize variations that depend on the location of the observer. The light of the aurora is emitted by the upper fringes of the Earth's atmosphere (heights of 100 to 400 km) as it is bombarded by electrons of the solar wind (solar wind protons contribute a smaller amount of energy). The modification of the trajectories of these particles by Earth's magnetic field restricts activity to high latitudes, producing the "aurora borealis" in the Northern Hemisphere and the "aurora australis" in the Southern Hemisphere. The wavelengths of four, atmospheric, molecular and atomic emission lines that can contribute strongly to auroral light are included in the list on p. 27. Whether aurorae appear coloured depends on their luminance—light that is too faint will not activate colour vision and appears white. When the luminance is sufficiently great, the relative contributions of blue, green, and red emission lines can result in a variety of auroral hues.

TIMES OF SUNRISE AND SUNSET

The tables on the next three pages give the times of sunrise and sunset at four-day intervals for locations ranging from 20° to 62° north latitude. "Rise" and "set" correspond to the upper limb of the Sun appearing at the horizon for an observer at sea level. The times are local mean time (LMT) for the Greenwich meridian (i.e. UT at 0° longitude), although for North American observers the stated values may be read directly as LMT at the observer's position without significant error. The tables may be interpolated linearly for both non-tabular latitudes and dates, and can be extrapolated beyond the 20° and 62° latitude limits a few degrees without significant loss of accuracy.

It is a common misconception that extreme values for sunrise and sunset times occur on the shortest and the longest days of the year. This is not the case and is due to the tilt of Earth's spin axis to the axis of its orbit and to Earth's varying speed along its elliptical orbit (as Kepler described in his second law). At midnorthern latitudes, the earliest sunset occurs early in December and the latest sunrise in early January, whereas the shortest day (in the sense of hours of daylight) is December 21 or 22. For more information see: *Sky & Telescope*, December 1988, p. 674, and July 1972, p. 20; and an article by Terence Hicks in *JRASC*, *88*, p. 86, February 1994.

The standard time of an event at a particular location must take account of the observer's longitude relative to his or her standard meridian (see STANDARD TIME ZONES on pp. 36–37). The **table below** lists the latitude and the longitude correction (in minutes of time) for a number of cities in Canada and the United States. For example, to find the time of sunrise at Toronto on February 15, 2001: the latitude is 44°, and from the table the time of sunrise at 0° longitude is 6:59 UT (after interpolating for latitude). Thus, at Toronto, the time of sunrise will be approximately 6:59 LMT. Toronto is in the Eastern time zone (E) and is 18 minutes of time west of the standard meridian for this zone (75°W). Thus, sunrise in Toronto will occur at 7:17 EST (Eastern Standard Time). The longitude correction for any location may be found by converting the difference between the longitude of the place and that of its standard meridian to time (1° = 4 minutes of time), the correction being + if the place is west of its standard meridian, – if east. **Note**: Due to a difference in height between the observer and the actual horizon, the observed time may differ by several minutes from the predicted time.

Canadian Cities				American Cities	
Brandon	50°+40C	Québec	47°–15E	Atlanta	34°+37E
Calgary	51°+36M	Regina	50°+58C	Boston	42°–16E
Charlottetown	46°+12A	Resolute	75°+20C	Chicago	42°–10C
Corner Brook	49°+22N	Rimouski	48°–26E	Cincinnati	39°+38E
Edmonton	54°+34M	Saint John	45°+24A	Denver	40° 00M
Halifax	45°+14A	St. John's	48°+01N	Fairbanks	65°+50A
Hamilton	43°+20E	Sarnia	43°+29E	Flagstaff	35°+27M
Kelowna	50°–03P	Saskatoon	52°+67C	Kansas City	39°+18C
Kingston, ON	44°+06E	Sudbury	47°+24E	Los Angeles	34°–07P
Kitchener	43°+22E	Thunder Bay	48°+57E	Miami	26°+21E
London	43°+25E	Toronto	44°+18E	Minneapolis	45°+13C
Moncton	46°+19A	Vancouver	49°+12P	New Orleans	30° 00C
Montreal	46°–06E	Victoria	48°+13P	New York	41°–04E
Niagara Falls	43°+16E	Whitehorse	61°+60P	San Francisco	38°+10P
Ottawa	45°+03E	Windsor, ON	42°+32E	Seattle	48°+09P
Pangnirtung	66°+23A	Winnipeg	50°+29C	Tucson	32°+24M
Prince George	54°+11P	Yellowknife	62°+38M	Washington	39°+08E

SUNRISE AND SUNSET, 2001 JANUARY–APRIL
UNIVERSAL TIME AT GREENWICH MERIDIAN

Latitude:	+20°		+30°		+35°		+40°		+45°		+50°		+54°		+58°		+62°	
Event:	RISE	SET	RISE	SET	RISE	SET	RISE	SET	RISE	SET	RISE	SET	RISE	SET	RISE	SET	RISE	SET
Jan. -2	6:34	17:30	6:55	17:09	7:07	16:57	7:21	16:43	7:38	16:27	7:58	16:06	8:19	15:45	8:46	15:18	9:24	14:40
2	6:35	17:33	6:56	17:12	7:08	17:00	7:22	16:46	7:38	16:30	7:58	16:10	8:19	15:50	8:45	15:23	9:22	14:46
6	6:37	17:35	6:57	17:15	7:09	17:03	7:22	16:50	7:38	16:34	7:58	16:15	8:17	15:55	8:43	15:30	9:18	14:54
10	6:37	17:38	6:57	17:18	7:08	17:07	7:22	16:54	7:37	16:39	7:56	16:20	8:15	16:01	8:39	15:36	9:13	15:03
14	6:38	17:41	6:57	17:22	7:08	17:11	7:20	16:58	7:35	16:43	7:53	16:25	8:11	16:07	8:35	15:44	9:06	15:12
18	6:38	17:43	6:56	17:25	7:07	17:15	7:19	17:03	7:33	16:48	7:50	16:31	8:07	16:14	8:29	15:52	8:59	15:23
22	6:38	17:46	6:55	17:29	7:05	17:19	7:16	17:07	7:30	16:54	7:46	16:38	8:02	16:21	8:23	16:01	8:50	15:34
26	6:37	17:48	6:53	17:32	7:03	17:23	7:14	17:12	7:26	16:59	7:42	16:44	7:57	16:29	8:16	16:10	8:41	15:45
30	6:36	17:51	6:51	17:36	7:00	17:27	7:10	17:17	7:22	17:05	7:36	16:51	7:50	16:37	8:08	16:20	8:31	15:57
Feb. 3	6:35	17:53	6:49	17:39	6:57	17:31	7:07	17:22	7:17	17:11	7:31	16:58	7:43	16:45	7:59	16:29	8:20	16:09
7	6:33	17:55	6:46	17:42	6:54	17:35	7:02	17:26	7:12	17:16	7:24	17:05	7:36	16:53	7:50	16:39	8:09	16:20
11	6:31	17:57	6:43	17:46	6:50	17:39	6:58	17:31	7:07	17:22	7:18	17:12	7:28	17:01	7:41	16:48	7:58	16:32
15	6:29	17:59	6:40	17:49	6:46	17:43	6:53	17:36	7:01	17:28	7:11	17:18	7:20	17:09	7:31	16:58	7:46	16:44
19	6:27	18:01	6:36	17:52	6:42	17:46	6:48	17:40	6:55	17:34	7:03	17:25	7:11	17:17	7:21	17:07	7:34	16:55
23	6:24	18:03	6:32	17:55	6:37	17:50	6:42	17:45	6:48	17:39	6:55	17:32	7:02	17:25	7:11	17:17	7:21	17:06
27	6:21	18:04	6:28	17:58	6:32	17:54	6:36	17:50	6:41	17:45	6:47	17:39	6:53	17:33	7:00	17:26	7:09	17:18
Mar. 3	6:18	18:06	6:24	18:00	6:27	17:57	6:30	17:54	6:34	17:50	6:39	17:45	6:44	17:41	6:49	17:36	6:56	17:29
7	6:15	18:07	6:19	18:03	6:22	18:01	6:24	17:58	6:27	17:55	6:31	17:52	6:34	17:49	6:38	17:45	6:43	17:40
11	6:12	18:08	6:15	18:06	6:16	18:04	6:18	18:03	6:20	18:01	6:22	17:58	6:25	17:56	6:27	17:54	6:31	17:51
15	6:08	18:10	6:10	18:08	6:11	18:08	6:12	18:07	6:13	18:06	6:14	18:05	6:15	18:04	6:16	18:03	6:18	18:02
19	6:05	18:11	6:05	18:11	6:05	18:11	6:05	18:11	6:05	18:11	6:05	18:11	6:05	18:12	6:05	18:12	6:05	18:12
23	6:02	18:12	6:00	18:13	6:00	18:14	5:59	18:15	5:58	18:16	5:56	18:18	5:55	18:19	5:54	18:21	5:52	18:23
27	5:58	18:13	5:55	18:16	5:54	18:17	5:52	18:19	5:50	18:21	5:48	18:24	5:45	18:27	5:42	18:30	5:38	18:34
31	5:55	18:14	5:51	18:18	5:48	18:20	5:46	18:23	5:43	18:26	5:39	18:30	5:35	18:34	5:31	18:39	5:25	18:44
Apr. 4	5:51	18:15	5:46	18:20	5:43	18:24	5:39	18:27	5:35	18:31	5:30	18:37	5:26	18:41	5:20	18:48	5:12	18:55
8	5:48	18:16	5:41	18:23	5:37	18:27	5:33	18:31	5:28	18:37	5:22	18:43	5:16	18:49	5:09	18:56	4:59	19:06
12	5:44	18:17	5:37	18:25	5:32	18:30	5:27	18:35	5:21	18:42	5:13	18:49	5:06	18:56	4:58	19:05	4:46	19:17
16	5:41	18:19	5:32	18:28	5:27	18:33	5:21	18:39	5:14	18:47	5:05	18:55	4:57	19:04	4:47	19:14	4:34	19:28
20	5:38	18:20	5:28	18:30	5:22	18:36	5:15	18:43	5:07	18:52	4:57	19:02	4:48	19:11	4:36	19:23	4:21	19:39
24	5:35	18:21	5:24	18:33	5:17	18:40	5:09	18:48	5:00	18:57	4:49	19:08	4:39	19:19	4:25	19:32	4:08	19:50
28	5:33	18:22	5:20	18:35	5:13	18:43	5:04	18:52	4:54	19:02	4:42	19:14	4:30	19:26	4:15	19:41	3:56	20:01

SUNRISE AND SUNSET, 2001 MAY–AUGUST
UNIVERSAL TIME AT GREENWICH MERIDIAN

Latitude: Event	+20° RISE	+20° SET	+30° RISE	+30° SET	+35° RISE	+35° SET	+40° RISE	+40° SET	+45° RISE	+45° SET	+50° RISE	+50° SET	+54° RISE	+54° SET	+58° RISE	+58° SET	+62° RISE	+62° SET
May 2	5:30	18:24	5:16	18:38	5:08	18:46	4:59	18:56	4:48	19:07	4:35	19:20	4:22	19:34	4:05	19:50	3:44	20:12
6	5:28	18:25	5:13	18:41	5:04	18:49	4:54	19:00	4:42	19:12	4:28	19:26	4:14	19:41	3:56	19:59	3:32	20:23
10	5:26	18:27	5:10	18:43	5:01	18:53	4:50	19:04	4:37	19:16	4:21	19:32	4:06	19:48	3:46	20:08	3:20	20:34
14	5:24	18:28	5:07	18:46	4:57	18:56	4:46	19:07	4:32	19:21	4:16	19:38	3:59	19:55	3:38	20:16	3:09	20:45
18	5:23	18:30	5:05	18:48	4:54	18:59	4:42	19:11	4:28	19:26	4:10	19:43	3:52	20:01	3:30	20:24	2:59	20:56
22	5:22	18:32	5:03	18:51	4:52	19:02	4:39	19:15	4:24	19:30	4:05	19:49	3:47	20:08	3:22	20:32	2:49	21:07
26	5:21	18:33	5:01	18:53	4:50	19:05	4:36	19:18	4:21	19:34	4:01	19:54	3:41	20:14	3:16	20:40	2:39	21:16
30	5:20	18:35	5:00	18:55	4:48	19:07	4:34	19:21	4:18	19:38	3:57	19:58	3:37	20:19	3:10	20:46	2:31	21:26
Jun. 3	5:20	18:37	4:59	18:57	4:47	19:10	4:32	19:24	4:16	19:41	3:55	20:02	3:33	20:24	3:05	20:52	2:24	21:34
7	5:20	18:38	4:58	18:59	4:46	19:12	4:31	19:27	4:14	19:44	3:52	20:06	3:30	20:28	3:01	20:58	2:18	21:41
11	5:20	18:39	4:58	19:01	4:45	19:14	4:31	19:29	4:13	19:46	3:51	20:09	3:28	20:31	2:58	21:02	2:13	21:47
15	5:20	18:41	4:58	19:03	4:46	19:15	4:31	19:30	4:13	19:48	3:50	20:11	3:27	20:34	2:56	21:05	2:10	21:51
19	5:21	18:42	4:59	19:04	4:46	19:17	4:31	19:32	4:13	19:50	3:50	20:12	3:27	20:36	2:56	21:07	2:09	21:54
23	5:22	18:42	5:00	19:04	4:47	19:18	4:32	19:33	4:14	19:51	3:51	20:13	3:28	20:36	2:57	21:07	2:10	21:54
27	5:23	18:43	5:01	19:05	4:48	19:18	4:33	19:33	4:15	19:51	3:53	20:13	3:30	20:36	2:59	21:07	2:13	21:53
Jul. 1	5:24	18:43	5:02	19:05	4:50	19:18	4:35	19:33	4:17	19:50	3:55	20:12	3:32	20:35	3:02	21:05	2:17	21:50
5	5:25	18:44	5:04	19:05	4:52	19:17	4:37	19:32	4:20	19:49	3:58	20:11	3:36	20:33	3:06	21:02	2:23	21:45
9	5:27	18:43	5:06	19:04	4:54	19:16	4:39	19:31	4:22	19:48	4:01	20:09	3:40	20:30	3:11	20:58	2:30	21:39
13	5:28	18:43	5:08	19:03	4:56	19:15	4:42	19:29	4:26	19:45	4:05	20:06	3:45	20:26	3:17	20:53	2:38	21:32
17	5:30	18:41	5:10	19:02	4:59	19:13	4:45	19:27	4:29	19:42	4:10	20:02	3:50	20:21	3:24	20:47	2:47	21:23
21	5:31	18:41	5:12	19:00	5:01	19:11	4:49	19:24	4:33	19:39	4:15	19:57	3:56	20:16	3:31	20:40	2:57	21:14
25	5:33	18:40	5:15	18:58	5:04	19:08	4:52	19:21	4:38	19:35	4:20	19:52	4:02	20:10	3:39	20:33	3:07	21:04
29	5:34	18:38	5:17	18:55	5:07	19:05	4:56	19:17	4:42	19:30	4:25	19:47	4:08	20:03	3:47	20:25	3:18	20:53
Aug. 2	5:36	18:36	5:20	18:53	5:10	19:02	4:59	19:13	4:46	19:25	4:31	19:41	4:15	19:56	3:55	20:16	3:29	20:42
6	5:37	18:34	5:22	18:49	5:13	18:58	5:03	19:08	4:51	19:20	4:36	19:34	4:22	19:49	4:04	20:07	3:39	20:30
10	5:38	18:32	5:24	18:46	5:16	18:54	5:07	19:03	4:56	19:14	4:42	19:27	4:29	19:41	4:12	19:57	3:50	20:18
14	5:40	18:29	5:27	18:42	5:19	18:50	5:11	18:58	5:00	19:08	4:48	19:20	4:36	19:32	4:21	19:47	4:01	20:06
18	5:41	18:27	5:29	18:38	5:22	18:45	5:14	18:53	5:05	19:02	4:54	19:13	4:43	19:23	4:30	19:37	4:12	19:54
22	5:42	18:23	5:31	18:34	5:25	18:40	5:18	18:47	5:10	18:55	5:00	19:05	4:50	19:14	4:38	19:26	4:23	19:41
26	5:43	18:20	5:34	18:29	5:28	18:35	5:22	18:41	5:15	18:48	5:06	18:57	4:57	19:05	4:47	19:15	4:33	19:28
30	5:44	18:17	5:36	18:25	5:31	18:29	5:26	18:35	5:20	18:41	5:12	18:48	5:05	18:55	4:56	19:04	4:44	19:15

SUNRISE AND SUNSET, 2001 SEPTEMBER–DECEMBER
UNIVERSAL TIME AT GREENWICH MERIDIAN

Latitude: Event	+20° RISE	SET	+30° RISE	SET	+35° RISE	SET	+40° RISE	SET	+45° RISE	SET	+50° RISE	SET	+54° RISE	SET	+58° RISE	SET	+62° RISE	SET
Sep. 3	5:45	18:14	5:38	18:20	5:34	18:24	5:30	18:28	5:24	18:34	5:18	18:40	5:12	18:46	5:04	18:53	4:54	19:02
7	5:46	18:10	5:40	18:15	5:37	18:18	5:33	18:22	5:29	18:26	5:24	18:31	5:19	18:36	5:13	18:42	5:05	18:49
11	5:47	18:06	5:42	18:10	5:40	18:13	5:37	18:15	5:34	18:19	5:30	18:22	5:26	18:26	5:21	18:31	5:15	18:36
15	5:47	18:03	5:44	18:05	5:43	18:07	5:41	18:09	5:39	18:11	5:36	18:14	5:33	18:16	5:30	18:19	5:26	18:23
19	5:48	17:59	5:47	18:00	5:46	18:01	5:45	18:02	5:43	18:03	5:42	18:05	5:40	18:06	5:38	18:08	5:36	18:10
23	5:49	17:55	5:49	17:55	5:49	17:55	5:48	17:56	5:48	17:56	5:48	17:56	5:47	17:56	5:47	17:57	5:46	17:57
27	5:50	17:52	5:51	17:50	5:52	17:50	5:52	17:49	5:53	17:48	5:54	17:47	5:55	17:46	5:55	17:45	5:57	17:44
Oct. 1	5:51	17:48	5:53	17:46	5:55	17:44	5:56	17:42	5:58	17:41	6:00	17:38	6:02	17:36	6:04	17:34	6:07	17:31
5	5:52	17:45	5:56	17:41	5:58	17:38	6:00	17:36	6:03	17:33	6:06	17:30	6:09	17:27	6:13	17:23	6:17	17:18
9	5:53	17:41	5:58	17:36	6:01	17:33	6:04	17:30	6:08	17:26	6:12	17:21	6:17	17:17	6:22	17:12	6:28	17:05
13	5:54	17:38	6:01	17:31	6:04	17:28	6:08	17:24	6:13	17:19	6:19	17:13	6:24	17:07	6:31	17:01	6:39	16:52
17	5:55	17:35	6:03	17:27	6:08	17:23	6:13	17:18	6:18	17:12	6:25	17:05	6:32	16:58	6:40	16:50	6:50	16:40
21	5:57	17:32	6:06	17:23	6:11	17:18	6:17	17:12	6:24	17:05	6:32	16:57	6:39	16:49	6:49	16:40	7:01	16:27
25	5:58	17:29	6:09	17:19	6:15	17:13	6:21	17:06	6:29	16:59	6:38	16:49	6:47	16:40	6:58	16:29	7:12	16:15
29	6:00	17:27	6:12	17:15	6:18	17:09	6:26	17:01	6:34	16:53	6:45	16:42	6:55	16:32	7:07	16:19	7:23	16:03
Nov. 2	6:02	17:25	6:15	17:12	6:22	17:05	6:30	16:57	6:40	16:47	6:51	16:35	7:03	16:24	7:16	16:10	7:34	15:52
6	6:04	17:23	6:18	17:09	6:26	17:01	6:35	16:52	6:45	16:41	6:58	16:29	7:10	16:16	7:26	16:01	7:46	15:41
10	6:06	17:22	6:21	17:07	6:30	16:58	6:39	16:48	6:51	16:37	7:05	16:23	7:18	16:09	7:35	15:52	7:57	15:30
14	6:08	17:20	6:24	17:04	6:33	16:55	6:44	16:45	6:56	16:32	7:11	16:17	7:26	16:02	7:44	15:44	8:09	15:20
18	6:11	17:20	6:28	17:03	6:37	16:53	6:49	16:42	7:02	16:28	7:18	16:12	7:33	15:56	7:53	15:37	8:20	15:10
22	6:13	17:19	6:31	17:01	6:41	16:51	6:53	16:39	7:07	16:25	7:24	16:08	7:41	15:51	8:02	15:30	8:31	15:01
26	6:15	17:19	6:34	17:00	6:45	16:49	6:57	16:37	7:12	16:22	7:30	16:05	7:48	15:47	8:10	15:24	8:41	14:53
30	6:18	17:19	6:37	17:00	6:49	16:49	7:02	16:36	7:17	16:20	7:35	16:02	7:54	15:43	8:18	15:19	8:51	14:46
Dec. 4	6:21	17:20	6:41	17:00	6:52	16:48	7:05	16:35	7:21	16:19	7:41	16:00	8:00	15:40	8:25	15:15	9:00	14:40
8	6:23	17:21	6:44	17:00	6:55	16:48	7:09	16:35	7:25	16:18	7:45	15:58	8:05	15:38	8:31	15:12	9:08	14:36
12	6:25	17:22	6:46	17:01	6:58	16:49	7:12	16:35	7:29	16:18	7:49	15:58	8:10	15:37	8:37	15:11	9:14	14:33
16	6:28	17:24	6:49	17:02	7:01	16:50	7:15	16:36	7:32	16:19	7:53	15:59	8:14	15:38	8:41	15:10	9:20	14:32
20	6:30	17:25	6:51	17:04	7:04	16:52	7:18	16:38	7:35	16:21	7:55	16:00	8:16	15:39	8:44	15:11	9:23	14:32
24	6:32	17:27	6:53	17:06	7:05	16:54	7:20	16:40	7:37	16:23	7:57	16:02	8:18	15:41	8:46	15:14	9:25	14:35
28	6:34	17:30	6:55	17:09	7:07	16:56	7:21	16:42	7:38	16:26	7:58	16:05	8:19	15:44	8:46	15:17	9:25	14:39
32	6:35	17:32	6:56	17:11	7:08	16:59	7:22	16:45	7:38	16:29	7:59	16:09	8:19	15:48	8:45	15:22	9:23	14:44

TWILIGHT

There are three definitions for the beginning of morning and ending of evening twilight: (1) *Civil twilight*—centre of the Sun 6° below the horizon, brightest stars visible, artificial illumination required for most outdoor activities, marks the ending or beginning of night for aviation purposes; (2) *Nautical twilight*—centre of the Sun 12° below the horizon, horizon no longer visible; (3) *Astronomical twilight*—centre of the Sun 18° below the horizon, amount of sunlight scattered by the atmosphere is negligible.

The table below gives the beginning of morning and ending of evening astronomical twilight in UT at 0° longitude. For observers in North America the times may be handled in the same way as those of sunrise and sunset (see p. 89).

Latitude / M-E	+20°		+30°		+35°		+40°		+45°		+50°		+54°		+58°		+62°	
	MORN	EVE	MORN	EVE	MORN	EVE	MORN	EVE	MORN	EVE	MORN	EVE	MORN	EVE	MORN	EVE	MORN	EVE
Jan. 0	5:16	18:50	5:30	18:36	5:37	18:29	5:44	18:22	5:52	18:15	6:00	18:07	6:06	18:00	6:14	17:53	6:23	17:44
10	5:19	18:56	5:33	18:43	5:39	18:37	5:45	18:30	5:52	18:24	5:59	18:17	6:05	18:11	6:11	18:05	6:18	17:57
20	5:21	19:01	5:32	18:50	5:38	18:45	5:43	18:40	5:48	18:34	5:54	18:29	5:58	18:25	6:03	18:20	6:08	18:15
30	5:20	19:07	5:29	18:58	5:33	18:54	5:37	18:50	5:41	18:46	5:44	18:43	5:47	18:40	5:50	18:38	5:52	18:36
Feb. 9	5:18	19:11	5:24	19:05	5:26	19:02	5:29	19:00	5:30	18:59	5:31	18:58	5:32	18:58	5:32	18:58	5:31	18:59
19	5:13	19:15	5:16	19:12	5:17	19:11	5:17	19:11	5:17	19:12	5:15	19:13	5:13	19:16	5:10	19:19	5:05	19:24
Mar. 1	5:07	19:18	5:07	19:19	5:06	19:20	5:04	19:22	5:01	19:25	4:56	19:30	4:51	19:35	4:44	19:42	4:35	19:52
11	4:59	19:22	4:55	19:25	4:52	19:28	4:48	19:32	4:42	19:39	4:35	19:47	4:26	19:55	4:15	20:07	4:00	20:22
21	4:50	19:25	4:43	19:32	4:38	19:37	4:31	19:44	4:23	19:53	4:11	20:05	3:59	20:17	3:43	20:34	3:20	20:57
31	4:41	19:28	4:30	19:39	4:23	19:47	4:13	19:56	4:01	20:08	3:46	20:24	3:29	20:41	3:06	21:05	2:33	21:39
Apr. 10	4:31	19:32	4:17	19:47	4:07	19:56	3:55	20:09	3:39	20:25	3:19	20:46	2:56	21:09	2:24	21:42	1:30	22:40
20	4:22	19:36	4:04	19:55	3:52	20:07	3:36	20:22	3:17	20:42	2:50	21:09	2:20	21:41	1:31	22:32		
30	4:14	19:41	3:52	20:03	3:37	20:18	3:19	20:37	2:55	21:01	2:20	21:36	1:38	22:21				
May 10	4:07	19:46	3:41	20:13	3:24	20:30	3:02	20:52	2:33	21:21	1:49	22:07	0:32	23:33				
20	4:01	19:52	3:32	20:22	3:13	20:41	2:48	21:06	2:13	21:42	1:13	22:43						
30	3:58	19:58	3:26	20:30	3:04	20:51	2:36	21:20	1:56	22:01	0:25	23:39						
Jun. 9	3:56	20:02	3:22	20:36	3:00	20:59	2:29	21:31	1:44	22:15								
19	3:57	20:06	3:22	20:40	2:59	21:04	2:28	21:35	1:40	22:23								
29	4:00	20:07	3:25	20:41	3:02	21:05	2:31	21:35	1:44	22:22								
Jul. 9	4:04	20:06	3:31	20:39	3:09	21:01	2:40	21:30	1:57	22:13								
19	4:09	20:03	3:38	20:34	3:18	20:54	2:51	21:20	2:14	21:57	1:04	23:05						
29	4:14	19:58	3:47	20:26	3:28	20:44	3:05	21:07	2:34	21:38	1:43	22:27						
Aug. 8	4:19	19:52	3:55	20:15	3:40	20:31	3:20	20:50	2:53	21:16	2:15	21:54	1:21	22:45				
18	4:24	19:43	4:04	20:03	3:50	20:16	3:34	20:33	3:12	20:54	2:42	21:23	2:06	21:58	0:58	23:01		
28	4:28	19:34	4:12	19:50	4:01	20:01	3:47	20:14	3:30	20:31	3:06	20:54	2:40	21:20	2:01	21:57	0:32	23:14
Sep. 7	4:31	19:24	4:19	19:37	4:10	19:45	3:59	19:55	3:46	20:09	3:28	20:27	3:08	20:46	2:41	21:12	2:00	21:52
17	4:34	19:14	4:25	19:23	4:19	19:29	4:11	19:37	4:01	19:47	3:47	20:00	3:33	20:14	3:13	20:33	2:46	21:00
27	4:37	19:05	4:31	19:10	4:27	19:14	4:22	19:19	4:15	19:26	4:05	19:36	3:55	19:46	3:41	19:59	3:22	20:17
Oct. 7	4:39	18:56	4:37	18:58	4:35	19:00	4:32	19:03	4:28	19:06	4:22	19:13	4:15	19:28	4:06	19:28	3:53	19:40
17	4:42	18:49	4:43	18:47	4:43	18:47	4:42	18:48	4:40	18:49	4:37	18:52	4:34	18:56	4:28	19:01	4:21	19:08
27	4:45	18:43	4:50	18:38	4:51	18:36	4:52	18:35	4:53	18:34	4:53	18:34	4:52	18:35	4:50	18:37	4:47	18:40
Nov. 6	4:49	18:38	4:56	18:31	4:59	18:27	5:02	18:24	5:05	18:22	5:07	18:19	5:09	18:18	5:10	18:17	5:10	18:16
16	4:53	18:36	5:03	18:26	5:08	18:21	5:12	18:17	5:17	18:12	5:21	18:08	5:25	18:04	5:28	18:01	5:32	17:57
26	4:58	18:36	5:10	18:24	5:16	18:18	5:22	18:13	5:28	18:07	5:34	18:00	5:39	17:55	5:45	17:49	5:51	17:43
Dec. 6	5:04	18:38	5:17	18:25	5:24	18:18	5:31	18:11	5:37	18:04	5:45	17:57	5:51	17:51	5:58	17:44	6:06	17:35
16	5:09	18:42	5:23	18:28	5:31	18:21	5:38	18:14	5:45	18:06	5:53	17:58	6:00	17:51	6:08	17:43	6:17	17:34
26	5:14	18:47	5:28	18:33	5:36	18:26	5:43	18:18	5:50	18:11	5:58	18:03	6:06	17:56	6:13	17:48	6:22	17:39
Jan. 5	5:18	18:53	5:32	18:39	5:38	18:32	5:45	18:26	5:52	18:19	6:00	18:11	6:06	18:05	6:13	17:58	6:21	17:50

MIDNIGHT TWILIGHT AND MIDNIGHT SUN
By Roy Bishop

Astronomers generally desire dark skies, free of moonlight and man-made light pollution. As mentioned on the previous page, the beginning or end of *astronomical twilight* corresponds to the centre of the Sun being 18° below the horizon. At that point the amount of sunlight scattered by the upper layers of Earth's atmosphere is negligible; i.e. it is less than the combined illuminance (about 2×10^{-3} lux) from starlight, airglow, and zodiacal light, the three main contributors to the light of the "dark" night sky.

For observers in countries at high latitudes (e.g. the United Kingdom, Norway, southern Argentina and Chile, and most of Canada) around the time of the summer solstice the Sun always lies less than 18° below the horizon, and the sky does not get dark at night! This "midnight twilight" phenomenon can be displayed in a graph as a function of latitude and time of year.

The **diagram** at the right indicates the brightness of the sky at local midnight at any time of the year for any latitude north of 45°N or south of 45°S. Below the lower curve the natural sky is dark. Between the two curves twilight prevails. Above the upper curve the Sun is in the sky. Place names in roman type (left-hand side) are in the Northern Hemisphere; place names in *italic* type (right-hand side) are in the *Southern Hemisphere*. On the horizontal axis use the roman-type months for the former, *italic*-type months for the latter. The diagram is simplified slightly in that the months are assumed to be of equal duration, and the seasonal pattern of months and summer solstices for Earth's two hemispheres are assumed to be identical except for a six-month phase shift.

The latitude of the Arctic and Antarctic Circles (90° subtract the obliquity of the ecliptic = 66°34′) is indicated by the dashed line. This line is *not* tangent to the Midnight Sun curve because at midnight on the summer solstice at either the Arctic or the Antarctic Circle the Sun is above the horizon. Atmospheric refraction raises the apparent Sun about 34′ above the true Sun. Also, rise/set is defined as the top limb of the Sun at a sea level horizon; thus the 16′ semidiameter of the Sun must also be taken into account. To see the top limb of the Sun on the horizon at local midnight on the summer solstice, an observer must be 34′ + 16′ = 50′ south of the Arctic Circle (or north of the Antarctic Circle), at latitude 65°44′.

By running a horizontal line across the chart at a selected latitude, the reader can determine the approximate dates when midnight twilight and, possibly, midnight Sun begin and end for any locality at north or south latitudes above 48.6°, the lower limit for midnight twilight on the summer solstice. (Remarkably, when rounded to the nearest degree, the latter figure is the latitude of the longest east-west international border: the 2000-km-long 49th parallel between the United States and western Canada.)

Some examples: The diagram indicates that at Grise Fiord (a hamlet on the stunning south coast of Ellesmere Island, and Canada's most northerly community) the sky is never dark from about March 10 until early October, and the "midnight Sun" lasts from late April until mid-August. Note that Cape Horn at midnight is bathed in dim Antarctic twilight from early November until early February. Even at the latitude of Vancouver there is a period of almost a month each year when the sky never gets astronomically dark — although the natural night sky is obliterated *every* night near any town or city unless there is an electrical power failure! Finally, note that Earth's poles are astronomically dark for less than 3 months of the year.

MIDNIGHT TWILIGHT AND MIDNIGHT SUN DIAGRAM

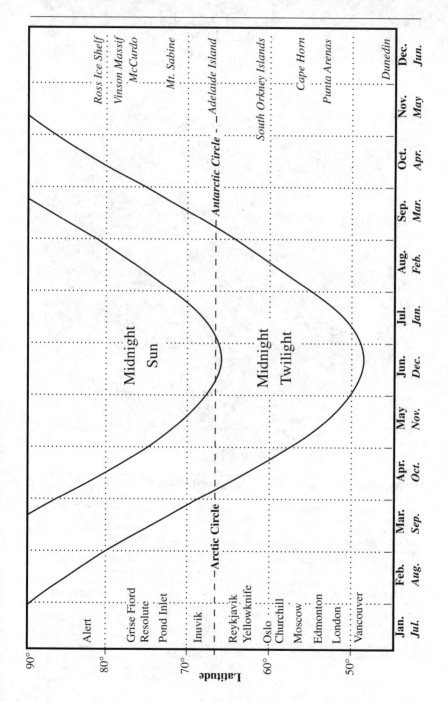

THE MOON

MAP OF MOON

By Roy Bishop

Maria

LS	Lacus Somniorum (Lake of Dreams) (330°)
MC	Mare Crisium (Sea of Crises) (300°)
MFe	Mare Fecunditatis (Sea of Fertility) (310°)
MFr	Mare Frigoris (Sea of Cold) (0°)
MH	Mare Humorum (Sea of Moisture) (40°)
MI	Mare Imbrium (Sea of Rains) (20°)
MNe	Mare Nectaris (Sea of Nectar) (325°)
MNu	Mare Nubium (Sea of Clouds) (15°)
MS	Mare Serenitatis (Sea of Serenity) (340°)
MT	Mare Tranquillitatis (Sea of Tranquillity) (330°)
MV	Mare Vaporum (Sea of Vapors) (355°)
OP	Oceanus Procellarum (Ocean of Storms) (50°)
SA	Sinus Aestuum (Seething Bay) (8°)
SI	Sinus Iridum (Bay of Rainbows) (32°)
SM	Sinus Medii (Central Bay) (0°)
SR	Sinus Roris (Bay of Dew) (60°)

Lunar Probes

2 *Luna 2*, First to reach Moon (1959.9.13) (0°)
7 *Ranger 7*, First close pictures (1964.7.31) (21°)
9 *Luna 9*, First soft landing (1966.2.3) (64°)
11 *Apollo 11*, First men on Moon (1969.7.20) (337°)
12 *Apollo 12* (1969.11.19) (23°)
14 *Apollo 14* (1971.2.5) (17°)
15 *Apollo 15* (1971.7.30) (356°)
16 *Apollo 16* (1972.4.21) (344°)
17 *Apollo 17* (1972.12.11) (329°)

Angles in parentheses equal (360°–λ), where λ is the selenographic longitude of the centre of the feature. 0° marks the mean centre of the lunar disk and the angles increase toward the observer's east (i.e. westward on the Moon). These angles facilitate locating the feature on the accompanying map, and may be correlated with the Sun's selenographic colongitude (see THE SKY MONTH BY MONTH (pp. 56–81)) to determine the optimum times for viewing the feature.

MAP OF MOON (continued)

Craters

21 Albategnius (356°)
22 Alphonsus (3°)
23 Arago (338°)
24 Archimedes (4°)
25 Aristarchus (47°)
26 Aristullus (358°)
27 Aristoteles (342°)
28 Arzachel (2°)
29 Atlas (315°)
31 Autolycus (358°)
32 Bessel (342°)
33 Bullialdus (22°)
34 Cassini (355°)
35 Catharina (336°)
36 Clavius (15°)
37 Cleomedes (304°)
38 Cook (311°)
39 Copernicus (20°)
41 Cyrillus (336°)
42 Delambre (342°)

43 Endymion (305°)
44 Eratosthenes (11°)
45 Eudoxus (343°)
46 Fracastorius (326°)
47 Furnerius (299°)
48 Gassendi (40°)
49 Grimaldi (68°)
51 Hercules (321°)
52 Hercules (321°)
53 Herschel (2°)
54 Hevelius (66°)
55 Hipparchus (354°)
56 Julius Caesar (345°)
57 Kepler (38°)
58 Langrenus (299°)
59 Lansberg (27°)
61 Longomontanus (21°)
62 Macrobius (314°)
63 Maginus (6°)
64 Manilius (351°)
65 Maskelyne (330°)
66 Maurolycus (345°)

67 Mersenius (49°)
68 Newcomb (316°)
69 Petavius (298°)
71 Piccolomini (327°)
72 Plato (10°)
73 Plinius (336°)
74 Posidonius (330°)
75 Ptolemaeus (2°)
76 Reinhold (23°)
77 Ross (338°)
78 Schickard (55°)
79 Schiller (40°)
81 Snellius (304°)
82 Stevinus (305°)
83 Taruntius (313°)
84 Theophilus (333°)
85 Timocharis (13°)
86 Tycho (11°)
87 Wilhelm (20°)

Mountains

A Alpine Valley (356°)
B Alps Mts. (359°)
E Altai Mts. (336°)
F Apennine Mts. (2°)
G Carpathian Mts. (24°)
H Caucasus Mts. (352°)
K Haemus Mts. (349°)
M Jura Mts. (34°)
N Pyrenees Mts. (319°)
R Rheita Valley (312°)
S Riphaeus Mts. (27°)
V Spitzbergen (5°)
W Straight Range (20°)
X Straight Wall (8°)
Y Taurus Mts. (319°)
Z Teneriffe Mts. (13°)

UNIVERSAL TIME OF NEW MOON DATES

2001			2002		
Jan. 24.5	May 23.1	Sep. 17.4	Jan. 13.6	May 12.4	Sep. 7.1
Feb. 23.3	Jun. 21.5	Oct. 16.8	Feb. 12.3	Jun. 11.0	Oct. 6.5
Mar. 25.1	Jul. 20.8	Nov. 15.3	Mar. 14.1	Jul. 10.4	Nov. 4.9
Apr. 23.6	Aug. 19.1	Dec. 14.9	Apr. 12.8	Aug. 8.8	Dec. 4.3

These dates will be useful for planning observing sessions, determining favourable dates for observing very thin lunar crescents, and setting moon dials on clocks. These dates are indicated to lower precision in the calendar on the inside back cover.

TIMES OF MOONRISE AND MOONSET

The following 12 pages of tables give the times of moonrise and moonset for each day of the year for locations ranging from 20° to 62° north latitude. The tables may be interpolated linearly for non-tabular latitudes, and can be extrapolated beyond the 20° and 62° latitude limits a few degrees without significant loss of accuracy. "Rise" and "set" correspond to the upper limb of the Moon appearing at the horizon for an observer at sea level. The times are local mean time (LMT) for the Greenwich meridian (i.e. UT at 0° longitude). Because of the relatively rapid eastward motion of the Moon, unlike the sunrise and sunset tables, for observers not near 0° longitude the times cannot be read directly as LMT. The table must be interpolated according to the observer's longitude. Also, to convert from the observer's LMT to standard time, the observer's longitude correction relative to his or her standard meridian must, of course, be applied. The chart at the right enables the sum of these two corrections to be determined easily in one step. However, the chart must first be set for your longitude.

To prepare the **Moonrise/Moonset Correction Diagram,** first mark your longitude on the *West or East Longitude* scale. Using a straight-edge, draw a diagonal line from this mark to the origin (the 0,0 point). Next, the *Correction in minutes* axis (which is subdivided at two-minute intervals) must be labelled. As a guide, the first three divisions have been tentatively labelled 0, ±2, ±4 (*use + if you are west of the prime meridian in Greenwich, England, − if east*); but, to these numbers must be added your longitude correction relative to your standard meridian (see the third paragraph on p. 89.) As an aid both for labelling and for reading the chart, the vertical lines at 10-minute intervals are wider. **Examples:** For Toronto (which is 4.5°W of its standard meridian of 75°) the longitude correction is +18 minutes, so an observer in Toronto would label the Correction axis divisions 18, 20, 22, 24,...; an observer in Boston (longitude correction −16) would label the axis −16, −14, −12,...; an observer in Hong Kong (east longitude, longitude correction +24) would label the axis: 24, 22, 20,...; an observer in Vienna (longitude correction −6) would label the axis: −6, −8, −10,....

The chart is now ready for use on any day from your position. Interpolating for non-tabular latitudes, from the table obtain today's time for the event (moonrise, or moonset) and tomorrow's time if you are west of Greenwich (yesterday's time if east), enter the difference on the Tabular Delay axis, and run horizontally across to meet the diagonal line. The correction, to the nearest minute, can then be read directly below off the Correction axis. This correction is applied to the tabular "today's time" and results in the standard time of the event for your position. **Note**: Due to a difference in height between the observer and the actual horizon, the observed time may differ by several minutes from the predicted time.

MOONRISE/MOONSET CORRECTION DIAGRAM

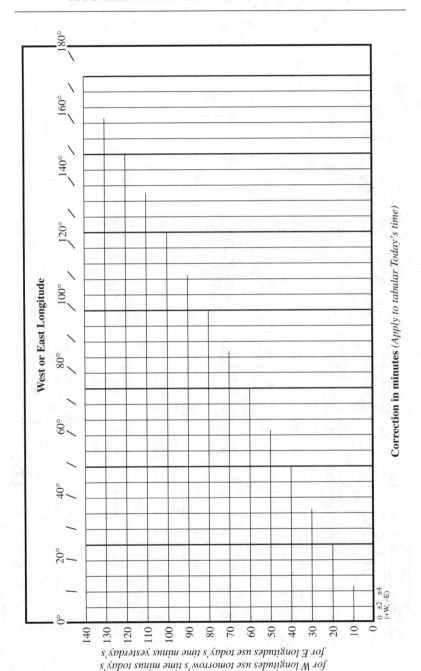

MOONRISE AND MOONSET, 2001 JANUARY
UNIVERSAL TIME AT GREENWICH MERIDIAN

Moon phases: ◑ Last Quarter ○ New Moon ◐ First Quarter ● Full Moon

Latitude:	+20°		+30°		+35°		+40°		+45°		+50°		+54°		+58°		+62°	
Event:	RISE	SET	RISE	SET	RISE	SET	RISE	SET	RISE	SET	RISE	SET	RISE	SET	RISE	SET	RISE	SET
Jan. 1	11:13	23:16	11:19	23:12	11:22	23:10	11:26	23:07	11:31	23:04	11:36	23:01	11:41	22:57	11:47	22:53	11:55	22:47
2	11:49	—	11:51	—	11:52	—	11:53	—	11:54	—	11:56	—	11:57	—	11:59	—	12:02	—
3	12:25	0:07	12:23	0:07	12:21	0:08	12:20	0:08	12:18	0:08	12:16	0:08	12:14	0:09	12:11	0:09	12:08	0:09
4	13:04	0:59	12:57	1:04	12:53	1:07	12:48	1:10	12:43	1:14	12:37	1:18	12:31	1:23	12:24	1:28	12:15	1:34
5	13:45	1:54	13:34	2:04	13:28	2:09	13:20	2:15	13:12	2:22	13:02	2:31	12:52	2:40	12:40	2:50	12:24	3:03
6	14:32	2:53	14:16	3:06	14:07	3:14	13:57	3:23	13:45	3:34	13:31	3:47	13:17	4:00	13:00	4:16	12:37	4:37
7	15:24	3:54	15:05	4:12	14:54	4:22	14:41	4:34	14:27	4:48	14:09	5:05	13:51	5:22	13:28	5:44	12:58	6:13
8	16:22	4:59	16:01	5:20	15:49	5:32	15:35	5:45	15:18	6:02	14:57	6:22	14:37	6:42	14:10	7:08	13:32	7:45
9	17:26	6:05	17:05	6:26	16:52	6:39	16:38	6:53	16:20	7:10	15:59	7:32	15:38	7:55	15:10	8:21	14:30	9:01
10	18:33	7:08	18:13	7:29	18:02	7:41	17:48	7:55	17:32	8:11	17:13	8:31	16:53	8:51	16:28	9:17	15:53	9:53
11	19:40	8:07	19:24	8:25	19:14	8:35	19:03	8:47	18:50	9:01	18:34	9:18	18:18	9:35	17:58	9:56	17:31	10:24
12	20:45	9:00	20:33	9:14	20:26	9:22	20:18	9:32	20:08	9:42	19:57	9:55	19:46	10:08	19:32	10:23	19:14	10:43
13	21:47	9:48	21:40	9:58	21:35	10:03	21:31	10:09	21:25	10:16	21:18	10:25	21:12	10:33	21:03	10:43	20:53	10:56
14	22:46	10:32	22:43	10:37	22:42	10:39	22:40	10:42	22:38	10:46	22:36	10:50	22:34	10:54	22:32	10:59	22:28	11:05
15	23:42	11:13	23:44	11:13	23:46	11:13	23:47	11:13	23:49	11:13	23:51	11:13	23:53	11:13	23:56	11:13	23:59	11:12
16	—	11:52	—	11:48	—	11:45	—	11:42	—	11:38	—	11:34	—	11:30	—	11:26	—	11:20
17	0:36	12:31	0:43	12:22	0:47	12:17	0:52	12:11	0:57	12:05	1:04	11:56	1:10	11:49	1:18	11:39	1:28	11:27
18	1:30	13:11	1:41	12:58	1:47	12:51	1:55	12:42	2:04	12:32	2:14	12:20	2:25	12:09	2:38	11:55	2:54	11:36
19	2:23	13:53	2:38	13:36	2:47	13:27	2:57	13:16	3:08	13:03	3:23	12:48	3:37	12:33	3:55	12:14	4:19	11:49
20	3:16	14:36	3:34	14:17	3:44	14:06	3:56	13:53	4:11	13:38	4:29	13:20	4:46	13:02	5:09	12:38	5:40	12:07
21	4:08	15:22	4:28	15:02	4:40	14:49	4:54	14:35	5:10	14:19	5:30	13:58	5:50	13:38	6:17	13:11	6:54	12:33
22	4:59	16:11	5:20	15:49	5:33	15:37	5:47	15:22	6:04	15:05	6:26	14:44	6:47	14:22	7:15	13:54	7:56	13:13
23	5:48	17:01	6:09	16:40	6:22	16:28	6:36	16:13	6:53	15:57	7:14	15:36	7:35	15:15	8:03	14:48	8:42	14:09
24	6:34	17:51	6:54	17:32	7:06	17:21	7:19	17:08	7:35	16:53	7:54	16:34	8:14	16:15	8:39	15:51	9:13	15:17
25	7:18	18:42	7:36	18:26	7:46	18:16	7:58	18:05	8:11	17:52	8:28	17:36	8:45	17:20	9:06	17:00	9:34	16:33
26	7:59	19:33	8:13	19:20	8:22	19:12	8:31	19:03	8:43	18:53	8:56	18:40	9:10	18:28	9:26	18:12	9:48	17:52
27	8:37	20:23	8:48	20:13	8:54	20:08	9:02	20:01	9:10	19:54	9:20	19:45	9:30	19:37	9:42	19:26	9:58	19:12
28	9:13	21:12	9:21	21:07	9:25	21:04	9:29	21:00	9:35	20:56	9:42	20:51	9:48	20:46	9:55	20:40	10:05	20:33
29	9:49	22:02	9:52	22:01	9:54	22:00	9:56	21:59	9:58	21:58	10:01	21:57	10:04	21:56	10:07	21:55	10:11	21:53
30	10:24	22:52	10:23	22:56	10:23	22:57	10:22	23:00	10:21	23:02	10:21	23:05	10:20	23:08	10:19	23:11	10:17	23:16
31	11:01	23:45	10:56	23:52	10:53	23:57	10:49	—	10:45	—	10:41	—	10:36	—	10:31	—	10:24	—

MOONRISE AND MOONSET, 2001 FEBRUARY
UNIVERSAL TIME AT GREENWICH MERIDIAN

Latitude:	+20°		+30°		+35°		+40°		+45°		+50°		+54°		+58°		+62°	
Event:	RISE	SET	RISE	SET	RISE	SET	RISE	SET	RISE	SET	RISE	SET	RISE	SET	RISE	SET	RISE	SET
Feb. 1	11:40	—	11:30	—	11:25	—	11:18	0:02	11:11	0:08	11:03	0:15	10:54	0:21	10:44	0:30	10:32	0:40
2	12:22	0:39	12:09	0:51	12:01	0:58	11:52	1:06	11:41	1:15	11:29	1:27	11:17	1:38	11:02	1:51	10:42	2:09
3	13:10	1:37	12:52	1:53	12:42	2:03	12:31	2:13	12:17	2:26	12:01	2:41	11:45	2:56	11:25	3:15	10:58	3:41
4	14:03	2:38	13:43	2:58	13:31	3:09	13:18	3:22	13:02	3:37	12:42	3:56	12:23	4:15	11:58	4:39	11:24	5:12
5	15:03	3:42	14:41	4:03	14:28	4:15	14:14	4:30	13:57	4:47	13:36	5:08	13:14	5:29	12:46	5:56	12:07	6:36
6	16:07	4:45	15:46	5:07	15:34	5:19	15:20	5:33	15:03	5:51	14:42	6:12	14:21	6:33	13:54	7:00	13:15	7:40
7	17:15	5:46	16:56	6:06	16:45	6:17	16:33	6:30	16:18	6:46	16:00	7:05	15:42	7:24	15:19	7:48	14:47	8:21
8	18:22	6:43	18:07	6:59	17:59	7:09	17:49	7:20	17:38	7:32	17:24	7:47	17:10	8:02	16:53	8:21	16:30	8:45
9	19:27	7:35	19:17	7:47	19:12	7:54	19:05	8:01	18:58	8:10	18:48	8:21	18:39	8:32	18:28	8:45	18:14	9:01
10	20:30	8:22	20:25	8:29	20:22	8:33	20:19	8:38	20:15	8:43	20:11	8:49	20:07	8:55	20:02	9:03	19:55	9:12
11	21:29	9:06	21:30	9:08	21:30	9:09	21:30	9:10	21:30	9:12	21:31	9:14	21:31	9:15	21:32	9:18	21:32	9:20
12	22:26	9:47	22:32	9:45	22:35	9:43	22:38	9:41	22:42	9:39	22:47	9:36	22:52	9:34	22:58	9:31	23:05	9:28
13	23:22	10:28	23:32	10:20	23:38	10:16	23:44	10:11	23:52	10:06	—	9:59	—	9:53	—	9:45	—	9:35
14	—	11:09	—	10:57	—	10:50	—	10:43	—	10:34	0:01	10:23	0:10	10:13	0:21	10:00	0:36	9:44
15	0:17	11:50	0:31	11:35	0:39	11:26	0:48	11:16	0:59	11:04	1:12	10:50	1:25	10:36	1:42	10:18	2:03	9:55
16	1:11	12:34	1:28	12:15	1:38	12:05	1:50	11:52	2:03	11:38	2:20	11:20	2:37	11:03	2:58	10:41	3:27	10:11
17	2:03	13:19	2:23	12:59	2:35	12:47	2:48	12:33	3:04	12:17	3:24	11:57	3:43	11:37	4:09	11:11	4:45	10:34
18	2:55	14:07	3:16	13:46	3:29	13:33	3:43	13:19	4:00	13:01	4:21	12:40	4:43	12:18	5:11	11:50	5:51	11:10
19	3:45	14:57	4:06	14:35	4:19	14:23	4:33	14:08	4:51	13:51	5:12	13:30	5:33	13:09	6:02	12:41	6:42	12:00
20	4:32	15:47	4:52	15:27	5:04	15:15	5:18	15:02	5:35	14:46	5:55	14:27	6:15	14:07	6:41	13:41	7:18	13:05
21	5:16	16:38	5:35	16:20	5:46	16:10	5:58	15:58	6:13	15:45	6:30	15:28	6:48	15:11	7:10	14:49	7:41	14:20
22	5:58	17:29	6:14	17:14	6:23	17:06	6:33	16:56	6:45	16:45	7:00	16:31	7:14	16:18	7:32	16:01	7:56	15:39
23	6:37	18:19	6:49	18:08	6:56	18:02	7:04	17:55	7:14	17:47	7:25	17:37	7:36	17:27	7:49	17:15	8:07	16:59
24	7:14	19:09	7:23	19:02	7:27	18:59	7:33	18:54	7:39	18:49	7:47	18:43	7:54	18:37	8:03	18:30	8:15	18:20
25	7:50	19:59	7:54	19:56	7:57	19:55	8:00	19:54	8:03	19:52	8:07	19:49	8:11	19:47	8:15	19:45	8:21	19:41
26	8:25	20:49	8:26	20:51	8:26	20:52	8:26	20:54	8:26	20:55	8:26	20:57	8:26	20:59	8:27	21:01	8:27	21:03
27	9:01	21:41	8:57	21:47	8:55	21:51	8:52	21:55	8:49	22:00	8:46	22:06	8:42	22:11	8:38	22:18	8:33	22:27
28	9:39	22:34	9:31	22:45	9:26	22:51	9:21	22:58	9:14	23:06	9:07	23:16	9:00	23:26	8:51	23:38	8:40	23:53

MOONRISE AND MOONSET, 2001 MARCH
UNIVERSAL TIME AT GREENWICH MERIDIAN

Latitude:	+20°		+30°		+35°		+40°		+45°		+50°		+54°		+58°		+62°	
Event:	RISE	SET	RISE	SET	RISE	SET	RISE	SET	RISE	SET	RISE	SET	RISE	SET	RISE	SET	RISE	SET
Mar. 1	10:19	23:29	10:07	23:44	10:00	23:53	9:52	—	9:42	—	9:31	—	9:20	—	9:06	—	8:49	—
2	11:04	—	10:47	—	10:38	—	10:27	0:03	10:15	0:14	10:00	0:28	9:45	0:42	9:26	1:00	9:02	1:23
3	11:53	0:28	11:34	0:46	11:22	0:57	11:09	1:09	10:54	1:23	10:36	1:41	10:17	1:59	9:54	2:22	9:22	2:53
4	12:48	1:28	12:27	1:49	12:14	2:01	12:00	2:15	11:43	2:31	11:22	2:52	11:01	3:13	10:34	3:39	9:55	4:18
5	13:48	2:29	13:26	2:51	13:14	3:03	12:59	3:18	12:42	3:35	12:20	3:57	11:59	4:19	11:30	4:47	10:50	5:28
6	14:52	3:29	14:32	3:50	14:20	4:02	14:07	4:16	13:51	4:33	13:31	4:53	13:11	5:13	12:45	5:40	12:09	6:17
7	15:58	4:26	15:41	4:45	15:31	4:55	15:20	5:07	15:07	5:22	14:51	5:39	14:34	5:56	14:14	6:18	13:46	6:47
8	17:04	5:19	16:51	5:34	16:44	5:42	16:36	5:52	16:26	6:03	16:14	6:16	16:03	6:29	15:48	6:45	15:30	7:05
9	18:08	6:08	18:00	6:18	17:56	6:24	17:51	6:30	17:45	6:37	17:39	6:46	17:32	6:55	17:24	7:05	17:13	7:18
10	19:10	6:54	19:08	6:59	19:06	7:01	19:05	7:05	19:03	7:08	19:01	7:12	18:59	7:16	18:57	7:21	18:54	7:27
11	20:10	7:37	20:13	7:37	20:14	7:37	20:16	7:36	20:19	7:36	20:21	7:36	20:24	7:35	20:27	7:35	20:32	7:34
12	21:08	8:19	21:16	8:14	21:20	8:11	21:26	8:07	21:32	8:03	21:39	7:59	21:46	7:54	21:55	7:49	22:06	7:42
13	22:05	9:01	22:17	8:51	22:25	8:45	22:33	8:39	22:42	8:31	22:54	8:22	23:06	8:14	23:20	8:03	23:39	7:50
14	23:01	9:44	23:17	9:30	23:27	9:22	23:38	9:12	23:50	9:01	—	8:48	—	8:36	—	8:20	—	8:00
15	23:56	10:28	—	10:10	—	10:00	—	9:48	—	9:35	0:06	9:18	0:22	9:02	0:41	8:41	1:08	8:13
16	—	11:14	0:15	10:54	0:26	10:42	0:39	10:28	0:55	10:13	1:13	9:53	1:32	9:33	1:57	9:08	2:31	8:33
17	0:49	12:02	1:10	11:40	1:22	11:27	1:37	11:13	1:54	10:56	2:15	10:34	2:36	10:13	3:04	9:45	3:44	9:04
18	1:40	12:51	2:02	12:29	2:15	12:16	2:29	12:02	2:47	11:44	3:09	11:23	3:31	11:01	4:00	10:32	4:41	9:50
19	2:28	13:41	2:50	13:21	3:02	13:09	3:16	12:55	3:33	12:38	3:54	12:17	4:15	11:57	4:43	11:29	5:22	10:51
20	3:14	14:32	3:33	14:14	3:45	14:03	3:58	13:50	4:13	13:35	4:32	13:17	4:51	12:59	5:15	12:36	5:48	12:03
21	3:56	15:23	4:13	15:08	4:23	14:58	4:34	14:48	4:47	14:36	5:03	14:21	5:19	14:06	5:39	13:47	6:05	13:22
22	4:36	16:14	4:50	16:02	4:58	15:55	5:07	15:47	5:17	15:37	5:30	15:26	5:42	15:15	5:57	15:01	6:17	14:43
23	5:14	17:04	5:24	16:56	5:29	16:51	5:36	16:46	5:43	16:40	5:52	16:32	6:01	16:25	6:11	16:16	6:25	16:04
24	5:50	17:54	5:56	17:51	5:59	17:48	6:03	17:46	6:07	17:43	6:13	17:39	6:18	17:36	6:24	17:32	6:31	17:26
25	6:26	18:45	6:27	18:46	6:28	18:46	6:29	18:46	6:31	18:47	6:32	18:47	6:33	18:48	6:35	18:48	6:37	18:49
26	7:02	19:37	6:59	19:42	6:58	19:45	6:56	19:48	6:54	19:52	6:51	19:57	6:49	20:01	6:46	20:07	6:43	20:14
27	7:39	20:30	7:32	20:40	7:28	20:45	7:23	20:51	7:18	20:59	7:12	21:08	7:06	21:16	6:58	21:27	6:49	21:41
28	8:19	21:25	8:08	21:39	8:01	21:47	7:53	21:56	7:45	22:07	7:34	22:20	7:24	22:33	7:12	22:49	6:57	23:10
29	9:02	22:23	8:47	22:40	8:38	22:51	8:28	23:02	8:16	23:16	8:01	23:33	7:47	23:50	7:30	—	7:07	—
30	9:49	23:22	9:31	23:42	9:20	23:54	9:07	—	8:53	—	8:35	—	8:17	—	7:54	0:12	7:24	0:41
31	10:42	—	10:21	—	10:08	—	9:54	0:08	9:37	0:24	9:17	0:44	8:56	1:05	8:29	1:31	7:51	2:08

MOONRISE AND MOONSET, 2001 APRIL
UNIVERSAL TIME AT GREENWICH MERIDIAN

Latitude: Event:	+20° RISE	+20° SET	+30° RISE	+30° SET	+35° RISE	+35° SET	+40° RISE	+40° SET	+45° RISE	+45° SET	+50° RISE	+50° SET	+54° RISE	+54° SET	+58° RISE	+58° SET	+62° RISE	+62° SET
Apr. 1	11:39	0:22	11:17	0:44	11:04	0:56	10:49	1:11	10:32	1:29	10:10	1:50	9:48	2:12	9:19	2:41	8:37	3:23
2	12:40	1:21	12:19	1:42	12:06	1:55	11:52	2:10	11:35	2:27	11:14	2:48	10:53	3:10	10:26	3:38	9:46	4:17
3	13:43	2:17	13:25	2:37	13:14	2:48	13:01	3:01	12:47	3:17	12:28	3:36	12:10	3:55	11:47	4:19	11:15	4:52
4	14:47	3:10	14:32	3:26	14:24	3:36	14:14	3:46	14:02	3:59	13:48	4:14	13:35	4:29	13:17	4:48	12:54	5:12
5	15:50	3:59	15:40	4:11	15:34	4:18	15:27	4:26	15:20	4:35	15:10	4:46	15:01	4:56	14:50	5:09	14:36	5:26
6	16:51	4:44	16:46	4:52	16:44	4:56	16:40	5:00	16:37	5:06	16:32	5:12	16:28	5:18	16:23	5:26	16:16	5:35
7	17:51	5:28	17:52	5:30	17:52	5:31	17:52	5:32	17:53	5:34	17:53	5:36	17:53	5:38	17:54	5:40	17:55	5:42
8	18:50	6:10	18:56	6:07	18:59	6:05	19:03	6:03	19:07	6:01	19:12	5:58	19:17	5:56	19:23	5:53	19:31	5:49
9	19:49	6:52	19:59	6:44	20:05	6:39	20:12	6:34	20:20	6:28	20:30	6:21	20:40	6:15	20:51	6:06	21:07	5:56
10	20:46	7:34	21:01	7:22	21:10	7:15	21:20	7:07	21:31	6:57	21:45	6:46	21:59	6:35	22:17	6:22	22:40	6:05
11	21:43	8:18	22:02	8:02	22:12	7:53	22:25	7:42	22:39	7:29	22:57	7:14	23:15	6:59	23:38	6:40	—	6:16
12	22:39	9:05	23:00	8:45	23:12	8:34	23:26	8:21	23:42	8:06	—	7:47	—	7:28	—	7:05	0:09	6:32
13	23:32	9:53	23:54	9:31	—	9:19	—	9:04	—	8:47	0:03	8:26	0:24	8:05	0:51	7:37	1:30	6:58
14	—	10:43	—	10:20	0:07	10:07	0:22	9:52	0:39	9:35	1:01	9:13	1:24	8:50	1:53	8:20	2:36	7:37
15	0:22	11:33	0:44	11:12	0:57	10:59	1:12	10:45	1:29	10:27	1:51	10:06	2:13	9:44	2:42	9:15	3:24	8:34
16	1:09	12:25	1:30	12:05	1:42	11:53	1:56	11:40	2:12	11:24	2:32	11:05	2:52	10:45	3:19	10:19	3:55	9:44
17	1:53	13:16	2:11	12:59	2:22	12:49	2:34	12:37	2:48	12:24	3:06	12:07	3:23	11:51	3:45	11:30	4:14	11:01
18	2:34	14:06	2:49	13:53	2:58	13:45	3:08	13:36	3:19	13:25	3:34	13:12	3:47	12:59	4:05	12:43	4:27	12:22
19	3:12	14:57	3:24	14:47	3:30	14:41	3:38	14:35	3:47	14:27	3:57	14:18	4:07	14:09	4:20	13:58	4:36	13:44
20	3:49	15:47	3:56	15:41	4:01	15:38	4:05	15:34	4:11	15:30	4:18	15:25	4:24	15:20	4:32	15:14	4:42	15:06
21	4:24	16:38	4:28	16:36	4:30	16:36	4:32	16:35	4:34	16:34	4:37	16:33	4:40	16:32	4:44	16:31	4:48	16:29
22	5:00	17:29	4:59	17:33	4:59	17:35	4:58	17:37	4:57	17:40	4:56	17:43	4:55	17:46	4:54	17:49	4:53	17:54
23	5:37	18:23	5:32	18:31	5:29	18:35	5:25	18:41	5:21	18:47	5:16	18:54	5:11	19:01	5:06	19:10	4:58	19:22
24	6:17	19:18	6:07	19:31	6:01	19:38	5:54	19:46	5:47	19:56	5:38	20:08	5:29	20:19	5:19	20:34	5:05	20:52
25	6:59	20:16	6:45	20:33	6:37	20:43	6:27	20:54	6:16	21:07	6:03	21:23	5:51	21:38	5:35	21:59	5:14	22:26
26	7:46	21:16	7:28	21:36	7:17	21:48	7:06	22:01	6:52	22:17	6:35	22:36	6:18	22:56	5:57	23:22	5:28	23:57
27	8:37	22:17	8:17	22:39	8:05	22:52	7:51	23:06	7:34	23:24	7:14	23:46	6:54	—	6:28	—	5:51	—
28	9:34	23:17	9:11	23:39	8:59	23:52	8:44	—	8:26	—	8:04	—	7:42	0:08	7:12	0:37	6:30	1:19
29	10:34	—	10:12	—	9:59	—	9:44	0:07	9:27	0:24	9:05	0:46	8:43	1:09	8:14	1:38	7:32	2:20
30	11:36	0:14	11:16	0:34	11:04	0:46	10:51	1:00	10:35	1:17	10:16	1:37	9:56	1:57	9:31	2:23	8:56	2:59

MOONRISE AND MOONSET, 2001 MAY
UNIVERSAL TIME AT GREENWICH MERIDIAN

Latitude:	+20°		+30°		+35°		+40°		+45°		+50°		+54°		+58°		+62°	
Event:	RISE	SET	RISE	SET	RISE	SET	RISE	SET	RISE	SET	RISE	SET	RISE	SET	RISE	SET	RISE	SET
May 1	12:38	1:07	12:22	1:24	12:12	1:35	12:02	1:46	11:49	2:00	11:33	2:17	11:18	2:34	10:58	2:54	10:32	3:22
2	13:40	1:55	13:28	2:09	13:21	2:17	13:13	2:26	13:04	2:37	12:53	2:49	12:42	3:02	12:28	3:17	12:11	3:36
3	14:40	2:41	14:33	2:50	14:29	2:55	14:24	3:01	14:19	3:08	14:13	3:16	14:06	3:24	13:59	3:34	13:49	3:46
4	15:39	3:23	15:37	3:27	15:36	3:30	15:35	3:33	15:33	3:36	15:32	3:40	15:30	3:43	15:28	3:48	15:26	3:53
5	16:37	4:04	16:40	4:04	16:42	4:03	16:44	4:03	16:47	4:02	16:50	4:01	16:53	4:01	16:56	4:00	17:01	3:59
6	17:34	4:45	17:43	4:39	17:47	4:36	17:53	4:32	17:59	4:28	18:07	4:23	18:14	4:18	18:24	4:13	18:36	4:05
7	18:32	5:26	18:45	5:16	18:52	5:10	19:01	5:03	19:11	4:56	19:23	4:46	19:35	4:37	19:50	4:26	20:10	4:12
8	19:29	6:10	19:46	5:55	19:56	5:47	20:07	5:37	20:21	5:26	20:37	5:12	20:53	4:59	21:14	4:43	21:42	4:21
9	20:26	6:55	20:46	6:37	20:58	6:26	21:11	6:14	21:27	6:00	21:47	5:42	22:07	5:25	22:33	5:04	23:09	4:34
10	21:21	7:43	21:43	7:22	21:56	7:10	22:11	6:56	22:28	6:39	22:50	6:19	23:12	5:58	23:42	5:32	—	4:55
11	22:14	8:32	22:36	8:10	22:49	7:57	23:04	7:42	23:22	7:24	23:45	7:02	—	6:40	—	6:10	0:24	5:27
12	23:03	9:24	23:24	9:01	23:37	8:48	23:52	8:33	—	8:16	—	7:53	0:08	7:31	0:38	7:01	1:22	6:17
13	23:48	10:15	—	9:55	—	9:42	—	9:28	0:09	9:11	0:30	8:51	0:51	8:29	1:20	8:02	1:59	7:23
14	—	11:07	0:08	10:49	0:19	10:38	0:32	10:25	0:48	10:11	1:07	9:52	1:26	9:34	1:50	9:11	2:23	8:39
15	0:30	11:58	0:47	11:43	0:57	11:34	1:08	11:23	1:21	11:11	1:37	10:57	1:52	10:42	2:12	10:24	2:37	9:59
16	1:09	12:48	1:23	12:37	1:30	12:30	1:39	12:22	1:49	12:13	2:01	12:02	2:13	11:51	2:28	11:38	2:47	11:21
17	1:46	13:38	1:56	13:31	2:01	13:26	2:07	13:21	2:14	13:15	2:23	13:08	2:31	13:02	2:41	12:53	2:54	12:43
18	2:22	14:28	2:27	14:25	2:30	14:23	2:34	14:21	2:38	14:19	2:42	14:16	2:47	14:13	2:52	14:09	2:59	14:05
19	2:57	15:19	2:58	15:20	2:59	15:21	2:59	15:22	3:00	15:23	3:01	15:24	3:02	15:25	3:03	15:27	3:04	15:29
20	3:34	16:12	3:30	16:18	3:28	16:21	3:26	16:25	3:23	16:30	3:20	16:35	3:17	16:40	3:13	16:47	3:09	16:55
21	4:12	17:07	4:04	17:17	3:59	17:23	3:54	17:30	3:48	17:38	3:41	17:48	3:34	17:58	3:25	18:10	3:15	18:25
22	4:53	18:04	4:41	18:19	4:33	18:28	4:25	18:38	4:16	18:50	4:04	19:04	3:53	19:18	3:40	19:36	3:22	20:00
23	5:39	19:05	5:22	19:24	5:12	19:35	5:01	19:47	4:49	20:02	4:33	20:21	4:18	20:39	3:59	21:03	3:34	21:35
24	6:29	20:07	6:09	20:29	5:58	20:41	5:44	20:56	5:29	21:13	5:10	21:34	4:50	21:56	4:26	22:24	3:52	23:05
25	7:25	21:09	7:03	21:32	6:50	21:45	6:36	22:00	6:18	22:18	5:56	22:40	5:34	23:03	5:06	23:33	4:25	—
26	8:26	22:09	8:03	22:30	7:50	22:43	7:35	22:57	7:17	23:14	6:55	23:36	6:32	23:57	6:03	—	5:19	0:16
27	9:29	23:04	9:08	23:23	8:56	23:34	8:42	23:47	8:25	—	8:05	—	7:44	—	7:17	0:25	6:38	1:04
28	10:32	23:54	10:14	—	10:04	—	9:52	—	9:38	0:01	9:21	0:20	9:04	0:38	8:43	1:00	8:13	1:31
29	11:34	—	11:21	0:10	11:13	0:18	11:04	0:28	10:54	0:40	10:41	0:54	10:28	1:08	10:13	1:25	9:52	1:47
30	12:34	0:40	12:26	0:51	12:21	0:57	12:15	1:04	12:08	1:13	12:00	1:22	11:53	1:32	11:43	1:43	11:31	1:58
31	13:33	1:23	13:29	1:29	13:27	1:33	13:24	1:36	13:22	1:41	13:18	1:46	13:15	1:51	13:11	1:57	13:06	2:05

MOONRISE AND MOONSET, 2001 JUNE
UNIVERSAL TIME AT GREENWICH MERIDIAN

Latitude:	+20°		+30°		+35°		+40°		+45°		+50°		+54°		+58°		+62°	
Event:	RISE	SET	RISE	SET	RISE	SET	RISE	SET	RISE	SET	RISE	SET	RISE	SET	RISE	SET	RISE	SET
Jun. 1	14:29	2:04	14:31	2:05	14:32	2:05	14:33	2:06	14:34	2:07	14:35	2:08	14:37	2:09	14:38	2:10	14:40	2:11
2	15:26	2:43	15:32	2:40	15:36	2:37	15:40	2:35	15:45	2:32	15:51	2:29	15:57	2:25	16:04	2:21	16:13	2:16
3	16:22	3:23	16:33	3:15	16:40	3:10	16:47	3:04	16:56	2:58	17:06	2:50	17:16	2:43	17:29	2:34	17:45	2:22
4	17:19	4:05	17:34	3:52	17:43	3:44	17:53	3:36	18:05	3:26	18:20	3:14	18:35	3:03	18:53	2:48	19:17	2:30
5	18:15	4:48	18:34	4:32	18:45	4:22	18:58	4:11	19:13	3:58	19:31	3:42	19:50	3:26	20:14	3:07	20:47	2:41
6	19:11	5:35	19:32	5:15	19:44	5:03	19:59	4:50	20:16	4:34	20:37	4:15	20:59	3:56	21:27	3:31	22:08	2:57
7	20:05	6:24	20:27	6:02	20:40	5:49	20:55	5:34	21:13	5:17	21:36	4:55	21:59	4:33	22:29	4:04	23:14	3:23
8	20:56	7:14	21:18	6:52	21:31	6:39	21:46	6:24	22:03	6:05	22:25	5:43	22:48	5:20	23:17	4:50	—	4:05
9	21:43	8:06	22:03	7:45	22:16	7:32	22:29	7:17	22:46	7:00	23:06	6:38	23:26	6:16	23:52	5:47	0:00	5:05
10	22:26	8:58	22:45	8:39	22:55	8:27	23:07	8:14	23:21	7:58	23:38	7:39	23:55	7:19	—	6:54	0:28	6:18
11	23:07	9:50	23:22	9:33	23:30	9:23	23:40	9:12	23:51	8:59	—	8:42	—	8:26	0:17	8:05	0:46	7:38
12	23:44	10:40	23:55	10:27	—	10:19	—	10:10	—	10:00	0:05	9:47	0:18	9:35	0:35	9:20	0:57	8:59
13	—	11:30	—	11:21	0:02	11:15	0:09	11:09	0:17	11:02	0:27	10:53	0:37	10:45	0:49	10:34	1:05	10:21
14	0:20	12:19	0:27	12:14	0:31	12:11	0:36	12:08	0:41	12:04	0:47	11:59	0:53	11:54	1:01	11:49	1:10	11:42
15	0:55	13:09	0:58	13:08	0:59	13:08	1:01	13:07	1:03	13:07	1:06	13:06	1:08	13:05	1:11	13:05	1:15	13:03
16	1:30	14:00	1:28	14:04	1:27	14:06	1:26	14:08	1:25	14:11	1:24	14:15	1:23	14:18	1:21	14:22	1:20	14:27
17	2:06	14:53	2:00	15:01	1:57	15:06	1:53	15:12	1:49	15:18	1:43	15:26	1:38	15:33	1:32	15:43	1:25	15:55
18	2:46	15:49	2:35	16:02	2:29	16:09	2:22	16:18	2:14	16:28	2:05	16:40	1:56	16:52	1:45	17:07	1:31	17:26
19	3:29	16:48	3:14	17:05	3:05	17:15	2:56	17:27	2:45	17:40	2:31	17:57	2:18	18:13	2:01	18:34	1:40	19:02
20	4:17	17:50	3:59	18:11	3:48	18:23	3:36	18:36	3:21	18:53	3:04	19:13	2:46	19:33	2:24	20:00	1:55	20:37
21	5:11	18:54	4:50	19:16	4:38	19:29	4:23	19:44	4:07	20:02	3:46	20:24	3:25	20:47	2:58	21:17	2:20	22:00
22	6:11	19:57	5:49	20:19	5:36	20:32	5:21	20:47	5:03	21:04	4:40	21:26	4:17	21:49	3:48	22:18	3:04	23:00
23	7:15	20:56	6:54	21:16	6:41	21:28	6:26	21:41	6:09	21:57	5:47	22:16	5:25	22:36	4:57	23:01	4:15	23:35
24	8:21	21:50	8:02	22:06	7:51	22:16	7:38	22:27	7:23	22:40	7:04	22:56	6:46	23:11	6:22	23:30	5:48	23:55
25	9:26	22:38	9:11	22:51	9:02	22:58	8:52	23:06	8:40	23:15	8:26	23:27	8:12	23:37	7:54	23:51	7:30	—
26	10:28	23:23	10:18	23:31	10:12	23:35	10:05	23:40	9:57	23:45	9:47	23:52	9:38	23:58	9:26	—	9:12	0:08
27	11:28	—	11:22	—	11:19	—	11:16	—	11:12	—	11:07	—	11:03	—	10:57	0:06	10:50	0:16
28	12:25	0:04	12:25	0:07	12:25	0:09	12:25	0:10	12:25	0:12	12:25	0:14	12:25	0:16	12:25	0:19	12:25	0:22
29	13:21	0:44	13:26	0:42	13:29	0:41	13:32	0:39	13:36	0:37	13:41	0:35	13:45	0:33	13:50	0:31	13:57	0:28
30	14:17	1:24	14:27	1:17	14:32	1:13	14:39	1:08	14:46	1:03	14:55	0:56	15:04	0:50	15:15	0:43	15:29	0:34

MOONRISE AND MOONSET, 2001 JULY
UNIVERSAL TIME AT GREENWICH MERIDIAN

Moon phase symbols across the top of the table: ○ ◐ ● ◑

Jul. / Event	+20° RISE	+20° SET	+30° RISE	+30° SET	+35° RISE	+35° SET	+40° RISE	+40° SET	+45° RISE	+45° SET	+50° RISE	+50° SET	+54° RISE	+54° SET	+58° RISE	+58° SET	+62° RISE	+62° SET
1	15:13	2:04	15:27	1:53	15:35	1:46	15:44	1:38	15:55	1:30	16:08	1:19	16:21	1:09	16:38	0:56	17:00	0:40
2	16:08	2:46	16:26	2:31	16:36	2:22	16:48	2:11	17:02	1:59	17:19	1:45	17:37	1:30	17:59	1:13	18:29	0:50
3	17:03	3:31	17:24	3:12	17:36	3:01	17:50	2:48	18:06	2:33	18:27	2:15	18:47	1:57	19:14	1:34	19:52	1:03
4	17:57	4:18	18:20	3:57	18:33	3:44	18:48	3:30	19:05	3:13	19:28	2:52	19:50	2:31	20:20	2:04	21:04	1:25
5	18:49	5:08	19:12	4:45	19:25	4:32	19:40	4:17	19:58	3:59	20:20	3:37	20:43	3:14	21:13	2:44	21:57	2:00
6	19:38	5:59	19:59	5:37	20:12	5:24	20:26	5:09	20:43	4:51	21:04	4:29	21:25	4:06	21:53	3:36	22:32	2:53
7	20:23	6:51	20:42	6:31	20:53	6:19	21:06	6:05	21:21	5:48	21:39	5:28	21:58	5:07	22:21	4:40	22:53	4:02
8	21:04	7:43	21:20	7:25	21:30	7:15	21:40	7:02	21:53	6:48	22:08	6:31	22:23	6:13	22:41	5:50	23:06	5:20
9	21:43	8:34	21:55	8:19	22:03	8:11	22:11	8:01	22:20	7:49	22:33	7:35	22:43	7:21	22:57	7:04	23:14	6:41
10	22:19	9:24	22:27	9:13	22:32	9:07	22:38	8:59	22:45	8:51	22:52	8:41	23:00	8:31	23:09	8:18	23:21	8:02
11	22:53	10:13	22:58	10:06	23:01	10:02	23:04	9:58	23:07	9:52	23:11	9:46	23:15	9:40	23:20	9:33	23:25	9:23
12	23:28	11:02	23:28	10:59	23:28	10:58	23:28	10:56	23:29	10:54	23:29	10:52	23:29	10:50	23:29	10:47	23:30	10:43
13	—	11:51	23:59	11:53	23:56	11:54	23:54	11:55	23:51	11:57	23:47	11:58	23:44	12:00	23:40	12:02	23:34	12:05
14	0:03	12:42	—	12:48	—	12:52	—	12:56	—	13:01	—	13:07	—	13:13	23:51	13:20	23:40	13:29
15	0:40	13:35	0:31	13:46	0:26	13:52	0:21	13:59	0:15	14:08	0:07	14:18	0:00	14:28	—	14:40	23:47	14:56
16	1:20	14:31	1:07	14:47	1:00	14:55	0:51	15:06	0:42	15:17	0:30	15:32	0:19	15:46	0:05	16:04	23:59	16:28
17	2:05	15:31	1:48	15:50	1:38	16:01	1:27	16:14	1:14	16:29	0:59	16:47	0:43	17:06	0:24	17:30	—	18:03
18	2:55	16:34	2:35	16:55	2:24	17:08	2:10	17:23	1:54	17:40	1:35	18:01	1:16	18:23	0:51	18:52	0:17	19:33
19	3:52	17:37	3:30	18:00	3:17	18:13	3:03	18:28	2:45	18:46	2:23	19:09	2:01	19:31	1:32	20:01	0:51	20:45
20	4:55	18:39	4:33	19:01	4:20	19:13	4:05	19:28	3:47	19:45	3:25	20:05	3:02	20:27	2:32	20:54	1:48	21:32
21	6:02	19:37	5:41	19:56	5:29	20:06	5:15	20:19	4:59	20:33	4:39	20:51	4:18	21:08	3:52	21:30	3:14	21:59
22	7:09	20:30	6:52	20:44	6:42	20:52	6:31	21:02	6:17	21:13	6:01	21:26	5:45	21:39	5:24	21:54	4:56	22:15
23	8:15	21:18	8:02	21:27	7:55	21:33	7:47	21:39	7:37	21:46	7:26	21:54	7:15	22:02	7:00	22:12	6:42	22:25
24	9:17	22:02	9:10	22:06	9:06	22:09	9:02	22:11	8:56	22:15	8:50	22:18	8:43	22:22	8:35	22:26	8:25	22:32
25	10:18	22:43	10:16	22:43	10:15	22:42	10:14	22:42	10:12	22:41	10:10	22:40	10:09	22:40	10:07	22:39	10:04	22:38
26	11:16	23:24	11:19	23:18	11:21	23:15	11:23	23:11	11:26	23:07	11:29	23:02	11:32	22:57	11:35	22:51	11:40	22:44
27	12:12	—	12:21	23:54	12:25	23:48	12:31	23:41	12:37	23:33	12:45	23:24	12:52	23:15	13:02	23:04	13:13	22:50
28	13:08	0:04	13:21	—	13:28	—	13:37	—	13:47	—	13:59	23:49	14:11	23:36	14:26	23:19	14:45	22:58
29	14:04	0:46	14:21	0:31	14:30	0:23	14:42	0:13	14:55	0:02	15:11	—	15:27	—	15:47	23:39	16:15	23:10
30	14:59	1:29	15:19	1:11	15:30	1:01	15:44	0:49	16:00	0:35	16:19	0:18	16:39	0:01	17:04	—	17:40	23:29
31	15:53	2:15	16:15	1:55	16:28	1:43	16:42	1:29	17:00	1:12	17:22	0:52	17:44	0:32	18:13	0:06	18:56	23:59

MOONRISE AND MOONSET, 2001 AUGUST
UNIVERSAL TIME AT GREENWICH MERIDIAN

○　　◐　　●　　◑

Latitude:	+20°		+30°		+35°		+40°		+45°		+50°		+54°		+58°		+62°	
Event:	RISE	SET	RISE	SET	RISE	SET	RISE	SET	RISE	SET	RISE	SET	RISE	SET	RISE	SET	RISE	SET
Aug. 1	16:45	3:04	17:08	2:42	17:21	2:29	17:36	2:14	17:54	1:56	18:17	1:34	18:40	1:11	19:10	0:42	19:55	—
2	17:34	3:55	17:56	3:32	18:09	3:19	18:24	3:04	18:41	2:46	19:03	2:23	19:25	2:00	19:53	1:30	20:34	0:46
3	18:20	4:46	18:40	4:25	18:52	4:12	19:05	3:58	19:21	3:41	19:40	3:20	20:00	2:58	20:25	2:30	20:59	1:50
4	19:03	5:38	19:20	5:19	19:30	5:08	19:41	4:55	19:55	4:40	20:11	4:21	20:27	4:03	20:47	3:39	21:14	3:05
5	19:42	6:29	19:56	6:13	20:04	6:04	20:13	5:54	20:23	5:41	20:36	5:26	20:49	5:11	21:04	4:52	21:24	4:26
6	20:19	7:19	20:29	7:07	20:35	7:00	20:41	6:52	20:49	6:43	20:58	6:31	21:06	6:20	21:17	6:06	21:30	5:48
7	20:54	8:09	21:00	8:00	21:03	7:56	21:07	7:50	21:11	7:44	21:17	7:37	21:22	7:29	21:28	7:20	21:35	7:09
8	21:28	8:57	21:30	8:53	21:31	8:51	21:32	8:48	21:33	8:45	21:34	8:42	21:36	8:38	21:38	8:34	21:40	8:29
9	22:02	9:46	21:59	9:46	21:58	9:46	21:56	9:47	21:54	9:47	21:52	9:48	21:50	9:48	21:47	9:48	21:44	9:49
10	22:37	10:35	22:31	10:40	22:27	10:43	22:22	10:46	22:17	10:50	22:11	10:54	22:05	10:59	21:58	11:04	21:49	11:11
11	23:15	11:26	23:04	11:36	22:58	11:41	22:50	11:47	22:42	11:54	22:32	12:03	22:22	12:11	22:10	12:22	21:55	12:35
12	23:57	12:20	23:41	12:33	23:33	12:41	23:23	12:50	23:11	13:01	22:57	13:14	22:43	13:26	22:26	13:42	22:04	14:03
13	—	13:17	—	13:34	—	13:44	—	13:56	23:46	14:10	23:28	14:27	23:11	14:43	22:48	15:05	22:18	15:34
14	0:43	14:16	0:24	14:37	0:13	14:49	0:01	15:03	—	15:19	—	15:39	23:48	16:00	23:21	16:27	22:42	17:05
15	1:36	15:18	1:14	15:40	1:02	15:53	0:47	16:08	0:30	16:26	0:09	16:49	—	17:11	—	17:41	23:26	18:25
16	2:35	16:20	2:12	16:42	1:59	16:55	1:44	17:10	1:25	17:28	1:03	17:50	0:40	18:12	0:10	18:42	—	19:24
17	3:39	17:19	3:17	17:40	3:04	17:51	2:49	18:05	2:32	18:21	2:10	18:40	1:48	19:00	1:19	19:25	0:38	19:59
18	4:46	18:15	4:27	18:32	4:16	18:41	4:03	18:52	3:48	19:05	3:29	19:20	3:11	19:35	2:47	19:54	2:13	20:19
19	5:53	19:06	5:38	19:18	5:30	19:25	5:20	19:33	5:09	19:41	4:54	19:52	4:41	20:03	4:23	20:15	4:00	20:31
20	6:59	19:53	6:49	20:00	6:44	20:03	6:37	20:08	6:30	20:13	6:21	20:19	6:12	20:24	6:02	20:31	5:48	20:40
21	8:02	20:37	7:58	20:38	7:56	20:39	7:53	20:40	7:50	20:41	7:46	20:42	7:43	20:43	7:38	20:45	7:32	20:46
22	9:04	21:19	9:05	21:15	9:06	21:13	9:06	21:10	9:07	21:08	9:09	21:04	9:10	21:01	9:11	20:57	9:13	20:52
23	10:03	22:01	10:09	21:52	10:13	21:47	10:17	21:41	10:22	21:35	10:28	21:27	10:34	21:19	10:42	21:10	10:51	20:58
24	11:01	22:43	11:12	22:30	11:19	22:22	11:26	22:13	11:35	22:03	11:46	21:51	11:56	21:39	12:09	21:25	12:26	21:06
25	11:58	23:27	12:13	23:10	12:23	23:00	12:33	22:48	12:45	22:35	13:00	22:19	13:15	22:03	13:34	21:43	13:59	21:16
26	12:54	—	13:13	23:52	13:24	23:41	13:37	23:27	13:52	23:11	14:11	22:52	14:30	22:32	14:54	22:07	15:28	21:32
27	13:49	0:13	14:10	—	14:23	—	14:38	—	14:55	23:53	15:16	23:31	15:38	23:09	16:07	22:40	16:48	21:58
28	14:42	1:01	15:04	0:39	15:18	0:26	15:33	0:11	15:51	—	16:14	—	16:37	23:56	17:08	23:25	17:53	22:39
29	15:32	1:51	15:54	1:28	16:07	1:15	16:22	1:00	16:40	0:41	17:02	0:19	17:25	—	17:55	—	18:38	23:39
30	16:19	2:42	16:40	2:20	16:52	2:07	17:06	1:53	17:22	1:35	17:42	1:13	18:03	0:51	18:29	0:22	19:06	—
31	17:02	3:34	17:20	3:14	17:31	3:02	17:43	2:49	17:57	2:33	18:15	2:13	18:32	1:54	18:53	1:28	19:23	0:52

MOONRISE AND MOONSET, 2001 SEPTEMBER
UNIVERSAL TIME AT GREENWICH MERIDIAN

Event	+62° RISE	+62° SET	+58° RISE	+58° SET	+54° RISE	+54° SET	+50° RISE	+50° SET	+45° RISE	+45° SET	+40° RISE	+40° SET	+35° RISE	+35° SET	+30° RISE	+30° SET	+20° RISE	+20° SET
Sep. 1	19:33	2:12	19:11	2:40	18:55	3:01	18:41	3:17	18:27	3:34	18:16	3:47	18:06	3:58	17:57	4:08	17:42	4:25
2	19:40	3:34	19:25	3:54	19:13	4:10	19:03	4:22	18:53	4:35	18:45	4:46	18:37	4:55	18:31	5:02	18:20	5:16
3	19:46	4:55	19:36	5:09	19:29	5:20	19:23	5:28	19:16	5:37	19:11	5:44	19:06	5:50	19:02	5:56	18:55	6:05
4	19:50	6:16	19:46	6:23	19:43	6:29	19:41	6:34	19:38	6:39	19:36	6:43	19:34	6:46	19:32	6:49	19:29	6:54
5	19:54	7:37	19:56	7:38	19:57	7:39	19:58	7:40	19:59	7:40	20:00	7:41	20:01	7:42	20:02	7:42	20:03	7:43
6	19:58	8:58	20:05	8:53	20:11	8:49	20:16	8:46	20:21	8:43	20:25	8:40	20:29	8:38	20:32	8:36	20:38	8:32
7	20:03	10:21	20:17	10:10	20:27	10:01	20:36	9:54	20:45	9:46	20:52	9:40	20:59	9:35	21:04	9:30	21:14	9:22
8	20:11	11:47	20:31	11:29	20:46	11:15	20:59	11:03	21:12	10:52	21:22	10:42	21:32	10:34	21:40	10:27	21:54	10:14
9	20:22	13:16	20:49	12:50	21:10	12:30	21:27	12:14	21:44	11:58	21:57	11:46	22:09	11:35	22:19	11:25	22:37	11:09
10	20:40	14:46	21:16	14:10	21:42	13:45	22:03	13:25	22:23	13:06	22:39	12:50	22:53	12:37	23:05	12:26	23:26	12:06
11	21:13	16:09	21:57	15:26	22:26	14:57	22:49	14:34	23:11	14:12	23:30	13:55	23:45	13:40	23:58	13:27	—	13:05
12	22:10	17:16	22:55	16:31	23:25	16:00	23:49	15:37	—	15:14	—	14:56	—	14:41	—	14:27	0:20	14:05
13	23:34	17:59	—	17:19	—	16:52	—	16:30	0:11	16:09	0:29	15:52	0:44	15:38	0:58	15:25	1:20	15:00
14	—	18:23	0:13	17:54	0:40	17:31	1:00	17:14	1:21	16:56	1:37	16:41	1:51	16:29	2:04	16:18	2:24	16:00
15	1:16	18:38	1:44	18:17	2:05	18:01	2:22	17:48	2:38	17:35	2:52	17:24	3:03	17:15	3:13	17:06	3:30	16:52
16	3:03	18:47	3:21	18:35	3:36	18:25	3:47	18:17	3:59	18:08	4:09	18:01	4:17	17:55	4:24	17:50	4:36	17:40
17	4:50	18:54	5:00	18:49	5:07	18:45	5:14	18:41	5:20	18:38	5:26	18:35	5:30	18:32	5:34	18:30	5:41	18:26
18	6:34	19:00	6:36	19:02	6:38	19:03	6:39	19:04	6:40	19:05	6:41	19:06	6:42	19:07	6:43	19:08	6:44	19:09
19	8:16	19:06	8:11	19:14	8:06	19:21	8:02	19:27	7:58	19:33	7:55	19:38	7:52	19:42	7:50	19:46	7:46	19:52
20	9:56	19:12	9:43	19:28	9:32	19:40	9:24	19:51	9:15	20:01	9:07	20:10	9:01	20:17	8:56	20:24	8:46	20:35
21	11:35	19:21	11:12	19:45	10:56	20:03	10:42	20:17	10:29	20:32	10:18	20:44	10:08	20:55	10:00	21:04	9:46	21:20
22	13:09	19:34	12:38	20:07	12:15	20:30	11:57	20:49	11:40	21:08	11:25	21:23	11:13	21:36	11:03	21:47	10:44	22:06
23	14:36	19:56	13:56	20:37	13:28	21:05	13:07	21:27	12:46	21:48	12:29	22:06	12:15	22:20	12:03	22:33	11:42	22:55
24	15:49	20:32	15:03	21:18	14:32	21:49	14:09	22:12	13:46	22:35	13:28	22:54	13:12	23:09	12:59	23:22	12:36	23:45
25	16:41	21:26	15:55	22:11	15:24	22:42	15:01	23:05	14:38	23:28	14:20	23:46	14:04	—	13:51	—	13:28	—
26	17:13	22:36	16:33	23:16	16:05	23:43	15:44	—	15:22	—	15:05	—	14:51	0:01	14:38	0:14	14:16	0:37
27	17:32	23:56	17:00	—	16:37	—	16:18	0:04	16:00	0:25	15:44	0:42	15:32	0:56	15:20	1:08	15:01	1:29
28	17:44	—	17:20	0:27	17:01	0:50	16:46	1:07	16:31	1:25	16:18	1:39	16:08	1:52	15:58	2:02	15:42	2:20
29	17:52	1:18	17:34	1:41	17:20	1:59	17:09	2:12	16:58	2:27	16:48	2:38	16:40	2:48	16:33	2:57	16:20	3:11
30	17:57	2:40	17:46	2:56	17:36	3:08	17:29	3:18	17:21	3:28	17:15	3:37	17:09	3:44	17:04	3:50	16:56	4:01

MOONRISE AND MOONSET, 2001 OCTOBER
UNIVERSAL TIME AT GREENWICH MERIDIAN

Event	+20° RISE	+20° SET	+30° RISE	+30° SET	+35° RISE	+35° SET	+40° RISE	+40° SET	+45° RISE	+45° SET	+50° RISE	+50° SET	+54° RISE	+54° SET	+58° RISE	+58° SET	+62° RISE	+62° SET
Oct. 1	17:30	4:50	17:35	4:44	17:37	4:40	17:40	4:36	17:43	4:30	17:47	4:24	17:51	4:18	17:55	4:11	18:01	4:02
2	18:05	5:39	18:05	5:37	18:05	5:36	18:05	5:34	18:05	5:33	18:05	5:31	18:05	5:29	18:05	5:26	18:05	5:23
3	18:39	6:29	18:35	6:31	18:32	6:32	18:29	6:34	18:26	6:35	18:22	6:37	18:18	6:39	18:14	6:42	18:08	6:45
4	19:15	7:19	19:06	7:26	19:01	7:30	18:56	7:34	18:49	7:39	18:41	7:45	18:33	7:52	18:24	7:59	18:13	8:08
5	19:54	8:11	19:40	8:22	19:33	8:28	19:24	8:36	19:15	8:45	19:03	8:55	18:51	9:05	18:37	9:18	18:19	9:35
6	20:36	9:05	20:19	9:20	20:09	9:29	19:58	9:39	19:45	9:51	19:29	10:06	19:13	10:21	18:53	10:39	18:28	11:03
7	21:22	10:01	21:02	10:20	20:50	10:31	20:37	10:44	20:21	10:59	20:01	11:18	19:42	11:36	19:17	12:00	18:43	12:34
8	22:14	10:59	21:51	11:20	21:38	11:33	21:23	11:48	21:05	12:05	20:43	12:27	20:21	12:49	19:51	13:18	19:09	14:00
9	23:10	11:57	22:47	12:20	22:34	12:34	22:18	12:49	22:00	13:08	21:37	13:31	21:13	13:54	20:42	14:26	19:55	15:12
10	—	12:55	23:49	13:17	23:36	13:30	23:22	13:46	23:04	14:04	22:42	14:26	22:20	14:49	21:51	15:18	21:08	16:01
11	0:11	13:50	—	14:10	—	14:22	—	14:36	—	14:52	23:58	15:11	23:39	15:31	23:15	15:56	22:41	16:30
12	1:14	14:42	0:55	14:58	0:44	15:08	0:31	15:19	0:16	15:32	—	15:47	—	16:03	—	16:22	—	16:46
13	2:18	15:30	2:03	15:42	1:55	15:49	1:45	15:57	1:33	16:06	1:19	16:17	1:05	16:27	0:47	16:40	0:24	16:57
14	3:22	16:15	3:12	16:22	3:06	16:26	3:00	16:31	2:52	16:36	2:43	16:42	2:34	16:48	2:23	16:55	2:09	17:03
15	4:24	16:59	4:20	17:00	4:17	17:01	4:15	17:02	4:11	17:03	4:07	17:04	4:04	17:06	3:59	17:07	3:53	17:09
16	5:26	17:42	5:27	17:38	5:28	17:35	5:29	17:33	5:30	17:30	5:31	17:26	5:32	17:23	5:34	17:19	5:36	17:14
17	6:27	18:25	6:34	18:16	6:38	18:10	6:42	18:04	6:48	17:57	6:54	17:49	7:00	17:41	7:08	17:31	7:17	17:19
18	7:28	19:09	7:40	18:55	7:47	18:47	7:55	18:38	8:04	18:27	8:16	18:14	8:27	18:02	8:41	17:46	8:59	17:26
19	8:29	19:56	8:45	19:38	8:55	19:27	9:06	19:15	9:19	19:01	9:35	18:44	9:51	18:27	10:11	18:05	10:39	17:37
20	9:28	20:45	9:48	20:24	10:00	20:11	10:14	19:57	10:30	19:40	10:50	19:19	11:10	18:59	11:36	18:32	12:13	17:54
21	10:26	21:36	10:48	21:13	11:01	20:59	11:17	20:44	11:35	20:26	11:57	20:03	12:21	19:39	12:51	19:08	13:37	18:22
22	11:20	22:28	11:44	22:05	11:57	21:52	12:13	21:36	12:32	21:17	12:55	20:54	13:19	20:30	13:51	19:58	14:40	19:10
23	12:11	23:21	12:34	22:59	12:47	22:46	13:02	22:32	13:20	22:14	13:43	21:52	14:05	21:29	14:35	21:00	15:19	20:16
24	12:58	—	13:18	23:54	13:30	23:43	13:44	23:29	14:00	23:14	14:20	22:55	14:40	22:35	15:06	22:10	15:42	21:35
25	13:40	0:14	13:58	—	14:08	—	14:20	—	14:34	—	14:50	—	15:07	23:44	15:28	23:24	15:55	22:58
26	14:19	1:05	14:33	0:49	14:42	0:39	14:51	0:28	15:02	0:15	15:15	0:00	15:27	—	15:43	—	16:04	—
27	14:56	1:55	15:06	1:43	15:12	1:35	15:18	1:27	15:26	1:17	15:35	1:06	15:44	0:54	15:55	0:40	16:09	0:21
28	15:30	2:45	15:36	2:36	15:40	2:31	15:44	2:26	15:48	2:19	15:54	2:12	15:59	2:04	16:05	1:55	16:13	1:43
29	16:05	3:34	16:06	3:30	16:07	3:27	16:08	3:25	16:09	3:22	16:11	3:18	16:12	3:15	16:14	3:10	16:16	3:05
30	16:39	4:23	16:36	4:23	16:34	4:24	16:33	4:24	16:31	4:24	16:28	4:25	16:26	4:25	16:23	4:26	16:19	4:27
31	17:14	5:13	17:07	5:18	17:03	5:21	16:58	5:25	16:53	5:29	16:46	5:33	16:40	5:38	16:33	5:43	16:23	5:51

MOONRISE AND MOONSET, 2001 NOVEMBER
UNIVERSAL TIME AT GREENWICH MERIDIAN

Latitude: Event:	+20° RISE	SET	+30° RISE	SET	+35° RISE	SET	+40° RISE	SET	+45° RISE	SET	+50° RISE	SET	+54° RISE	SET	+58° RISE	SET	+62° RISE	SET
Nov. 1	17:52	6:05	17:41	6:15	17:34	6:20	17:26	6:27	17:17	6:34	17:07	6:43	16:57	6:52	16:44	7:03	16:28	7:17
2	18:34	6:59	18:18	7:13	18:09	7:21	17:58	7:31	17:46	7:42	17:31	7:55	17:17	8:09	16:59	8:25	16:36	8:47
3	19:19	7:55	19:00	8:14	18:49	8:24	18:36	8:36	18:20	8:51	18:02	9:08	17:43	9:26	17:20	9:48	16:48	10:19
4	20:10	8:54	19:48	9:15	19:35	9:27	19:20	9:42	19:02	9:59	18:41	10:20	18:19	10:41	17:50	11:09	17:09	11:50
5	21:05	9:53	20:42	10:16	20:28	10:29	20:13	10:45	19:54	11:03	19:31	11:27	19:07	11:50	18:35	12:22	17:48	13:09
6	22:05	10:51	21:42	11:14	21:29	11:27	21:13	11:43	20:55	12:02	20:32	12:25	20:09	12:48	19:38	13:19	18:52	14:05
7	23:06	11:46	22:46	12:08	22:34	12:20	22:20	12:35	22:04	12:51	21:44	13:12	21:24	13:33	20:57	14:00	20:20	14:39
8	—	12:38	23:52	12:56	23:42	13:07	23:31	13:19	23:18	13:33	23:02	13:50	22:46	14:07	22:26	14:29	21:59	14:57
9	0:08	13:26	—	13:40	—	13:48	—	13:57	—	14:08	—	14:21	—	14:33	23:58	14:48	23:41	15:08
10	1:10	14:11	0:58	14:20	0:51	14:25	0:43	14:31	0:34	14:38	0:23	14:46	0:12	14:53	—	15:03	—	15:15
11	2:11	14:53	2:04	14:57	2:00	14:59	1:56	15:02	1:51	15:05	1:44	15:08	1:39	15:11	1:31	15:15	1:22	15:20
12	3:11	15:34	3:09	15:33	3:09	15:32	3:08	15:31	3:07	15:30	3:06	15:29	3:05	15:28	3:03	15:26	3:02	15:24
13	4:10	16:16	4:15	16:09	4:17	16:05	4:20	16:01	4:23	15:56	4:27	15:50	4:31	15:44	4:35	15:37	4:41	15:29
14	5:10	16:57	5:20	16:47	5:25	16:40	5:32	16:33	5:39	16:24	5:48	16:13	5:57	16:03	6:07	15:50	6:21	15:34
15	6:11	17:44	6:25	17:28	6:33	17:19	6:43	17:08	6:54	16:55	7:08	16:40	7:22	16:25	7:39	16:07	8:02	15:42
16	7:11	18:32	7:30	18:12	7:41	18:01	7:53	17:47	8:08	17:32	8:26	17:12	8:45	16:53	9:08	16:29	9:41	15:55
17	8:11	19:23	8:32	19:01	8:45	18:48	9:00	18:32	9:17	18:14	9:39	17:52	10:01	17:29	10:30	17:00	11:13	16:16
18	9:08	20:16	9:31	19:53	9:45	19:39	10:01	19:23	10:19	19:04	10:43	18:40	11:07	18:16	11:40	17:44	12:28	16:55
19	10:02	21:10	10:25	20:47	10:39	20:34	10:54	20:18	11:13	20:00	11:36	19:37	12:00	19:13	12:32	18:41	13:20	17:54
20	10:51	22:04	11:13	21:43	11:25	21:31	11:40	21:16	11:57	21:00	12:19	20:39	12:41	20:18	13:09	19:50	13:49	19:11
21	11:36	22:56	11:55	22:38	12:06	22:28	12:19	22:16	12:34	22:02	12:52	21:44	13:10	21:27	13:34	21:04	14:05	20:34
22	12:17	23:47	12:32	23:33	12:41	23:25	12:52	23:15	13:04	23:04	13:19	22:52	13:33	22:37	13:51	22:20	14:15	21:58
23	12:54	—	13:06	—	13:13	—	13:21	—	13:30	—	13:41	23:57	13:51	23:47	14:04	23:36	14:21	23:21
24	13:29	0:37	13:37	0:27	13:42	0:21	13:47	0:14	13:53	0:06	14:00	—	14:06	—	14:15	—	14:25	—
25	14:03	1:26	14:07	1:20	14:09	1:16	14:11	1:13	14:14	1:08	14:17	1:03	14:20	0:57	14:24	0:51	14:28	0:43
26	14:37	2:14	14:36	2:13	14:36	2:12	14:35	2:11	14:34	2:10	14:34	2:09	14:33	2:08	14:32	2:06	14:31	2:04
27	15:12	3:04	15:06	3:07	15:03	3:09	15:00	3:11	14:56	3:13	14:51	3:16	14:47	3:19	14:41	3:22	14:34	3:27
28	15:48	3:55	15:39	4:03	15:33	4:07	15:27	4:12	15:19	4:18	15:10	4:26	15:02	4:33	14:52	4:41	14:39	4:52
29	16:29	4:48	16:14	5:01	16:06	5:08	15:57	5:16	15:46	5:26	15:33	5:37	15:20	5:49	15:05	6:03	14:45	6:21
30	17:13	5:45	16:55	6:01	16:44	6:11	16:32	6:22	16:18	6:35	16:01	6:51	15:44	7:07	15:23	7:27	14:54	7:55

MOONRISE AND MOONSET, 2001 DECEMBER
UNIVERSAL TIME AT GREENWICH MERIDIAN

Moon phases (left to right across top): ◑ ● ◐ ○

Latitude:	+20°		+30°		+35°		+40°		+45°		+50°		+54°		+58°		+62°	
Event:	RISE	SET	RISE	SET	RISE	SET	RISE	SET	RISE	SET	RISE	SET	RISE	SET	RISE	SET	RISE	SET
Dec. 1	18:03	6:44	17:41	7:04	17:29	7:16	17:15	7:29	16:58	7:45	16:37	8:05	16:16	8:26	15:49	8:52	15:11	9:29
2	18:58	7:44	18:35	8:07	18:21	8:20	18:05	8:35	17:47	8:54	17:24	9:16	17:00	9:40	16:29	10:11	15:43	10:56
3	19:57	8:44	19:34	9:08	19:21	9:21	19:05	9:37	18:46	9:56	18:23	10:20	17:59	10:44	17:27	11:16	16:39	12:04
4	21:00	9:42	20:38	10:04	20:26	10:17	20:11	10:32	19:54	10:50	19:33	11:12	19:11	11:34	18:43	12:03	18:02	12:45
5	22:03	10:36	21:45	10:55	21:34	11:07	21:22	11:20	21:08	11:35	20:50	11:53	20:33	12:12	20:11	12:35	19:40	13:07
6	23:04	11:25	22:51	11:41	22:43	11:50	22:34	12:00	22:24	12:11	22:11	12:26	21:58	12:40	21:43	12:57	21:22	13:19
7	—	12:10	23:56	12:21	23:51	12:27	23:46	12:34	23:39	12:42	23:31	12:52	23:24	13:01	23:14	13:12	23:02	13:27
8	0:05	12:53	—	12:58	—	13:01	—	13:05	—	13:09	—	13:14	—	13:19	—	13:25	—	13:32
9	1:03	13:33	1:00	13:33	0:58	13:34	0:56	13:34	0:54	13:34	0:51	13:35	0:48	13:35	0:45	13:36	0:41	13:36
10	2:01	14:13	2:03	14:08	2:05	14:06	2:06	14:03	2:08	13:59	2:10	13:55	2:12	13:51	2:14	13:46	2:17	13:40
11	2:59	14:54	3:07	14:44	3:11	14:39	3:16	14:32	3:22	14:25	3:29	14:16	3:35	14:08	3:44	13:58	3:54	13:45
12	3:58	15:37	4:10	15:22	4:17	15:14	4:26	15:05	4:35	14:54	4:47	14:41	4:59	14:28	5:13	14:12	5:32	13:51
13	4:57	16:23	5:14	16:04	5:23	15:54	5:35	15:41	5:48	15:27	6:05	15:09	6:21	14:52	6:42	14:30	7:10	14:01
14	5:56	17:12	6:16	16:50	6:28	16:38	6:42	16:23	6:59	16:06	7:19	15:45	7:40	15:24	8:07	14:56	8:45	14:17
15	6:54	18:04	7:17	17:41	7:30	17:27	7:46	17:11	8:04	16:52	8:27	16:29	8:51	16:05	9:22	15:34	10:09	14:46
16	7:50	18:58	8:13	18:34	8:27	18:21	8:43	18:05	9:02	17:46	9:26	17:22	9:50	16:58	10:23	16:25	11:12	15:36
17	8:42	19:52	9:04	19:30	9:18	19:17	9:33	19:02	9:51	18:45	10:14	18:23	10:37	18:00	11:07	17:30	11:51	16:47
18	9:29	20:46	9:50	20:26	10:02	20:15	10:15	20:02	10:31	19:47	10:51	19:28	11:11	19:08	11:37	18:44	12:12	18:09
19	10:12	21:38	10:29	21:22	10:39	21:13	10:51	21:02	11:04	20:50	11:21	20:34	11:37	20:19	11:57	20:00	12:24	19:34
20	10:51	22:28	11:05	22:16	11:13	22:09	11:22	22:02	11:32	21:52	11:45	21:41	11:57	21:30	12:12	21:16	12:32	20:58
21	11:27	23:17	11:37	23:10	11:42	23:05	11:49	23:00	11:56	22:54	12:05	22:47	12:13	22:40	12:23	22:31	12:36	22:20
22	12:01	—	12:07	—	12:10	—	12:13	23:58	12:17	23:56	12:22	23:53	12:27	23:49	12:33	23:46	12:40	23:41
23	12:35	0:06	12:36	0:02	12:36	0:00	12:37	—	12:38	—	12:39	—	12:40	—	12:41	—	12:42	—
24	13:08	0:54	13:05	0:55	13:03	0:56	13:01	0:57	12:58	0:58	12:56	0:59	12:53	0:59	12:49	1:01	12:45	1:02
25	13:43	1:44	13:36	1:49	13:31	1:53	13:26	1:56	13:20	2:01	13:14	2:06	13:07	2:11	12:59	2:17	12:49	2:25
26	14:21	2:35	14:09	2:46	14:02	2:51	13:54	2:58	13:45	3:06	13:34	3:16	13:23	3:25	13:10	3:36	12:54	3:51
27	15:03	3:30	14:47	3:44	14:38	3:53	14:27	4:03	14:14	4:14	13:59	4:28	13:44	4:42	13:26	4:59	13:01	5:22
28	15:51	4:27	15:31	4:46	15:19	4:57	15:06	5:09	14:50	5:24	14:31	5:42	14:12	6:01	13:47	6:24	13:14	6:56
29	16:44	5:28	16:21	5:49	16:08	6:02	15:53	6:17	15:35	6:34	15:13	6:56	14:50	7:18	14:21	7:47	13:38	8:29
30	17:43	6:30	17:20	6:53	17:06	7:07	16:50	7:22	16:31	7:41	16:08	8:05	15:43	8:29	15:11	9:01	14:23	9:49
31	18:46	7:30	18:24	7:53	18:11	8:07	17:56	8:22	17:38	8:41	17:15	9:03	16:52	9:27	16:22	9:57	15:38	10:42

ECLIPSE PATTERNS
By Roy Bishop

Eclipse Seasons

The plane of the Moon's orbit is tilted about 5° to the plane of Earth's orbit, the ecliptic. Since 5° is considerably larger than the angular sizes of the Sun and Moon ($\approx$0.5°), eclipses can occur only when the Sun is near (within about ±15° to ±18° for solar eclipses) one of the two points (nodes) at which the Moon's orbit crosses the ecliptic. The *ascending* node is the one at which the Moon crosses to the *north* side of the ecliptic.

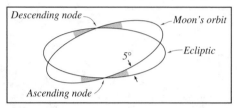

The Sun moves eastward along the ecliptic about 1° per day; thus the interval during which an eclipse can occur is at most about $(2 \times 18°) \div 1°/d = 36$ d, an *eclipse season*. Since the interval between new moons (29.5 days) is somewhat less, one or two solar eclipses will occur in each eclipse season. Six months later, when the Sun is near the other node, another eclipse season occurs. However, the plane of the Moon's orbit wobbles, making the nodes regress slowly westward along the ecliptic with a period of 18.61 years; thus the two eclipse seasons drift backward through the year, occurring about 19 days earlier each year.

The eclipse seasons of 2001 occur in January (part of an eclipse season which began in 2000 December), June/July, and December.

In a calendar year there can be as many as seven eclipses (solar and lunar combined, as last occurred in 1982), and as few as four (the usual number, as in 1999). In a calendar year there can be as many as five solar or lunar eclipses, and as few as two. The number of total or annular solar eclipses in a calendar year can range from zero to two, the number of total lunar eclipses from zero to three. *In 2001 there are five eclipses: three lunar (one each: total, partial, and penumbral), and two solar (one total and one annular).*

The Saros

Eclipses of the Sun and Moon recur with various periodicities that are more or less approximate. These periodicities are interesting both as numerical curiosities and because they may be used to predict eclipses. The most famous periodicity, the *Saros*, has been known since ancient times. It is a consequence of a remarkable commensurability among three lunar average periods:

Synodic month (S) (new to new)	$= 29.530\ 589$ d, $223S = 6585.3213$ d
Draconic month (N) (node to node)	$= 27.212\ 221$ d, $242N = 6585.3575$ d
Anomalistic month (P) (perigee to perigee)	$= 27.554\ 550$ d, $239P = 6585.5375$ d

Several aspects of this arithmetic are relevant to the pattern of eclipses (for brevity, the following comments are restricted primarily to the case of solar eclipses):

(1) An integer number of Ss (223) ensures a new Moon and hence the possibility of a second solar eclipse.

(2) $242N \approx 223S$ means that the new Moon will be almost at the same position relative to a node, ensuring that an eclipse *will* occur again and that it will occur somewhere near the same geographic latitude.

(3) The **Saros** $(223S) = 6585.3213$ d $= 18$ years $+ only$ 10.3213 d or 11.3213 d (depending on the number of intervening leap years). Thus one Saros later Earth will be at almost the same point in its elliptical orbit and hence at nearly the same distance from the Sun. Moreover, the inclination of Earth toward the Sun (season) will be nearly the same; thus the same latitude region of Earth will be exposed to the eclipse.

(4) $239P \approx 223S$ means that one Saros later the new Moon will be at almost the same point in its elliptical orbit and thus at the same distance from Earth. With the same lunar and solar distances, the type of eclipse (total or annular) will be the same. Since the eclipse will occur near the same geographic latitude (see (2) and (3)), the duration of totality or annularity, or the magnitude of partial eclipse if the eclipse is not central, will be almost the same as it was one Saros earlier.

(5) $242N - 223S = 0.0361$ d $= 0.87$ h. This, together with the 0.55°/h eastward speed of the Moon in its orbit means that, after one Saros, the Moon will be about 0.5° west of its former position relative to its node. Thus a Saros series does not last forever; there will be about $36°/0.5° \approx 72$ eclipses in a Saros series (the number ranges from 69 to 86). Furthermore any one Saros series will last for about $72 \times 18 \approx 1300$ years (the range is 1226 to 1532 years).

A Saros series begins with about 10 partial eclipses of increasing magnitude in the north or south polar region, depending upon whether the eclipses are occurring near the ascending or descending lunar node, respectively. These are followed by about 50 central eclipses (either total or annular), which over many centuries progressively shift southward or northward across Earth (about 300-km shift in latitude with each successive eclipse), and the series ends with 10 or so partial eclipses of decreasing magnitude in the opposite polar region.

Currently, for solar eclipses 39 Saros series are running simultaneously, numbers 117 through 155 (for lunar eclipses, 41 Saros series are running, numbers 109 through 149). That is, in any 18-year 11-day interval, one eclipse from each of these 39 (and 41) series takes place, after which the whole pattern repeats. Those series occurring at the lunar ascending node are given odd numbers; those at the descending node, even numbers (vice versa for lunar eclipses).

The eclipse sequence of the year 2001 is similar to that of the four-eclipse year 1983, except that the extra 11 days of the Saros cycle has bumped the next Saros member of the lunar eclipse of 1982 December 30 (Saros 134) into the year 2001, resulting in five eclipses in 2001.

(6) The Saros $= 223S = 6585.3213$ d, and the fractional 0.3213 d $\approx$ one-third of a day. Thus each successive solar eclipse in a Saros series will be shifted one-third of the way westward (120° in longitude) around Earth. After three Saros periods (54 years and 33 days, a cycle known as the *Exeligmos*), the eclipse will be back at approximately the same geographic longitude, although shifted about 1000 km in latitude. Two examples follow.

(a) The total lunar eclipse of 2001 January 9, visible from Europe, Africa and Asia, is the 26th of 73 eclipses belonging to Saros 134 (an even number, hence the Moon is near its ascending node on that date). One Saros later, on 2019 January 21 a nearly identical total lunar eclipse (the 27th of Saros 134) will be visible from longitudes centred about 120° further west, in the Americas.

(b) The total solar eclipse of 2024 April 8 (no. 30 of Saros 139), which sweeps northeastward across eastern North America, will be geographically similar to that of 1970 March 7 (no. 27 of Saros 139) which followed the eastern seaboard of North America, one Exeligmos earlier.

The Metonic Cycle

The sequence of lunar phases and the year repeat their relative pattern at 19-year intervals, a cycle known to astronomers in ancient Babylon and which was discovered independently around 430 BC by a Greek astronomer, Meton. We have

$235S = 235 \times 29.530\,589 = 6939.6884$ d;
19 years = 6939 d or 6940 d (depending on leap years).

Also, $255N$ is also very close to 19 years:

$255N = 255 \times 27.212\,221 = 6939.1164$ d.

Thus solar and lunar eclipses also repeat on a 19-year "Metonic" cycle. Since $255N$ is less than $235S$, the Moon does not reach the same phase (new or full for an eclipse) until it has moved eastward relative to the node by

$(235S - 255N) \times 24\text{h} \times 0.55°/\text{h} = 7.5°$.

Thus a Metonic eclipse series will have only

eclipse season width on the ecliptic $(36°) \div 7.5 \approx 4$ or 5 eclipses;

and the geographic latitude of successive solar eclipses in a series will change substantially (north or south, depending upon whether the Moon is at its ascending node or descending node, respectively).

What about the Moon's position in its orbit relative to its perigee? Using the anomalistic month P (the Moon returns to perigee on average every 27.554 550 d),

$235S \div P = 251.85$, which is *not* near an integer.

Thus in a Metonic series the Moon's distance is not the same from one eclipse to another. Hence the type of solar eclipse (total or annular) will vary within the series.

With only about four eclipses in a series, a mix of eclipse types, and scattered geographic occurrence, a Metonic eclipse series is not as elegant or useful as a Saros series. The main feature of a Metonic eclipse series is that, like lunar phases, the successive eclipses occur on (almost) the *same day* of the year.

Examples of the Metonic Cycle for a lunar phase, lunar eclipses, and two recent Western Hemisphere total solar eclipses are given below. The numbers in parentheses are Saros numbers.

Last Q Moon	Lunar Eclipses	Solar Eclipses
1944 May 15	1962 Jan. 20 (no eclipse)	1960 Feb. 26 (no eclipse)
1963 May 16	1981 Jan. 20 Pen. (114)	**1979** Feb. 26 Total (120)
1982 May 16	**2000** Jan. 21 Total (124)	**1998** Feb. 26 Total (130)
2001 May 15	2019 Jan. 21 Total (134)	2017 Feb. 26 Annular (140)
2020 May 14	2038 Jan. 21 Pen. (144)	2036 Feb. 27 Partial (150)
2039 May 15	2057 Jan. 21 (no eclipse)	2055 Feb. 27 (no eclipse)

ECLIPSES DURING 2001
BY FRED ESPENAK

Two central solar eclipses and three lunar eclipses occur in 2001 as follows:

2001 Jan. 9:	Total lunar eclipse
2001 Jun. 21:	Total solar eclipse
2001 Jul. 5:	Partial lunar eclipse
2001 Dec. 14:	Annular solar eclipse
2001 Dec. 30:	Penumbral lunar eclipse

Predictions for eclipses are summarized in Figures 1 through 7 (pp. 131–137). World maps show the regions of visibility for each eclipse. The lunar eclipse diagrams also include the path of the Moon through Earth's shadows. Contact times for each principal phase are tabulated along with the magnitudes and geocentric coordinates of the Sun and Moon at greatest eclipse.

Total Lunar Eclipse of January 9

The first lunar eclipse of the year is total and is well placed for Eastern Hemisphere observers. Nevertheless, the total phase can be seen from northeastern-most Canada. The event occurs just half a day before perigee. The Moon is in Gemini about one degree west of the bright star Delta Gem ($m_v = +3.53$).

Although the eclipse is not central (the Moon passes north of the shadow axis), the total phase still lasts 62 min. The eclipse begins at 17:43.6 UT with first penumbral contact. An hour later, the partial eclipse commences with first umbral contact at 18:42.1 UT. The total umbral eclipse begins at 19:49.6 UT and ends at 20:51.7 UT. The partial phase ends at 21:59.1 UT, and the Moon leaves the penumbral shadow at 22:57.7 UT. The Moon's path through Earth's shadows as well as a map showing worldwide visibility of the event is shown in Figure 1 (p. 131).

At the instant of mideclipse (20:20.6 UT), the Moon will lie in the zenith for observers in Saudi Arabia. At this time, the umbral magnitude[1] peaks at 1.1947 as the Moon's southern limb passes 6.1 arc-minutes north of the shadow's axis. In contrast, the Moon's northern limb will lie 6.5 arc-minutes from the northern edge of the umbra and 39.5 arc-minutes from the shadow centre. Thus, the northern sections of the Moon will appear much brighter than the southern part, which will lie deeper in the shadow. Since the Moon samples a large range of umbral depths during totality, its appearance will likely change dramatically with time. However, it is impossible to predict the exact brightness distribution in the umbra, so observers are encouraged to estimate the Danjon value at different times during totality (see Danjon Scale of Lunar Eclipse Brightness on p. 121). Note that it may also be necessary to assign different Danjon values to different portions of the Moon (i.e. north vs. south).

During totality, the winter Milky Way and constellations will be well placed for viewing. Castor and Pollux lie 8°–10° north of the eclipsed Moon, while the Beehive cluster (M44) in Cancer is 17° to the east. Jupiter, Saturn, and the Pleiades form an attractive trio in Taurus, about 50° west of the Moon.

The event will be widely visible from Europe, Africa, and Asia. The Moon sets in Australia during various stages of the eclipse. Observers in eastern Canada (Maritime provinces) will find totality already in progress at moonrise. Ontario, Quebec, and New England (U.S.) will witness the final partial phases as the moon rises.

Table 5 (p. 130) lists predicted umbral immersion and emersion times for 20

---

[1] Umbral magnitude of a lunar eclipse is defined as the fraction of the Moon's diameter covered by the umbral shadow. The magnitude is < 1.0 for partial eclipses, and ≥1.0 for total eclipses.

well-defined lunar craters. The timing of craters is useful in determining the atmospheric enlargement of Earth's shadow (see Crater Timings During Lunar Eclipses on p. 122).

Total Solar Eclipse of June 21

The first total solar eclipse of the third millennium will be visible from within a narrow corridor that traverses the Southern Hemisphere. The path of the Moon's umbral shadow begins in the South Atlantic, crosses southern Africa and Madagascar, and ends at sunset in the Indian Ocean. A partial eclipse will be seen within the much broader path of the Moon's penumbral shadow, which includes eastern South America and the southern two-thirds of Africa (Figure 2, p. 132).

The eclipse begins in the South Atlantic about 400 km southeast of Uruguay. The Moon's umbral shadow first touches down on Earth at 10:35:55 UT. Along the sunrise terminator, the duration is 2 min 6 s as seen from the centre of the 127-km-wide path. During the next two hours, the umbra sweeps across the South Atlantic with no major landfall. The central duration, path width and Sun's altitude all steadily increase as the Moon's shadow rushes along its northeastern transoceanic course.

The instant of greatest eclipse[2] occurs at 12:03:41 UT when the axis of the Moon's shadow passes closest to the centre of Earth (gamma[3] = −0.570). The length of totality reaches its maximum duration of 4 min 56 s, the Sun's altitude is 55°, the path width is 200 km and the umbra's velocity is 0.554 km/s. Unfortunately, these most favourable circumstances occur at sea some 1100 km west of equatorial Africa's South Atlantic coastline (Figure 3, p. 133).

Another half-hour will elapse before the umbra reaches southern Africa. During this period, the duration and path width will slowly wane as the curvature of Earth carries the projected eclipse path away from the Moon. As a result, the tapering shadow cone will present a progressively narrower cross section to Earth's surface along the path of totality. Nevertheless, the 2001 total solar eclipse is over twice as long as the last total eclipse in 1999 at all corresponding positions along the path.

Landfall finally occurs along the Atlantic coast of Angola at 12:36 UT. The centreline duration is 4 min 36 s, the path width is 193 km and the Sun's altitude is 49°. Travelling with a ground speed of 0.63 km/s, the umbra swiftly moves eastward through the civil war-torn nation. Although the weather prospects are excellent, Angola's political strife makes it a dangerous place for eclipse observers. By 12:57 UT, the shadow reaches the western border of Zambia, where totality lasts a maximum of 4 min 6 s. The umbra's path is now directed to the east-southeast as it heads toward the nation's capital city. Lying about 40 km south of the centreline, Lusaka enjoys a total eclipse lasting a respectable 3 min 14 s. Farther to the north, the centreline duration is 3 min 35 s and the Sun's altitude is 31°. Quickly crossing the Zambezi River, the path continues into Zimbabwe and Mozambique. The centreline runs near the border between these two nations for several hundred kilometres. Zimbabwe's capital city of Harare lies just 100 km south of the path, so its citizens will witness a partial eclipse of magnitude 0.976. As the umbra leaves Zimbabwe, it lies wholly within Mozambique for a minute before its leading edge reaches the shore of the Indian Ocean (≈13:20 UT). At nearly the same time, its northern edge just skirts

---

[2] The instant of greatest eclipse occurs when the distance between the Moon's shadow axis and Earth's geocentre reaches a minimum. Although greatest eclipse differs slightly from the instants of greatest magnitude and greatest duration (for total eclipses), the differences are quite small.

[3] Minimum distance of the Moon's shadow axis from Earth's centre in units of equatorial Earth radii.

the southern border of Malawi. The centreline duration is now 3 min 9 s as the Sun's altitude drops to 23°. The shadow's speed has increased to 1.7 km/s as it begins to leave the continent for the open waters of the Indian Ocean.

One last major landfall remains as the umbra races over southern Madagascar. The eclipse occurs quite late in the day with the Sun just 11° above the western horizon. The central duration now stands at 2 min 25 s (13:28 UT) as the shadow's long elliptical projection stretches across the entire east-west breadth of the island. Continuing into the Indian Ocean, the umbra leaves Earth's surface (13:31:33 UT) as the path ends. Over the course of 2 h 54 min, the Moon's umbra travels along a path approximately 12 000 km long and covering 0.3% of Earth's surface area. Path coordinates and centreline circumstances are presented in Table 1 (p. 125).

Local circumstances for cities throughout the path are given in Table 2 (p. 126). All times are given in Universal Time. The Sun's altitude and azimuth, the eclipse magnitude[4] and obscuration[5] are all given at the instant of maximum eclipse. An 88-page detailed report on this eclipse is available from NASA as Technical Publication 1999–209484 (see NASA Solar Eclipse Bulletins). Additional information is also available at the 2001 total solar eclipse web site:

http://sunearth.gsfc.nasa.gov/eclipse/TSE2001/TSE2001.html

Partial Lunar Eclipse of July 5

The second lunar eclipse of the year is partial and occurs in eastern Sagittarius 3° north of Nunki (σ Sagittarius). The event is a moderate partial eclipse with the Moon's northern limb dipping 15 arc-minutes into Earth's umbral shadow. The penumbral phase begins at 12:10.9 UT, but most observers will be unable to detect any shading during the first half hour or so. The partial eclipse commences with first umbral contact at 13:35.2 UT. Two hours and 40 minutes later, the partial eclipse ends at 16:15.3 UT. Although it cannot actually be observed, the eclipse technically ends when the Moon leaves the penumbral shadow at 17:39.8 UT.

At the instant of mideclipse (14:55.3 UT), the Moon will stand at the zenith for observers in central Australia. At that time, the umbral eclipse magnitude peaks at 0.4992 as the centre of the Moon passes along the southern edge of the umbra. Unfortunately, none of the partial phases will be visible from North America except from the Aleutian Islands. The eclipse is best seen from the western Pacific, Asia, and Australia. The Moon's path through Earth's shadow(s) as well as a map showing worldwide visibility of the event are shown in Figure 4 (p. 134).

Table 5 (p. 130) lists predicted umbral immersion and emersion times for 15 bright lunar craters. The timing of craters is useful in determining the atmospheric enlargement of Earth's shadow (see Crater Timings During Lunar Eclipses on p. 122).

Annular Solar Eclipse of December 14

The last solar eclipse of 2001 is an annular eclipse visible primarily from the western hemisphere (Figure 5, p. 135). The Moon's antumbral shadow first touches down on Earth at 19:08 UT near the International Date Line some 3000 km northwest of the Hawaiian Islands. Unfortunately, the path of annularity misses the island chain and passes about 500 km to its south. Still, the islands enjoy a deep partial eclipse with a magnitude exceeding 0.8.

Travelling along a southeastern track, the path begins curving northward as it reaches the Equator. Greatest eclipse occurs at 20:51:56 UT just half a degree north of

[4] Eclipse magnitude is defined as the fraction of the Sun's diameter occulted by the Moon.
[5] Eclipse obscuration is defined as the fraction of the Sun's surface area occulted by the Moon.

the Equator. The duration of the annular phase will last for 3 min 53 s, but the event takes place in open ocean with no landfall in sight.

As the path swings to the northeast, it finally makes its only major landfall as it quickly crosses the Central American nations of Costa Rica and Nicaragua. Figure 6 (p. 136) is a detailed map showing the path limits, centreline and curves of constant duration through these countries. Midannularity occurs along the Pacific coast of Costa Rica at 22:32 UT during the late afternoon. The Sun will stand 11° above the southwestern horizon during an annular phase lasting 3 min 19 s. The corresponding eclipse magnitude and obscuration (fraction of the Sun's surface) will be 0.956 and 0.915, respectively. Costa Rica's capital city of San Jose actually lies just inside the southern limit, where midannularity occurs at 23:33 UT.

Several minutes later, the antumbral shadow leaves Earth's surface at 22:35:53 UT. Over the course of 3 h 28 min, the Moon's antumbra travels along a path approximately 12 900 km long and covering 0.4% of Earth's surface area. Path coordinates and centreline circumstances are presented in Table 3 (p. 127).

Partial phases of the eclipse are visible from much of North America as well as northwestern South America. Local circumstances for a number of cities are listed in Table 4 (pp. 128–130). All times are given in Universal Time. The Sun's altitude and azimuth, the eclipse magnitude, and obscuration are all given at the instant of maximum eclipse. Additional information is also available at the 2001 annular solar eclipse web site:

http://sunearth.gsfc.nasa.gov/eclipse/ASE2001/ASE2001.html

Penumbral Lunar Eclipse of December 30

The final event of the year is a deep penumbral lunar eclipse visible from much of the Western Hemisphere. First and last penumbral contacts occur at 08:25.5 UT and 12:33.2 UT, respectively.

Greatest eclipse occurs at 10:29.3 UT with a maximum penumbral eclipse magnitude of 0.9190. Observers will note subtle yet distinct shading across the southern portions of the Moon. The Moon's southern limb actually lies 3.5 arc-minutes north of the umbra at its closest approach.

The Moon's path through Earth's penumbra as well as a map showing worldwide visibility of the event are shown in Figure 7 (p. 137).

Solar Eclipse Figures

For each solar eclipse, an orthographic projection map of Earth shows the path of penumbral (partial) and umbral (total or annular) eclipse. North is to the top in all cases and the daylight terminator is plotted for the instant of greatest eclipse. An asterisk symbol indicates the subsolar point[6] on Earth.

The limits of the Moon's penumbral shadow delineate the region of visibility of the partial solar eclipse. This irregular or saddle-shaped region often covers more than half of the daylight hemisphere of Earth and consists of several distinct zones or limits. At the northern and/or southern boundaries lie the limits of the penumbra's path. Partial eclipses have only one of these limits, as do central eclipses when the Moon's shadow axis falls no closer than about 0.45 radii from Earth's centre. Great loops at the western and eastern extremes of the penumbra's path identify the areas where the eclipse begins/ends at sunrise and sunset, respectively. If the penumbra has both a northern and southern limit, the rising and setting curves form two separate, closed loops. Otherwise, the curves are connected in a distorted figure 8. Bisecting

---

[6] The subsolar point is the geographic location where the Sun appears directly overhead (zenith).

the "eclipse begins/ends at sunrise and sunset" loops is the curve of maximum eclipse at sunrise (western loop) and sunset (eastern loop). The points P1 and P4 mark the coordinates where the penumbral shadow first contacts (partial eclipse begins) and last contacts (partial eclipse ends) Earth's surface. If the penumbral path has both a northern and southern limit, then points P2 and P3 are also plotted. These correspond to the coordinates where the penumbral shadow cone becomes internally tangent to Earth's disk.

A curve of maximum eclipse is the locus of all points where the eclipse is at maximum at a given time. Curves of maximum eclipse are plotted at each half hour Universal Time. They generally run between the penumbral limits in the north/south direction or from the "maximum eclipse at sunrise and sunset" curves to one of the limits. If the eclipse is central (i.e. total or annular), the curves of maximum eclipse run through the outlines of the umbral shadow, which are plotted at 10-min intervals. The curves of constant eclipse magnitude delineate the locus of all points where the magnitude at maximum eclipse is constant. These curves run exclusively between the curves of maximum eclipse at sunrise and sunset. Furthermore, they're parallel to the northern/southern penumbral limits and the umbral paths of central eclipses. In fact, the northern and southern limits of the penumbra can be thought of as curves of constant magnitude of 0.0. The adjacent curves are for magnitudes of 0.2, 0.4, 0.6, and 0.8 (i.e. 20%, 40%, 60% and 80%). For total eclipses, the northern and southern limits of the umbra are curves of constant magnitude of 1.0. Umbral path limits for annular eclipses are curves of maximum eclipse magnitude.

Greatest eclipse is defined as the instant when the axis of the Moon's shadow passes closest to Earth's centre. Although greatest eclipse differs slightly from the instants of greatest magnitude and greatest duration (for total eclipses), the differences are usually negligible. The point on Earth's surface intersected by the axis at greatest eclipse is marked by an asterisk symbol. For partial eclipses, the shadow axis misses Earth entirely. Therefore, the point of greatest eclipse lies on the day/night terminator and the Sun appears in the horizon.

Data pertinent to the eclipse appear with each map. At the top are listed the instant of conjunction of the Sun and Moon in right ascension and the instant of greatest eclipse, expressed as both Universal Times and Julian dates. The eclipse magnitude is defined as the fraction of the Sun's diameter obscured by the Moon at greatest eclipse. For central eclipses (total or annular), the magnitude is replaced by the geocentric ratio of diameters of the Moon and the Sun. Gamma is the minimum distance of the Moon's shadow axis from Earth's centre in Earth radii at greatest eclipse. The Saros series of the eclipse is listed, followed by the member position. The first member number identifies the sequence position of the eclipse in the Saros, while the second is the total number of eclipses in the series.

In the upper left and right corners are the geocentric coordinates of the Sun and the Moon, respectively, at the instant of greatest eclipse. They are:

RA   Right ascension
Dec   Declination
S.D. Apparent semi-diameter
H.P. Horizontal parallax

To the lower left are exterior/interior contact times of the Moon's penumbral shadow with Earth, which are defined:

P1   Instant of first exterior tangency of penumbra with Earth's limb
      (Partial eclipse begins)
P2   Instant of first interior tangency of penumbra with Earth's limb
P3   Instant of last interior tangency of penumbra with Earth's limb

P4 Instant of last exterior tangency of penumbra with Earth's limb
(Partial eclipse ends)

Not all eclipses have P2 and P3 penumbral contacts. They are only present in cases where the penumbral shadow falls completely within Earth's disk. For central eclipses, the lower right corner lists exterior/interior contact times of the Moon's umbral shadow with Earth's limb which are defined as follows:

U1 Instant of first exterior tangency of umbra with Earth's limb
(Umbral [total/annular] eclipse begins)
U2 Instant of first interior tangency of Umbra with Earth's limb
U3 Instant of last interior tangency of Umbra with Earth's limb
U4 Instant of last exterior tangency of Umbra with Earth's limb
(Umbral [total/annular] eclipse ends)

At bottom centre are the geographic coordinates of the position of greatest eclipse along with the local circumstances at that location (i.e. Sun altitude, Sun azimuth, path width, and duration of totality/annularity). At bottom left is a list of parameters used in the eclipse predictions while bottom right gives the Moon's geocentric libration (optical + physical) at greatest eclipse.

Lunar Eclipse Figures

Each lunar eclipse has two diagrams associated with it along with data pertinent to the eclipse. The top figure shows the path of the Moon through Earth's penumbral and umbral shadows. Above this figure are listed the instant of conjunction in right ascension of the Moon with Earth's shadow axis and the instant of greatest eclipse, expressed as both Universal Times and Julian dates. The penumbral and umbral magnitudes are defined as the fraction of the Moon's diameter immersed in the two shadows at greatest eclipse. The radii of the penumbral and umbral shadows P. Radius and U. Radius are also listed. Gamma is the minimum distance in Earth radii of the Moon's centre from Earth's shadow axis at greatest eclipse, while Axis is the same parameter expressed in degrees. The Saros series of the eclipse is listed, followed by a pair of numbers. The first number identifies the sequence position of the eclipse in the Saros, while the second is the total number of eclipses in the series.

In the upper left and right corners are the geocentric coordinates of the Sun and the Moon, respectively, at the instant of greatest eclipse. They are:

RA Right ascension
Dec Declination
S.D. Apparent semi-diameter
H.P. Horizontal parallax

To the lower left are the semi- or half durations of the penumbral, umbral (partial), and total eclipses. Below them are the Sun/Moon ephemerides used in the predictions, followed by the extrapolated value of ΔT (the difference between Terrestrial Time and Universal Time). To the lower right are the contact times of the Moon with Earth's penumbral and umbral shadows, defined as follows:

P1 Instant of first exterior tangency of Moon with penumbra
(Penumbral eclipse begins)
U1 Instant of first exterior tangency of Moon with umbra
(Partial umbral eclipse begins)
U2 Instant of first interior tangency of Moon with umbra
(Total umbral eclipse begins)

U3 Instant of last interior tangency of Moon with umbra
(Total umbral eclipse ends)

U4 Instant of last exterior tangency of Moon with umbra
(Partial umbral eclipse ends)

P4 Instant of last exterior tangency of Moon with penumbra
(Penumbral eclipse ends)

The bottom figure is a cylindrical equidistant projection map of Earth that shows regions of visibility for each stage of the eclipse. In particular, the moonrise/moonset terminator is plotted for each contact and is labelled accordingly. The Moon appears directly overhead (zenith) during greatest eclipse at the position indicated by an asterisk symbol. The region that is completely unshaded will observe the entire eclipse while the darkly shaded area will witness none of the event. The remaining lightly shaded areas will experience moonrise or moonset while the eclipse is in progress. The shaded zones east of the asterisk symbol will witness moonset before the eclipse ends while the shaded zones west will witness moonrise after the eclipse has begun.

Danjon Scale of Lunar Eclipse Brightness

The Moon's appearance during a total lunar eclipse can vary enormously from one eclipse to the next. Obviously, the geometry of the Moon's path through the umbra plays an important role. Not as apparent is the effect that Earth's atmosphere has on total eclipses. Although the physical mass of Earth blocks off all direct sunlight from the umbra, the planet's atmosphere refracts some of the Sun's rays into the shadow. Earth's atmosphere contains varying amounts of water (clouds, mist, precipitation) and solid particles (meteoric dust, organic debris, volcanic ash). This material significantly filters and attenuates the sunlight before it is refracted into the umbra. For instance, large or frequent volcanic eruptions dumping huge quantities of ash into the atmosphere are often followed by very dark, red eclipses for several years. Extensive cloud cover along Earth's limb also tends to darken the eclipse by blocking sunlight.

The French astronomer A. Danjon proposed a useful five-point scale for evaluating the visual appearance and brightness of the Moon during total lunar eclipses. The L values for various luminosities are defined as follows:

$L = 0$ Very dark eclipse
Moon almost invisible, especially at midtotality

$L = 1$ Dark eclipse, grey or brownish in coloration
Details distinguishable only with difficulty

$L = 2$ Deep red or rust-coloured eclipse
Very dark central shadow, while outer umbra is relatively bright

$L = 3$ Brick-red eclipse
Umbral shadow usually has a bright or yellow rim

$L = 4$ Very bright copper-red or orange eclipse
Umbral shadow has a bluish, very bright rim

The assignment of an L value to lunar eclipses is best done with the naked eye, binoculars, or a small telescope near the time of midtotality. It's also useful to examine the Moon's appearance just after the beginning and before the end of totality. The Moon is then near the edge of the shadow and provides an opportunity to assign an L value to the outer umbra. In making any evaluations, you should record both the instrumentation and the time. Also note any variations in colour and brightness in different parts of the umbra, as well as the apparent sharpness of the shadow's edge. Pay attention to the visibility of lunar features within the umbra. Notes and sketches made during the eclipse are often invaluable in recalling important details, events, and impressions.

Crater Timings During Lunar Eclipses

In 1702, Pierre de La Hire made a curious observation about Earth's umbra. To accurately predict the duration of a lunar eclipse, he found it necessary to increase the radius of the shadow one arc-minute more than warranted by geometric considerations. Although the effect is clearly related to Earth's atmosphere, it's not completely understood since the shadow enlargement seems to vary from one eclipse to the next. The enlargement can be measured through careful timings of lunar craters as they enter and exit the umbra.

Such observations are best made using a low-power telescope and a clock or watch synchronized with radio time signals. Timings should be made to a precision of 0.1 min. The basic idea is to record the instant when the most abrupt gradient at the umbra's edge crosses the apparent centre of the crater. In the case of large craters like Tycho and Copernicus, it's recommended that you record the times when the shadow touches the two opposite edges of the crater. The average of these times is equal to the instant of crater bisection.

As a planning guide, Table 5 lists several well-defined craters with predicted umbral immersion and emersion times during the two lunar eclipses of 2001. The predictions assume a 2% enlargement of the umbra and include the effects of Earth's oblateness. Naturally, you should be thoroughly familiar with these features before an eclipse in order to prevent confusion and misidentification. The four umbral contacts with the Moon's limb can also be used in determining the shadow's enlargement. However, these events are less distinct and difficult to time accurately. Observers are encouraged to make crater timings and to send their results to *Sky & Telescope* for analysis.

Eclipse Altitudes and Azimuths

The altitude a and azimuth A of the Sun or Moon during an eclipse depends on the time and the observer's geographic coordinates. They are calculated as follows:

$$h = 15\,(\text{GST} + \text{UT} - \alpha) + \lambda$$
$$a = \arcsin [\, \sin \delta \sin \phi + \cos \delta \cos h \cos \phi \,]$$
$$A = \arctan [\, -(\cos \delta \sin h) / (\sin \delta \cos \phi - \cos \delta \cos h \sin \phi) \,]$$

where:

h	=	Hour Angle of Sun or Moon
a	=	Altitude
A	=	Azimuth
GST	=	Greenwich Sidereal Time at 0:00 UT
UT	=	Universal Time
α	=	Right ascension of Sun or Moon
δ	=	Declination of Sun or Moon
λ	=	Observer's longitude (east +, west −)
ϕ	=	Observer's latitude (north +, south −)

During the eclipses of 2001, the values for GST and the geocentric right ascension and declination of the Sun or the Moon (at greatest eclipse) are as follows:

Eclipse	Date	GST	α	δ
Total lunar	2001 Jan. 9	7.296	7.419	22.380
Total solar	2001 Jun. 21	17.984	6.013	23.438
Partial lunar	2001 Jul. 5	18.911	18.988	−23.406
Annular solar	2001 Dec. 14	5.573	17.487	−23.251
Penumbral lunar	2001 Dec. 30	6.596	6.635	24.205

Eclipses During 2002

Next year, there will be two central solar and three penumbral lunar eclipses:

2002 May 26:	Penumbral lunar eclipse
2002 Jun. 10:	Annular solar eclipse
2002 Jun. 24:	Penumbral lunar eclipse
2002 Nov. 20:	Penumbral lunar eclipse
2002 Dec. 4:	Total solar eclipse

A full report on eclipses during 2002 will be published next year in the *Observer's Handbook 2002*.

Total Solar Eclipse of 2002 December 4

The next total eclipse of the Sun is also visible from southern Africa. The path of the Moon's umbral shadow begins in the South Atlantic, off the west coast of equatorial Africa. It crosses through Angola, Zambia, Namibia, Botswana, Zimbabwe, South Africa and Mozambique (Figure 8, p. 138). Totality takes place in the morning hours with a central duration ranging from 1 min to 1.5 min. The track continues across the Indian Ocean and ends in southern Australia north of Adelaide.

Complete details will eventually be posted on the NASA TSE2002 web site as well as in the next NASA bulletin scheduled for publication in late 2000. The TSE2002 web site address is:

http://sunearth.gsfc.nasa.gov/eclipse/TSE2002/TSE2002.html

NASA Solar Eclipse Bulletins

Special bulletins containing detailed predictions and meteorological data for future solar eclipses of interest are prepared by F. Espenak and J. Anderson, and are published through NASA's Publication series. The bulletins are provided as a public service to both the professional and lay communities, including educators and the media. A list of currently available bulletins and an order form can be found at:

http://sunearth.gsfc.nasa.gov/eclipse/Sepubs/RPrequest.html

Single copies of the eclipse bulletins are available at no cost by sending a 9 × 12-inch self-addressed envelope stamped with postage for 11 oz (310 g). Please print the eclipse year on the envelope's lower left corner. Use stamps only, since cash or cheques cannot be accepted. Requests from outside the United States and Canada may send 10 international postal coupons. Mail requests to: Fred Espenak, NASA/ Goddard Space Flight Center, Code 693, Greenbelt, Maryland 20771, USA.

The NASA eclipse bulletins are also available over the Internet, including out-of-print bulletins. Using a web browser, they can be read or downloaded from the GSFC/SDAC (Solar Data Analysis Center) eclipse page:

http://umbra.nascom.nasa.gov/eclipse/index.html

The original Microsoft Word text files and PICT figures (Macintosh format) are also available via anonymous ftp. They are stored as BinHex-encoded, StuffIt-compressed Mac folders with .hqx suffixes. For PCs, the text is available in a zip-compressed format in files with the .zip suffix. There are three subdirectories for figures (GIF format), maps (JPEG format), and tables.

Eclipse Web Sites

A special solar and lunar eclipse web site is available at:

http://sunearth.gsfc.nasa.gov/eclipse/eclipse.html

The site features predictions and maps for all solar and lunar eclipses well into the 21st century. Special emphasis is placed on eclipses occurring during the next two years with detailed path maps, tables, graphs and meteorological data. Additional catalogues list every solar and lunar eclipse over a 5000-year period.

Detailed information on solar and lunar eclipse photography, and tips on eclipse observing and eye safety may be found at:

http://www.MrEclipse.com

Acknowledgements

All eclipse predictions were generated on a Power Macintosh 8500/150 using algorithms developed from the *Explanatory Supplement* (1974) with additional algorithms from Meeus, Grosjean, and Vanderleen (1966). The solar and lunar ephemerides were generated from Newcomb and the *Improved Lunar Ephemeris*. A correction of –0.6″ was added to the Moon's ecliptic latitude to account for the difference between the Moon's centre of mass and centre of figure. For partial solar eclipses, the value used for the Moon's radius is $k = 0.272\ 488\ 0$. For lunar eclipses, the diameter of the umbral shadow was enlarged by 2% to compensate for Earth's atmosphere and the effects of oblateness have been included. Figure annotation was performed with Claris MacDraw Pro.

All calculations, diagrams, tables, and opinions presented in this section are those of the author and he assumes full responsibility for their accuracy.

This publication is available electronically along with additional information and updates at:

http://sunearth.gsfc.nasa.gov/eclipse/OH/OH2001.html

References

Espenak, F., 1988, *Fifty Year Canon of Solar Eclipses: 1986–2035*, Sky Publishing Corp., Cambridge, MA.

Espenak, F., 1989, *Fifty Year Canon of Lunar Eclipses: 1986–2035*, Sky Publishing Corp., Cambridge, MA.

Espenak, F. and J. Anderson, 1999, *Total Solar Eclipse of 2001 June 21*, NASA TP 1999–209484, Washington DC.

Explanatory Supplement to the Astronomical Ephemeris and the American Ephemeris and Nautical Almanac, 1974, Her Majesty's Nautical Almanac Office, London.

Improved Lunar Ephemeris 1952–1959, 1954, U.S. Naval Observatory, Washington, DC.

Littmann, M., K. Willcox and F. Espenak, 1999, *Totality – Eclipses of the Sun*, Oxford University Press, New York.

Meeus, J., C. C. Grosjean, and W. Vanderleen, 1966, *Canon of Solar Eclipses*, Pergamon Press, New York.

Meeus, J. and H. Mucke, 1979, *Canon of Lunar Eclipses: –2002 to +2526*, Astronomisches Buro, Wien.

Newcomb, S., 1895, "Tables of the Motion of the Earth on its Axis Around the Sun," *Astron. Papers Amer. Eph.*, Vol. 6, Part I.

TABLE 1—PATH OF THE UMBRAL SHADOW
TOTAL SOLAR ECLIPSE OF 2001 JUNE 21

Time UT	Northern Limit Lat.	Long.	Southern Limit Lat.	Long.	Centreline Lat.	Long.	Sun Alt °	Path Width km	Central Durat.
Limit	36°05′ S	50°19′ W	37°10′ S	49°48′ W	36°37′ S	50°03′ W	0	127	2m06s
10:40	29°38′ S	37°27′ W	31°52′ S	38°54′ W	30°43′ S	38°06′ W	12	140	2m34s
10:45	26°03′ S	30°57′ W	27°55′ S	31°28′ W	26°58′ S	31°11′ W	20	148	2m55s
10:50	23°35′ S	26°35′ W	25°20′ S	26°48′ W	24°27′ S	26°41′ W	25	155	3m11s
10:55	21°37′ S	23°10′ W	23°20′ S	23°13′ W	22°28′ S	23°11′ W	30	160	3m25s
11:00	19°58′ S	20°17′ W	21°40′ S	20°14′ W	20°49′ S	20°15′ W	34	165	3m38s
11:05	18°33′ S	17°46′ W	20°15′ S	17°39′ W	19°24′ S	17°42′ W	37	169	3m49s
11:10	17°19′ S	15°30′ W	19°01′ S	15°20′ W	18°10′ S	15°24′ W	40	173	3m59s
11:15	16°13′ S	13°25′ W	17°55′ S	13°13′ W	17°04′ S	13°19′ W	43	177	4m09s
11:20	15°15′ S	11°30′ W	16°57′ S	11°16′ W	16°06′ S	11°22′ W	45	180	4m17s
11:25	14°23′ S	09°40′ W	16°06′ S	09°26′ W	15°14′ S	9°33′ W	47	183	4m25s
11:30	13°36′ S	07°57′ W	15°20′ S	07°41′ W	14°28′ S	7°49′ W	49	187	4m32s
11:35	12°55′ S	06°17′ W	14°39′ S	06°01′ W	13°47′ S	6°09′ W	51	189	4m38s
11:40	12°18′ S	04°40′ W	14°03′ S	04°24′ W	13°10′ S	4°32′ W	52	192	4m44s
11:45	11°46′ S	03°06′ W	13°31′ S	02°50′ W	12°38′ S	2°58′ W	53	194	4m48s
11:50	11°18′ S	01°34′ W	13°04′ S	01°18′ W	12°11′ S	1°26′ W	54	196	4m52s
11:55	10°54′ S	00°03′ W	12°41′ S	00°13′ E	11°47′ S	0°06′ E	55	198	4m54s
12:00	10°34′ S	01°28′ E	12°21′ S	01°44′ E	11°27′ S	1°36′ E	55	199	4m56s
12:05	10°18′ S	02°58′ E	12°05′ S	03°14′ E	11°12′ S	3°06′ E	55	200	4m57s
12:10	10°06′ S	04°29′ E	11°54′ S	04°44′ E	11°00′ S	4°37′ E	55	200	4m56s
12:15	9°58′ S	06°01′ E	11°46′ S	06°15′ E	10°51′ S	6°08′ E	54	200	4m55s
12:20	9°53′ S	07°34′ E	11°41′ S	07°48′ E	10°47′ S	7°41′ E	54	200	4m53s
12:25	9°53′ S	09°09′ E	11°41′ S	09°23′ E	10°47′ S	9°15′ E	53	199	4m50s
12:30	9°57′ S	10°46′ E	11°45′ S	11°00′ E	10°51′ S	10°53′ E	51	197	4m46s
12:35	10°06′ S	12°27′ E	11°54′ S	12°40′ E	11°00′ S	12°33′ E	50	195	4m40s
12:40	10°19′ S	14°11′ E	12°07′ S	14°25′ E	11°13′ S	14°18′ E	48	193	4m34s
12:45	10°38′ S	16°01′ E	12°25′ S	16°14′ E	11°31′ S	16°07′ E	46	190	4m27s
12:50	11°02′ S	17°57′ E	12°49′ S	18°11′ E	11°55′ S	18°03′ E	44	186	4m19s
12:55	11°33′ S	20°00′ E	13°19′ S	20°15′ E	12°26′ S	20°07′ E	41	183	4m11s
13:00	12°11′ S	22°14′ E	13°57′ S	22°30′ E	13°04′ S	22°22′ E	39	179	4m01s
13:05	12°58′ S	24°40′ E	14°44′ S	24°59′ E	13°51′ S	24°49′ E	36	174	3m50s
13:10	13°56′ S	27°24′ E	15°43′ S	27°47′ E	14°49′ S	27°35′ E	32	170	3m38s
13:15	15°09′ S	30°34′ E	16°56′ S	31°03′ E	16°02′ S	30°47′ E	28	164	3m25s
13:20	16°43′ S	34°23′ E	18°33′ S	35°03′ E	17°38′ S	34°42′ E	23	158	3m09s
13:25	18°55′ S	39°27′ E	20°54′ S	40°32′ E	19°54′ S	39°57′ E	17	150	2m51s
13:30	23°07′ S	48°41′ E	—	—	24°42′ S	50°39′ E	5	136	2m20s
Limit	26°10′ S	55°24′ E	27°19′ S	55°01′ E	26°45′ S	55°13′ E	0	131	2m10s

TABLE 2—LOCAL CIRCUMSTANCES FOR
SOLAR ECLIPSE OF 2001 JUNE 21

Geographic Location	Eclipse Begins h:m	Maximum Eclipse h:m	Eclipse Ends h:m	Sun Alt °	Sun Az °	Ecl. Mag.	Ecl. Obs.	Dur. Total
ANGOLA								
Luanda	10:57	12:38	14:08	51	326	0.961	0.961	
ARGENTINA								
Buenos Aires	— r	11:01r	11:35	0	62	0.537	0.437	
BRAZIL								
Belo Horizonte	9:35	10:33	11:38	12	59	0.642	0.560	
Brasília	9:39	10:31	11:28	11	62	0.464	0.356	
Fortaleza	9:56	10:41	11:31	27	61	0.259	0.154	
Recife	9:45	10:42	11:47	28	58	0.442	0.332	
Rio de Janeiro	9:33	10:34	11:42	12	58	0.736	0.676	
São Paulo	— r	10:32	11:37	8	60	0.706	0.638	
CAMEROON								
Yaoundé	11:05	12:35	13:58	63	317	0.588	0.498	
DEM. REP. CONGO								
Kinshasa	11:07	12:45	14:12	52	319	0.823	0.787	
KENYA								
Nairobi	12:15	13:25	14:26	29	298	0.524	0.422	
MADAGASCAR								
Antananarivo	12:21	13:32	— s	10	299	0.900	0.882	
MOZAMBIQUE								
Maputo	11:50	13:12	14:22	21	311	0.784	0.737	
NIGERIA								
Ibadan	10:51	12:14	13:36	73	339	0.479	0.373	
Lagos	10:49	12:14	13:37	72	341	0.505	0.402	
REUNION								
St.-Denis	12:29	13:34	— s	2	296	0.854	0.823	
SOUTH AFRICA								
Cape Town	11:18	12:37	13:50	27	332	0.513	0.410	
Durban	11:46	13:06	14:15	20	314	0.677	0.604	
Johannesburg	11:40	13:04	14:17	25	316	0.735	0.675	
Pretoria	11:40	13:05	14:18	25	315	0.748	0.691	
SUDAN								
Khartoum	12:49	13:14	13:38	42	288	0.054	0.015	
TANZANIA								
Dar-es-Salaam	12:15	13:28	14:32	23	299	0.657	0.579	
URUGUAY								
Montevideo	— r	10:53r	11:37	0	62	0.689	0.617	
ZAMBIA								
Lusaka	11:42	13:11	14:27	31	310	1.013	1.000	3m14s
ZIMBABWE								
Harare	11:48	13:15	14:28	27	309	0.976	0.978	

All times are Universal Time.
"r" indicates eclipse in progress at sunrise. "s" indicates eclipse in progress at sunset.

TABLE 3—PATH OF THE ANTUMBRAL SHADOW OF THE ANNULAR SOLAR ECLIPSE OF 2001 DECEMBER 14

Time UT	Northern Limit Lat.	Long.	Southern Limit Lat.	Long.	Centreline Lat.	Long.	Sun Alt °	Path Width km	Central Durat.
Limit	30°49′ N	76°01′ E	29°22′ N	75°21′ E	30°05′ N	75°41′ E	0	171	3m08s
19:10	—	—	26°50′ N	79°08′ W	28°23′ N	79°23′ E	4	167	3m09s
19:15	23°11′ N	69°00′ W	21°33′ N	68°56′ W	22°21′ N	68°57′ W	17	153	3m14s
19:20	20°02′ N	63°37′ W	18°36′ N	63°50′ W	19°18′ N	63°43′ W	23	146	3m17s
19:25	17°39′ N	59°47′ W	16°20′ N	60°06′ W	16°59′ N	59°57′ W	29	141	3m19s
19:30	15°41′ N	56°43′ W	14°26′ N	57°06′ W	15°03′ N	56°54′ W	33	138	3m22s
19:35	13°59′ N	54°08′ W	12°47′ N	54°31′ W	13°23′ N	54°19′ W	37	135	3m25s
19:40	12°30′ N	51°51′ W	11°20′ N	52°16′ W	11°55′ N	52°03′ W	40	132	3m27s
19:45	11°09′ N	49°49′ W	10°01′ N	50°14′ W	10°35′ N	50°01′ W	44	130	3m29s
19:50	9°56′ N	47°57′ W	8°49′ N	48°22′ W	9°23′ N	48°09′ W	47	129	3m32s
19:55	8°50′ N	46°13′ W	7°44′ N	46°38′ W	8°17′ N	46°25′ W	49	127	3m34s
20:00	7°49′ N	44°36′ W	6°44′ N	45°00′ W	7°16′ N	44°48′ W	52	126	3m36s
20:05	6°53′ N	43°03′ W	5°48′ N	43°27′ W	6°20′ N	43°15′ W	54	125	3m38s
20:10	6°02′ N	41°35′ W	4°57′ N	41°59′ W	5°29′ N	41°47′ W	56	125	3m41s
20:15	5°14′ N	40°11′ W	4°10′ N	40°33′ W	4°42′ N	40°22′ W	58	124	3m43s
20:20	4°31′ N	38°48′ W	3°26′ N	39°10′ W	3°58′ N	38°59′ W	60	124	3m44s
20:25	3°51′ N	37°28′ W	2°46′ N	37°50′ W	3°18′ N	37°39′ W	62	124	3m46s
20:30	3°14′ N	36°10′ W	2°10′ N	36°30′ W	2°42′ N	36°20′ W	63	124	3m48s
20:35	2°41′ N	34°53′ W	1°36′ N	35°12′ W	2°08′ N	35°02′ W	64	124	3m49s
20:40	2°11′ N	33°36′ W	1°06′ N	33°55′ W	1°38′ N	33°45′ W	65	125	3m51s
20:45	1°44′ N	32°20′ W	0°38′ N	32°38′ W	1°11′ N	32°29′ W	66	125	3m52s
20:50	1°20′ N	31°04′ W	0°14′ N	31°21′ W	0°47′ N	31°12′ W	66	125	3m53s
20:55	0°59′ N	29°47′ W	0°08′ S	30°03′ W	0°25′ N	29°55′ W	66	126	3m53s
21:00	0°41′ N	28°30′ W	0°26′ S	28°45′ W	0°07′ N	28°38′ W	65	126	3m54s
21:05	0°26′ N	27°12′ W	0°42′ S	27°26′ W	0°08′ S	27°19′ W	65	127	3m54s
21:10	0°14′ N	25°53′ W	0°54′ S	26°06′ W	0°20′ S	26°00′ W	64	128	3m54s
21:15	0°05′ N	24°32′ W	1°04′ S	24°44′ W	0°29′ S	24°38′ W	63	128	3m54s
21:20	0°00′ S	23°09′ W	1°10′ S	23°21′ W	0°35′ S	23°15′ W	61	129	3m53s
21:25	0°02′ S	21°44′ W	1°13′ S	21°55′ W	0°38′ S	21°49′ W	60	130	3m53s
21:30	0°01′ S	20°16′ W	1°12′ S	20°25′ W	0°37′ S	20°21′ W	58	131	3m52s
21:35	0°05′ S	18°45′ W	1°08′ S	18°53′ W	0°32′ S	18°49′ W	56	132	3m50s
21:40	0°14′ N	17°09′ W	0°59′ S	17°16′ W	0°23′ S	17°13′ W	54	133	3m49s
21:45	0°28′ N	15°29′ W	0°47′ S	15°35′ W	0°10′ S	15°32′ W	51	134	3m47s
21:50	0°46′ N	13°42′ W	0°29′ S	13°48′ W	0°08′ N	13°45′ W	49	135	3m45s
21:55	1°10′ N	11°49′ W	0°07′ S	11°54′ W	0°32′ N	11°51′ W	46	137	3m43s
22:00	1°41′ N	09°46′ W	0°22′ N	09°51′ W	1°01′ N	09°49′ W	43	138	3m41s
22:05	2°18′ N	07°32′ W	0°58′ N	07°37′ W	1°38′ N	07°35′ W	40	140	3m38s
22:10	3°05′ N	05°04′ W	1°42′ N	05°09′ W	2°23′ N	05°06′ W	36	143	3m35s
22:15	4°03′ N	02°15′ W	2°37′ N	02°21′ W	3°20′ N	02°18′ W	32	146	3m32s
22:20	5°17′ N	98°57′ W	3°47′ N	99°06′ W	4°32′ N	99°02′ W	28	149	3m29s
22:25	6°56′ N	94°49′ W	5°20′ N	95°05′ W	6°07′ N	94°58′ W	22	154	3m25s
22:30	9°26′ N	88°56′ W	7°36′ N	89°32′ W	8°30′ N	89°15′ W	15	161	3m21s
Limit	14°59′ N	76°20′ W	13°27′ N	75°50′ W	14°13′ N	76°05′ W	0	177	3m13s

TABLE 4—LOCAL CIRCUMSTANCES FOR
SOLAR ECLIPSE OF 2001 DECEMBER 14

Geographic Location	Eclipse Begins h:m	Maximum Eclipse h:m	Eclipse Ends h:m	Sun Alt °	Sun Az °	Ecl. Mag.	Ecl. Obs.	Dur. Total
CANADA								
Hamilton, ON	21:11	21:44s	— s	0	238	0.224	0.121	
North York, ON	21:11	21:38s	— s	0	237	0.194	0.098	
Ottawa, ON	21:12	21:20s	— s	0	237	0.071	0.022	
Regina, SK	21:03	21:22	21:41	9	214	0.023	0.004	
Toronto, ON	21:11	21:41s	— s	0	238	0.208	0.109	
Vancouver, BC	20:24	20:45	21:06	17	189	0.024	0.004	
Victoria, BC	20:21	20:45	21:09	18	189	0.032	0.007	
Winnipeg, MB	21:06	21:35	22:02	6	223	0.058	0.017	
COLOMBIA								
Bogota	21:30	22:37	— s	2	247	0.689	0.601	
Cali	21:28	22:37	— s	4	246	0.687	0.598	
Medellín	21:27	22:37	— s	3	246	0.753	0.677	
COSTA RICA								
San Jose	21:14	22:33	— s	9	244	0.956	0.913	0m54s
ECUADOR								
Guayaquil	21:28	22:35	— s	10	247	0.571	0.464	
Quito	21:28	22:36	— s	8	247	0.609	0.508	
EL SALVADOR								
San Salvador	21:05	22:28	— s	13	242	0.840	0.784	
GUATEMALA								
Guatemala	21:02	22:27	23:37	14	241	0.801	0.736	
HONDURAS								
Tegucigalpa	21:08	22:29	— s	11	242	0.852	0.798	
JAMAICA								
Kingston	21:19	22:32	— s	0	246	0.867	0.816	
MEXICO								
Ciudad de Mexico	20:45	22:13	23:26	21	234	0.592	0.489	
Guadalajara	20:35	22:05	23:20	25	230	0.525	0.414	
Monterrey	20:45	22:05	23:14	20	230	0.438	0.320	
Puebla	20:47	22:15	23:28	20	235	0.610	0.509	
NETHERLANDS ANTILLES								
Willemstad, Curaca	21:29	22:10s	— s	0	246	0.571	0.464	
NICARAGUA								
Managua	21:10	22:31	— s	11	243	0.914	0.873	
PANAMA								
Panama City	21:21	22:35	— s	5	245	0.875	0.826	
PERU								
Lima	21:45	22:33	23:17	12	248	0.264	0.154	
PUERTO RICO								
San Juan	21:26	21:48s	— s	0	246	0.305	0.190	
UNITED STATES								
Akron, OH	21:11	21:59s	— s	0	239	0.287	0.174	
Albany, NY	21:13	21:21s	— s	0	238	0.082	0.028	
Allentown, PA	21:13	21:35s	— s	0	239	0.198	0.101	
Atlanta, GA	21:10	22:14	— s	2	240	0.410	0.291	
Austin, TX	20:53	22:04	23:06	15	231	0.362	0.244	

TABLE 4—LOCAL CIRCUMSTANCES FOR
SOLAR ECLIPSE OF 2001 DECEMBER 14 (continued)

Geographic Location	Eclipse Begins h:m	Maximum Eclipse h:m	Eclipse Ends h:m	Sun Alt °	Sun Az °	Ecl. Mag.	Ecl. Obs.	Dur. Total
UNITED STATES cont...								
Baltimore, MD	21:13	21:43s	— s	0	240	0.261	0.151	
Baton Rouge, LA	21:02	22:12	— s	9	236	0.416	0.297	
Birmingham, AL	21:08	22:12	— s	4	238	0.392	0.273	
Boise, ID	20:30	21:06	21:42	20	201	0.070	0.022	
Buffalo, NY	21:12	21:42s	— s	0	238	0.223	0.121	
Charleston, WV	21:11	22:07s	— s	0	241	0.342	0.224	
Chicago, IL	21:08	21:59	— s	3	235	0.228	0.125	
Cincinnati, OH	21:09	22:06	— s	1	239	0.302	0.188	
Cleveland, OH	21:11	21:58s	— s	0	239	0.278	0.166	
Columbia, SC	21:12	22:16	— s	0	242	0.437	0.318	
Columbus, OH	21:10	22:06	— s	0	240	0.300	0.186	
Dallas, TX	20:55	22:02	23:01	13	231	0.320	0.204	
Dayton, OH	21:10	22:05	— s	1	239	0.293	0.179	
Denver, CO	20:48	21:38	22:24	16	219	0.148	0.066	
Des Moines, IA	21:03	21:53	22:39	7	230	0.188	0.094	
Detroit, MI	21:10	22:01s	— s	0	239	0.257	0.148	
El Paso, TX	20:36	21:46	22:48	22	221	0.272	0.161	
Flint, MI	21:10	22:01	— s	0	238	0.240	0.134	
Grand Rapids, MI	21:09	21:59	— s	1	237	0.225	0.122	
Harrisburg, PA	21:13	21:42s	— s	0	240	0.247	0.140	
Hartford, CT	21:13	21:20s	— s	0	239	0.064	0.019	
Honolulu, HI	18:08	19:27	21:01	28	133	0.842	0.788	
Houston, TX	20:56	22:08	23:10	13	233	0.393	0.274	
Indianapolis, IN	21:08	22:04	— s	2	237	0.277	0.165	
Jackson, MS	21:04	22:11	— s	8	236	0.386	0.267	
Jacksonville, FL	21:12	22:20	— s	1	242	0.511	0.398	
Kansas City, MO	21:01	21:56	22:46	9	230	0.222	0.120	
Lansing, MI	21:09	22:00	— s	0	238	0.238	0.133	
Lincoln, NE	21:00	21:50	22:37	10	227	0.180	0.088	
Little Rock, AR	21:02	22:05	— s	9	234	0.319	0.203	
Los Angeles, CA	20:05	21:10	22:12	29	202	0.199	0.102	
Louisville, KY	21:09	22:07	— s	2	238	0.308	0.193	
Madison, WI	21:07	21:56	— s	4	233	0.195	0.099	
Memphis, TN	21:05	22:07	— s	7	236	0.330	0.214	
Miami, FL	21:14	22:25	— s	1	244	0.633	0.535	
Milwaukee, WI	21:08	21:57	— s	3	235	0.207	0.108	
Minneapolis, MN	21:05	21:48	22:29	6	229	0.140	0.061	
Montgomery, AL	21:08	22:14	— s	4	239	0.421	0.302	
Nashville, TN	21:08	22:09	— s	4	238	0.339	0.222	
New Haven, CT	21:13	21:21s	— s	0	239	0.079	0.026	
New Orleans, LA	21:04	22:14	— s	8	237	0.437	0.319	
New York, NY	21:13	21:28s	— s	0	239	0.142	0.062	
Norfolk, VA	21:14	21:47s	— s	0	241	0.312	0.196	
Oklahoma City, OK	20:56	21:57	22:52	13	229	0.264	0.154	
Omaha, NE	21:01	21:51	22:37	9	228	0.178	0.086	
Orlando, FL	21:13	22:22	— s	1	243	0.555	0.446	
Philadelphia, PA	21:13	21:34s	— s	0	239	0.192	0.097	
Phoenix, AZ	20:23	21:29	22:30	26	212	0.218	0.117	
Pittsburgh, PA	21:12	21:54s	— s	0	240	0.296	0.182	
Portland, OR	20:15	20:48	21:21	21	190	0.057	0.016	
Providence, RI	21:13	21:14s	— s	0	239	0.003	0.000	
Raleigh, NC	21:13	22:01s	— s	0	241	0.394	0.275	
Richmond, VA	21:13	21:51s	— s	0	241	0.326	0.210	
Riverside, CA	20:07	21:13	22:15	29	203	0.201	0.104	

TABLE 4—LOCAL CIRCUMSTANCES FOR
SOLAR ECLIPSE OF 2001 DECEMBER 14 (continued)

Geographic Location	Eclipse Begins h:m	Maximum Eclipse h:m	Eclipse Ends h:m	Sun Alt °	Sun Az °	Ecl. Mag.	Ecl. Obs.	Dur. Total
UNITED STATES cont...								
Rochester, NY	21:12	21:36s	— s	0	238	0.190	0.095	
Sacramento, CA	20:02	20:56	21:49	27	194	0.137	0.059	
St. Paul, MN	21:05	21:48	22:29	5	229	0.142	0.062	
St. Louis, MO	21:05	22:02	— s	6	234	0.264	0.154	
St. Petersburg, FL	21:12	22:22	— s	3	242	0.56	0.451	
Salem, OR	20:12	20:48	21:23	21	190	0.064	0.019	
Salt Lake City, UT	20:35	21:21	22:04	20	209	0.109	0.042	
San Antonio, TX	20:51	22:04	23:07	16	231	0.373	0.255	
San Diego, CA	20:06	21:15	22:20	30	204	0.221	0.119	
San Francisco, CA	19:57	20:54	21:49	28	193	0.150	0.067	
San Jose, CA	19:58	20:56	21:52	28	194	0.155	0.071	
Seattle, WA	20:22	20:48	21:14	19	191	0.036	0.008	
Springfield, IL	21:06	22:01	— s	5	234	0.248	0.14	
Syracuse, NY	21:12	21:30s	— s	0	238	0.153	0.069	
Tallahassee, FL	21:10	22:18	— s	3	241	0.483	0.367	
Tampa, FL	21:12	22:22	— s	2	242	0.558	0.449	
Toledo, OH	21:10	22:03	— s	0	239	0.265	0.155	
Topeka, KS	21:00	21:55	22:44	10	229	0.215	0.114	
Tulsa, OK	20:58	21:59	22:53	11	230	0.263	0.153	
Washington, DC	21:13	21:45s	— s	0	240	0.275	0.164	
VENEZUELA								
Caracas	21:31	22:10s	— s	0	247	0.531	0.419	
Maracaibo	21:28	22:24s	— s	0	246	0.743	0.665	

All times are Universal Time.
"r" indicates eclipse in progress at sunrise. "s" indicates eclipse in progress at sunset.

TABLE 5—CRATER IMMERSION AND EMERSION TIMES FOR THE
TOTAL LUNAR ECLIPSES OF 2001 JANUARY 9 AND JULY 5

2001 JANUARY 9

Immersion		Emersion	
UT	Crater	UT	Crater
18:45	Grimaldi	21:02	Aristarchus
18:49	Billy	21:05	Plato
18:57	Kepler	21:06	Grimaldi
18:57	Campanus	21:10	Kepler
18:59	Aristarchus	21:12	Aristoteles
19:04	Tycho	21:13	Pytheas
19:06	Copernicus	21:13	Billy
19:09	Pytheas	21:13	Timocharis
19:14	Timocharis	21:15	Eudoxus
19:22	Manilius	21:17	Copernicus
19:23	Dionysius	21:25	Campanus
19:26	Menelaus	21:27	Manilius
19:26	Plato	21:29	Menelaus
19:29	Plinius	21:33	Plinius
19:32	Goclenius	21:35	Tycho
19:33	Eudoxus	21:36	Dionysius
19:35	Aristoteles	21:40	Proclus
19:36	Taruntius	21:45	Taruntius
19:37	Langrenus	21:50	Goclenius
19:39	Proclus	21:54	Langrenus

2001 JULY 5

Immersion		Emersion	
UT	Crater	UT	Crater
13:45	Aristarchus	14:37	Grimaldi
13:54	Plato	15:09	Kepler
14:00	Pytheas	15:13	Dionysius
14:00	Timocharis	15:17	Copernicus
14:01	Kepler	15:23	Aristarchus
14:04	Aristoteles	15:25	Taruntius
14:07	Eudoxus	15:29	Pytheas
14:10	Copernicus	15:34	Manilius
14:13	Grimaldi	15:38	Timocharis
14:24	Manilius	15:39	Menelaus
14:27	Menelaus	15:41	Plinius
14:33	Plinius	15:49	Proclus
14:46	Proclus	15:55	Plato
14:53	Dionysius	16:00	Eudoxus
15:09	Taruntius	16:02	Aristoteles

FIGURE 1—TOTAL LUNAR ECLIPSE OF 2001 JANUARY 9

Geocentric Conjunction = 20:18:50.3 UT   J.D. = 2451919.346416
Greatest Eclipse = 20:20:36.3 UT   J.D. = 2451919.347642

Penumbral Magnitude = 2.18677   P. Radius = 1.3203°   Gamma = 0.37203
Umbral Magnitude = 1.19438   U. Radius = 0.7673°   Axis = 0.38036°

Saros Series = 134   Member = 26 of 73

Sun at Greatest Eclipse
(Geocentric Coordinates)

RA = 19h25m03.4s
Dec = –21°59'58.5"
S.D. = 00°16'15.9"
H.P. = 00°00'08.9"

Moon at Greatest Eclipse
(Geocentric Coordinates)

RA = 07h25m07.9s
Dec = +22°22'46.4"
S.D. = 00°16'43.0"
H.P. = 01°01'21.1"

Eclipse Semi-Durations

Penumbral = 02h37m02s
Umbral =   01h38m30s
Total =   00h31m01s

Eph. = Newcomb/ILE
ΔT =   64.3 s

F. Espenak, NASA/GSFC - 2000 Apr 27

Eclipse Contacts

P1 = 17:43:34 UT
U1 = 18:42:06 UT
U2 = 19:49:36 UT
U3 = 20:51:38 UT
U4 = 21:59:07 UT
P4 = 22:57:37 UT

FIGURE 2—TOTAL SOLAR ECLIPSE OF 2001 JUNE 21

Geocentric Conjunction = 11:57:53.4 UT   J.D. = 2452081.998535
Greatest Eclipse = 12:03:45.6 UT   J.D. = 2452082.002611

Eclipse Magnitude = 1.04954   Gamma = –0.57010

Saros Series = 127   Member = 57 of 82

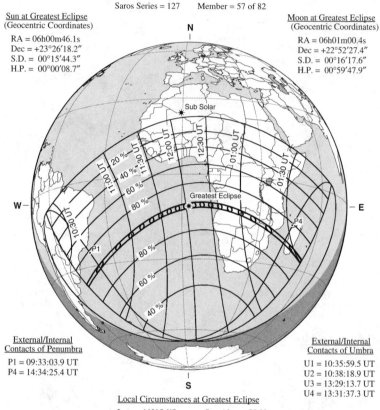

Sun at Greatest Eclipse
(Geocentric Coordinates)

RA = 06h00m46.1s
Dec = +23°26′18.2″
S.D. = 00°15′44.3″
H.P. = 00°00′08.7″

Moon at Greatest Eclipse
(Geocentric Coordinates)

RA = 06h01m00.4s
Dec = +22°52′27.4″
S.D. = 00°16′17.6″
H.P. = 00°59′47.9″

External/Internal
Contacts of Penumbra

P1 = 09:33:03.9 UT
P4 = 14:34:25.4 UT

External/Internal
Contacts of Umbra

U1 = 10:35:59.5 UT
U2 = 10:38:18.9 UT
U3 = 13:29:13.7 UT
U4 = 13:31:37.3 UT

Local Circumstances at Greatest Eclipse

Lat. = 11°15.1′S   Sun Alt. = 55.2°
Long. = 002°43.7′E   Sun Azm. = 354.8°
Path Width = 200.0 km   Duration = 04m56.5s

Ephemeris & Constants

Eph. = Newcomb/ILE
ΔT =   64.5 s
k1 = 0.2724880
k2 = 0.2722810
Δb = 0.0″   Δl = 0.0″

Geocentric Libration
(Optical + Physical)

l = –3.83°
b = 0.76°
c = 1.61°

Brown Lun. No. = 971

0   1000   2000   3000   4000   5000
Kilometers

F. Espenak, NASA/GSFC - 2000 Apr 27

FIGURE 3—THE PATH OF THE 2001 JUNE 21 TOTAL SOLAR ECLISPE THROUGH AFRICA

Courtesy of *Total Solar Eclipse of 2001 June 21*, NASA TP 1999-209484, by F. Espanak and Jay Anderson.

FIGURE 4—PARTIAL LUNAR ECLIPSE OF 2001 JULY 5

Geocentric Conjunction = 14:55:04.9 UT   J.D. = 2452096.121584
Greatest Eclipse = 14:55:18.8 UT   J.D. = 2452096.121746

Penumbral Magnitude = 1.57336   P. Radius = 1.2006°   Gamma = −0.72874
Umbral Magnitude = 0.49949   U. Radius = 0.6658°   Axis = 0.66601°

Saros Series = 139   Member = 21 of 81

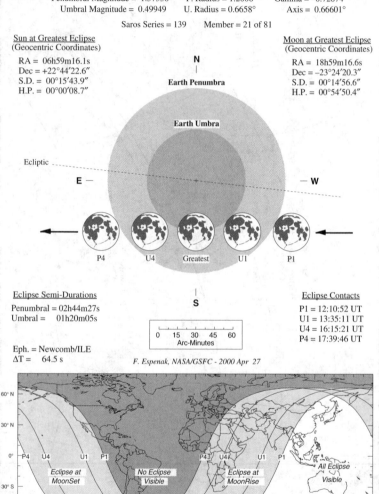

Sun at Greatest Eclipse
(Geocentric Coordinates)

RA = 06h59m16.1s
Dec = +22°44′22.6″
S.D. = 00°15′43.9″
H.P. = 00°00′08.7″

N

Earth Penumbra

Earth Umbra

Ecliptic

E —

— W

Moon at Greatest Eclipse
(Geocentric Coordinates)

RA = 18h59m16.6s
Dec = −23°24′20.3″
S.D. = 00°14′56.6″
H.P. = 00°54′50.4″

P4   U4   Greatest   U1   P1

Eclipse Semi-Durations

Penumbral = 02h44m27s
Umbral =   01h20m05s

Eph. = Newcomb/ILE
ΔT =   64.5 s

S

| 0 | 15 | 30 | 45 | 60 |
Arc-Minutes

Eclipse Contacts

P1 = 12:10:52 UT
U1 = 13:35:11 UT
U4 = 16:15:21 UT
P4 = 17:39:46 UT

F. Espenak, NASA/GSFC - 2000 Apr 27

Eclipse at MoonSet

No Eclipse Visible

Eclipse at MoonRise

All Eclipse Visible

FIGURE 5—ANNULAR SOLAR ECLIPSE OF 2001 DECEMBER 14

Geocentric Conjunction = 20:44:53.4 UT   J.D. = 2452258.364507
Greatest Eclipse = 20:51:56.4 UT   J.D. = 2452258.369402

Eclipse Magnitude = 0.96811   Gamma = 0.40880

Saros Series = 132   Member = 45 of 71

Sun at Greatest Eclipse
(Geocentric Coordinates)
RA = 17h29m14.1s
Dec = –23°15′02.0″
S.D. = 00°16′14.9″
H.P. = 00°00′08.9″

Moon at Greatest Eclipse
(Geocentric Coordinates)
RA = 17h29m29.4s
Dec = –22°52′06.1″
S.D. = 00°15′30.3″
H.P. = 00°56′54.2″

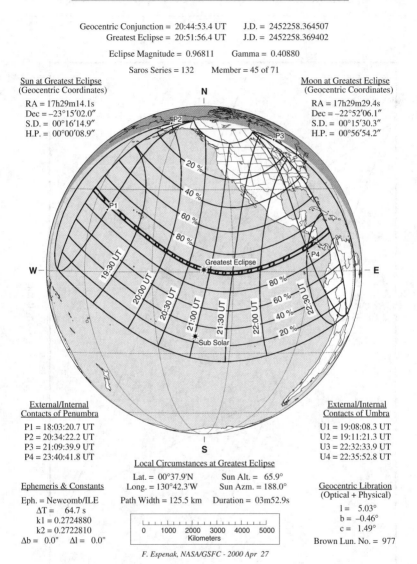

External/Internal
Contacts of Penumbra
P1 = 18:03:20.7 UT
P2 = 20:34:22.2 UT
P3 = 21:09:39.9 UT
P4 = 23:40:41.8 UT

External/Internal
Contacts of Umbra
U1 = 19:08:08.3 UT
U2 = 19:11:21.3 UT
U3 = 22:32:33.9 UT
U4 = 22:35:52.8 UT

Ephemeris & Constants
Eph. = Newcomb/ILE
ΔT =   64.7 s
k1 = 0.2724880
k2 = 0.2722810
Δb = 0.0″   Δl = 0.0″

Local Circumstances at Greatest Eclipse
Lat. = 00°37.9′N   Sun Alt. = 65.9°
Long. = 130°42.3′W   Sun Azm. = 188.0°
Path Width = 125.5 km   Duration = 03m52.9s

Geocentric Libration
(Optical + Physical)
l = 5.03°
b = –0.46°
c = 1.49°
Brown Lun. No. = 977

```
|  |  |  |  |  |  |
0   1000  2000  3000  4000  5000
        Kilometers
```

F. Espenak, NASA/GSFC - 2000 Apr 27

FIGURE 6—THE PATH OF THE 2001 DECEMBER 14 ANNULAR SOLAR ECLISPE THROUGH CENTRAL AMERICA

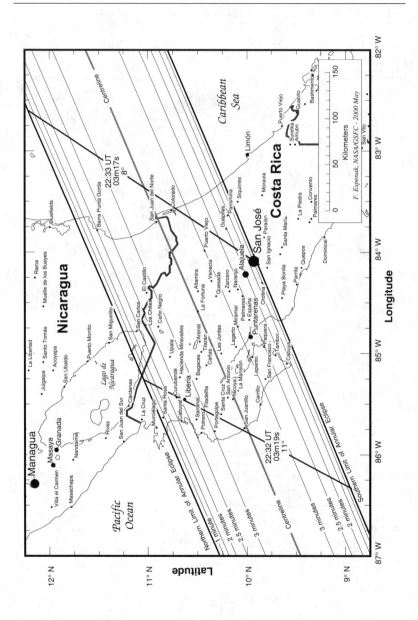

FIGURE 7—PENUMBRAL LUNAR ECLIPSE OF 2001 DECEMBER 30

Geocentric Conjunction = 10:32:53.3 UT   J.D. = 2452273.939506
Greatest Eclipse = 10:29:19.1 UT   J.D. = 2452273.937027

Penumbral Magnitude = 0.91866   P. Radius = 1.2833°   Gamma = 1.07323
Umbral Magnitude = −0.11035   U. Radius = 0.7303°   Axis = 1.05828°

Saros Series = 144   Member = 15 of 71

Sun at Greatest Eclipse
(Geocentric Coordinates)

RA = 18h38m16.2s
Dec = −23°08′50.8″
S.D. = 00°16′15.9″
H.P. = 00°00′08.9″

N

Moon at Greatest Eclipse
(Geocentric Coordinates)

RA = 06h38m07.6s
Dec = +24°12′19.0″
S.D. = 00°16′07.4″
H.P. = 00°59′10.2″

P4   Greatest   P1

E —   — **W**

Ecliptic

Earth Umbra

Earth Penumbra

S

Eclipse Semi-Durations

Penumbral = 02h03m51s

Eclipse Contacts

P1 = 08:25:31 UT
P4 = 12:33:13 UT

0   15   30   45   60
Arc-Minutes

Eph. = Newcomb/ILE
ΔT = 64.7 s

F. Espenak, NASA/GSFC - 2000 Apr 27

60° N

30° N

0°

30° S

60° S

P4   P1   P4   P1

All Eclipse Visible   *Eclipse at MoonSet*   *No Eclipse Visible*   *Eclipse at MoonRise*

180° W   120° W   60° W   0°   60° E   120° E   180° E

Longitude

Latitude

FIGURE 8—THE PATH OF THE 2002 DECEMBER 4 TOTAL SOLAR ECLISPE THROUGH AFRICA

Courtesy of *Total Solar Eclipse of 2001 June 21*, NASA TP 1999-209484, by F. Espanak and Jay Anderson.

ECLIPSE WEATHER PROSPECTS
BY JAY ANDERSON

2001 JUNE 21 SOLAR ECLIPSE OVERVIEW

The interior of southern Africa is a vast plateau lying about 1000 m above sea level with a cool and pleasant winter climate. Surrounding this plateau is a jumble of hilly and mountainous terrain ending abruptly in a narrow coastal belt that hugs the Atlantic Ocean on one side and the Indian Ocean on the other.

Mean June daytime cloud cover in percent over southern Africa. The data for this chart were collected from satellite imagery on a $1° × 1°$ grid over a 13-year period ending in 1994. Lighter areas represent lower mean cloud amounts and thus more favourable viewing conditions for the eclipse

Weather prospects decrease along the eclipse track, with nearly perfect conditions in Angola and western Zambia, good possibilities in eastern Zambia and Zimbabwe, and poor chances in Mozambique. The island of Madagascar repeats this trend, with excellent prospects on the western side of the island and poorer chances in the east where the moist trade winds from the Indian Ocean bring a rainy environment.

2001 JUNE 21 SOLAR ECLIPSE IN DETAIL

Angola

In Angola, a narrow coastal plain rises rapidly to a broad plateau lying above 1000 m altitude. The two regions—plain and plateau—have distinct temperature regimes, but are equally blessed with fine eclipse skies in June. During the winter months there is little flow from the Atlantic over the Angolan plateau, and skies are clear with little or no precipitation. While climatological statistics are in short supply due to the decades-long civil war, measurements from satellite suggest that the best skies along the eclipse track are to be expected on the plateau. The mean cloudiness in this region is less than 10% and occasionally below 5%. Much of this may be academic, since the ongoing Angolan civil war makes travel into the interior hazardous, in spite of a U.N.-brokered cease-fire.

Zambia

Access to the centreline is relatively easy in Zambia. The highway from Lusaka west to Mongu (M9) stays within the umbral shadow for over 300 km, although well to the south of the centreline. This route is described as being in "protracted repair" by one guide book, but is the main route to Kafue National Park and the western half of the country. Two other highways head north from Lusaka to cross the centreline in two places. Landless Corner, 69 km north of the capital, lies just beyond the middle of the shadow path on the Great North Road. To the northeast, the Great East Road to Chipata crosses the centreline at about 60 km distance. Both of these roads are in excellent condition.

Winter months in Zambia are virtually rainless. The circulation associated with the anticyclones to the south dries the midlevels of the atmosphere and suppresses any tendency to form rain-bearing clouds. The southeast trade winds, blowing first across Madagascar and then Mozambique, carry little moisture into the midcontinent in June, blocked in large part by the Eastern Highlands.

Cloud reaches the eclipse track from the east, spreading into the interior along the course of the Zambezi River. The cloud tends to be high-based and thin, unless a fresh disturbance has just arrived from the coast. Satellite pictures show that small patches of morning cloudiness tend to expand and become more convective as the day progresses, sometimes bringing an extensive blanket of thin cumulus cloud through which the Sun is often visible. The cloud tends to have numerous holes, which will greatly aid those who are mobile and for whom information from other sites is available.

The Zambezi cloudiness tends to slosh around in the middle of the Zambian plains, moving slowly to the south and west over a period of days and gradually dissipating. Conditions may be similar for several days in a row. Lusaka and the Great North Road tend to mark the western edge of the heaviest cloudiness, so movement should usually be planned toward destinations farther to the west. Eclipse sites in western Zambia are virtually guaranteed clear skies, although travel in the area is more difficult.

Temperatures on the Zambia-Zimbabwe plateau are pleasant but cool in June, with daytime highs generally in the low- to mid-20s and morning lows between 5°C and 10°C. The dry air and generally cloudless skies should bring a significant drop in ground temperatures during the eclipse, especially on the plateau west of Lusaka.

Zimbabwe

After crossing the Zambezi, the umbral path is shared by Zimbabwe and Mozambique for 400 km until it passes entirely into Mozambique near Changara. The south side of the shared track and most of the centreline belong to Zimbabwe, while the north half crosses the length of western Mozambique. In Zimbabwe the track traverses the lip of the Zambezi escarpment, looking down on Lago de Cahora Bassa in Mozambique. The heights of the escarpment are quite substantial, rising more than 1500 m above the river valley in the Mavuradonha Mountains north of Centenary. Perhaps the greatest limitation to Zimbabwean sites may be the lack of convenient routes for movement to sunnier locations should the selected site suddenly turn cloudy, since all roads tend to run across rather than along the track.

For the most part, the weather through northern Zimbabwe is similar to that in eastern Zambia. Cloudiness is only slightly higher and the percent of possible sunshine correspondingly lower by a few percentage points. June precipitation is higher than in Zambia, but barely so (less than 1 mm at Mount Darwin), at least in the vicinity of the shadow track. Because the Zimbabwean half of the track lies on the heights of the Zambezi escarpment, it escapes the larger part of the cloud that traverses the valley below and which gives a distinctly higher cloud cover to the Mozambican half of the track.

From a climatological point of view, the best sites in Zimbabwe are those in the west, close to the Zambia border. In this area, Kariba and Karoi, both just outside the path of totality, show 82% and 76% of the maximum possible sunshine respectively. Slightly farther along the track, Mount Darwin reports 74%, while Tete (Mozambique), much lower in the valley and farther east, reports a meagre 58%.

Mozambique

Mozambique is the cloudiest location from which to attempt to see the eclipse, but access to the track is relatively easy in western sections. The highway from Blantyre in Malawi to Harare (through the Tete corridor) is well travelled and in good condition, allowing easy access to the eclipse. In the east near the delta of the Zambezi, the highway from Beira to Quelimane reaches the centreline just south of the river. This area has been heavily damaged by recent floods and is a challenging route to the track.

The climate of Mozambique is primarily a lowland one, with higher precipitation, temperature, and cloud cover than the inland plateau. Cloud statistics favour areas near the coast, with lighter cloud in Quelimane and Beira than in Tete. Average sunshine is 8.4 hours per day at Beira, on the coast south of the track, but declines to 6.5 hours per day at Tete, 420 km inland. Satellite images show that most cloud in the area seems to form over the land, with much sunnier conditions over the waters along the coast.

Madagascar

Exotic Madagascar, lying in the path of the Indian Ocean trade winds, would seem to be poorly served for the eclipse observer, but its mountainous terrain blocks the moisture-laden easterly flow and forms a delightful pocket of clear skies on the southwest coast. Much of the moisture is trapped in the lower levels of the east coast, and even the central highlands, near Ihosy, offer fairly good weather prospects.

The centre of the eclipse comes ashore north of Morombe, into a landscape of dry scrub forest and occasional rivers. The town, small and dusty with a bustling beach waterfront, lies far enough south of the central track that the loss of time might be a concern (17 s), but the pleasant surroundings and supporting infrastructure are likely to make it a more attractive spot than nearby Ambahikily.

Ambahikily lies on the south side of the Mangoky River, where the road from Toliara to Morombe reaches its most northerly point, a few kilometres from the centreline. Open spaces are at a premium, but there are a number of sites in and around the village that will lend themselves to a good view of totality. It will be difficult to follow the eclipse right to the horizon, so those dedicated to seeing as close to fourth contact as possible should remain at the beach in Morombe.

Sunshine records for Toliara, on the west coast, promise an average of 9.2 hours per day in June, 86% of the maximum possible, bettered only by the exceptionally dry conditions in Zambia and Angola. The fact that the eclipse comes late in June is also an advantage, for July is an even drier month on the island, and the statistics for June probably slightly overestimate the cloudiness that is likely on eclipse day.

The prospects are not so bright for the windward side of the island's mountain backbone. Cloudiness is common, with over 15% of observations at eclipse time reporting precipitation. The percent of possible sunshine has declined to 66% at Fort Dauphin and the frequency of broken or greater cloudiness is nearly 50%. This high frequency of broken cloudiness is further aggravated by the low sun angle, less than 10°, which further increases the chances of the eclipse view being blocked. With only a day needed to reach the much more suitable conditions in western Madagascar, it is likely that the southeast will not appeal to many travellers.

2001 DECEMBER 14 ANNULAR ECLIPSE

The weather of Nicaragua and Costa Rica is strongly influenced by the northeasterly trade winds that carry moisture-laden air from the Caribbean Sea onto the land. The mountainous central backbone of the country intercepts these winds, forcing the air upward where it cools and becoming saturated. Because of the interaction of the wind and topography, the middle elevations of the Caribbean-facing slopes have an annual precipitation that exceeds 4000 mm.

The eastern slopes have two rainy seasons, one from June to August and a second in November and December. Mornings typically begin with several hours of sunshine, but as the land warms and the winds increase, it then begins to cloud over and rain for the afternoon. More ominously, from September to February, major storms, called "temporales del Atlantico," occasionally buffet the slopes, bringing several days of continuous rain. Hurricanes are rare at Costa Rica's latitude but slightly more likely in Nicaragua.

Fortunately for this eclipse, a quite different climatology persists on the Pacific side of the Cordillera. Here, the northeast winds are moving downhill after losing their moisture on the Atlantic slopes; the air is drier with fewer clouds to block the Sun. The table below shows that Puntarenas in the west is much less cloudy than Limon on the Atlantic coast, as is Managua in comparison to Bluefields. Satellite cloud measurements show that the trend continues toward the Pacific coast. In contrast to the east side of the mountains, the rainy season in the west comes to an end in November, and December is in the early stages of the winter dry season.

Distant hurricanes can influence the weather on the Pacific coast, by reversing the normal tradewind flow so that west coast winds now blow uphill and mimic the cloud and rain patterns described above for the east coast. These "temporales del Pacifico" are uncommon but can last for two days or more.

The dynamic climatology of Costa Rica suggests that eclipse chasers should head for the Pacific coast for the best weather prospects. Exactly where will depend on personal preferences, for many observers believe that an annular eclipse is best seen from the edge of the track, where beading phenomena are much more pronounced. Satellite observations show that sunshine is most abundant in the northern part of Costa Rica's Pacific coast, likely because of the additional influence of coastal mountains to the south. Those most interested in Baily's beads should head for the north limit of the track on the Pacific coast where the very best prospects are to be found.

Location	Clear	Percent frequency of			Percent of observations with rain
		Scattered	Broken	Overcast	
Costa Rica					
Limon	2.6	16.9	19.7	60.8	18.9
Puntarenas	28.3	26.5	32.9	12.3	3.3
Nicaragua					
Bluefields	0	28.5	33.3	38.2	9.9
Managua	2.7	44.3	34.4	18.7	2.9
Panama					
David	0	42.9	18.7	38.5	32.0

Climatological statistics for selected sites along the eclipse track at 6:00 p.m. local standard time. Scattered cloud occupies 1/10 to 5/10 of the sky, broken, 6/10 to 9/10.

VIEWING A SOLAR ECLIPSE—A WARNING

Solar eclipses are among the most widely publicized and observed celestial events. It is essential to be aware of the visual danger associated with a solar eclipse. The safety rule is simple but not widely appreciated: **Never look at the dazzling surface of the Sun, either directly with the unaided eyes or through binoculars or a telescope.** To do so one risks permanent partial blindness, and this can occur almost instantly in the case of telescopic viewing. Viewing our Sun is just as dangerous on any clear day, but at the time of an eclipse people have a reason to want to look at it—and often resort to dangerous methods.

A **direct view of the Sun is safe only if a suitable filter is used in a proper manner.** In the case of binoculars or a telescope, the filter must be one that attaches *securely* to the *front* end of the instrument, never one that attaches to the eyepiece end (the heat developed near the eyepiece can shatter such a filter).

Filters specifically designed for solar viewing include aluminized Mylar and glass filters plated with a slightly transparent, metallic film. Such filters may be purchased at telescope supply stores. Shade #14 (no other shade) rectangular welder's glass may be used; however, since these filters are of low optical quality, they are useful only for views not involving binoculars or a telescope. All of these are commercial items and cannot be replaced with ordinary household items. For example, layers of photographic colour film, coloured glass, stacked sunglasses, crossed polarizers, smoked glass, or photographic neutral density filters must never be used. Although one may devise a combination that dims the *visible* sunlight to a comfortable level, the make-shift filter may be quite transparent in the infrared part of the solar spectrum, and this invisible radiation will damage the retina of the observer's eye. For the same reason, one must never rely on clouds or heavy atmospheric haze to dim the solar image when using a telescope. Two layers of fully exposed and developed, silver-based, black and white photographic film provides adequate protection, but many modern films, including all colour films, are based on dyes that do not provide protection in the infrared. Thus it is best to avoid using filters made of photographic film.

One of the simplest, safest, and least known ways to observe the partial phases of a solar eclipse is *pinhole mirror projection*. Take a small pocket mirror and, with masking tape, cover all but a small section of the mirror's surface. The shape and size of the small opening are not critical, but a square about 6 mm on a side works well. Prop the mirror up on a sunny window sill and orient the mirror so the reflected sunlight shines on the ceiling or a wall of the room—but not directly into anyone's eyes! The spot of light on the viewing surface will be a *pinhole image* of the solar disk. The mirror has a great advantage over the usual "pinhole-in-a-box arrangement" in that the image can be aimed across a substantial distance to a convenient viewing screen. The greater the projection distance, the larger, but dimmer, will be the Sun's image. The size of the mirror aperture should be adjusted for the best compromise between image brightness and image sharpness. With this simple device, the progress of a solar eclipse can be viewed in complete safety by a group of children in a darkened room.

A sharper and brighter image of the solar disk may be projected onto a white viewing screen placed 30 cm or 40 cm behind the eyepiece of binoculars or a small telescope (the telescope aperture should be stopped down to about 50 mm in order to limit the intensity of sunlight passing through the instrument, and the viewing screen should be shielded from direct sunlight). However, one must *not* look through the instrument when aiming it, and, especially if children are present, a physical barrier should be used to prevent anyone from attempting to look into the eyepiece. If the telescope has a finderscope, it should be either covered or removed.

OCCULTATIONS BY THE MOON

The Moon often passes between Earth and a star, an event called an *occultation*. During an occultation a star suddenly disappears as the east limb of the Moon crosses the line between the star and the observer. The star reappears from behind the west limb some time later. Because the Moon moves through an angle about equal to its own diameter every hour, the longest time for an occultation is about an hour. The time is shorter if the occultation is not central. Occultations are equivalent to total solar eclipses, except they are eclipses of stars other than our own.

Since observing occultations is rather easy, amateur astronomers should try this activity. The slow, majestic drift of the Moon in its orbit is an interesting part of such observations, and the disappearance or reappearance of a star at the Moon's limb is a remarkable sight, particularly when it occurs as a *graze* near the Moon's northern or southern limb. During a graze a star may disappear and reappear several times in succession as mountains and valleys in the Moon's polar regions drift by it. On rarer occasions the Moon occults a planet.

Lunar occultation and graze observations are used to refine our knowledge of the Moon's orbit, the shape of the lunar profile, and the fundamental star coordinate system. These observations complement those made by other techniques, such as laser-ranging and photographs. Improved knowledge of the lunar profile is useful in determinations of the Sun's diameter from solar eclipse records. Occultation observations are also useful for detecting double stars and measuring their separations. Binaries with separations as small as 0.02″ have been discovered visually during grazes. Doubles with separations in this range are useful for filling the gap between doubles that can be directly resolved visually and those whose duplicity has been discovered spectroscopically.

Observations

The **International Lunar Occultation Centre (ILOC)** analyzes lunar occultation observations and is the world clearing house for such observations. Anyone interested in pursuing a systematic program of lunar occultation observations should write to the ILOC (address on the inside front cover) for their booklet *Guide to Lunar Occultation Observations*.

Observers in North America should also contact the **International Occultation Timing Association (IOTA)**, 2760 SW Jewell Ave., Topeka, KS 66611-1614, USA; email: iota@inlandnet.net. IOTA provides predictions and coordination services for occultation observers. Detailed predictions for any grazing occultation are available ($1.50 U.S. each; free by email); instructions explaining the use of predictions are also available ($5.00 U.S.). Annual membership in IOTA is $30 U.S. in North America, $35 U.S. overseas. Less expensive online rates are available. Membership includes free graze predictions, descriptive materials, and a subscription to *Occultation Newsletter* (available separately for $20 U.S. in North America, $25 overseas). IOTA's web address is http://www.lunar-occultations.com/iota.

For observers in the southwestern Pacific (New Zealand, Australia, Papua New Guinea, and nearby areas), The Royal Astronomical Society of New Zealand (RASNZ) provides occultation data (total lunar, lunar grazing, planetary, and Jupiter satellite), plus comprehensive instructions for new observers. See the RASNZ web site: http://occsec.wellington-net.nz/sitemap.htm.

The main information required in a lunar occultation observation is the time of the event and the observer's location. Supplementary data include the seeing conditions, telescope size, timing method, estimate of the observer's reaction time and the accuracy of the timing, and whether or not the reaction time correction has been applied. The timing should be accurate to 0.5 s or better (a shortwave radio time signal and tape recorder provide a simple, permanent time record; but a video record provides higher accuracy). The observer's longitude, latitude, and altitude should be reported to the nearest tenth of a second of arc and 10 m, respectively, and should be accurate to at least 0.5" or 16 m. These can be determined from either GPS measurements (10 minutes of position averaging and an unobstructed view of the sky above 15° altitude are needed) or a suitable topographical map. For Canada the maps are available from the Canada Map Office, 615 Booth Street, Ottawa, ON, K1A 0E9. In the United States (except Alaska) write to U.S. Geological Survey, Map Sales, Box 25286, Denver, CO 80225, asking for an index to topographical maps in your state, or call (800) USA-MAPS. For Alaska write to U.S. Geological Survey, Map Sales, 101-12th Ave., #12, Fairbanks, AK 99701.

Observers are encouraged to develop a video capability for recording occultations in order to obtain reliable and accurate timings. Inexpensive yet sensitive video cameras are now available. Visual timings must be accurate to ±0.2 s to be good enough for further improvement of the lunar profile and other parameters, except for grazes, where ±0.5 s is adequate. For asteroidal occultations, especially the shorter duration events of 10 s or less, video or photoelectric observations are much preferred.

Pages 150–158 give tables of occultation predictions and a table and maps of northern or southern limits for grazing occultations.

1. TOTAL OCCULTATION PREDICTIONS

PREDICTIONS BY THE INTERNATIONAL LUNAR OCCULTATION CENTRE, JAPAN

The total occultation predictions, as given in the **tables** on pp. 150–152, are for the 18 standard stations identified on the map below; the longitudes and latitudes of these stations are given in the table headings.

The predictions are limited to stars of magnitude 5.0 and brighter. The first five columns give for each occultation the date, the Zodiacal Catalogue (ZC) number of the star, its magnitude, the phenomenon (DD or DB = disappearance at dark limb or bright limb, respectively; RD or RB = reappearance at dark limb or bright limb,

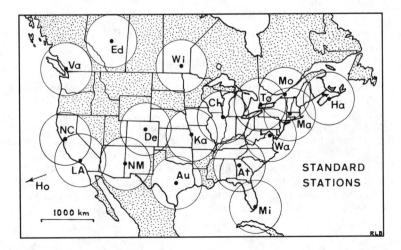

respectively), and the elongation of the Moon from the Sun in degrees (see the middle of p. 56). Under each station are given the Universal Time of the event, factors A and B (see below), and the position angle P (from the north point, eastward around the Moon's limb to the point of occurrence of the phenomenon). In several places, predictions have been replaced by the cryptic notations GBG (after moonset), GSM (before moonrise), NB2 (Sun's altitude greater than −6°), NSG (after sunrise), and NBM (before sunset). If A and B give an unrealistic representation, as in the case of near grazes, they are omitted.

The terms A and B are for determining corrections to the times of the events for stations within 500 km of the standard stations. If Lo* and La* represent the longitude and latitude of the standard station, and Lo and La those of the observer, then for the observer,

UT of event =
UT of event at the standard station + $A(Lo - Lo^*) + B(La - La^*)$,

where Lo, etc., are expressed in degrees, and A and B are in minutes of time per degree. Longitude measured *west* of Greenwich is assumed to be *positive* (which is opposite to the IAU convention and that used by IOTA's *Occult* software). Due regard must be paid to the algebraic signs of the terms. To convert UT to the standard time of the observer, see the section STANDARD TIME ZONES on pp. 36–37.

As an example, consider the occultation of ZC 648 (δ Tau) on 2001 January 6 as seen from Ottawa. For Ottawa, Lo = 75.72° and La = 45.40°. The nearest standard station is Montreal, for which Lo* = 73.60° and La* = 45.50°. Therefore, the UT of the disappearance at the dark limb (DD) is 22:01.3 − 0.4 × (75.72° − 73.60°) min + 1.8 × (45.40° − 45.50°) min = 22:00.3. (Almost the same result is obtained using Toronto as the standard station.) The elongation of the Moon is 139°, which corresponds to the waxing gibbous phase (between first quarter and full). The position angle of disappearance is approximately 65°.

The number of events observable from any location increases *rapidly* as predictions are extended to fainter stars. Observers who wish to pursue such work can obtain software or more extensive lists from Walter Robinson, 515 W. Kump, Bonner Springs, KS 66012–1439, USA, by providing accurate geographical coordinates and a long, self-addressed envelope (with postage); or, better, write to the email address webmaster@lunar-occultations.com.

2. GRAZE PREDICTIONS AND DATA ON OCCULTED STARS
By Eberhard Riedel and David W. Dunham

(A) GRAZE PREDICTIONS

The **table** on pp. 153–154 lists lunar grazing occultation predictions for much of North America for 2001. The events are limited to stars of magnitude 7.0 or brighter (paths for stars down to magnitude 7.5 are shown when the Moon is 40% or less sunlit) that will graze the limb of the Moon when it is at a favourable elongation from the Sun and at least as high above a land horizon in degrees as the star's magnitude (e.g. a 3rd-magnitude star is included only if its altitude is at least 3°). The star's USNO reference number is the Zodiacal Catalogue (ZC) number, unless the number is prefixed with an X. In the latter case, the star is not in the ZC, and its number is from the XZ catalogue, a more extensive catalogue of zodiacal stars prepared at the USNO.

The **maps** on pp. 155–158 show the predicted graze tracks. The maps are "false" projections, since the latitude and longitude scales are both linear. This makes it much easier for measuring coordinates or plotting locations with known coordinates than is possible with any other type of projection. The longitude scale is compressed by a factor of cosine 50°. The maps are not detailed enough for locating oneself in the 2- or 3-km-wide zone where multiple disappearances of the star may occur. To obtain detailed predictions of any graze for plotting on larger-scale maps of your region, write to (or email) IOTA (see p. 144).

Each track is keyed to the sequential number in the table. The computer-drawn number appears at the east and west ends of the track, and is aligned parallel to it. Some overlapping numbers have been omitted for legibility; in these cases, check the other end of the track for the number. Conditions are represented by three different types of lines:

Solid line = Dark limb, night
Dashed line = Bright limb, night
Dotted line = Dark or bright limb, day

Thicker lines are drawn for 1st-magnitude stars and planets. Many tracks begin and/or end with a letter A, B, or S. A denotes that the Moon is at a low altitude, B that the bright limb interferes, and S that sunlight or twilight interferes. The tick marks along the tracks indicate multiples of 10 min of every hour. For example, if the time for the west end of the track is 3:16.2, the tick marks proceeding eastward correspond to 3:20, 3:30, etc. Time always increases from west to east along the path. *The time ticks, track numbers, and the A, B, and S letters are on the side of the limit with an occultation*, that is north of southern limits and south of northern limits. The locations for the North American standard stations for lunar total occultation predictions are indicated by asterisks on the graze maps (see the map on p. 145). For grazes of planets, a *partial occultation* of the object will occur at the northern or southern limit. The line plotted is the centre of the partial occultation zone, typically several kilometres wide.

(B) NAMES OF OCCULTED STARS

The stars that are occulted by the Moon are stars that lie along the zodiac; hence they are known by their number in the Zodiacal Catalogue (ZC) compiled by James Robertson and published in the *Astronomical Papers Prepared for the Use of the American Ephemeris and Nautical Almanac*, vol. 10, pt. 2 (U.S. Government Printing Office, Washington, 1940). Robertson's Zodiacal Catalogue has been out of print for several years. In 1986 Isao Sato, a member of the Lunar Occultation Observers Group in Japan, republished the ZC. This new edition is based on the epoch J2000 and includes much new data, particularly on double stars. Since stars are not usually recognized by their ZC numbers, the equivalent Bayer designations or Flamsteed numbers of the stars occulted during the year are given in the table on the next page. The last four stars are not in the ZC, so their XZ numbers are given. The ZC and XZ catalogues are available via IOTA's web site.

ZC	Name	ZC	Name	ZC/XZ	Name
5	33 Psc	931	4 Gem	1813	FW Vir
118	20 Cet	942	6 Gem	1950	80 Vir
170	33 Cet	946	eta Gem (Propus)	2020	94 Vir
322	64 Cet	954	8 Gem	2193	o Lib
327	ξ¹ Cet	956	9 Gem	2196	30 Lib
401	85 (Cet)/Ari	960	10 Gem	2213	34 Lib
405	μ Cet	962	11 Gem	2218	ζ Lib
648	δ Tau (Hyadum II)	964	12 Gem	2322	ν Sco (Jabbah)
653	64 Tau	976	μ Gem (Tejat)	2597	V1947 Sgr
658	V776 Tau	1047	36 Gem	2630	1 Sgr
668	ε Tau (Ain)	1070	ω Gem	2659	V4028 Sgr
697	SZ Tau	1092	48 Gem	2836	χ² Sgr
700	HU Tau	1110	δ Gem (Wasat)	2872	53 Sgr
752	ι Tau	1129	63 Gem	3031	17 Cap
765	106 Tau	1178	82 Gem	3089	χ Cap
766	105 Tau	1215	7 Cnc	3090	26 Cap
769	107 Tau	1221	9 Cnc	3092	27 Cap
784	108 Tau	1277	η Cnc	3106	φ Cap
792	109 Tau	1295	39 Cnc	3164	ε Cap
817	114 Tau	1296	40 Cnc	3304	56 Aqr
847	ζ Tau	1299	ε Cnc (Praesepe)	3343	τ¹ Aqr
911	141 (Tau)/Ori	1504	37 Leo	3349	τ² Aqr
916	1 Gem	1544	46 Leo	3536	30 Psc
923	2 Gem	1702	ν Vir	X08546	WY Gem
929	3 Gem	1773	16 Vir	X23045	V1349 Oph

(C) OCCULTED STARS KNOWN TO BE DOUBLE

In the table at the right are data on double stars for which graze predictions are given. This information is from DSFILE, a comprehensive file of zodiacal double star data compiled by Don Stockbauer, Henk Bulder, Mitsuru Sôma, and David Dunham; most of the data for the ZC stars are in the Sato ZC catalogue. The successive columns give the USNO reference number of the star, the number of the graze track, the double star code (d), the magnitudes of the brighter (A) and dimmer (B) components, the separation in seconds of arc, and the position angle of B from A measured eastward from north. If the star is triple, the third component's magnitude is given under C, and its separation and position angle from A are given in the last columns.

The parameters are given for the epoch of the occultation, computed from orbital elements when available or from extrapolations from a long series of observations. If there is little change in the available observations, the last-observed separation and P.A. are used. Components fainter than magnitude 11.5 are not listed, and some very close doubles whose parameters are not known, generally with separations less than 0.2″, are also not listed. The latter include spectroscopic binaries (code J, U, or sometimes V) and visual occultation doubles (most codes K and X, and many Vs).

The codes have the following meanings: A or C or G, visual double; B or V, close double, usually discovered by occultation; D, primary of wide pair, secondary has separate catalogue entry; E, secondary star of wide pair; F, prediction is for the following component of a visual double; H, triple, with close occultation pair and third visual component, prediction uses a mean position; I, data for B component computed from orbital elements, but the B component is itself a close double, with data for the C component referred to B rather than A; K, possible double from occultation; J or U, L, M, and V, visual double, prediction uses a mean position; O, data computed from orbital elements; Q = O, but A component may be close double (if triple,

C-component data are computed from orbital elements); R, triple, close pair = O and C component also has orbit relative to centre of close pair; W = A or C, but A component is a spectroscopic binary; X, probable double from occultation; Y, triple, K or X (B component) and A or C (C component); and Z, triple, O (B component) and V (C component). Some close pairs have rapid orbital motion so the current position angle is unknown.

USNO	Graze #	d	A	B	Sep. "	P.A. °	C	Sep. "	P.A. °
210	221	A	6.6	8.6	6.0	328			
368	30, 243	M	6.2	9.8	1.5	141			
398	5, 61, 122	V	6.9	8.5	0.01	298			
401	6, 62, 121	V	6.9	7.2	0.01	21			
405	4	V	4.5	8.5	0.05	133			
648	33	L	3.9	9.5	0.05	190			
653	34	X	5.6	5.6	0.04	53			
658	124	T	4.3	8.4	1.8	338	8.7	84.6	232
663	65	A	6.9	8.7	18.9	58			
684	8	V	6.9	7.0	3.1	97			
760	35	M	7.1	7.5	1.0	298			
765	37, 87	X	5.7	6.7	0.01	349			
766	193	K	6.8	6.8	0.3	270			
817	67, 196	T	5.6	5.6	0.1	90	10.9	37.8	348
843	128, 156	O	7.2	7.8	3.9	276			
916	197, 226	Q	4.9	5.1	0.2	?			
929	139, 199	M	5.9	8.5	0.6	346			
931	90, 140	M	7.5	7.8	0.21	231			
946	39, 70, 92, 93, 143	Q	3.4	5.4	0.03	?	8.8	1.5	255
964	176, 204	C	7	8.5	59.6	87	9.5	62.8	59
976	71, 72	G	3.2	9.8	113.5	141	10.7	113.3	141
982	177	T	7.3	7.9	0.13	162	8.0	0.22	163
1047	52	X	6.1	6.1	0.1	132			
1110	40, 74, 94	O	3.5	8.2	5.7	221			
1128	75	A	6.9	12.1	11.3	22	9.9	35.6	276
1129	41	L	5.9	7.5	0.05	124			
1144	76	A	6.6	8.4	11.5	178			
1178	161, 229	T	6.8	7.3	0.3	45	13.5	4.0	34
1221	208, 230	V	5.9	10	0.4	110			
1293	79	V	6.8	9.9	0.5	226			
1295	115	C	6.5	6.5	149.8	151			
1304	81, 116	M	7	8.4	0.5	85			
1773	42	V	5.8	5.8	0.6	76			
1856	215	M	7.5	7.6	1	99			
1923	43	M	7.0	10.8	0.4	239			
2193	148	C	6.1	8.3	42.5	349			
2322	106	Y	4.9	5.4	1.3	2			
2331	20	V	7.0	7.3	0.03	324			
2432	82	M	7.3	7.6	0.3	13			
2597	22	D	7.5	8.8	10.7	212			
2630	149	A	5.1	10.8	42.1	287			
2872	84	O	6.9	7.1	0.2	327			
3089	184	C	5.3	11.0	67	66			
3343	239	A	5.8	9.0	20.2	123	10.0	63.4	34
3413	24, 109	A	6.4	10.9	3.5	256			
X01775	44	C	6.9	9.5	36.9	100			

TABLE OF TOTAL LUNAR OCCULTATIONS

DATE	ZC	MAG	PH	ELG °	HALIFAX 63.6°W, 44.6°N TIME (UT)	A m	B m	P °	MONTREAL 73.6°W, 45.5°N TIME (UT)	A m	B m	P °	TORONTO 79.4°W, 43.7°N TIME (UT)	A m	B m	P °
Jan. 6	648	3.9	DD	139	22:06.2	-0.9	1.5	78	22:01.3	-0.4	1.8	65	NBM			
6	653	4.8	DD	140	22:50.2	...	...	130	22:33.9	-1.2	0.8	109	22:26.3	-0.9	0.9	105
6	658	4.2	DD	140	23:35.6	-1	2	50	23:30.2	-0.5	2.5	34	23:23.4	-0.3	2.6	31
8	847	3	DD	157	5:03.2	-1.4	-0.1	66	4:48.1	-1.6	0.3	66	4:38	-1.7	0.3	72
8	847	3	RB	158	6:07.9	-0.8	-1.7	286	5:56.5	-1.2	-1.5	283	5:51.2	-1.4	-1	27
14	1702	4.2	RD	240	3:08.3	-0.3	0.6	296	GSM				GSM			
Feb. 6	1110	3.5	DD	151	6:35.5	-0.8	-0.9	76	6:25.4	-1	-1	84	6:21.1	-1.1	-1.2	95
Mar. 3	847	3	DD	101	23:05.9	-2.1	-1.6	121	22:44.5	-1.9	-0.4	110	22:33.7	-2	-0.2	110
3	847	3	RB	102	24:07.4	-1.7	1.9	221	23:52.5	-1.6	1.8	228	23:39.9	-1.5	2.2	225
31	976	3.2	DD	84	23:40.9	-1.7	-0.4	80	NBM				NBM			
Apr. 28	946	3.2	DD	56	2:35.9	-0.2	-0.4	53	2:32.9	-0.3	-0.7	63	2:32.4	-0.4	-0.9	74
Jul. 10	3349	4.2	RD	231	5:51.4	-1.1	2.4	201	5:42	-1.1	2.3	209	5:31.1	-1.1	2.6	208
17	VEN	-4.1	DD	319	18:41.7	-0.8	0.6	35	18:33	-1	0.3	43	18:26.8	-1.1	-0.1	54
17	VEN	-4.1	RD	319	19:22.4	0.5	-2.8	314	19:23.2	0.1	-2.6	305	19:27.3	-0.2	-2.2	293
Aug. 8	3536	4.7	RD	222	2:48.6	...	...	318	GSM				GSM			
8	5	4.7	RD	224	5:30.1	-2	0.9	270	5:11.9	-1.8	1	284	5:00.6	-1.5	1	287
27	2589	4.8	DD	115	23:19.3	-2.1	0.4	84	NBM				NBM			
Sep. 10	SAT	0.1	DB	267	13:39.6	-1.3	1.1	35	13:26.6	-1.5	1.2	37	13:16	-1.6	0.9	47
10	SAT	0.1	RD	268	14:23.8	-0.1	-3.1	313	14:17.8	-0.6	-3	307	14:18.4	-0.9	-2.3	295
29	3349	4.2	DD	151	23:55.1	...	...	138	23:37.8	...	...	128	23:31.3	...	...	133
Oct. 7	668	3.6	RD	234	....				6:54.5	-0.4	3.8	195	6:45.8	-0.4	3.5	199
8	817	4.8	RD	247	....				8:53.5	-1	4.7	197	8:40.1	...	...	195
28	3536	4.7	DD	142	21:39.7	-0.4	3.1	6	NBM				GSM			
28	5	4.7	DD	143	23:39.1	-1.2	1.9	44	23:30.8	-0.9	2.3	33	23:21.9	-0.8	2.4	32
Nov. 5	916	4.3	RD	228	5:17.5	-1.4	1.3	258	5:05.7	-1.2	1.1	270	4:57.2	-1	1.2	272
Dec. 1	SAT	-0.4	DB	183	0:55.3	-0.6	2.1	52	0:54.1	-0.1	2.4	37	0:49.8	0.1	2.4	33
1	SAT	-0.4	RD	183	2:02.5	-1.4	1.1	264	1:49.9	-1.3	0.9	281	1:41	-1.2	0.9	285
8	1702	4.2	RD	277	9:35.4	...	...	241	9:06.8	...	...	216	....			
21	3349	4.2	DD	70	0:44.4	-1.8	-3.2	117	0:25.6	-1.6	-1.5	95	0:17.9	-1.8	-1.1	91
28	SAT	-0.3	DD	153	....				....				9:01.6	-0.9	1.3	24
28	SAT	-0.3	RB	154	....				....				9:31.2	0.7	-3.3	322

DATE	ZC	MAG	PH	ELG °	WINNIPEG 97.2°W, 49.9°N TIME (UT)	A m	B m	P °	EDMONTON 113.4°W, 53.6°N TIME (UT)	A m	B m	P °	VANCOUVER 123.1°W, 49.2°N TIME (UT)	A m	B m	P °
Jan. 8	847	3	DD	157	4:18.9	-1.2	2.1	42	4:21.4			2	4:00.5	...	...	11
8	847	3	RB	157	5:16.5	-1.6	-1.4	298	4:38.1	...	...	334	4:28.8	...	...	322
29	3536	4.7	DD	50	2:06.3	...	...	137	1:31.5	-1.3	-1.5	95	1:22	-1.8	-1.2	95
Feb. 3	648	3.9	DD	113	GBG				9:42.2	0.2	-1.5	97	9:52.2	0.3	-2.1	117
6	1110	3.5	DD	151	5:52.1	-1.4	-0.5	90	5:28.9	-1.4	0.4	82	5:13.6	-1.5	0.4	96
Mar. 3	847	3	DD	101	22:15.2	-0.8	1.6	74	22:14.3	-0.2	2.2	50	22:04.1	0	2.1	48
3	847	3	RB	101	23:25.3	-1.2	1.2	259	23:11.2	-1	1	283	22:57.8	-0.8	1.1	284
31	847	3	DD	75	6:01.1	0.4	-2	123	5:57.3	0.1	-2.5	129	6:16.6	...	...	165
31	847	3	RB	75	GBG				6:40.7	-0.3	-0.5	228	6:31.1	...	...	193
Apr. 28	946	3.2	DD	56	2:15.9	-0.8	-1	75	NSG				NSG			
28	976	3.2	DD	58	5:39.7	0	-0.5	51	5:35.4	-0.2	-0.9	60	5:37.6	-0.3	-1.2	79
Jul. 17	VEN	-4.1	DB	318	18:06.3	-1.4	1.2	38	17:52.3	-1.2	3.5	18	17:27.6	-1.3	2.6	32
17	VEN	-4.1	RD	319	19:03.7	-0.8	-2.9	302	18:34	-1.4	-4.1	316	18:30.9	-1.9	-2.1	296
19	MER	-0.6	DB	341	....				11:43.4	-0.2	0.6	135	GSM			
19	MER	-0.6	RD	342	....				12:19.6	0.6	2.7	212	12:15.1	0.8	2.4	213
Aug. 8	5	4.7	RD	223	4:47.1	...	...	310	GSM				GSM			
15	JUP	-2	DB	315	20:42.2	...	...	20	20:23.5	-1.3	0.7	35	20:11.2	-1.2	-0.3	62
15	JUP	-2	RD	315	20:58	...	...	348	20:55.9	0.3	-3.5	332	21:07.8	-0.3	-2.3	305
26	2353	4.6	DD	95	GBG				GBG				5:06.7	-1.2	-1	75
Sep. 4	3536	4.7	RD	198	10:45.1	-0.1	1.8	189	10:40.2	-0.8	0.3	222	10:28.8	-1.1	0.7	223
10	SAT	0.1	DB	267	13:03.2	...	...	13	....				....			
10	SAT	0.1	RD	267	13:37.4	...	...	321	....				....			
Oct. 7	668	3.6	RD	234	6:49.5	-0.7	1.9	240	6:46.1	-0.5	1.6	264	6:35	-0.3	1.5	267
8	817	4.8	RD	247	8:40.3	-1	1.9	240	8:32	-0.8	1.5	264	8:18.7	-0.6	1.5	266
Nov. 5	916	4.3	RD	228	4:44.1	-1.1	0.1	315	....				....			
22	3164	4.7	DD	81	3:06.6	-1.7	-2.5	116	2:36.4	-1.4	-0.7	84	2:23.1	-1.7	-0.2	80
25	3536	4.7	DD	115	GBG				7:29.4	-0.5	-0.8	63	7:26.9	-0.8	-0.8	69
Dec. 2	916	4.3	RD	201	NB2				13:36.2	-0.3	-1.7	281	13:37.8	-0.7	-1.1	261
8	1702	4.2	RD	277	8:52.5	...	...	224	8:58.2	-0.2	2.7	245	GSM			
20	3349	4.2	DD	70	23:48.9	-1.3	0.5	52	NBM				NBM			
28	SAT	-0.3	DD	153	8:52.9	...	...	12	....				8:18.4	-1.3	1.9	29
28	SAT	-0.3	RB	154	9:16.1	...	...	329	....				9:07.9	-1	-2.9	304
32	1308	4.7	RD	207	....				....				10:50.1	...	...	347

TABLE OF TOTAL LUNAR OCCULTATIONS (continued)

					MASSACHUSETTS 72.5°W, 42.5°N				WASHINGTON, D.C. 77.0°W, 38.9°N				CHICAGO 87.7°W, 41.9°N			
DATE	ZC	MAG	PH	ELG °	TIME (UT)	A m	B m	P °	TIME (UT)	A m	B m	P °	TIME (UT)	A m	B m	P °
Jan. 6	648	3.9	DD	139	21:56.8	−0.5	1.6	72	NBM				NBM			
6	653	4.8	DD	140	22:33.7	−1.5	0.3	119	22:26.3	−1.5	0	122	NBM			
6	658	4.2	DD	140	23:23.8	−0.7	2.2	44	23:13	−0.6	2.2	46	23:17.8	0.1	2.8	22
8	847	3	DD	157	4:49.6	−1.7	−0.1	76	4:42.5	−1.9	−0.4	89	4:22.6	−1.8	0.6	75
8	847	3	RB	157	6:01.7	−1.2	−1.1	274	5:58.5	−1.5	−0.5	260	5:39.5	−1.7	−0.5	267
Feb. 6	1110	3.5	DD	151	6:29.7	−1	−1.1	91	6:30	−1	−1.5	106	6:13.3	−1.3	−1.4	108
Mar. 3	847	3	DD	101	22:49.3	−2.3	−1.4	123	22:44.5	−2.9	−2.6	135	22:18.1	−1.7	0.4	106
3	847	3	RB	102	23:47.6	−1.6	2.8	215	23:28	−1.1	4.7	199	23:24.1	−1.3	2.4	226
Apr. 28	946	3.2	DD	56	2:35.4	−0.2	−0.8	70	2:37.7	−0.2	−1	84	2:30.9	−0.5	−1.2	88
Jul. 10	3349	4.2	RD	231	5:35.8	−1.2	2.6	204	5:20.2	−1.1	3.2	197	5:17.7	−1	2.8	205
17	VEN	−4.1	DB	319	18:33.8	−0.9	−0.1	53	18:30.8	−1	−0.6	69	18:17	−1.3	−0.3	65
17	VEN	−4.1	RD	319	19:30.2	0.1	−2.2	296	19:36.7	−0.2	−1.6	280	19:27.9	−0.5	−1.7	280
Aug. 8	3536	4.7	RD	222	2:42.7	...	...	313	GSM				GSM			
8	5	4.7	RD	224	5:10.8	−1.8	1.1	278	4:59.1	−1.6	1.2	276	4:48	−1.1	1	289
15	JUP	−2	DB	315	....				GBG				20:45.4	−0.7	0.3	39
15	JUP	−2	RD	315	....				GBG				21:15.5	0.9	−2.6	331
Sep. 10	SAT	0.1	DB	267	13:25.7	−1.5	0.5	50	13:17.6	−1.7	0.1	65	13:00.4	−1.8	0.9	54
10	SAT	0.1	RD	268	14:26.3	−0.6	−2.3	296	14:29.8	−0.9	−1.6	280	14:12.9	−1.3	−1.7	285
29	3349	4.2	DD	151	23:39.4	...	...	138	....				NBM			
Oct. 7	668	3.6	RD	234	6:39.4	...	...	175	....				6:36.8	−0.4	2.9	209
8	817	4.8	RD	247	....				....				8:27.3	−0.5	4.1	200
28	5	4.7	DD	143	23:25.1	−1	2.2	38	23:12.6	−0.9	2.3	41	23:11.8	−0.6	2.5	30
Nov. 5	916	4.3	DD	228	5:03.3	−1.2	1.4	261	4:53.3	−1	1.5	257	4:47.3	−0.8	1	278
28	327	4.5	DD	148	6:00.9	...	...	359	5:46.6	−0.9	2.4	17	....			
Dec. 1	SAT	−0.4	DB	183	0:47.4	−0.2	2.2	45	0:39.1	−0.1	2.1	47	0:47.5	0.4	2.5	25
1	SAT	−0.4	RD	183	1:48.2	−1.3	1.1	272	1:38.8	−1.1	1.2	269	1:30.2	−1.1	0.7	294
21	3349	4.2	DD	70	0:33.2	−2	−2.3	108	0:31.6	−2.7	−2.7	113	0:03.3	−2	−0.4	81
28	SAT	−0.3	DD	154	9:06.2	...	...	18	9:00	−0.6	0.3	42	8:53.6	−0.8	0.3	43
28	SAT	−0.3	RB	154	9:29.1	...	...	329	9:42.2	0.5	−2.1	305	9:39.8	0.2	−2.3	302

					MIAMI 80.3°W, 25.8°N				ATLANTA 84.3°W, 33.8°N				AUSTIN 97.8°W, 30.2°N			
DATE	ZC	MAG	PH	ELG °	TIME (UT)	A m	B m	P °	TIME (UT)	A m	B m	P °	TIME (UT)	A m	B m	P °
Jan. 6	658	4.2	DD	140	NBM				22:58.9	−0.4	2	48	NBM			
8	847	3	DD	157	5:01.7	...	...	150	4:30.7	−2.3	−1	106	4:00.4	−2.5	−0.6	109
8	847	3	RB	157	5:34.8	...	...	197	5:44.9	−2	0.8	239	5:11.3	−2	2.1	226
Feb. 6	1110	3.5	DD	152	6:58.6	0.2	−4.1	159	6:32.4	−0.9	−2.4	131	6:39.6	...	...	179
15	2271	4.3	RD	273	8:48.5	−0.2	−2.1	340	RB				8:37.9	−0.2	−0.8	323
Mar. 3	847	3	DD	101	....				....				22:02	...	...	135
3	847	3	RB	101	....				....				22:36.5	...	...	191
30	668	3.6	DD	60	1:25.2	−1.7	2.6	26	....				1:07.8	...	...	10
Apr. 28	946	3.2	DD	56	2:55	0.3	−1.8	125	2:42.6	−0.1	−1.4	106	2:47.8	0	−2.6	136
Jul. 10	3349	4.2	RD	230	....				4:50.2	...	...	175	....			
17	VEN	−4.1	DB	319	18:44.6	−0.6	−2.2	118	18:27.5	−1.2	−1.2	91	18:13.5	−1.9	−2.2	112
17	VEN	−4.1	RD	319	19:44.1	−0.8	0.4	233	19:39.9	−0.6	−0.7	257	19:26.1	−1.5	0.7	232
Aug. 8	5	4.7	RD	223	4:36.7	−1.3	1.6	252	4:42.8	−1.2	1.2	271	4:27.2	−0.5	1.2	267
15	JUP	−2	DB	315	GBG				20:47.1	−0.2	−0.3	62	20:46.3	−0.3	−0.9	90
15	JUP	−2	RD	315	GBG				GBG				21:41.4	0.2	−1.1	283
Sep. 10	SAT	0.1	DB	267	13:23	−1.9	−2.1	115	13:05.1	−2.1	−0.4	84	12:34.5	−2.7	−0.3	92
10	SAT	0.1	RD	268	14:31.6	−1.7	1	230	14:26.7	−1.4	−0.5	258	14:01.6	−2.2	0.8	240
Oct. 7	668	3.6	RD	234	....				....				5:59.3	0.6	3.7	190
Nov. 4	752	4.7	RD	214	2:53.1	...	...	314	....				....			
5	916	4.3	RD	228	4:26.4	−0.2	2.3	224	4:39.5	−0.6	1.5	253	4:28.6	−0.3	1.1	263
28	327	4.5	DD	148	5:25.1	−1.9	0.5	63	5:28.2	−1.3	1.9	30	5:02.7	−1.2	2.8	21
Dec. 1	SAT	−0.4	DB	182	0:16.4	−0.2	1.3	72	0:29	0.1	1.9	48	0:26.4	0.5	1.8	40
1	SAT	−0.4	RD	183	1:17.9	−0.6	1.6	243	1:25.9	−0.8	1.1	268	1:14.2	−0.4	0.7	279
21	3349	4.2	DD	70	....				0:22.4	...	...	116	NBM			
28	SAT	−0.3	DD	153	9:03.1	−0.2	−0.8	90	8:56.6	−0.5	−0.4	68	8:50.4	−0.8	−1.1	92
28	SAT	−0.3	RB	154	GBG				9:53	0.2	−1.2	279	9:54.3	−0.5	−0.5	253
32	1308	4.7	RD	208	NB2				RB				11:59.7	−0.4	−2.3	320

See pp. 145–146 for an explanation of this table.

TABLE OF TOTAL LUNAR OCCULTATION PREDICTIONS (continued)

DATE	ZC	MAG	PH	ELG °	KANSAS CITY 94.5°W, 39.0°N TIME (UT)	A m	B m	P °	DENVER 105.0°W, 39.8°N TIME (UT)	A m	B m	P °	NEW MEX., ARIZ. 109.0°W, 34.0°N TIME (UT)	A m	B m	P °
Jan. 8	847	3	DD	156	4:08.3	-1.9	0.6	81	3:51.2	-1.5	1.4	69	3:37.9	-1.6	1	82
8	847	3	RB	157	5:27.5	-1.9	0.2	258	5:07.3	-1.9	0.3	265	4:55.2	-1.9	1.2	249
Feb. 6	1110	3.5	DD	151	6:09	-1.4	-2	124	5:51.2	-1.7	-2	128	6:04	...	...	163
Mar. 3	847	3	DD	101	22:05.7	-1.5	0.5	106	21:54.2	-0.8	1.2	89	21:44.8	-0.9	0.8	99
3	847	3	RB	101	23:08.9	-1	2.6	223	23:00.2	-0.9	2	240	22:44.8	-0.6	2.3	228
Apr. 28	946	3.2	DD	56	2:31.5	-0.5	-1.5	103	2:23.2	-0.8	-1.9	112	2:34.1	-0.5	-3	138
Jul. 17	VEN	-4.1	DB	318	18:08.2	-1.6	-0.6	78	17:48.6	-2	-0.1	76	17:42.5	-2.5	-0.9	95
17	VEN	-4.1	RD	319	19:27.1	-0.9	-1.1	265	19:13.9	-1.4	-0.9	262	19:09.2	-1.8	0.4	240
Aug. 8	5	4.7	RD	223	4:39	-0.7	1	286	GSM				GSM			
15	JUP	-2	DB	315	20:41.7	-0.5	-0.4	60	20:34.7	-0.7	-0.7	72	20:37.4	-0.6	-1.1	93
15	JUP	-2	RD	315	21:26.7	0.5	-2	311	21:28.7	0.2	-1.8	300	21:37.7	-0.1	-1.2	280
26	2353	4.6	DD	95	GBG				GBG				5:41	-0.9	-1.6	108
Sep. 10	SAT	0.1	DB	267	12:45	-2	0.9	63	12:26	-1.8	1.8	52	12:09.5	-2.1	1.3	67
10	SAT	0.1	RD	268	14:06.5	-1.7	-1	272	13:45.7	-2.1	-0.9	276	13:38.5	-2.3	0.3	257
Oct. 7	668	3.6	RD	234	6:26.2	-0.3	2.7	212	6:24.6	-0.3	2.1	230	6:11.3	-0.1	2.2	222
8	817	4.8	RD	247	8:13.2	-0.2	4	200	8:11.3	-0.5	2.6	221	7:54.1	0	3	210
Nov. 5	916	4.3	RD	228	4:39.4	-0.6	1	280	4:33.9	-0.5	0.5	297	4:29	-0.2	0.6	287
28	327	4.5	DD	148	5:42.2	...	...	340	....				....			
Dec. 1	SAT	-0.4	DD	182	0:43.6	0.6	2.5	22	0:55.8	...	...	357	GSM			
1	SAT	-0.4	RD	183	1:21.9	-0.9	0.5	298	1:11.3	...	...	324	1:10.8	-0.5	-0.1	308
20	3349	4.2	DD	70	23:49.3	-2.2	0.1	76	NBM				NBM			
28	SAT	-0.3	DD	153	8:47.7	-0.9	-0.2	60	8:36.5	-1.2	-0.2	63	8:34.3	-1.4	-0.8	86
28	SAT	-0.3	RB	154	9:45.8	-0.1	-1.7	285	9:41.4	-0.5	-1.5	278	9:45	-0.8	-0.6	256
32	1308	4.7	RD	207	11:30.4	...	...	3	11:31.3	-0.2	-3.2	338	11:44.1	-0.9	-2.1	312

DATE	ZC	MAG	PH	ELG °	LOS ANGELES 118.3°W, 34.1°N TIME (UT)	A m	B m	P °	N. CALIFORNIA 122.0°W, 38.0°N TIME (UT)	A m	B m	P °	HONOLULU 157.9°W, 21.3°N TIME (UT)	A m	B m	P °
Jan. 8	847	3	DD	156	3:25.3	-1.1	1.5	70	3:28.9	-0.7	2	54	2:54.3	0.4	1.5	50
8	847	3	RB	157	4:38.2	-1.7	1	259	4:34.8	-1.7	0.5	276	3:43.3	-0.4	0.4	278
Feb. 5	976	3.2	DD	139	....				....				8:35.5	-2.6	0.5	75
6	1110	3.5	DD	151	5:48.6	...	...	170	5:22.9	-2.1	-2.3	139	GSM			
10	1702	4.2	RD	213	....				....				15:11.6	-0.8	-2.6	333
Mar. 3	847	3	DD	100	21:39.5	-0.3	1.1	86	21:43.8	-0.1	1.5	73	GSM			
3	847	3	RB	101	22:39.9	-0.5	1.8	242	22:44.3	-0.6	1.5	256	GSM			
Apr. 6	1702	4.2	DD	157	....				....				11:57.6	...	...	43
28	976	3.2	DD	58	5:57	0.2	-1.4	110	5:52	0.1	-1.4	104	....			
Jun. 14	3536	4.7	RD	274	NB2				NB2				12:27.7	-0.9	0.3	284
14	5	4.7	RD	275	NB2				NB2				15:00.5	-2.3	1.5	249
27	1702	4.2	DD	79	6:56.8	-0.4	0	55	6:56.1	...	...	43	6:35.7	-1.1	-2	135
Jul. 17	VEN	-4.1	DB	318	17:18.1	-2.7	-0.1	89	17:10.6	-2.3	0.9	72	15:44.4	-0.8	1.6	65
17	VEN	-4.1	RD	319	18:50.4	-2.1	0.8	240	18:44	-2.1	0.1	254	17:03.3	-1.6	1.7	244
Aug. 15	946	3.2	RD	310	....				12:43.1	...	...	198	GSM			
15	JUP	-2	DB	314	20:30.5	-0.8	-1.5	104	20:21.5	-1.1	-1.3	96	....			
15	JUP	-2	RD	315	21:34.8	-0.5	-1	268	21:28.3	-0.6	-1.3	275	....			
26	2353	4.6	DD	95	5:30.4	-1.3	-1.4	102	5:20.3	-1.4	-1.2	93	NSG			
Sep. 4	3536	4.7	DD	197	RB				10:13	-0.5	2.6	191	8:47.7	-1.4	2.6	216
10	SAT	0.1	DB	266	11:53	-1.5	2	54	11:57.7	-1	2.8	36	11:05	0.6	2.7	23
10	SAT	0.1	RD	267	13:16.4	-2.4	0.3	265	13:07.2	-2.5	-0.4	283	11:49.5	-1.5	-0.2	293
24	2589	4.8	DD	89	GBG				GBG				7:30.1	-1.6	-0.5	83
Oct. 4	327	4.5	RD	204	GBG				GBG				15:47.4	-1.1	1.6	217
7	668	3.6	RD	234	6:11.1	0	1.8	235	6:17.6	-0.1	1.6	247	GSM			
8	817	4.8	RD	247	7:53.4	-0.1	2.2	226	8:00.4	-0.3	1.9	241	GSM			
11	1308	4.7	RD	289	....				....				15:09.2	-2	-0.6	297
Nov. 5	916	4.3	RD	228	4:27.2	-0.2	0.2	301	GSM				GSM			
22	3164	4.7	DD	81	2:50.7	...	...	127	2:30.5	-2.9	-1	103	NSG			
22	3175	4.8	DD	82	....				GBG				5:38.7	-4	-1.8	109
25	3536	4.7	DD	115	....				7:45.3	-1.6	-3	113	6:28.7	-4.1	-0.4	95
Dec. 2	916	4.3	RD	201	13:45.9	-1.7	1.6	214	13:44.2	-1.3	0.5	226	....			
6	1484	3.6	RD	253	....				....				12:57.4	-1.6	-3.2	339
28	SAT	-0.3	DD	153	8:19.5	-1.8	-0.7	87	8:11.3	-1.8	-0.1	73	6:42.3	-2.4	0.5	90
28	SAT	-0.3	RB	154	9:35.3	-1.3	-0.3	250	9:28.5	-1.3	-0.8	262	8:00.3	-1.7	2.6	219
32	1308	4.7	RD	207	11:32.7	-1.5	-1.6	298	11:20.5	-1.4	-1.8	305	9:40.7	...	...	204

See pp. 145–146 for an explanation of this table.

TABLE OF GRAZING LUNAR OCCULTATION PREDICTIONS

The table below and on the next page lists lunar grazing occultation predictions for much of North America for 2001. The four maps following the table show the graze tracks (see the descriptive text on pp. 146–147).

For each graze is given:

No.   A chronological sequential number used on the maps

Date   The date

USNO d   The star's USNO (U.S. Naval Observatory) reference number (see the bottom of p. 146) and its duplicity code (in the "**d**" column—see section (C) on pp. 148–149 concerning double stars)

m   Its visual magnitude

%sl   The percent of the Moon sunlit (+ for waxing, – for waning)

L   Whether the track is a northern (N) or southern (S) limit

W.U.T.   The Universal Time at the west end of the track

Lo., La.   The longitude and latitude of the west end of the track

No.	Date	USNO	d	m	%sl	L	W.U.T.	Lo.	La.	No.	Date	USNO	d	m	%sl	L	W.U.T.	Lo.	La.
1	Jan. 1	3458		6.2	31+	S	1:37.2	–123	27	50	Mar. 4	1021		6.1	70+	S	23:09.1	–78	46
2	1	18	K	5.8	40+	S	23:03.2	–86	29	51	5	X09801		7.0	72+	S	2:14.2	–121	37
3	2	118		4.8	49+	S	20:52.2	–68	47	52	5	1047	X	5.3	72+	S	5:32.2	–60	55
4	5	405	V	4.3	72+	S	4:47.9	–130	50	53	5	1059	X	6.9	74+	N	7:48.5	–130	51
5	5	398	V	6.5	72+	N	4:46.2	–74	49	54	6	1191		6.8	82+	S	5:03.4	–91	55
6	5	401	V	6.3	72+	N	5:10.5	–80	40	55	13	2097		6.8	83–	S	9:01.1	–90	55
7	6	523	K	6.4	81+	N	5:51.5	–90	29	56	13	2110		6.3	82–	S	12:10.9	–110	55
8	7	684	V	6.2	89+	S	2:27.9	–130	32	57	14	2210		6.8	75–	S	5:23.3	–88	41
9	7	718		6.0	91+	S	9:43.9	–130	47	58	19	2921		6.0	27–	S	10:58.8	–112	29
10	8	847	J	3.0	96+	S	4:07.0	–106	20	59	22	3304		6.4	6–	S	12:05.3	–101	24
11	8	847	J	3.0	96+	N	4:07.4	–130	49	60	27	286		7.5	4+	S	1:46.7	–110	24
12	9	X11153		7.5	100E	N	20:48.7	–58	53	61	28	398	V	6.5	8+	S	0:22.4	–87	45
13	12	1504		5.4	89–	S	14:49.2	–130	42	62	28	401	V	6.3	8+	S	0:45.3	–94	36
14	16	1976		7.0	50–	S	14:00.1	–102	55	63	29	523	K	6.4	16+	S	2:38.9	–124	27
15	17	2072		6.6	41–	S	8:16.2	–101	32	64	29	X04680		7.3	16+	S	2:43.7	–121	47
16	18	2196		6.5	31–	S	11:43.7	–109	55	65	30	663	A	6.9	23+	S	0:11.8	–81	52
17	18	2210		6.8	29–	S	15:02.8	–121	55	66	30	668		3.5	24+	N	0:48.9	–116	30
18	19	2313		7.0	22–	S	9:20.6	–72	51	67	31	817	T	4.9	34+	N	1:51.3	–112	22
19	19	2316		6.4	22–	S	10:10.3	–86	50	68	31	847	J	3.0	36+	S	6:18.9	–130	51
20	19	2331	V	6.3	22–	S	12:15.0	–122	44	69	31	851	K	6.4	37+	N	7:16.8	–130	44
21	20	X23045		7.0	14–	S	12:45.2	–106	50	70	31	946	Q	3.5	43+	N	19:03.3	–107	33
22	21	2597	D	7.5	8–	S	15:12.8	–130	47	71	31	976	G	2.9	44+	S	22:26.2	–113	20
23	26	3284	K	7.0	5+	S	22:28.1	–76	41	72	31	976	G	2.9	44+	N	22:52.6	–130	53
24	28	3413	A	6.1	10+	S	0:49.1	–115	47	73	Apr. 1	997	A	7.0	46+	N	3:27.7	–73	55
25	29	3529	K	6.5	17+	S	1:02.9	–103	20	74	1	1110	O	3.5	55+	S	20:58.8	–125	44
26	29	3536		4.4	17+	S	1:45.2	–127	38	75	2	1128	A	6.8	56+	S	1:11.2	–98	42
27	29	5	L	4.6	18+	S	3:56.5	–130	50	76	2	1144	A	6.6	57+	N	3:24.7	–118	25
28	32	X03132		6.8	43+	S	0:12.0	–93	23	77	2	1152	X	7.0	59+	N	5:34.4	–130	50
29	Feb. 1	X03361		7.0	46+	S	6:37.6	–130	45	78	3	1277		5.3	68+	S	2:26.9	–119	38
30	1	368	M	6.2	46+	N	7:07.7	–116	44	79	3	1293	V	6.8	70+	S	6:42.8	–70	55
31	2	464	K	6.1	54+	S	2:15.9	–84	20	80	3	1299	V	6.3	70+	S	6:57.1	–82	55
32	3	620		6.1	67+	S	4:57.2	–130	27	81	3	1304	M	6.8	70+	N	6:44.3	–130	39
33	3	648	L	3.8	69+	S	10:22.7	–130	42	82	12	2432	M	6.7	81–	S	7:00.1	–87	55
34	3	653	X	4.8	69+	S	10:36.4	–130	53	83	12	X23043		7.0	79–	S	11:55.0	–130	52
35	4	760	M	6.6	76+	S	1:41.9	–118	30	84	15	2872	O	6.3	53–	S	8:21.9	–106	25
36	4	769	X	6.5	76+	S	3:23.5	–130	39	85	15	2875		6.0	53–	S	8:30.5	–108	26
37	4	765	X	5.3	76+	N	4:02.6	–103	41	86	26	617		6.6	6+	N	0:06.4	–83	22
38	5	928		5.9	85+	N	3:46.3	–96	41	87	26	765	X	5.3	12+	S	23:42.0	–68	46
39	5	946	Q	3.5	86+	N	5:38.9	–130	28	88	27	782		7.2	13+	N	2:23.0	–107	44
40	6	1110	O	3.5	93+	S	5:30.9	–130	33	89	28	928		5.9	20+	S	0:35.7	–80	46
41	6	1129	L	5.3	94+	S	9:32.5	–122	55	90	28	931	M	6.9	21+	N	1:03.5	–93	31
42	11	1773	V	5.0	88–	N	3:44.9	–100	40	91	28	942		6.5	21+	N	1:43.0	–102	38
43	12	1923	M	7.0	78–	S	10:23.5	–130	55	92	28	946	Q	3.5	21+	S	2:42.8	–62	55
44	26	X01775	C	7.3	12+	S	23:37.6	–84	42	93	28	946	Q	3.5	21+	S	2:27.7	–130	34
45	27	208		7.0	13+	S	4:25.0	–130	41	94	29	1110	O	3.5	32+	S	4:30.2	–65	55
46	28	306		6.8	19+	S	0:27.9	–95	37	95	30	1250		5.8	43+	S	4:11.6	–110	55
47	Mar. 2	581		6.8	40+	N	5:03.9	–100	42	96	May 1	1377		7.0	54+	S	2:11.5	–98	52
48	2	697	K	6.5	48+	S	22:17.7	–65	47	97	12	2811		6.2	79–	S	5:53.2	–89	40
49	3	847	J	3.0	59+	S	21:52.6	–113	20	98	12	2823		6.8	78–	S	8:25.4	–117	47

TABLE OF GRAZING LUNAR OCCULTATION PREDICTIONS (continued)

No.	Date	USNO d	m	%sl	L	W.U.T.	Lo.	La.	No.	Date	USNO d	m	%sl	L	W.U.T.	Lo.	La.
99	May 14	3090	6.7	60-	N	12:09.5	-115	41	174	Oct. 8	828	6.3	70-	N	9:05.8	-130	36
100	17	3458	6.2	32-	N	11:02.3	-97	36	175	9	962	6.9	60-	N	4:54.0	-94	31
101	25	X07846	7.2	5+	N	2:00.8	-98	39	176	9	964 C	7.0	60-	N	5:12.2	-107	45
102	25	911 K	6.4	5+	N	4:19.1	-114	55	177	9	982 T	6.8	60-	N	7:35.8	-130	41
103	26	1059 X	6.9	11+	S	2:22.1	-95	48	178	13	1535	6.8	16-	N	9:23.4	-100	39
104	27	1215	6.8	20+	N	3:29.4	-116	44	179	13	1544	5.4	16-	N	10:43.5	-119	34
105	29	1479	6.4	41+	N	4:20.5	-130	43	180	19	2213	5.8	6+	N	0:02.9	-97	33
106	Jun. 5	2322 Y	4.1	99+	S	5:18.7	-92	55	181	19	2218 X	5.5	6+	N	0:51.7	-112	40
107	10	3031	5.9	84-	N	8:23.4	-120	54	182	21	2504	7.4	20+	N	0:12.6	-98	30
108	11	X29870	6.9	76-	N	9:22.9	-109	49	183	22	2659	6.2	29+	S	1:08.3	-107	35
109	13	3413 A	6.1	57-	N	11:18.8	-130	26	184	25	3089 C	5.3	60+	S	5:01.0	-130	46
110	16	208	7.0	29-	N	8:31.2	-96	30	185	25	3092	6.2	60+	S	6:41.3	-104	20
111	19	590	6.3	6-	N	10:08.3	-77	20	186	26	3214	6.8	69+	S	4:33.6	-130	25
112	19	600	6.6	5-	N	11:49.5	-112	20	187	28	3458	6.2	85+	S	5:57.9	-96	20
113	23	1167	6.2	4+	N	3:36.9	-110	48	188	28	3536	4.4	89+	N	21:56.6	-78	49
114	24	1296	6.6	9+	S	1:16.6	-64	55	189	29	18 K	5.8	90+	S	2:17.1	-98	20
115	24	1295 C	6.4	9+	S	1:18.7	-69	52	190	Nov. 3	668	3.5	95-	S	14:01.0	-92	55
116	24	1304 M	6.8	9+	N	1:27.2	-65	55	191	4	752 K	4.6	91-	N	2:31.6	-96	20
117	24	X13328	7.5	10+	N	3:39.4	-114	43	192	4	755 K	6.2	91-	N	3:33.6	-128	48
118	27	1702	4.0	40+	N	6:54.8	-130	42	193	4	766 K	5.8	91-	N	4:39.1	-130	26
119	Jul. 10	3349	4.0	82-	S	4:38.8	-92	34	194	4	784 C	6.3	90-	N	8:31.2	-130	31
120	12	60	6.9	63-	N	11:23.4	-130	21	195	4	792	5.0	90-	S	11:30.5	-109	29
121	15	401 V	6.3	34-	N	7:51.7	-101	32	196	4	817 T	4.9	88-	S	15:13.4	-130	55
122	15	398 V	6.5	35-	N	7:59.8	-107	50	197	5	916 Q	4.3	84-	N	4:17.7	-124	40
123	16	523 K	6.4	24-	N	9:52.0	-122	33	198	5	923 K	6.7	84-	N	5:03.5	-121	20
124	17	658 T	4.3	16-	S	6:49.4	-78	50	199	5	929 M	5.8	83-	N	7:56.4	-60	51
125	17	X05851	7.4	15-	N	9:48.2	-91	20	200	5	954 K	6.1	82-	N	9:43.2	-130	31
126	17	Venus	-3.6	13-	S	17:26.5	-126	20	201	5	956	6.2	82-	N	10:17.2	-130	49
127	17	Venus	-3.6	13-	N	17:50.5	-130	54	202	5	960	6.6	82-	S	12:11.8	-106	28
128	18	843 O	7.0	8-	N	11:26.8	-118	25	203	5	962	6.9	82-	S	12:23.0	-105	36
129	19	1014	7.0	3-	N	10:31.6	-93	31	204	5	964 C	7.0	82-	S	12:27.3	-96	47
130	19	Mercury	-0.5	3-	S	11:47.1	-122	42	205	5	1050	5.7	76-	N	23:58.5	-59	54
131	25	1755	6.9	24+	N	1:33.7	-98	25	206	6	1080	6.7	75-	N	5:28.4	-98	20
132	Aug. 2	2836	5.5	97+	S	10:03.4	-128	20	207	6	1092	5.8	74-	N	7:31.6	-129	20
133	7	3458	6.2	92-	N	9:34.1	-130	42	208	7	1221 V	6.0	64-	N	5:27.1	-114	45
134	8	3536	4.4	87-	N	2:35.6	-74	46	209	11	1739 V	6.4	19-	N	10:00.9	-106	22
135	13	600	6.6	40-	N	6:28.4	-92	30	210	11	X18000	7.1	19-	N	10:46.9	-99	21
136	13	617	6.6	39-	N	9:56.7	-78	20	211	11	X18000	7.1	19-	N	10:51.7	-119	53
137	15	911 K	6.4	19-	N	7:43.8	-102	53	212	11	X18067 V	7.5	18-	S	12:16.7	-121	24
138	15	X08347	7.4	19-	N	9:45.3	-118	38	213	11	X18067 V	7.5	18-	N	12:36.5	-105	55
139	15	929 M	5.8	19-	N	10:19.3	-102	20	214	11	1755	6.9	17-	N	14:29.8	-130	55
140	15	931 M	6.9	19-	N	10:34.9	-123	22	215	12	1856 M	6.8	10-	N	10:48.1	-70	55
141	15	X08546 V	7.2	19-	N	11:15.2	-108	20	216	12	1867	7.5	10-	N	12:06.5	-118	48
142	15	942	6.5	19-	N	11:26.1	-130	33	217	19	X26108	7.4	15+	S	1:31.2	-120	21
143	15	946 Q	3.5	18-	S	12:14.6	-130	31	218	22	3164 U	4.5	41+	S	2:37.9	-130	23
144	15	Jupiter	-1.6	16-	N	20:40.6	-106	55	219	23	3374	6.1	58+	S	20:11.8	-58	50
145	17	1253 X	7.3	4-	N	11:58.4	-113	24	220	25	3536	4.4	71+	S	7:58.9	-130	32
146	20	1702	4.0	5+	N	23:57.5	-82	26	221	27	210 A	6.6	86+	S	4:58.1	-106	20
147	23	1950	5.2	5+	N	0:21.7	-82	38	222	28	322 K	5.6	92+	N	4:43.9	-89	43
148	25	2193 C	6.1	41+	N	0:32.5	-67	55	223	28	327 K	4.4	92+	S	5:45.9	-97	38
149	28	2630 A	5.0	73+	N	5:58.7	-130	28	224	29	454	5.6	97+	S	6:56.6	-130	51
150	30	2921	6.0	89+	N	9:00.0	-120	21	225	Dec. 1	Saturn	-0.2	100-	N	1:00.3	-117	35
151	31	3031	5.9	93+	N	3:52.6	-130	47	226	2	916 Q	4.3	97-	S	13:15.5	-130	35
152	Sep. 7	322 K	5.6	83-	N	7:02.3	-78	20	227	3	1050	5.7	93-	S	6:55.9	-82	47
153	7	327 K	4.4	83-	N	8:24.2	-82	20	228	3	1070	5.2	92-	N	11:19.9	-130	41
154	9	577	6.0	65-	N	8:21.2	-107	20	229	4	1178 T	5.8	87-	N	4:17.0	-130	50
155	10	Saturn	0.3	54-	N	12:26.5	-130	44	230	4	1221 V	6.0	85-	S	12:43.8	-130	33
156	11	843 O	7.0	45-	N	5:39.1	-101	52	231	6	1479	6.4	65-	S	13:10.2	-130	54
157	11	861	6.3	44-	N	7:25.9	-95	20	232	8	X17638	6.9	44-	N	8:11.4	-112	44
158	12	1014	7.0	34-	N	5:55.0	-92	52	233	8	1702	4.0	44-	S	8:32.6	-122	48
159	12	1036	6.5	33-	N	9:14.9	-128	35	234	9	1813	5.7	33-	N	8:01.5	-95	21
160	12	1050	5.7	32-	N	11:34.8	-130	32	235	10	1950	5.7	22-	S	11:27.7	-128	35
161	13	1178 T	6.3	23-	N	9:14.3	-90	20	236	19	3106	5.2	16+	S	1:34.1	-110	20
162	14	1315	7.1	14-	N	7:53.4	-86	50	237	19	3116	6.6	17+	S	3:21.1	-113	20
163	15	1462	7.3	6-	N	11:40.1	-119	48	238	19	3227	6.3	23+	S	23:31.2	-103	42
164	20	2020 K	6.5	9+	N	0:06.1	-87	47	239	20	3343 A	5.7	32+	S	22:46.7	-90	40
165	26	2857	6.5	65+	N	0:48.0	-102	28	240	21	3349	4.0	32+	S	0:02.9	-99	20
166	27	2991	6.1	75+	N	2:15.0	-124	43	241	22	3484	6.9	42+	S	2:36.5	-112	20
167	28	3106	5.2	82+	S	0:29.3	-80	44	242	24	170	6.0	63+	N	6:54.4	-111	20
168	28	3116	6.9	82+	N	2:04.7	-89	28	243	25	368 M	6.2	78+	S	21:08.9	-65	40
169	Oct. 4	322 K	5.6	96-	N	14:21.2	-130	53	244	26	393 K	6.7	79+	S	1:51.4	-129	30
170	6	527 A	6.2	87-	N	7:31.2	-126	20	245	27	527 A	6.2	89+	N	9:20.1	-128	53
171	7	668	3.5	80-	N	5:23.3	-108	20	246	28	654 K	6.0	93+	S	3:25.8	-130	39
172	7	700 U	5.8	78-	N	11:34.7	-125	20	247	28	Saturn	-0.1	94+	N	8:32.9	-130	54
173	8	792	5.0	71-	N	3:46.9	-83	20	248	29	792	5.0	98+	S	2:13.2	-92	20

GRAZING OCCULTATION MAPS

JANUARY 1 – FEBRUARY 15

FEBRUARY 16 – MARCH 31

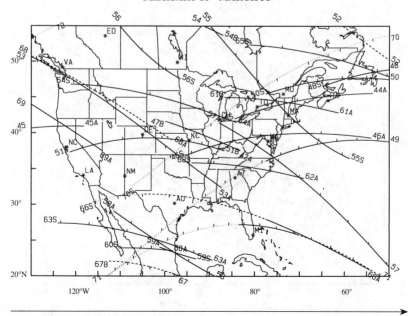

GRAZING OCCULTATION MAPS (continued)

APRIL 1 – MAY 15

MAY 16 – JUNE 30

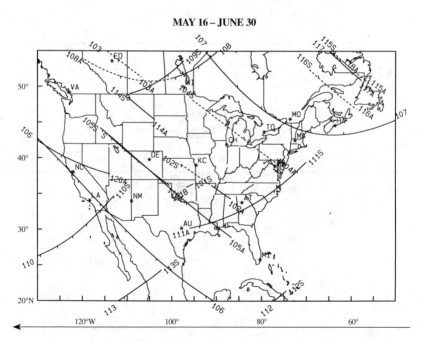

GRAZING OCCULTATION MAPS (continued)

JULY 1 – AUGUST 15

AUGUST 16 – OCTOBER 15

GRAZING OCCULTATION MAPS (continued)

OCTOBER 16 – NOVEMBER 15

NOVEMBER 16 – DECEMBER 31

TIDES AND THE EARTH–MOON SYSTEM
BY ROY BISHOP

The tidal aspect of gravitation produces some of the most interesting phenomena in the universe, from the structure of interacting galaxies, such as M51, to the volcanoes of Io, the fragmentation of Comet Shoemaker-Levy 9 by Jupiter in 1994, the synchronous rotation of our Moon, and the pulse of the seas on our planet. Perhaps because they occur at our feet, the tides of the oceans are often overlooked when considering the heavens. These tides were known to the ancients, but an understanding of their origin came only three centuries ago with the publication of Newton's *Principia*.

In the Newtonian context, tides originate in the fact that the force of gravity decreases with distance from a massive body. The Moon exerts a force on Earth, and Earth responds by accelerating toward the Moon; however, the waters on the hemisphere facing the Moon, being closer to the Moon, accelerate more and fall ahead of Earth. Similarly, Earth itself accelerates more than the waters on the other hemisphere and falls ahead of these waters. Thus two aqueous bulges are produced, one on the side of Earth facing the Moon and one on the side facing away from the Moon:

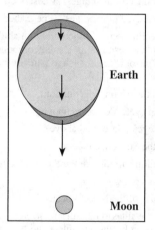

In order of decreasing length, the arrows indicate the force per unit mass (acceleration) produced by the Moon's gravity on the near side, centre, and far side of Earth. It is the resulting horizontal flow of the water toward the two points nearest and farthest from the Moon that forms the two tidal bulges (indicated by heavy shading).

As Earth rotates on its axis beneath these two bulges, the rise and fall of the oceans results. If Earth had no rigidity, the entire planet would flex freely in the same fashion, and there would be virtually no water tides. The very existence of the tides indicates that on a time scale of several hours our planet displays considerable rigidity.

Because of the Moon's orbital motion, it transits on the average 50.47 min later each day. Thus on successive days, high tides recur about 50 min later (or for the many regions experiencing two high tides daily, these tides recur at intervals of 12 h 25 min).

Although the Sun exerts a gravitational force 180 times as strong as does the Moon on Earth, because the Moon is so much closer, the *variation* in the Moon's force across Earth's diameter is about 2.2 times larger than the variation in the Sun's force. As described above, it is this variation that produces tides; thus the pair of bulges raised by the Moon are considerably larger than the pair raised by the Sun. As the Moon goes through its monthly cycle of phases, these two pairs of tidal bulges get in and out of step, combining in step to produce *spring tides* (no connection with the season) when the Moon is new or full and out of step to produce *neap tides* when the Moon is at first or last quarter.

Another factor having a substantial influence on tidal ranges is the elliptical shape of the Moon's orbit. Although the Moon is only 9% to 14% closer at perigee than at apogee, because the *variation* in its gravitational force varies inversely as the cube of its distance (the force itself varies inversely as the square of the distance), the Moon's tidal influence is 30% to 48% greater at perigee than at apogee. Because the Sun tidally influences the shape of the Moon's orbit, exceptionally close perigees coincide with full or new Moon, and the resulting extreme tides are known as *perigean spring tides*. In some areas, such as the Bay of Fundy in eastern Canada, the perigee–apogee influence is greater than the spring–neap influence. Although the variation of the Moon's distance is not readily apparent to observers viewing the Moon directly, to observers on the shores near the head of the Bay of Fundy, the 3 m to 6 m *increase* in the vertical tidal range makes it obvious when the Moon is near perigee, clear skies or cloudy!

There are many astronomical factors influencing the tides. These can be sorted out according to the periods they produce. The periods of the more important factors are:

(1) semidiurnal, 12 h 00 min (two solar-induced tidal bulges, as described above);

(2) semidiurnal, 12 h 25 min (two lunar-induced tidal bulges, as described above);

(3) diurnal, 24 h 50 min (the changing declinations of Moon and Sun shift the pairs of tidal bulges out of Earth's equatorial plane resulting in a tidal component with a one-day period—this is the dominant tide in some areas, such as parts of the southern coast of Canada's Gulf of St. Lawrence);

(4) semimonthly, 13.66 days (variation in the Moon's declination);

(5) semimonthly, 14.77 days (spring–neap cycle, described above);

(6) monthly, 27.55 days (perigee-apogee cycle, described above);

(7) semiannual, 182.6 days (variation in the Sun's declination);

(8) annual, 365.26 days (perihelion–aphelion variation in the Sun's tidal influence);

(9) 8.8 years (rotation period of the Moon's perigee); and

(10) 18.6 years (rotation period of the nodes of the Moon's orbit).

In addition to astronomical factors, the tides on Earth are strongly influenced by the sizes, boundaries, and depths of ocean basins and inlets and by Earth's rotation, winds, and barometric pressure fluctuations. Tides typically have ranges (vertical high-to-low) of a metre or two, but there are regions in the oceans where the various influences conspire to produce virtually no tides at all, and others where the tides are greatly amplified. Among the latter regions are the Sea of Okhotsk, the northern coast of Australia, the English channel, and in Canada—Ungava Bay in northern Quebec and the Bay of Fundy between New Brunswick and Nova Scotia. The tidal ranges in these regions are of the order of 10 m.

The highest ocean tides on Earth occur in Minas Basin, the eastern extremity of the Bay of Fundy, where the mean tide range is 12 m and can reach 16 m when the various factors affecting the tides are in phase (although the highest tides occur typically a day or two after the astronomical influences reach their peak). The most dramatic view of this vertical range is at the government wharf in the town of Hantsport, Nova Scotia. Remarkably, this site is practically unknown; it is not advertised, and no special provisions have been made to accommodate spectators.

The primary cause of the immense tides of Fundy is a resonance of the Bay of Fundy–Gulf of Maine system. The system is effectively bounded at its outer end by the edge of the continental shelf with its approximately 40:1 increase in depth. The system has a natural period of approximately 12.7 hours, a Q-value of about 5, and is driven near resonance by the dominant semidiurnal tides of the Atlantic Ocean. Like a father pushing his daughter on a swing, the gentle Atlantic tidal pulse pushes the waters of the Bay of Fundy–Gulf of Maine basin at nearly the optimum frequency to cause a large oscillation.

Perhaps the most awesome display of the tides on our planet occurs at Cape Split, Nova Scotia, on the southern side of the entrance to Minas Basin (Cape Split may be reached by a pleasant two-hour walk along a popular hiking trail from the village of Scots Bay). Here, at the time of the midpoint of an incoming tide, for a considerable distance the forest on the towering cliffs is filled with a hollow roar produced by the turbulence of the waters surging over the submarine ridges below. The currents exceed 8 knots (4 m/s), and the flow in the deep, 5-km-wide channel on the north side of Cape Split equals the combined flow of all the streams and rivers of Earth ($\approx$4 km³/h). Three hours later the spectacle pauses and then begins flowing in the opposite direction.

Through friction, the tides convert Earth's rotational kinetic energy into heat at a rate of about 4 TW, comparable to humankind's total rate of energy use. Approximately 1% of this occurs in the Bay of Fundy and, since 1984, a tiny portion of this (20 MW peak) is being turned into commercial electric power at the Annapolis Basin tidal power plant in Nova Scotia. The only other large-scale tidal power installation is in France on the Rance estuary (240 MW peak).

Tidal friction also transfers angular momentum from Earth to the Moon, lengthening the day and increasing the size of the orbit of the Moon. The day is lengthening by about 1 second every 40 000 years—imperceptible on a human time scale, but of profound significance to Earth's rotation over a few billion years. (For example 900 million years ago when Earth was already 80% of its present age, there were about 480 18-hour days in a year.) The Moon is receding about 3.8 cm per year, with the result that within 600 million years total solar eclipses will cease. Presently we are well into the transitional phase: annular eclipses already outnumber total solar eclipses. New moons occur, on average, almost one day earlier each successive month; however, because of the increasing size of the lunar orbit, in about 300 million years the lunar (synodic) month will have lengthened to equal the average calendar month (although the average month will then contain only about twenty-eight 26-hour days).

If the Sun does not first incinerate our planet, there will come a day that is as long as the lunar month (each then equal to about 40 present days), and a more distant Moon will stand stationary in the sky, as does Earth now in the lunar sky. But this situation will not endure, for solar tides will still be present and will reduce the angular momentum of the Earth–Moon system, causing the Moon to approach Earth once more.

For more information, see the superb introduction is *The Tides* by E. P. Clancy, Anchor Books, Doubleday and Co., 1969 (now, unfortunately, out of print). An excellent article dealing specifically with the tides of Fundy and tidal power installations has been written by Christopher Garrett (1984, *Endeavour* 8, #2, 58–64). The major astronomical factors influencing the tides (the phases, perigees and apogees of the Moon) are tabulated in THE SKY MONTH BY MONTH section (pp. 58–81) of this Handbook. These may be scanned to determine days favourable for large tides. Detailed predictions for tides in Canadian waters are published in *Canadian Tide and Current Table*s, the six volumes of which are individually available from Canadian Government bookstores or by mail from Hydrographic Chart Distribution Office, Fisheries and Oceans Canada, 1675 Russell Road, P.O. Box 8080, Ottawa, ON, Canada K1G 3H6.

PLANETS AND SATELLITES

GENERAL INTRODUCTION

PLANETARY HELIOCENTRIC LONGITUDES, 2001

The heliocentric longitude of a planet is the angle between the vernal equinox and the planet, as seen from the Sun. It is measured in the ecliptic plane, in the direction of the orbital motion of the planet (counterclockwise as viewed from the north side of the ecliptic plane). Knowing the heliocentric longitudes and distances of the planets from the Sun (see p. 18), one can construct a diagram or model showing the relative orientations of the Sun and planets on any date.

UT	Me °	V °	E °	Ma °	J °	S °	U °	N °	P °
Jan. 1.0	292	47	101	182	69	59	320	306	253
Feb. 1.0	73	97	132	196	72	60	321	306	253
Mar. 1.0	209	142	160	209	74	61	321	306	253
Apr. 1.0	299	192	191	224	77	62	321	307	254
May 1.0	80	241	221	239	80	63	322	307	254
Jun. 1.0	222	290	251	256	82	65	322	307	254
Jul. 1.0	308	337	279	273	85	66	322	307	254
Aug. 1.0	105	27	309	290	87	67	323	307	254
Sep. 1.0	234	76	339	310	90	68	323	308	254
Oct. 1.0	323	125	8	329	93	69	323	308	255
Nov. 1.0	129	175	39	348	95	70	324	308	255
Dec. 1.0	242	224	69	7	98	71	324	308	255
Jan. 1.0	338	273	100	26	101	72	324	308	255

MAGNITUDES OF NAKED–EYE PLANETS IN 2001

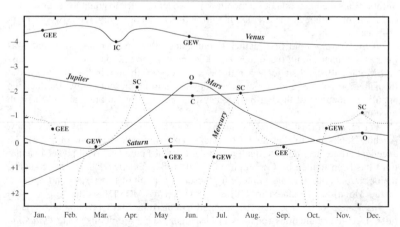

The visual magnitudes of the five, classical (naked-eye) planets during 2001 are given. Oppositions (O), conjunctions (C), inferior and superior conjunctions (IC, SC), and greatest elongations east and west (GEE, GEW) are indicated. See the diagram explaining these terms at the right.

PRONUNCIATION OF PLANET NAMES

Mercury	mûr′kū–rē
Venus	vē′nŭs
Earth	ûrth
Mars	màrz
Jupiter	jōo′pĭ–tĕr
Saturn	sàt′ûrn
Uranus	yoor′à–nŭs
Neptune	nĕp′tyōon
Pluto	plōo′tō

à àsk;   ē wē; ĕ mĕt; ē makēr;   ĭ bĭt;
ō gō; oo book; ōo mōon;   ū ūnite; ŭ ŭp; û ûrn

SOLAR SYSTEM GEOMETRY

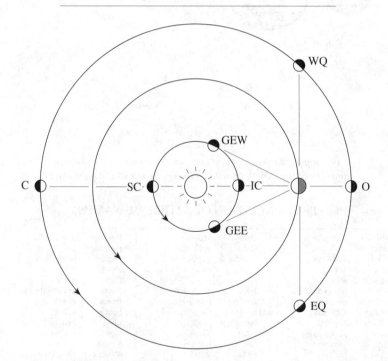

The diagram is a simplified view of our solar system, from the north side. Earth is shown (middle orbit) together with an inferior planet (i.e. Mercury or Venus) and a superior planet (e.g. Mars). Four special geometrical configurations of the inferior planet relative to Earth are shown; in counterclockwise chronological sequence they are inferior conjunction (IC), greatest elongation west (GEW), superior conjunction (SC), and greatest elongation west (GEW). Four special configurations of the superior planet relative to Earth are also shown; in clockwise chronological sequence they are opposition (O), eastern quadrature (EQ), conjunction (C), and western quadrature (WQ).

TELESCOPIC APPEARANCE OF THE PLANETS

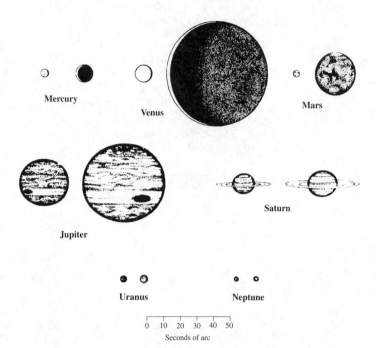

Mercury

Venus

Mars

Jupiter

Saturn

Uranus   Neptune

```
0    10   20   30   40   50
         Seconds of arc
```

*The apparent maximum and minimum observable size of seven
planets is illustrated along with charateristic telescopic appearance.*

PRONUNCIATION OF SATELLITE NAMES

Adrastea	à-drăs'tē-à	Europa	yoo-rō'pà	Pandora	păn-dôr'à
Amalthea	ăm''l-thē'à	Galatea	găl'à-tē'à	Pasiphae	pà-sĭf'à-ē'
Ananke	à'năn-kē	Ganymede	găn'ĕ-mēd'	Phobos	fō'bŏs
Ariel	âr'ē-ĕl	Helene	hà-lēn'	Phoebe	fē'bē
Atlas	ăt'lăs	Himalia	hĭm'à-lĭ-à	Portia	pôr'shà
Belinda	bà-lĭn'dà	Hyperion	hī-pēr'ĭ-ŏn	Prometheus	prŏ-mē'thē-ŭs
Bianca	bē-āng'kà	Iapetus	ī-ăp'ĕ-tŭs	Proteus	prō'tē-ŭs
Caliban	kăl'ĭ-băn	Io	ī'ō	Puck	pŭk
Callisto	kà-lĭs'tō	Janus	jā'nŭs	Rhea	rē'à
Calypso	kà-lĭp'sō	Juliet	joo'lē-ĕt	Rosalind	rŏz'à-lĭnd
Carme	kàr'mē	Larissa	là-rĭs'à	Sinope	sĭ-nō'pē
Charon	kâr'ĕn	Leda	lē'dà	Sycorax	sĭk'ō-răks
Cordelia	kôr-dĕl'yà	Lysithea	lĭs'ĭ-thē'à	Telesto	tà-lĕs'tō
Cressida	krĕs'ĭ-dà	Metis	mē'tĭs	Tethys	tē'thĭs
Deimos	dī'mŏs	Mimas	mī'măs	Thalassa	thà-làs'à
Desdemona	dĕz'dà-mō'nà	Miranda	mĭ-răn'dà	Thebe	thē'be
Despina	dĭs-pĭn'à	Moon	moon	Titan	ti't'n
Dione	dī-ō'nē	Naiad	nī'àd	Titania	tī'tā'nē-à
Elara	ē'làr-à	Nereid	nēr'ē-ĭd	Triton	trī't'n
Enceladus	ĕn-sĕl'à-dŭs	Oberon	ō'bà-rŏn	Umbriel	ŭm'brē-ĕl'
Epimetheus	ĕp'à-mē'thē-ŭs	Ophelia	ō-fēl'yà		

ā dāte; ă tăp; â câre; à àsk; ē wē; ĕ mĕt; ī īce; ĭ bĭt; ō gō; ŏ hŏt; ô ôrb; oo book; o͞o mo͞on; ŭ ŭp

RIGHT ASCENSIONS OF THE SUN AND PLANETS IN 2001

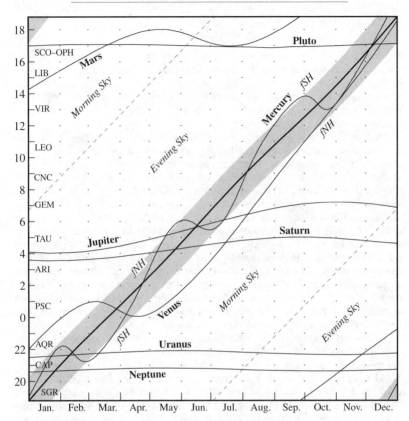

This diagram shows the variation during the year in the right ascension (vertical axis) of the Sun and the planets. The slightly curved, heavy diagonal line represents the Sun; the shaded regions approximately indicate parts of the night sky affected by twilight. The two dashed diagonal lines represent the boundary between the evening sky and the morning sky.

The diagram may be used as a quick reference to determine in what part of the sky a planet may be found (including in which constellation—note the names along the vertical axis), when a superior planet is in conjunction with the Sun or at opposition (opposition is approximately where its curve intersects the dashed diagonal lines, and note that, due to retrograde motion, this point is also where the planet's curve has its maximum negative slope), when Mercury and Venus have their various greatest elongations and conjunctions, and when there are conjunctions of planets. For example, the mid-June opposition of Mars can be read from the top of the diagram. Also note the close approach of Mercury and Venus during late October and early November; the curves come very close to each other but do not cross, so this is not, technically, a conjunction.

For observers in midlatitudes, at certain times of the year the ecliptic stands steeply to the horizon in the western evening sky or the eastern morning sky, making apparitions of planets in these parts of the sky favourable from the Northern Hemisphere ("fNH" on the diagram) or favourable from the Southern Hemisphere ("fSH"). For example, this year observers in the Northern Hemisphere will get their best chance to see Mercury in mid-May (evening sky) or late October and early November (morning sky).

For more information on all these events, see THE SKY MONTH BY MONTH *(pp. 56–81) and* THE PLANETS FOR 2001 *(immediately following).*

THE PLANETS FOR 2001
By Terence Dickinson

INTRODUCTION

Planetary observing is perhaps the most widely accessible and diversified category of amateur astronomical pursuits. Planets can be seen on almost any clear night of the year. Indeed, in heavily light-polluted cities they are sometimes the *only* celestial objects visible. With dark skies ever more remote from population centres, planetary observing is returning—partly by default—to take its place as an important part of the amateur astronomer's repertoire.

But a more important factor than sky conditions is needed to explain the expanding interest in planetary observing. It is the widespread recognition among amateur astronomers that high-quality optics are essential for good views of the planets. That, combined with the increased commercial availability of such instruments—especially previously unavailable systems such as apochromatic refractors and Maksutov-Newtonians—means that planetary observing is more accessible than ever.

Planetary observing divides into three distinct categories, each with its opportunities and limitations. *Unaided-eye* observing consists of detecting, identifying, and monitoring the night-to-night and week-to-week motion and visibility of the five brighter planets. *Binoculars* add Uranus and Neptune along with the Galilean satellites of Jupiter. Binoculars are ideal for tracking planetary motion against the backdrop of stars, many of which are too faint for naked-eye detection. But it is only through *telescopic* observing that the planets reveal their uniqueness, and this section concentrates on that aspect. For a listing of unaided-eye highlights such as conjunctions, see THE SKY MONTH BY MONTH section on pp. 56–81.

Urban and suburban locales unsuited for many aspects of astronomy can be perfectly acceptable for telescopic planetary observing. Atmospheric turbulence—seeing—is often no worse, and sometimes better, in urban areas. However, observers should avoid using telescopes on pavement, balconies, or immediately beside a house or substantial building due to the heat radiated to the surrounding atmosphere from these structures. Also, avoid looking over these objects if possible. A typical grassed backyard is fine in most instances. For optimum performance, all telescopes (except small refractors) require from 10 min to an hour to cool to outside temperature when taken outdoors. Hazy but otherwise cloudless nights are usually just as good as, and sometimes better than, clear skies for steady telescopic images of planets.

More than any other class of telescopic observing, planetary observing is most affected by seeing. Many nights are rendered useless for planet watching by ever-present ripples and undulations in Earth's atmosphere. Planets within 15° of the horizon are virtually always afflicted. Minimum altitude for expectations of reasonable seeing is 25°. A further problem with low-altitude planetary targets is dispersion associated with atmospheric refraction. Refraction causes celestial objects to appear displaced to higher altitudes. Since the effect is wavelength dependent (being less for longer wavelengths), for planets at low altitudes this produces a red fringe on the lower side of the planet and a green (or blue) fringe on the upper, as well as introducing chromatic smearing to the whole image.

Regardless of the type of telescope used for planetary observing, optical quality is far more critical than aperture. In no other type of observing are the effects of less-than-perfect optics more apparent. Other factors that significantly degrade a telescope's planetary performance include a large *central obstruction* in the optical system (all Schmidt-Cassegrains, Maksutov-Cassegrains, and Newtonians with secondary mirror diameters exceeding 20% of their apertures), *secondary mirror supports* (most Newtonians), *chromatic aberration* (most achromatic refractors over 90 mm), *internal air currents* (all types, refractors least), optical component *cool-down time* (mostly aperture-dependent, telescopes over 200 mm can take hours), and *dirty optics*.

In the remarks below, when a planetary phenomenon is stated as being visible in a certain minimum aperture, good seeing and a moderate level of observer experience are assumed. When a specific minimum aperture is cited, an unobstructed optical system (i.e. a refractor) is assumed. Somewhat larger apertures are often required if centrally obstructed systems are used, or the observer is inexperienced.

Editor's Note: The boxed tables that appear in this section were prepared by the Editor, and he assumes full responsibility for their accuracy.

MERCURY

Of the five planets visible to the unaided eye, Mercury is by far the most difficult to observe and is seldom conveniently located for either unaided eye or telescopic observation. The problem for observers is Mercury's tight orbit, which constrains the planet to a small zone on either side of the Sun as viewed from Earth. When Mercury is east of the Sun we may see it as an evening "star" low in the west just after sunset. When it is west of the Sun we might view Mercury as a morning "star" in the east before sunrise. But due to celestial geometry involving the tilt of Earth's axis and Mercury's orbit, we get much better views of Mercury at certain times of the year.

MERCURY—MOST FAVOURABLE EVENING VIEW IN 2001 FROM NORTHERN LATITUDES

Date 0h UT	Mag.	Angular Diameter "	Percent Illuminated	Elongation from Sun °	RA (2001) h m	Dec ° '
May 2	−1.4	5.4	91	10	3 16	+19 11
6	−1.1	5.6	86	14	3 48	+21 42
10	−0.7	6.2	70	17	4 19	+23 33
14	−0.3	6.7	58	20	4 46	+24 45
18	+0.1	7.3	47	21	5 11	+25 21
22	+0.5	8.1	37	22	5 30	+25 26

From midlatitudes, the best time to see the planet in the *evening* sky is within a month or two of the spring equinox and in the *morning* sky within a month or two of the autumn equinox (this applies to both northern and southern latitudes, although the respective seasons are six months out of phase). Binoculars are of great assistance in searching for the planet about 40 min to an hour after sunset or before sunrise during the periods when it is visible. The planet's brightness, which varies by more than two magnitudes, is a more important factor influencing its visibility than its angular distance from the Sun during any particular elongation. Mercury's true colour is almost pure white, but absorption from Earth's atmosphere within 15° of the horizon, where Mercury is most easily seen, usually imparts a yellow or ochre hue to the planet.

Telescopic observers will find the rapidly changing phases of Mercury of interest. The planet appears to zip from gibbous to crescent phase in about three weeks during each of its evening elongations. The phases are accessible to users of 75-mm or larger telescopes; the 30% phase can be detected at 50×. Large apertures (over

200 mm) rarely offer an advantage due to the crippling effects of poor seeing at lower altitudes, especially following sunset when the planet is most frequently observed. Experienced planetary observers often report their most satisfying telescopic observations of Mercury in the morning sky. Near favourable western elongations, the planet may be easily located at least an hour before sunrise, then followed to higher altitudes into the daytime sky. Seeing often remains steady more than an hour after sunrise by which time the planet may be 30° above the horizon. Under such conditions the phase is sharply defined, and the small disk takes on a unique appearance, paler than Venus, with a vaguely textured surface. Surface details, though suspected in moments of fine seeing, are always elusive. Contrasts among the planet's surface features are lower than on the lunar surface, although in other respects the two bodies are similar.

VENUS

Venus is the only world in the solar system that closely resembles Earth in size and mass. It also comes nearer to Earth than any other planet, at times approaching as close as 0.27 AU. Despite the fundamental similarity, surface conditions on Earth and Venus differ greatly. The clouds and haze that cloak the planet are highly reflective, making Venus the brightest natural celestial object in the nighttime sky apart from our Moon. Whenever it is visible, it is readily recognized. Because its orbit is within that of Earth's, Venus is never separated from the Sun by an angle greater than 47°. However, this is more than sufficient for the dazzling object to dominate the morning or evening sky.

Like Mercury, Venus exhibits phases, although they are much more easily detected in small telescopes because of Venus' greater size. When it is far from us near the other side of its orbit, we see the planet nearly fully illuminated, but because of its distance, it appears small—about 10″ in diameter. As Venus moves closer to Earth, the phase decreases (we see less of the illuminated portion of the planet), but the diameter increases until it is a thin slice nearly a minute of arc in diameter. It takes Venus several months to move from one of these extremes to the other, compared to just a few weeks for Mercury.

As 2001 opens, Venus is a dazzling beacon in the southwest at dusk, very favourably positioned for northern observers (although much less so for southern observers; see THE SKY MONTH BY MONTH). For northerners, the brilliant planet continues to dominate the early evening sky until mid-March when it plunges toward the Sun and inferior conjunction on March 30. At inferior conjunction, Venus will be 8° north of the Sun, distant enough so that it can be followed by telescope in the daytime sky by experienced observers—using extreme caution to avoid an accidental unprotected solar-viewing encounter. The planet will appear as a 1% illuminated crescent at this time, one minute in diameter. During the half-century centred on 2001, Venus is never more than 8.5° of the Sun at inferior conjunction so this one presents a favourable observing opportunity.

At high northern latitudes near inferior conjunction, observers may be able to make the rare sighting of Venus in *both* the evening sky and the morning sky, at opposite ends of the same night. The celestial geometry will be most favourable for this on the night of March 27/28, although even with the aid of binoculars, this will be a difficult observation. Following inferior conjunction, the overall observing conditions reverse, with southern observers gaining a fine morning sky viewing apparition while northern sky watchers will find Venus hugging the morning sky eastern horizon until midsummer. From then through to the end of the year, Venus' elevation in morning twilight tends to favour northern observers.

VENUS—FAVOURABLE INFERIOR CONJUNCTION, 2001

Date 0h UT	Mag.	Angular Diameter "	Percent Illuminated	Elongation from Sun °	RA (2001) h m	Dec ° '
Jan. 21	–4.4	25.3	49.2	47	23 16	–4 35
Feb. 10	–4.6	32.6	36.8	45	0 17	+4 49
22	–4.6	38.9	27.4	40	0 43	+9 37
Mar. 6	–4.6	46.9	16.6	33	0 54	+12 58
14	–4.5	52.6	9.4	24	0 51	+13 52
22	–4.3	57.2	3.6	15	0 40	+13 17
26	–4.1	58.6	1.8	11	0 31	+12 25
*30	–4.0	59.2	1.0	8	0 23	+11 12
Apr. 3	–4.1	58.6	1.5	9	0 14	+9 46
7	–4.2	57.2	3.0	14	0 07	+8 15
15	–4.4	52.4	8.4	24	23 59	+5 30
23	–4.5	46.5	15.6	32	0 01	+3 40
May 5	–4.5	38.3	26.2	39	0 18	+2 59
17	–4.5	31.8	35.6	43	0 48	+4 18
Jun. 6	–4.5	24.4	48.4	46	1 53	+9 06

* Inferior conjunction occurs March 30 4h UT with Venus 8°01′ N of the Sun and 0.282 AU from Earth.

Favourable inferior conjunctions such as this occur at almost exactly 8-year intervals; Venus will be an even greater 8°10′ N of the Sun at its 2009 March 27 inferior conjunction. See "Recurrent Phenomena of Venus and the Venus/Earth Orbital Resonance" by David Chapman, *JRASC*, *80*, 336, 1986.

Telescopic observing information for the prime observing period near inferior conjunction is given in the above table. For other times, the following information will be useful: On January 1 Venus is 58% illuminated and 20″ in apparent diameter; June 1, 45%, 25″; July 1, 60%, 18″; August 1, 72%, 14″; September 1, 82%, 12″.

When Venus is about a 20% crescent, even rigidly held, good quality binoculars can be used to distinguish that the planet is not spherical or a point source. The new generation of image-stabilized binoculars beautifully display the crescent Venus. A 60-mm refractor should be capable of revealing the shape of all but the gibbous and full phases. Experienced observers prefer to observe Venus during the daytime, and indeed the planet is bright enough to be seen with the unaided eye if one knows where to look.

Because of Venus' high surface brightness (about 40 times greater than Jupiter's), Venus can accommodate the highest magnifications a telescope can deliver. The author has used magnifications over 4× per millimetre of aperture on occasion and regularly employs 1.5× to 3× per millimetre on the planet, particularly in bright twilight when the sky is moderately dark but Venus is still high enough to avoid low-altitude seeing degradation. Venus' cloud-shrouded surface appears to most observers to be featureless no matter what type of telescope is used or what the planet's phase. Broad streaks and splotches in the clouds, revealed in blue-filtered and ultraviolet images of Venus, may be vaguely detected telescopically using a violet filter (#38A or #47), although sketches of these features seldom match among different observers.

MARS

In many ways Mars is the most interesting planet to observe with the unaided eye. It moves rapidly among the stars—its motion can often be detected after an interval of less than a week—and it varies in brightness over a far greater range than any other planet. Mars may be distinguished by its pale orange-red colour, a hue that originates with rust-coloured dust that covers much of the planet. As 2001 opens, Mars is a morning-sky object on the Virgo/Libra border. During the next five months it moves eastward through Libra and Scorpius as it brightens from magnitude +1 to −2 and its ochre glow dominates the southern sky (low in the south for northerners, high in the south for southerners). Mars is brightest and closest to Earth in June, in Ophiuchus, where it is visible throughout the night. In the evening sky from July to the end of the year, Mars moves from Ophiuchus eastward into Sagittarius in September, into Capricornus in October, and on into Aquarius in December. During this period it remains a conspicuous naked-eye object, fading from magnitude +2 to zero.

Telescopically Mars is usually a disappointingly small featureless ochre disk except within a few months of opposition when its distance from Earth is then near minimum. If Mars is at perihelion at these times the separation can be as little as 56 million kilometres. Such close approaches occur at intervals of 15 to 17 years; the most recent was in 1988, the next will be in 2003. At a perihelion opposition the telescopic disk of Mars is 25″ in diameter and much detail on the planet can be distinguished with telescopes of 100-mm aperture or greater. At oppositions other than when Mars is near perihelion, the disk is correspondingly smaller (see the diagram at the right).

Observers using 100-mm or larger telescopes can record enough detail to note changes in the planet's dark regions from one opposition to the next. These alterations are caused by high-velocity winds in the thin Martian atmosphere that transport vast quantities of dust, both dark and light, across the desert planet. Most of Mars looks like a peach-coloured desert with darker greyish zones (also deserts) of varying size and prominence. The clarity of the surface features—white polar caps and dark, irregular patches on a peach-coloured sphere—depends to a large extent on the transparency of the Martian atmosphere. Dust storms, clouds, and haze can lower contrast across large sectors of the disk. But when the Martian air is clear and the seeing conditions on Earth permit, the subtle colour and fine detail of the planet's surface are exquisite and compelling in a telescope.

This year, Mars will be closer to Earth than it has been since 1988. Minimum distance of 67.34 million kilometres (.4502 AU) is reached on June 21, more than a week after opposition on June 13. This difference is caused by the substantial eccentricity of the Martian orbit, which is carrying Mars toward the Sun around opposition time. At closest approach, Mars will be 20.8″ in apparent diameter, somewhat greater than the average closest approach apparent diameter of 18″. From the Southern Hemisphere, Mars rides near overhead around midnight during the weeks around opposition. That, combined with the planet's relatively large apparent diameter, makes this is a very favourable opposition for southerners. But for northern observers, Mars will be bright but low—very low. During the prime observing window, May through July, Mars will be between declination −24° and −27°. This places the planet no more than 21° above the southern horizon for an observer at latitude +45°. Rarely is the seeing at such low elevation steady enough to resolve fine planetary detail.

Even so, northern observers will still want to make the best of this year's close approach of the red planet because the most distinctive Martian surface features (Syrtis Major, Sabaeus Sinus, and Meridiani Sinus) near the equator are well displayed. Throughout the prime observing window, the Martian equator is within a few

(text continued on p. 174)

OPPOSITIONS OF MARS, 1997–2010

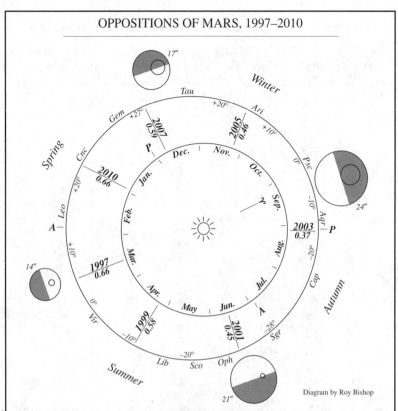

Diagram by Roy Bishop

*The above diagram represents the orbits of Earth and Mars as viewed from the north eclip-
tic pole. Straight lines link simultaneous positions of the two planets for seven successive
oppositions of Mars, beginning with that of the year 1997. The separation of the two planets
(in astronomical units) at the various oppositions is indicated beside each of the connecting
lines. The months inside of Earth's orbit indicate the position of Earth during the year (both
planets orbit counterclockwise). For each orbit, two tick marks labeled A and P indicate the
aphelion point and the perihelion point, respectively. The direction of the vernal equinox is
shown (toward the late September position of Earth). Around the orbit of Mars is indicated
its declination (ranges between +27° and –28°) and the constellation in which Mars resides
when at opposition.*

    *Four views of Mars are shown—at its two equinoxes and two solstices. These views
show the portion of Mars illuminated by the Sun, the location and approximate size of its
north polar cap, and the apparent size of Mars (labelled in arc-seconds) for oppositions
occurring at these points in its orbit. The seasons of the Martian northern hemisphere are
indicated around the outer margin of the diagram, and are very nearly one season ahead
of those on Earth at the same orbital position. (For the southern hemisphere of Mars, the
season and the configuration of the south polar cap are the same as those of the diametri-
cally opposite view.) Note that the maximum angular diameter Mars can attain (25″) occurs
near its perihelion, at a late-August opposition (as in the year 2003).*

    *As an example of the information that can be read from this diagram: the 2001 opposi-
tion of Mars occurs in mid-June with Mars 0.45 AU from Earth. Mars will be about 21″ in
angular diameter and located near declination –26°, near the Ophiuchus-Sagittarius border.
It will be the northern hemisphere autumn equinox on Mars, with a tiny north polar cap and
a large south polar cap on the limb of Mars.*

MARS—EPHEMERIS FOR PHYSICAL OBSERVATIONS, 2001

Date 0h UT	Dist. AU	Mag.	Equat. Diam. "	Percent Illum.	Position Angle °	Incl. °	L(1) °	Δ °/d
Jan. 13	1.673	+1.2	5.6	91	38	+16	152.9	9.61
Feb. 14	1.353	+0.8	6.9	90	37	+9	205.4	9.53
Mar. 18	1.034	+0.2	9.1	89	33	+3	260.3	9.41
Apr. 19	0.747	−0.6	12.5	92	28	−1	319.1	9.29
27	0.684	−1.0	13.7	93	28	−2	244.8	9.22
May 5	0.627	−1.2	14.9	94	27	−2	171.0	9.15
13	0.576	−1.4	16.3	96	27	−2	97.9	9.06
21	0.532	−1.7	17.6	97	27	−1	25.4	8.98
29	0.497	−2.0	18.9	99	28	0	313.5	8.91
Jun. 6	0.471	−2.2	19.9	100	29	+2	242.3	8.86
14	0.455	−2.4	20.6	100	30	+3	171.4	8.84
22	0.450	−2.3	20.8	100	31	+5	100.7	8.87
30	0.455	−2.2	20.6	98	32	+6	29.7	8.93
Jul. 8	0.469	−2.0	20.0	97	33	+7	318.3	9.02
16	0.490	−1.8	19.1	95	33	+7	246.1	9.12
24	0.518	−1.6	18.1	93	33	+7	173.2	9.21
Aug. 1	0.550	−1.5	17.0	91	33	+7	99.5	9.30
9	0.586	−1.4	16.0	89	32	+6	25.1	9.38
17	0.625	−1.2	15.0	88	31	+5	310.1	9.44
25	0.666	−1.0	14.1	87	30	+3	234.5	9.50
Sep. 2	0.709	−0.8	13.2	86	28	+2	158.5	9.55
10	0.753	−0.7	12.4	85	26	0	82.1	9.64
Oct.. 12	0.941	−0.2	10.0	85	16	−9	133.6	9.77
Nov. 13	1.148	+0.2	8.2	86	2	−18	181.1	9.87
Dec. 15	1.370	+0.6	6.8	87	348	−24	225.3	

The above table gives information useful for observers of Mars during 2001. Data are given at 8-day intervals while Mars is greater than 12″ in equatorial diameter (Apr. 19 to Sep. 10), otherwise the intervals are approximately one-month. The columns give (1) the date; (2) the distance of Mars from Earth in astronomical units; (3) the visual magnitude of Mars; (4) its apparent equatorial angular diameter; (5) the percent of its disk illuminated; (6) the position angle of its rotation axis, measured counterclockwise from north (clockwise in telescopes having an odd number of reflections); (7) the inclination of its rotation axis to the plane of the sky, positive if its north pole is tipped toward Earth; and two quantities, (8) $L(1)$ and (9) Δ, that can be used to calculate the planetographic longitude L of the central meridian of the observed geometric disk of Mars at any moment. L increases westward on Mars (eastward on the celestial sphere).

For a given date and time (UT) of observation, L is equal to $L(1)$ for the nearest preceding date in the table, less Δ multiplied by the number of complete days elapsed since that date. To the result, add 14.6° multiplied by the time in hours elapsed since 0h UT. If the result is less than 0°, add 360°; if the result is 360° or larger, subtract 360°. The answer is accurate to better than 1°, provided the time of observation is accurate to ±2 minutes. This value of L can then be used to orient the map at the right to the view of Mars seen in a telescope.

MAP OF MARS

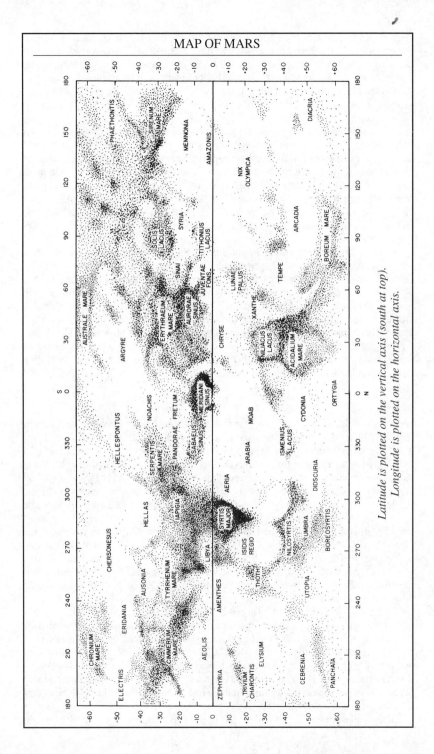

Latitude is plotted on the vertical axis (south at top).
Longitude is plotted on the horizontal axis.

degrees of the centre of the Martian disk, unlike the past four oppositions when the more featureless northern hemisphere was tilted Earthward. The sector of Mars that includes the features mentioned above will be aligned toward the Americas during late evening hours from about May 23 to June 12, and again from about June 28 to July 16. This is merely a guideline useful near the opposition; for accurate predictions of the visibility of specific Martian features on any date, use the table and map on the previous two pages.

By coincidence, the Martian northern hemisphere autumn equinox occurs on June 17, very close to the date of closest approach. That means the north polar cap will be at its minimum size and the southern cap will be close to its maximum. Telescopic observers on Earth therefore should more easily see part of the expanded south polar cap. Polar cap observations will be affected by the date of observation. From late March through to early June, we will see Mars' equator within 2° of the centre of the disk, giving us an equal viewing angle of both polar regions. During June, the angle increases to expose more of the northern hemisphere, reaching an angle of 7° by mid-July. This again reduces to zero in early September.

Coloured eyepiece filters can improve the visibility of darker Martian surface features and reduce glare in larger aperture telescopes. Deep yellow, orange, or red filters enhance the contrast of the dark areas. Smaller telescopes benefit most from a #21 or #23A filter; for larger instruments try #23A or #25. These filters also slightly improve the seeing by eliminating shorter (mostly blue) wavelengths of light, which are more susceptible to atmospheric turbulence. Optimum magnification for Mars varies with telescope type and seeing conditions, but because Mars has a higher surface brightness than Jupiter or Saturn, powers about 1.3× to 1.5× those typically used for observing the giant planets usually offer an ideal compromise between decreasing contrast and higher resolution as magnification increases.

JUPITER

Jupiter, the solar system's largest planet, is a colossal ball of hydrogen and helium without any solid surface comparable to land masses on Earth. Jupiter likely has a small rocky core encased in a thick mantle of metallic hydrogen which is enveloped by a massive atmospheric cloak topped by a quilt of multicoloured clouds. These clouds are the visible surface of Jupiter—a realm of constant change characterized by alternating dark belts and brighter zones. The zones are ammonia ice-crystal clouds, the belts mainly ammonium hydrosulphide clouds. Frequently the belts intrude on the zones with dark rifts or loops called festoons.

The equatorial region of Jupiter's clouds rotates 5 min faster than the rest of the planet: 9 h 50 min compared to 9 h 55 min. This means constant interaction as one region slips by the other at about 400 km/h. It also means that there are basically two rotational systems from the viewpoint of week-to-week telescopic observation (see the table at the right). Jupiter's rapid rotation also makes the great globe markedly bulged at the equator.

Two dark belts, the North Equatorial Belt and the South Equatorial Belt, are obvious in the smallest telescopes. Larger instruments reveal several more narrow dark belts along with the famous Great Red Spot, a salmon-coloured oval vortex observed for centuries on the south edge of the South Equatorial Belt. Historically, the Red Spot has varied from being blatantly obvious to nearly invisible. For example, in 1997 it was detectable with 100-mm aperture, but could hardly be described as prominent because it closely matched its surroundings in hue and contrast. In 2001 observers should find the Red Spot near longitude 75° in System II.

The smallest of telescopes will reveal Jupiter's four large satellites, each of which

JUPITER—EPHEMERIS FOR PHYSICAL OBSERVATIONS, 2001

Date UT	Mag.	Equat. Diam. "	System I L(0) °	ω °/d	System II L(0) °	ω °/d
Jan. 0.0	−2.7	47	116.9	877.87	192.1	870.24
Feb. 0.0	−2.5	43	330.7	877.76	169.5	870.13
Mar. 0.0	−2.3	39	67.9	877.68	53.0	870.05
Apr. 0.0	−2.1	36	276.0	877.65	24.6	870.02
May 0.0	−2.0	33	325.4	877.65	205.1	870.02
Jun. 0.0	−1.9	32	172.4	877.67	175.6	870.04
Jul. 0.0	−1.9	32	222.5	877.71	356.8	870.08
Aug. 0.0	−2.0	33	71.4	877.76	329.2	870.13
Sep. 0.0	−2.1	35	282.1	877.84	303.3	870.20
Oct. 0.0	−2.2	38	337.2	877.92	129.5	870.29
Nov. 0.0	−2.4	42	192.7	877.00	108.4	870.37
Dec. 0.0	−2.6	45	252.7	877.04	299.6	870.41
Jan. 0.0	−2.7	47				

In the above table, the two quantities $L(0)$ and ω can be used to calculate the longitude L of the central meridian of the observed disk of Jupiter at any instant to an accuracy of ±0.5°. System I is the most rapidly rotating region between the middle of the North Equatorial Belt and the middle of the South Equatorial Belt. System II applies to the rest of the planet. Here $L(0)$ is the longitude of the central meridian at 0:00 UT on the 0th day of the month (i.e. at the beginning of the last day of the previous month) and ω is the apparent average angular speed of Jupiter during the month, taking into account both the transit time of light and the motion of Jupiter relative to Earth.

For a given date and time (UT) of observation, L is equal to $L(0)$ for the month in question plus ω multiplied by the decimal date (retaining 4 figures past the decimal point in the date). The result will usually exceed 360°; if so, divide the result by 360 and then multiply the decimal portion of the quotient by 360°.

Example: At
23:40 EDT Oct. 16 = 3:40 UT Oct. 17 = Oct. 17.1528,
the longitude of the central meridian at the latitude of the Great Red Spot (System II) is:
$$L = (129.5 + (870.29 \times 17.1528)) \div 360 = 41.8261 \times 360 = 297°.$$

is equal to or larger than Earth's satellite. They provide a never-ending fascination for amateur astronomers. (For the configurations of these four Galilean satellites, see the right-side of the pages in the THE SKY MONTH BY MONTH section.) Sometimes the satellites are paired on either side of the belted planet; frequently one is missing—either behind Jupiter, in the planet's shadow, or in front of Jupiter. In the latter case the satellite usually blends in against Jupiter's bright clouds and is difficult to see (more on this below). Even more interesting are the occasions when one of the satellites casts its shadow on the disk of the planet (see PHENOMENA OF THE GALILEAN SATELLITES on pp. 182–188). The tiny black shadow can be particularly evident if it is cast on one of the bright zones of Jupiter. This phenomenon sometimes is evident in a 60-mm refractor under good seeing conditions. On rarer occasions, *two* shadows

GREAT RED SPOT—TIME OF TRANSIT

The table on the previous page may be used to determine when the Great Red Spot (GRS) (near longitude 63° in System II) will cross the central meridian of the disk of Jupiter.

Example: Suppose an observer in Ontario, Canada (time zone: Eastern Standard, −5 h) is viewing Jupiter on the night of 2001 Dec. 3. At 0h UT Dec. 4 (19h EST December 3) the table gives

$$(299.6° + (870.41 \times 4)) \div 360° = 10.5034 \times 360° = 181°$$

for the longitude of the meridian in System II. A further rotation of

$$(360° − 181°) + 63° = 242°$$

will bring the GRS to the central meridian, which will require

$$242° \div 870.41°/d = 0.2780 \text{ d} = 6\text{h } 40\text{m}.$$

Thus the GRS will transit at

6:40 UT Dec. 4 = 1:40 EST Dec. 4.

Note that the GRS slowly drifts in longitude, so the 63° figure is only a guide. By timing a transit of the GRS and using the table, you can update its longitude.

are cast upon the face of Jupiter. These "double shadow transits" are included on the right-hand pages of THE SKY MONTH BY MONTH section.

The satellite umbral shadows vary significantly in size from one to another. Mean opposition angular diameters are: Io 0.9″, Europa 0.6″, Ganymede 1.1″, and Callisto 0.5″. The enormous contrast between the dark shadows and the bright Jovian clouds makes these tiny features visible even though they are smaller than the nominal resolution limit of a small telescope. Furthermore, the satellites' penumbral shadows are quite large, especially Callisto's, which adds a few tenths of an arc-second to their effective visual diameters. The satellites themselves have the following mean opposition apparent diameters: Io 1.2″, Europa 1.0″, Ganymede 1.7″, and Callisto 1.6″. A 150-mm telescope reveals the size differences as well as colour variations among the satellites.

When the Galilean satellites transit the disk of Jupiter, they are seldom visible in telescopes under 100 mm and are best seen near the planet's limb when entering or leaving the disk. Tracking a satellite transit completely across Jupiter is a challenging observation. Each satellite has a characteristic appearance when superimposed on the Jovian cloudscape. Europa is bright white, similar to the brightest Jovian clouds. When traversing a white cloud zone in the central sector of Jupiter, Europa is usually invisible. However, it stands out well when near the limb or against a dark belt. Callisto, the darkest satellite, is best seen in the reverse circumstances. When seen against a pale zone this greyish satellite can be mistaken for a satellite shadow, but it is often lost against a dark belt. Ganymede is intermediate in surface brightness, but because of its great size, it is the easiest of the four to track completely across Jupiter's face. Io, innermost of the Galilean satellites, is also the most frequently seen in transit. It is close to Europa in brightness but is generally easier to follow over typical cloud features, probably due to its slightly greater diameter. Near opposition, a transiting satellite often appears adjacent to its own shadow. These events are especially worth a look. Jupiter's other satellites are photographic objects for large instruments.

As 2001 opens, Jupiter is in Taurus high in the southeastern evening sky after dusk. For southern observers it is near the meridian in the north. By mid-May Jupiter becomes lost in the solar glare, conjunction with the Sun occurring on May 8. By late-July, Jupiter peeks above the eastern horizon in dawn twilight for both northern and southern observers. By August it is a prominent early-morning sky luminary in Gemini, in which constellation it remains for the rest of the year. In November and December, Jupiter dominates the eastern late-evening sky. Opposition occurs on 2002 January 1. Late this year, Jupiter is at declination $+22°$, close to its maximum possible altitude for northern observers.

SATURN

Saturn is the telescopic showpiece of the night sky. The chilling beauty of the small pale orb floating in a field of velvet is something no photographs or descriptions can adequately duplicate. Any telescope magnifying more than 30× will show the rings. The view is exquisite in 100- to 200-mm instruments. The rings consist of billions of particles—largely water ice—that range in size from microscopic specks to flying mountains kilometres across. The reason "rings" is plural is that gaps and brightness differences define hundreds of distinct rings. However, from Earth only the three most prominent components—known simply as rings A, B, and C—can be distinguished visually. (See the diagram Saturn—Main Ring Features Visible From Earth on the next page.)

Cassini's division, a gap between rings A and B discovered in 1675, is visible in small telescopes when the ring system is well inclined to our view. Cassini's division is a region less densely populated with ring particles than adjacent rings. Ring B, the brightest, overpowers ring C to such an extent that ring C, also known as the *crepe ring*, is seen only with difficulty in small telescopes. A Saturn phenomenon easily seen with backyard telescopes is the shadow of the planet on the rings. From one to four months before or after opposition the shadow falling on the rings is very apparent, often giving the scene a powerful three-dimensional aura.

In addition to the rings, Saturn has a family of at least 18 satellites. Titan, the largest, is easily seen in any telescope as an 8th-magnitude object orbiting Saturn in about 16 days. At east and west elongation Titan appears about five ring diameters from the planet. Telescopes over 60-mm aperture should reveal Rhea at 10th magnitude less than two ring diameters from Saturn. The satellite Iapetus has the peculiar property of being five times brighter at western elongation (magnitude 10.1) than at eastern elongation (11.9). One side of the satellite has the reflectivity of snow while the other resembles dark rock. When brightest, Iapetus is located about 12 ring diameters west of the parent planet. Of the remaining satellites Tethys and Dione may be glimpsed in a 150-mm telescope, but the others require larger apertures. (See CONFIGURATIONS OF SATURN'S BRIGHTEST SATELLITES starting on pp. 189–192.)

The disk of Saturn appears about one-sixth the area of Jupiter through the same telescope with the same magnification. In telescopes less than 75-mm aperture, probably no features will ever be seen on the cloud deck of the planet other than the shadow cast by the rings. As the size of the telescope is increased, the pale equatorial region, a dusky equatorial band, and the darker polar regions become evident. Saturn has a belt system like Jupiter's but it is much less active and the contrast is reduced. Seldom in telescopes less than 100-mm aperture do more than one or two belts come into view. Saturn is approaching its 2003 perihelion and its angular diameter in 2001 exceeds that of any opposition in more than a quarter of a century.

Saturn begins the year in the evening sky in Taurus, near Jupiter, but becomes lost in the solar glare by early May. It is in conjunction with the Sun on May 25 and is not well placed for telescopic observing until August in the morning sky. Saturn is at opposition in Taurus on December 3 when it is 8.08 AU or 67 light-min from Earth, 20.6″ in diameter, and the rings are 46.6″ across.

SATURN—MAIN RING FEATURES VISIBLE FROM EARTH

EARTH
(to same scale)

$1.00 = 60\,330$ km $= 9.74''$ (at mean opposition distance)

RADII

Diagram by Roy Bishop

SATURN'S RING SYSTEM—MAIN STRUCTURAL REGIONS

Ring	Radius**	Discoverer
D	1.11–1.23 ⎱	⎰ *Voyager 1* (1980)
C*	1.23–1.52 ⎰	⎱ W. C. & G . P. Bond, W. R. Dawes (1850)
B*	1.52–1.95	Galileo (1610), C. Huygens (1659),
A*	2.02–2.26	G. D. Cassini (1675)
F	2.33	*Pioneer 11* (1979)
G	2.8	*Voyager 1* (1980)
E	3.–8.	W.A. Feibelman (1966)

* Visible from Earth. Also, the E ring can be detected when Saturn's ring system appears edge-on

** In units of Saturn's equatorial radius (60 330 km)

After having been edge-on to Earth in February of 1996, Saturn's rings are now open very close to their maximum possible extent with their south side facing Earth. During January the ring tilt is about 23° as seen from Earth. By September, the rings have opened to 26°. The tilt remains near this value for the remainder of the year. This makes 2001 an excellent year for examining the divisions and structural subtleties of the rings.

URANUS

At magnitude 5.7, Uranus can be seen with the unaided eye under a clear, dark sky. However, it is much more easily located with binoculars. A 75-mm telescope will reveal its small, greenish, featureless disk.

Unlike the three other giant planets, the axis of Uranus is tipped almost parallel to the plane of the solar system. This means that we view Uranus nearly pole-on at certain points in its 84-year orbit. The southern (and counterclockwise turning) hemisphere of Uranus is now angled slightly toward Earth. Its south pole appeared nearest to (and slightly south of) the centre of its disk in 1985. Uranus has at least 15 satellites, all smaller than Earth's Moon, none of which can be detected in small or moderate-sized telescopes.

Uranus is at opposition in Capricornus on August 15, when it is 18.965 AU or 2.6 light-h from Earth. It is then magnitude 5.7 and 3.7″ in apparent diameter. Use the chart below to locate this distant planet.

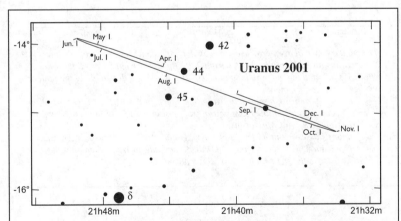

The finder chart above, provided by David Lane, shows the path of Uranus in Capricornus, over the nine-month period 2001 April–December. Coordinates are in epoch 2000.0, and the magnitude limit is 9.0. Tick marks are drawn along the path at the beginning of each month.

The bright, 3rd-magnitude star at the bottom of the chart is δ Cap. This is the easternmost star in Capricornus that is marked in the JULY ALL-SKY MAP on p. 280, the 3rd star left of the small letter "F."

Along the five-month retrograde portion of its track, from May 30 to October 31 and centred at the mid-August opposition, Uranus remains brighter than magnitude 5.8 and is well placed for observation. It is comparable in magnitude to the stars marked "44" and "45" in this chart.

NEPTUNE

Neptune is an 8th-magnitude binocular object—an easy target in 7 × 50 or larger glasses—but seeing the planet as a disk rather than a point of light is a different matter. Magnifications over 200× are usually necessary, and even then Neptune is just a tiny bluish dot with no hard edge due to limb darkening. Neptune's large satellite Triton can be seen by an experienced observer using a 300-mm telescope. Triton varies from 8″ to 17″ from Neptune.

In 2001 Neptune is in Capricornus and may be easily identified using the chart below. At opposition on July 30, Neptune is magnitude 7.8, 29.08 AU or 4.04 light-hours from Earth and 2.3″ in diameter.

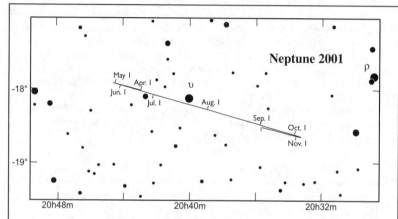

The finder chart above, provided by David Lane, shows the path of Neptune in Capricornus, over the eight-month period 2001 April–November. Coordinates are in epoch 2000.0, and the magnitude limit is 9.0. Tick marks are drawn along the path at the beginning of each month.

The stars ρ and υ Cap are marked on the chart. In the JULY ALL-SKY MAP on p. 280, ρ is the leftmost of the close pair of stars just above the ecliptic and along the western (right) edge of Capricornus.

Neptune passes within 6′ (0.1°) of 5.1-magnitude υ Cap around July 21, shortly before opposition. For several days, it will be possible to frame Neptune and this naked-eye star in the same high-power telescopic field.

PLUTO

Besides being the solar system's smallest planet, Pluto is different from the other eight in almost every respect. Its unique characteristics include its orbit, which is so elliptical that the planet was closer to the Sun than was Neptune from 1980 through 1999.

Opposition is on June 4 when the planet will be at visual magnitude 13.8 and 29.39 AU or 4.08 light-h from Earth. It can be identified using the chart at the right and a 200-mm or larger telescope. Pluto was near perihelion throughout the 1980s and 1990s, and as bright as it ever gets. A few observers (with good optics, transparent skies, steady seeing, and high magnifications) succeeded in sighting Pluto with telescopes as small as 100-mm refractors.

FINDER CHART FOR PLUTO, 2001
By Ian Cameron

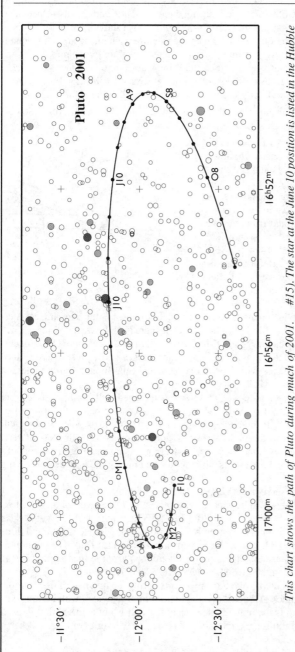

This chart shows the path of Pluto during much of 2001. Pluto's position is marked at 10-day intervals beginning February 10 (F10) and extending until October 28.

To locate the field: The filled disks all appear on Uranometria Vol. II Chart #292, and only the dark gray ones appear in Tirion's Sky Atlas 2000.0 (1st edition chart

#15). The star at the June 10 position is listed in the Hubble Guide Star Catalog as magnitude 6.5 and the two brightest stars nearby are listed as magnitude 8.3. Pluto is at opposition on June 4 at magnitude 13.8. The chart limit is magnitude 14.5 using the Guide Star magnitudes as the criterion. Caution is thus advised when star hopping, since not all faint visible stars appear in this catalogue.

PHENOMENA OF THE GALILEAN SATELLITES

The tables on the next six pages give the various transits, occultations, and eclipses of the four great satellites of Jupiter during January–April and August–December. Jupiter is not well-placed for observations during the other three months since it is in conjunction with the Sun on June 14. Since the satellite phenomena are not instantaneous but require up to several minutes, the predicted times are for the middle of each event. The predictions were generated by the Bureau des Longitudes in Paris.

Satellites are denoted using the standard designations: I = Io, II = Europa, III = Ganymede, IV = Callisto. Events are denoted using the following abbreviations:

Ec = eclipse, **Oc** = occultation, **Tr** = transit of satellite, **Sh** = transit of shadow; **I** = ingress, **E** = egress, **D** = disappearance, **R** = reappearance.

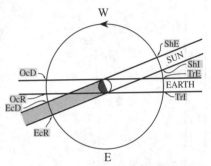

The general motion of the satellites and the successive phenomena are shown in the diagram at right, which is a view of Jupiter and the orbit of one of its satellites looking down from the north side. Satellites move from east to west across the face of the planet, and from west to east behind it ("east" and "west" are here used in the sense of the observer's sky, not in the Jovian sense). Before opposition, shadows fall to the west, and after opposition, to the east (as in the diagram).

The sequence of phenomena for the outer satellite shown in the diagram, counterclockwise beginning at the lower right, is transit ingress (TrI), transit egress (TrE), shadow ingress (ShI), shadow egress (ShE), occultation disappearance (OcD), occultation reappearance (OcR), eclipse disappearance (EcD), and eclipse reappearance (EcR). The actual sequence will depend on the actual Sun–Jupiter–Earth angle and the size of the satellite's orbit.

Approximately three-quarters of the phenomena listed will not be visible from any one locality because they occur when Jupiter is near or below the horizon or when daylight interferes. In practice, an observer usually knows when Jupiter will be conveniently placed in the night sky or, if not, can check in THE SKY MONTH BY MONTH section of this Handbook (pp. 56–81) for this information. The table can then be scanned to select those events which will occur during the intended observing period.

For example, an observer near Victoria, British Columbia, on the evening of 2001 December 2 would know that Jupiter is well placed in the late evening sky. If he planned to observe from 10 p.m. to 1:00 a.m. PST (8h behind UT), he could scan the table for events in the interval December 3, 6:00 to 9:00 UT. He would find three events, at 22:12, 0:00, 0:32, and 0:41 PST, involving Io and Callisto. The configuration of the four Galilean satellites during that evening is given in the diagram on the right-hand side of p. 81 in the THE SKY MONTH BY MONTH section.

Note that Callisto is not involved in any events during the first half of the year; the occultation disappearance of August 8 is the first event of the year involving this outlying satellite. Callisto is the only Galilean satellites that is not eclipsed during each of its revolutions. The eclipse of September 27 is the first of a series of 66 eclipses that ends 2004 September 20.

SATELLITES OF JUPITER, UT OF 2001 GEOCENTRIC PHENOMENA

JANUARY

```
 0  3:21  I   OcD
    6:20  I   EcR
   19:20  III TrI
   21:19  III TrE
   22:34  III ShI
 1  0:29  I   TrI
    0:42  III ShE
    1:17  I   ShI
    2:39  I   TrE
    3:28  I   ShE
   13:01  II  TrI
   14:39  II  ShI
   15:35  II  TrE
   17:15  II  ShE
   21:48  I   OcD
 2  0:49  I   EcR
   18:55  I   TrI
   19:46  I   ShI
   21:05  I   TrE
   21:57  I   ShE
 3  7:05  II  OcD
   11:27  II  EcR
   16:15  I   OcD
   19:18  I   EcR
 4  9:00  III OcD
   11:03  III OcR
   12:33  III EcD
   13:22  I   TrI
   14:15  I   ShI
   14:43  III EcR
   15:32  I   TrE
   16:26  I   ShE
 5  2:11  II  TrI
    3:57  II  ShI
    4:45  II  TrE
    6:33  II  ShE
   10:42  I   OcD
   13:47  I   EcR
 6  7:49  I   TrI
    8:44  I   ShI
    9:59  I   TrE
   10:55  I   ShE
   20:16  II  OcD
 7  0:46  II  EcR
    5:08  I   OcD
    8:16  I   EcR
   22:48  III TrI
 8  0:50  III TrE
    2:16  I   TrI
    2:35  III ShI
    3:13  I   ShI
    4:26  I   TrE
    4:44  III ShE
    5:24  I   ShE
   15:22  II  TrI
   17:15  II  ShI
   17:56  II  TrE
   19:51  II  ShE
   23:35  I   OcD
 9  2:44  I   EcR
   20:43  I   TrI
```

```
 9 21:42  I   ShI
   22:53  I   TrE
   23:52  I   ShE
10  9:27  II  OcD
   14:05  II  EcR
   18:02  I   OcD
   21:13  I   EcR
11 12:30  III OcD
   14:35  III OcR
   15:11  I   TrI
   16:11  I   ShI
   16:34  III EcD
   17:21  I   TrE
   18:21  I   ShE
   18:45  III EcR
12  4:33  II  TrI
    6:33  II  ShI
    7:07  II  TrE
    9:09  II  ShE
   12:30  I   OcD
   15:42  I   EcR
13  9:38  I   TrI
   10:39  I   ShI
   11:48  I   TrE
   12:50  I   ShE
   22:39  II  OcD
14  3:24  II  EcR
    6:57  I   OcD
   10:11  I   EcR
15  2:20  III TrI
    4:05  I   TrI
    4:25  III TrE
    5:08  I   ShI
    6:15  I   TrE
    6:36  III ShI
    7:19  I   ShE
    8:46  III ShE
   17:45  II  TrI
   19:52  II  ShI
   20:19  II  TrE
   22:27  II  ShE
16  1:24  I   OcD
    4:40  I   EcR
   22:32  I   TrI
   23:37  I   ShI
17  0:42  I   TrE
    1:48  I   ShE
   11:52  II  OcD
   16:43  II  EcR
   19:51  I   OcD
   23:08  I   EcR
18 16:04  III OcD
   17:00  I   TrI
   18:06  I   ShI
   18:12  III OcR
   19:10  I   TrE
   20:17  I   ShE
   20:34  III EcD
   22:46  III EcR
19  6:57  II  TrI
    9:10  II  ShI
    9:32  II  TrE
```

```
19 11:45  II  ShE
   14:19  I   OcD
   17:37  I   EcR
20 11:27  I   TrI
   12:35  I   ShI
   13:38  I   TrE
   14:46  I   ShE
21  1:05  II  OcD
    6:02  II  EcR
    8:46  I   OcD
   12:06  I   EcR
22  5:55  I   TrI
    5:59  III TrI
    7:04  I   ShI
    8:05  I   TrE
    8:06  III TrE
    9:15  I   ShE
   10:38  III ShI
   12:48  III ShE
   20:10  II  TrI
   22:28  II  ShI
   22:45  II  TrE
23  1:03  II  ShE
    3:14  I   OcD
    6:35  I   EcR
24  0:23  I   TrI
    1:33  I   ShI
    2:33  I   TrE
    3:43  I   ShE
   14:19  II  OcD
   19:22  II  EcR
   21:42  I   OcD
25  1:04  I   EcR
   18:51  I   TrI
   19:44  III OcD
   20:02  I   ShI
   21:01  I   TrE
   21:54  III OcR
   22:12  I   ShE
26  0:35  III EcD
    2:47  III EcR
    9:24  II  TrI
   11:46  II  ShI
   11:59  II  TrE
   14:21  II  ShE
   16:09  I   OcD
   19:32  I   EcR
27 13:19  I   TrI
   14:31  I   ShI
   15:29  I   TrE
   16:41  I   ShE
28  3:33  II  OcD
    8:41  II  EcR
   10:37  I   OcD
   14:01  I   EcR
29  7:47  I   TrI
    9:00  I   ShI
    9:42  III TrI
    9:57  I   TrE
   11:10  I   ShE
   11:51  III TrE
   14:39  III ShI
```

```
29 16:50  III ShE
   22:38  II  TrI
30  1:04  II  ShI
    1:13  II  TrE
    3:39  II  ShE
    5:05  I   OcD
    8:30  I   EcR
31  2:14  I   TrI
    3:28  I   ShI
    4:25  I   TrE
    5:39  I   ShE
   16:49  II  OcD
   22:00  II  EcR
   23:33  I   OcD
```

FEBRUARY

```
 1  2:59  I   EcR
   20:43  I   TrI
   21:57  I   ShI
   22:53  I   TrE
   23:29  III OcD
 2  0:08  I   ShE
    1:42  III OcR
    4:36  III EcD
    6:49  III EcR
   11:53  II  TrI
   14:22  II  ShI
   14:28  II  TrE
   16:57  II  ShE
   18:01  I   OcD
   21:28  I   EcR
 3 15:11  I   TrI
   16:26  I   ShI
   17:21  I   TrE
   18:37  I   ShE
 4  6:04  II  OcD
   11:19  II  EcR
   12:29  I   OcD
   15:57  I   EcR
 5  9:39  I   TrI
   10:55  I   ShI
   11:49  I   TrE
   13:06  I   ShE
   13:30  III TrI
   15:41  III TrE
   18:40  III ShI
   20:52  III ShE
 6  1:09  II  TrI
    3:40  II  ShI
    3:44  II  TrE
    6:15  II  ShE
    6:57  I   OcD
   10:25  I   EcR
 7  4:07  I   TrI
    5:24  I   ShI
    6:18  I   TrE
    7:35  I   ShE
   19:21  II  OcD
 8  0:39  II  EcR
    1:26  I   OcD
    4:54  I   EcR
   22:36  I   TrI
```

```
 8 23:53  I   ShI
 9  0:46  I   TrE
    2:04  I   ShE
    3:19  III OcD
    5:34  III OcR
    8:37  III EcD
   10:51  III EcR
   14:25  II  TrI
   16:58  II  ShI
   17:00  II  TrE
   19:33  II  ShE
   19:54  II  OcD
   23:23  I   EcR
10 17:04  I   TrI
   18:22  I   ShI
   19:15  I   TrE
   20:33  I   ShE
11  8:38  II  OcD
   11:17  II  OcR
   11:18  II  EcD
   13:58  II  EcR
   14:22  I   OcD
   17:52  I   EcR
12 11:33  I   TrI
   12:51  I   ShI
   13:43  I   TrE
   15:02  I   ShE
   17:22  III TrI
   19:36  III TrE
   22:41  III ShI
13  0:54  III ShE
    3:41  II  TrI
    6:16  I   ShI
    6:16  II  TrE
    8:51  I   OcD
    8:51  II  ShE
   12:21  I   EcR
14  6:02  I   TrI
    7:20  I   ShI
    8:12  I   TrE
    9:31  I   ShE
   21:56  II  OcD
15  0:35  II  OcR
    0:38  II  EcD
    3:18  II  EcR
    3:19  I   OcD
    6:50  I   EcR
```

SATELLITES OF JUPITER, UT OF 2001 GEOCENTRIC PHENOMENA (ct'd)

FEBRUARY (ct'd)

Date	Time	Sat	Ph
16	0:30	I	TrI
	1:49	I	ShI
	2:41	I	TrE
	4:00	I	ShE
	7:15	III	OcD
	9:32	III	OcR
	12:38	III	EcD
	14:54	III	EcR
	16:58	II	TrI
	19:33	II	TrE
	19:34	II	ShI
	21:48	I	OcD
	22:09	II	ShE
17	1:18	I	EcR
	18:59	I	TrI
	20:18	I	ShI
	21:10	I	TrE
	22:29	I	ShE
18	11:14	II	OcD
	13:54	II	OcR
	13:57	II	EcD
	16:17	I	OcD
	16:37	II	EcR
	19:47	I	EcR
19	13:28	I	TrI
	14:47	I	ShI
	15:38	I	TrE
	16:58	I	ShE
	21:19	III	TrI
	23:35	III	TrE
20	2:42	III	ShI
	4:55	III	ShE
	6:16	II	TrI
	8:51	II	TrE
	8:52	II	ShI
	10:45	I	OcD
	11:27	II	ShE
	14:16	I	EcR
21	7:57	I	TrI
	9:16	I	ShI
	10:07	I	TrE
	11:27	I	ShE
22	0:34	II	OcD
	3:13	II	OcR
	3:16	II	EcD
	5:14	I	OcD
	5:56	II	EcR
	8:45	I	EcR
23	2:26	I	TrI
	3:45	I	ShI
	4:36	I	TrE
	5:56	I	ShE
	11:14	III	OcD
	13:33	III	OcR
	16:39	III	EcD
	18:56	III	EcR
	19:34	II	TrI
	22:09	II	TrE
	22:10	II	ShI
	23:43	I	OcD
24	0:45	II	ShE
	3:14	I	EcR
	20:55	I	TrI
	22:14	I	ShI
	23:05	I	TrE
25	0:25	I	ShE
	13:53	II	OcD
	16:32	II	OcR
	16:35	II	EcD
	18:12	I	OcD
	19:15	II	EcR
	21:42	I	EcR
26	15:24	I	TrI
	16:43	I	ShI
	17:35	I	TrE
	18:54	I	ShE
27	1:21	III	TrI
	3:38	III	TrE
	6:43	III	ShI
	8:52	II	TrI
	8:58	III	ShE
	11:27	II	ShI
	11:28	II	TrE
	12:41	I	OcD
	14:03	II	ShE
	16:11	I	EcR
28	9:53	I	TrI
	11:12	I	ShI
	12:04	I	TrE
	13:23	I	ShE

MARCH

Date	Time	Sat	Ph
1	3:13	II	OcD
	5:53	II	OcR
	5:55	II	EcD
	7:10	I	OcD
	8:35	II	EcR
	10:40	I	EcR
2	4:22	I	TrI
	5:41	I	ShI
	6:33	I	TrE
	7:52	I	ShE
	15:18	III	OcD
	17:39	III	OcR
	20:40	III	EcD
	22:11	II	TrI
	22:58	III	EcR
3	0:45	II	ShI
	0:47	II	TrE
	1:39	I	OcD
	3:21	II	ShE
	5:09	I	EcR
	22:51	I	TrI
4	0:10	I	ShI
	1:02	I	TrE
	2:21	I	ShE
	16:33	II	OcD
	19:13	II	OcR
	19:14	II	EcD
	20:08	I	OcD
	21:54	II	EcR
	23:38	I	EcR
5	17:21	I	TrI
	18:39	I	ShI
	19:32	I	TrE
	20:50	I	ShE
6	5:27	III	TrI
	7:46	III	TrE
	10:44	III	ShI
	11:30	II	TrI
	13:00	III	ShE
	14:03	II	ShI
	14:07	II	TrE
	14:38	I	OcD
	16:39	II	ShE
	18:07	I	EcR
7	11:50	I	TrI
	13:08	I	ShI
	14:01	I	TrE
	15:18	I	ShE
8	5:55	II	OcD
	9:07	I	OcD
	11:14	II	EcR
	12:35	I	EcR
9	6:20	I	TrI
	7:37	I	ShI
	8:31	I	TrE
	9:48	I	ShE
	19:25	III	OcD
	21:47	III	OcR
10	0:40	III	EcD
	0:50	II	TrI
	2:59	III	EcR
	3:21	II	ShI
	3:26	II	TrE
	3:36	I	OcD
	5:57	II	ShE
	7:04	I	EcR
11	0:49	I	TrI
	2:05	I	ShI
	3:00	I	TrE
	4:16	I	ShE
	19:16	II	OcD
	22:05	I	OcD
12	0:33	II	EcR
	1:33	I	EcR
	19:19	I	TrI
	20:34	I	ShI
	21:30	I	TrE
	22:46	I	ShE
13	9:38	III	TrI
	11:58	III	TrE
	14:10	II	TrI
	14:46	III	ShI
	16:35	I	OcD
	16:39	II	ShI
	16:47	II	TrE
	17:03	III	ShE
	19:15	II	ShE
	20:02	I	EcR
14	13:48	I	TrI
	15:03	I	ShI
	15:59	I	TrE
	17:14	I	ShE
15	8:38	II	OcD
	11:04	I	OcD
	13:53	II	EcR
	14:31	I	EcR
16	8:18	I	TrI
	9:32	I	ShI
	10:29	I	TrE
	11:43	I	ShE
	23:36	III	OcD
17	1:59	III	OcR
	3:31	II	TrI
	4:41	III	EcD
	5:34	I	OcD
	5:56	II	ShI
	6:07	II	TrE
	7:00	III	EcR
	8:33	II	ShE
	8:59	I	EcR
18	2:47	I	TrI
	4:01	I	ShI
	4:59	I	TrE
	6:12	I	ShE
	22:00	II	OcD
19	0:03	I	OcD
	3:12	II	EcR
	3:28	I	EcR
	21:17	I	TrI
	22:30	I	ShI
	23:29	I	TrE
20	0:41	I	ShE
	13:51	III	TrI
	16:12	III	TrE
	16:52	II	TrI
	18:33	I	OcD
	18:47	III	ShI
	19:14	II	ShI
	19:29	II	TrE
	21:05	III	ShE
	21:51	II	ShE
	21:57	I	EcR
21	15:47	I	TrI
	16:59	I	ShI
	17:58	I	TrE
	19:10	I	ShE
22	11:23	II	OcD
	13:03	I	OcD
	16:26	I	EcR
	16:32	II	EcR
23	10:17	I	TrI
	11:28	I	ShI
	12:28	I	TrE
	13:39	I	ShE
24	3:50	III	OcD
	6:13	II	TrI
	6:15	III	OcR
	7:32	I	OcD
	8:32	II	ShI
	8:42	II	EcD
	8:50	II	TrE
	10:55	I	EcR
	11:02	III	EcR
	11:09	II	ShE
25	4:47	I	TrI
	5:57	I	ShI
	6:58	I	TrE
	8:08	I	ShE
26	0:46	II	OcD
	2:02	I	OcD
	5:23	I	EcR
	5:51	II	EcR
	23:17	I	TrI
27	0:26	I	ShI
	1:28	I	TrE
	2:37	I	ShE
	18:07	III	TrI
	19:34	II	TrI
	20:30	III	TrE
	20:32	I	OcD
	21:50	II	ShI
	22:12	II	TrE
	22:48	III	ShI
	23:52	I	EcR
28	0:27	II	ShE
	1:07	III	ShE
	17:46	I	TrI
	18:55	I	ShI
	19:58	I	TrE
	21:06	I	ShE
29	14:10	II	OcD
	15:01	I	OcD
	18:21	I	EcR
	19:11	II	EcR
30	12:16	I	TrI
	13:24	I	ShI
	14:28	I	TrE
	15:35	I	ShE
31	8:08	III	OcD
	8:56	II	TrI
	9:31	I	OcD
	10:33	III	OcR
	11:07	II	ShI
	11:34	II	TrE
	12:42	III	EcD
	12:50	I	EcR
	13:45	II	ShE
	15:04	III	EcR

SATELLITES OF JUPITER, UT OF 2001 GEOCENTRIC PHENOMENA (ct'd)

APRIL

1	6:46	I	TrI
	7:53	I	ShI
	8:58	I	TrE
	10:04	I	ShE
2	3:33	II	OcD
	4:01	I	OcD
	7:18	I	EcR
	8:30	II	EcR
3	1:16	I	TrI
	2:22	I	ShI
	3:28	I	TrE
	4:33	I	ShE
	22:18	II	TrI
	22:25	III	TrI
	22:31	I	OcD
4	0:25	II	ShI
	0:49	III	TrE
	0:56	II	TrE
	1:47	I	EcR
	2:48	III	ShI
	3:03	II	ShE
	5:09	III	ShE
	19:46	I	TrI
	20:51	I	ShI
	21:58	I	TrE
	23:02	I	ShE
5	16:57	II	OcD
	17:01	I	OcD
	20:16	I	EcR
	21:50	II	EcR
6	14:17	I	TrI
	15:20	I	ShI
	16:28	I	TrE
	17:31	I	ShE
7	11:31	I	OcD
	11:40	II	TrI
	12:28	III	OcD
	13:43	II	ShI
	14:18	II	TrE
	14:45	I	EcR
	14:55	III	OcR
	16:20	II	ShE
	16:43	III	EcD
	19:06	III	EcR
8	8:47	I	TrI
	9:48	I	ShI
	10:59	I	TrE
	12:00	I	ShE
9	6:01	I	OcD
	6:21	II	OcD
	9:13	I	EcR
	11:08	II	EcR
10	3:17	I	TrI
	4:17	I	ShI
	5:29	I	TrE
	6:29	I	ShE
11	0:31	I	OcD
	1:03	II	TrI
	2:45	III	TrI
	3:00	II	ShI

11	3:41	II	TrE
	3:42	I	EcR
	5:11	III	TrE
	5:38	II	ShE
	6:49	III	ShI
	9:10	III	ShE
	21:47	I	TrI
	22:46	I	ShI
12	23:59	I	TrE
	0:58	I	ShE
	19:01	I	OcD
	19:46	II	OcD
	22:11	I	EcR
13	0:28	II	EcR
	16:17	I	TrI
	17:15	I	ShI
	18:29	I	TrE
	19:27	I	ShE
14	13:31	I	OcD
	14:26	II	TrI
	16:18	II	ShI
	16:40	I	EcR
	16:50	III	OcD
	17:04	II	TrE
	18:56	II	ShE
	19:17	III	OcR
	20:44	III	EcD
	23:08	III	EcR
15	10:47	I	TrI
	11:44	I	ShI
	13:00	I	TrE
	13:56	I	ShE
16	8:01	I	OcD
	9:11	II	OcD
	11:08	I	EcR
	13:47	II	EcR
17	5:18	I	TrI
	6:13	I	ShI
	7:30	I	TrE
	8:25	I	ShE
18	2:31	I	OcD
	3:49	II	TrI
	5:36	II	ShI
	5:37	I	EcR
	6:28	II	TrE
	7:08	III	TrI
	8:14	II	ShE
	9:35	III	TrE
	10:50	III	ShI
	13:13	III	ShE
	23:48	I	TrI
19	0:42	I	ShI
	2:00	I	TrE
	2:54	I	ShE
	21:01	I	OcD
	22:36	II	OcD
20	0:06	I	EcR
	3:07	II	EcR
	18:18	I	TrI
	19:11	I	ShI
	20:31	I	TrE
	21:23	I	ShE

21	15:31	I	OcD
	17:12	II	TrI
	18:35	I	EcR
	18:54	II	ShI
	19:51	II	TrE
	21:14	III	OcD
	21:32	II	ShE
	23:42	III	OcR
22	0:44	III	EcD
	3:09	III	EcR
	12:49	I	TrI
	13:39	I	ShI
	15:01	I	TrE
	15:52	I	ShE
23	10:02	I	OcD
	12:01	II	OcD
	13:03	I	EcR
	16:25	II	EcR
24	7:19	I	TrI
	8:08	I	ShI
	9:31	I	TrE
	10:21	I	ShE
25	4:32	I	OcD
	6:36	II	TrI
	7:32	I	EcR
	8:11	II	ShI
	9:15	II	TrE
	10:50	II	ShE
	11:33	III	TrI
	14:01	III	TrE
	14:50	III	ShI
	17:14	III	ShE
26	1:49	I	TrI
	2:37	I	ShI
	4:02	I	TrE
	4:49	I	ShE
	23:02	I	OcD
27	1:26	II	OcD
	2:01	I	EcR
	5:45	II	EcR
	20:20	I	TrI
	21:06	I	ShI
	22:32	I	TrE
	23:18	I	ShE
28	17:32	I	OcD
	19:59	II	TrI
	20:30	I	EcR
	21:29	II	ShI
	22:38	II	TrE
29	0:08	II	ShE
	1:38	III	OcD
	4:08	III	OcR
	4:44	III	EcD
	7:10	III	EcR
	14:50	I	TrI
	15:35	I	ShI
	17:03	I	TrE
	17:47	I	ShE
30	12:02	I	OcD
	14:51	II	OcD
	14:58	I	EcR
	19:04	II	EcR

MAY TO JULY
SUPPRESSED

AUGUST

1	2:17	II	EcD
	6:33	II	OcR
	10:55	I	ShI
	11:40	I	TrI
	13:08	I	ShE
	13:54	I	TrE
2	8:02	I	EcD
	11:03	I	OcR
	20:28	II	ShI
	22:03	II	TrI
	23:11	II	ShE
3	0:48	II	TrE
	5:23	I	ShI
	6:10	I	TrI
	7:36	I	ShE
	8:24	I	TrE
	22:48	III	ShI
4	1:28	III	ShE
	2:00	III	TrI
	2:31	I	EcD
	4:47	III	TrE
	5:33	I	OcR
	15:35	II	EcD
	19:57	II	OcR
	23:52	I	ShI
5	0:40	I	TrI
	2:04	I	ShE
	2:53	I	TrE
	20:59	I	EcD
6	0:03	I	OcR
	9:46	II	ShI
	11:27	II	TrI
	12:29	II	ShE
	14:12	II	TrE
	18:20	I	ShI
	19:10	I	TrI
	20:33	I	ShE
	21:23	I	TrE
7	12:40	III	EcD
	15:22	III	EcR
	15:28	I	EcD
	16:06	III	OcD
	18:33	I	OcR
	18:55	III	OcR
8	4:52	II	EcD
	8:41	IV	OcD
	9:12	IV	OcR
	9:20	II	OcR
	12:49	I	ShI
	13:40	I	TrI
	15:01	I	ShE
	15:53	I	TrE
9	9:56	I	EcD
	13:03	I	OcR
	23:04	II	ShI
10	0:51	II	TrI
	1:47	II	ShE
	3:36	II	TrE

10	7:17	I	ShI
	8:10	I	TrI
	9:30	I	ShE
	10:23	I	TrE
11	2:48	III	ShI
	4:25	I	EcD
	5:28	III	ShE
	6:23	III	TrI
	7:33	I	OcR
	9:11	III	TrE
	18:10	II	EcD
	22:43	II	OcR
12	1:46	I	ShI
	2:40	I	TrI
	3:58	I	ShE
	4:53	I	TrE
	22:53	I	EcD
13	2:03	I	OcR
	12:22	II	ShI
	14:14	II	TrI
	15:05	II	ShE
	16:59	II	TrE
	20:14	I	ShI
	21:09	I	TrI
	22:27	I	ShE
	23:23	I	TrE
14	16:39	III	EcD
	17:22	I	EcD
	19:21	III	EcR
	20:27	III	OcD
	20:33	I	OcR
	23:18	III	OcR
15	7:27	II	EcD
	12:06	II	OcR
	14:43	I	ShI
	15:39	I	TrI
	16:55	I	ShE
	17:52	I	TrE

SATELLITES OF JUPITER, UT OF 2001 GEOCENTRIC PHENOMENA (ct'd)

AUGUST (ct'd)

Day	Time	Sat	Ph
16	11:50	I	EcD
	15:03	I	OcR
	20:19	IV	TrI
	21:22	IV	TrE
17	1:40	II	ShI
	3:38	II	TrI
	4:24	II	ShE
	6:23	II	TrE
	9:11	I	ShI
	10:09	I	TrI
	11:24	I	ShE
	12:22	I	TrE
18	6:19	I	EcD
	6:47	III	ShI
	9:28	III	ShE
	9:33	I	OcR
	10:43	III	TrI
	13:33	III	TrE
	20:44	II	EcD
19	1:28	II	OcR
	3:39	I	ShI
	4:38	I	TrI
	5:52	I	ShE
	6:52	I	TrE
20	0:47	I	EcD
	4:03	I	OcR
	14:58	II	ShI
	17:01	II	TrI
	17:42	II	ShE
	19:46	II	TrE
	22:08	I	ShI
	23:08	I	TrI
21	0:20	I	ShE
	1:21	I	TrE
	19:16	I	EcD
	20:38	III	EcD
	22:33	I	OcR
	23:22	III	EcR
22	0:48	III	OcD
	3:40	III	OcR
	10:01	II	EcD
	14:50	II	OcR
	16:36	I	ShI
	17:38	I	TrI
	18:49	I	ShE
	19:51	I	TrE
23	13:44	I	EcD
	17:02	I	OcR
24	4:16	II	ShI
	6:24	II	TrI
	7:00	II	ShE
	9:10	II	TrE
	11:05	I	ShI
	12:07	I	TrI
	13:17	I	ShE
	14:20	I	TrE
25	4:17	IV	OcD
	5:43	IV	OcR
	8:13	I	EcD
	10:45	III	ShI
	11:32	I	OcR
25	13:28	III	ShE
	15:01	III	TrI
	17:52	III	TrE
	23:19	II	EcD
26	4:12	II	OcR
	5:33	I	ShI
	6:37	I	TrI
	7:46	I	ShE
	8:50	I	TrE
27	2:41	I	EcD
	6:02	I	OcR
	17:34	II	ShI
	19:46	II	TrI
	20:18	II	ShE
	22:32	II	TrE
28	0:02	I	ShI
	1:06	I	TrI
	2:14	I	ShE
	3:19	I	TrE
	21:09	I	EcD
29	0:31	I	OcR
	0:37	III	EcD
	3:22	III	EcR
	5:05	III	OcD
	7:59	III	OcR
	12:36	II	EcD
	17:33	II	OcR
	18:30	I	ShI
	19:36	I	TrI
	20:43	I	ShE
	21:49	I	TrE
30	15:38	I	EcD
	19:01	I	OcR
31	6:52	II	ShI
	9:09	II	TrI
	9:36	II	ShE
	11:55	II	TrE
	12:58	I	ShI
	14:05	I	TrI
	15:11	I	ShE
	16:18	I	TrE

SEPTEMBER

Day	Time	Sat	Ph
1	10:06	I	EcD
	13:30	I	OcR
	14:44	III	ShI
	17:27	III	ShE
	19:17	III	TrI
	22:08	III	TrE
2	1:53	II	EcD
	6:54	II	OcR
	7:27	I	ShI
	8:34	I	TrI
	9:39	I	ShE
	10:48	I	TrE
	15:49	IV	TrI
	17:29	IV	TrE
3	4:35	I	EcD
	8:00	I	OcR
	20:10	II	ShI
	22:31	II	TrI
	22:54	II	ShE
4	1:17	II	TrE
	1:55	I	ShI
	3:04	I	TrI
	4:08	I	ShE
	5:17	I	TrE
	23:03	I	EcD
5	2:29	I	OcR
	4:37	III	EcD
	7:23	III	EcR
	9:21	III	OcD
	12:16	III	OcR
	15:10	III	EcD
	20:15	II	OcR
	20:24	I	ShI
	21:33	I	TrI
	22:36	I	ShE
	23:46	I	TrE
6	17:32	I	EcD
	20:59	I	OcR
7	9:29	II	ShI
	11:53	II	TrI
	12:13	II	ShE
	14:39	II	TrE
	14:52	I	ShI
	16:02	I	TrI
	17:04	I	ShE
	18:15	I	TrE
8	12:00	I	EcD
	15:28	I	OcR
	18:42	III	ShI
	21:26	III	ShE
	23:30	III	TrI
9	2:23	III	TrE
	4:27	II	EcD
	9:20	I	ShI
	9:35	II	OcR
	10:31	I	TrI
	11:33	I	ShE
	12:44	I	TrE
10	6:29	I	EcD
	9:57	I	OcR
	22:47	II	ShI
	23:36	IV	OcD
11	1:14	II	TrI
	1:31	IV	OcR
	1:31	II	ShE
	3:49	I	ShI
	4:00	II	TrE
	5:00	I	TrI
	6:01	I	ShE
	7:14	I	TrE
12	0:57	I	EcD
	4:27	I	OcR
	8:36	III	EcD
	11:23	III	EcR
	13:33	III	OcD
	16:29	III	OcR
	17:44	II	EcD
	22:17	I	ShI
	22:55	II	OcR
	23:30	I	TrI
13	0:30	I	ShE
	1:43	I	TrE
13	19:26	I	EcD
	22:56	I	OcR
14	12:05	II	ShI
	14:36	II	TrI
	14:49	II	ShE
	16:46	I	ShI
	17:22	II	TrE
	17:59	I	TrI
	18:58	I	ShE
	20:12	I	TrE
15	13:54	I	EcD
	17:25	I	OcR
	22:41	III	ShI
16	1:26	III	ShE
	3:40	III	TrI
	6:34	III	TrE
	7:01	II	EcD
	11:14	I	ShI
	12:15	II	OcR
	12:28	I	TrI
	13:26	I	ShE
	14:41	I	TrE
17	8:23	I	EcD
	11:54	I	OcR
18	1:23	II	ShI
	3:56	II	TrI
	4:07	II	ShE
	5:42	I	ShI
	6:42	II	TrE
	6:56	I	TrI
	7:55	I	ShE
	9:10	I	TrE
19	2:51	I	EcD
	6:23	I	OcR
	10:51	IV	TrI
	12:34	III	EcD
	12:54	IV	TrE
	15:23	III	EcR
	17:42	III	OcD
	20:17	II	EcD
	20:40	III	OcR
20	0:11	I	ShI
	1:25	I	TrI
	1:34	II	OcR
	2:23	I	ShE
	3:38	I	TrE
	21:20	I	EcD
21	0:52	I	OcR
	14:41	II	ShI
	17:17	II	TrI
	17:26	II	ShE
	18:39	I	ShI
	19:54	I	TrI
	20:03	II	TrE
	20:51	I	ShE
	22:07	I	TrE
22	15:48	I	EcD
	19:21	I	OcR
23	2:39	III	ShI
	5:26	III	ShE
	7:47	III	TrI
	9:34	II	EcD
23	10:42	III	TrE
	13:07	I	ShI
	14:23	I	TrI
	14:53	II	OcR
	15:20	I	ShE
	16:36	I	TrE
24	10:17	I	EcD
	13:50	I	OcR
25	3:59	II	ShI
	6:36	II	TrI
	6:44	II	ShE
	7:36	I	ShI
	8:52	I	TrI
	9:23	II	TrE
	9:48	I	ShE
	11:05	I	TrE
26	4:45	I	EcD
	8:19	I	OcR
	16:33	III	EcD
	19:22	III	EcR
	21:48	III	OcD
	22:51	II	EcD
27	0:46	III	OcR
	2:04	I	ShI
	3:20	I	TrI
	4:11	II	OcR
	4:16	I	ShE
	5:33	I	TrE
	6:37	IV	EcD
	7:24	IV	EcR
	18:21	IV	OcD
	20:35	IV	OcR
	23:14	I	EcD
28	2:48	I	OcR
	17:18	II	ShI
	19:56	II	TrI
	20:02	II	ShE
	20:32	I	ShI
	21:49	I	TrI
	22:43	II	TrE
	22:45	I	ShE
29	0:02	I	TrE
	17:42	I	EcD
	21:17	I	OcR
30	6:39	III	ShI
	9:26	III	ShE
	11:52	III	TrI
	12:08	II	EcD
	14:48	III	TrE
	15:01	I	ShI
	16:17	I	TrI
	17:13	I	ShE
	17:29	II	OcR
	18:30	I	TrE

SATELLITES OF JUPITER, UT OF 2001 GEOCENTRIC PHENOMENA (ct'd)

OCTOBER

Date	Time	Sat.	Phen.
1	12:10	I	EcD
	15:45	I	OcR
2	6:36	II	ShI
	9:15	II	TrI
	9:20	II	ShE
	9:29	I	ShI
	10:46	I	TrI
	11:41	I	ShE
	12:01	II	TrE
	12:59	I	TrE
3	6:39	I	EcD
	10:14	I	OcR
	20:31	III	EcD
	23:22	III	EcR
4	1:25	II	EcD
	1:49	III	OcD
	3:57	I	ShI
	4:49	III	OcR
	5:14	I	TrI
	6:10	I	ShE
	6:46	II	OcR
	7:27	I	TrE
5	1:07	I	EcD
	4:43	I	OcR
	17:23	IV	ShI
	18:25	IV	ShE
	19:54	II	ShI
	22:26	I	ShI
	22:34	II	TrI
	22:39	II	ShE
	23:43	I	TrI
6	0:38	I	ShE
	1:20	II	TrE
	1:56	I	TrE
	5:12	IV	TrI
	7:31	IV	TrE
	19:36	I	EcD
	23:11	I	OcR
7	10:37	III	ShI
	13:25	III	ShE
	14:41	II	EcD
	15:51	III	TrI
	16:54	I	ShI
	18:11	I	TrI
	18:48	III	TrE
	19:06	I	ShE
	20:03	II	OcR
	20:24	I	TrE
8	14:04	I	EcD
	17:40	I	OcR
9	9:12	II	ShI
	11:22	I	ShI
	11:51	II	TrI
	11:57	II	ShE
	12:39	I	TrI
	13:35	I	ShE
	14:38	II	TrE
	14:52	I	TrE
10	8:33	I	EcD
	12:08	I	OcR
11	0:30	III	EcD
	3:22	III	EcR
	3:58	II	EcD
	5:48	III	OcD
	5:51	I	ShI
	7:07	I	TrI
	8:03	I	ShE
	8:48	III	OcR
	9:19	II	OcR
	9:20	I	TrE
12	3:01	I	EcD
	6:36	I	OcR
	22:30	II	ShI
13	0:19	I	ShI
	1:09	II	TrI
	1:16	II	ShE
	1:35	I	TrI
	2:31	I	ShE
	3:49	I	TrE
	3:56	II	TrE
	21:30	I	EcD
14	0:25	IV	EcD
	1:05	I	OcR
	1:46	IV	EcR
	12:20	IV	OcD
	14:35	III	ShI
	14:48	IV	OcR
	17:15	II	EcD
	17:25	III	ShE
	18:47	I	ShI
	19:46	III	TrI
	20:03	I	TrI
	21:00	I	ShE
	22:17	I	TrE
	22:35	II	OcR
	22:44	III	TrE
15	15:58	I	EcD
	19:33	I	OcR
16	11:48	II	ShI
	13:15	I	ShI
	14:26	II	TrI
	14:31	I	TrI
	14:34	II	ShE
	15:28	I	ShE
	16:45	I	TrE
	17:13	II	TrE
17	10:27	I	EcD
	14:01	I	OcR
18	4:29	III	EcD
	6:32	II	EcD
	7:22	III	EcR
	7:44	I	ShI
	8:59	I	TrI
	9:42	III	OcD
	9:56	I	ShE
	11:13	I	TrE
	11:51	II	OcR
	12:43	III	OcR
19	4:55	I	EcD
	8:29	I	OcR
20	1:07	II	ShI
	2:12	I	ShI
	3:27	I	TrI
	3:43	II	TrI
	3:52	II	ShE
	4:25	I	ShE
	5:40	I	TrE
	6:30	II	TrE
	23:24	I	EcD
21	2:57	I	OcR
	18:33	III	ShI
	19:48	II	EcD
	20:40	I	ShI
	21:24	III	ShE
	21:55	I	TrI
	22:53	I	ShE
	23:37	III	TrI
22	0:08	I	TrE
	1:05	II	OcR
	2:36	III	TrE
	11:14	IV	ShI
	12:44	IV	ShE
	17:52	I	EcD
	21:25	I	OcR
	22:45	IV	TrI
23	0:25	IV	EcD
	1:15	IV	TrE
	14:25	II	ShI
	15:09	I	ShI
	16:23	I	TrI
	16:58	II	TrI
	17:10	II	ShE
	17:21	I	ShE
	18:36	I	TrE
	19:45	II	TrE
24	12:21	I	EcD
	15:53	I	OcR
25	8:29	III	EcD
	9:05	II	EcD
	9:37	I	ShI
	10:50	I	TrI
	11:23	III	EcR
	11:50	I	ShE
	13:04	I	TrE
	13:32	III	OcD
	14:19	II	OcR
	16:34	III	OcR
26	6:49	I	EcD
	10:20	I	OcR
27	3:43	II	ShI
	4:05	I	ShI
	5:18	I	TrI
	6:14	II	TrI
	6:18	I	ShE
	6:29	II	ShE
	7:31	I	TrE
	9:01	II	TrE
28	1:18	I	EcD
	4:48	I	OcR
	22:22	II	EcD
	22:31	III	ShI
	22:33	I	ShI
	23:45	I	TrI
29	0:46	I	ShE
	1:23	III	ShE
	1:59	I	TrE
	3:23	III	TrI
	3:33	II	OcR
	6:23	III	TrE
	19:46	I	EcD
	23:16	I	OcR
30	17:01	II	ShI
	17:02	I	ShI
	18:13	I	TrI
	18:19	IV	EcD
	19:15	I	ShE
	19:28	II	TrI
	19:47	II	ShE
	20:03	IV	EcR
	20:26	I	TrE
	22:15	II	TrE
31	5:25	IV	OcD
	8:02	IV	OcR
	14:15	I	EcD
	17:43	I	OcR

NOVEMBER

Date	Time	Sat.	Phen.
1	11:30	I	ShI
	11:38	II	EcD
	12:27	III	EcD
	12:40	I	TrI
	13:43	I	ShE
	14:54	I	TrE
	15:22	III	EcR
	16:46	II	OcR
	17:16	III	OcD
	20:19	III	OcR
2	8:43	I	EcD
	12:11	I	OcR
3	5:58	I	ShI
	6:20	II	ShI
	7:07	I	TrI
	8:11	I	ShE
	8:43	II	TrI
	9:06	II	ShE
	9:21	I	TrE
	11:30	II	TrE
4	3:12	I	EcD
	6:38	I	OcR
5	0:27	I	ShI
	0:55	II	EcD
	1:35	I	TrI
	2:29	III	ShI
	2:40	I	ShE
	3:48	I	TrE
	5:22	III	ShE
	5:59	II	OcR
	7:06	III	TrI
	10:05	III	TrE
	21:40	I	EcD
6	1:05	I	OcR
	18:55	I	ShI
	19:37	II	ShI
	20:02	I	TrI
	21:08	I	ShE
	21:56	II	TrI
	22:15	I	TrE
	22:24	II	ShE
7	0:43	II	TrE
	16:09	I	EcD
	19:33	I	OcR
8	5:08	IV	ShI
	7:00	IV	ShE
	13:23	I	ShI
	14:12	II	EcD
	14:29	I	TrI
	15:20	IV	TrI
	15:36	I	ShE
	16:26	III	EcD
	16:42	I	TrE
	17:56	IV	TrE
	19:11	II	OcR
	19:22	III	EcR
	20:56	III	OcD
	23:59	III	OcR
9	10:37	I	EcD
	14:00	I	OcR
10	7:51	I	ShI
	8:56	I	TrI
	8:56	II	ShI
	10:05	I	ShE
	11:09	II	TrI
	11:10	I	TrE
	11:42	II	ShE
	13:57	II	TrE
11	5:06	I	EcD
	8:27	I	OcR
12	2:20	I	ShI
	3:23	I	TrI
	3:29	II	EcD
	4:33	I	ShE
	5:36	I	TrE
	6:27	III	ShI
	8:22	II	OcR
	9:22	III	ShE
	10:43	III	TrI
	13:43	III	TrE
	23:34	I	EcD
13	2:54	I	OcR
	20:48	I	ShI
	21:50	I	TrI
	22:14	II	ShI
	23:01	I	ShE
14	0:03	I	TrE
	0:21	II	TrI
	1:00	II	ShE
	3:09	II	TrE
	18:03	I	EcD
	21:21	I	OcR
15	15:16	I	ShI
	16:16	I	TrI
	16:45	II	EcD
	17:30	I	ShE
	18:30	I	TrE
	20:24	III	EcD
	21:33	II	OcR
	23:21	III	EcR

SATELLITES OF JUPITER, UT OF 2001 GEOCENTRIC PHENOMENA (ct'd)

NOVEMBER (ct'd)

Date	UT	Sat	Phen
16	0:30	III	OcD
	3:33	III	OcR
	12:15	IV	EcD
	12:31	I	EcD
	14:18	IV	EcR
	15:48	I	OcR
	21:30	IV	OcD
17	0:12	IV	OcR
	9:45	I	ShI
	10:43	I	TrI
	11:32	II	ShI
	11:58	I	ShE
	12:57	I	TrE
	13:33	II	TrI
	14:19	II	ShE
	16:21	II	TrE
18	7:00	I	EcD
	10:15	I	OcR
19	4:13	I	ShI
	5:10	I	TrI
	6:02	II	EcD
	6:26	I	ShE
	7:24	I	TrE
	10:26	III	ShI
	10:43	II	OcR
	13:22	III	ShE
	14:16	III	TrI
	17:17	III	TrE
20	1:28	I	EcD
	4:41	I	OcR
	22:41	I	ShI
	23:36	I	TrI
21	0:50	II	ShI
	0:55	I	ShE
	1:50	I	TrE
	2:44	II	TrI
	3:37	II	ShE
	5:32	II	TrE
	19:57	I	EcD
	23:08	I	OcR
22	17:10	I	ShI
	18:03	I	TrI
	19:19	II	EcD
	19:23	I	ShE
	20:17	I	TrE
	23:53	II	OcR
23	0:23	III	EcD
	3:21	III	EcR
	4:01	III	OcD
	7:04	III	OcR
	14:25	I	EcD
	17:35	I	OcR
24	11:38	I	ShI
	12:29	I	TrI
	13:52	I	ShE
	14:09	II	ShI
	14:44	I	TrE
	15:55	II	TrI
	16:56	II	ShE
	18:43	II	TrE
	23:04	IV	ShI
25	1:13	IV	ShE
	6:56	IV	TrI
	8:54	I	EcD
	9:36	IV	TrE
	12:01	I	OcR
26	6:06	I	ShI
	6:56	I	TrI
	8:20	I	ShE
	8:36	II	EcD
	9:10	I	TrE
	13:02	II	OcR
	14:25	III	ShI
	17:21	III	ShE
	17:44	III	TrI
	20:45	III	TrE
27	3:22	I	EcD
	6:28	I	OcR
28	0:35	I	ShI
	1:22	I	TrI
	2:48	I	ShE
	3:27	II	ShI
	3:36	I	TrE
	5:04	II	TrI
	6:14	II	ShE
	7:52	II	TrE
	21:51	I	EcD
29	0:54	I	OcR
	19:03	I	ShI
	19:49	I	TrI
	21:17	I	ShE
	21:53	II	EcD
	22:03	I	TrE
30	2:11	II	OcR
	4:22	III	EcD
	7:22	III	EcR
	7:27	III	OcD
	10:30	III	OcR
	16:19	I	EcD
	19:21	I	OcR

DECEMBER

Date	UT	Sat	Phen
1	13:31	I	ShI
	14:15	I	TrI
	15:45	I	ShE
	16:29	I	TrE
	16:45	II	ShI
	18:14	II	TrI
	19:33	II	ShE
	21:02	II	TrE
2	10:48	I	EcD
	13:47	I	OcR
3	6:12	IV	EcD
	8:00	I	ShI
	8:32	IV	EcR
	8:41	I	TrI
	10:14	I	ShE
	10:55	I	TrE
	11:10	II	EcD
	12:38	IV	OcD
	15:19	II	OcR
	15:22	IV	OcR
	18:23	III	ShI
	21:07	III	TrI
	21:21	III	ShE
4	0:09	III	TrE
	5:16	I	EcD
	8:13	I	OcR
5	2:28	I	ShI
	3:07	I	TrI
	4:42	I	ShE
	5:21	I	TrE
	6:03	II	ShI
	7:23	II	TrI
	8:51	II	ShE
	10:11	II	TrE
	23:45	I	EcD
6	2:40	I	OcR
	20:56	I	ShI
	21:33	I	TrI
	23:11	I	ShE
	23:48	I	TrE
7	0:27	II	EcD
	4:27	II	OcR
	8:22	III	EcD
	13:53	III	OcR
	18:14	I	EcD
	21:06	I	OcR
8	15:25	I	ShI
	15:59	I	TrI
	17:39	I	ShE
	18:14	I	TrE
	19:22	II	ShI
	20:32	II	TrI
	22:10	II	ShE
	23:20	II	TrE
9	12:42	I	EcD
	15:32	I	OcR
10	9:53	I	ShI
	10:25	I	TrI
	12:08	I	ShE
	12:40	I	TrE
	13:44	II	EcD
	17:34	II	OcR
	22:21	III	ShI
11	0:27	III	TrI
	1:20	III	ShE
	3:29	III	TrE
	7:11	I	EcD
	9:58	I	OcR
	17:01	IV	ShI
	19:26	IV	ShE
	21:41	IV	TrI
12	0:22	IV	TrE
	4:22	I	ShI
	4:51	I	TrI
	6:36	I	ShE
	7:06	I	TrE
	8:40	II	ShI
	9:40	II	TrI
	11:28	II	ShE
	12:28	II	TrE
13	1:39	I	EcD
	4:24	I	OcR
	22:50	I	ShI
	23:17	I	TrI
14	1:05	I	ShE
	1:32	I	TrE
	3:01	II	EcD
	6:42	II	OcR
	12:21	III	EcD
	17:12	III	OcR
	20:08	I	EcD
	22:50	I	OcR
15	17:19	I	ShI
	17:43	I	TrI
	19:33	I	ShE
	19:58	I	TrE
	21:58	II	ShI
	22:48	II	TrI
16	0:46	II	ShE
	1:36	II	TrE
	14:37	I	EcD
	17:16	I	OcR
17	11:47	I	ShI
	12:09	I	TrI
	14:02	I	ShE
	14:24	I	TrE
	16:18	II	EcD
	19:49	II	OcR
18	2:19	III	ShI
	3:45	III	TrI
	5:20	III	ShE
	6:47	III	TrE
	9:05	I	EcD
	11:42	I	OcR
19	6:15	I	ShI
	6:35	I	TrI
	8:30	I	ShE
	8:50	I	TrE
	11:16	II	ShI
	11:56	II	TrI
	14:04	II	ShE
	14:44	II	TrE
20	0:11	IV	EcD
	2:45	IV	EcR
	3:03	IV	OcD
	3:34	I	EcD
	5:45	IV	OcR
	6:08	I	OcR
21	0:44	I	ShI
	1:01	I	TrI
	2:59	I	ShE
	3:15	I	TrE
	5:35	II	EcD
	8:55	II	OcR
	16:21	III	EcD
	20:29	III	OcR
	22:02	I	EcD
22	0:34	I	OcR
	19:12	I	ShI
	19:27	I	TrI
	21:27	I	ShE
	21:41	I	TrE
23	0:35	II	ShI
	1:04	II	TrI
	3:23	II	ShE
	3:52	II	TrE
	16:31	I	EcD
	19:00	I	OcR
24	13:41	I	ShI
	13:53	I	TrI
	15:56	I	ShE
	16:07	I	TrE
	18:53	II	EcD
	22:02	II	OcR
25	6:18	III	ShI
	7:01	III	TrI
	9:20	III	ShE
	10:03	III	TrE
	11:00	I	EcD
	13:26	I	OcR
26	8:09	I	ShI
	8:18	I	TrI
	10:24	I	ShE
	10:33	I	TrE
	13:53	II	ShI
	14:11	II	TrI
	16:41	II	ShE
	16:59	II	TrE
27	5:28	I	EcD
	7:52	I	OcR
28	2:38	I	ShI
	2:44	I	TrI
	4:53	I	ShE
	4:59	I	TrE
	8:10	II	EcD
	11:00	IV	ShI
	11:09	II	OcR
	11:53	IV	TrI
	13:38	IV	ShE
	14:33	IV	TrE
	20:20	III	EcD
	23:44	III	OcR
	23:57	I	EcD
29	2:17	I	OcR
	21:06	I	ShI
	21:10	I	TrI
	23:21	I	ShE
	23:25	I	TrE
30	3:12	II	ShI
	3:18	II	TrI
	6:00	II	ShE
	6:06	II	TrE
	18:26	I	EcD
	20:43	I	OcR
31	15:35	I	ShI
	15:36	I	TrI
	17:50	I	ShE
	17:51	I	TrE
	21:27	II	EcD
32	0:15	II	OcR
	10:16	III	TrI
	10:17	III	ShI
	12:54	I	OcD
	13:18	III	TrE
	13:20	III	ShE
	15:10	I	EcR

CONFIGURATIONS OF SATURN'S BRIGHTEST SATELLITES
By Larry D. Bogan

The diagrams on the next three pages give the relative locations of the five brightest satellites of Saturn during January, February, March, and July through December 2001. The names and magnitudes of these satellites, in order of increasing distance from Saturn, are Enceladus 11.8, Tethys 10.3, Dione 10.4, Rhea 9.7, and Titan 8.4. **The curves** in the diagrams show the elongations of the satellites from Saturn for day 0.0 UT to day 32.0 UT for each month. The curves for Enceladus and Dione, the first and third out from Saturn, are drawn dashed to facilitate identification. The narrow, central, vertical band represents the disk of Saturn, while the wider, vertical band represents the outer edge of Saturn's "A" ring.

At the top of each monthly diagram is a **scale drawing** of Saturn, its rings, and the orbits of four of the five brightest satellites as seen through an inverting telescope (in the Northern Hemisphere). South is up. Because of the small size of the scale drawing, no orbit is shown for the innermost satellite, Enceladus. Due to its faintness and proximity to the bright rings, Enceladus is best seen when near a maximum elongation—but even then good seeing, good optics, and an aperture of at least 250 mm are required.

During 2001 we see Saturn and its satellites from south of the ring plane. The maximum tilt for 2001 will be 26.2° on September 1. The direction of motion of the satellites is clockwise (indicated by arrow on the orbit of Titan) as viewed with a telescope having an even number (0, 2, 4,…) of reflections in its optics.

A particular **configuration of the satellites** may be determined by drawing a horizontal line across the monthly curves at the time (UT) of interest. The intersection of this line with the curves gives the relative elongations of the satellites. Project these elongations onto the drawing of the orbits at the top of the diagram. The east side of the "A" ring vertical band has been extended up to the drawing to facilitate transfer of each elongation. The March diagram shows an example configuration for March 4 at 9 p.m. EST (March 5 at 2h UT).

The direction of the orbital motion of a satellite determines on which side of its orbit (north or south) a satellite is located. A satellite *moving right* (east) will be *above* (south of) Saturn in the scale drawing, and a satellite *moving left* (west) will be *below* (north of) Saturn in the drawing.

Greatest Elongations and Conjunctions for Iapetus

Iapetus has a magnitude comparable to the five satellites plotted in the diagrams, but varies from magnitude 10.1 (western elongation) to 11.9 (eastern elongation). Iapetus' orbit is about 2.9 times the size of Titan's, is tilted 15° to Saturn's ring plane, and its period is 79 days. Iapetus is easiest to find near conjunctions when it is just north or south of Saturn. The table lists times of greatest elongations and conjunctions for Iapetus during 2001.

Eastern Elong.		Inferior Conj.		Western Elong.		Superior Conj.	
Jan. 15	12.9h	Feb. 5	9.7h	Feb. 25	9.8h	Mar. 16	13.2h
Apr. 5	20.7h	Apr. 27	7.3h	May. 17	13.7h	June 5	23.4h
June 26	14.5h	July 17	23.8h	Aug. 6	22.3h	Aug. 26	2.5h
Sept. 15	10.8h	Oct. 6	5.9h	Oct. 25	13.7h	Nov. 13	5.1h
Dec. 02	23.7h	Dec. 23	10.1h				

Note: Dan Bruton has created a free DOS program called SATSAT2 that calculates and displays the positions of eight of the brightest satellites of Saturn for any time and date. It is available at http://www.physics.sfasu.edu/astro/dansoftware.html.

CONFIGURATIONS OF SATURN'S SATELLITES
2001 JANUARY–MARCH

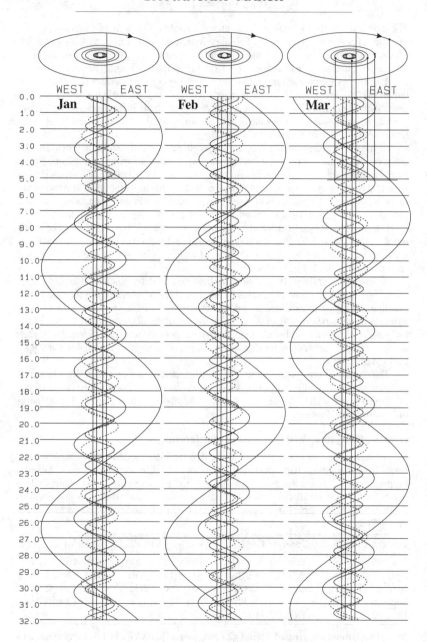

CONFIGURATIONS OF SATURN'S SATELLITES
2001 JULY–SEPTEMBER

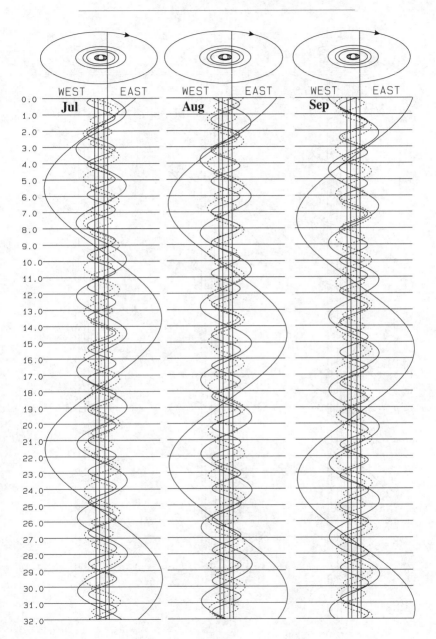

CONFIGURATIONS OF SATURN'S SATELLITES
2001 OCTOBER–DECEMBER

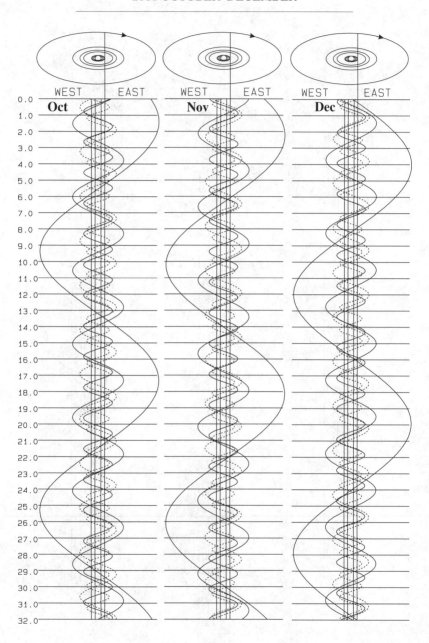

ASTEROIDS

THE BRIGHTEST ASTEROIDS

On the next two pages are ephemerides for asteroids (identified by number and name) that will be brighter than or equal to visual magnitude 10.0 and more than 90° from the Sun during 2001. The positions are based on TT, although the equivalent but older designation "ET" appears on the tables. TT differs by about one minute from UT (see TIME AND TIME SCALES on pp. 30–34). "Mag" is visual magnitude. These data were derived from current osculating elements.

Using the ephemerides provided and an appropriate star atlas, charts displaying the motion of each asteroid can be produced. For example, the chart below, provided by David Lane, shows the path of Vesta as it moves through its retrograde loop in Taurus and Orion from September to December. The coordinates are for epoch 2000.0.

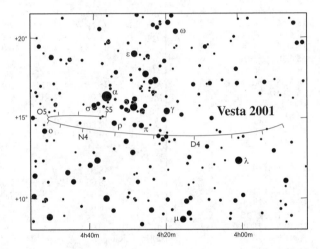

The chart magnitude limit is 8.0. Tick marks along Vesta's path locate its position at ten-day intervals, beginning with September 5 (S5) and ending with 2002 January 3. The field is very easy to locate—the brightest star in the chart is Aldebaran. At the start of its displayed track, Vesta lies approximately 1° south of Aldebaran.

Vesta brightens to visual magnitude 6.5 when at opposition on November 27, making it the brightest asteroid in 2001. With its unusually high albedo (≈30%) and small orbit, Vesta is the only asteroid that becomes bright enough to be seen without optical aid, but this will however be a challenging observation in 2001. With a diameter of 538 km and a distance of 1.59 AU at its 2001 opposition, Vesta will have an angular diameter of 0.47″, which will make it very difficult to resolve with Earth-based telescopes. Ceres, with a diameter of 1003 km and opposition distance of 1.89 AU, will have an angular diameter of 0.65″, but northern observers will also find it difficult to resolve because of its southern declination.

Vesta was the fourth asteroid discovered, by Heinrich Olbers in 1807, hence its designation (4) Vesta. Because of its brightness, Vesta was thought to be the largest asteroid until 1895 when E. E. Barnard, using a filar micrometer on the 36-inch (0.91-m) refractor at Lick Observatory, found Vesta to be smaller than Ceres.

EPHEMERIDES FOR THE BRIGHTEST ASTEROIDS IN 2001
BY BRIAN MARSDEN

Date 0h ET	RA(2000) h m	Dec ° ′	Mag.	Date 0h ET	RA(2000) h m	Dec ° ′	Mag.
(1) Ceres				**(4) Vesta (continued)**			
Apr. 11	19 24.0	−23 40	8.8	Oct. 8	4 52.0	+15 04	7.4
21	19 31.6	−23 56	8.6	18	4 51.0	+14 52	7.2
May 1	19 37.1	−24 17	8.5	28	4 47.0	+14 39	7.0
11	19 40.3	−24 46	8.4	Nov. 7	4 40.1	+14 26	6.8
21	19 41.1	−25 24	8.2	17	4 30.9	+14 15	6.6
31	19 39.2	−26 10	8.0	27	4 20.3	+14 07	6.5
Jun. 10	19 34.7	−27 02	7.8	Dec. 7	4 09.6	+14 05	6.6
20	19 27.8	−27 57	7.6	17	4 00.0	+14 11	6.8
30	19 19.2	−28 50	7.4	27	3 52.5	+14 25	7.0
Jul. 10	19 09.6	−29 37	7.3				
20	19 00.1	−30 15	7.5	**(6) Hebe**			
30	18 51.8	−30 42	7.8	Mar. 12	12 58.3	+10 38	10.0
Aug. 9	18 45.4	−30 59	8.0	22	12 50.7	+12 14	9.9
19	18 41.6	−31 06	8.2	Apr. 1	12 42.2	+13 39	9.9
29	18 40.5	−31 06	8.4	11	12 33.8	+14 46	10.0
Sep. 8	18 42.0	−31 01	8.6				
18	18 46.1	−30 51	8.7	**(7) Iris**			
28	18 52.5	−30 38	8.8	Apr. 21	15 16.6	−22 57	9.9
				May 1	15 07.4	−22 15	9.6
(2) Pallas				11	14 57.6	−21 24	9.5
Mar. 12	17 05.4	+11 25	9.5	21	14 48.1	−20 28	9.7
22	17 11.0	+13 38	9.5	31	14 39.9	−19 32	9.9
Apr. 1	17 14.4	+15 57	9.4				
11	17 15.4	+18 17	9.3	**(9) Metis**			
21	17 14.0	+20 31	9.2	Nov. 17	8 04.1	+23 45	9.9
May 1	17 10.1	+22 33	9.2	27	8 08.3	+24 15	9.6
11	17 04.1	+24 14	9.2	Dec. 7	8 08.9	+24 58	9.4
21	16 56.6	+25 29	9.2	17	8 05.6	+25 53	9.2
31	16 48.1	+26 13	9.2	27	7 58.8	+26 55	8.9
Jun. 10	16 39.6	+26 22	9.2				
20	16 31.8	+26 00	9.3	**(10) Hygiea**			
30	16 25.5	+25 09	9.4	Aug. 19	22 44.0	−3 13	10.0
Jul. 10	16 21.0	+23 54	9.6	29	22 36.6	−3 49	9.8
20	16 18.5	+22 22	9.7	Sep. 8	22 29.2	−4 29	9.9
30	16 18.2	+20 39	9.8				
Aug. 9	16 20.0	+18 48	9.9	**(11) Parthenope**			
19	16 23.7	+16 55	10.0	Nov. 7	4 03.5	+13 24	9.9
				17	3 53.7	+12 56	9.7
(3) Juno				27	3 43.5	+12 34	9.8
Nov. 17	9 30.3	+2 19	9.4	Dec. 7	3 34.2	+12 22	10.0
27	9 39.3	+1 18	9.3				
Dec. 7	9 46.0	+0 30	9.2	**(14) Irene**			
17	9 50.0	−0 01	9.1	May 1	17 46.7	−19 08	10.0
27	9 51.1	−0 11	9.0	11	17 43.0	−19 35	9.8
				21	17 36.4	−20 05	9.6
(4) Vesta				31	17 27.4	−20 38	9.4
Sep. 8	4 38.6	+15 16	7.9	Jun. 10	17 17.3	−21 11	9.1
18	4 45.5	+15 17	7.7	20	17 07.1	−21 44	9.4
28	4 50.0	+15 12	7.6	30	16 58.3	−22 15	9.7
				Jul. 10	16 51.8	−22 45	10.0

EPHEMERIDES FOR THE BRIGHTEST ASTEROIDS IN 2001 (cont.)

Date 0h ET	RA(2000) h m	Dec ° ′	Mag.
(15) Eunomia			
May 1	16 08.7	−35 08	9.9
11	15 59.7	−34 49	9.7
21	15 49.5	−34 14	9.6
31	15 39.4	−33 23	9.6
Jun. 10	15 30.4	−32 22	9.8
20	15 23.3	−31 15	9.9
(19) Fortuna			
Sep. 8	0 29.5	+4 56	9.8
18	0 22.6	+4 05	9.4
28	0 14.4	+3 03	9.0
Oct. 8	0 06.3	+1 58	9.4
18	23 59.5	+1 01	9.7
28	23 55.2	+0 19	10.0
(22) Kalliope			
Dec. 7	5 34.3	+28 53	10.0
17	5 23.6	+29 39	9.9
(29) Amphitrite			
Mar. 12	13 24.8	−11 37	9.9
22	13 17.5	−11 22	9.7
Apr. 1	13 08.6	−10 55	9.5
11	12 59.2	−10 20	9.4
21	12 50.2	−9 43	9.6
May 1	12 42.6	−9 09	9.8
(39) Laetitia			
Sep. 8	1 51.0	+1 59	10.0
18	1 48.5	+0 39	9.7
28	1 43.6	−0 50	9.5
Oct. 8	1 37.0	−2 19	9.4
18	1 29.6	−3 41	9.4
28	1 22.3	−4 45	9.6
Nov. 7	1 16.3	−5 28	9.8
17	1 12.1	−5 46	10.0
(40) Harmonia			
Dec. 7	6 01.1	+22 03	9.8
17	5 49.7	+22 23	9.4
27	5 38.1	+22 42	9.7
(42) Isis			
May 31	17 12.0	−20 05	9.8
Jun. 10	17 01.5	−20 46	9.5
20	16 50.8	−21 29	9.8
(43) Ariadne			
May 1	14 56.5	−21 39	9.7
11	14 46.7	−20 38	9.6
21	14 37.5	−19 29	9.9

Date 0h ET	RA(2000) h m	Dec ° ′	Mag.
(68) Leto			
Jul. 20	20 04.8	−33 41	9.9
30	19 55.0	−34 13	10.0
(89) Julia			
Sep. 28	2 49.4	+42 36	10.0
Oct. 8	2 44.0	+43 49	9.9
18	2 35.0	+44 28	9.7
28	2 23.6	+44 25	9.6
Nov. 7	2 11.9	+43 40	9.6
17	2 01.8	+42 20	9.7
27	1 54.8	+40 36	9.8
Dec. 7	1 51.7	+38 46	10.0
(349) Dembowska			
Jul. 20	22 09.8	−24 13	10.0
30	22 03.6	−25 00	9.8
Aug 9	21 55.7	−25 44	9.7
.19	21 46.9	−26 18	9.7
29	21 38.1	−26 38	9.8
Sep. 8	21 30.5	−26 40	10.0
(354) Eleonora			
Feb. 20	11 59.5	+13 54	9.9
Mar. 2	11 54.2	+16 08	9.8
12	11 47.5	+18 15	9.7
22	11 40.3	+20 04	9.8
Apr. 1	11 33.8	+21 26	10.0
(532) Herculina			
Jan. 31	14 26.2	+5 45	10.0
Feb. 10	14 36.8	+6 18	9.9
20	14 45.1	+7 07	9.7
Mar. 2	14 50.8	+8 10	9.6
12	14 53.7	+9 23	9.4
22	14 53.4	+10 41	9.2
Apr. 1	14 50.1	+11 56	9.1
11	14 44.2	+12 57	9.0
21	14 36.3	+13 37	8.9
May 1	14 27.7	+13 47	9.0
11	14 19.5	+13 24	9.1
21	14 12.7	+12 31	9.3
31	14 08.1	+11 11	9.5
Jun. 10	14 06.0	+9 30	9.7
20	14 06.5	+7 36	9.8
30	14 09.5	+5 32	10.0
(704) Interamnia			
Oct. 8	0 21.2	+32 16	10.0
18	0 13.5	+31 09	10.0

PLANETARY APPULSES AND OCCULTATIONS
By David W. Dunham

As planets, satellites, asteroids, and comets move across the sky, they will on occasion pass near an observer's line of sight to a distant star. Such close passes are called appulses. More rarely, the moving object's trajectory will carry it directly between the observer and the star, thereby producing an occultation. Astronomers have learned much about various solar system bodies by carefully monitoring the changing apparent brightness of stars during the immersion and emersion phases of occultations. If the occulting body does not have an atmosphere, the occultation is virtually instantaneous; an atmosphere causes the star's disappearance and reappearance to occur gradually. The rate of disappearance/reappearance is related to the temperature and composition of the atmosphere. If a planet has rings or other debris in its environs, the extent and degree of transparency of this material can be precisely mapped. The rings of Uranus, the ring arcs of Neptune, and the atmosphere of Pluto were all discovered by occultation observations. In addition, if an occultation can be observed at several appropriately distributed sites, it is often possible to determine the size and shape of the occulting body more accurately than by other Earth-based techniques.

Amateur astronomers can sometimes contribute importantly to occultation observing campaigns. This is particularly true for asteroid occultations where the strip across Earth from which an event is observable is often very narrow and uncertain in location (due to uncertainties in both the star's position and the ephemeris of the asteroid). By recording the times of the star's disappearance and reappearance as seen from several sites (i.e. by noting the edges of the asteroid's shadow as it sweeps across Earth), the asteroid's profile can be directly determined. Often timings of adequate accuracy can be made by visual observers using modest telescopes.

When observing an occultation, it is important that an observer know his location to within a fraction of a kilometre. Geographic longitude and latitude as well as the altitude of an observing site can be determined from a high-quality topographic map. If observations are to be of maximum value, the times of immersion and emersion must be determined as accurately as possible—certainly to better than 0.5 s, and better than 0.2 s for the shortest events (those less than about 10 s duration). **Photoelectric equipment** with high-speed digital recording systems are well suited for this work. Attaching a low light-level **video camera**, especially one with an image intensifier, to a telescope is another good method for accurately timing these events. **Visual observers** equipped with tape recorders and short wave time signal receivers can also be useful. Even simple measurements of the duration of an occultation made with an ordinary stopwatch can be of value. **CCD observers** should beware that most of these systems are incapable of timing accuracies better than about 2 s; hence visual observation may be better. But a trick that some CCD observers have used is to turn off the telescope clock drive shortly before the predicted time and let the images trail. The occultation will appear as a break in the trail that can be measured to a few tenths of a second, depending on seeing conditions, if the moment the drive is turned off is accurately timed.

Occultation observations are coordinated in North America by the International Occultation Timing Association (IOTA). Whether you are a member of IOTA or not, this organization wants to inform you and others in your area who can locate 9th- and 10th-magnitude stars, of last-minute prediction updates. Please send the approximate (or accurate) longitude and latitude (or location from the nearest town if in the United States) of convenient observing sites; telescope size(s); and whether mobile or not, by email to dunham@erols.com. IOTA publishes a newsletter and maintains a "hotline" for disseminating last-minute prediction updates; within a few days of each event, improved predictions may be obtained from recorded telephone messages at

(301) 474-4945 (Greenbelt, Md.) or from the asteroidal occultation secion of IOTA's web site at http://www.lunar-occultations.com/iota. Individuals interested in joining IOTA should refer to p. 144 in the section OCCULTATIONS BY THE MOON in this Handbook.

Other sources of occultation information include the *Solar System Photometry Handbook* (published by Willmann-Bell, Inc., 1983), *Sky & Telescope* (particularly the February issue), and occasional papers in the *Astronomical Journal, Icarus,* and other scientific journals.

Observations of this type of occultation, *including* negative observations, should be sent to Jan Manek, Stefanik Observatory, Petrin 205, 118 46 Praha (Prague) 1, Czech Republic (email: jmanek@mbox.vol.cz) for publication by IOTA. When reporting timings, describe your geographic longitude, latitude, and altitude (to the nearest second of arc and 30 m, respectively), telescope size, timing method, an estimate of the observer's reaction time (if applicable), the accuracy of the timing, and whether or not the reaction time correction has been applied.

The following two-page table of predictions of asteroidal and planetary occultations visible from North America for 2001 has been provided by Jim Stamm of IOTA. The predictions are by Edwin Goffin in Belgium.

The successive columns in the table list (1) the date and time of the event; (2) the name of the occulting body; (3) the apparent magnitude of the asteroid or planet; (4) the catalogue number of the occulted star; (5) the apparent visual magnitude of the star; (6) the right ascension and (7) declination of the star; (8) the expected magnitude change from the combined brightness; (9) the predicted maximum duration of the occultation in seconds; and (10) the approximate region from which the occultation is predicted to be visible. Due to uncertainties in the catalogue positions of the stars and the ephemerides of the asteroids from which these predictions are derived, the exact region of visibility of an occultation cannot be derived until CCD observations link the star and asteroid to the new HIPPARCOS reference frame, usually about a week prior to the event.

For North American observers, finder charts and further details on these and other occultations can be found in the *2001 Planetary Occultation Supplement to Occultation Newsletter* available from IOTA. (See p. 144 in this Handbook for information on IOTA and on The Royal Astronomical Society of New Zealand. The latter organization provides information on occultations visible from the southwestern Pacific region.)

Notes regarding some of the events in the table:

(1) May 25: The star is ZC 3260 = HIP 109647 = HR 8467 and is a spectroscopic binary that can probably be resolved during this occultation.

(2) Sep. 7: The star is ZC 983 = HIP 30570 = HR 2304. It is a close double star with magnitude 6.5 and 6.9 components separated by about 0.08″ in position angle (PA) 140°. Since Metis will subtend 0.11″, some observers can see occultations of both stars. If only the primary star is covered, there will appear to be a 0.9-magnitude drop since the pair cannot be resolved directly. If only the secondary star is occulted, the apparent magnitude drop will be only 0.5, more difficult to detect if the seeing is poor.

(3) Sep. 20: The star was resolved into 7.4- and 8.4-magnitude components by HIPPARCOS. The separation in 1991 was 0.12″ in PA 336°. Since Lucia subtends only 0.03″ and its motion is almost perpendicular to the component separation, there will be separate occultations of the two stars along separate paths. Since the stars can not be resolved directly, there will appear to be a 1.4-magnitude drop if the primary is occulted but only a 0.4-magnitude drop if the secondary star is covered.

IOTA SELECTED LIST OF NORTH AMERICAN OCCULTATIONS BY SOLAR SYSTEM OBJECTS FOR THE YEAR 2001

Date	UT	Occulting Body (mag.)	Star	(mag.)	RA (2000) h m s	Dec ° ′ ″	ΔMag	Dur. s	Nominal Path
Jan. 10	9:11	162 Laurentia 12.9	TYC 2390-01259-1	11.8	5 22 56.47	+30 46 17.7	1.4	12	Florida to Oregon
19	7:23	91 Aegina 11.7	TYC 1941-01637-1	11.2	8 24 48.12	+22 45 51.3	1.0	11	Yucatan to Baja Sur to Hawaii
27	6:12	83 Beatrix 11.5	TYC 1945-00581-1	10.4	8 39 15.72	+27 09 08.1	1.4	8	Cape Breton to Ketchikan
28	4:01	596 Scheila 13.4	TYC 2505-00780-1	11.7	9 50 00.58	+33 43 13.8	2.0	9	Cape Breton to Vancouver
Feb. 6	1:56	346 Hermentaria 11.5	TYC 1901-01583-1	11.8	6 47 05.49	+27 30 33.1	0.6	16	Florida Keys to Baja Sur
6	23:34	173 Ino 12.6	SAO 110692	7.7	2 41 58.98	+0 33 01.1	4.9	6	San Francisco, CA to Winnipeg
13	6:02	432 Pythia 12.4	SAO 100028	7.7	12 18 04.15	+18 26 06.4	4.7	6	Cuba to Oregon
16	4:26	83 Beatrix 12	SAO 80084	9.1	8 18 48.08	+27 48 21.4	2.9	11	Southern Florida to Baja Sur
16	5:11	174 Phaedra 12.7	SAO 98586	8.9	9 27 56.53	+16 59 01.0	3.8	5	Wash. D.C. to San Francisco, CA
22	0:45	372 Palma 11.9	TYC 2856-00064-1	9.9	3 11 03.66	+41 29 02.7	2.2	8	San Diego, CA to El Paso, TX
Mar. 6	7:06	238 Hypatia 12.6	SAO 138387	9.5	11 44 52.18	−2 02 18.0	3.2	11	Florida to Alaska
8	3:37	57 Mnemosyne 12.3	TYC 1541551	9.9	6 33 30.10	+5 02 03.3	2.5	12	San Francisco, CA to Nunavut
31	4:05	238 Hypatia 12.8	SAO 118870	7.6	11 27 33.48	+1 18 05.6	5.2	12	Newfoundland to Nunavut
Apr. 9	3:05	324 Bamberga 12.0	TYC 2390-01625-1	11.7	5 18 36.36	+30 07 59.0	0.9	7	British Columbia to South Carolina
17	1:33	423 Diotima 11.7	PPM 159577	11.0	13 13 28.23	+6 12 35.0	1.2	17	Guatemala and Honduras
May 7	9:13	345 Tercidina 13.0	TYC 5714-00335-1	11.8	19 00 59.02	−12 01 10.6	1.5	17	Guatemala to Hudson Bay
8	4:41	337 Devosa 12.1	SAO 182707	8.4	14 37 04.89	−25 48 09.3	3.7	5	Georgia to Idaho
25	10:21	97 Klotho 13.0	SAO 145940	6.5	22 12 43.87	−4 43 14.7	6.5	5	Guadalajara, Mexico to So. Florida
31	11:56	200 Dynamene 13.1	PPM 735851	10.9	20 02 32.55	−26 57 52.3	2.3	40	Central Mexico to Baja Sur
Jun. 10	6:47	34 Circe 12.6	TAC −14°07591	11.9	18 36 50.38	−14 42 41.6	1.2	11	Southern Florida to Baja Norte
19	8:43	51 Nemausa 11.9	PPM 709417	11.2	22 22 43.18	+0 53 15.4	1.1	25	Mexico City to Central Florida
22	10:37	564 Dudu 12.5	SAO 210513	7.9	18 44 40.10	−38 07 42.8	4.6	5	Central Mexico
Jul. 11	9:51	54 Alexandra 11.7	TYC 0589-01102-1	11.8	23 44 53.29	+4 13 40.6	0.7	18	Guatemala to Eastern North Carolina
12	3:06	702 Alauda 11.5	SAO 188447	8.7	19 41 28.50	−20 05 06.5	2.8	14	Puerto Rico to Louisiana
28	12:01	712 Boliviana 13.2	TYC 1814-00205-1	11.9	4 11 01.51	+23 15 24.9	1.6	4	San Diego, CA to NW Arizona
Aug. 2	10:24	176 Iduna 12.5	TYC 1082-00137-1	10.9	20 22 08.88	+13 01 53.0	1.8	10	Central Mexico to South of Hawaii

IOTA SELECTED LIST OF NORTH AMERICAN OCCULTATIONS BY SOLAR SYSTEM OBJECTS FOR THE YEAR 2001 (continued)

Date	UT	Occulting Body (mag.)	Star	(mag.)	RA (2000) h m s	Dec ° ' "	ΔMag	Dur. s	Nominal Path
Aug. 8	7:27	392 Wilhelmina 13.7	TYC 5000921	9.9	20 21 00.79	+3 08 44.0	3.9	6	Northern Quebec to Vancouver
17	9:00	5 Astraea 11.1	TYC 6360-00349-1	11.1	21 22 31.92	−15 10 29.3	0.8	9	Wisconsin to South of Hawaii
19	6:10	233 Asterope 11.4	PPM 204764	10.5	21 03 56.47	−03 17 16.3	1.3	12	Central Bahamas to Guatemala
22	6:25	713 Luscinia 13.2	TYC 1169-00037-1	11.3	23 31 03.29	+9 54 44.5	2.1	15	Newfoundland to Baja Sur
Sep. 7	9:40	9 Metis 10.8	SAO 78349	6.1	6 25 32.94	+23 19 37.8	4.7	6	Central Quebec to No. California
9	4:17	129 Antigone 10.9	SAO 165635	8.4	23 20 19.37	−14 23 44.3	2.7	9	Hudson Bay to Central Baja
17	3:59	225 Henrietta 12.6	TYC 1119-01857-1	11.5	21 33 14.52	+7 41 29.7	1.5	11	Nunavut to Southern Mexico
20	3:15	222 Lucia 14.4	SAO 110328	7.0	2 05 23.31	+10 04 36.5	7.3	6	Southern Florida to Central Mexico
24	7:48	253 Mathilde 12.1	TAC −03°17274	11.6	23 11 24.66	+3 49 16.6	1.1	10	Northern Quebec to San Diego, CA
Oct. 4	5:08	446 Aeternitas 12.8	SAO 191094	9.3	22 22 40.73	−24 41 32.9	3.6	7	Yucatan to Saskatchewan
10	22:46	407 Arachne 12.6	TYC 0570-00048-1	10.8	22 38 41.02	+2 32 31.5	2.0	19	Greenland to Washington, D.C.
12	4:25	222 Lucia 13.9	SAO 110171	9.2	1 51 24.40	+8 47 20.8	4.8	4	Virginia to Baja Sur
18	4:53	225 Henrietta 13.2	TYC 0543-00855-1	10.6	21 37 42.83	+1 35 26.6	2.7	10	Victoria Island to Panama
24	1:18	410 Chloris 12.9	TYC 6886-00413-1	11.9	19 10 08.97	−28 36 23.2	1.4	4	Los Angeles, CA to Wisconsin
24	6:39	36 Atalante 10.6	TYC 2830-01557-1	11.1	2 18 59.02	39 13 39.8	0.5	12	Tip of Yucatan to San Francisco, CA
Nov. 10	5:14	266 Aline 12.2	TYC 1196-01360-1	11.6	1 11 14.00	+17 02 48.9	1.0	12	No. Labrador thru Central Mexico
Dec. 2	1:36	241 Germania 12.8	TYC 5234-01098-1	11.1	22 42 37.55	−01 43 52.3	2.0	10	Guadalajara, Mexico to So. Florida
8	11:58	105 Artemis 13.3	SAO 155160	9.2	9 24 59.03	−10 21 47.1	4.1	13	SW Yukon to San Francisco, CA
9	2:00	395 Delia 14.5	PPM 93658	9.8	4 39 06.68	+22 42 43.4	4.7	4	So. Greenland to San Francisco, CA
10	6:24	712 Boliviana 11.1	TYC 0734-00123-1	10.9	6 13 33.49	+09 53 33.5	0.8	14	Northern Bahamas thru Yucatan
15	10:06	105 Artemis 13.2	TYC 5463-01466-1	11.6	9 26 19.03	−11 13 00.3	1.8	17	Vancouver thru Baja Peninsula
19	3:29	712 Boliviana 11.0	TYC 0717-00435-1	11.0	6 04 56.52	+8 50 59.5	0.7	14	Central Newfoundland to Cent. Baja
21	3:18	117 Lomia 12.7	PPM 67617	10.6	2 40 46.40	+36 26 47.5	2.2	21	Southern Greenland to Baja Sur
27	12:47	488 Kreusa 12.3	TYC 1427-01247-1	11.7	10 31 00.60	+21 50 38.7	1.1	24	Vancouver to Southeastern Nunavut
30	8:27	654 Zelinda 10.0	SAO 97104	9.5	7 38 23.56	+16 34 48.0	1.0	13	No. Bahamas to Chiapas, Mexico
31	1:09	1303 Luthera 13.4	SAO 59812	6.4	7 08 36.24	+37 26 42.4	7.1	6	Northern Quebec to Saskatoon

METEORS, COMETS, AND DUST

METEORS

BY ROBERT L. HAWKES

The term *meteor* applies to the streak of light (and related phenomena such as ionization) produced when an interplanetary particle (a *meteoroid*) enters Earth's upper atmosphere and the meteoroid material ablates (evaporates). Heights of ablation for typical meteors are 60–125 km above Earth's surface (higher-speed meteors ablate at greater heights). Evaporated meteoroid atoms undergo high speed atomic collisions with atmospheric constituents, and it is the decay of these excited states that produces the meteor luminosity. Most meteoroids are very small—a bright visual meteor is typically produced by a grain smaller than a pea. Very bright meteors are termed *fireballs* (see the section FIREBALLS on p. 204). If a solid object reaches the ground, it is termed a *meteorite*.

The meteoroid complex can be conveniently divided into two parts—a *stream* component made up of particles in highly correlated orbits and a more or less random *sporadic* component. About 5 to 10 sporadic meteors per hour are visible (by a single observer with dark adapted eyes) from a dark sky location on any given night. When Earth's orbit intersects a meteor stream an enhancement of the meteor rate, a meteor *shower*, is observed. Perspective causes the parallel paths of shower meteors to appear to radiate from a point when plotted on a star map. The constellation in which this point of divergence, or *radiant*, seems to lie is used in naming the meteor shower. When two or more meteor showers have radiants in the same constellation, a nearby bright star is used in the designation (e.g. the η-Aquarids). The Quadrantid shower is named after an obsolete constellation.

The sporadic meteor component is derived from the shower component by gradual loss of orbital coherence due to collisions with smaller meteoroids, radiative effects, and differential gravitational perturbations. The division between shower and sporadic meteors is not precise, and there continues to be debate regarding the validity of some minor meteor showers. A detailed list of meteor showers, including the minor showers, is available in the annual meteor shower calendar published by the International Meteor Organization (IMO) (http://www.imo.net/).

The activity of a meteor shower is usually specified by the *zenithal hourly rate* (ZHR). The ZHR is the number of meteors a single experienced observer would see per hour from a shower with a radiant directly overhead in a dark sky location under exceptional conditions where +6.5 magnitude stars are visible.

Several research groups have produced sophisticated models of the Leonid stream which predict very strong activity again in 2001, perhaps considerably stronger than in 1999 when ZHR rates were several thousand per hour, for a brief one-hour maximum. In 2001 Earth will pass very close to the dust ejected from Comet Tempel-Tuttle in 1866, and rates up to ZHR = 15 000 have been predicted. It is anticipated that there will be two (or possibly three) maxima due to contributions from different years (1767, 1699, 1866) of cometary release. The two most prominent are listed in the table. The times of maxima are believed to be well determined, but the strengths at maximum are much less certain. The best location for viewing the 2001 Leonids will be the western Pacific and Asia. Extensive information on the Leonid shower is available at http://leonid.arc.nasa.gov/.

In a number of cases orbital similarity permits a link between a meteor shower and a parent object. For example, the η-Aquarids and Orionids are derived from

Comet Halley, the Leonids from Comet Tempel-Tuttle, the Perseids from Comet Swift-Tuttle, the Taurid complex from Comet Encke and the Geminids from Asteroid Phaethon. Dedicated amateur meteor astronomers contribute the majority of visual observations. For visual observations it is critical to choose a dark sky location free from obstructions and allow at least 20 min for dark adaptation. In general, one should not observe near the horizon (at least 40° elevation) and should look roughly 40° away from the radiant of the shower. Carefully estimate your limiting magnitude to the nearest tenth of a magnitude (see the SKY TRANSPARENCY section on p. 51), and record it, the UT of the observing session, and observing direction (centre of field of view). The simplest observation method involves making an instantaneous decision regarding whether each individual meteor belongs to a shower (from the radiant and apparent speed). The shower association, brightness, and time for each meteor can be recorded orally on a tape recorder for uninterrupted observing periods. Visual observations of this type (after application of correction factors) are valuable for determining rate profiles and population indices of showers. Extensive information on observing meteors by visual, as well as other methods, is available from the IMO, the North American Meteor Network (http://web.infoave.net/~meteorobs/), and the American Meteor Society (http://www.amsmeteors.org). These organizations also collect and analyze visual observations from amateurs.

Telescopic observations of meteors (usually employing binoculars) allow the plotting of trails with more precision, as well as emphasizing those showers rich in faint meteors (although generally at faint magnitudes the meteor population is dominated by sporadic meteors). Photographic observations can be made with normal or wide angle lenses, and using exposures of typically 5 to 30 min. A rotating shutter permits determination of apparent angular velocity. Increasingly amateurs are using video equipment for meteor observations. A standard home camcorder is limited to about magnitude +2 and will lead to very low rates (several hours per meteor) except during a strong meteor shower. Image intensifiers (which are now available as reasonably priced second-hand units) coupled to video cameras can extend the sensitivity to magnitude +8, with sporadic meteor rates of 15/hour.

Any of the techniques can be extended to simultaneous observations from two stations, and triangulation will yield the precise trajectory and orbital information. Baselines of 20 to 150 km are appropriate, with intersection heights at about 90 km. Addition of a diffraction grating (preferably a blazed grating which concentrates visible light in the first order spectrum) in front of the objective lens can be used to make meteor spectra with the photographic or video observation techniques. Typically gratings with 200 to 800 lines per millimetre are used for this work. A meteor produces an ionization trail in the atmosphere, which can be used to reflect electromagnetic waves from distant television or radio transmitters. Meteors will be detected using this forward scatter radio technique as brief (usually a few tenths of a second) reception of the signal from the distant station which is normally blocked by the curvature of the Earth. See RADIO DETECTION OF METEORS on p. 203 for more details.

In addition to the URLs listed earlier, *The Handbook for Visual Meteor Observers* is available from the International Meteor Organization, and Neil Bone's book *Meteors* (Sky Publishing, 1993) provides an excellent introduction to visual, telescopic, and photographic meteor observation.

TABLE OF METEOR SHOWERS 2001

The more prominent night time showers visible from the Northern Hemisphere are included in the following table. Explanations of the entries in the various column are given following the table.

Shower	Max (UT)	λ (2000)	D (d)	ZHR	R	Moon (%)	r	RA h m	Dec (°)	v (km/s)
Quadrantid	Jan. 3 12h	283.16	0.8	90	√	56	2.1	15 30	+50	42
Lyrid	Apr. 22 4h	32.1	6	15	√	3	2.9	18 16	+34	48
η–Aquarid	May 4 23h	44.5	8	20	>03	92	2.7	22 27	00	65
S δ–Aquarid	Jul. 28 18h	125.7	12	20	>23	65	3.2	22 38	−16	41
Perseid	Aug. 12 10h	139.8	5	100	√	49	2.2	3 06	+58	60
Orionid	Oct. 22 2h	208.7	8	20	>23	30	2.8	6 22	+16	66
S Taurid	Nov. 3 2h	220.7	30	10	√	96	2.3	3 24	+14	28
N Taurid	Nov. 13 1h	230.7	30	15	√	7	2.3	3 55	+23	29
Leonid 1	Nov. 18 10h	236.11	0.2	1000?	>00	11	2.7?	10 18	+22	71
Leonid 2	Nov. 18 18h	236.45	0.2	10,000?	>00	11	2.8?	10 18	+22	71
Geminid	Dec. 14 4h	262.2	3	95	√	1	2.6	7 30	+33	35
Ursid	Dec. 22 12h	270.7	2	20	√	47	3.0	14 28	+75	34

The column labelled **Max** lists the hour and date (universal time, UT) of the 2001 intersection of Earth with the most dense region of the stream. These maxima are based on the solar longitude values (λ) for each shower given in the third column (epoch 2000). Many streams have a complex rate profile—e.g. the Orionid shower has an earlier peak for faint meteors (λ = 207.5) than for bright meteors (λ = 209.8). Most showers show activity over a number of days, and the duration of each shower, D (defined as the duration in days of 1/4 peak activity or more), is given in the next column. Some showers (e.g. the Quadrantids) are highly concentrated with strong displays lasting only a few hours, while others are spread over weeks (e.g. the Taurid complex). Concentrated showers are more likely to be of recent formation. There are no records of the Quadrantid shower before the 19th century, while several showers have been observed for hundreds or thousands of years (e.g. the Perseids). Some showers (such as the Leonids) have meteoroids concentrated in a small region of the orbit, and hence have much higher peak rates in certain years.

The column labelled **ZHR** gives the predicted zenithal hourly rate.

The higher the radiant is in the sky, the more direct the projection of the stream cross-section on the sky area above the observer, and the apparent activity will be higher. The column labelled R indicates when the radiant is above the horizon for an observer at 43°N latitude; for example >23 means that the shower can be observed after 11 p.m. local time. A √ means that the radiant is above the horizon throughout night hours. The number of meteors observed varies strongly with limiting magnitude—therefore, effective meteor observations must be made in the absence of significant moonlight. In the column labelled **Moon** the percentage illumination of the Moon at the date of shower maximum is given.

The relative number of bright and faint meteors is given by the *population index*, r, which is defined as the ratio of the number of meteors of magnitude $M + 1$ to the number of magnitude M. The number of meteors that can be observed is a strong function of limiting sensitivity. For example, for a limiting magnitude of +3.5, a shower with a ZHR of 60 and a population index $r = 2.8$ would have the number of observable meteors per hour reduced by a factor of $(2.8)^3$ to a rate of only 2.7 meteors per hour. Thus the ZHR figures are *not* expected visual meteor rates.

The next two columns give the right ascension (**RA**) and declination (**Dec**) of the shower radiant. A typical meteor shower is active over several days, and the apparent radiant moves somewhat during this period. The tables published by the International Meteor Organization give the daily motion of the radiant. Meteors can only be observed when the radiant is above the local horizon (or nearly so). The geocentric speed v of the meteors in each shower is given in kilometres per second in the final column.

RADIO DETECTION OF METEORS
By Philip Gebhardt

The term *meteor* applies not only to the streak of light produced by a meteoroid, but also to the column of ionized atoms and molecules along the path behind the meteoroid. These meteor trails are capable of scattering radio signals from terrestrial stations, which include those broadcast by commercial FM and TV stations. Unlike visual observation, radio detection of sporadic meteors or shower meteors can be undertaken in daylight and during inclement weather. Similarly, a night sky illuminated by the full Moon has no adverse effect on radio detection. Radio detection rates of meteors tend to be higher than visual observation rates. This occurs because particles down to 10^{-5} kg can be detected visually, while particles down to 10^{-10} kg can be detected by radio. *(Editor's Note:* Assuming a density of 1 t/m^3, these mass limits correspond to diameters of about 3 mm and 0.06 mm, respectively.)

Two types of meteor trails exist, *underdense* and *overdense*, determined by the line density of free electrons. Reradiated signals from underdense trails (fewer than 2×10^{14} electrons per metre) rise above the receiver noise almost instantaneously and then decay exponentially. The duration of these received signals is about a second or less. Reflected signals from overdense trails may reach a higher amplitude and last longer, but destructive interference due to reflection from different parts of the trail can produce fluctuations in the signal..

Data for selected meteor showers appear in the table at the left. These data are for visual observations and should be considered only general guidelines for radio purposes.

Sporadic meteors peak in number near 6 a.m. local time (i.e. on the advancing side of Earth in its orbit), and are at a minimum near 6 p.m. At midlatitudes the ratio of meteors detected at these two times is approximately 3:1. There is also an annual cycle with a minimum in February and a maximum in August.

Frequencies between 20 MHz and 150 MHz are used for meteor detection. Both duration and amplitude of meteor signals are frequency dependent—both decrease with increasing frequency. At the lower frequencies, however, galactic as well as man-made noise (particularly in urban areas) become limiting factors. Also, as the wavelength becomes comparable to the width of the meteor trail, the echo strength decreases.

The commercial FM broadcast band (88 to 108 MHz) provides the best introductory opportunity for meteor detection. The abundance of broadcast stations transmitting 24 hours a day ensures that a return signal can usually be heard from a suitably positioned meteor regardless of the time of day. Commercial FM and TV stations can be received at much greater distances than normal—up to about 2000 km. The technique involves listening on a frequency not used by a local FM station. When a suitably positioned meteor occurs, a reflected signal from a distant FM station will be heard briefly. The rate will vary from a few per hour for off-peak times for sporadic meteors to several hundred per hour during a very active shower. Other means of signal propagation may be heard on the FM band, but only meteor signals will have their characteristic fast rise-time and short duration.

Any FM receiver will detect signals scattered by meteor trails. Signals can be heard using nothing more than a car radio; however, more signals will be detected using an outdoor FM or FM/TV antenna and a more sensitive receiver. Antenna direction is determined by the shower radiant position. For example, when the radiant is in the northeast, aim the antenna northwest or southeast; if the radiant is in the west, aim south or north.

Further information can be found on the following web sites: http://www.odxa.on.ca, http://www.imo.net/calendar/cal01.html.

FIREBALLS

BY JEREMY TATUM AND DAMIEN LEMAY

A *fireball* is defined as a meteor that is brighter than −4 in apparent magnitude (i.e. as bright as or brighter than Venus). With camera networks and satellite-based detections now providing statistical information on entry of fireballs into Earth's atmosphere, the main reason to collect fireball reports is to assist with meteorite recovery or to provide orbital information for recovered meteorites. Rapid recovery of meteorites is vital for the study of short-lived radioactive isotopes produced by cosmic ray bombardment of the meteorite while in interplanetary space. Small but potentially recoverable meteorites can be produced by fireballs at least as faint as magnitude −6. A very slow fireball with no indication of terminal breakup is a good candidate for meteorite survival. The presence of delayed sound indicates penetration into the lower atmosphere and probable meteorite fall. The value of a meteorite is significantly greater when we know something of its atmospheric trajectory and orbit. Visual data can, under favourable circumstances, be used to obtain an approximate atmospheric trajectory. The Meteorites and Impacts Advisory Committee, MIAC (Comité consultatif sur les météorites et les impacts, CCMI) of the Canadian Space Agency maintains a web site with images and information on fireballs, meteorites, and impact craters at http://miac.uqac.uquebec.ca/. If you want information on recent Canadian fireball or meteorite events, check the MIAC/CCMI bulletin board at:

> http://miac.uqac.uquebec.ca/MIAC/wwwboard/wwwboard.html

The preferred method for submitting fireball reports is by completion of an electronic fireball reporting form at one of the following locations:

Canada (only): http://miac.uqac.uquebec.ca/MIAC/fireball.htm
United States (AMS): http://www.amsmeteors.org/
Global (IMO): http://www.imo.net/fireball/report.html
North American Meteor Network (NAMN):
> *visual observations*: http://web.infoave.net/~meteorobs/fireball_form.html
> *photographic observations*: http://web.infoave.net/~meteorobs/photo_form.html

If you do not have access to the web, write a brief report with the following information:

(1) The name, telephone number, and address of the observer(s).
(2) The time of occurrence (and uncertainty in this time).
(3) The location of the observer at the time the fireball was seen (preferably in precise longitude and latitude).
(4) The beginning and ending points of the fireball, either in terms of right ascension and declination or in terms of azimuth and elevation. If possible, indicate the uncertainty in these angles. Indicate whether the true beginning was observed and whether the ending point was blocked by horizon objects.
(5) If possible, a direct apparent magnitude estimate. If not, indicate if the fireball was brighter than, approximately equal to, or fainter than the full Moon.
(6) The duration of the fireball and the persistent train (if any).
(7) A qualitative description of the event (colour, flares, fragmentation, and sound). Indicate the absence as well as the presence of features such as sound and fragmentation. In the case of sound, indicate the delay between the fireball appearance and the sound.
(8) The existence of any video or photographic records.

Email your report to fireball@mta.ca (MIAC/CCMI) (within Canada) or fidac@imo.net (IMO) (outside Canada).

METEORITE IDENTIFICATION
BY RICHARD K. HERD

Meteorites are rocks that have fallen to Earth from space. Those that are observed to fall, and are recovered based on those observations, are called meteorite *falls*. For the majority however, there is no record of their fiery passage through the atmosphere. When recognized, they are called meteorite *finds*. Both falls and finds are important for scientific research. They are samples of the extraterrestrial material of our Solar system, and the main source of information about it. Some even contain extrasolar mineral grains and primordial compounds made in other stars, and yield information about the origin of the Universe. Identified meteorites are quite rare in Canada; less than 60 are known, but there have been 3 falls recovered since 1994. About 25 000 meteorites are known worldwide; 18 000 come from Antarctica and 2000 from deserts in Africa and Asia.

Often there is confusion about when and where meteorites may fall or be preserved, and about what they are and look like. Samples sent to experts for identification, even by other scientists, are usually "meteorwrongs"—terrestrial rocks or man-made debris such as slag, that do not really resemble meteorites.

Popular ideas about when and where meteorites fall are connected to the observation of *meteors* ("shooting stars" or "falling stars"). The term meteor applies to the brief streak of light produced when a high-speed, interplanetary particle enters Earth's upper atmosphere. Although the submission of material for identification sometimes coincides with the publicity surrounding annual meteor showers, these showers do not result in meteorites. Meteor showers are associated with cometary debris which is probably too fragile to yield samples—the fragments are reduced to dust high in the atmosphere. In contrast, stronger rocky/metallic fragments the size of a fist and larger can survive passage through the atmosphere and result in meteorites. These first appear as bright *fireballs*. The vast majority are relatively small, are slowed to terminal speeds by atmospheric friction, and cease to show a bright trail long before they reach Earth's surface.

Several meteorites have now been shown to have had orbits that included the Asteroid Belt; most meteorites may begin their Earthbound journey as fragments (*meteoroids*) from collisions among asteroidal objects, but that may not be their ultimate origin in either space or time. About 20 meteorites are known to have come from the Moon, and a similar number from Mars, probably blasted off their surfaces by impacts. The provenance of the rest is not yet known. All are believed to originate within our solar system, and to be samples of its rocky materials, showing their development, from primitive beginnings to the present. In the absence of extensive space exploration, and to prepare for it, they are invaluable.

Rare meteoroids of masses exceeding 100 tonnes are not slowed appreciably by Earth's atmosphere and produce craters upon impact (100 tonnes is also an estimate of the total mass of meteoritic material entering the atmosphere each day, mainly as dust). The larger impacts may have dramatically altered the history of life on our planet, but they do not result in meteorites—the kinetic energy is sufficiently high to vaporize the impacting body completely and to deform and melt the target area in a fraction of a second. Crater diameters are typically about ten times the diameter of the impacting body. Glassy *tektites* found scattered over several continents may record such impacts, but they do not have meteorite compositions or characteristics.

Bright meteors which may seem very close are usually quite high in the atmosphere, 50 km or further away from the observer. Even if an extraterrestrial object does reach the surface, it is likely to plunge into the 70% that is water, or be lost among forests, jungles, or mountainous regions. In only a dozen or so recorded cases have meteorites landed within a few metres of a human being (see "Possible Hazards of Meteorite Falls" by

C. E. Spratt, *JRASC*, *85*, p. 263, October 1991). Many meteorites have been recovered from open areas such as deserts, farmland, and the Antarctic ice cap. Some have lain on Earth for many thousands of years. The best general reference on meteorites currently is *Rocks from Space* by O. Richard Norton, 2nd Edition, Mountain Press, 1998. Information about meteorites, tektites, and impacts is also increasingly available on the World Wide Web.

Meteorites are divided into three groups, which vary widely both in appearance and properties: *stones* or *stony meteorites* (*aerolites*); *stony-irons* (*siderolites*); and *irons* or *iron meteorites* (*siderites*). All usually contain metallic iron compounds (involving nickel and traces of other metals) and are mildly to strongly magnetic. Those that have lain on Earth's surface for long periods may be rusted almost beyond recognition.

Despite many resemblances to natural rocks, minerals, slags and metals, meteorites usually possess a number of distinctive characteristics. However, some may not exhibit these characteristics and may require laboratory tests to confirm their identity. Specimens generally have a fusion crust, which is dull black to brown in colour, and quite soft. The crust is more prevalent on stones and stony-irons and may have partially flaked off.

Stones are the most abundant and resemble some terrestrial rocks, but are denser. They contain scattered grains of metallic iron that are visible on broken or polished surfaces, in a silicate matrix. Most (called *chondrites*) also contain spheres of silicate minerals called *chondrules*; these are generally visible to the naked eye in broken or cut specimens. Chrondrites are the oldest, most primitive, least altered, meteorites. Rare stony meteorites without chondrules are called *achondrites*; these are thought to be melt products from chondrites, samples of younger volcanic planetary surfaces. In August 1996, NASA announced that a research team had found fossil and chemical evidence of bacterial life in an ancient achondrite from Mars, but other scientists disagree. This controversial discovery has resulted in renewed interest in space missions to Mars and in finding water and life on Mars and elsewhere, e.g. in extreme conditions even on Earth.

Irons and stony-irons are dense, with up to equal amounts of silicates and iron, and are often irregular in shape. They are thought to be core/mantle material of planets formed by melting chondrites.

Meteorites are never porous (i.e. do not have bubble-like cavities), nor are they ever almost perfectly spherical and smooth. During atmospheric entry, only their surface is affected. Surfaces of irons and stony-irons are dimpled (shallow depressions) rather than being bulbous. Also, they rust easily so that there may be no bright metal showing. Stony meteorites do not show protuberances, and weathered varieties are rusty even on broken surfaces. Fresh stony meteorites may have a whitish rock interior, with bright whitish metal specks; their surfaces are black or smoky grey, varying in lustre from quite glassy to dull, and perhaps with telltale lines from their flight through the air.

The best way to determine if an object is a possible meteorite is to compare it with a known meteorites. The Geological Survey of Canada (GSC) maintains the National Meteorite Collection of over 1900 specimens, and supports research on them. It also offers to pay the owner a minimum of $500 for the first specimen of any new Canadian meteorite. Should you find a suspected meteorite, you may forward it to: **Geological Survey of Canada, 601 Booth St., Ottawa, ON, K1A 0E8, Attention: Meteorite Identification**. The specimen will be examined and reported on free of charge. If it is too large for mailing, a description of its appearance, or a photograph, and its exact location should be sent. The GSC also makes available, free of charge, a brochure on meteorites, with pictures of meteorites and comparative pictures of non-meteorites. Write to the GSC's Publication Office at the above address. Meteorites of Canadian origin are subject to the provisions of the Cultural Property Import and Export Act and may not be exported from Canada without a permit.

METEORITE IMPACT CRATERS OF NORTH AMERICA
BY R. A. F. GRIEVE

The first recognition of meteorite impact craters on Earth, and the basis of their scientific investigation, occurred in North America. Daniel Barringer, an American engineer and entrepreneur, first argued in 1905 that a 1-km-diameter hole in the Arizona desert was the result of the impact of a large iron meteorite. Barringer had hoped to exploit the several million tonnes of iron meteorite that he believed lay buried beneath the crater floor. Unfortunately, virtually all of the impacting body had been destroyed as a consequence of the extreme pressures and temperatures generated by the impact. Although the numerous, small fragments of the "Cañon Diablo" meteorite found strewn about the surrounding terrain did indeed come from the impacting body, they owed their survival to having split off the impacting body before impact. Barringer's ideas were controversial, and it was not until 1960, when Ed Chao and Gene Shoemaker discovered coesite, the high pressure form of the mineral quartz, that what is now known as Barringer or Meteor Crater was unequivocally proven to be of impact origin. It was 30 years after Barringer's proposal for an impact origin for Meteor Crater that American scientists John Boon and Claude Albritton Jr. suggested that several other puzzling, generally circular, features in the American midwest were, in fact, further evidence of meteorite impact on Earth rather than the result of explosive volcanism. The lack of a crater rim and meteorite fragments at any of these sites led to the realization that these were no longer prerequisite evidence for defining an ancient meteorite impact crater.

Crater investigations in Canada also stemmed from an interest in their economic potential. Discovery of the New Quebec Crater in the 1940s on military air photographs prompted Fred Chubb, a prospector, to seek support for a visit to this remote, circular landmark. He hoped to confirm that it was a large kimberlite "pipe," similar to the diamond-bearing ones of South Africa. Vic Meen of the Royal Ontario Museum led two expeditions to the site in 1950 and 1951 and concluded, based on its morphology and lack of volcanic evidence, that meteorite impact was the most likely cause of the crater. On the strength of Meen's discovery, Carlyle Beals, the Dominion Astronomer for Canada, instituted a crater research program at the Dominion Observatory, which included a systematic search of aerial photographs and led to confirmation of the Holleford crater. As the observatory program became known, word was received from other scientists and laymen of unusual, circular topographic features in Canada (e.g. Brent, Clearwater).

Worldwide research programs have, as of 2000, confirmed over 160 impact sites on Earth. Only a small fraction (10%) retain meteorite fragments. In craters larger than approximately 1 km in diameter, the extreme shock pressures and temperatures vaporize and melt the impacting body. The bulk of these impact sites are identified by characteristic deformation features in the target rocks—features uniquely produced in nature only by hypervelocity impact and known as shock metamorphic features.

Approximately five new confirmed meteorite craters are added to the world list each year. Many of the recent additions to the list have been identified through the discovery of shock features, which in turn led to recognition of a degraded and sometimes partially buried, circular structure. Approximately one-third of the known structures are completely buried beneath postimpact sediments. They were discovered initially as geophysical anomalies and subsequently drilled. In a few cases, such as Beaverhead (#4 on the accompanying table and map), where shatter cones are simply found within an intensely disturbed oval zone, no circular morphologic feature is yet apparent. In the following table, therefore, values for crater diameter may represent a defined outer margin, whether an upraised rim or a peripheral fault, or the diameter may be a reconstruction from geologic and geophysical data with no obvious, morphologic counterpart.

For more information and images of many craters, visit http://gdcinfo.agg.nrcan.gc.ca.

TABLE OF METEORITE IMPACT CRATERS OF NORTH AMERICA

#	Name, Location	Lat. (N)	Long. (W)	Diam. km	Age* Ma	Surface Expression	Visible Geologic Features
1	Ames, Oklahoma, USA	36° 15′	98° 12′	16.	470. (30)	buried 3 km	none
2	Avak, Alaska, USA	71 15	156 38	12.	100. (5)	buried 30 m	none
3	Barringer (Meteor) Crater, Arizona, USA	35 02	111 01	1.2	0.049 (0.003)	rimmed polygonal crater highly shocked sandstone	fragments of meteorite,
4	Beaverhead, Montana, USA	44 36	113 00	60.	≈600.	oval area of crushed sandstone, and shatter cones	shatter cones
5	Brent, Ontario	46 05	78 29	3.8	450. (30)	sediment-filled shallow depression	fracturing
6	Calvin, Michigan, USA	41 50	85 57	8.5	450. (10)	buried 400 m	none
7	Carswell, Saskatchewan	58 27	109 30	39.	115. (10)	discontinuous circular ridge impact melt	shatter cones, breccia,
8	Charlevoix, Quebec	47 32	70 18	54.	357. (15)	semi-circular trough, central peak	breccia, shatter cones, impact melt
9	Chesapeake Bay, Virginia, USA	37 17	76 01	85	35.5 (0.6)	buried 400–500 m, ring structure	none
10	Chicxulub, Mexico	21 20	89 30	180.	64.98 (0.05)	buried 1 km, ring of sink holes	none (related to the K/T mass extinction event)
11	Clearwater East, Quebec	56 05	74 07	26.	290. (20)	circular lake	sedimentary float
12	Clearwater West, Quebec	56 13	74 30	36.	290. (20)	island ring in circular lake	impact melt, breccias
13	Couture, Quebec	60 08	75 20	8.	430. (25)	circular lake	breccia float
14	Crooked Creek, Missouri, USA	37 50	91 23	7.	320. (80)	oval area of disturbed rocks, shallow marginal depression	breccia, shatter cones
15	Decatureville, Missouri, USA	37 54	92 43	6.	<300.	slight oval depression	breccia, shatter cones
16	Deep Bay, Saskatchewan	56 24	102 59	13.	100. (50)	circular bay	sedimentary float
17	Des Plaines, Illinois, USA	42 03	87 52	8.	<280.	buried, 15–100 m	none
18	Eagle Butte, Alberta	49 42	110 30	10.	<65.	minor structural disturbance	shatter cones
19	Elbow, Saskatchewan	50 59	106 43	8.	395. (25)	buried, small mound	none
20	Flynn Creek, Tennessee, USA	36 17	85 40	3.8	360. (20)	sediment-filled shallow depression with small central peak	breccia, shatter cones
21	Glasford, Illinois, USA	40 36	89 47	4.	<430.	buried 350 m	none
22	Glover Bluff, Wisconsin, USA	43 58	89 32	8.	<500.	disturbed dolomite exposed	shatter cones
23	Gow, Saskatchewan	56 27	104 29	5.	<250.	lake and central island	breccia, impact melt
24	Haughton, N.W.T.	75 22	89 41	24.	23.4 (1.0)	shallow circular depression	shatter cones, breccia
25	Haviland, Kansas, USA	37 35	99 10	0.015	<0.001	excavated depression	fragments of meteorite
26	Holleford, Ontario	44 28	76 38	2.4	550. (100)	sediment-filled shallow depression	sedimentary fill
27	Ile Rouleau, Quebec	50 41	73 53	4.	<300.	island is central peak of submerged structure	shatter cones, breccia dykes

* Numbers in parentheses are possible errors.

TABLE OF METEORITE IMPACT CRATERS OF NORTH AMERICA (ct'd)

#	Name, Location	Lat. (N)	Long. (W)	Diam. km	Age* Ma	Surface Expression	Visible Geologic Features
28	Kentland, Indiana, USA	40 45	87 24	13.	<97.	central peak exposed in quarries, rest buried	breccia, shatter cones, disturbed rocks
29	La Moinerie, Quebec	57 26	66 37	8.	400. (50)	lake-filled, depression	breccia float
30	Manicouagan, Quebec	51 23	68 42	100.	214. (1)	circumferential lake, central peak	impact melt, breccia
31	Manson, Iowa, USA	42 35	94 33	35.	73.8 (0.3)	none, central elevation buried 30 m	none
32	Maple Creek, Saskatchewan	49 48	109 06	6.	<75.	buried, small mound	disturbed rocks
33	Marquez, Texas, USA	31 17	96 18	12.7	58. (2)	circular area of disturbed rock	shatter cones
34	Middlesboro, Kentucky, USA	36 37	83 44	6.	<300.	circular depression	disturbed rocks
35	Mistastin, Labrador	55 53	63 18	28.	38. (4)	elliptical lake and central island	breccia, impact melt
36	Montagnais, Nova Scotia	42 53	64 13	45.	50.5 (0.8)	none, under water (115 m) and sediment	none
37	New Quebec, Quebec	61 17	73 40	3.4	1.4 (0.1)	rimmed, circular lake	raised rim, impact melt
38	Newporte, North Dakota, USA	48 58	101 58	3.	<500.	none, buried 3 km	none
39	Nicholson, N.W.T.	62 40	102 41	12.5	<400.	irregular lake with islands	breccia
40	Odessa, Texas, USA	31 45	102 29	0.17	<0.05	sediment-filled depression with very slight rim, 4 others buried & smaller	fragments of meteorite
41	Pilot, N.W.T.	60 17	111 01	6.	445. (2)	circular lake fracturing,	breccia float
42	Presqu'ile, Quebec	49 43	74 48	24.	<500.	none, heavily eroded	shatter cones
43	Red Wing, North Dakota, USA	47 36	103 33	9.	200. (25)	none, buried 1.5 km	none
44	St. Martin, Manitoba	51 47	98 32	40.	220. (32)	none, partially buried	impact melt
45	Serpent Mound, Ohio, USA	39 02	83 24	8.	<320.	circular area of disturbed rock, slight central peak	breccia, shatter cones
46	Sierra Madera, Texas, USA	30 36	102 55	13.	<100.	central hills, annular depression, outer ring of hills	breccia, shatter cones
47	Slate Islands, Ontario	48 40	87 00	30.	≈450.	islands are central peak of submerged structure	shatter cones, breccia dykes
48	Steen River, Alberta	59 30	117 38	25.	95. (7)	none, buried 200 m	none
49	Sudbury, Ontario	46 36	81 11	250.	1850. (3)	deformed elliptical basin	breccia, impact melt, shatter cones, breccia dykes
50	Upheaval Dome, Utah, USA	38 26	109 54	10.	<65.	circular area of disturbed rock buried 1 km	breccia dykes
51	Viewfield, Saskatchewan	49 35	103 34	25.	190. (20)	lake-filled, depression	none
52	Wanapitei, Ontario	46 45	80 45	7.5	37. (2)	circular lake	breccia float
53	Wells Creek, Tennessee, USA	36 23	87 40	12.	200. (100)	basin with central hill, inner and outer annular valleys, ridges	breccia, shatter cones
54	West Hawk, Manitoba	49 46	95 11	2.4	100. (50)	circular lake	none

* Numbers in parentheses are possible errors.

MAP OF NORTH AMERICAN METEORITE IMPACT STRUCTURES

Of the 160 impact structures identified on Earth (as of 1999), 54 are located in North America (29 in Canada, 24 in the United States, and 1 in Mexico). These are indicated on the above map. The numbers correspond to the listing in the table on the preceding two pages. The latest discoveries are Elbow (#19), Maple Creek (#32) and Viewfield (#51). All are in Saskatchewan, Canada, with Viewfield being an oil-producing structure. Although the oceans cover 70% of Earth, only two impact structures have been identified on the seafloor (#36 and Mjølnir in the Barents Sea). Also, with the exception of structure #49, all of those shown occurred within approximately the last 10% of Earth's history. Evidence of many earlier craters has been erased by geologic processes. It is possible, however, to calculate a terrestrial cratering rate by focusing only on geologically stable areas of Earth (known as cratons), with low erosion and sedimentation rate. One such area is the North American craton. These rate calculations indicate that Earth has received at least 10 000 impacts sufficient to result in craters greater than 20 km in diameter over the last 3.5 billion years. Very early in Earth history, the cratering rate was even higher, perhaps reaching 100 times the current rate. Doubtless some of these impacts have had profound influence upon the evolution of life on this planet. For example, the very large structure in Mexico, Chicxulub (#10), is linked to a major extinction event 65 million years ago. Some impact craters are the source of considerable economic resources. In North America, hydrocarbons are extracted from #1, 2, 6, 32, 33, 38, 43, 46, 48; #7 produces uranium, and #49 is the site of a world class Ni-Cu mining camp.

COMETS IN 2001

BY BRIAN MARSDEN

Listed below are the periodic comets expected at perihelion in 2001. The orbital elements are given with sufficient precision to allow an ephemeris computation good to about one arcminute (1'). The angular elements are referred to the ecliptic and mean equinox J2000.0.

Comet	Perihelion Date T TT	Perihelion Dist. q AU	Eccen. e	Rev. Per. P a	Arg. Peri. ω °	Asc. Node Ω °	Incl. i °
47P/Ashbrook-Jackson	Jan. 6.50	2.3054	0.3961	7.5	348.88	2.60	12.51
41P/Tuttle-Giac.-K.	6.98	1.0523	0.6593	5.4	62.18	141.10	9.23
74P/Smirnova-Chernykh	15.65	3.5458	0.1483	8.5	86.65	77.16	6.65
73P/Schwass.-Wach. 3	27.73	0.9374	0.6938	5.4	198.78	69.92	11.41
P/1992 G3 (Mueller 4)	Feb. 7.86	2.6470	0.3885	9.0	43.67	145.37	29.75
44P/Reinmuth 2	20.00	1.8897	0.4645	6.6	46.10	296.07	6.98
113P/Spitaler	25.88	2.1273	0.4235	7.1	50.06	14.53	5.78
75P/Kohoutek	27.35	1.7873	0.4962	6.7	175.69	269.68	5.91
110P/Hartley 3	Mar. 21.40	2.4783	0.3147	6.9	167.94	287.75	11.69
45P/Honda-Mrkos-Paj.	29.89	0.5284	0.8251	5.3	326.14	89.08	4.26
97P/Metcalf-Brewington	Apr. 10.24	2.6054	0.4571	10.5	229.59	186.43	17.95
P/1993 X1 (Kushida-M.)	29.55	2.7526	0.2774	7.4	347.57	93.69	2.37
24P/Schaumasse	May 2.66	1.2050	0.7048	8.2	57.87	79.83	11.75
61P/Shajn-Schaldach	8.99	2.3301	0.3895	7.5	216.62	166.88	6.08
51P/Harrington	Jun. 5.89	1.5681	0.5618	6.8	233.60	119.18	8.66
86P/Wild 3	18.60	2.3103	0.3645	6.9	179.16	72.61	15.44
P/1994 A1 (Kushida)	27.79	1.4313	0.6290	7.6	216.02	245.62	4.12
16P/Brooks 2	Jul. 19.83	1.8349	0.4919	6.9	198.11	176.91	5.55
82P/Gehrels 3	Sep. 3.07	3.6266	0.1257	8.4	227.95	239.69	1.13
19P/Borrelly	14.73	1.3582	0.6239	6.9	353.38	75.42	30.32
P/1987 Q3 (Helin)	24.75	2.5308	0.5657	14.1	215.42	143.54	4.72

The returns of 16P/Brooks 2, 74P/Smirnova-Chernykh, 82P/Gehrels 3, 86P/Wild 3, P/1987 Q3 (Helin) and P/1992 G3 (Mueller 4) are favourable, while those of 19P/Borrelly, 47P/Ashbrook-Jackson, 61P/Shajn-Schaldach, 110P/Hartley 3, and P/1993 X1 (Kushida-Murumatsu) are fair. The returns of 24P/Schaumasse, 44P/Reinmuth 2, 51P/Harrington, 75P/Kohoutek, 97P/Metcalf-Brewington, 113P/Spitaler and P/1994 A1 (Kushida) are poor, while those of 41P/Tuttle-Giacobini-Kresak, 45P/Honda-Mrkos-Pajdusakova, and 73P/Schwassmann-Wachmann 3 are very poor.

OBSERVING COMETS
By David H. Levy

Comets are interesting and fun to observe because each is unique, differing in appearance from other comets. Most comets also change their own appearance as the weeks of their apparition pass by. Comets like Halley (1986), Hyakutake (1996), and Hale-Bopp (1997) changed frequently with varying amounts of gaseous emission and the flaring of dust jets.

Observationally, comets are very much like deep-sky objects. Even in large telescopes an observer can confuse a comet with a galaxy or a diffuse planetary nebula. Comets near a telescope's limit are virtually impossible to spot without an accurate position extracted from a detailed atlas like *Uranometria* or *Millennium*. It is difficult to define a telescope's limiting magnitude for comets because the more diffuse a comet is, the more difficult it is to find. Typically, under a dark sky a 150-mm telescope will catch a 9th magnitude comet, a 200-mm telescope will see 10th, and a 400 mm should have no trouble with a 13th magnitude comet.

Magnitude Estimates

The brightness of the coma can be estimated using a variety of methods, the most common of which is the "In-Out" method devised by Sidgwick:

(1) Study the coma until you become familiar with its "average" brightness, an easy process if the coma is of uniform brightness, but rather difficult if there is a strong central condensation.

(2) Using a variable star chart or some source on which star magnitudes are listed, find a comparison star at approximately the same altitude as the comet.

(3) Defocus the star to the size of the in-focus coma.

(4) Compare the star's out-of-focus brightness with that of the coma.

Repeat the last three steps with a second star, or more if needed, until an interpolation can be made.

Coma Size

A comet magnitude estimate becomes more useful if an estimate of the coma diameter is made at the same time. An observer seeing a 3' (3 minutes of arc) coma, for example, will estimate much brighter than another observer who sees only a 1' coma at the same time. The simplest way of estimating coma size is to draw the coma with the embedded and surrounding field stars and then compare the drawing to an atlas, using its scale to determine the size.

Degree of Condensation

A nightly measurement of a comet's degree of condensation is a good way of studying its changing behaviour. A comet undergoing an outburst of dust from its nucleus might begin its display by showing almost overnight the development of an increased condensation. Use an integer scale from 0 to 9, where 0 means a diffuse coma with absolutely uniform brightness, 3 means a diffuse coma with gradually increasing brightness toward the centre, 6 involves a definite central condensation, and 9 refers to an almost stellar image.

Tail

Because of the changing Earth–Sun–comet geometry, and also because of changing activity in a comet, the length and position angle of a tail should be measured. A rough way to measure the length of a tail is to sketch it and compare with a detailed atlas, as with the coma. Observers can also measure the position angle using an atlas and a protractor.

Visual Comet Hunting

The key ingredient to a successful comet search is perseverance. Although there are stories of people finding comets very quickly (Mark Whitaker discovered Comet Whitaker-Thomas 1968 V after three nights of comet hunting), these are the exception. Don Machholz searched for some 1700 hours for each of his first two comets, and I spent more than 917 hours before my first discovery. In contrast, neither Alan Hale nor Tom Bopp were comet hunting when they independently discovered what later became the Great Comet of 1997.

Although it is important to know the sky well before beginning a comet search program, it is more important to know the difference between the fuzzy appearances of comets compared to galaxies, neb- ulae, and clusters. Observing all the objects in Messier's Catalogue (see pp. 256–259) provides an excel- lent education in what these distant objects look like, and observing as many known comets as possible is good preparation for recognizing an unknown interloper. Generally, comets lack the bilateral symmetry of spiral galaxies and the mottled

Comet Levy 1990c *Photo by the author using the 18-inch Schmidt camera at Mount Palomar Observatory.*

appearance of globular clusters. More important, they usually have unsharp edges, fading off into space so that it is often difficult to tell where the comet ends and the sky begins.

Although most comet hunters still use traditional star atlases to check their sus- pects, some are moving into a new mode of comet hunting. These hunters have attached encoders to their telescopes that allow an instant reading of the suspect's position in right ascension and declination. If the telescope has been properly set up, this approach allows faster checking of suspicious objects. However, a sense of the nature of the fuzzy object in the field of view is still important since thousands of non- stellar objects dot the sky.

Search Procedure

Although comets may appear at any time, they are usually found within 90° of the Sun. A good area to search is in the evening western sky during the week after full Moon, and in the morning eastern sky before dawn around new Moon. Although comet hunters differ in their approaches to searching, one way is to use an altazimuth mount and make horizontal sweeps. In the western sky, begin near the end of twilight at the horizon, sweep across, then return to the point of origin, move upward about half a field of view and sweep again, etc. In the morning reverse the process.

If you are sure you have discovered a comet, follow the procedure given in this Handbook (see REPORTING OF ASTRONOMICAL DISCOVERIES on p. 9). For more information on comet observing and hunting, read *Observing Comets, Asteroids, Meteors, and the Zodiacal Light* by Stephen J. Edberg and David H. Levy (Cambridge University Press, 1994).

Designation of Comets

At the International Astronomical Union's 22nd General Assembly in The Hague in 1994, Commission 20 of the IAU approved a resolution that changes the way comets are designated. Under the old system, a comet was designated according to its order of discovery or recovery in a given year (e.g. 1982i, Comet Halley, was the ninth comet to appear in 1982). After cometary information was complete for a given year, each comet also received a Roman numeral designation based on the order of perihelion passage (e.g. Halley at its last return was also known as 1986 III).

Under the new system, which went into effect in January 1995 but which is retroactive to every comet for which a reasonable orbit is available, a comet is assigned only one designation which is similar to, although not identical to, the provisional designation system for asteroids. The year is divided into periods called "half-months" beginning with A (the first half of January) and concluding with Y (the last half of December), leaving out the letter I. In addition, there is a letter indicating the comet's status: C for a long period comet, P for a "periodic comet" (defined as having a period of less than 200 years), X for a comet for which a reasonable orbit cannot be computed, or D for a disappeared comet. Once the orbit of a periodic comet is well known, that comet receives a permanent number according to the order in which the comet's periodicity was recognized. Thus the new designation for Comet Halley is 1P/Halley. Comet Shoemaker-Levy 9 was 1993e; its new designation is D/1993 F2. Except for the numbered periodic comets, the system is based on a cumbersome provisional designation system for asteroids (asteroids get simple numbers when their orbits are well known), and uses it as a final designation system for all but the periodic comets.

However, the vast majority of scientists, press, and public ignore the cumbersome new designation, preferring instead to use the more easily remembered proper names. Our experience with comets Hale-Bopp and Hyakutake showed clearly that people were far more comfortable with their proper names, largely ignoring the obscure C/1995 O1 and C/1996 B2 designations.

One manifestation of the designation change is that on the IAU circulars, comet names are placed in parentheses, for example, 1995 O1 (Hale-Bopp). This is a style change adopted by the editor of the circulars and was not part of the IAU resolution. Other publications are free to use variations, such as Comet Hale-Bopp (1995 O1), an approach closer to the traditional format.

Editor's Note: David Levy is the discoverer of 21 comets, 8 by visual searches (comets Levy-Rudenko 1984t, Levy 1987a, Levy 1987y, Levy 1988e, Okazaki-Levy-Rudenko 1989r, Levy 1990c, P/Levy 1991q, and Takamizawa-Levy 1994f) plus 13 comets discovered photographically at Palomar under the combined name Shoemaker-Levy. One of these, Shoemaker-Levy 9 (D/1993 F2), collided with Jupiter in July 1994. Brief descriptions of the first twelve to be discovered are given in *JRASC*, 85, 384, 1991. In 1990 David Levy and H. E. Holt discovered the first Martian Trojan asteroid: 1990MB.

INTERPLANETARY DUST
By Roy Bishop

Outside of the astronomical community it is not generally realized that the inner solar system contains a vast cloud of dust. The particles in this cloud are concentrated near the plane of the ecliptic and toward the Sun, their spatial particle density in the ecliptic falling off somewhat more rapidly than the reciprocal of their distance from the Sun. Measurements from spacecraft indicate that the cloud extends well beyond the orbit of Mars but is negligible in the vicinity of Jupiter's orbit and beyond.

The particles composing the cloud have a continuum of sizes, from pebble-sized clumps down to specks with diameters comparable to the wavelength of visible light and smaller. The smaller particles are the more numerous, although the mass distribution appears to peak near 10^{-8} kg, corresponding to a particle diameter of a few tenths of a millimetre. The total mass of the cloud is small, amounting to perhaps 10^{-14} of the mass of the solar system. It is as if the satellites of Mars had been pulverized and spread throughout the inner solar system.

Like the planetary system, the interplanetary dust cloud is not static. Its particles generally move in orbits about the Sun. In addition, the particles undergo continual fragmentation due to collisions, sputtering associated with bombardment by the solar wind, electrostatic bursting, and sublimation. This progression toward smaller and smaller sizes is of crucial significance for the cloud, since particles with diameters appreciably less than a tenth of a millimetre have a sufficiently large surface-to-volume ratio that the radiation pressure of sunlight has a significant effect upon their motion—aberration of sunlight results in a small backward force which slows the dust particles (the Poynting–Robertson Effect), and they slowly spiral inward toward the Sun. During a total solar eclipse in 1983, instruments carried by a balloon detected a ring-like concentration of dust only a couple of solar diameters from the Sun. Its inner edge apparently marks the point at which solar heat vaporizes the infalling particles. The resulting tiny gas molecules, like the smallest particles of dust, are blown out of the solar system by the dominant radiation pressure and interactions with the solar wind.

Because of the above-mentioned influences on the sizes and motions of the dust particles, the estimated mean life of a cloud particle is about 10^4 years. Since this is much less than the age of the solar system, it is obvious that the cloud must be in a dynamic equilibrium—that is, it must be gaining new material as it loses the old. Part of the tail of a bright comet is the result of significant quantities of dust ejected from its nucleus, and it is generally assumed that comets provide a sizeable fraction of the supply of new dust to the cloud. Since comet nuclei are believed to consist of the undifferentiated matter that the solar system formed out of, much of the dust of the interplanetary cloud is most likely composed of this same low-density, fragile, primitive material. IRAS (Infrared Astronomical Satellite) data indicate that collisions of asteroids are also a significant source of dust, but it is not yet known whether comets or asteroids provide the greater input of dust to the cloud.

To an observer on Earth, the most noticeable aspect of the dust cloud is meteors—larger particles of the cloud that encounter Earth at high speeds and vaporize in the upper atmosphere. In addition, sunlight scattered by the dust cloud appears as a faint (fortunately!) glow in the vicinity of the ecliptic. This glow is brightest toward the Sun, is due primarily to particles with diameters between a few micrometres and a millimetre, and is referred to as the *zodiacal light*. A slight brightening in the sky opposite the Sun, called the Gegenschein (German for "counterglow"), is due to a phase effect (analogous to full moon) and also, possibly, to a concentration of dust at the L3 Lagrangian Point of the Earth–Sun system. As astronomical objects, the zodiacal light and the Gegenschein are unusual in that they can be seen only with the unaided eye. Both are invisible in binoculars or a telescope.

The Zodiacal Light

Poetic references to the zodiacal light go back several centuries (e.g. see *The Observatory*, *108*, 181, 1988). The 19th-century poet Edward FitzGerald is noted for his translation of the famous poem "Rubaiyat" by the Persian Omar Khayyam. In one of the stanzas, Khayyam's reference to the morning was altered by FitzGerald into haunting references to the zodiacal light: "Dreaming when Dawn's Left Hand was in the Sky" (in midnorthern latitudes, the zodiacal light and the first glow of the early autumn dawn combine to produce a large, glowing, ghostly figure having an upraised left arm); and "Before the phantom of False morning died" (the zodiacal light soon vanishes in the glow of the true dawn).

When conditions are favourable, the zodiacal light is indeed a mysterious and beautiful sight. Because the zodiacal light is brightest nearest the Sun, it is best seen after the end of evening twilight and before the beginning of morning twilight (for times of twilight, see the index) and when the ecliptic is at a steep angle relative to the horizon. In the tropics the ecliptic is always at a steep angle to the horizon, and the short duration of twilight is an added advantage. In midnorthern latitudes the optimum geometry occurs in the evening western sky in February and March, and in the morning eastern sky in September and October. The zodiacal light appears as a huge, softly radiant pyramid of white light with its base near the horizon and its axis centred on the zodiac. In its brightest parts it exceeds the luminance of the central Milky Way.

Despite its brightness, most people have not seen the zodiacal light. As mentioned above, certain times of night and year are more favourable than others. In addition, moonlight, haze, or light pollution rule out any chance of seeing this phenomenon. Even with a dark, transparent sky the inexperienced observer may confuse the zodiacal light with twilight and thus ignore it, or may not notice it because he or she is expecting a much smaller object.

The Gegenschein

Photometric measurements indicate that the zodiacal light extends all around the zodiac with a shallow minimum in brightness some 120° to 150° from the Sun; nevertheless, this "zodiacal band" or "light bridge" is exceedingly faint and hence seldom visible. However, the slight brightening in the vicinity of the antisolar point can be seen under the right conditions.

The Gegenschein is very faint. The slightest haze, moonlight, bright nearby stars, planets, or light pollution will hide it completely. Most observers, including experienced ones, have not seen it. The Gegenschein is sufficiently faint that one will not see it without making a special effort to *look* for it. It is a ghostly apparition best seen near midnight, and in midnorthern latitudes, in the autumn or winter when the antisolar point is nearest the zenith. To avoid interference from bright stars or the Milky Way observations should be restricted to the periods late September to early November, and late January to early February, when the Gegenschein is in Pisces and Cancer, respectively. It appears as a faint yet distinct, somewhat elliptical glow perhaps 10° in diameter. The luminance of the Gegenschein is about 10^{-4} cd/m^2, some 10 orders of magnitude dimmer than the brightest light the human eye can tolerate.

Don't determine the antisolar point before you look—imagination is too powerful. Find the antisolar point by locating the Gegenschein, and *then* check your star charts!

STARS

CONSTELLATIONS—NAMES AND ABBREVIATIONS

Nominative & Pronunciation	Genitive & Pronunciation	Abbr.	Meaning
Andromeda, ăn-drŏm'ē-dà	Andromedae, ăn-drŏm'ē-dē'	And	Daughter of Cassiopeia
Antlia, ănt'lĭ-à	Antliae, ănt'lē-ē'	Ant	The Air Pump
Apus, ā'pŭs	Apodis, ăp'ă-dĭs	Aps	Bird of Paradise
Aquarius, à-kwâr'ē-ŭs	Aquarii, à-kwâr'ē-ī'	Aqr	The Water-bearer
Aquila, à-kwĭl'à	Aquilae, à-kwĭl'ē	Aql	The Eagle
Ara, ā'rà	Arae, ā'rē	Ara	The Altar
Aries, âr'ēz	Arietis, à-rī'ē-tĭs	Ari	The Ram
Auriga, ô-rī'gà	Aurigae, ô-rī'jē	Aur	The Charioteer
Bootes, bō-ō'tēz	Bootis, bō-ō'tĭs	Boo	The Herdsman
Caelum, sē'lŭm	Caeli, sē'lī	Cae	The Chisel
Camelopardalis kà-mĕl'ō-pàr'dà-lĭs	Camelopardalis kà-mĕl'ō-pàr'dà-lĭs	Cam	The Giraffe
Cancer, kăn'sēr	Cancri, kăn'krē	Cnc	The Crab
Canes Venatici kā'nēz vē-năt'ĭ-sī	Canum Venaticorum kā'nŭm vē-năt'ĭ-kôr'ŭm	CVn	The Hunting Dogs
Canis Major, kā'nĭs mā'jēr	Canis Majoris, kā'nĭs mā-jôr'ĭs	CMa	The Big Dog
Canis Minor, kā'nĭs mī'nēr	Canis Minoris, kā'nĭs mī-ñôr'ĭs	CMi	The Little Dog
Capricornus, kăp'rĭ-kôr-nŭs	Capricorni, kăp'rĭ-kôr-nī	Cap	The Goat
Carina, kà-rī'-nà	Carinae, kà-rī'-nē	Car	The Keel
Cassiopeia, kăs'ĭ-ō-pē'yà	Cassiopeiae, kăs'ĭ-ō-pē'yē	Cas	The Queen
Centaurus, sĕn-tôr'ŭs	Centauri, sĕn-tôr'ī	Cen	The Centaur
Cepheus, sē'fē-ŭs	Cephei, sē'fē-ī'	Cep	The King
Cetus, sē'tŭs	Ceti, sē'tī	Cet	The Whale
Chamaeleon, kà-mē'lē-ŭs	Chamaeleontis, kà-mē'lē-ŏn'tĭs	Cha	The Chameleon
Circinus, sûr'sĭ-nŭs	Circini, sûr'sĭ-nī	Cir	The Compasses
Columba, kō-lŭm'bà	Columbae, kō-lŭm'bē	Col	The Dove
Coma Berenices kō'mà bĕr'ĕ-nī'sēz	Comae Berenices kō'mē bĕr'ĕ-nī'sēz	Corn	Berenice's Hair
Corona Australis kō-rō'nà ôs-trā'lĭs	Coronae Australis kō-rō'nē ôs-trā'lĭs	CrA	The Southern Crown
Corona Borealis kō-rō'nà bôr'ē-ăl'ĭs	Coronae Borealis kō-rō'nē bôr'ē-ăl'ĭs	CrB	The Northern Crown
Corvus, kôr'vŭs	Corvi, kôr'vī	Crv	The Crow
Crater, krā'tēr	Crateris, krā-tēr'ĭs	Crt	The Cup
Crux, krŭks	Crucis, krōo'sĭs	Cru	The Cross
Cygnus, sĭg'nŭs	Cygni, sĭg'nī	Cyg	The Swan
Delphinus, dĕl-fī'nŭs	Delphini, dĕl-fī'nī	Del	The Dolphin
Dorado, dō-rà'dō	Doradus, dō-rà'dŭs	Dor	The Swordfish
Draco, drā'kō	Draconis, drā'kō'nĭs	Dra	The Dragon
Equuleus, ē-kwōo'lē-ŭs	Equulei, ē-kwōo'lē-ī'	Equ	The Little Horse
Eridanus, ē-rĭd'à-nŭs	Eridani, ē-rĭd'à-nī'	Eri	The River
Fornax, fôr'năks	Fornacis, fôr-năs'ĭs	For	The Furnace
Gemini, jĕm'ĭ-nī	Geminorum, jĕm'ĭ-nôr'ŭm	Gem	The Twins
Grus, grŭs	Gruis, grōo'ĭs	Gru	The Crane (bird)
Hercules, hûr'kū-lēz	Herculis, hûr'kū-lĭs	Her	The Son of Zeus
Horologium, hŏr'ō-lō'jĭ-ŭm	Horologii, hŏr'ō-lō'jĭ-ī	Hor	The Clock
Hydra, hī'drà	Hydrae, hī'drē	Hya	The Water Snake (♀)
Hydrus, hī'drŭs	Hydri, hī'drī	Hyi	The Water Snake (♂)
Indus, ĭn'dŭs	Indi, ĭn'dī	Ind	The Indian
Lacerta, là-sûr'tà	Lacertae, là-sûr'tē	Lac	The Lizard

CONSTELLATIONS—NAMES AND PRONUNCIATIONS (continued)

Nominative & Pronunciation	Genitive & Pronunciation	Abbr.	Meaning
Leo, lē′ō	Leonis, lē′ō′nĭs	Leo	The Lion
Leo Minor, lē′ō mī′nēr	Leonis Minoris lē′ō′nĭs mī–nôr′ĭs	LMi	The Little Lion
Lepus, lē′pŭs	Leporis, lĕp′ôr–ĭs	Lep	The Hare
Libra, lē′brà	Librae, lē′brē	Lib	The Balance
Lupus, lōō′pŭs	Lupi, lōō′pī	Lup	The Wolf
Lynx, lĭnks	Lyncis, lĭn′sĭs	Lyn	The Lynx
Lyra, lī′rà	Lyrae, lī′rē	Lyr	The Lyre
Mensa, mĕn′sà	Mensae, mĕn′sē	Men	The Table
Microscopium mī′krō–skō′pē–ŭm	Microscopii mī′krō–skō′pē–ī′	Mic	The Microscope
Monoceros, mō–nŏs′ēr–ŏs	Monocerotis, mō–nŏs′ēr–ō′tĭs	Mon	The Unicorn
Musca, mŭs′kà	Muscae, mŭs′ē	Mus	The Fly
Norma, nôr′mà	Normae, nôr′mē	Nor	The Square
Octans, ŏk′tănz	Octantis, ŏk′tăn′tĭs	Oct	The Octant
Ophiuchus, ō′fē–ū′kŭs	Ophiuchi, ō′fē–ū′kī	Oph	The Serpent-bearer
Orion, ō–rī′ŏn	Orionis, ôr′ē–ō′nĭs	Ori	The Hunter
Pavo, pā′vō	Pavonis, pà–vō′nĭs	Pav	The Peacock
Pegasus, pĕg′à–sŭs	Pegasi, pĕg′à–sī	Peg	The Winged Horse
Perseus, pûr′sē–ŭs	Persei, pûr′sē–ī′	Per	Rescuer of Andromeda
Phoenix, fē′nĭks	Phoenicis, fē–nī′cĭs	Phe	The Phoenix
Pictor, pĭk′tēr	Pictonis, pĭk–tor′ĭs	Pic	The Painter
Pisces, pī′sēz	Piscium, pĭsh′ē–ŭm	Psc	The Fishes
Piscis Austrinus, pī′sĭs ôs–trī′nŭs	Piscis Austrini, pī′sĭs ôs–trī′nī	PsA	The Southern Fish
Puppis, pŭp′ĭs	Puppis, pŭp′ĭs	Pup	The Stern
Pyxis, pĭk′sĭs	Pyxidis, pĭk′sĭ–dĭs	Pyx	The Compass
Reticulum, rē–tĭk′–ū–lŭm	Reticuli, rē–tĭk′–ū–lī	Ret	The Reticle
Sagitta, sà–jĭt′à	Sagittae, sà–jĭt′ē	Sge	The Arrow
Sagittarius, săj′ĭ–târ′ē–ŭs	Sagittarii, săj′ĭ–târ′ē–ī′	Sgr	The Archer
Scorpius, skôr′pē–ŭs	Scorpii, skôr′pē–ī	Sco	The Scorpion
Sculptor, skŭlp′tēr	Sculptoris, skŭlp′tôr′ĭs	Scl	The Sculptor
Scutum, skū′tŭm	Scuti, skōō′tī	Sct	The Shield
Serpens, sûr′pĕnz	Serpentis, sûr–pĕn′tĭs	Ser	The Serpent
Sextans, sĕks′tănz	Sextantis, sĕks–tăn′tĭs	Sex	The Sextant
Taurus, tôr′ŭs	Tauri, tôr′ī	Tau	The Bull
Telescopium tĕl′à–skō′pē–ŭm	Telescopii, tĕl′à–skō′pē–ī	Tel	The Telescope
Triangulum, trī–ăng′gū–lŭm	Trianguli, trī–ăng′gū–lī′	Tri	The Triangle
Triangulum Australe trī–ăng′gū–lŭm ôs–trā′lē	Trianguli Australis trī–ăng′gū–lī′ ôs–trā′lĭs	TrA	The Southern Triangle
Tucana, tōō–kăn′à	Tucanae, tōō–kăn′ē	Tuc	The Toucan
Ursa Major, ûr′sà mā′jēr	Ursae Majoris, ûr′sē mà–jôr′ĭs	UMa	The Great Bear
Ursa Minor, ûr′sà mī′nēr	Ursae Minoris, ûr′sē mī–nôr′ĭs	UMi	The Little Bear
Vela, vē′là	Velorum, vē–lôr′ŭm	Vet	The Sails
Virgo, vûr′gō	Virginis, vûr′jĭn–ĭs	Vir	The Maiden
Volans, vō′lănz	Volantis, vō–lăn′tĭs	Vol	The Hying Fish
Vulpecula, vŭl–pĕk′ū–là	Vulpeculae, vŭl–pĕk′ū–lē′	Vul	The Fox

ā dāte; ă tăp; â câre; à àsk;   ē wē; ĕ mĕt; ē makēr;   ī īce; ĭ bĭt;   ō gō; ŏ hŏt; ô ôrb; ōō mōōn; ū ūnite; ŭ ŭp; û ûrn

In terms of area (based on the official IAU boundaries), of the 88 constellations the 3 largest are Hydra (1303 square degrees), Virgo (1294), and Ursa Major (1280); the 3 smallest: Sagitta (80), Equueleus (72), and Crux (68). A complete list of the areas of the constellations appears in the 1972 edition of *The Handbook of the British Astronomical Association*, and was reproduced in the June 1976 issue of *Sky and Telescope* (p. 408).

FINDING LIST OF SOME NAMED STARS

Name & Pronunciation	Con.	RA	Name & Pronunciation	Con.	RA
Acamar, ā′kà-màr	θ Eri	2	Gienah, jē′nà	γ Crv	12
Achernar, ā′kĕr-nàr	α Eri	1	Hadar, hăd′ar	β Cen	14
Acrux, ā′krŭks	α Cru	12	Hamal, hăm′al	α Ari	2
Adara, à-dā′rà	ε CMa	6	Kaus Australis,	ε Sgr	18
Al Na'ir, ăl-nâr′	α Gru	22	kôs ôs-trā′lĭs		
Albireo, ăl-bĭr′ē-ō	β Cyg	19	Kochab, kō′kăb	β UMi	14
Alcor, ăl-kôr′	80 UMa	13	Markab, màr′kăb	α Peg	23
Alcyone, ăl-sī′ō-nē	η Tau	3	Megrez, me′grĕz	δ UMa	12
Aldebaran,	α Tau	4	Menkar, mĕn′kàr	α Cet	3
ăl-dĕb′à-ràn			Menkent, mĕn′kĕnt	τ Cen	14
Alderamin,	α Cep	21	Merak, mē′răk	β UMa	11
ăl-dĕr′à-mĭn			Merope, mĕr′ō-pē	23 Tau	3
Algeiba, ăl-jē′bà	γ Leo	10	Miaplacidus,	β Car	9
Algenib, ăl-jē′nĭb	γ Peg	0	mī′à-plăs′ĭ-dŭs		
Algol, ăl′gŏl	β Per	3	Mintaka, mĭn-tà′kà	δ Ori	5
Alioth, ăl′ĭ-ŏth	ε UMa	12	Mira, mī′rà	o Cet	2
Alkaid, ăl-kād′	η UMa	13	Mirach, mī′răk	β And	1
Almach, ăl′măk	γ And	2	Mirfak, mir′făk	α Per	3
Alnilam, ăl-nī′lăm	ε Ori	5	Mizar, mi′zàr	ζ UMa	13
Alphard, ăl′fàrd	α Hya	9	Nunki, nŭn′kē	σ Sgr	18
Alphecca, ăl-fĕk′à	α CrB	15	Peacock, pē′kŏk	α Pav	20
Alpheratz, ăl-fē′răts	α And	0	Phecda, fĕk′dà	γ UMa	11
Altair, ăl-târ′	α Aqi	19	Polaris, pō-lâr′ĭs	α UMi	1
Ankaa, ăn′kà	α Phe	0	Pollux, pŏl′ŭks	β Gem	7
Antares, ăn-tā′rēs	α Sco	16	Procyon, prō′sĭ-ŏn	α CMi	7
Arcturus, ark-tū′rŭs	α Boo	14	Pulcherrima,	ε Boo	14
Atria, ā′trĭ-a	α TrA	16	pŭl-kĕr′ĭ-mà		
Avior, ă-vĭ-ôr′	ε Car	8	Ras-Algethi,	α Her	17
Bellatrix, bĕ-lā′trĭks	γ Ori	5	ràs′ăl-jē′thē		
Betelgeuse, bĕt′ĕt-jūz	α Ori	5	Rasalhague, ràs′ăl-hā′gwē	α Oph	17
Canopus, kà-nō′pŭs	α Car	6	Regulus, rĕg′ū-lŭs	α Leo	10
Capella, kàp-pĕl′à	α Aur	5	Rigel, rī′gĕl	β Ori	5
Caph, kăf	β Cas	0	Rigil Kentaurus,	α Cen	14
Castor, kàs′tēr	α Gem	7	rī′jĭl kĕn-tô′rŭs		
Con Caroli, kôr kăr′ŏ-lī	α CVn	12	Sabik, sā′bĭk	η Oph	17
Deneb, dĕn′ĕb	α Cyg	20	Scheat, shē′ăt	β Peg	23
Denebola, dĕn-nĕb′ō-la	β Leo	11	Schedar, shĕd′àr	α Cas	1
Diphda, dĭf′dà	β Cet	0	Shaula, shô′là	λ Sco	17
Dubhe, dŭb′ē	α UMa	11	Sirius, sĭr′ĭ-ŭs	α CMa	6
Elnath, ĕl′năth	β Tau	5	Spica, spī′kà	α Vir	13
Eltanin, ĕl-tā′nĭn	γ Dra	17	Suhail, sŭ-hāl′	λ Vel	9
Enif, ĕn′ĭf	ε Peg	21	Thuban, thoo′ban	α Dra	14
Fomaihaut, fō′măl-ôt	α PsA	22	Vega, ve′gà	α Lyr	18
Gacrux, gà′krŭks	γ Cru	12	Zubenelgenubi,	α Lib	14
Gemma, jĕm′à	α CrB	15	zoo-bĕn′ĕl-jĕ-nū′bē		

Key to pronunciation on previous page.

THE BRIGHTEST STARS
By Robert F. Garrison

The 314 stars brighter than apparent magnitude 3.55 are listed with 2001.5 positions. **Star Name**: If the star is a visual double, the letter A indicates that the data are for the brighter component. The brightness and separation of the second component (B) are given in the last column. Sometimes the double is too close to be conveniently resolved and the data refer to the combined light (AB); in interpreting such data the magnitudes of the two components must be considered.

Apparent Visual Magnitude (**V**): These magnitudes are based on photoelectric observations compiled for the HIPPARCOS catalogue. The *V* filter is yellow and corresponds roughly to the response of the eye. The photometric system is that of Johnson and Morgan in *Ap. J.*, *117*, p. 313, 1953. It is as likely as not that the true magnitude is within 0.03 of the quoted figure, on the average. Variability, range and period of variable stars are given in the remarks.

Colour Index (**B–V**): The blue magnitude, *B*, is the brightness of a star as observed photoelectrically through a blue filter. The difference *B–V* is therefore a measure of the colour of a star. There is a close relation between *B–V* and the spectral type, but some of the stars are reddened by interstellar dust. The probable error of a value of *B–V* is about 0.02 at most. The (*B–V*) values are from the HIPPARCOS catalogue.

Spectral Classification (**MK Type**): A "temperature" type (O, B, A, F, G, K, M) is given first, followed by a finer subtype (0–9) and a "luminosity" class (Roman numerals I–V, with an "a" or "b" added occasionally to indicate slightly brighter or fainter). The sequences are in the sense that the O stars are hottest, M stars are coolest, Ia stars are the most luminous supergiants, III stars are giants, and V stars are the most numerous; the Vs are known as dwarfs or main-sequence stars. Other symbols used in the column are "p" for peculiar, "e" for hydrogen emission, "m" for strong metallic lines, "f" for broad, nonhydrogen emission in hot stars, and "n" or "nn" for unusually broad lines (= rotation). The table contains the best types available, either from the literature or from my own plates.

Parallax (**π**): Parallaxes are shown in milli-arcseconds (mas) and have been taken from the HIPPARCOS catalogue.

Absolute Visual Magnitude (**M$_V$**) and *Distance in Light-Years* (**D**): The absolute magnitudes and distances are newly derived from the parallaxes. The exceptions are marked by a colon following the absolute magnitude and are determined from a calibration of the spectral classification. The effect of the absorption of light was corrected by comparing the spectral classification and the *B–V*, using an intrinsic-colour calibration by the author (unpublished).

Proper Motion (**μ**) and *Position Angle* (**PA**): From *The Bright Star Catalogue* by Hoffleit and Jaschek, Yale University Press, 1982. Proper motions given are the absolute value of the vector resultant from the individual-coordinate proper motions given in *The Bright Star Catalogue*. The position angle indicates the direction of the proper motion with an angle measured in degrees from the north through east.

Radial Velocity (**RV**): From *The Bright Star Catalogue* referenced above. The symbol "V" indicates a variable velocity and an orbit is usually not known. On the other hand, "SB" indicates a spectroscopic binary, which is an unresolved system whose duplicity is revealed by periodic oscillations of the lines in its spectrum and for which an orbit is generally known. If the lines of both stars are detectable, the symbol "SB2" is used; "+" indicates motion away from, "–" towards, the observer.

Remarks: These contain data on companions and variability as well as notes on the spectra. Traditional names have been selected from *The Bright Star Catalogue*. The navigation stars are in bold type.

TABLE OF BRIGHTEST STARS

Star Name	RA (2001.5) h m	Dec ° '	V	B-V	MK Type	π mas	Mv	D ly	μ "/yr	PA °	RV km/s	Remarks
Sun			-26.75	0.63	G2 V	—	4.8	8 lm	—	—	varies	Sun
α And	0 08.5	+29 06	2.07	-0.04	B9p IV:(HgMn)	34	-0.5	97	0.209	139	-12 SB	Alpheratz
β Cas	0 09.3	+59 10	2.28	0.38	F2 III	60	1.2	54	0.555	109	+11 SB	Caph	var: 2.25-2.31, 0.10d
γ Peg	0 13.4	+15 12	2.83	-0.19	B2 IV	10	-2.4	333	0.008	176	+4 SB	Algenib; var: 2.80-2.87, 0.15d
β Hyi	0 25.6	-77 15	2.82	0.62	G1 IV	134	3.4	24	2.255	82	23	
α Phe	0 26.4	-42 18	2.40	1.08	K0 IIIb	42	-0.3	77	0.442	152	+75 SB	Ankaa
δ And A	0 39.5	+30 52	3.27	1.27	K3 III	32	0.9	101	0.161	122	-7 SB	
α Cas	0 40.6	+56 33	2.24	1.17	K0 IIIa	14	-2.5	228	0.058	117	-4 V?	Schedar
β Cet	0 43.7	-17 59	2.04	1.02	K0 III	34	-1.0	96	0.234	81	13	Diphda
η Cas A	0 49.2	+57 50	3.46	0.59	G0 V	168	4.6	19	1.218	115	+9 SB	B: 7.51, K4 Ve, 12"
γ Cas	0 56.9	+60 44	2.15	-0.05	B0 IVnpe(shell)	5	-5.0	613	0.026	90	-7 SB	var: 1.6-3.0; B: 8.8, 2"
β Phe AB	1 06.1	-46 42	3.32	0.89	G8 III	16	0.3:	147	0.030	279	-1	AB similar in light, spectrum, 1"
η Cet	1 08.8	-10 10	3.46	1.16	K1.5 III CN1	28	-0.1	118	0.250	122	12	
β And	1 09.8	+35 38	2.07	1.58	M0 IIIa	16	-1.9	199	0.210	121	+3 V	Mirach
δ Cas	1 25.9	+60 14	2.66	0.16	A5 IV	33	-0.2	99	0.303	99	+7 SB	Ruchbah; ecl.? 2.68-2.76, 759d
γ Phe	1 28.5	-43 19	3.41	1.54	K7 IIIa	14	-1.6	234	0.204	184	+26 SB	var: 3.39-3.49
α Eri	1 37.7	-57 14	0.45	-0.16	B3 Vnp (shell)	23	-2.9	144	0.108	105	+16 V	Achernar
τ Cet	1 44.2	-15 57	3.49	0.73	G8 V	274	5.7	12	1.921	296	-16	
α Tri	1 53.2	+29 35	3.42	0.49	F6 IV	51	1.8	64	0.230	177	-13 SB	Metallah
ε Cas	1 54.5	+63 40	3.35	-0.15	B3 V:p(shell)	7	-2.5	442	0.036	114	-8 V	Segin
β Ari	1 54.8	+20 48	2.64	0.17	A4 V	55	1.3	60	0.145	138	-2 SB	Sharatan
α Hyi	1 58.8	-61 34	2.86	0.29	F0 III-IVn	46	1.1	71	0.271	83	+1 V	
γ And A	2 04.1	+42 20	2.10	1.87	K3 Ib	9	-3.0	355	0.066	136	-12 SB	Almaak; B: 5.4, B9 V, 10"; C: 6.2, A0 V; BC: 1"
α Ari	2 07.3	+23 28	2.01	1.15	K2 IIIab	49	0.5	66	0.238	127	-14 SB	Hamal; Calcium weak?
β Tri	2 09.7	+34 59	3.01	1.04	A5 IV	26	0.1	124	0.153	104	+10 SB2	
o Cet A	2 19.5	-2 59	6.47	0.97	M5-10 IIIe	8	3.0	418	0.232	183	+64 V	Mira; LPV, 2-10; B: VZ Cet, 9.5v, Bpe, 1"
α UMi A	2 33.4	+89 16	1.97	0.64	F5-8 Ib	8	-4.1	431	0.046	95	-17 SB	Polaris; low amp Cep, 4d: B: 8.2, F3 V, 18"
γ Cet AB	2 43.5	+3 15	3.56	0.11	A2 Va	40	1.3	82	0.203	224	-5 V	Kaffaljidhma; A: 3.57; B: 6.23, 3"
θ Eri A	2 58.3	-40 18	3.28	0.17	A5 IV	20	-0.3	161	0.065	294	+12 SB2	Acamar; B: 4.35, A1 Va, 8"
α Cet	3 02.4	+4 06	2.54	1.63	M2 III	15	-1.7	220	0.075	189	-26	Menkar
γ Per	3 04.9	+53 31	2.91	0.72	G8 III + A2 V	13	-0.8:	196	0.002	180	+3 SB	composite spectrum
ρ Per	3 05.3	+38 51	3.32	1.53	M4 II	10	-1.3	325	0.165	128	28	semi-regular var: 3.3-4.0

TABLE OF BRIGHTEST STARS (continued)

Star Name	RA (2001.5) h m	Dec ° '	V	B–V	MK Type	π mas	Mv	D ly	μ "/yr	PA °	RV km/s	Remarks	
β Per	3 08.3	+40 58	2.09	0.00	B8 V + F:	35	-0.5	93	0.004	124	+4 SB	ecl: 2.12–3.4,2.87d; composite	Algol
α Per	3 24.5	+49 51	1.79	0.48	F5 Ib	6	-4.9	592	0.033	131	-2 V	in cluster	Mirphak
δ Per	3 43.1	+47 47	3.01	-0.13	B5 IIIn	6	-3.1	528	0.042	139	+4 SB		
δ Eri	3 43.3	-9 46	3.52	0.92	K0 IV	111	3.4	29	0.752	352	-6		
γ Hyi	3 47.2	-74 14	3.26	1.59	M2 III	15	-1.0	214	0.128	24	16		
η Tau	3 47.7	+24 06	2.85	-0.09	B7 IIIn	9	-1.6:	212	0.048	157	+10 V?	in Pleiades	Alcyone
ζ Per A	3 54.3	+31 53	2.84	0.27	B1 Ib	3	-6.0	982	0.011	146	+20 SB	B: 9.16, B8 V, 13"	
ε Per A	3 57.9	+40 01	2.90	-0.20	B0.5 IV	6	-3.4	538	0.029	145	+1 SB2	B: 7.39, B9.5 V, 9"	
γ Eri	3 58.1	-13 30	2.97	1.59	M1 IIIb	15	-1.6	221	0.124	153	62	Calcium, Chromium weak	Zaurak
λ Tau A	4 00.8	+12 30	3.41	-0.10	B3 V	9	-2.3	370	0.011	218	+18 SB2	ecl: 3.3–3.8, 3.95d; B: A4 IV	
α Ret A	4 14.4	-62 28	3.33	0.92	G8 II–III	20	-0.5	163	0.068	43	+36 SB?		
θ² Tau	4 28.7	+15 52	3.40	0.18	A7 III	22	0.2	149	0.105	103	+40 SB	in Hyades	
ε Tau	4 28.8	+19 10	3.53	1.01	K0 III	21	0.1	155	0.114	108	39	in Hyades	Ain
α Dor AB	4 34.0	-55 03	3.62	-0.08	A0p V:(Si)	19	0.2	176	0.051	89	26	A: 3.8; B: 4.3, B9 IV, 0.2"	
α Tau A	4 36.0	+16 30	0.87	1.54	K5 III	50	-0.8	65	0.200	161	+54 SB	var: 0.75–0.95	Aldebaran
π³ Ori	4 50.0	+6 58	3.19	0.48	F6 V	125	3.7	26	0.463	88	+24 SB2		
ι Aur	4 57.1	+33 10	2.69	1.49	K3 II	6	-3.6	512	0.018	167	18	var?	Hassaleh
ε Aur A	5 02.1	+43 50	3.03	0.54	A9 Iae + B	2	-8.0:	7824	0.004	166	-3 SB	ecl: 2.94–3.83, 9892d	Al Anz
ε Lep	5 05.5	-22 22	3.19	1.46	K4 III	14	-2.0	227	0.073	166	1		
η Aur	5 06.7	+41 14	3.18	-0.15	B3 V	15	-1.2	219	0.073	157	+7 V?		Hoedus II
β Eri	5 07.9	-5 05	2.78	0.16	A3 IVn	37	0.4	89	0.128	231	-9		Kursa
μ Lep	5 13.0	-16 12	3.29	-0.11	B9p IV:(HgMn)	18	-0.4	184	0.043	129	28	var: 2.97–3.36, 2d	
β Ori A	5 14.6	-8 12	0.18	-0.03	B8 Ia	4	-6.6	773	0.004	236	+21 SB	B: 7.6,B5 V,9"; C: 7.6; BC: 0.1"	Rigel
α Aur AB	5 16.8	+46 00	0.08	0.80	G6:III + G2:III	77	-0.8	42	0.430	169	+30 SB	composite; A: 0.6; B: 1.1, 0.04"	Capella
η Ori AB	5 24.6	-2 23	3.35	-0.24	B0.5 V + B	4	-3.9	901	0.003	288	+20 SB2	ecl: 3.14–3.35,8d; A: 3.6; B: 5.0, 1.6"	
γ Ori	5 25.3	+6 21	1.64	-0.22	B2 III	13	-2.8	243	0.018	221	+18 SB?		Bellatrix
β Tau	5 26.5	+28 37	1.65	-0.13	B7 III	25	-1.3	131	0.178	172	+9 V		Alnath
β Lep A	5 28.4	-20 45	2.81	0.81	G5 II	20	-0.7	159	0.090	185	-14	B: 7.4, 2.6"	
δ Ori A	5 32.2	-0 18	2.25	-0.18	O9.5 II	4	-5.4	916	0.002	252	+16 SB	ecl: 1.94–2.13, 5.7d	Mintaka
α Lep	5 32.9	-17 50	2.58	0.21	F0 Ib	3	-5.5	1283	0.006	279	24		Arneb
β Dor	5 33.6	-62 30	3.76	0.64	F7–G2 Ib	3	-4.2	1038	0.007	8	+7 V	Cepheid: 3.43–4.06, 9.8d	
λ Ori A	5 35.3	+9 56	3.39	-0.16	O8 III	3	-4.6	1055	0.006	191	34	B: 5.61, B0 V, 4"	Meissa

TABLE OF BRIGHTEST STARS (continued)

Star Name	RA (2001.5) h m	Dec ° ′	V	B–V	MK Type	π mas	Mv	D ly	μ ″/yr	PA °	RV km/s	Remarks
ι Ori A	5 35.5	−5 55	2.75	−0.21	O9 III	2	−5.6	1325	0.005	284	+22 SB2	B: 7.3, B7 IIIp(He wk), 11″; Nair al Saif
ε Ori	5 36.4	−1 12	1.69	−0.18	B0 Ia	2	−6.6	1342	0.004	236	+26 SB	Alnilam
ζ Tau	5 37.8	+21 08	2.97	−0.15	B2 IIIpe(shell)	8	−2.8	417	0.023	177	+20 SB	var: 2.90–3.03; B: 5.0, 0.007″
α Col A	5 39.7	−34 05	2.65	−0.12	B7 IV	12	−1.9	268	0.026	178	+35 V?	Phaet
ζ Ori A	5 40.9	−1 57	1.74	−0.20	O9.5 Ib	4	−5.5	817	0.002	207	+18 SB	B: 4.2, B0 III, 2.4″; Alnitak
ζ Lep	5 47.1	−14 50	3.55	0.10	A2 Vann	46	1.7	70	0.023	263	+20 SB?	
κ Ori	5 47.9	−9 40	2.07	−0.17	B0.5 Ia	5	−5.0:	815	0.006	211	+21 V?	Saiph
β Col	5 51.0	−35 46	3.12	1.15	K1.5 III	38	0.2	86	0.405	7	+89 V	Wezn
α Ori	5 55.3	+7 24	0.45	1.50	M2 Iab	8	−5.0:	522	0.028	68	+21 SB	Betelgeuse; var: 0.4–1.3
β Aur	5 59.7	+44 57	1.90	0.08	A1 IV	40	−0.2	82	0.055	269	−18 SB2	Menkalinan; ecl: 1.93–2.02, 4d(=mags)
θ Aur AB	5 59.8	+37 13	2.65	−0.08	A0p II:(Si)	19	−1.0	173	0.097	149	+30 SB	B: 7.2, G2 V, 4″
η Gem	6 15.0	+22 31	3.31	1.60	M3 III	9	−1.8	349	0.068	259	+19 SB	Propus; var: 3.3–3.9; B: 8.8, 1.6″
ζ CMa	6 20.3	−30 03	3.02	−0.16	B2.5 V	10	−2.2	336	0.006	59	+32 SB	Phurud
β CMa	6 22.8	−17 57	1.98	−0.24	B1 II-III	7	−4.0	499	0.014	253	+34 SB	Murzim; var: 1.93–2.00, 0.25d
μ Gem	6 23.1	+22 31	2.87	1.62	M3 IIIab	14	−1.5	232	0.125	154	55	Tejat Posterior; var: 2.76–3.02
α Car	6 23.9	−52 41	−0.62	0.16	A9 Ib	10	−5.4	313	0.034	50	21	Canopus
ν Pup	6 37.7	−43 12	3.17	−0.10	B8 IIIn	8	−2.4	423	0.010	234	+28 SB	
γ Gem	6 37.8	+16 24	1.93	0.00	A1 IVs	31	−0.6	105	0.061	136	−13 SB	Alhena
ε Gem	6 44.1	+25 08	3.06	1.38	G8 Ib	4	−5.0	903	0.016	195	+10 SB	Mebsuta
α CMa A	6 45.3	−16 43	−1.44	0.01	A0mA1 Va	379	1.5	9	1.324	204	−8 SB	Sirius; B: 8.5, WDA, 50y, 10″(1980)
ξ Gem	6 45.4	+12 53	3.35	0.44	F5 IV	57	2.2	57	0.224	211	+25 V?	Alzirr
α Pic	6 48.2	−61 57	3.24	0.23	A6 Vn	33	0.7	99	0.275	345	21	
τ Pup	6 50.0	−50 37	2.94	1.21	K1 III	18	−1.9	183	0.079	157	+36 SB	
ε CMa A	6 58.6	−28 58	1.50	−0.21	B2 II	8	−4.1	431	0.002	27	27	Adara
σ CMa	7 01.2	−27 56	3.49	1.73	K7 Ib	3	−4.7	1216	0.008	284	22	var: 3.43–3.49
o² CMa	7 03.2	−23 50	3.02	−0.08	B3 Ia	1	−6.6	2567	0.007	262	+48 SB	
δ CMa	7 08.4	−26 24	1.83	0.67	F8 Ia	2	−7.2	1791	0.008	291	+34 SB	Wezen
L₂ Pup	7 13.5	−44 38	4.42	1.33	M5 IIIe	16	1.5	198	0.346	18	+53 V?	Long Period Var: 2.6–6.2; HR2748
π Pup	7 17.2	−37 06	2.86	1.62	K3 Ib	3	−5.1	1094	0.012	284	16	
δ Gem AB	7 20.3	+21 59	3.50	0.37	F0 IV	55	2.2	59	0.029	241	+4 SB	B: 8.2, K3 V, 0.2″
η CMa	7 24.1	−29 18	2.45	−0.08	B5 Ia	1	−7.5	3196	0.008	284	+41 V	Aludra
β CMi	7 27.3	+8 18	2.89	−0.10	B8 V	19	−0.8	170	0.065	233	+22 SB	Gomeisa

TABLE OF BRIGHTEST STARS (continued)

Star Name	RA (2001.5) h m	Dec °′	V	B-V	MK Type	π mas	Mv	D ly	μ "/yr	PA °	RV km/s	Remarks	
σ Pup A	7 29.2	−43 18	3.25	1.51	K5 III	18	−1.6	184	0.195	342	+88 SB	B: 8.6, G5: V, 22″	
α Gem A	7 34.7	+31 53	1.58	0.03	A1mA2 Va	63	0.6	52	0.199	239	+6 SB	AB: 3″ separation	Castor
α Gem B	7 34.8	+31 53	1.93	0.03	A2mA5 V:	63	1.0	52	0.199	239	−1 SB	BA: 3″ separation	Castor
α CMi A	7 39.5	+5 13	0.41	0.43	F5 IV–V	286	2.8	11	1.248	214	−3 SB	B: 10.3, 4″	**Procyon**
β Gem	7 45.5	+28 01	1.16	0.99	K0 IIIb	97	1.1	34	0.629	265	+3 V		**Pollux**
ξ Pup	7 49.5	−24 52	3.34	1.22	G6 Ia	2	−7.5:	3260	0.033	240	+3 SB		
χ Car	7 56.8	−52 59	3.46	−0.18	B3 IVp(note)	8	−2.0	387	0.042	306	+19 V	Si II strong	
ζ Pup	8 03.6	−40 00	2.21	−0.27	O5 Iafn	2	−6.1	1399	0.033	290	−24 V?		Naos
ρ Pup	8 07.7	−24 18	2.83	0.46	F2mF5 II:(var)	52	1.4	63	0.100	299	+46 SB	delta Del spec; var: 2.68–2.78, 0.14d	
γ² Vel	8 09.5	−47 20	1.75	−0.15	WC8 + O9 I:	4	−5.8	840	0.007	304	+35 SB2	var: 1.6–1.8, 154s	Suhail al Muhlif
β Cnc	8 16.6	+9 11	3.59	1.48	K4 III	11	−1.2	290	0.068	220	22		Altarf
ε Car	8 22.5	−59 31	2.17	1.20	K3:III + B2:V	5	−4.8	632	0.030	301	2	ecl? 3.1–3.4p, 785d	Avior
o UMa A	8 30.3	+60 43	3.35	0.86	G5 III	18	−0.3	184	0.171	230	20	var: 3.3–3.8, 358d	
δ Vel AB	8 44.7	−54 42	1.99	0.04	A1 Va	41	0.0	80	0.082	164	+ 2 V?	B: 5.0, 2″	
ε Hya ABC	8 46.9	+6 25	3.38	0.69	G5:III + A:	24	0.0	135	0.198	254	+36 SB	composite A: 3.8; B: 4.7, 0.2″; C: 7.8,3″	
ζ Hya	8 55.5	+5 56	3.11	0.98	G9 II–III	22	−0.2	151	0.101	277	23		
ι UMa A	8 59.4	+48 02	3.12	0.22	A7 IVn	68	2.2	48	0.501	242	+9 SB	BC: 10.8, M1 V, 4″	Talitha
λ Vel	9 08.0	−43 26	2.23	1.67	K4 Ib–IIa	6	−4.8	573	0.026	299	18	var: 2.14–2.22	Suhail
a Car	9 11.0	−58 58	3.43	−0.19	B2 IV–V	8	−2.2	418	0.028	283	+23 SB2	ecl: 3.2–3.6, 6.7d	HR3659
β Car	9 13.2	−69 43	1.67	0.07	A1 III	29	−1.1	111	0.183	304	−5 V?		Miaplacidus
ι Car	9 17.1	−59 17	2.21	0.19	A7 Ib	5	−4.4	694	0.019	285	13	var: 2.2–2.5	Turais
α Lyn	9 21.2	+34 23	3.14	1.55	K7 IIIab	15	−1.3	222	0.223	273	38		
κ Vel	9 22.1	−55 01	2.47	−0.14	B2 IV–V	6	−3.9	539	0.012	315	+22 SB		
α Hya	9 27.7	−8 40	1.99	1.44	K3 II–III	18	−2.1	177	0.034	327	−4 V?		Alphard
N Vel	9 31.1	−57 02	3.16	1.54	K5 III	14	−1.6	238	0.034	268	−14		
θ UMa	9 33.0	+51 41	3.17	0.48	F6 IV	74	2.6	44	1.094	240	+15 SB		HR3803
o Leo AB	9 41.3	+9 53	3.52	0.52	F5 II + A5?	24	0.1	135	0.149	254	+27 SB	A: occ.bin.(=mags)	Subra
1 Car	9 45.3	−62 31	3.69	1.01	F9–G5 Ib	2	−5.8	1509	0.016	281	+4 V	Cepheid var: 3.39–4.12, 35.5d	HR3884
ε Leo	9 46.0	+23 46	2.97	0.81	G1 II	13	−1.6	251	0.048	252	+4 V?		Ras Elased Australis
υ Car AB	9 47.1	−65 04	3.10	0.29	A6 II	2	−2.5:	326	0.012	305	14	B: 6.26, B7 III, 5″	
φ Vel	9 56.9	−54 34	3.52	−0.07	B5 Ib	2	−5.5	1929	0.013	293	14		
η Leo	10 07.5	+16 46	3.48	−0.03	A0 Ib	2	−5.5	2131	0.006	189	+3 V	B: 4.5, 0.1″	

TABLE OF BRIGHTEST STARS (continued)

Star Name	RA (2001.5) h m	Dec ° '	V	B–V	MK Type	π mas	Mv	D ly	μ "/yr	PA °	RV km/s	Remarks	
α Leo A	10 08.5	+11 58	1.36	−0.09	B7 Vn	42	−0.6	77	0.248	271	+6 SB		**Regulus**
ω Car	10 13.8	−70 03	3.29	−0.07	B8 IIIn	9	−2.1	370	0.032	275	+7 V		
ζ Leo	10 16.8	+23 25	3.43	0.31	F0 IIIa	13	−1.1	260	0.023	124	−16 SB		Adhafera
q Car	10 17.1	−61 20	3.39	1.54	K3 IIa	4	−4.2	736	0.027	276	8	var: 3.36–3.42	HR4050
λ UMa	10 17.3	+42 55	3.45	0.03	A1 IV	24	0.4	134	0.170	255	+18 V		Tania Borealis
γ Leo A	10 20.1	+19 51	2.61	1.13	K1 IIIb Fe-0.5	26	−0.7	126	0.342	116	−37 SB	AB: 5" separation	Algieba
γ Leo B	10 20.1	+19 51	3.16	1.42	G7 III Fe-1	26	−1.9	126	0.358	119	−36 V	BA: 5" separation	
μ UMa	10 22.5	+41 30	3.06	1.60	M0 IIIp	13	−1.5	249	0.088	290	−21 SB	Ca II emission	Tania Australis
p Car	10 32.0	−61 41	3.30	−0.09	B4 Vne	7	−2.0:	326	0.021	287	26	var: 3.27–3.37	HR4140
θ Car	10 43.0	−64 23	2.74	−0.22	B0.5 Vp	7	−3.1	439	0.022	291	+24 SB	Nitrogen enhanced	
μ Vel AB	10 46.9	−49 25	2.90	1.07	G5 III + F8:V	28	0.0	116	0.085	125	+6 SB	B: 6.4, 2"	
ν Hya	10 49.7	−16 12	3.11	1.20	K2 III	24	−0.3	138	0.215	24	−1		
β UMa	11 02.0	+56 22	2.34	0.03	A0mA1 IV-V	41	0.4	79	0.087	70	−12 SB		Merak
α UMa AB	11 03.9	+61 44	1.81	1.06	K0 IIIa	26	−1.3	124	0.138	239	−9 SB	A: 1.86, B: 4.8, A8 V, <1"	Dubhe
ψ UMa	11 09.8	+44 29	3.00	1.14	K1 III	22	−0.5	147	0.075	245	−4		
δ Leo	11 14.3	+20 31	2.56	0.13	A4 IV	57	1.3	58	0.197	133	−20 V		Zosma
θ Leo	11 14.3	+15 25	3.33	0.00	A2 IV(K var)	18	−0.2	178	0.104	216	+8 V	B: 9.5, 7"	Chort
ν UMa	11 18.6	+33 05	3.49	1.40	K3 III Ba0.3	8	−3.2	421	0.036	309	−9 SB		Alula Borealis
ξ Hya	11 33.1	−31 52	3.54	0.95	G7 III	25	0.0	129	0.211	259	−5 V		
λ Cen	11 35.9	−63 02	3.11	−0.04	B9.5 IIn	8	−2.5	410	0.039	258	−1 V		
β Leo	11 49.2	+14 34	2.14	0.09	A3 Va	90	1.9	36	0.511	257	0 V		Denebola
γ UMa	11 54.0	+53 41	2.41	0.04	A0 Van	39	0.2	84	0.094	86	−13 SB		Phad
δ Cen	12 08.5	−50 44	2.58	−0.13	B2 IVne	8	−3.1	395	0.034	249	+11 V	var: 2.51–2.65	
ε Crv	12 10.3	−22 38	3.02	1.33	K2 III	11	−2.3	303	0.073	278	5		Minkar
δ Cru	12 15.3	−58 45	2.79	−0.19	B2 IV	8	−2.6	364	0.039	255	+22 V?	var: 2.25–2.31p, 3.7h	
δ UMa	12 15.5	+57 01	3.32	0.08	A2 Van	40	1.4	81	0.102	88	−13 V		Megrez
γ Crv	12 16.0	−17 33	2.58	−0.11	B8 III	20	−0.9	165	0.163	276	−4 SB	sp. var?	Gienah Ghurab
α Cru A	12 26.7	−63 06	1.25	−0.20	B0.5 IV	10	−4.0	321	0.030	236	−11 SB	AB: 5"	**Acrux**
α Cru B	12 26.7	−63 06	1.64	−0.18	B1 Vn	10	−3.6	321	0.031	248	−1	BA: 5"	
α Crv A	12 30.0	−16 31	2.94	−0.01	B9.5 IVn	37	−2.0	88	0.255	236	+9 V	B: 8.26, K2 V, 24"	Algorab
γ Cru	12 31.3	−57 07	1.59	1.60	M3.5 III	37	−0.7	88	0.269	174	21	var: 1.6–1.9	Gacrux
β Crv	12 34.5	−23 24	2.65	0.89	G5 II	23	−0.5	140	0.059	179	−8		Kraz

TABLE OF BRIGHTEST STARS (continued)

Star Name	RA (2001.5) h m	Dec ° '	V	B-V	MK Type	π mas	M_v	D ly	μ "/yr	PA °	RV km/s	Remarks
α Mus	12 37.3	-69 09	2.69	-0.18	B2 IV-V	11	-2.3	306	0.043	248	+13 V	var: 2.17-2.24p, 2h
γ Cen A	12 41.6	-48 58	2.95	-0.02	A1 IV	25	-0.1	130	0.190	268	-6 SB	AB: 5"
γ Cen B	12 41.6	-48 58	2.85	-0.02	A0 IV	25	-0.1	130	0.190	268	-6 SB	BA: 5"
γ Vir AB	12 41.8	-1 29	2.74	0.37	F1 V + F0mF2 V	85	2.2	39	0.567	271	-20 SB	A: 3.48, B: 3.50, 4" Porrima
β Mus AB	12 46.4	-68 07	3.51	-0.18	B2 V + B2.5 V	10	-2.2:	424	0.041	233	+42 V	A: 3.58, B: 4.10, 1"
β Cru	12 47.8	-59 42	1.25	-0.24	B0.5 III	9	-4.0	352	0.042	246	+16 SB	var: 1.23-1.31, 0.7d? **Becrux**
ε UMa	12 54.2	+55 57	1.76	-0.02	A0p IV:(CrEu)	40	-0.2	81	0.109	95	-9 SB?	var: 1.76-1.79, 5.1d **Alioth**
δ Vir	12 55.7	+3 23	3.39	1.57	M3 III	16	-0.5	202	0.474	263	-18 V?	Auva
α² CVn A	12 56.1	+38 18	2.85	-0.06	A0p (SiEu)	30	0.4	110	0.242	282	-3 V	B: 5.6, F0 V, 20" Cor Caroli
ε Vir	13 02.4	+10 57	2.85	0.93	G9 IIIab	32	0.4	102	0.274	274	-14	Vindamiatrix
γ Hya	13 19.0	-23 10	2.99	0.92	G8 IIIa	25	-0.6	132	0.081	127	-5 V?	
ι Cen	13 20.7	-36 42	2.75	0.07	A2 Va	56	1.4	59	0.351	255	0	
ζ UMa A	13 23.9	+54 57	2.23	0.06	A1 Va	42	0.3	78	0.122	102	-6 SB2	B: 3.94, A1mA7 IV-V, 14" Mizar
α Vir	13 25.3	-11 09	0.98	-0.24	B1 V	12	-3.6	262	0.054	232	+1 SB2	var: 0.97-1.04; mult. 3.1,4.5,7.5 **Spica**
ζ Vir	13 34.9	-0 36	3.38	0.11	A2 IV	45	1.6	73	0.287	277	-13	Heze
ε Cen	13 40.0	-53 28	2.29	-0.17	B1 III	9	-3.3	376	0.028	232	3	
η UMa	13 47.5	+49 19	1.85	0.19	B3 V	32	-1.8	101	0.127	264	-11 SB?	Alkaid
ν Cen	13 49.7	-41 41	3.41	-0.23	B2 IV	7	-2.4	475	0.035	227	+9 SB	
μ Cen	13 49.8	-42 28	3.47	-0.17	B2 IV-V pne	6	-2.8	527	0.034	220	+9 SB	variable shell: 2.92-3.43
η Boo	13 54.8	+18 24	2.68	0.58	G0 IV	88	2.4	37	0.370	190	0 SB	Mufrid
ζ Cen	13 55.7	-47 17	2.55	-0.18	B2.5 IV	8	-2.9	384	0.072	232	+7 SB2	var: 0.61-0.68; B: 3.9, 1"
β Cen AB	14 04.0	-60 22	0.58	-0.23	B1 III	6	-5.5	526	0.030	221	+6 SB	**Hadar**
π Hya	14 06.5	-26 41	3.25	1.09	K2 IIIb	32	0.2	101	0.049	163	27	
θ Cen	14 06.9	-36 22	2.06	1.01	K0 IIIb	54	0.1	61	0.738	225	0 SB	Menkent
α Boo	14 15.8	+19 11	-0.05	1.24	K1.5 III Fe-0.5	89	-0.6	37	2.281	209	-5 V?	high space velocity Arcturus
ι Lup	14 19.5	-46 04	3.55	-0.18	B2.5 IVn	9	-1.7	352	0.014	266	22	
γ Boo	14 32.1	+38 18	3.04	0.19	A7 IV+	38	1.0	85	0.189	322	-37 V	Seginus
η Cen	14 35.6	-42 10	2.33	-0.16	B1.5 IV pne	11	-2.8	308	0.049	226	0 SB	variable shell
α Cen A	14 39.8	-60 50	0.14	0.71	G2 V	742	4.2	4	3.678	281	-25 SB	AB: 21" **Rigil Kentaurus**
α Cen B	14 39.8	-60 51	1.24	0.90	K1 V	742	6.2	4	3.678	281	-21 V?	BA: 21"; C: Proxima, 12.4, M5e, 2°
α Lup	14 42.0	-47 24	2.30	-0.15	B1.5 III	6	-4.1	548	0.026	220	+5 SB	var: 2.28-2.31, 0.26d
α Cir	14 42.6	-64 59	3.18	0.26	A7p (Sr)	61	1.9	53	0.302	218	+7 SB?	B: 8.6, K5 V, 16"

TABLE OF BRIGHTEST STARS (continued)

Star Name	RA (2001.5) Dec h m ° ′		V	B–V	MK Type	π mas	Mv	D ly	μ ″/yr	PA °	RV km/s	Remarks	
ε Boo AB	14 45.0	+27 04	2.65	1.34	K0 II-III+A0 V	16	−2.6	210	0.054	289	−17 V	A: 2.70; B: 5.12, 3″	Izar
β UMi	14 50.7	+74 09	2.07	1.97	K4 III	26	−1.1	126	0.036	286	+17 V		Kocab
α Lib A	14 51.0	−16 03	2.75	0.15	A3 III–IV	42	0.7	77	0.130	237	−23 SB		Zuben Elgenubi
β Lup	14 58.6	−43 09	2.68	−0.18	B2 IV	6	−3.5	523	0.057	221	0 SB		
κ Cen	14 59.3	−42 07	3.34	−0.21	B2 V	15	−2.8	539	0.033	215	+8 SB		
β Boo	15 01.9	+40 23	3.49	0.96	G8 IIIa(note)	15	−0.7	219	0.056	235	−20	Ba 0.4, Fe −0.5	Nekkar
σ Lib	15 04.0	−25 17	3.25	1.67	M2.5 III	11	−1.9	292	0.087	237	−4	var: 3.20–3.36	Brachium
ζ Lup	15 12.4	−52 06	3.41	0.92	G8 III	28	0.1	116	0.128	237	−10		
δ Boo	15 15.5	+33 19	3.46	0.96	G8 III Fe-1	28	0.6	117	0.143	144	−12 SB		
β Lib	15 17.1	−9 23	2.61	−0.07	B8 IIIn	20	−1.0	160	0.101	275	−35 SB		Zuben Elschemali
γ TrA	15 19.0	−68 40	2.87	0.01	A1 IIIn	18	−0.8	183	0.067	243	−3 V		
γ UMi	15 20.7	+71 50	3.01	0.06	A3 III	7	−0.1:	147	0.031	308	−4 V		Pherkad
δ Lup	15 21.5	−40 39	3.22	−0.23	B1.5 IVn	6	−2.8	510	0.036	207	0 V?		
ε Lup AB	15 22.8	−44 41	3.56	−0.19	B2 IV-V	6	−2.5	504	0.024	232	+8 SB2	A: 3.5; B: 5.0, <1″	
ι Dra	15 24.9	+58 58	3.29	1.17	K2 III	32	0.8	102	0.020	311	−11		Ed Asich
α CrB	15 34.8	+26 43	2.22	0.03	A0 IV(composite)	44	0.3	75	0.151	127	+2 SB	ecl: 2.21–2.32, 17.4d	Alphekka
γ Lup AB	15 35.2	−41 10	3.40	−0.22	B2 IVn	6	−2.8	567	0.035	207	+2 V	A: 3.5; B: 3.6, <1″; similar spectra	
α Ser	15 44.3	+6 25	2.63	1.17	K2 IIIb CN1	45	0.9	73	0.143	72	+3 V?	var?	Unukalhai
μ Ser	15 49.8	−3 26	3.54	−0.04	A0 III	21	0.3	156	0.094	253	−9 SB		
β TrA	15 55.3	−63 26	2.83	0.32	F0 IV	81	2.3	40	0.438	205	0		
π Sco A	15 59.1	−26 07	2.89	−0.18	B1 V + B2 V	7	−3.0	459	0.028	198	−3 SB2	A: occ.bin: 3.4 + 4.5, 0.0003″ sep.	
T CrB	15 59.5	+25 55	10.08	1.34	gM3: + Bep	0	−9.3	...	0.013	327	−29 SB	recurrent nova 1866, 1946; now V=11	
η Lup A	16 00.2	−38 24	3.42	−0.21	B2.5 IVn	7	−2.5	493	0.040	213	+8 V	A: 3.47, B: 7.70, 15″	
δ Sco AB	16 00.5	−22 38	2.29	−0.12	B0.3 IV	8	−4.4:	522	0.027	202	−7 SB	AB: mult<1″, C: 4.9, B2 IV–V, 8″	Dschubba
β Sco AB	16 05.5	−19 49	2.56	−0.07	B0.5 V	6	−4.2	530	0.022	196	−1 SB	A: 2.78; B: 5.04, 1″; C: 4.93, 14″	Grafias
δ Oph	16 14.5	−3 42	2.73	1.58	M1 III	19	−0.8	170	0.153	198	−20 V		Yed Prior
ε Oph	16 18.5	−4 42	3.23	0.97	G9.5 IIIb	30	0.8	107	0.089	64	−10 V		Yed Posterior
σ Sco A	16 21.3	−25 36	2.91	0.13	B1 III	4	−4.8:	522	0.025	201	+3 SB	var: 2.94–3.06, 0.25d; B: 8.3, B9 V, 20″	
η Dra A	16 24.0	+61 31	2.73	0.91	G8 IIIab	37	0.7	88	0.064	338	−14 SB?	B: 8.7, 6″	
α Sco A	16 29.6	−26 26	1.06	1.87	M1.5 Iab	5	−5.8	604	0.024	197	−3 SB	B: 5.37 V, 3″	**Antares**
β Her	16 30.4	+21 30	2.78	0.95	G7 IIIa	22	−0.5	148	0.100	260	−26 SB		Kornephoros
τ Sco	16 36.0	−28 13	2.82	−0.21	B0 V	8	−3.1	430	0.026	198	+2 V		

TABLE OF BRIGHTEST STARS (continued)

Star Name	RA (2001.5) Dec h m ° '	V	B–V	MK Type	π mas	Mv	D ly	μ "/yr	PA °	RV km/s	Remarks
ζ Oph	16 37.3 −10 34	2.54	0.04	O9.5 Vn	7	−4.3	458	0.026	28	−15 V	
ζ Her AB	16 41.3 +31 36	2.81	0.65	G1 IV	93	2.5	35	0.614	310	−70 SB	A: 2.90; B: 5.53, G7 V, 1.1"
η Her	16 42.9 +38 56	3.48	0.92	G7.5 IIIb Fe-1	29	0.1	112	0.089	158	+8 V?	
α TrA	16 48.8 −69 02	1.91	1.45	K2 IIb–IIIa	8	−5.0	415	0.044	141	−3	Atria
ε Sco	16 50.3 −34 17	2.29	1.14	K2 III	50	0.1	65	0.661	247	−3 &	cr
μ¹ Sco	16 52.0 −38 03	3.00	−0.20	B1.5 IVn	4	−4.1	821	0.031	202	−25 SB2	ecl: 2.80–3.08, 1.4d
κ Oph	16 57.8 +9 22	3.19	1.16	K2 III	38	1.1	86	0.293	268	−56	
ζ Ara	16 58.7 −55 59	3.12	1.55	K4 III	6	−4.5	574	0.037	200	−6	
ζ Dra	17 08.8 +65 43	3.17	−0.12	B6 III	10	−2.0	340	0.033	310	−17 V	Aldhibah
η Oph AB	17 10.5 −15 44	2.43	0.06	A2.5 Va	39	0.8	84	0.102	22	−1 SB	Sabik; A: 3.0; B: 3.5, A3 V, 1"
μ Sco	17 12.3 −43 15	3.30	0.44	F2p (Cr)	46	1.4	72	0.286	175	−27	
α Her AB	17 14.8 +14 23	2.78	1.16	M5 Ib–II	9	−3.5:	1369	0.035	348	−33 V	Ras Algethi; var: 3.0–4.0; B: 5.4, 5"
π Her	17 15.1 +36 48	3.16	1.44	K3 IIab	9	−2.2	367	0.029	276	−26	
δ Her	17 15.2 +24 50	3.12	0.08	A1 Vann	42	1.2	78	0.159	188	−40 SB	Sarin; B: 8.8, 9"
θ Oph	17 22.2 −25 00	3.27	−0.19	B2 IV	6	−3.1	563	0.021	188	−2 SB	occ.bin: 3.4, 5.4; var: 3.25–3.29, 0.14d
β Ara	17 25.4 −55 32	2.84	1.48	K3 Ib–IIa	5	−4.1	603	0.024	182	0	
γ Ara A	17 25.5 −56 23	3.31	−0.15	B1 Ib	3	−5.7:	652	0.011	170	−3 V	broad lines for Ib; B: 10.0, 18"
β Dra A	17 30.4 +52 19	2.79	0.95	G2 Ib–IIa	3	−2.9	361	0.026	301	−20 V	Restaban; B: 11.5, 4"
υ Sco	17 30.9 −37 17	2.70	−0.18	B2 IV	6	−3.5	518	0.032	182	8 SB	
α Ara	17 32.0 −49 52	2.84	−0.14	B2 Vne	13	−1.8	242	0.075	199	0 SB	
λ Sco	17 33.7 −37 06	1.62	−0.23	B1.5 IV	5	−3.6:	359	0.029	178	−3 SB2	Shaula; var: 1.59–1.65, 0.21d
α Oph	17 35.1 +12 34	2.08	0.16	A5 Vnn	70	1.3	47	0.255	157	+13 SB?	Rasalhague
θ Sco	17 37.5 −43 00	1.97	0.41	F1 III	12	−3.0	272	0.016	90	1	Sargas
ξ Ser	17 37.7 −15 24	3.54	0.26	F0 IIIb	31	0.9	105	0.076	216	−43 SB	
κ Sco	17 42.7 −39 02	2.39	−0.17	B1.5 III	7	−3.6	464	0.030	194	−14 SB	var: 2.39–2.42, 0.2d
β Oph	17 43.5 +4 34	2.76	1.17	K2 III	40	0.7	82	0.164	345	−12 V	Cebalrai
μ Her A	17 46.4 +27 44	3.42	0.75	G5 IV	119	3.6	27	0.808	202	−16 V	BC: 9.78, 33"
ι¹ Sco	17 47.8 −40 07	2.99	0.51	F2 Ia	2	−8.0:	3619	0.006	171	−28 SB	
G Sco	17 49.9 −37 02	3.19	1.19	K2 III	26	−0.6	127	0.064	58	25	HR6630
γ Dra	17 56.7 +51 29	2.24	1.52	K5 III	22	−1.1	148	0.025	213	−28	Etamin
ν Oph	17 59.1 −9 46	3.32	0.99	G9.5 IIIa	21	0.0	153	0.118	184	13	
γ² Sgr	18 05.9 −30 25	2.98	0.98	K0 III	34	0.1	96	0.192	196	+22 SB	Nash

TABLE OF BRIGHTEST STARS (continued)

Star Name	RA (2001.5) h m	Dec ° '	V	B–V	MK Type	π mas	Mv	D ly	μ "/yr	PA °	RV km/s	Remarks
η Sgr A	18 17.7	–36 46	3.10	1.50	M3.5 IIab	22	–0.1	149	0.210	218	+1 V?	var: 3.08-3.12; B: 8.33, G8: IV:, 4"
δ Sgr	18 21.1	–29 50	2.72	1.38	K2.5 IIIa	11	–3.3	306	0.050	127	–20	Kaus Meridionalis
η Ser	18 21.5	–2 54	3.23	0.94	K0 III–IV	53	1.4	62	0.890	218	+9 V?	
ε Sgr	18 24.3	–34 23	1.79	–0.03	A0 II:n(shell?)	23	–1.4	145	0.129	194	–15	Kaus Australis
α Tel	18 27.1	–45 58	3.49	–0.18	B3 IV	13	–1.0	249	0.048	198	0 V?	
λ Sgr	18 28.1	–25 26	2.82	1.03	K1 IIIb	42	0.4	77	0.190	193	–43	Kaus Borealis
α Lyr	18 37.0	+38 47	0.03	0.00	A0 Va	129	0.6	25	0.348	35	–14 V	**Vega**
φ Sgr	18 45.8	–26 59	3.17	–0.11	B8 III	14	–1.0	231	0.052	89	+22 SB	similar companion, 0.1"
β Lyr	18 50.1	+33 22	3.52	0.00	B7 Vpe (shell)	4	–4.1	881	0.002	180	–19 SB	Sheliak ecl: 3.34–4.34, 12.9d
σ Sgr	18 55.4	–26 18	2.05	–0.13	B3 IV	15	–2.4	224	0.056	166	–11 V	Nunki
ξ² Sgr	18 57.9	–21 06	3.52	1.15	K1 III	3	0.1	913	0.035	111	–20	
γ Lyr	18 58.9	+32 41	3.25	–0.05	B9 II	5	–3.3	634	0.007	288	–21 V	Sulaphat
ζ Sgr AB	19 02.7	–29 53	3.27	0.06	A2 IV–V + A4:V:	37	1.1	89	0.014	266	+22 SB	Ascella A: 3.2; B: 3.5, <1"
ζ Aql A	19 05.5	+13 52	2.99	0.01	A0 Vann	39	0.9	83	0.095	184	–25 SB	
λ Aql	19 06.4	–4 53	3.43	–0.10	B9 Vnp (kB7HeA0)	26	0.6	125	0.090	193	–12 V	
τ Sgr	19 07.1	–27 40	3.32	1.17	K1.5 IIIb	27	–0.4	120	0.255	192	+45 SB	
π Sgr ABC	19 09.9	–21 01	2.88	0.38	F2 II–III	7	–3.1	440	0.035	180	–10	A: 3.7; B: 3.8; C: 6.0, <1"
δ Dra	19 12.6	+67 40	3.07	0.99	G9 III	33	0.6	100	0.130	44	25	Nodus Secundus
δ Aql	19 25.6	+3 07	3.36	0.32	F2 IV	65	2.6	50	0.267	72	–30 SB	
β Cyg A	19 30.7	+27 57	3.36	1.09	K3 II + B9.5 V	8	–2.3	385	0.002	153	–24 V	Albireo B: 5.11, 35"; C: Δm=1.5, 0.4"
δ Cyg AB	19 44.9	+45 08	2.86	0.00	B9.5 III	19	–0.7	171	0.069	45	–20 SB	B: 6.4, F1 V, 2"
γ Aql	19 46.3	+10 37	2.72	1.51	K3 II	7	–2.6:	326	0.016	83	–2 V	Tarazed
α Aql	19 50.9	+8 52	0.76	0.22	A7 Vnn	194	2.1	17	0.662	54	–26	**Altair**
η Aql	19 52.6	+1 01	3.87	0.63	F6–G1 Ib	3	–4.3	1173	0.009	131	–15 SB	Cepheid var: 3.53–4.33, 7.2d
γ Sge	19 58.9	+19 30	3.51	1.57	M0 III	12	–0.9	274	0.070	69	–33	
θ Aql	20 11.5	–0 49	3.24	–0.07	B9.5 III	11	–1.4	287	0.037	79	–27 SB2	
β Cap A	20 21.1	–14 47	3.05	0.79	K0: II: + A5: V:n	9	–1.4	344	0.039	86	–19 SB	Dabih A: mult: 4.0+4.3+4.8+6.7, <1"
γ Cyg	20 22.2	+40 15	2.23	0.67	F8 Ib	2	–4.1:	522	0.001	27	–8	Sadr
α Pav	20 25.8	–56 44	1.94	–0.12	B2.5 V	18	–2.1	183	0.087	169	+2 SB	Peacock
α Ind	20 37.7	–47 18	3.11	1.00	K0 III CN–1	32	0.1	101	0.090	39	–1	
α Cyg	20 41.5	+45 17	1.25	0.09	A2 Ia	1	–7.5:	1467	0.005	11	–5 V	**Deneb**
β Pav	20 45.1	–66 12	3.42	0.16	A6 IV	23	0.6	141	0.041	295	10	

TABLE OF BRIGHTEST STARS (continued)

Star Name	RA (2001.5) h m	Dec ° ′	V	B–V	MK Type	π mas	M_v	D ly	μ ″/yr	PA °	RV km/s	Remarks
η Cep	20 45.3	+61 50	3.41	0.91	K0 IV	70	2.7	47	0.827	6	–87	
ε Cyg	20 46.2	+33 58	2.48	1.02	K0 III	45	0.7	72	0.484	47	–11 SB	
ζ Cyg	21 13.1	+30 14	3.21	0.99	G8 IIIa Ba 0.6	22	0.2	151	0.052	181	+17 SB	
α Cep	21 18.6	+62 35	2.45	0.26	A7 Van	67	1.4	49	0.159	71	–10 V	Alderamin
β Cep	21 28.6	+70 34	3.23	–0.20	B1 III	5	–4.0:	815	0.016	38	–8 SB	var: 3.16–3.27, 0.2d; B: 7.8, 13″; Alphirk
β Aqr	21 31.7	–5 34	2.91	0.83	G0 Ib	5	–3.5	612	0.020	105	7	Sadalsuud
ε Peg	21 44.2	+9 52	2.38	1.52	K2 Ib	5	–5.2	672	0.030	81	+5 V	var: 0.7–3.5 (flare in 1972); Enif
δ Cap	21 47.2	–16 08	2.85	0.18	A3mF2 IV:	85	2.2	39	0.394	138	–6 SB	var: 2.83–3.05, 1d; occ.bin: 3.2 + 5.2
γ Gru	21 54.1	–37 22	3.00	–0.08	B8 IV–Vs	16	–1.1	203	0.104	99	–2 V?	
α Aqr	22 05.9	–0 19	2.95	0.97	G2 Ib	4	–4.3	756	0.016	104	+8 V?	Sadalmelik
α Gru	22 08.3	–46 58	1.73	–0.07	B7 Vn	32	–0.9	101	0.198	139	12	Al Nair
θ Peg	22 10.4	+6 12	3.52	0.09	A2mA1 IV–V	34	1.0	97	0.277	83	–6 SB2	Baham
ζ Cep	22 10.9	+58 12	3.39	1.56	K1.5 Ib	4	–4.2	726	0.015	58	–18 SB	
α Tuc	22 18.6	–60 16	2.87	1.39	K3 III	16	–2.2	199	0.071	237	+42 SB	
δ Cep A	22 29.2	+58 25	4.07	0.78	F5–G2 Ib	3	–4.4	950	0.012	67	–16 SB	Cepheid variable: 3.55–4.41, 5.4d
ζ Peg	22 41.5	+10 50	3.41	–0.09	B8.5 III	16	–0.7	208	0.080	96	+7 V?	Homam
β Gru	22 42.8	–46 53	2.07	1.60	M5 III	19	–1.4	170	0.138	92	2	var: 2.0–2.3
η Peg	22 43.1	+30 13	2.93	0.85	G8 II + F0 V	3	–1.2	1113	0.025	148	+4 SB	Matar
ε Gru	22 48.7	–51 19	3.49	0.08	A2 Va	25	0.4	130	0.126	120	0 V	
ι Cep	22 49.7	+66 13	3.51	1.05	K0 III	28	0.6	115	0.137	209	–12	
μ Peg	22 50.1	+24 37	3.51	0.93	G8 III	28	0.8	117	0.152	104	14	
δ Aqr	22 54.9	–15 49	3.27	0.07	A3p (weak 4481)	20	–0.1	159	0.047	242	+18 V	Skat
α PsA	22 57.8	–29 37	1.17	0.15	A3 Va	130	1.6	25	0.373	116	7	Fomalhaut
β Peg	23 03.9	+28 06	2.44	1.66	M2 II–III	16	–1.7	199	0.236	53	+9 V	var: 2.31–2.74; Scheat
α Peg	23 04.8	+15 13	2.49	0.00	A0 III–IV	23	–0.9	140	0.073	121	–4 SB	Markab
γ Cep	23 39.5	+77 38	3.21	1.03	K1 III–IV	72	2.1	4.5	0.168	337	–42	Alrai

THE NEAREST STARS
By Alan H. Batten

The *annual parallax* of a star is the difference between its direction as seen from Earth and the Sun. Astronomers began to look for stellar parallax as soon as they began to take seriously the idea that the Sun, and not Earth, is the centre of the planetary system. The great distances of the other stars ensured, however, that determination of parallax would be beyond the powers of early telescopes. James Bradley (1693–1762) came close to succeeding and correctly deduced that even the largest parallaxes must be less than 2″, but about another century was to elapse before success was achieved. Then, between 1838 and 1840, Bessel, Struve, and Henderson all published trustworthy parallaxes for three different stars. Two of those star systems, α Centauri (Henderson) and 61 Cygni (Bessel), are indeed so close to us that they appear in this table. Struve measured the parallax of Vega, which, although a relatively close neighbour of the Sun, lies some distance beyond the limit adopted here. Progress in measuring other parallaxes remained rather slow until it became possible, toward the end of the 19th century, to apply photography to the problem.

We usually present this table of the nearest stars as a static list, but it is only a snapshot of how the solar neighbourhood is at present. All the stars are moving, relative to each other, and Proxima Centauri neither always has been nor always will be our nearest stellar neighbour. Some years ago, in the *Quarterly Journal of the Royal Astronomical Society*, R.A.J. Matthews discussed how long Proxima has been and will be the nearest star to our Sun. The answer is this: for much longer than recorded human history. He estimates that Proxima first became our closest neighbour about 32 000 years ago. Before then, the system L726-8 was closer, and after another 33 000 years, Ross 248 will be closer. At present, Proxima and α Centauri are still approaching us. In about 27 000 years, they will be at their minimum distance from the Sun, and, assuming they are indeed a bound triple system, will all have parallaxes greater than 1″. Of course, these figures are all approximate because of uncertainties in our knowledge of both the present distances and motions of these stars.

The table emphasizes the relative rarity of massive hot stars. Ignoring the white dwarfs, which are not massive, only Sirius, Procyon, and Altair are hotter and more massive than the Sun, and only α Centauri equals the Sun in these respects. Most of the objects in the table are very faint, cool stars. On the other hand, there is only one example of a "brown dwarf": LP 944-20 (at 16.22 ly in the table). These objects are not massive enough to shine by the light of thermonuclear reactions, and they derive their energy from their gravitational contraction. They are necessarily difficult to detect, and there may be others still to be found within the region covered by this table, including some of the suspected unseen companions to some of the stars. Another known brown dwarf, Gliese 229B, lies just beyond the limit of this table.

The HIPPARCOS-based table

The table has been thoroughly revised to include recent results from HIPPARCOS, the satellite launched to obtain high-precision parallaxes and proper motions for a large number of stars down to an approximate limiting magnitude $V = 12.5$. The results largely confirm earlier ground-based work, at least for nearby stars. Parallaxes are now more precisely known, so the order of stars in the list has been changed—but mostly not by very much, and not at all until ε Eridani. According to HIPPARCOS, however, the next star in this list, CD −36°15693, is a whole light-year nearer than we thought; the last star in the old table, AC +79°3888, now lies beyond the arbitrary adopted limit of 17 ly. HIPPARCOS has added six new stars to the table and recent ground-based observations a seventh (L372-58 or LHS 1565). We still rely on ground-based observations for stars fainter than $V = 12.5$ and for BD +20°2465, close in the sky to the much brighter (but much more distant) γ Leonis. Most data for stars not observed by HIPPARCOS are from the *Yale Catalogue of Trigonometrical Parallaxes*.

We can either incorporate the HIPPARCOS data in weighted means with the ground-based data or assume that the new values are definitive. Although the latter course is somewhat unfair to the earlier work, I have adopted it, to make immediately clear what HIPPARCOS has achieved. There are few significant differences between the results of the two treatments. The satellite's results have been published in 16 volumes, also available on CD-ROM. Table 3.6.1 of Volume 1 lists the 150 stars closest to the Sun measured by HIPPARCOS and contains all the information presented here, except the radial velocities. I have taken all the stars from that table, out to and including Altair, and interspersed stars from the *Yale Catalogue* that have parallaxes within the same limit, and L372-58. Our new table contains 39 single stars, 11 pairs (including common-proper-motion pairs), and 4 triples (α Centauri A and B, with Proxima, o² Eridani A, B and C, G208-45 and 44 which has a known unresolved companion, and L789-6, a pair whose brighter component has recently been found to be a spectroscopic binary), 73 objects in all.

HIPPARCOS parallaxes are quoted in milliarcseconds (mas, 0″.001) rather than the arcseconds formerly used. I have adopted the new units since the elimination of the zero and decimal point before the significant figures makes room for more information, as described below. I have given HIPPARCOS parallaxes to the nearest tenth of a mas. They are not that precise, even though the HIPPARCOS catalogue quotes them to five significant figures. The best determined values have uncertainties of several tenths of a mas, most are uncertain by one or two mas—better than ground-based observations, but not outstandingly so. A few are considerably less certain than good ground-based determinations. Most *Yale Catalogue* parallaxes are given to the nearest tenth of a mas, but I have always rounded them off. Readers, therefore, may tell at once, by the appearance of a figure after the decimal point, whether or not a given parallax was determined from HIPPARCOS. The order in which stars appear, however, is decided by that fourth significant figure, even if it is suppressed. That is why the star LP731-58 appears, at first sight, to be out of order in the table.

Recently we have learned more about LP 944-20, the least luminous object known near the Sun and, as mentioned above, a brown dwarf. The spectral type of such a cool object is necessarily uncertain and M9V is the earliest this can be. There are no good photometric measurements of the visual magnitude of the star, but from measurements in the red and infrared its absolute bolometric magnitude is found to be 14.32. Again, the bolometric correction for so cool an object is uncertain, but I have tried to give an approximate estimate of the likely absolute visual magnitude (17*). Another star in the table that has been in the news recently is BD−15°6290 (at 15.34 ly in the table, and also known as Gliese 876). Precise radial-velocity measurements show that this star has a planet of at least two Jupiter masses and an orbital period of 60.8 days. Although several other stars have been suspected of having unseen companions (including Proxima Centauri and Barnard's star), this is the first definite planetary system found in the solar neighbourhood. The star BD+20°2465 is very close in the sky to a 10.2 magnitude star with almost the same proper motion and a parallax of 183 mas. The two may well form a common-proper-motion pair, but the fainter one at a distance of 17.8 ly falls outside the scope of the present table.

Subject to these comments, the table is arranged as previously. Successive columns give the name or designation of the star, the right ascension (RA) and declination (Dec) for the equinox 2000, the parallax (π) in mas, the distance (*D*) in light-years (if you prefer the scientific unit of parsecs, just take the reciprocal of the parallax; one parsec is approximately 3.26 ly). Subsequent columns give the spectral type (**Sp.**, on the MK system whenever possible), the total proper motion (μ) in *mas*/yr, the position angle of the proper motion (θ) measured in degrees from north through east, the total space motion *(W)* in kilometres per second for those stars with known radial velocities, and the apparent and absolute visual magnitudes *(V* and M_V respectively). Distances of HIPPARCOS stars are given to 0.01 ly and of the others to 0.1 ly. Again, I stress that we rarely know distances that precisely. Except for stars new to the list, I have usually retained the spectral types previously used. The K and M stars were classified by R.F. Wing some years ago. Recent reclassification resulted in few significant changes. Many M-type stars are flare stars, variable in both magnitude and spectral type. The space motion is given the same sign as the radial velocity (+ for recession). This is a little misleading for the two components of BD+59°1915, whose radial velocities are small, and which are travelling together, despite the difference in sign of their space motions. Only the radial velocity of o² Eridani C is given, but B and C are a known orbital pair. Several of the radial velocities are based on only one or two observations and are the least reliable data in the table. The velocities of the centres of mass of the binaries α Centauri, Sirius, Procyon, and 70 Ophiuchi are, however, reasonably well known. I have taken magnitudes from HIPPARCOS whenever possible, except for 70 Ophiuchi, for which the HIPPARCOS value appears to refer to the total light of the system. Magnitudes quoted to only one decimal are not photoelectrically determined.

HIPPARCOS has determined parallaxes and proper motions separately for each component of some binary systems. The components of α Centauri have the same parallax, but those of 61 Cygni are different; the components of Procyon are between them in distance, and BD +59°1915B turns out to be closer than its brighter companion. The two components of the common-proper-motion pair CD−25°10553, included in earlier versions of this table, have been removed because further analysis makes it doubtful that they are as close as previously thought. I have suppressed parallax and proper-motion entries for those components of binaries for which separate determinations were *not* made, sometimes condensing the entry to a single line. Only the B components of two BD stars are in the table: they form optical pairs with their respective brighter and more distant components.

Unfortunately, there is no uniform nomenclature for these predominantly faint stars; for some, names exist in several different systems. Preferred designations are as follows: proper names and Bayer Greek letters, Bonn or Cordoba *Durchmusterungen* numbers and a miscellany of designations for fainter stars; usually I chose the one I thought most familiar. HIP denotes the serial number in the HIPPARCOS catalogue.

With so much new data, some errors are likely to have made their way into the table. Either I or the Editor will be pleased to have them pointed out. The preparation of this table was greatly assisted by access to the HIPPARCOS and SIMBAD catalogues provided by the Canadian Astronomy Data Centre. I am grateful to Ian Ridpath for comments on the 2000 table.

Editor's Note: For more information see "Our Changing Views of the Solar Neighbourhood," Batten, A.H. 1998, *JRASC*, *92*, 231–237.

TABLE OF NEAREST STARS

Name	RA (2000) h m	Dec ° '	π mas	D ly	Sp.	μ mas/y	θ °	W km/s	V	M_V
Sun					G2V				−26.72	4.85
Proxima	14 30	−62 41	772.3	4.22	M5.5Ve	3853	281	−29	11.01	15.45
α Cen A	14 40	−60 50	742.1	4.40	G2V	3709	277	−32	−0.01	4.34
B			742.1	4.40	K1V	3724	285	−32	1.35	5.70
Barnard's	17 58	+4 41	549.0	5.94	M5V	10358	356	−139	9.54	13.24
Wolf 359	10 56	+7 01	419	7.79	M6.5Ve	4702	235	+55	13.46	16.57
BD+36°2147	11 03	+35 58	392.4	8.31	M2+V	4802	187	−104	7.49	10.46
Sirius A	6 45	−16 43	379.2	8.60	A1Vm	1339	204	−18	−1.44	1.45
B					DA2				8.44	11.33
L726–8A	1 39	−17 56	373	8.7	M5.5Ve	3360	80	+52	12.56	15.42
B					M5.5Ve			+53	12.96	15.82
Ross 154	18 50	−23 50	336.5	9.69	M3.6Ve	6660	107	−10	10.37	13.00
Ross 248	23 42	+44 09	316	10.3	M5.5Ve	1588	176	−84	12.27	14.77
ε Eri	3 33	−9 27	310.8	10.50	K2V	977	271	+22	3.72	6.18
CD−36°15693	23 06	−35 51	303.9	10.73	M2V	6896	79	+108	7.35	9.76
Ross 128	11 48	+0 48	299.6	10.89	M4+V	1361	154	−26	11.12	13.50
L789–6ABC	22 39	−15 17	290	11.2	M5+Ve	3256	47	−80	12.32	14.63
61 Cyg A	21 07	+38 45	287.1	11.36	K5V	5281	52	−108	5.20	7.49
Procyon A	7 39	+5 13	285.9	11.41	F5IV–V	1259	215	−21	0.40	2.68
B					DF				10.7	13.0
61 Cyg B	21 07	+38 45	285.4	11.43	K7V	5172	53	−107	6.05	8.33
BD+59°1915B	18 43	+59 38	284.5	11.47	M4V	2312	323	+39	9.70	11.97
A			280.3	11.64	M3.5V	2238	324	−38	8.94	11.18
BD+43°44A	0 18	+44 01	280.3	11.64	M2V	2918	82	+51	8.09	10.33
B					M4V			+54	11.10	13.34
G51–15	08 30	+26 48	276	11.8	M6.5Ve	1270	242		14.81	17.01
ε Ind	22 03	−56 47	275.8	11.83	K4Ve	4704	123	−90	4.69	6.89
τ Cet	1 44	−15 56	274.2	11.90	G8V	1922	296	−37	3.49	5.68
L372–58	3 36	−44 30	273	11.9	M4.5V	831	119		13.03	15.21
L725–32	1 12	−17 00	269.1	12.12	M5.5Ve	1372	62	+37	12.10	14.25
BD+5°1668	7 27	+5 14	263.3	12.39	M4V	3738	171	+72	9.84	11.94
Kapteyn's	5 12	−45 01	255.3	12.78	M1VIp	8671	131	+294	8.86	10.89
CD−39°14192	21 17	−38 52	253.4	12.87	M0Ve	3455	251	+69	6.69	8.71
Krüger 60A	22 28	+57 42	249.5	13.07	M3.5V	990	242	−30	9.59	11.58
B					M4Ve			−37	11.3	13.3
Ross 614A	6 29	−2 49	242.9	13.43	M4Ve	930	132	+30	11.12	13.05
B									14	15.9
BD−12°4523	16 30	−12 40	234.5	13.91	M4V	1189	185	−27	10.10	11.95
CD−37°15492	0 05	−37 21	229.3	14.23	M2V	6100	113	+128	8.56	10.36
Wolf 424A	12 33	+09 03	228	14.3	M5+Ve	1811	277	−38	13.10	14.89
B									13.4	15.2

TABLE OF NEAREST STARS (continued)

Name	RA (2000) Dec h m ° ′		π mas	D ly	Sp.	μ mas/y	θ °	W km/s	V	M_V
BD–13°637B	3 22	–13 16	227.5	14.34		320	201		12.16	13.94
van Maanen's	0 49	+5 23	227.0	14.37	DG	2978	156	+82	12.37	14.15
L1159–16	2 00	+13 01	224	14.6	M4.5Ve	2096	148		12.26	14.01
L143–23	10 45	–61 10	222	14.7	M4	1657	348		13.87	15.60
BD+68°946	17 36	+68 20	220.9	14.77	M3.5V	1310	194	–36	9.15	10.87
LP731–58	10 48	–11 21	221	14.8	M6.5V	1645	158		15.60	17.32
CD–46°11540	17 29	–46 53	220.4	14.80	M3V	1050	147		9.38	11.10
G208–45	19 54	+44 24	220	14.8	M6Ve	616	139		13.99	15.70
44AB					M6Ve	681	142		13.41	15.12
BD–15°6346B	23 07	–14 52	216.5	15.07		140	53		12.24	13.92
L145–141	11 46	–64 50	216.4	15.07	DC:	2688	97		11.50	13.18
G158–27	0 07	–7 34	213	15.3	M5–5.5V	2028	204		13.74	15.38
BD–15°6290	22 53	–14 16	212.7	15.34	M5V	1174	125	+28	10.16	11.80
BD+44°2051A	11 05	+43 32	206.9	15.77	M1V	4511	282	+122	8.82	10.40
B					M5de				14.40	15.93
BD+50°1725	10 11	+49 27	205.2	15.90	K7V	1452	250	–42	6.60	8.16
BD+20°2465	10 20	+19 52	205	15.9	M3.5Ve	491	264	+16	9.43	10.99
HIP 82725	16 55	–62 24	203.0	16.07		308	56		11.72	13.26
HIP 85605	17 30	+24 39	202.7	16.09		362	16		11.39	12.92
CD–49°13515	21 34	–49 00	202.5	16.11	M2V	819	183	+22	8.66	10.19
LP944-20	3 40	–35 26	201	16.22	≥M9V	439	176	+14		17.*
CD–44°11909	17 37	–44 18	198.3	16.43	M4V	1176	217	–66	10.94	12.43
o² EriA	4 15	–7 39	198.2	16.46	K1V	4088	213	–106	4.43	5.92
B					DA	4070	212	–100	9.52	11.01
C					M4.5Ve			(–45)	11.17	12.66
BD+43°4305A	22 47	+44 20	198.1	16.47	M4–Ve	841	237	–20	10.29	11.77
70 Oph A	18 05	+2 30	196.6	16.59	K0V	971	173	–24	4.20	5.67
B					K4V				5.99	7.46
Altair	19 51	+8 52	194.4	16.78	A7V	661	54	–31	0.76	2.20

DOUBLE AND MULTIPLE STARS
By Brian D. Mason

Approximately 85% of stars are found in double or multiple systems. While the first detection of these double systems dates back to the early 17th century, it was not until systematic work with large aperture telescopes was done (notably by William Herschel) that the physical rather than optical nature of these systems was ascertained. The larger the aperture of the telescope, the closer the stars that can be separated under good conditions. The resolving power in arcseconds can be estimated as $120/D$, where D is the diameter of the telescope objective in millimetres.

The double stars in the table (two pages ahead) were selected to cover a wide variety of interests. While wide or slow moving pairs are good for evaluating optical performance or estimating seeing, with the preponderance of inexpensive, large-aperture telescopes and the availability of interferometry for the amateur (see p. 91 of the March 1997 and p. 34 of the November 1996 issues of *Sky & Telescope*), closer systems have been added to the list. Of the 36 listed systems, 10 have separations less than one arcsecond, and ten more between one and two arcseconds. A pair of binaries with white dwarf secondaries (α CMa and α CMi) are included to demonstrate the detection difficulty imposed by a large magnitude difference. Also, one-quarter of the list consists of stars south of the equator. Since many of the stars selected exhibit significant motion, the predicted position angles and separations are given for both 2001.0 and 2002.0. P.A. (Position Angle) is the angular direction of the fainter star (B) from the brighter (A), measured counterclockwise from north (*clockwise* in an optical system having an *odd* number of reflections). Note that data for 2001.0 have been changed for some systems due to improvements in orbits or more recent measurements. Also included are notes on selected systems discussing some of their aspects.

Other double stars appear in THE NEAREST STARS (pp. 231–235) and THE BRIGHTEST STARS (pp. 220–230) sections in this Handbook. For more information about observing double stars, see the aforementioned articles by A. Maurer and H.A. McAlister and the following articles in *Sky & Telescope*: R. Tanguay (Feb. 1999, 116); J. Mullaney (Mar. 1993, 112); J. Ashbrook (Nov. 1980, 379); J. Meeus (Jan. and Feb. 1971, 21, 88); and C.E. Worley (Aug., Sep. & Nov. 1961, 73, 140, 261).

Notes on some double stars in the table:

α Psc: Also known as *Al Rischa*, the cord (binding the fish of Pisces together). Discovered by William Herschel. While the motion of the binary is certain, the characterization of the orbit and it's period are less so.

γ And: The AB system is striking in colour, the brighter star golden, and the secondary blue. The B component is itself a triple system consisting of a close (2.7 day) spectroscopic binary and the wider BC pair also listed in the table. (In the NOVEMBER ALL-SKY MAP on p. 282, γ And is the bright star immediately west of the word "Algol.")

α CMa: The companion to Sirius is a difficult target, usually observable only during periods of exceptional seeing when you can use the highest magnification and move the primary off the field of view. The white dwarf secondary, predicted by Bessel and first observed by Alvan Clark, remains a challenging target for visual observers.

α CMi: Like Sirius, Procyon has a white dwarf companion. As it is significantly closer (1.2" compared to 4.6"), it is correspondingly more difficult to observe. It was first detected in 1840 by the variation in the proper motion of the star, but not resolved until 1896.

ζ **Cnc:** A gorgeous and easily seen triple system, the wide C component is quite bright, and is well separated (6°). While its period is very uncertain, preliminary orbital analysis yields a period of about 1150 years. A new, close component to "C" has been found by infrared adaptive optics.

ξ **UMa:** Many "firsts" are associated with this system. It was one of the first discovered systems (Herschel), one of the first systems whose motion led to the discovery of the physical (rather than optical) nature of double stars (Struve), and was the first star to have an orbit calculated for it (Savary). Always relatively wide, this is a system that will never fail to please, observing season to observing season, having an obvious mean motion of 6° per year. (In the MAY ALL-SKY MAP on p. 279, ξ UMa is the star nearest to the letter "S" in the word "BERENICES.")

α **Cru:** This brilliant double star is located at the bottom of the Southern Cross. According to Allen, it was "discovered to be double by some Jesuit missionaries sent by King Louis XIV to Siam in 1685."

γ **Vir:** This system had the second orbit ever determined for a double star (John Herschel) and was unresolved by him at the Cape in 1836. It reached its widest separation of 6.2″, and is closing to another periastron passage around 2007. Observations over the next ten years will allow its orbit to be refined and become very well characterized.

α **Cen:** Our closest neighbour is a quick moving double star. The brighter component is a near twin of the Sun, while the B component is cooler. The C component, Proxima, which is slightly closer to the Sun, is an extremely faint red dwarf, 2.2° away.

ζ **Her:** While the period of this binary is short, it is also quite close to the Sun (about 30 light-years), so the angular separation is often quite large.

α **Her:** A slow moving, easy to separate system, this binary has a significant colour difference between the two companions, A being reddish and B appearing green. The period is very uncertain. See also the *Variable Star of the Year* in the 1998 *Observer's Handbook*. (In the JULY ALL-SKY MAP on p. 280, α Her is the star in the stick pattern of HERCULES closest to OPHIUCHUS.)

β **Cyg:** Also known as Albireo. If a neophyte doubts the colour of stars, this jewel of the summer sky should change their view. Appearing as brilliant yellow and a deep blue, this wide double has shown no apparent motion. The A component also has a close interferometric companion at a separation of about 0.4″. (In the JULY ALL-SKY MAP on p. 280, β Cyg lies at the south end of the stick pattern for CYGNUS.)

16 Cyg: The fainter component of this double star system, 16 Cygni B (which is the same type as the Sun) has one of the recently discovered extra-solar planets orbiting it. See the March 1998 *Sky & Telescope* (p. 30) article by Marcy and Butler. (In the SEPTEMBER ALL-SKY MAP on p. 281, note the line of three stars just north of the letter "S" in the word "CYGNUS." 16 Cyg lies 1° ENE of the eastern star of this trio.)

τ **Cyg:** This system was originally thought to have a close spectroscopic companion; however, that radial velocity variation is now attributed to the 2–3 hour δ Scuti nature of the A component. The large Δm makes this system challenging.

ζ **Aqr:** This central star in the "Water Jar" asterism saw closest approach in the mid-70s and is now opening up again. The A component also has an astrometric binary with a period of 26 years, described by Wulff Heintz.

TABLE OF DOUBLE AND MULTIPLE STARS

Star	RA (2000) h m	Dec ° ′	Magnitudes comb. A B	2001.0 P.A. °	Sep. ″	2002.0 P.A. °	Sep. ″	Period years
85 Peg	0 02.2	+27 05	5.7 5.8 8.8	193	0.7	204	0.7	26
γ Ari	1 35.3	+19 18	3.8 3.9 3.9	0	7.7			
α Psc*	2 02.0	+02 46	3.9 4.3 5.2	271	1.8	270	1.8	930
γ And AB*	2 03.9	+42 20	2.0 2.1 4.8	64	9.8			
γ And BC*	2 03.9	+42 20	4.5 4.8 6.0	103	0.4	102	0.4	61
γ Per	3 04.8	+53 30	2.9 3.2 4.4	63	0.2	63	0.2	15
33 Ori	5 31.2	+03 18	5.5 5.8 6.9	27	1.9			
α CMa*	6 45.1	−16 43	−1.5 −1.5 8.5	139	5.0	131	5.4	50
α Gem	7 34.6	+31 53	1.6 2.0 2.9	65	4.0	64	4.0	470
α Cmi*	7 39.3	+5 14	0.4 0.4 10.8	77	1.2	84	1.2	41
ζ Cnc AB*	8 12.2	+17 39	5.0 5.6 6.0	77	0.8	71	0.9	60
ι Cnc	8 46.7	+28 46	3.9 4.0 6.6	307	30.6			
10 UMa	9 00.6	+41 47	3.9 4.1 6.1	34	0.7	25	0.7	22
σ² UMa	9 10.4	+67 08	4.8 4.9 7.9	353	3.8	353	3.9	1100
ψ Vel	9 30.7	−40 28	3.6 4.0 4.8	269	0.5	281	0.5	34
γ Leo	10 20.0	+19 50	2.3 2.6 3.8	125	4.4	125	4.4	620
ξ Uma*	11 18.2	+31 32	3.8 4.3 4.8	269	1.8	263	1.8	60
α Cru*	12 26.6	−63 06	0.2 0.8 1.2	114	4.0			
γ Vir*	12 41.7	−1 27	2.7 3.4 3.5	253	1.3	244	1.1	170
α Cen*	14 39.6	−60 50	−0.3 0.0 1.3	223	13.5	224	12.8	80
ε Boo	14 45.0	+27 04	2.0 2.3 4.5	341	2.6			
η CrB	15 23.2	+30 17	5.1 5.6 6.1	70	0.7	79	0.6	42
α Sco	16 29.4	−26 26	1.0 1.0 5.4	274	2.6	274	2.6	880
λ Oph	16 30.9	+01 59	3.6 4.0 5.0	30	1.4	31	1.4	130
ζ Her*	16 41.3	+31 36	3.0 3.0 6.5	341	0.5	296	0.5	34
α Her*	17 14.6	+14 23	3.3 3.5 5.4	105	4.7	104	4.6	3600
τ Oph	18 03.1	−8 11	4.8 5.3 5.8	281	1.7	282	1.7	260
70 Oph	18 05.5	+02 30	3.8 4.0 6.0	145	3.9	143	4.2	88
ε Lyr AB	18 44.3	+39 40	4.7 5.0 6.1	351	2.6	350	2.6	1200
ε Lyr CD	18 44.4	+39 37	4.6 5.2 5.5	82	2.3	82	2.3	720
ζ Sgr	19 02.6	−29 53	2.6 3.3 3.5	194	0.2	149	0.2	21
β Cyg*	19 30.7	+27 58	2.9 3.1 5.1	52	34.3			
16 Cyg*	19 41.8	+50 32	5.3 6.0 6.2	133	39.5			
δ Cyg	19 45.0	+45 08	2.9 2.9 7.9	225	2.6	224	2.6	780
π Aql	19 48.7	+11 49	5.7 6.1 6.9	105	1.4			
β Cap	20 21	−14 47	2.9 3.0 6.1	267	205.			
τ Cyg*	21 14.8	+38 03	3.7 3.8 6.3	298	0.8	291	0.8	50
μ Cyg	21 44.1	+28 45	4.4 4.7 6.1	309	1.8	310	1.8	790
ζ Aqr*	22 28.8	−0 01	3.7 4.4 4.6	184	2.0	182	2.0	760
σ Cas	23 59.0	+55 45	4.8 5.0 7.0	327	3.2			

* See the note concerning this double star on the preceding page.

VARIABLE STARS

BY JANET MATTEI

Variable stars provide information about many stellar properties. Depending upon their type, variables can reveal the mass, radius, temperature, luminosity, internal and external structure, composition, and evolution history of stars. The systematic observation of variable stars is an area in which an amateur astronomer can make a valuable contribution to astronomy.

For beginning observers, charts of the fields of four different types of bright variable stars are printed below. On each chart, the magnitudes (with decimal point omitted) of several suitable comparison stars are shown. A brightness estimate of the variable is made using two comparison stars, one brighter, one fainter than the variable. The magnitude, date, and time of each observation are recorded. When a number of observations have been made, a graph of magnitude versus date can be plotted. The shape of this "light curve" depends on the type of variable. Further information about variable star observing may be obtained from the American Association of Variable Star Observers (AAVSO), 25 Birch St., Cambridge, Massachusetts 02138-1205, U.S.A. (email: **aavso@aavso.org**, web site: **http://www.aavso.org**).

Table 1 is a list of long-period variables, brighter than magnitude 8.0 at maximum, and north of −20°. The first column (the Harvard designation of the star) gives the position for the year 1900: the first four figures give the hours and minutes of right ascension, the last three figures the declination in degrees. The column headed "**Max**" gives the mean maximum magnitude. The period "**Per.**" is in days. The "**Epoch**" gives the predicted date of the earliest maximum occurring this year; by adding multiples of the period to this epoch, the dates of subsequent maxima may be found. These variables may reach maximum two or three weeks before or after the epoch and may remain at maximum for several weeks. This table is prepared using the observations of the American Association of Variable Star Observers.

Table 2 contains stars that are representative of some other types of variables. The data for the preparation of the predicted epoch of maximum or minimum are taken from the *General Catalogue of Variable Stars*, Vols. 1 and II, 4th ed., for eclipsing binaries and RR Lyrae variables from *Rocznik Astronomiczny Obserwatorium Krakowskiego 2000, International Supplement*.

TABLE 1—LONG-PERIOD VARIABLE STARS NORTH OF −20°

Variable		Max m_v	Per. d	Epoch 2001	Variable		Max m_v	Per. d	Epoch 2001
0017+55	T Cas	7.8	445	Jul. 3	1432+27	R Boo	7.2	223	Jan. 2
0018+38	R And	7.0	409	Oct. 2	1517+31	S CrB	7.3	361	Oct. 20
0211+43A	W And	7.0	397	Nov. 1	1546+39	V CrB	7.5	358	Apr. 28
0214−03	o Cet	3.4	332	Sep. 4	1546+15	R Ser	6.9	357	Jan. 14
0228−13	U Cet	7.5	235	Mar. 20	1606+25	RU Her	8.0	484	Dec. 22
0231+33	R Tri	6.2	266	Sep. 2	1621+19	U Her	7.5	406	—
0430+65	T Cam	8.0	374	May 15	1621−12	V Oph	7.5	298	Jan. 7
0455−14	R Lep	6.8	432	Jul. 26	1632+66	R Dra	7.6	245	Jan. 4
0509+53	R Aur	7.7	459	Nov. 16	1647+15	S Her	7.6	307	Jul. 28
0549+20A	U Ori	6.3	372	Dec. 4	1702−15	R Oph	7.9	302	Oct. 10
0617−02	V Mon	7.0	335	Mar. 13	1717+23	RS Her	7.9	219	Feb. 19
0653+55	R Lyn	7.9	379	Mar. 11	1805+31	T Her	8.0	165	May 16
0701+22	R Gem	7.1	370	Nov. 17	1811+36	W Lyr	7.9	196	Mar. 8
0703+10	R CMi	8.0	338	Jul. 5	1833+08	X Oph	6.8	334	Jul. 10
0727+08	S CMi	7.5	332	Oct. 4	1901+08A	R Aql	6.1	270	Jul. 15
0811+12	R Cnc	6.8	362	Oct. 14	1910−17	T Sgr	8.0	392	—
0816+17	V Cnc	7.9	272	Feb. 14	1910−19	R Sgr	7.3	269	Feb. 12
0848+03	S Hya	7.8	257	May 2	1934+49	R Cyg	7.5	426	Dec. 8
0850−08	T Hya	7.8	288	Jun. 3	1940+48	RT Cyg	7.3	190	Mar. 29
0939+34	R LMi	7.1	372	Oct. 11	1946+32	χ Cyg	5.2	407	Feb. 2
0942+11	R Leo	5.8	313	Mar. 11	2016+47	U Cyg	7.2	465	Feb. 25
1037+69	R UMa	7.5	302	Oct. 19	2044−05	T Aqr	7.7	202	Apr. 12
1214−18	R Crv	7.5	317	Mar. 17	2108+68	T Cep	6.0	390	Aug. 6
1220+01	SS Vir	6.8	355	Sep. 21	2137+53	RU Cyg	8.0	234	†
1231+60	T UMa	7.7	257	May 13	2301+10	R Peg	7.8	378	Oct. 24
1233+07	R Vir	6.9	146	Mar. 21	2307+59	V Cas	7.9	228	Aug. 14
1239+61	S UMa	7.8	226	Jun. 1	2315+08	S Peg	8.0	319	Apr. 9
1315+46	V CVn	6.8	192	May 1?	2338−15	R Aqr	6.5	387	Jul. 10
1327+06	S Vir	7.0	378	Dec. 12	2353+50	R Cas	7.0	431	Nov. 14
1344+40	R CVn	7.7	328	Jul. 10	2357−15	W Cet	7.6	351	Nov. 6
1425+84	R Cam	7.9	270	Jun. 17					
1425+39	V Boo	7.9	258	Mar. 14					

† Variability too small to predict.

TABLE 2—OTHER TYPES OF VARIABLE STARS

Variable		Max m_v	Min m_v	Type	Sp. Cl.	Period d	Epoch 2001 UT
0053+81	U Cep	6.7	9.8	Ecl.	B8 + gG2	2.493080	Jan. 1.65*
0258+38	ρ Per	3.3	4.0	Semi R	M4	33–55, 1100	—
0301+40	β Per	2.1	3.3	Ecl.	B8 + G	2.867315	†
0355+12	λ Tau	3.5	4.0	Ecl.	B3	3.952952	Jan. 3.49*
0608+22	η Gem	3.1	3.9	Semi R	M3	233.4	—
0619+07	T Mon	5.6	6.6	Cep	F7–K1	27.024649	Jan. 9.53
0658+20	ζ Gem	3.6	4.2	Cep	F7–G3	10.15073	Jan. 6.86
1544+28	R CrB	5.8	14.8	R CrB	cFpep		—
1710+14	α Her	3.0	4.0	Semi R	M5	50–130, 6 y	—
1842–05	R Sct	5.0	7.0	RV Tau	G0e–K0p	144	—
1846+33	β Lyr	3.4	4.3	Ecl.	B8	12.939854‡	Jan. 5.40*
1922+42	RR Lyr	6.9	8.0	RR Lyr	A2–F1	0.566839	Jan. 1.17
1947+00	η Aql	3.5	4.3	Cep	F6–G4	7.176641	Jan. 6.82
2225+57	δ Cep	3.5	4.4	Cep	F5–G2	5.366341	Jan. 2.02

* Minimum.

† Predictions for all minima in 2001 are given in THE SKY MONTH BY MONTH section.

‡ Changing period (period revised for 2001).

DESCRIPTION OF VARIABLE STAR TYPES

Variable stars are divided into four main classes: (1) pulsating and (2) eruptive variables, where variability is intrinsic due to physical changes in the star or stellar system; (3) eclipsing binary and (4) rotating stars where variability is extrinsic due to an eclipse of one star by another or the effect of stellar rotation. A brief and general description of the major types in each class is given below.

(1) Pulsating Variables

Cepheids are variables that pulsate with periods from 1 to 70 days. They have high luminosity, and the amplitude of light variation ranges from 0.1 to 2 magnitudes. The prototypes of the group are located in open clusters and obey the well-known period–luminosity relation. They are of F spectral class at maximum and G to K at minimum. The later (cooler) the spectral class of a Cepheid, the longer is its period. Typical representative: δ Cephei.

RR Lyrae types are pulsating, giant variables with periods ranging from 0.05 to 1.2 days with amplitude of light variation between 1 and 2 magnitudes. They are usually of A spectral class. Typical representative: RR Lyrae.

RV Tauri types are supergiant variables with a characteristic light curve of alternating deep and shallow minima. The periods, defined as the interval between two deep minima, range from 30 to 150 days. The amplitude of light variation may be as much as 3 magnitudes. Many show long-term cyclic variation of 500 to 9000 days. Generally the spectral classes range from G to K. Typical representative: R Scuti.

Long-period—Mira Ceti variables are giant variables that vary with amplitudes from 2.5 to 5 magnitudes or more. They have well-defined periodicity, ranging from 80 to 1000 days. They show characteristic emission spectra of late spectral classes M, C, and S. Typical representative: o Ceti (Mira).

Semiregular variables are giants or supergiants showing appreciable periodicity accompanied by intervals of irregularity of light variation. The periods range from 30 to 1000 days with amplitudes not more than 1 to 2 magnitudes in general. Typical representative: R Ursae Minoris.

Irregular variables are stars that at times show only a trace of periodicity or none at all. Typical representative: RX Leporis.

(2) Eruptive Variables

Novae are close binary systems consisting of a normal star and a white dwarf that increase 7 to 16 magnitudes in brightness in one to several hundred days. After the outburst, the star fades slowly until the initial brightness is reached in several years or decades. Near maximum brightness, the spectrum is generally similar to A or F giants. Typical representative: CP Puppis (Nova 1942).

Supernovae increase in brightness by 20 or more magnitudes due to a gigantic stellar explosion. The general appearance of the light curve is similar to novae. Typical representative: CM Tauri (Supernova of 1054 AD and the central star of the Crab Nebula).

R Coronae Borealis types are highly luminous variables that have nonperiodic drops in brightness from 1 to 9 magnitudes, due to the formation of "carbon soot" in the stars' atmosphere. The duration of minima varies from a few months to years. Members of this group have F to K and R spectral class. Typical representative: R Coronae Borealis.

U Geminorum types are dwarf novae that have long intervals of quiescence at minimum with sudden rises to maximum. Depending upon the star, the amplitude of eruptions ranges from 2 to 6 magnitudes, and the duration between outbursts tens to thousands of days. Most of these stars are spectroscopic binaries with periods of a few hours. Typical representative: SS Cygni.

Z Camelopardalis types are variables similar to U Gem stars in their physical and spectroscopic properties. They show cyclic variations interrupted by intervals of constant brightness (stillstands) lasting for several cycles, approximately one-third of the way from maximum to minimum. Typical representative: Z Camelopardalis.

(3) Eclipsing Binaries

These are binary stars with the orbital plane lying near the line of sight of the observer. The components periodically eclipse each other, causing a decrease in the apparent brightness of the system. The period of the eclipses coincides with the period of the orbital motion. Typical representative: β Persei (Algol).

(4) Rotating Variables

These are rapidly rotating stars, usually close binary systems, which undergo small amplitude changes in light that may be due to dark or bright spots on their surface. Eclipses may also be present in such systems. Typical representative: RS Canum Venaticorum.

VARIABLE STAR OF THE YEAR—R HYDRAE
By Janet Mattei and John R. Percy

R Hydrae (HR 5080, HD 117287, SpT M7IIIe, RA (2000) 13h 29.7m, Dec (2000) −23°17′) is a remarkable southern Mira star (pulsating red giant)—a challenge for most Canadian observers, but much easier for observers below latitude +40°. Situated 12° south of Spica and 2.5° east of Gamma Hydrae, it stands out because of its red colour, as all Mira stars do. The maximum brightness of individual cycles can vary significantly from magnitude 4.0 to 6.0, and minimum from magnitude 8.5 to 10. This is one of the reasons why this and other Mira type variables need observing over a long period—no two cycles are exactly alike. Also of interest is a "wandering" hump seen on the rising branch of the light curve during some of the cycles. R Hydrae should be near maximum in late June 2001, and visible with binoculars or a small telescope through late spring and early summer. **Figure 1** shows a light curve for R Hydrae, based on observations from the American Association of Variable Star Observers (AAVSO) International Database.

Figure 1 *AAVSO light curve of R Hydrae from 1988 to mid-2000. The points are individual visual observations in the AAVSO International Database. They represent 2842 observations from 198 observers worldwide.*

The variability of R Hydrae was discovered almost 300 years ago, in 1704, by the Italian astronomer G.F. Maraldi, although the star had been recorded as early as 1662, by J. Hevelius. Thanks to the efforts of countless visual observers, the times and magnitudes of maximum brightness have been recorded regularly. These can be used to detect and measure changes in the period of the star. Imagine the analogy of a clock that is speeding up by one second per day. Compared with a perfect clock, it is "ahead" by one second at the end of day 1, by 1 + 2 = 3 s at the end of day 2, by 3 + 3 = 6 s at the end of day 3, by 6 + 4 = 10 s at the end of day 4, etc. The error accumulates as the *square* of the elapsed time; from the exact statistical relation, the period—and its rate of change—can be determined.

Observations of R Hydrae have revealed a remarkable behaviour in this star. From 1785 to 1937, the pulsation period decreased from 495 days to 389 days. Since 1937, it has remained approximately constant. The likely explanation is that R Hydrae has undergone a "helium shell flash." Mira stars are sun-like stars in an advanced stage of evolution. They have exhausted all of the hydrogen fuel in their core. They are now generating energy by fusing helium into carbon, and building up a core of this element. Around the carbon core is a thin shell of helium fusion, which is thermally unstable; every thousand to ten thousand years or so, this shell ignites—it "flashes," and the star shrinks and adjusts its size and luminosity. Since the pulsation period depends on the size, it also changes over a few hundred years.

Of the hundreds of Miras that are being monitored by variable star observers, only a handful show evidence of helium flashes—so far. But these help astronomers test their theories and models of stellar evolution. This is one of many ways in which amateur astronomers, with small telescopes, can contribute to forefront astronomy research.

A finder chart for R Hydrae is shown in **Figure 2**. The visual magnitudes of some constant comparison stars are given to the nearest tenth of a magnitude, with the decimal points removed. You can estimate the brightness of R Hydrae by comparing it with the constant stars and estimating its magnitude by interpolation.

For more information about R Hydrae, see the article by John Isles in *Sky & Telescope*, May 1996, p. 68. For more information about observing this and other variable stars, contact AAVSO (see the contact information on p. 239).

FIGURE 2—FINDER CHART FOR R HYDRAE

Finder chart for R Hydrae and some constant comparison stars in its vicinity. The numbers beside the comparison stars are their visual magnitudes, with the decimal point removed. North is up, and east is to the left. You can estimate the magnitude of R Hydrae, relative to the comparison stars, by interpolation.

STAR CLUSTERS
BY ANTHONY MOFFAT

The study of star clusters is crucial for the understanding of stellar structure and evolution. For most purposes, it can be assumed that the stars seen in a given cluster formed nearly simultaneously from the same parent cloud of gas and dust; thus, the basic factor that distinguishes one star from another is the quantity of matter each contains. Comparing one cluster with another, it is essentially only the age and the chemical composition of their stars that differ. But what makes one cluster *appear* different from another in the sky is mainly the degree of concentration and regularity, the spread in magnitude and colour of the member stars, all of which vary mainly with age, and the total number of stars. Extremely young clusters are often irregular in shape with clumps of newly formed stars, pervaded by lanes of obscuring dust and bright nebulosity (e.g. the Orion Nebula around the Trapezium Cluster), while the oldest clusters, if they were fortunate enough not to have already dissipated or been torn apart by external forces, tend to be symmetric in shape, with only the slower-burning, low-mass stars remaining visible; the massive stars will have spent their nuclear fuel and passed to the degenerate graveyard of white dwarfs, neutron stars, or black holes, depending on their original mass.

The star clusters in the following lists were selected as the most conspicuous. Two types can be recognized: *open* and *globular*. Open clusters often appear as irregular aggregates of tens to thousands of stars, sometimes barely distinguishable from random fluctuations of the general field; they are concentrated toward the Galactic disk and generally contain stars of chemical abundance like the Sun. They range in age from very young to very old.

Sometimes we observe loose, extended groups of very young stars. When precise methods of photometry, spectroscopy, and kinematics are applied, we see that these stars often have a common, but not necessarily strictly coeval, origin. Such loose concentrations of stars are referred to as *associations*. Dynamically, they are generally unbound over time scales of the order of ten million years, being subject to the strong tidal forces of passing clouds and the background Milky Way Galaxy. Often, they contain subconcentrations of young open clusters (e.g. the double cluster h and χ Persei of slightly different ages despite their proximity, in the association Per OB1, which stretches over some $6°$ on the sky) with a strong gradient in age as the star formation process rips through them from one edge to another. In view of their sparse nature, we do not consider it appropriate here to list any of the over 100-odd catalogued associations in the Milky Way Galaxy.

Globular clusters, on the other hand, are highly symmetric, extremely old and rich agglomerations of up to several million stars, distributed throughout the Galactic halo but concentrated toward the centre of the Milky Way Galaxy. Compared to the Sun and other disk stars, they tend to be much less abundant in elements heavier than hydrogen and helium.

The first table includes all well-defined Galactic open clusters with diameters greater than 40' and/or integrated magnitudes brighter than 5.0, as well as the richest clusters and some of special interest. The apparent integrated photographic magnitude (m_{pg}) is from Collinder, the angular diameter (**Diam.**) is generally from Trumpler, and the photographic magnitude of the fifth-brightest star (m_5) is from Shapley, except where in italics, which are new data. The distance (**Dist.**) is mainly from Becker and Fenkart *(Astr. Astrophys. Suppl. 4,* 241 (1971))*. The earliest spectral type of cluster stars (**Sp**) is a measure of the age as follows: expressed in millions of years, O5 = 2, B0 = 8, B5 = 70, A0 = 400, A5 = 1000, F0 = 3000, and F5 = 10 000.

OPEN CLUSTERS

NGC/ other†	RA (2000) h m	Dec ° '	Mag. m_{pg}	Diam. '	m_5	Dist. 10^3 ly	Sp	Remarks
188	0 44.0	+85 21	9.3	14	14.6	5.0	F2	Oldest known
752	1 57.8	+37 41	6.6	45	9.6	1.2	A5	
869	2 19.0	+57 10	4.3	30	9.5	7.0	B1	h Per
884	2 22.4	+57 07	4.4	30	9.5	8.1	B0	χ Per, M supergiants
Perseus	3 22	+48 36	2.3	240	5	0.6	B1	Moving cl.; α Per
Pleiades	3 47.1	+24 08	1.6	120	4.2	0.41	B6	M45, best known
Hyades	4 20	+15 38	0.8	400	3.9	0.15	A2	Moving cl. **, in Taurus
1912	5 28.6	+35 50	7.0	18	9.7	4.6	B5	M38
1976/80	5 35.4	−5 23	2.5	50	5.5	1.3	O5	Trapezium, very young
2099	5 52.4	+32 32	6.2	24	9.7	4.2	B8	M37
2168	6 08.8	+24 21	5.6	29	9.0	2.8	B5	M35
2232	6 26.5	−4 45	4.1	20	7	1.6	B1	
2244	6 32.4	+4 52	5.2	27	8.0	5.3	O5	Rosette, very young
2264	6 41.0	+9 53	4.1	30	8.0	2.4	O8	S Mon
2287	6 47.1	−20 44	5.0	32	8.8	2.2	B4	M41
2362	7 18.8	−24 56	3.8	7	9.4	5.4	O9	τ CMa
2422	7 35.6	−14 30	4.3	30	9.8	1.6	B3	
2437	7 41.8	−14 49	6.6	27	10.8	5.4	B8	M46
2451	7 45.4	−37 58	3.7	37	6	1.0	B5	
2516	7 58.3	−60 54	3.3	50	10.1	1.2	B8	
2546	8 12.5	−37 39	5.0	45	7	2.7	B0	
2632	8 40.1	+20 00	3.9	90	7.5	0.59	A0	Praesepe, M44
IC2391	8 40.3	−53 03	2.6	45	3.5	0.5	B4	
IC2395	8 41.0	−48 11	4.6	20	10.1	2.9	B2	
2682	8 50.4	+11 50	7.4	18	10.8	2.7	F2	M67, very old
3114	10 02.6	−60 07	4.5	37	7	2.8	B5	
IC2602	10 43.3	−64 23	1.6	65	6	0.5	B1	θ Car
Tr16	10 45.2	−59 42	6.7	10	10	9.6	O3	η Car and Nebula
3532	11 06.4	−58 39	3.4	55	8.1	1.4	B8	
3766	11 36.1	−61 37	4.4	12	8.1	5.8	B1	
Coma	12 25.1	+26 06	2.9	300	5.5	0.3	A1	Very sparse
4755	12 53.6	−60 20	5.2	12	7	6.8	B3	κ Cru, "jewel box"
6067	16 13.3	−54 13	6.5	16	10.9	4.7	B3	G, K supergiants
6231	16 54.0	−41 48	3.5	16	7.5	5.8	O9	O supergiants, WR stars
Tr 24	16 57.0	−40 40	3.5	60	7.3	5.2	O5	
6405	17 40.1	−32 13	4.6	26	8.3	1.5	B4	M6
IC4665	17 46.7	+5 44	5.4	50	7	1.1	B8	
6475	17 53.9	−34 48	3.3	50	7.4	0.8	B5	M7
6494	17 56.9	−19 01	5.9	27	10.2	1.4	B8	M23
6523	18 03.1	−24 23	5.2	45	7	5.1	O5	M8, Lagoon Neb.
6611	18 18.9	−13 47	6.6	8	10.6	5.5	O7	M16, nebula
IC4725	18 31.7	−19 15	6.2	35	9.3	2.0	B3	M25, Cepheid U Sgr
IC4756	18 39.3	+5 27	5.4	50	8.5	1.4	A3	
6705	18 51.1	−6 17	6.8	12.5	12	5.6	B8	M11,very rich
Mel 227	20 11.2	−79 19	5.2	60	9	0.8	B9	
IC1396	21 38.9	+57 30	5.1	60	8.5	2.3	O6	Tr 37
7790	23 58.4	+61 13	7.1	4.5	11.7	10.3	B1	Cepheids CEa, CEb and CF Cas

† IC = Index Catalogue; Tr = Trumpler; Mel = Melotte   ** Basic for distance determination

The table below includes all globular clusters with a total apparent photographic magnitude brighter than about 7.5. The data are taken from a compilation by Arp *(Galactic Structure,* ed. Blaauw and Schmidt, U. Chicago, 1965), supplemented by H. S. Hogg's Bibliography *(Publ. David Dunlap Obs. 2,* No. 12, 1963). The apparent diameter **(Diam.)** given contains 90% of the stars, except values in italics, which are from miscellaneous sources. The concentration class **(Conc.)** is such that I is the most compact, XII is least. The integrated spectral type **(Int. Sp.T.)** varies mainly with the abundances, and **m(25)** refers to the mean blue magnitude of the 25 brightest stars excluding the 5 brightest, which are liable to fluctuate more. The number of variables **(No. Var.)** known in the cluster is also given. A more detailed, recent catalogue of fundamental data for galactic globular clusters can be found in reviews by Harris and Racine *(Annual Review of Astronomy and Astrophysics, 17,* 241, 1979) and by Webbink *(IAU Symposium No. 113.,* p. 541, 1985).

GLOBULAR CLUSTERS

NGC	M/ other	RA (2000) h m	Dec ° '	Mag. m_{pg}	Diam. '	Conc.	Int. Sp.T.	m(25)	No. Var.	Dist. 10^3 ly
104†	47 Tuc	0 24.0	−72 04	4.35	*44*	III	G3	13.54	11	16
1851*		5 14.0	−40 01	7.72	*11.5*	II	F7		3	46
2808		9 11.9	−64 47	7.4	*18.8*	1	F8	15.09	4	30
5139†	ω Cen	13 26.8	−47 18	4.5	*65.4*	VIII	F7	13.01	165	17
5272†	3	13 42.2	+28 23	6.86	9.3	VI	F7	14.35	189	35
5904	5	15 18.5	+2 06	6.69	10.7	V	F6	14.07	97	26
6121	4	16 23.6	−26 31	7.05	22.6	IX	G0	13.21	43	14
6205	13	16 41.7	+36 28	6.43	12.9	V	F6	13.85	10	21
6218	12	16 47.1	−1 57	7.58	21.5	IX	F8	14.07	1	24
6254	10	16 57.1	−4 07	7.26	16.2	VII	G1	14.17	3	20
6341	92	17 17.1	+43 09	6.94	12.3	IV	Fl	13.96	16	26
6397		17 40.8	−53 41	6.9	*19*	IX	F5	12.71	3	9
6541†		18 08.0	−43 45	7.5	*23.2*	III	F6	13.45	1	13
6656†	22	18 36.3	−23 55	6.15	26.2	VII	F7	13.73	24	10
6723		18 59.6	−36 37	7.37	11.7	VII	G4	14.32	19	24
6752		19 10.9	−59 59	6.8	*41.9*	VI	F6	13.36	1	17
6809	55	19 40.1	−30 56	6.72	21.1	XI	F5	13.68	6	20
7078*	15	21 30.1	+12 10	6.96	9.4	IV	F2	14.44	103	34
7089	2	21 33.4	−0 50	6.94	6.8	II	F4	14.77	22	40

* Bright, compact X-ray sources were discovered in these clusters in 1975.
† These clusters contain dim X-ray sources.

AN EXAMPLE: M15
AN OLD, METAL-POOR GLOBULAR CLUSTER

The globular cluster M15 is one of the oldest known type of object. At declination +12°, it is well located for observation from both the Northern and Southern Hemispheres.

As confirmed by the recent comprehensive photometric study by P. R. Durrell and W. E. Harris (1993, *AJ, 105,* 1420), M15 is one of the most metal-poor globulars known. (In astronomy, "metal" means any chemical element other than hydrogen and helium.) Situated at a "mere" 34 000 ly in the Galactic halo some 27° below the Cygnus portion of the Galactic disk, its age is 15±3 billion years, a lower limit to the age of the Milky Way Galaxy (and in a broad sense to the universe itself). M15 is also the prototype of Galactic globulars that exhibit a central cusp in brightness, with the HST (Hubble Space Telescope) estimate of its core radius a mere 0.3 ly. Since this is actually larger than expected for a cluster at maximum collapse, it is believed that the M15 core is currently in the process of either collapsing or re-expanding. M15 furthermore enjoys the privilege of harbouring several exotic objects: a planetary nebula, some five millisecond pulsars, and an X-ray binary, not to mention a large number of RR Lyrae variables.

Durrell and Harris' ground-based CCD study was limited to a peripheral region of the cluster. The figure below illustrates the composite colour-magnitude diagram (CMD) they obtained by combining their very faint work with previous studies in larger areas of the brighter stars. Note that this combined CMD prevents it from being representative of the relative populations of stars of different luminosity (e.g. M15 must contain proportionately many more fainter stars than in the figure; see the combined analysis using the Canada-France-Hawaii Telescope and the prerefurbished HST of the central region of M15 to $V = 20$ by Stetson: 1994, *PASP, 106*, 250, Fig. 11). Nevertheless, the figure clearly shows the basic evolutionary phases of stars in globulars, from the faint red dwarf main sequence through the red subgiant and giant branches, jumping to the blue horizontal branch and a relatively sparsely populated asymptotic branch leading up to the potentially brightest red supergiants. Of special note is the extended blue horizontal branch, which has many RR Lyrae variables on its red edge, a signature of low metallicity.

It is interesting to note that, while Durrell and Harris find no "blue stragglers" (between the upper main sequence and the horizontal branch) in their ground-based study of the outer regions of M15, Stetson does find an increasing number of such stars toward the very centre. This is yet another case in which the HST is revealing that it is primarily the dense centres of globular clusters that exhibit significant numbers of blue stragglers, that therefore must be forming by stellar collisions.

Colour-magnitude diagram for the globular cluster M15
(from Durrell and Harris, 1993, AJ, 105, 1420).

AMATEUR SUPERNOVA HUNTING
BY REV. ROBERT EVANS

The first discoveries of supernovae by amateur astronomers were made by using photography through a telescope. However, it has been much simpler and cheaper for amateurs to operate visually, and supernova searching of this kind soon began, often using the most elementary backyard telescopes.

By the 1980s most of the supernovae brighter than 15th magnitude were being found visually by amateurs. In the early 1990s when professional astronomers were beginning to use supernova studies to address major problems in cosmology, they had to rely very much upon amateur searches to provide them with the best and brightest supernovae in nearby galaxies. These nearby supernovae provided much of the benchmark information needed for studying supernovae at remote distances, in order to arrive at independent estimates for the expansion, age, and fate of the universe.

CCD Supernova Hunting

In the last few years, the cost of charge-coupled devices (CCDs) has fallen to the point where many amateurs can afford to use them on computer-controlled telescopes. Some of these amateurs are hunting supernovae with resounding successes. Telescopes with CCDs and computer-control have a number of advantages:

(1) You can observe in locations with some light pollution or in the presence of fairly strong moonlight.

(2) With a computer to direct the telescope to individual galaxies, it is no longer necessary to know the sky well.

(3) With appropriate computer control of the telescope, you can sit in a warm room facing the computer screen.

(4) If your equipment is good enough, it will find supernovae without your presence.

Stars as faint as 18th or 19th magnitude become accessible, which includes most supernovae in nearby galaxies, plus the brighter supernovae in many distant galaxies, out to about 300 million light-years. Indeed, there are so many thousands of galaxies within range of your equipment that you will never have enough time to observe them all! However, you will need reference materials for all the galaxies on your observing list, even if you make the reference images yourself, so that you can tell when a new object appears near a galaxy.

Visual Supernova Hunting

Visual supernova hunting has special requirements, but it has a number of advantages over using a CCD. The requirements are as follows:

(1) A reasonably dark observing site is needed.

(2) Your telescope needs to be easily manageable so that you can locate objects quickly, and the aperture needs to be big enough so that you can see down to about 15th magnitude. You can then observe all the nearby galaxies (out to, say, 100 million light-years). You will then be able to see most supernovae in galaxies out to about 25 million light-years, and the brighter supernovae out to 100 million light-years or more. But, naturally, your chances of success decline with the distance of the galaxy. Fainter supernovae in any given galaxy may be more numerous than the brighter ones, although the latter are the most interesting, scientifically.

(3) As in CCD searches, charts or suitable photographs of all your target galaxies are needed, so that you can tell when a new object appears.

The advantages of visual searching are the following:

(**1**) You can be successful with much less expensive equipment than is needed for CCD work.

(**2**) An experienced visual observer usually knows the location and the normal appearance of many target galaxies and thus can work through observations of galaxies at 10 times the speed of anyone using a CCD on an amateur telescope. Professional-standard CCDs are quicker, but are still much more expensive than ones used by amateurs.

(**3**) You become very familiar with the night sky. Personally, I think this is a great benefit of visual searching.

(**4**) Amateurs who rely on computers to find galaxies are deceived by technology into being ignorant of the sky. Thus, when the technology fails (as it does from time to time), the search halts since the observer does not know where to locate target galaxies. A visual observer who knows the sky is immune to this problem.

Verification and Reporting

Verification of any suspected new discovery is vitally important. The first step is to check any suspect against all available photographs, CCD images, or charts of that galaxy. Measure carefully the offset of the new star from the nucleus of the galaxy. Watch the object for any possible movement against nearby stars. Note the time of your discovery (UT). It is necessary to have a team of other observers who can make independent observations of the new object, and who will do so immediately, if asked. These other observers must also have enough galaxy resources so that they can eliminate anything that is not a supernova, and they should live in a number of locations in case bad weather puts any one observer out of action.

The Central Bureau for Astronomical Telegrams has issued instructions describing how much verification they want about any possible new supernova, and these should be consulted. CCD observers need at least five observations covering 24 hours. A visual observer should have independent observations by people who know what they are doing. Even after the Central Bureau has been notified, spectra will probably need to be obtained through one of the main observatories before the Bureau will finally announce a discovery.

When the Central Bureau is notified, full details of all observations of the new object should be provided: the name and location of the person making the report, the discoverer's name and location, details of the reference materials consulted, details concerning the equipment used, universal time of all observations, name and position of the galaxy, offset and brightness of the supernova, and similar details about each verifying observation. Observers who are not already known at the Bureau should take special care and be especially thorough in detailing and supporting their report. For all discoveries, the email address of the Central Bureau is cbat@cfa.harvard.edu.

Much helpful advice is available in the *AAVSO Supernova Search Manual*, which is available from the AAVSO, 25 Birch Street, Cambridge, MA 02138, USA, for the cost of postage only. It can also be downloaded through the Internet (aavso@aavso.org).

Editor's Note: Robert Evans holds the all-time record for visual discoveries of supernovae: 32. His first discovery was in 1981. Ten of these were found using a 250-mm telescope, one using a 310-mm telescope, 18 with a 410-mm instrument (all three telescopes were "back-yard" variety newtonians), and 3 using the 1.02-m telescope at Siding Spring Observatory (Australian National University). In addition, he has discovered 4 supernovae (plus a comet!) on U.K. Schmidt films especially exposed by Anglo Australian Observatory staff in a Pro-Am project which Evans shared with Dr. Brian Schmidt of Mount Stromlo Observatory, and with Robert McNaught.

EXPIRED STARS
BY ROY BISHOP

Stars are where the action is, and the action is fuelled by gravitation and thermonuclear fusion. Gravitation, the midwife and undertaker, forms a star, heats the star to the temperatures necessary to ignite successive stages of fusion reactions, and when nuclear fuel runs out, crushes the ashes of the star into one of three final states: white dwarf, neutron star, or black hole. Thermonuclear fusion merely delays the onset of further collapse and higher temperatures. In the case of our Sun, the first and by far the longest delay, the "hang-up" provided by hydrogen-to-helium fusion, is already half over.

White Dwarfs

Stars comparable to our Sun have insufficient gravity to reach the temperatures necessary to form nuclei heavier than carbon or oxygen. When the thermal support pressure generated by fusion wanes, gravity gradually crushes the central portion of the star. If the mass of this core is less than 1.4 solar masses (a limit discovered by a leading astrophysicist of the 20th century, Subramanyan Chandrasekhar), the collapse halts at a very hot, Earth-sized remnant known as a white dwarf. At this point the squeeze of gravity is offset by *electron degeneracy pressure*, an intrinsic aspect of the wave–particle nature of matter, and the same pressure responsible for the stability and size of an atom. However, in the case of a white dwarf the pressure is such that the electrons are not tied to individual atomic nuclei but occupy the whole star. In this sense, the star has become a giant atom. In physics jargon: electrons are fermions (i.e. they obey Fermi–Dirac quantum statistics) and, hence, abide by the Pauli Exclusion Principle, which dictates that no two electrons can occupy the same quantum state. This results in an immense pressure, sufficient to prevent further collapse, provided the mass is less than the Chandrasekhar limit. White dwarf diameters are about 1% that of our Sun, which has a nearly water-like average density (1 g/cm^3). Thus a cubic centimetre of white dwarf material has a mass near $(100)^3$ g or one tonne (like a Honda Civic crushed into a sugar cube).

Because of their immense thermal energy and small surface area, white dwarfs cool extremely slowly. Also, they are intrinsically very faint and thus only those close to the solar system can be seen.

Only one white dwarf is easily observable with a small telescope: **Omicron 2 Eridani B** (also designated 40 Eridani B), located 16.5 light-years from Earth. Omicron 2 Eridani A, the bright (mag. 4.4) companion to the dim (mag. 9.5) white dwarf, is shown on the JANUARY ALL-SKY CHART on p. 277: o^2 Eri A is the eastern (left-hand) member of the close pair of stars located due west of the word "Rigel." Omicron 2 Eridani B, the white dwarf, is located only 83″ east-southeast of o^2 Eri A (position angle ≈110°). Remarkably, stars A and B are accompanied by a third star, a faint (mag. 11.2) red dwarf star, o^2 Eri C, which resides only 9″ north of B. (There is a brighter and closer white dwarf, the companion of Sirius, α CMa B, but it is usually lost in the glare of Sirius. See THE NEAREST STARS (pp. 231–235) and DOUBLE AND MULTIPLE STARS (pp. 236–238) for more information on both of these stellar systems.)

For the observer with a small telescope, o^2 Eri B is the only Earth-sized object visible in the depths of interstellar space, the only visible object with a mass density far exceeding that of ordinary matter, the only accessible star no longer powered by nuclear reactions, the only star that has expired and can still be seen.

Neutron Stars

For a large star of about eight or more solar masses, energy-releasing reactions end in its centre with the fusion of silicon nuclei into iron. Iron has the most tightly bound nucleus (per nuclear particle) and, hence, is no good as a fuel for further fusion. Electron degeneracy pressure supports the inert iron core until silicon fusion in a surrounding shell supplies enough additional iron to push the inert core over the Chandrasekhar limit. Gravity then overwhelms electron degeneracy pressure and the core collapses in less than a second. Gravitation-induced temperatures rise past 10^{10} K, sufficient to disassemble heavy nuclei synthesized over the life of the star. This absorbs energy, accelerating the collapse. Also, electrons attain sufficient energy to combine with protons to form neutrons and neutrinos, another energy-absorbing reaction that also removes electrons, further hastening the collapse.

Provided the infalling mass is less than about three solar masses, like a hammer striking an anvil, when the core reaches a diameter of about 20 km the infall is violently arrested by a combination of *neutron* degeneracy pressure and the short-range repulsive nature of the strong nuclear force, the same agents that govern the size and structure of the nuclei of atoms of ordinary matter. With a diameter 500 times smaller than that of a white dwarf, the density at this stage is $(500)^3$ larger, 100 million tonnes per cubic centimetre (like an aircraft carrier crushed to the size of the ball of a ballpoint pen). This is the density of ordinary atomic nuclei. The star's core has become effectively a gigantic nucleus, composed primarily of neutrons.

The abrupt rebound of the nearly rigid central core reverses the infall of the outer layers, turning the implosion into a spectacular explosion, a Type II supernova. The subsequent steps are complex and not yet well understood, but appear to involve interactions with the immense numbers of neutrinos generated in the neutron production. The gravitational energy released in the sudden collapse of the couple of solar masses now locked in the central neutron star is about 10^{46} J. This is far more energy than our Sun will produce in its entire 10-billion-year lifetime.

Over the next several thousand years, the remnants of the outer layers of the star form an expanding, glowing cloud of gas and dust, seeding interstellar space with the heavy chemical elements (oxygen, silicon, iron, uranium, etc.) synthesized in its outer layers both before and during the supernova explosion. The potassium ions moving in the neurons of your brain as you read these words emerged from such a conflagration some 5 billion years ago.

No neutron stars are visible in a small telescope, although one is *indirectly* visible in the Crab Nebula, M1. The Crab supernova was a bright naked-eye star in the skies of Earth in the year 1054 AD, although it had taken 6000 years for the light of the explosion to reach our planet. The nebula we see today is the expanding debris cloud as it was nearly 1000 years after the initial explosion.

The Crab Nebula glows across the electromagnetic spectrum, from radio waves to gamma rays, powered by the energy contained in the gravitational field and the rapid but decreasing spin of the neutron star at its centre. The glow of the debris cloud is like the glow of a red-hot disk brake slowing the spin of a wheel. The visible light from the cloud is *synchrotron radiation* emitted by electrons as they spiral in the tangled magnetic field of the neutron star. Nowhere else in the heavens is such an exotic light visible in a small telescope, polarized light with the brilliance of a thousand suns, emitted not by atoms but by free electrons being flung about by a spinning neutron star. The neutron star itself is known as a *pulsar* because it flashes 30 times per second, in step with its spin. However, even if the Crab pulsar were bright enough to be visible in a small telescope, the flashing would not be apparent because, as in a motion picture or cathode-ray tube monitor, the flicker is too rapid for the eye to follow.

Colour photographs of the Crab Nebula reveal a celestial gift: a package of bluish synchrotron radiation wrapped in the loops of a tattered red ribbon—fragments of the shattered star, fluorescing in hydrogen-alpha light. Unfortunately, the luminance of the fluorescence is below the threshold for retinal cone vision, and rod vision is blind to H-alpha light. Thus all we can see is the ghostly cloud of synchrotron radiation.

The Crab Nebula is located 1° northwest of the star at the tip of the east horn of the constellation Taurus, ζ Tau. In the JANUARY ALL-SKY CHART on p. 277, the nebula is the tiny circle of dots 5 mm to the right of the cross marking the summer solstice (SS). In a telescope the nebula appears merely as a small glowing cloud, but to the knowledgeable observer this synchrotron radiation brake of a spinning neutron star is an object for profound contemplation.

Black Holes

Stars whose masses are greater than about 20 suns likely retain more than 3 solar masses in their imploding cores. This is sufficient that gravitation will overwhelm not only the degeneracy pressure of electrons, but also the highly incompressible nature of nuclear matter. Within seconds, space-time itself closes around the imploding stellar core, removing all but the core's gravitational field from the observable universe. The star has become a black hole.

The earliest and best candidate for a stellar black hole is **Cygnus X-1**, one of the strongest galactic X-ray sources in the sky. Cygnus X-1 is the invisible companion of a star that can be seen in a small telescope: HDE 226868, an O9.7Iab star, a very luminous very hot supergiant located several thousand light-years from the Sun. It orbits its nearby, unseen companion with a 5.6-day period. The mass of the companion is between 10 and 16 solar masses, far too large for it to be a white dwarf or neutron star. X-rays are generated as material from the supergiant falls toward the invisible companion. The X-rays extend to energies of 100 keV and vary on time scales as short as milliseconds, indicative of a very compact companion.

At 9th magnitude, the supergiant HDE 226868 is visible in any small telescope. It is less than half a degree from the 4th magnitude star Eta Cygni. Eta Cygni is the star in the neck of the swan, next to the "C" in CYGNUS on the SEPTEMBER ALL-SKY CHART on p. 281. Any low magnification will more than encompass the field

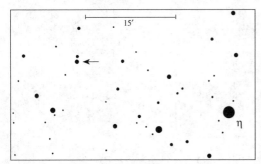

shown in the **finder chart** at the left. North is upward, Eta Cygni is at the lower right, and HDE 226868 is indicated by the small arrow. The chart magnitude limit is about 13. Although HDE 226868 is a blue supergiant, in telescopes of sufficient aperture this star appears orange because of interstellar dust between us and the star.

All that is to be seen is the hot supergiant, but the view will be worth the search if you know that at this same location in the field of your telescope lurks one of the most likely candidates for a black hole, a knot in the fabric of space-time where a giant star has vanished. No painting, computer simulation, or Hollywood movie can match this observation.

NEBULAE AND GALAXIES
GALACTIC NEBULAE
By William Herbst

The following objects were selected from the brightest and largest of the various classes to illustrate the different types of interactions between stars and interstellar matter in our galaxy. *Emission regions* (HII) are excited by the strong ultraviolet flux of young, hot stars and are characterized by the lines of hydrogen in their spectra. *Reflection nebulae* (Ref) result from the diffusion of starlight by clouds of interstellar dust. At certain stages of their evolution stars become unstable and explode, shedding their outer layers into what becomes a *planetary nebula* (Pl) or a *supernova remnant* (SN). *Protostellar nebulae* (PrS) are objects still poorly understood; they are somewhat similar to the reflection nebulae, but their associated stars, often variable, are very luminous infrared stars which may be in the earliest stages of stellar evolution. Also included in the selection are three *extended complexes* (Comp) of special interest for their rich population of dark and bright nebulosities of various types. In the table S is the optical surface brightness in magnitude per square second of arc of representative regions of the nebula, and $m*$ is the magnitude of the associated star.

NGC	M	Con	RA (2000) h m	Dec ° ′	Type	Size ′	S mag/sq″	$m*$	Dist. 10^3 ly	Remarks
1435		Tau	3 47.5	+24 05	Ref	15	20	4	0.4	Merope nebula
1535		Eri	4 14.2	−12 45	Pl	0.5	17	12		
1952	1	Tau	5 34.5	+22 01	SN	5	19	16v	4	"Crab" + pulsar
1976	42	Ori	5 35.3	−5 24	HII	30	18	4	1.5	Orion Nebula
2070		Dor	5 38.6	−69 05	HII	20	—	13	200	Tarantula Neb.
ζ Ori		Ori	5 40.8	−1 56	Comp	2°			1.5	Incl. "Horsehead"
2068	78	Ori	5 46.8	+0 02	Ref	5	20		1.5	
1C443		Gem	6 17.6	+22 36	SN	40			2	
2244		Mon	6 32.4	+4 52	HII	50	21	7	3	Rosette Neb.
2261		Mon	6 39.1	+8 43	PrS	2		12v	4	Hubble's Var. Neb.
2392		Gem	7 29.2	+2054	Pl	0.3	18	10	10	Clown Face Neb.
2626		Vel	8 35.6	−40 38	Ref	2	—	10	3	
3132		Vel	10 07.0	−40 25	Pl	1	17	10	—	Eight-Burst
3324		Car	10 37.5	−58 38	HII	15	—	8	9	
3372		Car	10 45.1	−59 41	HII	80	—	6v	9	Carina Neb.
3503		Car	11 01.3	−60 43	Ref	3	—	11	9	
3587	97	UMa	11 14.8	+55 01	Pl	3	21	13	12	Owl Nebula
—		Cru	12 51	−63	Dark	6°	—	—	0.5	Coal Sack
5189		Mus	13 33.8	−66 00	HII	150	—	10	—	
ρ Oph		Oph	16 25.6	−23 27	Comp	4°			0.5	Bright + dark neb.
6514	20	Sgr	18 02.4	−23 02	HII	15	19		3.5	Trifid Nebula
6523	8	Sgr	18 03.6	−24 23	HII	40	18		4.5	Lagoon Nebula
6543		Dra	17 58.6	+66 37	Pl	0.4	15	11	3.5	
6618	17	Sgr	18 20.9	−16 11	HII	20	19		3	Horseshoe Neb.
6720	57	Lyr	18 53.6	+33 03	Pl	1.2	18	15	5	Ring Nebula
6726		CrA	19 01.7	−36 54	PrS	5	—	7	0.5	
6853	27	Vul	19 59.5	+22 43	Pl	7	19	13	3.5	Dumbbell Neb.
6888		Cyg	20 12.3	+38 25	HII	15				
γ Cyg		Cyg	20 22.2	+40 16	Comp	6°				HII + dark neb.
6960/95		Cyg	20 45.6	+30 42	SN	150			2.5	Cygnus loop
7000		Cyg	20 58.9	+44 19	HII	100	22		3.5	N. America Neb.
7009		Aqr	21 04.1	−11 23	Pl	0.5	16	12	3	Saturn Nebula
7027		Cyg	21 07.1	+42 14	Pl	0.2	15	13		
7129		Cep	21 43.0	+65 06	Ref	3	21	10	2.5	Small cluster
7293		Aqr	22 29.6	−20 48	Pl	13	22	13		Helix Nebula

DEEP-SKY OBSERVING HINTS
BY ALAN DYER

In the 1960s and 1970s, few observers owned telescopes larger than 200-mm aperture. Today, 250-mm to 600-mm Dobsonian-mounted reflectors are commonplace. Using computerized telescopes, observers can now find thousands of objects at the push of a button. As a result, deep-sky observing has soared in popularity.

However, owners of less sophisticated, small-aperture instruments shouldn't think they are shut out of deep-sky viewing. In a dark sky, an 80-mm to 100-mm telescope will show all the Messier objects, and reveal hundreds of brighter NGC (New General Catalogue) objects. In fact, many large objects are best seen in fast (f/4 to f/6), small-aperture telescopes or in giant 70-mm and 80-mm binoculars. Contrary to popular belief, even slow f-ratio instruments (f/11 to f/16) are useful; their only disadvantage is the difficulty of achieving a low-power wide field. No matter what telescope you use, here are a few techniques for getting the most out of a night of deep-sky exploring:

- Always plan each night's observing. Prepare a list of a dozen or so objects for the night. Hunt them down on star charts or with computer programs first during the day to become familiar with their location.
- Seek out dark skies. A black sky improves contrast and makes up for a lack of aperture.
- To preserve night vision, always use a dim red flashlight for reading charts at the telescope.
- Avoid prolonged exposure to bright sunlight earlier in the day (such as a day at the beach). It will reduce your ability to dark adapt and make for tired eyes at night.
- Use averted vision. Look to one side of an object to place it on a more sensitive part of the retina.
- Another technique for picking out faint objects is to jiggle the telescope (and the image) slightly.
- Don't be afraid to use high power. It often brings out small, faint objects such as planetary nebulas and galaxies, plus resolves detail in globulars, small rich open clusters, and bright galaxies.
- Use a nebula filter on emission and planetary nebulas. Even in a dark sky, filters can dramatically enhance the view of these kinds of objects, often making obvious an otherwise elusive nebula.
- Be comfortable. Sit down while at the eyepiece and be sure to dress warmly.
- Collimate and clean your optics. A poorly maintained telescope will produce distorted star images, reduce image contrast, and make it more difficult to see faint stars and other threshold objects.
- Don't expect to use analog setting circles. In a portable telescope "dial-type" circles will rarely be accurate.
- Digital setting circles and "Go To" telescopes can find objects precisely. While they are wonderful observing aids, they can overwhelm observers with thousands of possible targets, often supplying scant information about each one. When making a list for a night's viewing, books such as the three-volume *Burnham's Celestial Handbook* and the two-volume *Night Sky Observer's Guide* by Kepple and Sanner are still the best guides.
- Don't be in a rush to check off targets. Take time to examine each object. Take notes or make drawings. Both will help train your eye to see subtle detail; you'll learn to see the most through your telescope.

THE MESSIER CATALOGUE
By Alan Dyer

Charles Messier's Catalogue provides a selection of the best and brightest deep-sky wonders for Northern Hemisphere viewers. Messier compiled his list in the late 1700s to aid prospective comet hunters. Some of these objects he discovered himself, some were first seen by other astronomers of the day, while a few (the Pleiades and the Beehive) were known since antiquity. The Messier numbers do not follow an ordered sequence across the sky. Rather, they are numbered in the order he discovered and catalogued them. Although he intended to, Messier never did publish a list with entries renumbered in order of right ascension.

In our version of the Messier Catalogue, we've listed the objects by season *for the evening observer*, grouping the objects within their respective constellations. The constellations are then listed roughly in order of increasing right ascension, that is constellations farther to the east and which rise later in the night are farther down the list. This is to help plan the sequence of an evening's Messier hunt.

The identity of some Messier objects is controversial. There is evidence that M91 and M102 are mistaken observations of M58 and M101, respectively. M104 and M109 were found by a colleague, Pierre Mechain, and reported to Messier for inclusion in his Catalogue. NGC 205, one of the companion galaxies to M31, the Andromeda Galaxy, was apparently found by Messier but never included in his Catalogue. Modern-day observers have dubbed this object M110. In our list, we have included 110 entries, including two objects that some have suggested as alternative candidates for M91 and M102.

Modern-day Messier hunters often wonder what telescopes Messier used. The largest were 190-mm and 200-mm reflectors. However, their speculum metal mirrors would have had the equivalent light gathering power of a modern 80-mm to 100-mm reflector. He also used a number of 90-mm refractors. Today, a dark site and a good 80-mm refractor or 100-mm reflector should be sufficient for completing the entire list. Objects M6 and M7 are the most southerly, while M74 and M76 are often considered the faintest and most difficult. M83's low altitude and diffuse appearance make it a challenge for Canadian observers north of 50° latitude

The columns contain the Messier number, the object's NGC (New General Catalogue) number, the constellation, the type of object, its epoch 2000 coordinates, visual magnitude m_v, and angular size in minutes of arc (planetary nebula sizes are given in seconds of arc ″). Entries marked "!!" are showpiece objects. OC = open cluster; GC = globular cluster; PN = planetary nebula; EN = emission nebula; RN = reflection nebula; E/RN = combination of emission and reflection nebula; SNR = supernova remnant; G = galaxy (E = elliptical, I = irregular, SA = normal spiral, SB = barred spiral, S0 = lenticular). Data are taken from *The Deep Sky Field Guide to Uranometria 2000.0* (published by Willmann-Bell, Inc., 1993), compiled by Murray Cragin, James Lucyk, and Barry Rappaport from a variety of contemporary catalogues. Some sizes have been rounded to two significant figures. Also recommended as an excellent guide is *The Messier Objects*, by Stephen James O'Meara (Cambridge University Press, 1998).

R.A.S.C. members who observe all 110 objects on this list
or all 110 objects on the following Finest NGC Objects list
are eligible for an R.A.S.C. "Messier Certificate" or "NGC certificate."
Contact your local Centre or the R.A.S.C. National Office for details.

NUMERICAL LISTING OF MESSIER OBJECTS

M#	Sky	Con	M#	Sky	Con	M#	Sky	Con	M#	Sky	Con	M#	Sky	Con
1	WIN	Tau	23	SUM	Sgr	45	WIN	Tau	67	SPR	Cnc	89	SPR	Vir
2	AUT	Aqr	24	SUM	Sgr	46	WIN	Pup	68	SPR	Hya	90	SPR	Vir
3	SPR	CVn	25	SUM	Sgr	47	WIN	Pup	69	SUM	Sgr	91	SPR	Com
4	SUM	Sco	26	SUM	Sct	48	WIN	Hya	70	SUM	Sgr	92	SUM	Her
5	SPR	Ser	27	SUM	Vul	49	SPR	Vir	71	SUM	Sge	93	WIN	Pup
6	SUM	Sco	28	SUM	Sgr	50	WIN	Mon	72	AUT	Aqr	94	SPR	CVn
7	SUM	Sco	29	SUM	Cyg	51	SPR	CVn	73	AUT	Aqr	95	SPR	Leo
8	SUM	Sgr	30	AUT	Cap	52	AUT	Cas	74	AUT	Psc	96	SPR	Leo
9	SUM	Oph	31	AUT	And	53	SPR	Com	75	SUM	Sgr	97	SPR	UMa
10	SUM	Oph	32	AUT	And	54	SUM	Sgr	76	AUT	Per	98	SPR	Com
11	SUM	Sct	33	AUT	Tri	55	SUM	Sgr	77	AUT	Cet	99	SPR	Com
12	SUM	Oph	34	AUT	Per	56	SUM	Lyr	78	WIN	Ori	100	SPR	Com
13	SUM	Her	35	WIN	Gem	57	SUM	Lyr	79	WIN	Lep	101	SPR	UMa
14	SUM	Oph	36	WIN	Aur	58	SPR	Vir	80	SUM	Sco	102	SPR	Dra?
15	AUT	Peg	37	WIN	Aur	59	SPR	Vir	81	SPR	UMa	103	AUT	Cas
16	SUM	Ser	38	WIN	Aur	60	SPR	Vir	82	SPR	UMa	104	SPR	Vir
17	SUM	Sgr	39	SUM	Cyg	61	SPR	Vir	83	SPR	Hya	105	SPR	Leo
18	SUM	Sgr	40	SPR	UMa	62	SUM	Oph	84	SPR	Vir	106	SPR	CVn
19	SUM	Oph	41	WIN	CMa	63	SPR	CVn	85	SPR	Com	107	SUM	Oph
20	SUM	Sgr	42	WIN	Ori	64	SPR	Com	86	SPR	Vir	108	SPR	UM
21	SUM	Sgr	43	WIN	Ori	65	SPR	Leo	87	SPR	Vir	109	SPR	UMa
22	SUM	Sgr	44	SPR	Cnc	66	SPR	Leo	88	SPR	Com	110	AUT	And

SEASONAL LISTING OF MESSIER OBJECTS

M#	NGC	Con	Type	RA (2000) h m	Dec ° '	m_v	Size '	Remarks
The Winter Sky								
1	1952	Tau	SNR	5 34.5	+22 01	8.4	6 × 4	!! famous Crab Neb. supernova remnant
45	—	Tau	OC	3 47.0	+24 07	1.2	110	!! Pleiades; look for subtle nebulosity
36	1960	Aur	OC	5 36.1	+34 08	6.0	12	bright but scattered group; use low pow.
37	2099	Aur	OC	5 52.4	+32 33	5.6	20	!! finest of 3 Auriga clusters; very rich
38	1912	Aur	OC	5 28.7	+35 50	6.4	21	look for small cluster NGC 1907 1/2° S
42	1976	Ori	E/RN	5 35.4	−5 27	—	65 × 60	!! Orion Nebula; finest in northern sky
43	1982	Ori	E/RN	5 35.6	−5 16	—	20 × 15	detached part of Orion Nebula
78	2068	Ori	RN	5 46.7	+0 03	—	8 × 6	bright featureless reflection nebula
79	1904	Lep	GC	5 24.5	−24 33	7.8	8.7	20-cm telescope needed to resolve
35	2168	Gem	OC	6 08.9	+24 20	5.1	28	!! look for sm. cluster NGC 2158 1/4° S
41	2287	CMa	OC	6 47.0	−20 44	4.5	38	4° south of Sirius; bright but coarse
50	2323	Mon	OC	7 03.2	−8 20	5.9	16	between Sirius & Procyon; use low mag.
46	2437	Pup	OC	7 41.8	−14 49	6.1	27	!! contains planetary nebula NGC 2438
47	2422	Pup	OC	7 36.6	−14 30	4.4	29	coarse cluster 1.5° west of M46
93	2447	Pup	OC	7 44.6	−23 52	≈6.2	22	compact, bright cluster; fairly rich
48	2548	Hya	OC	8 13.8	−5 48	5.8	54	former "lost" Messier; large, sparse cl.

SEASONAL LISTING OF MESSIER OBJECTS (continued)

M#	NGC	Con	Type	RA (2000) Dec h m ° '	m_v	Size '	Remarks
The Spring Sky							
44	2632	Cnc	OC	8 40.1 +19 59	3.1	95	!! Beehive or Praesepe; use low power
67	2682	Cnc	OC	8 50.4 +11 49	6.9	29	one of the oldest star clusters known
40	—	UMa	2 stars	12 22.4 +58 05	8.0	—	double star Winnecke 4; separation 50″
81	3031	UMa	G-SAab	9 55.6 +69 04	6.9	24 × 13	!! bright spiral visible in binoculars
82	3034	UMa	G-I0	9 55.8 +69 41	8.4	12 × 6	!! the "exploding" galaxy; M81 1/2° S
97	3587	UMa	PN	11 14.8 +55 01	9.9	194″	!! Owl Nebula; distinct grey oval
101	5457	UMa	G-SABcd	14 03.2 +54 21	7.9	26 × 26	!! Pinwheel Gal.; diffuse face-on spiral
108	3556	UMa	G-SBcd	11 11.5 +55 40	10.0	8.1 × 2.1	nearly edge-on; paired with M97 3/4° SE
109	3992	UMa	G-SBbc	11 57.6 +53 23	9.8	7.6 × 4.3	barred spiral near γ UMa
65	3623	Leo	G-SABa	11 18.9 +13 05	9.3	8.7 × 2.2	!! bright elongated spiral
66	3627	Leo	G-SABb	11 20.2 +12 59	8.9	8.2 × 3.9	!! M65 and NGC 3628 in same field
95	3351	Leo	G-SBb	10 44.0 +11 42	9.7	7.8 × 4.6	bright barred spiral
96	3368	Leo	G-SABab	10 46.8 +11 49	9.2	6.9 × 4.6	M95 in same field
105	3379	Leo	G-E1	10 47.8 +12 35	9.3	3.9 × 3.9	bright elliptical near M95 and M96
53	5024	Com	GC	13 12.9 +18 10	7.5	12.6	15-cm telescope needed to resolve
64	4826	Com	G-SAab	12 56.7 +21 41	8.5	9.2 × 4.6	!! Black Eye Gal.; eye needs big scope
85	4382	Com	G-SA0+	12 25.4 +18 11	9.1	7.5 × 5.7	bright elliptical shape
88	4501	Com	G-SAb	12 32.0 +14 25	9.6	6.1 × 2.8	bright multiple-arm spiral
91	4548	Com	G-SBb	12 35.4 +14 30	10.2	5.0 × 4.1	some lists say M9 = M58, not NGC4548
98	4192	Com	G-SABab	12 13.8 +14 54	10.1	9.1 × 2.1	nearly edge-on spiral near star 6 Com. B.
99	4254	Com	G-SAc	12 18.8 +14 25	9.9	4.6 × 4.3	nearly face-on spiral near M98
100	4321	Com	G-SABbc	12 22.9 +15 49	9.3	6.2 × 5.3	face-on spiral with starlike nucleus
49	4472	Vir	G-E2	12 29.8 +8 00	8.4	8.1 × 7.1	very bright elliptical
58	4579	Vir	G-SABb	12 37.7 +11 49	9.7	5.5 × 4.6	bright barred spiral; M59 and M60 1° E
59	4621	Vir	G-E5	12 42.0 +11 39	9.6	4.6 × 3.6	bright elliptical paired with M60
60	4649	Vir	G-E2	12 43.7 +11 33	8.8	7.1 × 6.1	bright elliptical with M59 and NGC 4647
61	4303	Vir	G-SABbc	12 21.9 +4 28	9.7	6.0 × 5.9	face-on two-armed spiral
84	4374	Vir	G-E1	12 25.1 +12 53	9.1	5.1 × 4.1	!! w/ M86 in Markarian's Chain
86	4406	Vir	G-E3	12 26.2 +12 57	8.9	12 × 9	!! w/ many NGC galaxies in Chain
87	4486	Vir	G-E0-1	12 30.8 +12 24	8.6	7.1 × 7.1	the one with famous jet and black hole
89	4552	Vir	G-E	12 35.7 +12 33	9.8	3.4 × 3.4	elliptical; resembles M87 but smaller
90	4569	Vir	G-SABab	12 36.8 +13 10	9.5	10 × 4	bright barred spiral near M89
104	4594	Vir	G-SA	12 40.0 −11 37	8.0	7.1 × 4.4	!! Sombrero Galaxy; look for dust lane
3	5272	CVn	GC	13 42.2 +28 23	5.9	16.2	!! contains many variable stars
51	5194/5	CVn	G-SAbc	13 29.9 +47 12	8.4	8 × 7	!! Whirlpool Galaxy; superb in big scope
63	5055	CVn	G-SAbc	13 15.8 +42 02	8.6	14 × 8	!! Sunflower Galaxy; bright, elongated
94	4736	CVn	G-SAab	12 50.9 +41 07	8.2	13 × 11	very bright and comet-like
106	4258	CVn	G-SABbc	12 19.0 +47 18	8.4	20 × 8	!! superb large, bright spiral
68	4590	Hya	GC	12 39.5 −26 45	7.7	12	15-cm telescope needed to resolve
83	5236	Hya	G-SABc	13 37.0 −29 52	7.6	16 × 13	large and diffuse; superb from far south
102	5866?	Dra	G-SA0+	15 06.5 +55 46	9.9	6.6 × 3.2	or is M102 = M101? (look for 5907)
5	5904	Ser	GC	15 18.6 +2 05	5.7	17.4	!! one of the sky's finest globulars
The Summer Sky							
13	6205	Her	GC	16 41.7 +36 28	5.7	16.6	!! Hercules Cluster; NGC 6207 1/2° NE
92	6341	Her	GC	17 17.1 +43 08	6.4	11.2	9° NE of M13; fine but often overlooked
9	6333	Oph	GC	17 19.2 −18 31	7.6	9.3	smallest of Ophiuchus globulars
10	6254	Oph	GC	16 57.1 −4 06	6.6	15.1	rich globular cluster; M12 is 3° NW
12	6218	Oph	GC	16 47.2 −1 57	6.8	14.5	loose globular cluster near M10
14	6402	Oph	GC	17 37.6 −3 15	7.6	11.7	20-cm telescope needed to resolve
19	6273	Oph	GC	17 02.6 −26 16	6.7	13.5	oblate globular; M62 4° south
62	6266	Oph	GC	17 01.2 −30 07	6.7	14.1	unsymmetrical; in rich field

SEASONAL LISTING OF MESSIER OBJECTS (continued)

M#	NGC	Con	Type	RA (2000) Dec h m ° '		m_v	Size '	Remarks
Summer Sky continued…								
107	6171	Oph	GC	16 32.5	−13 03	8.1	10.0	small, faint globular
4	6121	Sco	GC	16 23.6	−26 32	5.8	26.3	bright globular near Antares
6	6405	Sco	OC	17 40.1	−32 13	4.2	33	!! Butterfly Cluster; best at low power
7	6475	Sco	OC	17 53.9	−34 49	3.3	80	!! excellent in binocs or rich-field scope
80	6093	Sco	GC	16 17.0	−22 59	7.3	8.9	very compressed globular
16	6611	Ser	EN + OC	18 18.6	−13 58	—	35 × 28	Eagle Neb. w/ open cl.; use neb. filter
8	6523	Sgr	EN	18 03.8	−24 23	—	45 × 30	!! Lagoon Nebula w/ open cl. NGC 6530
17	6618	Sgr	EN	18 20.8	−16 11	—	20 × 15	!! Swan or Omega Nebula; use neb. filter
18	6613	Sgr	OC	18 19.9	−17 08	6.9	10	sparse cluster; 1° south of M17
20	6514	Sgr	E/RN	18 02.3	−23 02	—	20 × 20	!! Trifid nebula; look for dark lanes
21	6531	Sgr	OC	18 04.6	−22 30	5.9	13	0.7° NE of M20; sparse cluster
22	6656	Sgr	GC	18 36.4	−23 54	5.1	24	spectacular from southern latitude
23	6494	Sgr	OC	17 56.8	−19 01	5.5	27	bright, loose open cluster
24	—	Sgr	starcloud	18 16.5	−18 50	4.6	95 × 35	rich star cloud; best in big binoculars
25	IC4725	Sgr	OC	18 31.6	−19 15	4.6	32	bright but sparse open cluster
28	6626	Sgr	GC	18 24.5	−24 52	6.8	11.2	compact globular near M22
54	6715	Sgr	GC	18 55.1	−30 29	7.6	9.1	not easily resolved
55	6809	Sgr	GC	19 40.0	−30 58	6.4	19.0	bright, loose globular cluster
69	6637	Sgr	GC	18 31.4	−32 21	7.6	7.1	small, poor globular cluster
70	6681	Sgr	GC	18 43.2	−32 18	8.0	7.8	small globular 2° east of M69
75	6864	Sgr	GC	20 06.1	−21 55	8.5	6	small and distant; 59 000 ly away
11	6705	Sct	OC	18 51.1	−6 16	5.8	13	!! Wild Duck Cl.; the best open cluster?
26	6694	Sct	OC	18 45.2	−9 24	8.0	14	bright, coarse cluster
56	6779	Lyr	GC	19 16.6	+30 11	8.3	7.1	within a rich starfield
57	6720	Lyr	PN	18 53.6	+33 02	8.8	>71″	!! Ring Nebula; an amazing smoke ring
71	6838	Sge	GC	19 53.8	+18 47	8.0	7.2	loose globular; looks like an open cluster
27	6853	Vul	PN	19 59.6	+22 43	7.3	>348″	!! Dumbbell Nebula; a superb object
29	6913	Cyg	OC	20 23.9	+38 32	6.6	6	small, poor open cluster 2° S of γ Cygni
39	7092	Cyg	OC	21 32.2	+48 26	4.6	31	very sparse cluster; use low power

The Autumn Sky

M#	NGC	Con	Type	RA (2000) Dec h m ° '		m_v	Size '	Remarks
2	7089	Aqr	GC	21 33.5	−0 49	6.4	12.9	20-cm telescope needed to resolve
72	6981	Aqr	GC	20 53.5	−12 32	9.3	5.9	near the Saturn Nebula, NGC 7009
73	6994	Aqr	OC	20 59.0	−12 38	8.9p	2.8	group of 4 stars only; an "asterism"
15	7078	Peg	GC	21 30.0	+12 10	6.0	12.3	rich, compact globular
30	7099	Cap	GC	21 40.4	−23 11	7.3	11	toughest in 1-night Messier marathon
52	7654	Cas	OC	23 24.2	+61 35	6.9	12	young, rich cl.; faint Bubble Neb. nearby
103	581	Cas	OC	1 33.2	+60 42	7.4	6	three NGC open clusters nearby
31	224	And	G-SAb	0 42.7	+41 16	3.4	185 × 75	!! Andromeda Gal.; look for dust lanes
32	221	And	G-E5 pec	0 42.7	+40 52	8.1	11 × 7	closest companion to M31
110	205	And	G-E3 pec	0 40.4	+41 41	8.1	20 × 12	more distant companion to M31
33	598	Tri	G-SAcd	1 33.9	+30 39	5.7	67 × 42	large, diffuse spiral; requires dark sky
74	628	Psc	G-SAc	1 36.7	+15 47	9.4	11 × 11	faint, elusive spiral; tough in small scope
77	1068	Cet	G-SABab	2 42.7	−0 01	8.9	8.2 × 7.3	a Seyfert galaxy; with starlike nucleus
34	1039	Per	OC	2 42.0	+42 47	5.2	35	best at low power
76	650/51	Per	PN	1 42.4	+51 34	10.1	>65″	Little Dumbbell; faint but distinct

THE FINEST NGC OBJECTS
By Alan Dyer

Those looking for an observing project beyond the Messier Catalogue turn to the New General Catalogue (NGC). The NGC contains 7840 entries and forms the core database of today's computerized backyard telescopes. To match the Messier Catalogue, this list contains 110 of the finest NGC objects visible from midnorthern latitudes. The seasonal order is similar to that used in the Messier list, and there is no overlap. While the brightness of the best NGCs rivals many Messier targets, at least a 20-cm telescope is required to see all 110 objects on this list. Most are easy; a few are challenging.

The NGC was originally published by J.L.E. Dreyer in 1888, a work that expanded upon John Herschel's 1864 "General Catalogue." Supplementary "Index Catalogues" were published by Dreyer in 1895 and 1908. The first IC extends the NGC with another 1529 objects discovered visually between 1888 and 1894. Most are faint, elusive targets. (To provide a flavour of this extension to the NGC, one entry from the first IC is included on this list, IC 289.) The Second Index Catalogue contains 3857 entries, most discovered photographically between 1895 and 1907.

The *Sky Atlas 2000.0*, the sets of index card charts called *AstroCards*, *The Night Sky Observer's Guide Vol. 1 and 2* by Kepple and Sanner, and the *Uranometria 2000.0* star atlas (the latter two published by Willmann-Bell, Inc.) are recommended finder aids. Most planetarium and deep-sky charting computer programs, as well as computerized telescopes, include all the objects on this list and many more.

Notation below is as in the Messier list. Magnitudes (m_v) are visual, with the exception of those marked "p," which are photographic, or blue, magnitudes. Most galaxies appear smaller than the sizes listed. For open clusters, the number of stars (*) is also given. Data are taken from *The Deep Sky Field Guide to Uranometria 2000.0* (see the introduction to the Messier list), with some sizes rounded to two significant figures.

SEASONAL LISTING OF FINEST NGC OBJECTS

#	NGC	Con	Type	RA (2000) Dec h m ° ′	m_v	Size ′	Remarks
The Autumn Sky							
1	7009	Aqr	PN	21 04.2 −11 22	8.3p	>25″	!! Saturn Nebula; small bright oval
2	7293	Aqr	PN	22 29.6 −20 48	7.3	>769″	!! Helix Nebula; large, diffuse; use filter
3	7331	Peg	G-SAb	22 37.1 +34 25	9.5	10 × 4	!! large, bright spiral galaxy
4	7635	Cas	EN	23 20.7 +61 12	—	15 × 8	Bubble Neb.; very faint; 1/2° SW of M52
5	7789	Cas	OC	23 57.0 +56 44	6.7	15	!! 300*; faint but very rich cluster
6	185	Cas	G-E3	0 39.0 +48 20	9.2	14 × 12	companion to M31; small and faint
7	281	Cas	EN	0 52.8 +56 37	—	35 × 30	!! large faint nebulosity near η Cas
8	457	Cas	OC	1 19.1 +58 20	6.4	13	80*; rich; one of the best Cas. clusters
9	663	Cas	OC	1 46.0 +61 15	7.1	16	80*; look for NGCs 654 and 659 nearby
10	IC 289	Cas	PN	3 10.3 +61 19	13.3	>34″	dim oval smudge; use nebula filter!
11	7662	And	PN	23 25.9 +42 33	8.3	>12″	!! Blue Snowball; annular at high power
12	891	And	G-SAb	2 22.6 +42 21	9.9	13 × 3	!! faint, classic edge-on with dust lane
13	253	Scl	G-SABc	0 47.6 −25 17	7.6	30 × 7	!! very large and bright but at low altitude
14	772	Ari	G-SAb	1 59.3 +19 01	10.3	7.3 × 4.6	diffuse spiral galaxy
15	246	Cet	PN	0 47.0 −11 53	10.9	225″	large and faint with mottled structure
16	936	Cet	G-SB	2 27.6 −1 09	10.2	5.7 × 4.6	near M77; NGC 941 in the same field

SEASONAL LISTING OF FINEST NGC OBJECTS (continued)

#	NGC	Con	Type	RA (2000) h m	Dec ° '	m_v	Size '	Remarks
	Autumn Sky continued…							
17	869/884	Per	OC	2 21.0	+57 08	≈5	30/30	!! Double Cluster; 315*; use low power
18	1023	Per	G-SB0-	2 40.4	+39 04	9.3	8.6 × 4.2	bright lens-shaped galaxy near M34
19	1491	Per	EN	4 03.4	+51 19	—	25 × 25	visually small and faint emission nebula
20	1501	Cam	PN	4 07.0	+60 55	11.5	52″	faint; dark centre; look for NGC 1502
21	1232	Eri	G-SABc	3 09.8	−20 35	10.0	6.8 × 5.6	face-on spiral; look for NGC 1300 nearby
22	1535	Eri	PN	4 14.2	−12 44	9.6p	>18″	bright planetary with blue-grey disk

The Winter Sky

#	NGC	Con	Type	RA (2000) h m	Dec ° '	m_v	Size '	Remarks
23	1514	Tau	PN	4 09.2	+30 47	10.9	>114″	faint glow around 9.4^m central star
24	1931	Aur	E/RN	5 31.4	+34 15	—	4 × 4	haze surrounding four close stars
25	1788	Ori	RN	5 06.9	−3 21	—	5 × 3	fairly bright but diffuse reflection nebula
26	1973+	Ori	E/RN	5 35.1	−4 44	—	≈20 × 10	NGC 1973-5-7 just N. of M42 and M43
27	2022	Ori	PN	5 42.1	+9 05	11.9	>18″	small, faint & distinct with annular form
28	2024	Ori	EN	5 41.9	−1 51	—	30 × 30	bright but masked by glow from ζ Ori
29	2194	Ori	OC	6 13.8	+12 48	8.5	8	80*, fairly rich; look for 2169 nearby
30	2371/2	Gem	PN	7 25.6	+29 29	11.3	>55″	faint double-lobed planetary; use filter
31	2392	Gem	PN	7 29.2	+20 55	9.2	>15″	!! Clown Face or Eskimo Nebula
32	2237+	Mon	EN	6 32.3	+5 03	—	80 × 60	!! Rosette Neb.; very large; use filter
33	2261	Mon	E/RN	6 39.2	+8 44	var	3.5 × 1.5	Hubble's Variable Neb.; comet-shaped
34	2359	CMa	EN	7 18.6	−13 12	—	9 × 6	bright; look for 2360 & 2362 nearby
35	2440	Pup	PN	7 41.9	−18 13	9.4	>14″	almost starlike; irregular at high power
36	2539	Pup	OC	8 10.7	−12 50	6.5	21	50*; rich cluster; near M46 and M47
37	2403	Cam	G-SABc	7 36.9	+65 36	8.5	26 × 13	!! very large & bright; visible in binocs.
38	2655	Cam	G-SAB0	8 55.6	+78 13	10.1	6.0 × 5.3	bright ellipse with starlike nucleus

The Spring Sky

#	NGC	Con	Type	RA (2000) h m	Dec ° '	m_v	Size '	Remarks
39	2683	Lyn	G-SAb	8 52.7	+33 25	9.8	8.4 × 2.4	nearly edge-on spiral; very bright
40	2841	UMa	G-SAb	9 22.0	+50 58	9.2	6.8 × 3.3	!! classic elongated spiral; very bright
41	3079	UMa	G-SBc	10 02.2	+55 41	10.9	8.0 × 1.5	edge-on spiral; NGC 2950 nearby
42	3184	UMa	G-SABc	10 18.3	+41 25	9.8	7.8 × 7.2	large, diffuse face-on spiral
43	3877	UMa	G-SAc	11 46.1	+47 30	11.0	5.1 × 1.1	edge-on; same field as χ UMa
44	3941	UMa	G-SB0°	11 52.9	+36 59	10.3	3.7 × 2.6	small, bright and elliptical
45	4026	UMa	G-S0	11 59.4	+50 58	10.8	4.6 × 1.2	lens-shaped edge-on near γ UMa
46	4088	UMa	G-SABbc	12 05.6	+50 33	10.6	5.4 × 2.1	nearly edge-on; NGC 4085 in same field
47	4157	UMa	G-SABb	12 11.1	+50 29	11.3	7.1 × 1.2	a thin sliver; NGC 4026 and 4088 nearby
48	4605	UMa	G-SBcp	12 40.0	+61 37	10.3	6.4 × 2.3	bright, distinct edge-on spiral
49	3115	Sex	G-S0-	10 05.2	−7 43	8.9	8.1 × 2.8	Spindle Galaxy; bright and elongated
50	3242	Hya	PN	10 24.8	−18 38	7.8	>16″	!! Ghost of Jupiter; small but bright
51	3003	LMi	G-Sbc?	9 48.6	+33 25	11.9	5.2 × 1.6	faint elongated streak
52	3344	LMi	G-SABbc	10 43.5	+24 55	9.9	6.9 × 6.4	diffuse face-on barred spiral
53	3432	LMi	G-SBm	10 52.5	+36 37	11.2	6.9 × 1.9	nearly edge-on; faint flat streak
54	2903	Leo	G-SABbc	09 32.2	+21 30	9.0	12 × 6	!! very large, bright elongated spiral
55	3384	Leo	G-SB0-	10 48.3	+12 38	9.9	5.5 × 2.9	same field as M105 and NGC 3389
56	3521	Leo	G-SAb	11 05.8	−0 02	9.0	12 × 6	very large, bright spiral
57	3607	Leo	G-SA0°	11 16.9	+18 03	9.9	4.6 × 4.1	NGC 3605 & 3608 in same field
58	3628	Leo	G-Sb pec	11 20.3	+13 36	9.5	14 × 4	large edge-on; same field as M65 & M66
59	4111	CVn	G-SA0+	12 07.1	+43 04	10.7	4.4 × 0.9	bright lens-shaped edge-on spiral
60	4214	CVn	G-I AB	12 15.6	+36 20	9.8	10 × 8	large irregular galaxy
61	4244	CVn	G-SAcd	12 17.5	+37 49	10.4	17 × 2	!! large distinct edge-on spiral

SEASONAL LISTING OF FINEST NGC OBJECTS (continued)

#	NGC	Con	Type	RA (2000) Dec h m ° ′		m_v	Size ′	Remarks
Spring Sky continued …								
62	4449	CVn	G-I Bm	12 28.2	+44 06	9.6	5.5 × 4.1	bright with odd rectangular shape
63	4490	CVn	G-SBd p	12 30.6	+41 38	9.8	6.4 × 3.3	Cocoon Gal.; bright spiral; 4485 in field
64	4631	CVn	G-SBd	12 42.1	+32 32	9.2	16 × 3	!! large edge-on; with companion 4627
65	4656/7	CVn	G-SBm p	12 44.0	+32 10	10.5	20 × 3	!! in field with 4631; NE end curves up
66	5005	CVn	G-SABbc	13 10.9	+37 03	9.8	5.8 × 2.8	bright elongated spiral near α CVn
67	5033	CVn	G-SAc	13 13.4	+36 36	10.2	10 × 5	large bright spiral near NGC 5005
68	4274	Com	G-SBab	2 19.8	+29 37	10.4	6.7 × 2.5	NGCs 4278/83/86 in same field
69	4414	Com	G-SAc	12 26.4	+31 13	10.1	4.4 × 3.0	bright spiral with starlike nucleus
70	4494	Com	G-E1-2	12 31.4	+25 47	9.8	4.6 × 4.4	small bright elliptical
71	4559	Com	G-SABc	12 36.0	+27 58	10.0	12 × 5	large spiral with coarse structure
72	4565	Com	G-SAb	12 36.3	+25 59	9.6	14 × 2	!! superb edge-on spiral with dust lane
73	4725	Com	G-SABab	12 50.4	+25 30	9.4	10 × 8	very bright, large spiral
74	4038/9	Crv	G-SB/IB	12 01.9	−18 52	≈10.4	≈5 × 5 ea.	"Antennae" interacting galaxies
75	4361	Crv	PN	12 24.5	−18 48	10.9	>45″	small and bright; with 13ᵐ central star
76	4216	Vir	G-SABb	12 15.9	+13 09	10.0	7.8 × 1.6	nearly edge-on; with NGC 4206 and 4222
77	4388	Vir	G-SAb	12 25.8	+12 40	11.0	5.7 × 1.6	with M84 and M86 in Markarian's Chain
78	4438	Vir	G-SA0/a	12 27.8	+13 01	10.2	8.9 × 3.6	paired w/ NGC 4435 to form the "Eyes"
79	4517	Vir	G-Scd	12 32.8	+0 07	10.4	9.9 × 1.4	faint edge-on spiral
80	4526	Vir	G-SAB0°	12 34.0	+7 42	9.7	7.1 × 2.9	between 2 7th mag. stars
81	4535	Vir	G-SABc	12 34.3	+8 12	10.0	7.1 × 6.4	near M49 and 3/4° N of NGC 4526
82	4567/8	Vir	G-SAbc	12 36.5	+11 15	≈11	≈3 × 2 ea.	"Siamese Twins" interacting galaxies
83	4699	Vir	G-Sab	12 49.0	−8 40	9.5	4.4 × 3.2	small & bright; look for NGC 4697 3° N
84	4762	Vir	G-SB0°?	12 52.9	+11 14	10.3	9.1 × 2.2	flattest galaxy known!; 4754 in same field
85	5746	Vir	G-SA?b	14 44.9	+1 57	10.3	6.8 × 1.0	fine edge-on near 109 Virginis
86	5466	Boo	GC	14 05.5	+28 32	9.0	11	loose class XII; like rich open cl.; faint
87	5907	Dra	G-SAc	15 15.9	+56 20	10.3	12 × 2	!! fine edge-on with dust lane; near 5866
88	6503	Dra	G-SAcd	17 49.4	+70 09	10.2	7.3 × 2.4	bright elongated spiral
89	6543	Dra	PN	17 58.6	+66 38	8.1	>18″	Cat's Eye Nebula; with 10.9ᵐ central star
The Summer Sky								
90	6210	Her	PN	16 44.5	+23 49	8.8	>14″	blue starlike planetary
91	6369	Oph	PN	17 29.3	−23 46	11.4	>30″	"Little Ghost"; look for 6309 nearby
92	6572	Oph	PN	18 12.1	+6 51	8.1	8″	tiny bright blue oval
93	6633	Oph	OC	18 27.7	+6 34	4.6	27	sparse wide field cluster; IC 4756 nearby
94	6712	Sct	GC	18 53.1	−8 42	8.2	7.2	small globular; look for IC 1295 in field
95	6781	Aql	PN	19 18.4	+6 33	11.4	>109″	pale version of the Owl Nebula, M97
96	6819	Cyg	OC	19 41.3	+40 11	7.3	9.5	150*; faint but rich cluster in Milky Way
97	6826	Cyg	PN	19 44.8	+50 31	8.8	>25″	!! Blinking Planetary; 10.6ᵐ central star
98	6888	Cyg	EN	20 12.0	+38 21	—	18 × 13	Crescent Nebula; faint; use nebula filter
99a	6960	Cyg	SNR	20 45.7	+30 43	—	70 × 6	!! Veil Nebula west half; use filter!
99b	6992/5	Cyg	SNR	20 56.4	+31 43	—	72 × 8	!! Veil Nebula east half; use filter!
100	7000	Cyg	EN	20 58.8	+44 20	—	120 × 100	!! North America; use filter & low power
101	7027	Cyg	PN	21 07.1	+42 14	8.5	15″	unusual protoplanetary nebula
102	6445	Sgr	PN	17 49.2	−20 01	11.2	>34″	small, bright and annular; near M23
103	6520	Sgr	OC	18 03.4	−27 54	7.6p	6	60*; small; dark nebula B86 in same field
104	6818	Sgr	PN	19 44.0	−14 09	9.3	>17″	"Little Gem"; annular; NGC 6822 0.75° S
105	6802	Vul	OC	19 30.6	+20 16	8.8	3.2	50*, at east end of Brocchi's Cluster
106	6940	Vul	OC	20 34.6	+28 18	6.3	31	60*; fairly rich cluster in Milky Way
107	6939	Cep	OC	20 31.4	+60 38	7.8	7	80*; very rich; NGC 6946 in same field
108	6946	Cep	G-SABcd	20 34.8	+60 09	8.8	13 × 13	faint, diffuse face-on spiral near 6939
109	7129	Cep	RN	21 42.8	+66 06	—	7 × 7	faint reflection neb. around sparse cluster
110	40	Cep	PN	0 13.0	+72 32	12.4	>37″	unusual red planetary; 11.6ᵐ central star

DEEP-SKY CHALLENGE OBJECTS
BY ALAN DYER AND ALISTER LING

For those who wish to get a taste of the unusual, here is a selection of 45 "challenge" targets. Most require a 25- to 45-cm telescope. However, for detecting challenge objects, the quality of sky, quality of the optics, use of an appropriate filter, and the observer's experience are often more important than sheer aperture. Don't be afraid to tackle some of these with a smaller telescope.

Objects are listed in order of right ascension. Abbreviations are the same as in the Messier and NGC lists. Two columns have been added: one lists the page where you'll find that object in the *Uranometria 2000.0*; the last column suggests the minimum aperture in cm needed to see that object. Most data are taken from *Sky Catalogue 2000.0 Vol. 2*. Some visual magnitudes are from other sources.

#	Object	Con	Type	RA (2000) h m	Dec ° '	m_v	Size '	pg	Min Aperture
1	NGC 7822	Cep	E/RN	0 03.6	+68 37	—	60 × 30	15	30
	large, faint emission neb.; rated 'eeF'; also look for E/R nebula Ced 214 (assoc'd with star cluster Berkeley 59) 1° S								
2	IC 59	Cas	E/RN	0 56.7	+61 04	—	10 × 5	36	20–25
	faint emission/reflection nebula paired with IC 63 very close to γ Cas.; requires clean optics; rated as 'pF'								
3	NGC 609	Cas	OC	1 37.2	+64 33	11.0	3.0	16	25–30
	faint patch at low power; high power needed to resolve this rich cluster (also look for Trumpler 1 cluster 3° S)								
4	IC 1795	Cas	EN	2 24.7	+61 54	—	27 × 13	17	20
	brightest part of a complex of nebulosity that includes IC 1805 and IC 1848; use a nebula filter								
5	Maffei I	Cas	G–E3	2 36.3	+59 39	≈14	5 × 3	38	30
	heavily reddened galaxy; very faint; requires large aperture and black skies; nearby Maffei II for extremists								
6	NGC 1049	For	GC	2 39.7	–34 29	11.0	0.6	354	25–30
	Class V globular in dwarf 'Fornax System' Local Group galaxy 630 000 ly away; galaxy itself invisible?								
7	Abell 426	Per	G's	3 19.8	+41 31	12–16	≈30'	63	20–40
	Perseus galaxy cluster 300 million ly away; mag. 11.6 NGC 1275 Perseus A at centre; see Webb Vol. 5								
8	NGC 1432/35	Tau	RN	3 46.1	+23 47	—	30 × 30	132	10–15
	Pleiades nebulosity (also includes IC 349); brightest around Merope; requires transparent skies and clean optics								
9	IC 342	Cam	G–SBc	3 46.8	+68 06	≈12	17 × 17	18	20–30
	large and diffuse face-on spiral; member of UMa–Cam cloud (Kemble's Cascade of stars also on this chart)								
10	NGC 1499	Per	EN	4 00.7	+36 37	—	145 × 40	95	8–12.5 RFT
	California Nebula; very large and faint; use a wide–field telescope or big binoculars plus H–Beta filter								
11	NGC 1554/5	Tau	RN	4 21.8	+19 32	—	var.	133	20?
	Hind's Variable Neb.; small reflect. neb. around 9^m–13^m var. star T Tau; use high power; difficulty varies								
12	IC 405	Aur	E/RN	5 16.2	+34 16	—	30 × 19	97	20
	Flaming Star Neb. assoc'd with runaway star AE Aurigae; see Burnham's Handbk p. 285 (also look for IC 410)								
13	IC 434 / B 33	Ori	E/DN	5 40.9	–2 28	—	60 × 10	226	10–15 in dark sky!
	B33 is the Horsehead Nebula, a dark neb. superimposed on a very faint emission neb. IC 434; use H–Beta filter								
14	Sh 2–276	Ori	EN	5 48	+1 —	—	600 × 30!	226	10–15 RFT
	Barnard's Loop; SNR or interstellar bubble?; difficult to detect due to size; use filter and sweep with wide field								
15	Abell 12	Ori	PN	6 02.4	+9 39	≈13	37"	181	25–30
	also called PK 198 –6.1; faint; not plotted on Uranometria but is on NW edge of μ Orionis; OIII filter required								
16	IC 443	Gem	SNR	6 16.9	+22 47	—	50 × 40	137	25–30
	faint supernova remnant very close to η Gem.; use filter (also look for NGC 2174 and Sh 2–247 on this chart)								
17	J 900	Gem	PN	6 25.9	+17 47	12.2	8"	137	20
	Jonckheere 900; bright starlike planetary; plotted as PK 194 +2.1 in Uranometria; use OIII filter & high power								
18	IC 2177	Mon	E/RN	7 05.1	–10 42	—	120 × 40	273	20–25
	Seagull Nebula; large, faint; contains bright patches Gum 1 (–10°28'), NGC 2327 (–11°18') & Ced 90 (–12°20')								
19	PK 205 +14.1	Gem	PN	7 29.0	+13 15	≈13	≈700"	184	20–25
	Medusa Nebula or Abell 21; much larger than plotted in Uranometria; impressive in large aperture w/ OIII filter								
20	PK 164 +31.1	Lyn	PN	7 57.8	+53 25	≈14	400"	43	25
	extremely faint with two small components; use OIII filter; sometimes confused with nearby NGC 2474–75								

DEEP-SKY CHALLENGE OBJECTS (continued)

#	Object	Con	Type	RA (2000) h m	Dec ° ′	m_v	Size ′	pg	Min Aperture
21	**Leo I**	Leo	G–E3	10 08.4	+12 18	9.8	10.7 × 8.3	189	30

dwarf elliptical; satellite of Milky Way; very low surface brightness; 0.3° N of Regulus!; requires clean optics

22	**Abell 1367**	Leo	G's	11 44.0	+19 57	13–16	≈60	147	30–40

cluster of some 30 or more galaxies within a 1 degree field near 93 Leonis; see Webb Handbook Vol. 5, p. 139

23	**NGC 3172**	UMi	G-?	11 50.2	+89 07	13.6	0.7 × 0.7	2	25

'Polarissima Borealis'—closest galaxy to the North Celestial Pole; small, faint and otherwise unremarkable

24	**NGC 4236**	Dra	G-SBb	12 16.7	+69 28	9.6	18.6 × 6.9	25	20–25

very large, dim barred spiral; a diffuse glow (NGC 4395 on Chart #108 a similar large diffuse face-on)

25	**Mrk 205**	Dra	Quasar	12 21.6	+75 18	14.5	stellar	9	30

Markarian 205; a faint star on SW edge of NGC 4319; plotted as a radio source; centre of red-shift controversy

26	**3C 273**	Vir	Quasar	12 29.1	+2 03	12≈13	stellar	238	25–30

at 2 to 3 billon ly away one of the most distant objects visible in amateur telescopes; magnitude variable

27	**NGC 4676**	Com	G's	12 46.2	+30 44	14.lp	2 × 1	108	25

'The Mice' or VV 224—two classic interacting galaxies; very faint double nature detectable at high power

28	**Abell 1656**	Com	G's	13 00.1	+27 58	12–16	≈60	149	25–30

Coma Berenices gal. cl.; very rich; 400 million ly away; brightest member NGC 4889; see Webb Vol. 5

29	**NGC 5053**	Com	GC	13 16.4	+17 42	9.8	10.5	150	10–20

faint and very loose globular 1° SE of M53; requires large aperture to resolve; difficult in hazy skies; Class XI

30	**NGC 5897**	Lib	GC	15 17.4	–21 01	8.6	12.6	334	15–20

large, faint and loose globular; mag. 10.9 in Atlas Coeli Catalogue; requires large aperture to resolve; Class XI

31	**Abel 2065**	CrB	G's	15 22.7	–27 43	≈16	≈30	154	50 in superb sky!

Corona Borealis gal. cluster; perhaps the most difficult object for amateur telescopes; 1.5 billion ly away

32	**NGC 6027**	Ser	G's	15 59.2	+20 45	≈15	2 × 1	155	40

Seyfert's Sextet (6027 A–F); compact group of 6 small and very faint galaxies; see Burnham's Handbk p. 1793

33	**B 72**	Oph	DN	17 23.5	–23 38		30	338	8–12.5 RFT

Barnard's dark S-Nebula or 'The Snake'; opacity of 6/6; 1.5° NNE of θ Ophiuchi; area rich in dark nebulas

34	**NGC 6791**	Lyr	OC	19 20.7	+37 51	9.5	16	118	20–25

large, faint but very rich open cluster with 300 stars; a faint smear in smaller instruments; Type II 3 r

35	**PK 64 +5.l**	Cyg	PN	19 34.8	+30 31	9.6	8″	118	20

Campbell's Hydrogen Star; very bright but very starlike; also catalogued as star BD +30°3639

36	**M 1-92**	Cyg	RN	19 36.3	+29 33	11.0	12″ × 6″	118	25–30

Minkowski 92 or Footprint Nebula; bright, starlike reflection neb.; double at high mag.; assoc'd star invisible

37	**NGC 6822**	Sgr	G-Irr	19 44.9	–14 48	≈11	10.2 × 9.5	297	10–15

Barnard's Galaxy; member of the Local Group; large but very low surface brightness; requires transparent skies

38	**Palomar 11**	Aql	GC	19 45.2	–8 00	9.8	3.2′	297	20–30

Brightest of 15 heavily reddened GCs found on Sky Survey; magnitude is misleading; 11 Terzan GCs more challenging

39	**IC 4997**	Sge	PN	20 20.2	+16 45	10.9	2″	163	20

bright but starlike planetary; the challenge is to see the disk!; blink the field with and without a nebula filter

40	**IC 1318**	Cyg	EN	20 26.2	+40 30	—	large	84	8–15 RFT

complex of nebulosity around γ Cygni; multitude of patches in rich starfield; use a very wide field plus filter

41	**PK 80 –6.1**	Cyg	PN?	21 02.3	+36 42	13.5	16″	121	25

the 'Egg Nebula'; a very small proto-planetary nebula; can owners of large telescopes detect polarization?

42	**IC 1396**	Cep	EN	21 39.1	+57 30	—	170 × 140	57	10–12.5 RFT

extremely large and diffuse area of emission nebulosity; use nebula filter and very wide field optics in dark sky

43	**IC 5146**	Cyg	E/RN	21 53.5	+47 16	—	12 × 12	86	20–25

Cocoon Nebula; faint and diffuse; use H-Beta filter; at the end of the long filamentary dark nebula Barnard 168

44	**NGC 7317–20**	Peg	G's	22 36.1	+33 57	13–14	≈1′ ea.	123	25–30

Stephan's Quintet; 0.5° SSW of NGC 7331; easy to pick out 3 or 4 (also look for 'companions' to 7331)

45	**Jones 1**	Peg	PN	23 35.9	+30 28	12.1	332″	124	25–30

plotted as PK 104 –29.1 (from Perek & Kohoutek catalogue) in Uranometria; large dim glow; OIII filter required

GALAXIES: BRIGHTEST AND NEAREST
BY BARRY F. MADORE

External galaxies are generally of such low surface brightness that they often prove disappointing objects for the amateur observer. However, it must be remembered that many of these galaxies were discovered with very small telescopes and that the enjoyment of their discovery can be recaptured. In addition, the central concentration of light varies from galaxy to galaxy, making a visual classification of the types possible at the telescope. Indeed the type of galaxy as listed in the first table is in part based on the fraction of light coming from the central bulge of the galaxy as compared to the contribution from a disk component. Disk galaxies with dominant bulges are classified as Sa; as the nuclear contribution declines, types of Sb, Sc, and Sd are assigned until the nucleus is absent at type Sm. Often the disks of these galaxies show spiral symmetry, the coherence and strength of which is denoted by Roman numerals I through V, smaller numbers indicating well-formed global spiral patterns. Those spirals with central bars are designated SB while those with only a hint of a disk embedded in the bulge are called SO. A separate class of galaxies that possess no disk component are called ellipticals and can only be further classified numerically by their apparent flattening: EO being apparently round, E7 being the most flattened.

Environment appears to play an important role in the determining of the types of galaxies we see at the present epoch. Rich clusters of galaxies such as the system in Coma are dominated by ellipticals and gas-free SO galaxies. The less dense clusters and groups tend to be dominated by the spiral, disk galaxies. Remarkably, in pairs of galaxies the two types are much more frequently of the same Hubble type than random selection would predict. Encounters between disk galaxies may in some cases result in the instabilities necessary to form the spiral structure we often see. M51, the Whirlpool and its companion NGC 5195 are an often-cited example of this type of interaction. In the past when the universe was much more densely packed, interactions and collisions may have been sufficiently frequent that entire galaxies merged to form a single large new system; it has been suggested that some elliptical galaxies formed in this way.

The following table presents the 40 brightest galaxies taken from the Revised Shapley-Ames Catalog. As well as their designations, positions, and types, the table lists the total blue magnitudes, major and minor axis lengths (to the nearest minute of arc), one modern estimate of their distances in thousands of parsecs, and finally their radial velocities corrected for the motion of our Sun about the galactic centre. Although the universe as a whole is in expansion, there are parts that are still bound together (or at very least, held back in their expansion) by gravity. These groups and clusters are, in essence, representative of the largest material structures in the universe. Recently, large-scale flows of material have been reported, far in excess of the velocities expected due to the perturbing presence of other galaxies and clusters of galaxies. Either there are exceedingly large concentrations of matter yet to be discovered just beyond our limited view of the world, or the universe has had a much more interesting history than our present theories indicate. The brightest and nearest galaxies in the following table may be moving not only as a result of the universal expansion but also through very complex interactions with distant parts as yet only postulated but not seen.

THE 40 OPTICALLY BRIGHTEST SHAPLEY-AMES GALAXIES

NGC/IC	Other	RA (2000) Dec h m s	° ′	Type	Mag. B_T	Size ′	Distance kpc	Rad. Vel. km/s
55		0 15 08	−39 13.2	Sc	8.22	25 × 3	3100	+115
205	M110	0 40 23	+41 41.3	S0/E5pec	8.83	8 × 3	730	+49
221	M32	0 42 41	+40 51.9	E2	9.01	3 × 3	730	+86
224	M31	0 42 45	+41 16.5	Sb I–II	4.38	160 × 40	730	−10
247		0 47 10	−20 45.6	Sc III–IV	9.51	18 × 5	3100	+604
253		0 47 36	−25 17.4	Sc	8.13	22 × 6	4200	+504
SMC		0 52 38	−72 48.0	Im IV–V	2.79	216 × 216	60	+359
300		0 54 53	−37 41.2	Sc III	8.70	20 × 10	2400	+625
598	M33	1 33 53	+30 39.2	Sc II–III	6.26	60 × 40	670	+506
628	M74	1 36 42	+15 47.2	Sc I	9.77	8 × 8	17 000	+507
1068	M77	2 42 41	−0 00.9	Sb II	9.55	3 × 2	25 000	+510
1291		3 17 19	−41 06.5	SBa	9.42	5 × 2	15 000	+512
1313		3 18 16	−66 29.9	SBc III–IV	9.37	5 × 3	5200	+261
1316	Fornax A	3 22 42	−37 12.5	Sa (pec)	9.60	4 × 3	30 000	+1713
LMC		5 23 36	−69 45.4	SBm III	0.63	432 × 432	50	+34
2403		7 36 54	+65 35.9	Sc III	8.89	16 × 10	3 600	+299
2903		9 32 10	+21 29.9	Sc I–III	9.50	11 × 5	9400	+472
3031	M81	9 55 34	+69 04.1	SbI–II	7.86	16 × 10	3600	+124
3034	M82	9 55 54	+69 40.7	Amorphous	9.28	7 × 2	3600	+409
3521		11 05 49	−0 02.0	Sb II–III	9.64	7 × 2	13 000	+627
3627	M66	11 20 15	+12 59.1	Sb II	9.74	8 × 3	12 000	+593
4258	M106	12 18 57	+47 18.4	Sb II	8.95	20 × 6	10 000	+520
4449		12 28 12	+44 05.8	Sm IV	9.85	5 × 3	5000	+250
4472	M49	12 29 47	+7 59.8	E1/S0	9.32	5 × 4	22 000	+822
4486	M87	12 30 50	+12 23.6	E0	9.62	3 × 3	22 000	+1136
4594	M104	12 40 00	−11 37.4	Sa/b	9.28	7 × 2	17 000	+873
4631		12 42 05	+32 32.4	Sc	9.84	12 × 1	12 000	+606
4649	M60	12 43 40	+11 33.1	S0	9.83	4 × 3	22 000	+1142
4736	M94	12 50 54	+41 07.1	Sab	8.92	5 × 4	6900	+345
4826	M64	12 56 45	+21 41.0	Sab II	9.37	8 × 4	7000	+350
4945		13 05 26	−49 28.0	Sc	9.60	12 × 2	7000	+275
5055	M63	13 15 50	+42 01.7	Sbc II–III	9.33	8 × 3	11 000	+550
5128	Cen A	13 25 29	−43 01.0	S0 (pec)	7.89	10 × 3	6900	+251
5194	M51	13 29 53	+47 11.9	Sbc I–II	8.57	12 × 6	11 000	+541
5236	M83	13 37 00	−29 52.0	SBc II	8.51	10 × 8	6900	+275
5457	M101	14 03 13	+54 21.0	Sc I	8.18	22 × 22	7600	+372
6744		19 09 46	−63 51.3	Sbc II	9.24	9 × 9	13 000	+663
6822		19 44 57	−14 47.7	Im IV–V	9.35	20 × 10	680	+15
6946		20 34 51	+60 09.4	Sc II	9.68	13 × 9	6700	+336
7793		23 57 49	−32 35.4	Sd IV	9.65	6 × 4	4200	+241

The nearest galaxies, listed below, form what is known as the Local Group of Galaxies. Many of the distances are still quite uncertain. However, in the present Hubble Space Telescope era these galaxies are prime targets for a generation of astronomers intent on accurately determining each of their distances to the best possible precision.

THE NEAREST GALAXIES—OUR LOCAL GROUP

Name	RA (2000.0) Dec h m ° '		Mag. B_T	Type	Distance kpc
M31 = NGC 224	0 42.7	+41 16	4.38	Sb I–II	730
Milky Way Galaxy	—	—	—	Sb/c	—
M33 = NGC 598	1 33.9	+30 39	6.26	Sc II–III	670
LMC	5 23.7	–69 45	0.63	SBm III	50
SMC	0 52.7	–72 49	2.79	Im IV–V	60
NGC 6822	19 45.0	–14 48	9.35	Im IV–V	520
IC 1613	1 04.8	+02 07	10.00	Im V	740
M110 = NGC 205	0 40.4	+41 41	8.83	S0/E5 pec	730
M32 = NGC 221	0 42.7	+40 52	9.01	E2	730
NGC 185	0 38.9	+48 20	10.13	dE3 pec	730
NGC 147	0 33.2	+48 30	10.36	dE5	610
Fornax	2 39.9	–34 32	9.1	dE	130
Sculptor	1 00.2	–33 42	10.5	dE	85
Leo I	10 08.5	+12 19	11.27	dE	230
Leo II	11 13.5	+22 09	12.85	dE	230
Draco	17 20.1	+57 55	—	dE	80
Ursa Minor	15 08.8	+67 12	—	dE	75
Carina	6 41.6	–50 58	—	dE	170
And I	0 45.7	+38 01	13.5	dE	790
And II	1 16.5	+33 26	13.5	dE	730
And III	0 35.3	+36 31	13.5	dE	730
LGS 3	1 03.8	+21 53	—	?	730
Sextans	10 13.0	–1 36	—	dE	85
Antlia	10 04.0	–27 20	—	dE	1200
IC 10	0 20.4	+59 17	11.8	IBm	800

Editor's Notes:

(i) Aside from those famous companions of the Milky Way Galaxy, the Large Magellanic Cloud (LMC) and the Small Magellanic Cloud (SMC), there is only one galaxy beyond our own which is easily visible to unaided human eyes: **M31, the Andromeda Galaxy** (730 kpc or 2.4 Mly distant). M33, the Triangulum Galaxy, can also be seen, but this is a difficult observation. To locate M31, see the NOVEMBER ALL-SKY MAP on p. 280, where the tiny cluster of six dots above the first "A" of "ANDROMEDA" indicates its location. With modest optical aid (e.g. binoculars) a dozen or more of the galaxies listed in the brightest galaxies table can be seen by experienced observers under dark skies. With a 200 mm telescope, the quasar 3C273 at one thousand times the distance of M31 can elicit a noticeable signal in the visual cortex (see the section VARIABLE GALAXIES on p. 275).

(ii) An interesting article by G. Lake entitled "Cosmology of the Local Group" appears in *Sky & Telescope*, December 1992, p. 613.

GALAXIES WITH PROPER NAMES
By Barry F. Madore

Below are the catalogue designations and positions of galaxies known to have proper names which usually honour the discoverer (e.g. McLeish's Object), identify the constellation in which the galaxy is found (e.g. Andromeda Galaxy), or describe the galaxy in some easily remembered way (e.g. Whirlpool Galaxy).

Galaxy Name	Other Names / Remarks	RA (2000) h m	Dec ° ′
Ambartsumian's Knot	NGC 3561, UGC 06224, ARP 105	11 11.2	+28 42
Andromeda Galaxy	M31, NGC 224, UGC 00454	0 42.7	+41 16
Andromeda I		0 45.7	+38 01
Andromeda II		1 16.5	+33 26
Andromeda III		0 35.3	+36 31
Antennae Galaxy	Ring Tail, NGC 4038/39, ARP 244	12 01.9	−18 52
Antlia Dwarf	AM 1001-270	10 04.0	−27 20
Aquarius Dwarf	DDO 210	20 46.9	−12 51
Arp's Galaxy		11 19.6	+51 30
Atoms For Peace	NGC 7252, ARP 226	22 20.8	−24 41
Baade's Galaxies A & B	MCG+07-02-018/19	0 49.9	+42 35
Barbon's Galaxy	Markarian 328, ZWG 497.042	23 37.7	+30 08
Barnard's Galaxy	NGC 6822, IC 4895, DDO 209	19 44.9	−14 48
Bear's Paw (Claw)	NGC 2537, UGC 04274, ARP 6	8 13.2	+46 00
BL Lacertae		22 02.7	+42 17
Black Eye Galaxy	M64, NGC 4826, UGC 08062	12 56.7	+21 41
Bode's Galaxies	M81/82, NGC 3031/4, UGC 05318/22	9 55.7	+69 23
Burbidge Chain	MCG-04-03-010 to 13	0 47.5	−20 26
BW Tauri	UGC 03087, MCG+01-12-009	4 33.2	+5 21
Capricorn Dwarf	MCG−04-51-013, Palomar 12	21 46.5	−21 14
Carafe Galaxy	Cannon's Carafe, near NGC 1595/98	4 28.0	−47 54
Carina Dwarf		6 41.6	−50 58
Cartwheel Galaxy	Zwicky's Cartwheel, MCG-06-02-022a	0 37.4	−33 44
Centaurus A	NGC 5128, ARP 153	13 25.5	−43 01
Circinus Galaxy		14 13.2	−65 20
Coddington's Nebula	IC 2574, UGC 05666, DDO 81	10 28.4	+68 25
Copeland Septet	MCG+04-28-004/05/07 to 11, UGC 06597, UGC 06602, ARP 320, NGC 3745/46/48/50/51/53/54†	11 37.8	+21 59
Cygnus A	MCG+07-41-003	19 59.4	+40 43
Draco Dwarf	UGC 10822, DDO 208	17 20.2	+57 55
Exclamation Mark Galaxy		0 39.3	−43 06
The Eyes	NGC 4435/8, UGC 07574/5, ARP 120a,b	12 27.7	+13 03

† Position errors caused these to be historically marked as non-existent in the NGC and RNGC.

GALAXIES WITH PROPER NAMES (continued)

Galaxy Name	Other Names / Remarks	RA (2000) Dec h m ° ′
Fath 703	NGC 5892	15 13.7 −15 29
Fornax A	NGC 1316, ARP 154	3 22.7 −37 12
Fornax Dwarf	MCG-06-07-001	2 39.9 −34 32
Fourcade-Figueroa	MCG-07-28-004	13 34.8 −45 33
The Garland	S of NGC 3077 = UGC 05398	10 04.2 +68 40
Grus Quartet	NGC 7552/82/90/99	23 17.8 −42 26
GR 8 (Gibson Reaves)	UGC 08091, DDO 155	12 58.7 +14 13
Hardcastle's Galaxy	MCG-05-31-039	13 13.0 −32 41
Helix Galaxy	NGC 2685, UGC 04666, ARP 336	8 55.6 +58 44
Hercules A	MCG+01-43-006	16 51.2 +4 59
Hoag's Object		15 17.2 +21 35
Holmberg I	UGC 05139, DDO 63	9 40.5 +71 11
Holmberg II	UGC 04305, DDO 50, ARP 268	8 19.3 +70 43
Holmberg III	UGC 04841	9 14.6 +74 14
Holmberg IV	UGC 08837, DDO 185	13 54.7 +53 54
Holmberg V	UGC 08658	13 40.6 +54 20
Holmberg VI	NGC 1325a	3 24.9 −21 20
Holmberg VII	UGC 07739, DDO 137	12 34.7 +06 17
Holmberg VIII	UGC 08303, DDO 166	13 13.3 +36 12
Holmberg IX	UGC 05336, DDO 66	9 57.6 +69 03
Horologium Dwarf	Schuster's Spiral	3 59.2 −45 52
Hydra A	MCG-02-24-007	9 18.1 −12 06
Integral Sign Galaxy	UGC 03697, MCG+12-07-028	7 11.4 +71 50
Keenan's System	NGC 5216/16a/18, UGC 08528/9, ARP 104	13 32.2 +62 43
Kowal's Object		19 29.9 −17 41
Large Magellanic Cloud	Nubecula Major	5 23.6 −69 45
Leo I	Regulus Dwarf, UGC 05470, DDO 74, Harrington-Wilson #1	10 08.5 +12 18
Leo II	Leo B, UGC 06253, DDO 93, Harrington-Wilson #2	11 13.4 +22 10
Leo III	Leo A, UGC 05364, DDO 69	9 59.3 +30 45
Lindsay-Shapley Ring	Graham A	6 42.8 −74 15
Lost Galaxy	NGC 4535, UGC 07727	12 34.3 +8 11
McLeish's Object		20 09.7 −66 13
Maffei I	UGCA 34	2 36.3 +59 39
Maffei II	UGCA 39	2 42.0 +59 37
Malin 1		12 37.0 +14 20
Mayall's Object	MCG+07-23-019, ARP 148	11 03.9 +40 50

GALAXIES WITH PROPER NAMES (continued)

Galaxy Name	Other Names / Remarks	RA (2000) h m	Dec ° ′
Mice	NGC 4676a/b, UGC 07938/9, IC 819/20, ARP 242	12 46.1	+30 44
Miniature Spiral	NGC 3928, UGC 06834	11 51.8	+48 41
Minkowski's Object	ARP 133 (NE of NGC 541)	1 25.8	–01 21
Pancake	NGC 2685, UGC 04666, ARP 336	8 55.6	+58 44
Papillon	IC 708, UGC 06549	11 33.9	+49 03
Pegasus Dwarf	UGC 12613, DDO 216	23 28.5	+14 44
Perseus A	NGC 1275/6, UGC 02669	3 19.8	+41 31
Phoenix Dwarf Irr.		1 51.1	–44 26
Pinwheel Galaxy	see also Triangulum Galaxy	1 33.9	+30 39
Pinwheel Galaxy	M99, NGC 4254, UGC 07345	12 18.8	+14 25
Pinwheel Galaxy	M101, NGC 5457, UGC 08981, ARP 26	14 03.3	+54 22
Pisces Cloud	NGC 379/80/82-85, UGC 00682/3/6-9, ARP 331	1 07.5	+32 25
Pisces Dwarf	LGS 3	0 03.8	+21 54
Polarissima Australis	NGC 2573	1 42.0‡	–89 20
Polarissima Borealis	NGC 3172, ZWG 370.002	11 50.3‡	+89 07
Reinmuth 80	NGC 4517a, UGC 07685	12 32.5	+0 23
Reticulum Dwarf	Sersic 040.03	4 36.2	–58 50
Sagittarius Dwarf		19 30.0	–17 41
Sculptor Dwarf	MCG-06-03-015	1 00.2	–33 42
Sculptor Dwarf Irr.		0 08.1	–34 34
Seashell Galaxy	Companion to NGC 5291	13 47.4	–30 23
Serpens Dwarf	UGC 09792, Palomar 5	15 16.1	–0 08
Sextans A	UGCA 205, MCG-01-26-030, DDO 75	10 11.0	–4 41
Sextans B	UGC 05373, DDO 70	10 00.0	+5 19
Sextans C	UGC 05439	10 05.6	+00 04
Sextans Dwarf		10 13.1	–1 37
Seyfert's Sextet	Serpens Sextet, NGC 6027/6027a-e, UGC 10116	15 59.2	+20 46
Shapley-Ames 1		1 05.1	–6 13
Shapley-Ames 2	NGC 4507	12 35.1	–39 55
Shapley-Ames 3	MCG-02-33-015	12 49.4	–10 07
Shapley-Ames 4	UGC 08041	12 55.2	+0 07
Shapley-Ames 5	MCG-07-42-001	20 24.0	–44 00
Shapley-Ames 6		21 23.2	45 46
Siamese Twins	NGC 4567/4568	12 36.5	+11 15
Silver Coin	Sculptor Galaxy, NGC 253, UGCA 13	0 47.6	–25 18

‡ The high declination of these objects makes the RA particularly uncertain.

GALAXIES WITH PROPER NAMES (continued)

Galaxy Name	Other Names / Remarks	RA (2000) Dec h m ° '
Small Magellanic Cloud	Nubecula Minor	0 52.7 −72 50
Sombrero Galaxy	M104, NGC 4594	12 39.9 −11 37
Spider	UGC 05829, DDO 84	10 42.6 +34 27
Spindle Galaxy	NGC 3115	10 05.2 −7 42
Stephan's Quintet	NGC 7317-20, UGC 12099-102, ARP 319	22 36.0 +33 58
Sunflower Galaxy	M63, NGC 5055, UGC 08334	13 15.8 +42 02
Triangulum Galaxy	Pinwheel, M33, NGC 598, UGC 01117	1 33.9 +30 39
Ursa Minor Dwarf	UGC 09749, DDO 199	15 08.8 +67 12
Virgo A	M87, NGC 4486, UGC 07654, ARP 152	12 30.8 +12 23
Whirlpool Galaxy	Rosse's Galaxy, Question Mark Galaxy, M51, NGC 5194/5, UGC 08493/4, ARP 85	13 29.9 +47 12
Wild's Triplet	MCG-01-30-032 to 34, ARP 248	11 46.8 −3 49
Wolf-Lundmark-Melotte	MCG-03-01-015, DDO 221	0 02.0 −15 28
Zwicky #2	UGC 06955, DDO 105	11 58.4 +38 03
Zwicky's Triplet	UGC 10586, ARP 103	16 49.5 +45 30

Catalogues:

AM *Catalogue of Southern Peculiar Galaxies and Associations*, Arp, H.C. and Madore, B.F., Cambridge University Press (1987).

ARP *Atlas of Peculiar Galaxies*, Arp, H., *Ap.J.Suppl. 14*, 1 (1966).

DDO *David Dunlap Observatory Publ.*, van den Bergh, S., II, No. 5, 147 (1959).

IC *Index Catalogue*, Dreyer, J.L.E., *Mem. R.A.S.* (1895 - 1910).

MCG *Morphological Catalogue of Galaxies*, Vorontsov-Velyaminov, B.A. et al., Moscow State University, Moscow (1961 - 1974).

NGC *New General Catalogue of Nebulae and Clusters of Stars*, Dreyer, J.L.E., *Mem. R.A.S.* (1888).

RNGC *The Revised New General Catalogue of Nonstellar Astronomical Objects*, Sulentic, J.W. and Tifft, W.G., U. of Arizona Press (1973).

UGC *Uppsala General Catalogue of Galaxies*, Nilson, P., *Nova Acta Regiae Societatis Scientiarum Upsaliensis*, Ser. V:A, Vol. 1,

Uppsala, Sweden (1973).

UGCA *Catalogue of Selected Non-UGC Galaxies*, Nilson, P., Uppsala Astronomical Observatory (1974).

ZWG *Catalogue of Galaxies and Clusters of Galaxies*, Zwicky, F. et al., Vol 1-6, California Institute of Technology (1961 - 1968).

THE NASA/IPAC EXTRAGALACTIC DATABASE

BY BARRY F. MADORE

The *National Aeronautics and Space Administration/Infrared Processing and Analysis Center* (NASA/IPAC) Extragalactic Database (NED) has been providing computer-network access to a broad range of published extragalactic data since June 1990. NED offers: (1) an X-Windows Graphical User Interface (GUI) with point-and-click, mouse-driven menus, as well as graphics and image-display capabilities; (2) a VT100 ASCII-character menu; (3) a server mode; and (4) a web-based version. The GUI interface provides greater functionality and display capabilities, but its speed is critically dependent upon the network bandwidth; the VT100 mode and the web-based versions are generally faster.

NED represents the systematic merger of both major catalogues of extragalactic objects covering all wavelengths and also scores of shorter lists, culled from published journal articles. New catalogues and lists are continually being folded into NED, with each undergoing a detailed process of cross-identification for individual objects. Important recent additions include extragalactic supernovae, the *Hubble Deep Field (HDF)*, the *FIRST, 7C, MRC, B3, Texas, PMN* and *PMNM* radio source surveys, the *APM Bright Galaxy Catalogue, the ENOC* Catalogue, *Southern Ringed Galaxies,* and the *Las Campanas Redshift Survey (LCRS)*. Multi-million object catalogues such as *NVSS* and *APMUKS* are slowly being assimilated.

NED supports searches for objects and references, and offers browsing capabilities for abstracts of articles of extragalactic interest that have appeared in *A&A, AJ, ApJ, MNRAS,* and *PASP* since 1988, and in *Publications of the Astronomical Society of Japan, Astronomy Reports* and *Astronomy Letters* (formerly *Soviet Astronomy* and *Soviet Astronomy Letters*), *Nature,* and *IAU Circulars* since 1992.

Also on-line are over a million detailed photographic measurements, as well as thesis abstracts of doctoral dissertations on extragalactic topics. It is also possible to search the main NED database for objects selected by redshift, in addition to selection by catalogue prefix, position or type. Once found, plots can be produced for the objects and saved as Postscript files, or displayed directly within the GUI.

Since January 1997 NED has been available over the World Wide Web. To use this version of NED point your web browser at http://nedwww.ipac.caltech.edu. Because of the form-based nature of this interface, certain interactive plotting features of the X interface are not yet supported; however, new functionality is provided and the response of the interface as seen by the user is much enhanced.

NED can also still be accessed using a VT100 terminal (or VT100 emulation software) for the character-based interface, or X-Windows running on workstations for the GUI. A connection can be obtained with the command: <telnet ned.ipac.caltech.edu>. Once connected to the NED platform and prompted for a login, respond with <NED> (no password is required) and follow the interface options and instructions provided.

At any time during a session NED will forward to the user, upon request, files containing data retrieved during that session. Alternatively, NED also provides batch processing capabilities on input files submitted through electronic mail (see the *Batch Job* option and associated *Help* in the Main Menu).

This work is being carried out by the *Jet Propulsion Laboratory, California Institute of Technology*, under contract with the *National Aeronautics and Space Administration* (Astrophysics Division, Science Operations Branch).

RADIO SOURCES
BY KEN TAPPING

There are many types of cosmic radio source, driven by a wide variety of processes. Some are thermal, that is, producing radio emissions through their temperature. Others involve the interaction of high-energy electrons with magnetic fields, or complicated interactions of waves with plasmas. There are radio spectral lines from some atoms (such as the 21-cm emission from cosmic hydrogen) and an ever-increasing number of discovered molecular lines originating in cold, dense parts of the interstellar medium.

The list below is not complete; nor does it include only the strongest sources. It is intended to show a representative sample of the types of source that have been discovered. Some sources within reach of small (amateur-built) radio telescopes are included. Where possible, the flux densities at 100, 500 and 1000 MHz are given. The unit of flux density used is the "jansky" (Jy), where $1 \text{ Jy} = 10^{-26} \text{ Wm}^{-2}\text{Hz}^{-1}$. In the Remarks column, m denotes visual magnitude, z redshift, and P period.

For information on radio astronomy, see *Radio Astronomy*, by J.D. Kraus (Cygnus-Quasar Books, Powell, Ohio, USA, 1986). Some maps of the radio sky can be found in *Sky & Telescope*, *63*, 230, (1982). Information for amateur radio astronomers can be found in *Astronomy*, 5, no. 12, 50 (1977), in a series of articles in *JRASC, 72*, L5, L22, L38,… (1978), and in *Sky & Telescope, 55*, 385 and 475, and *56*, 28 and 114 (1978). A number of small, simple radio telescopes and some projects to try are described in *Radio Astronomy Projects*, by William Lonc, Radio-Sky Publishing, 1997.

TABLE OF RADIO SOURCES

Source	RA (2000) Dec h m ° ′	Flux Density (Jy) 100, 500, 1000 MHz Remarks
3C10	0 25.3 +64 08	180, 85, 56 Remnant of Tycho's Supernova (1572)
W3	2 25.4 +62 06	—, 80, 150 IC1795; Multiple HII region; OH Source
Algol	3 07.9 +40 56	* Eclipsing binary star
3C84	3 19.8 +41 32	70, 25, 17 NGC1725; Seyfert gal.; $m = 12.7$, $z = 0.018$
Fornax A	3 20.4 −37 22	900, 160, 110 NGC 1316; galaxy; $m = 10.1$; $z = 0.006$
Pictor-A	5 19.9 −45 47	440, 140, 100 Galaxy; $m = 15.8$, $z = 0.034$
V371 Orionis	5 33.7 +1 55	* Red dwarf (flare) star
Taurus A	5 34.5 +22 01	1450, 1250, 1000 Crab Nebula; remnant of 1054 Supernova
NP0532	5 34.5 +22 01	15, 0.5, 1 Crab Pulsar; $P = 0.0331$ s
Orion A	5 35.3 −5 25	90, 200, 360 Orion Nebula; HII region. OH, IR source
3C157	6 17.6 +22 42	360, 195, 180 IC443; Supernova remnant

TABLE OF RADIO SOURCES (continued)

Source	RA (2000) Dec h m ° ′	Flux Density (Jy) 100, 500, 1000 MHz Remarks
VY CMa	7 23.1 −20 44	* Optical variable start; OH, IR source
Puppis-A	8 20.3 −42 48	650, 300, 100 Supernova remnant
Hydra-A	9 18.1 −12 05	390, 110, 65 Galaxy; $m = 14.8$, $z = 0.052$
3C273	12 29.1 +2 03	150, 57, 49 Strongest quasar; $m = 13.0$, $z = 0.158$
Virgo-A	12 30.8 +12 23	1950, 450, 300 M87; elliptical galaxy with jet
Centaurus-A	13 25.4 −43 02	8500, 2500, 1400 NGC 5128; galaxy; $m = 7.5$, $z = 0.002$
3C295	14 11.4 +52 12	95, 60, 28 Galaxy; $m = 20.5$, $z = 0.461$
OQ172	14 45.3 +9 59	10, 4, 2 Quasar; $m = 18.4$, $z = 3.53$
Scorpius X1	16 19.9 −15 38	* X-ray, radio and optical variable star
Hercules-A	16 51.2 +5 01	800, 120, 65 Galaxy; $m = 18.5$, $z = 0.154$
Galactic Centre	17 42.0 −28 50	4400, 2900, 1800 Strong, diffuse emission
Sagittarius-A	17 42.5 −28 55	100, 250, 200 Associated with galactic centre
Sagittarius-B2	17 47.3 −28 24	—, 10, 70 Contains many molecules
SS433	19 11.9 +4 58	* Compact object with high-velocity jets
CP1919	19 21.6 +21 52	0.08, 0.03, 0.005(?) First pulsar discovered; $P = 1.3375$ s
PSR 1937+21	19 39.6 +21 35	5, 0.2(?), 0.04(?) Millisecond pulsar; $P = 0.001558$ s
Cygnus-A	19 59.5 +40 44	15 500, 4000, 2100 Strong radio galaxy
Cygnus-X	20 22.6 +40 23	400, 150, 30 Complex region
BL-Lacertae	22 02.7 +42 17	—, 5, 4 Radio galaxy; $m = 14.0$, $z = 0.07$
Cassiopeia-A	23 23.4 +58 49	25 000, 4500, 2800 Supernova remnant
Jupiter		Bursts at metre wavelengths
Moon		Thermal source ($\approx$225 K)
Sun		20 000, 300 000, 900 000 Also intense bursts and strong, varying emissions.

* Important source, although emission is weak and/or sporadic. Mean flux density less than one jansky.

VARIABLE GALAXIES

Some peculiar galaxies (Seyfert galaxies, BL Lacertae objects, and quasars) have bright, star-like nuclei which vary in brightness by up to several magnitudes on a time scale of months to years. These variations can be studied by amateurs and students, especially using photographic or electronic techniques. The table below lists the brightest variable galaxies. For more information, see *Sky & Telescope, 55*, 372 (1978), which gives finder charts and comparison stars for the four brightest Seyfert galaxies (indicated with asterisks in the table).

3C 273, the brightest quasar, was also the first quasar to be identified (in 1963). Charts for finding 3C 273 are at the bottom of this page. Start with the right-hand chart, which shows a "binocular-sized" field of view down to nearly 10th magnitude. The stars η Vir (mag 3.9), 16 Vir (mag 5.0), and 17 Vir (mag 6.5) are labelled. η Vir is the star immediately east of the autumnal equinox on the MARCH ALL-SKY MAP on p. 278. The two "bright" stars about 0.5° west of the small rectangle are of 7.6 magnitude (the small rectangle shows the area covered by the left-hand chart). On the left-hand chart, nine stars have their visual magnitudes indicated (on their west sides) to the nearest tenth of a magnitude, with the decimal point omitted. The position of 3C 273 is indicated by a small cross. With a red-shift $z = 0.158$, 3C 273 is receding from us at 44 000 km/s and is probably 2 or 3 billion light-years from Earth, making it, by far, the intrinsically brightest (output $\approx 10^{39}$ W), most distant object that can be seen in a small telescope.

Name	Type	RA (2000) Dec h m	° '	Magnitude
NGC 1275*	Seyfert?	3 19.8	+41 31	11–13
3C 120	Seyfert	4 33.2	+5 21	14–16
OJ 287	BL Lac	8 54.9	+20 07	12–16
NGC 4151*	Seyfert	12 10.5	+39 24	10–12
3C 273	Quasar	12 29.2	+2 03	12–13
3C 345	Quasar	16 43.0	+39 48	14–17
Mkn. 509*	Seyfert	20 44.2	−10 43	12–13
BL Lac	BL Lac	22 02.8	+42 17	14–17
NGC 7469*	Seyfert	23 03.2	+8 52	12–13

MAPS OF THE NIGHT SKY
By Roy Bishop

The maps on the next seven pages cover the entire sky. Stars are shown down to a magnitude of 4.5 or 5, that is. those that are readily apparent to the unaided eye on a reasonably dark night.

The first six maps are drawn for latitude 45°N, but are useful for latitudes several degrees north or south of this. They show the hemisphere of sky visible at various times of year. Because the aspect of the night sky changes continuously with both longitude and time, while time zones change discontinuously with both longitude and time of year, it is not possible to state simply when a particular observer will find that his or her sky fits exactly one of the six maps. The month indicated below each map is the time of year when the map will match the "late evening" sky. On any particular night, successive maps will represent the sky as it appears every four hours later. For example, at 2 a.m. or 3 a.m. on a March night, the May map should be used. Just after dinner on a January night, the November map will be appropriate. The centre of each map is the zenith, the point directly overhead; the circumference is the horizon. To identify the stars, hold the map in front of you so that the part of the horizon that you are facing (west, for instance) is downward. (The four letters around the periphery of each map indicate compass directions.)

The southern sky map is centred on the south celestial pole and extends to 20°S declination at its periphery. Thus there is considerable overlap with the southern areas of the other maps. Note that the orientation of the various names is generally inverted compared to that on the first six maps. This is in recognition that most users of this Handbook will be residents of the Northern Hemisphere and will make use of the southern sky map when they make trips to the tropics. Thus in "normal" use this map will be read in an area above its centre, unlike the first six maps which are normally read below their centres. The months indicated around the edge of the map may be used to orient it to each of the preceding six maps, and have the same "late evening" significance as explained above. Tick marks around the edge of the map indicate hours of right ascension, with hours 0, 3, 6, etc., labelled. Starting at the centre of the map, the series of small crosses along 0h right ascension indicates southern declinations 90°, 80°, 70°,..., 20°. With the aid of a drawing compass, an observer in the Northern Hemisphere can quickly locate a circle, centred on the south celestial pole, which represents the southern limit of his or her sky.

On all seven maps, stars forming the usual constellation patterns are linked by straight lines, constellation names being given in uppercase letters. Three constellations (Horologium, Mensa, and Microscopium) consist of faint stars; hence no patterns are indicated and the names are placed in parentheses. Small clusters of dots indicate the positions of bright star clusters, nebulae, or galaxies. The pair of wavy dotted lines indicates roughly the borders of the Milky Way. Small asterisks locate the directions of the galactic centre (GC), the north galactic pole (NGP), and the south galactic pole (SGP). LMC, SMC, and CS signify, respectively, the Large Magellanic Cloud, the Small Magellanic Cloud, and the Coal Sack. Two dashed lines appear on each of the first six maps. The one with more dashes is the celestial equator. Tick marks along this indicate hours of right ascension, the odd hours being labelled. The line with fewer dashes is the ecliptic, the apparent annual path of the Sun across the heavens. Letters along this line indicate the approximate position of the Sun at the beginning of each month. Also located along the ecliptic are the Northern Hemisphere vernal equinox (VE), summer solstice (SS), autumnal equinox (AE), and winter solstice (WS).

JANUARY ALL-SKY MAP

Observing notes

MARCH ALL-SKY MAP

Observing notes

MAY ALL-SKY MAP

Observing notes

JULY ALL-SKY MAP

Observing notes

SEPTEMBER ALL-SKY MAP

Observing notes

NOVEMBER ALL-SKY MAP

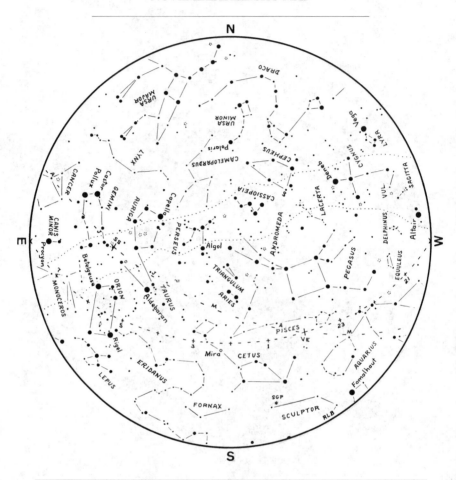

Observing notes

SOUTHERN ALL-SKY MAP

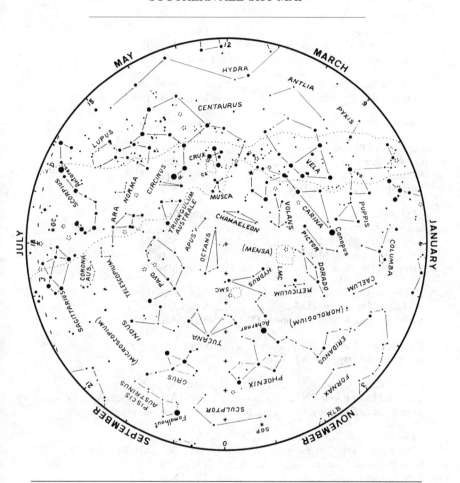

Observing notes

SOME HOLIDAYS AND SPECIAL DATES, 2001

New Year's Day .... Mon. Jan. 1
Martin Luther King Jr.'s Birthday (U.S.A.) ..... Mon. Jan. 15
Chinese New Year .... Wed. Jan. 24

Valentine's Day .... Wed. Feb. 14
Winter Star Party, Florida .... Mon. Feb. 19 – Sun. Feb. 25

Islamic New Year .... Mon. Mar. 26

First Day of Passover (Pesach) .... Sun. Apr. 8
Good Friday .... Fri. Apr. 13
Easter Sunday .... Sun. Apr. 15
International Astronomy Day .... Sat. Apr. 28

Mother's Day .... Sun. May 13
Texas Star Party .... Sun. May 13 – Sun. May 20
Victoria Day (Canada) .... Mon. May 21
Riverside Telescope Makers Conference .... Fri. May 25 – Sun. May 27
Memorial Day (U.S.A.) .... Mon. May 28

Father's Day .... Sun. Jun. 17
St.-Jean-Baptiste Day (Québec) .... Sun. Jun. 24
RASC General Assembly (London ON) .... Fri. Jun. 1 – Sun. Jul. 1

Canada Day .... Sun. Jul. 1
Independence Day (U.S.A.) .... Wed. Jul. 4

Civic Holiday (Canada) .... Mon. Aug. 6
Starfest, Mount Forest ON .... Thu. Aug. 16 – Sun. Aug. 19
Mount Kobau Star Party, BC .... Fri. Aug. 18 – Sun. Aug. 26

Labour Day .... Mon. Sep. 3
Alberta Star Party, Caroline AB .... Wed. Sep. 12 – Sun. Sep. 16
Rosh Hashanah .... Tue. Sep. 18
Yom Kippur .... Thu. Sep. 27

Thanksgiving Day (Canada) .... Mon. Oct. 8
Halloween .... Wed. Oct. 31

Remembrance Day (Canada)
Veteran's Day (U.S.A.) .... Sun. Nov. 11
First day of Ramadân .... Sat. Nov. 17
Thanksgiving Day (U.S.A.) .... Thu. Nov. 22

Christmas Day .... Tue. Dec. 25

See the inside back cover for 2001 and 2002 calendars.

OBSERVER'S HANDBOOK 2002
ORDER FORM

(The Observer's Handbook for the year 2002 will be
available in September 2001.)

Price per copy
Includes handling and shipping

# copies	Canada*	United States	Elsewhere†
1–4	$23.56	$22.95 US	$25.00 US
5–19	$14.98	$14.00 US	
20–99	$14.45	$13.50 US	
100+	$13.91	$13.00 US	

* includes GST; GST registration number 119126282
† Shipped via airmail

To: The Royal Astronomical Society of Canada
    136 Dupont Street
    Toronto ON M5R 1V2
    Canada

    Tel: (416) 924-7973; fax: (416) 924-2911; email: orders@rasc.ca
    Web site: http://www.rasc.ca

Please send .... copies of the Observer's Handbook 2002

Name   ....

Address   ....

           ....

           ....

Payment Enclosed $ ....   [ ] Cheque   [ ] Money Order

               [ ] VISA   [ ] Mastercard   [ ] Amex

    Name   ....

    Expiry .... Signature...

    Telephone (.........)..

    Email   ....

Please invoice‡ $ ....

‡Bulk orders for 5 or more copies only.
Shipment will be made upon receipt of payment.

To order any of the other publications of the RASC, including the award-winning
RASC Observer's Calendar, please contact the Society.

This page intentionally left blank.

SELECTED INDEX OF WEB ADDRESSES

INDEX